TENTH EDITION

Communication Works

Teri Kwal Gamble
COLLEGE OF NEW ROCHELLE

Michael Gamble
NEW YORK INSTITUTE OF TECHNOLOGY

Connect
Learn
Succeed™

The McGraw-Hill Companies

Connect
Learn
Succeed™

Published by McGraw-Hill, an imprint of The McGraw-Hill Companies, Inc., 1221 Avenue of the Americas, New York, NY 10020. Copyright © 2010, 2008, 2005, 2002, 1999, 1996, 1993, 1990, 1988, and 1984 by The McGraw-Hill Companies. All rights reserved. No part of this publication may be reproduced or distributed in any form or by any means, or stored in a database or retrieval system, without the prior written consent of The McGraw-Hill Companies, Inc., including, but not limited to, in any network or other electronic storage or transmission, or broadcast for distance learning.

This book is printed on acid-free paper.

1 2 3 4 5 6 7 8 9 0 WCK/WCK 0 9

ISBN: 978-0-07-340672-5
MHID: 0-07-340672-4

Publisher: *Michael Ryan*
Executive Editor: *Beth Mejia*
Executive Sponsoring Editor: *Katie Stevens*
Senior Developmental Editor: *Jennie Katsaros*
Editorial Coordinator: *Erika Lake*
Executive Marketing Manager: *Leslie Oberhuber*
Text Permissions Coordinator: *Karyn L. Morrison*
Senior Production Editor: *Leslie LaDow*

Manuscript Editor: *Amy Marks*
Designers: *Ashley Bedell & Elise Lansdon*
Cover: *Ashley Bedell*
Senior Photo Research Coordinator: *Natalia Peschiera*
Photo Researcher: *Editorial Image, LLC*
Senior Production Supervisor: *Rich DeVitto*
Composition: *10/12 Goudy by Aptara®, Inc.*
Printing: *45# Publisher's Matte Plus by World Color USA*

Cover: Clockwise from top left: © Stockbyte/Getty Images, © BananaStock/JupiterImages, © Digital Vision, © Stockbyte/PictureQuest, © Simon Marcus/Corbis

Library of Congress Cataloging-in-Publication Data

Gamble, Teri Kwal.
  Communication works/Teri Kwal Gamble, Michael Gamble.—10th ed.
       p. cm.
  Includes index
  ISBN-13: 978-0-07-340672-5 (softcover: alk. paper)
  ISBN-10: 0-07-340672-4 (softcover: alk. paper)
I. Communication.   I. Gamble, Michael,   1943–   II. Title
  P90.G299 2009
  302.2—dc22   2009935314

The Internet addresses listed in the text were accurate at the time of publication. The inclusion of a Web site does not indicate an endorsement by the authors or McGraw-Hill, and McGraw-Hill does not guarantee the accuracy of the information presented at these sites.

www.mhhe.com

For Matthew Jon and Lindsay Michele, our children, who grew up with this book and who continue to exert more influence on its contents than they can imagine. Wonderful students of life and always there when it matters, they embody communication at its best.

For Martha and Marcel Kwal and Nan and Wesley Gamble, our parents, who live on in our memories and were instrumental in helping us learn how and why communication works.

Brief Contents

Contents

PART FOUR
Communicating to the Public

About the Authors

Teri Kwal Gamble and Michael W. Gamble both earned PhDs in communication from New York University. They are full professors of communication and award-winning teachers, with Teri at the College of New Rochelle and Michael at the New York Institute of Technology in Manhattan. As co-founders of Interact Training Systems, a communication consulting firm, they have conducted seminars, workshops, and short courses for numerous business and professional organizations across the United States.

The Gambles are co-authors of several textbooks and training systems, including *Public Speaking in the Age of Diversity*; *Interpersonal Communication in Theory, Practice and Context*; and *Literature Alive!* Their trade books include *Sales Scripts That Sell*, *Phone Power*, and *The Answer Book*.

Teri and Michael live in New Jersey and spend much of their time exploring how and why communication works. Their personal favorite communicators are their children—their son, Matthew Jon, who has his doctorate in biochemistry and is now a scientist, and their daughter, Lindsay Michele, who received her MBA in marketing, ran the New York City Marathon, teaches this course, and works in real estate.

Teri and Michael Gamble with son Matthew and daughter Lindsay.

Preface

In this new edition, we continue to dedicate ourselves to exploring how communication works and why we benefit from becoming more skillful communicators.

We retained and revised the text's signature interactive approach, and updated the discussions on technology, media, and popular culture. Our objective remains to help students observe, think ethically and critically about communication, and assess which means of communication work best in their lives. We also reveal more precisely how technological advances are altering both the nature of our communication experiences and the ways we approach communication challenges.

NEW TO THIS EDITION

■ Skills section in each chapter: *Communication Skills in Practice* provides guidelines for developing communication skills for personal and professional success.

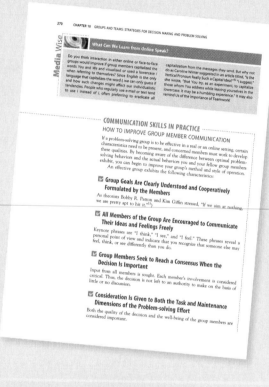

■ *Work It Out* activities help students comfortably begin building communication (interpersonal, group, and public presentation) skills.

- All new student speech examples cover topics such as health/wellness, climate change, diversity, immigration, and ethics.
- Interviewing and Developing Professional Relationships Appendix focuses on the job applicant and the job interview.
- Coverage of intergenerational communication includes the relationship between age and self-concept.
- The Toulmin model is discussed in the persuasion chapter.

SIGNATURE FEATURES AND THEMES

All the features in the book are designed to create a pedagogical environment that compels students to ask questions and become involved in individual or group assignments and class discussions.

Skill Builders:

We continue to offer a wide selection of Skill Builders—learning activities for use in or out of class. These activities encourage students to observe and consider communication, to assess its effects, and to experience the insights and practice they need to become effective communicators.

Exploring Diversity; Ethics and Communication; Thinking Critically:

To reflect the needs of an increasingly diverse student audience, and to encourage critical inquiry, we continue to pay significant attention to the influence of culture, the importance of communication ethics, and critical thinking in these feature boxes.

Media Wise and Resources for Further Inquiry and Reflection:

Because of the myriad ways in which communication and technology are linked, we have retained and updated the *Media Wise* boxes. Content for the end-of-chapter feature, *Listen to Me, View Me, Read Me, and Tell Me,* has been updated. This resource section encourages students to demonstrate and apply their understanding of chapter content to popular media, such as music, movies, and books.

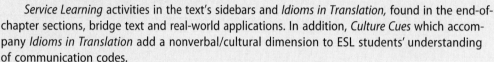

Service Learning activities in the text's sidebars and *Idioms in Translation,* found in the end-of-chapter sections, bridge text and real-world applications. In addition, *Culture Cues* which accompany *Idioms in Translation* add a nonverbal/cultural dimension to ESL students' understanding of communication codes.

Online Unit: Mass Communication and Media Literacy

We enhanced our coverage of cyber relationships to include how social networking media and online venues for self-expression are altering the communication mix.

COMMUNICATION WORKS ONLINE LEARNING CENTER:

The Online Learning Center at www.mhhe.com/gamble10e, an integral part of the book, was produced to appeal to a variety of learning styles. Margin icons, throughout the book and in the end-of-chapter sections, prompt readers to view relevant video clips and interacting learning tools. Features include chapter quizzes with feedback, key terminology flash cards, Communication Concepts videos, PowerPoint tutorials, and outline tutor.

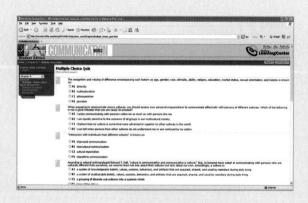

TEGRITY CAMPUS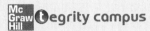

Tegrity Campus is a service that makes class time available all the time by automatically capturing every lecture in a searchable format for students to review when they study and complete assignments. With a simple one-click start-and-stop process, you capture all computer screens and corresponding audio. Students replay any part of any class with easy-to-use browser-based viewing on a PC or Mac.

Educators know that the more students can see, hear, and experience class resources, the better they learn. With Tegrity Campus, students quickly recall key moments by using Tegrity Campus's unique search feature. This search helps students efficiently find what they need, when they need it across an entire semester of class recordings. Help turn all your students' study time into learning moments immediately supported by your lecture.

To learn more about Tegrity watch a 2-minute Flash demo at http://tegritycampus.mhhe.com

COURSESMART

CourseSmart is a new way for faculty to find and review eTextbooks. It's also a great option for students who are interested in accessing their course materials digitally and saving money. CourseSmart offers thousands of the most commonly adopted textbooks across hundreds of courses from a wide variety of higher education publishers. It is the only place for faculty to review and compare the full text of a textbook online, providing immediate access without the environmental impact of requesting a print exam copy. At CourseSmart, students can save up to 50% off the cost of a print book, reduce their impact on the environment, and gain access to powerful Web tools for learning including full text search, notes and highlighting, and e-mail tools for sharing notes between classmates.

Acknowledgments

The contributions of many people, including past and present students, the instructors who have been so loyal over the years, and the wonderful professionals at McGraw-Hill, demonstrate that it takes a team to produce a text. We are so grateful to all those people for the attention, nurturing, and care they have given *Communication Works*.

We want to recognize the extremely talented editing team at McGraw-Hill. We are especially thankful to Frank Mortimer for his vision and business acumen, Katie Stevens for her belief in *Communication Works*, Jennie Katsaros, our tireless development editor, for again taking this book under her artful wing, understanding it, and providing friendship as well as keen insight into the market. We also want to thank Valerie Raymond for her close reading, wonderful ideas, organizational flair, and good decisions; Leslie LaDow, the text's production editor; and Ashley Bedell for the text's fresh design.

We especially thank our reviewers for their insightful advice that has resulted in this edition's improvements:

Jason E. Combs, *University of Dayton*
Karen Hamburg, *Camden County College*
Cheryl Hebert, *Estrella Mountain Community College*
Thaddeus J. Herron, *James Madison University*
Amy K. Lenoce, *Naugatuck Valley Community College*
John Marlow, *Hawaii Community College*
Donna Munde, *Mercer County Community College*
Jessica A. Nodulman, *Bowling Green State University*
Luann Okel Adams, *Mid-State Technical College*
Sergey Samoylenko, *George Mason University*
Ray Tipton, *Walters State Community College*
Don Wallace, *Brewton-Parker College*
Dan Warren, *Bellevue University*
Catherine Wright, *George Mason University*

Finally, we thank Matthew and Lindsay, our children, for their insights and support. When all is said and done, they are our reasons for loving life.

Teri Kwal Gamble
Michael W. Gamble

Communication Works

CHAPTER 1

After finishing this chapter, you should be able to

1. Define *communication*.

2. List the essential elements of communication and explain their interaction using representative communication models.

3. Describe the core principles of communication.

4. Discuss how digital media are transforming communication.

5. Explain what being a good communicator can do for you.

6. Identify guidelines for improving your effectiveness as a communicator.

Communication:
The Starting Line

Is it possible to communicate without talking to anyone else? Well, have you ever used Slydial? This technology lets you call someone's cell phone but go directly into voice mail. Why would anyone want to do this? For some, connecting with another person carries the risk of actually having to talk to—communicate with—the person reached. Another technology that makes it possible to contact someone without having to speak to the person is texting. Texting frees us to say anything we want to without fear of being interrupted. To be sure, texting and Slydial have advantages, too, but if taken to extremes and used unthinkingly, both technologies can make it easier for us not to have to listen to and interact with others. Communication, however, frequently involves a give and take, a back-and-forth exchange of ideas. That's part of what we think makes communication work.

So, welcome to *Communication Works!* If you're reading this textbook, most likely you're in college. Perhaps you're a traditional student between 20 and 30 years of age. Or maybe you're a nontraditional student between the ages of 30 and 50, or even older than that, especially if you are hoping to acquire new skills or are thinking about changing careers. If you are like many twenty-first-century individuals, you interact with others both face-to-face and in cyberspace. The cell phone lets you reach anyone at any time. You use it to text and to access Twitter in an effort to keep others informed. You may also log on to Facebook, MySpace, and Classmates or Reunion.com to connect. You live your life and maybe even have a "second life," a fantasy or alternative life you create and live online. Like most of us, your goal is to live as fulfilling a life as possible. And to do so, you will need to communicate effectively.

Today, job-specific talent, technical expertise, and graduation from a prestigious school do not carry any guarantees for upward mobility or attainment of goals. Many of us get our jobs because of our **social capital,** that is, our social connections or social networks—the people we know—rather than our human capital—what we know.[1] Our workplaces are prime environments for connecting with others. The Internet has democratized information. Finding out what we don't know has gotten a lot easier. Anyone with a computer is able to gather nearly as much intelligence as the CIA, access as much data as exists in the Library of Congress, and engage in conversations with people around the world at any hour.[2]

One factor shared by people who ascend both the professional and the personal ladders of success is superior communication skills. When you are a skilled communicator, you can sell ideas to people who otherwise might not have been open to them.[3] While not guaranteed, people with good communication skills are more likely to be promoted rapidly, happy in

social capital
social connections or networks

relationships, and believe their lives are rich and fulfilling. That is why this book can be of value to you. Whatever your age, sex, marital status, or employment history, it is never too late to learn skills that will enrich and improve the quality of your life. You are not born knowing how to make communication work. You learn and develop communication skills, a process that will continue throughout your life. That is why we designed this book to provide a program for lifelong learning. If you desire to improve your ability to relate to people in your social life, job, or academic life, now is the time to start making communication work!

WHAT IS COMMUNICATION?

We are all communicators. We engage in intrapersonal (with ourselves), dyadic (one to one), small-group (one to a few), public (one to many), and mass communication (communication that is shared across great distances with potentially large audiences through a technological device or mass medium). We also engage in computer-assisted or online communication. Every time we knowingly or unknowingly send a verbal or nonverbal message to anyone, communication takes place.[4] We define **communication** as the deliberate or accidental transfer of meaning. It is the process that occurs whenever someone observes or experiences behavior and attributes meaning to that behavior. As long as what someone does or says (his or her symbolic behavior) is interpreted as a message—as long as the behavior of one person affects or influences the behavior of another—communication is occurring. Since we spend more time communicating than doing anything else, our communication skill level helps shape our personal, social, work, and professional relationships. Communication is our link to the rest of humanity and serves a number of purposes, as these examples reveal:

communication

the deliberate or accidental transfer of meaning

> Talk and change the world.
>
> —Slogan espoused by a group of U.S. senators who happened to be female

> Communication is the vehicle which allows humans to recall the past, think in the present, and plan for the future.
>
> —ROY BERKO

> I once had a boyfriend who was Mr. Text-o-Rama. He never wanted to talk but he always wanted to text. To him the only way to communicate was via thumb. . . . New media professor Barb Iverson says, "Digital natives instinctively emote through their thumbs and don't consider a relationship 'official' until their Facebook or MySpace profile says it is."
>
> —As reported by NATALIE Y. MOORE on *Chicago Public Radio*

Which of these observations do you agree with? Which do you find most applicable to your own communication experiences?

Because our focus is communication, it makes sense to define and distinguish among the types of communication also used.

intrapersonal communication

communication with the self

- During **intrapersonal communication,** you think about, talk with, learn about, reason with, and evaluate yourself.

interpersonal communication

the relationship level of communication

- When you engage in **interpersonal communication,** you interact with another, learn about him or her, and act in ways that help sustain or terminate your relationship.

Contacts!

Identify five people with whom you recently had a sustained communication contact. (Note: The contact need not have been initiated by you.) For each contact, indicate the nature of your communication (the subject or message), the context or environment in which it occurred (classroom, office, home, voice mail, online, etc.), the type of interaction experienced (interpersonal, virtual, small-group, or public), and the outcome (what happened as a result of the interaction). Finally—and this is important—as an assessment of your communication effectiveness, rate each contact on a scale of 1 (extremely ineffective) to 5 (extremely effective), and give your rationale for each rating.

Extremely ineffective	1	2	3	4	5	Extremely effective

Now, how would you replay each contact if you were given the opportunity? If possible, would you prefer to increase or decrease the percentage of contacts you have that are virtual as opposed to face-to-face? Why?

- When you participate in **group communication,** you interact with a limited number of others, work to share information, develop ideas, make decisions, solve problems, offer support, or have fun.

- Through **public communication,** you inform and persuade the members of an audience to hold certain attitudes, values, or beliefs so that they will think, believe, or act in a particular way. You can also function as a member of an audience, in which case another person will do the same for you.

- During **mass communication,** the media entertain, inform, and persuade you. You, in turn, have the ability to use your viewing and buying habits to influence the media.

- During **online, or machine-assisted, communication,** you navigate cyberspace as you converse, research, and exchange ideas, and you build relationships with others using computers and the Internet.

Whatever the nature or type of communication, however, the communicative act itself is characterized by the interplay of certain elements.

group communication
interaction with a limited number of persons

public communication
communication designed to inform, persuade, or entertain audience members

mass communication
the transmission of messages that may be processed by gatekeepers prior to being sent to large audiences via a channel of broad diffusion

online, or machine-assisted, communication
the building of relationships using computers and the Internet

ELEMENTS OF COMMUNICATION: PICTURING THE COMMUNICATION MODEL

All communication interactions have certain common elements that together help define the communication process. The better you understand these elements, the easier it will be for you to develop your own communicative abilities. Let's begin by examining the **essentials of communication,** those components present during every communication event.

> Which type of communication do you use most? Least? Which do you enjoy most? Least? Why?

essentials of communication
those components present during every communication event

People

Obviously, human communication involves people. Interpersonal, small-group, and public communication encounters take place between and among all types of **senders** (persons who encode messages) and **receivers** (persons who decode messages). Senders and receivers, respectively, are individuals who give out and take in messages. Although it is easy to picture a communication experience beginning with a sender and ending with a receiver, it is important to understand that during communication the role of sender does not belong exclusively to one person

senders
persons who formulate, encode, and transmit a message

receivers
persons who receive, decode, and interpret a message

and the role of receiver to another. Instead, the processes of sending and receiving are constantly being reversed. Reflecting this fact, in *That's Not What I Meant!* linguist Deborah Tannen writes, "Communication is a continuous stream in which everything is simultaneously a reaction and an instigation, an instigation and a reaction."[5] Thus, when we communicate with one or more people, we simultaneously send and receive.

Messages

During every communication encounter, we all send and receive both verbal and nonverbal messages. What you talk about, the words you use to express your thoughts and feelings, the sounds you make, the way you sit and gesture, your facial expressions, and perhaps even your touch or your smell all communicate information. In effect, a **message** is the content of a communicative act. Some messages we send are private (a kiss accompanied by "I love you"); others are public and may be directed at hundreds or thousands of people. We send some messages purposefully ("I want you to realize . . . ") and others accidentally ("I had no idea you were watching . . . or 'lurking'"). Everything a sender or receiver does or says is a potential message as long as someone is there to interpret the behavior. When you smile, frown, shout, whisper, or turn away, you are communicating, and your communication is having some effect.

message
the content of a
communicative act

Channels

Channels are the media we use to carry messages. We can classify channels according to (1) which of our senses carries or receives the message, (2) whether the message is being delivered verbally, nonverbally, or both, and (3) the primary means of communication we use to deliver the message, that is, whether we use face-to-face interaction, computer-mediated communication including e-mail and instant messaging, telephone communication and text messaging, or a mass medium such as television or film. Thus, we are multichannel communicators. Let's see how this works.

channels
media through which messages
are sent

We receive sound messages (we hear noises from the street), sight messages (we see how someone looks), taste messages (we enjoy the flavor of a particular food), smell messages (we smell the cologne a friend is wearing), and touch messages (we feel the roughness of a fabric). Which channel are you most attuned to? Why? To what extent do you rely on one or more channels while excluding or ignoring others? Effective communicators are adept at switching channels. They recognize that communication is a multichannel experience.

The following dialogue between a husband and a wife illustrates the multichannel nature of communication:

> *Wife:* What's the matter with you? You're late again. We'll never get to the Adamses' on time.
>
> *Husband:* I tried my best.
>
> *Wife:* (Sarcastically) Sure, you tried your best. You always try your best, don't you? (Shaking her finger) I'm not going to put up with this much longer.
>
> *Husband:* (Raising his voice) You don't say! I happen to have been tied up at the office.
>
> *Wife:* My job is every bit as demanding as yours, you know.

Husband: (*Lowering his voice*) OK. OK. I know you work hard too. I don't question that. Listen, I really did get stuck in a conference. (*Puts his hand on her shoulder*) Let's not blow this up. Come on. I'll tell you about it on the way to Bill and Ellen's.

What message is the wife (the initial source-encoder) sending to her husband (the receiver-decoder)? She is letting him know with her words, her voice, and her physical actions that she is upset and angry. Her husband responds in kind, using words, vocal cues, and gestures in an effort to explain his behavior. Both are affected by the nature of the situation (they are late for an appointment), by their attitudes (how they feel about what is occurring), and by their past experiences.

Inventory each message you receive during a two-minute period, and note the channel through which it came.

Noise

In the context of communication, **noise** is anything that interferes with or distorts our ability to send or receive messages. Although we are accustomed to thinking of noise as a particular sound or group of sounds, the perceptive communicator realizes that noise can have both internal and external causes. Internal noise is attributed to the psychological makeup, intellectual ability, or physical condition of the communicators. External noise is attributed to the environment. Thus, noise includes distractions such as a loud siren, a disturbing odor, and a hot room; personal factors such as prejudices, daydreaming, and feelings of inadequacy; and semantic factors such as uncertainty about what another person's words are supposed to mean.

noise
anything that interferes with or distorts the ability to send and receive messages

Context

Communication always takes place in a **context,** or setting. Sometimes a context is so natural that we hardly notice it. At other times, however, the context makes such an impression on us that it exerts considerable control over our behavior. Consider the extent to which your present environment influences the way you act toward others or determines the nature of the communication encounters you share with them. Consider as well the extent to which certain environments might cause you to alter your posture, manner of speaking, attire, or means of interacting. Take into account the fact that sometimes conditions of place and time—that is, context—can affect our communications without our consciously realizing it.

context
the setting

Feedback

Whenever we communicate with one or more persons, we receive information in return. The verbal and nonverbal cues that we perceive in reaction to our communication function as **feedback.** Feedback tells us how we are coming across. A smile, a frown, a chuckle, a sarcastic remark, a muttered thought, or simply silence in response to something

feedback
information returned to a message source

What positive and negative feedback have you recently given to others? What positive and negative feedback have you received?

Contact in Context

Compare and contrast the types of communication that would be most likely to occur in each of the following contexts. Include a description of the nature of each interaction, the probable attire of each person, and his or her demeanor.

1. the first few minutes of a party
2. a business meeting
3. a coffeehouse
4. a funeral home
5. a college classroom
6. a political rally
7. a football stadium
8. a computer chat room

positive feedback
a behavior-enhancing response

negative feedback
a response that extinguishes behavior in progress

internal feedback
a response you give yourself

external feedback
a response from another

effect
the communication outcome

we did or said can cause us to change, continue, or end a transaction. Feedback that encourages us to continue behaving as we are is **positive feedback;** it enhances whatever behavior is in progress. In contrast, **negative feedback** extinguishes a behavior; it serves a corrective rather than a reinforcing function. Thus, negative feedback can help eliminate unwanted, ineffective behaviors. Note that the terms *positive* and *negative* should not be interpreted as "good" and "bad"; these terms simply reflect the way the responses affect behavior.

Both positive and negative feedback can emanate from internal or external sources. **Internal feedback** is feedback you give yourself as you monitor your own behavior or performance during a transaction. **External feedback** is feedback from others who are involved in the communication event. To be an effective communicator, you must be sensitive to both types of feedback. You must pay attention to your own reactions as well as the reactions of others.

Effect

As people communicate, they are changed in some way by the interaction, which in turn influences what follows. In other words, communication has an **effect** and can be viewed as an exchange of influences.

An effect can be emotional, physical, cognitive, or any combination of the three. An interpersonal, small-group, or public communication contact can elicit feelings of joy, anger, or sadness (emotional); communication can cause you to fight, argue, become apathetic, or evade an issue (physical); or it can lead to new insights, increased knowledge, the formulation or reconsideration of opinions, silence, or confusion (cognitive). The result of a communication encounter can also be any combination of the three effects just mentioned. Since effects are not always visible or immediately observable, there is obviously more to a communication reaction than meets the eye, or the ear.

MODELS OF COMMUNICATION

Now that we have examined the basic elements of communication, we are ready to see how our understanding can be reflected in a picture, or model, of the communication process.

Through communication, we share meaning with others by sending and receiving messages—sometimes

Communication can cause us to feel happy and loved.

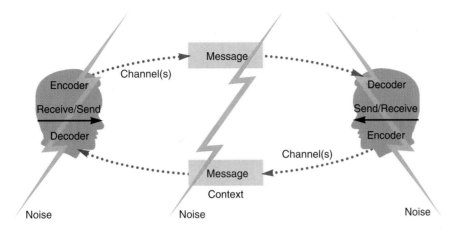

FIGURE 1.1

Gamble and Gamble's Model of Communication.

intentionally and sometimes unintentionally. Communication thus includes every element that could affect two or more people as they knowingly or unknowingly relate to one another.

At this point, we need to reiterate that communication occurs whenever one person assigns significance or meaning to the behavior of another. But, you might ask, will knowing this enable you to understand or establish better and more satisfying relationships with your friends, spouse, employer, parents? The answer is yes. If you understand the processes that permit people to contact and influence each other, if you understand the forces that can impede or foster the development of every kind of effective communication, then you stand a better chance of communicating effectively yourself. Models of communication, like the ones in Figures 1.1 and 1.2, explain and help you visualize the process we employ to initiate and maintain communicative relationships with others. You will find these models useful tools in discovering how communication operates and in examining your own communication encounters.

The model in Figure 1.1 shows that communication is a circle and that the sending and receiving responsibilities are shared by the communicators. A message or messages may be sent through one or more channels, and the interaction occurs in and is affected by a definite context. Note that noise can enter the interaction at any point and can affect either the sending or the receiving abilities of the communicators. Furthermore, noise can be caused by the context, can be present in the channel, or can pop up in the message itself.

Another model of communication, devised by communication theorist Frank Dance[6] (see Figure 1.2), depicts the communication process in a more abstract way. Dance's spiral, or helix, represents the way communication evolves or progresses in a person from birth to the present moment. This model emphasizes the fact that each person's present behavior is affected by his or her past experience and, likewise, that present behavior will have an impact on future actions. Thus, Dance's helix indicates that communication has no clearly observable beginning and no clearly observable end.

By playing with Dance's model, we can picture two communication spirals as meeting in a number of different ways, one of which is shown in

Work It Out

Bring to class a variety of materials with which to create an original model of communication. Explain what your model suggests about the state of communication today.

FIGURE 1.2 Dance's Communication Helix.

Source: From *Human Communication Theory: Original Essays* by Frank E. X. Dance. Holt, Rinehart & Winston. Copyright © 1967 by Frank E. X. Dance. Used by permission of the author.

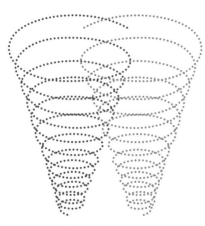

FIGURE 1.3   Meeting of Helixes.

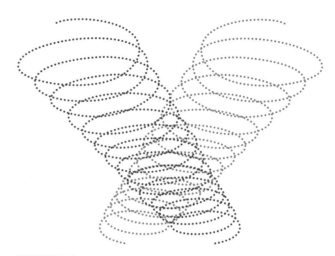

FIGURE 1.4   Model of Communication in Relationships.

Figure 1.3. The point where the spirals touch is the point of contact; each time a contact occurs, messages are sent and received by the interactants. Some helical spirals touch each other only once during a lifetime, whereas others crisscross or intertwine in a pattern that indicates an enduring relationship. Furthermore, the spirals (interactants) may sometimes develop in similar ways (grow together) and sometimes develop in different ways (grow apart; see Figure 1.4).

The understanding you now have should provide you with some of the background you will need as you work to increase your effectiveness as a communicator.

HOW GOOD A COMMUNICATOR ARE YOU? MASTERING CORE COMMUNICATION PRINCIPLES

Simply communicating frequently does not mean that you are as effective a communicator as you could be. Too often, we neglect problems that plague our communicative relationships. When we lack sensitivity and fail to consider the feelings of others, for example, our relationships suffer. There is no such thing as being too effective at establishing, maintaining, and controlling personal and public contacts with others. Being mindful of the principles discussed in this section can help you to improve your communication skills.

Communication Is Dynamic

When we call communication a dynamic process, we mean that all its elements constantly interact with and affect each other.[7] Since all people are interconnected, whatever happens to one person determines in part what happens to others.

Like the humans who compose them, relationships constantly evolve. Nothing about communication is static. Everything is accumulative. We communicate as long as we are alive. Thus, every interaction we engage in is part of connected happenings. As we learned from Dance's model, our present communication experiences may be thought of as points of arrival from past encounters and as points of departure for future ones. Do your experiences support this?

Can you think of an interpersonal, small-group, or public communication encounter you had that affected a later encounter?

Can you describe a work-related or personal situation in which the irreversibility of communication caused difficulties for you?

Communication Is Unrepeatable and Irreversible

Every human contact you experience is unique. It has never happened before, and never again will it happen in just the same way. Our interpretation of the adage "You can never step into the same river twice" is that the experience changes both you and the river forever. Similarly, a communication encounter affects and changes people so that the encounter can never happen in exactly the same way again. Thus, communication is both unrepeatable and irreversible. We can neither take back something we have said nor erase the effects of something we have done. And although we may be greatly influenced by our past, we can never reclaim it. In the words of a Chinese proverb, "Even the emperor cannot buy back one single day." Do you think this proverb is accurate?

Experience changes us forever.

Communication Has No Opposite

People often assume that communication is purposeful and that we communicate only because we want to communicate. While this is sometimes true, it is also true that sometimes we communicate without any awareness of doing so—and just as often even without wanting to.

Whenever we are involved in an interaction, we respond in some way. Even if we choose not to respond verbally, even if we maintain absolute silence and attempt not to move a muscle, our lack of response is itself a response, constitutes a message, influences others, and communicates. We can never voluntarily stop behaving—because behavior has no opposite. No matter how hard we try, we cannot *not* communicate, because all behavior is communication and therefore is a message.

What does the following observation by Koji Yanase, a Japanese bar-association official, suggest about the nature of communication?

If an American is hit on the head by a ball at the ballpark, he sues. If a Japanese person is hit on the head, he says, "It's my honor. It's my fault. I shouldn't have been standing there."
—Newsweek,
February 26, 1996

Communication Is Affected by Culture

As we will learn in Chapter 2, how we formulate and interpret messages depends on our culture. Cultural diversity, including race, ethnicity, gender, and age, influences the meanings we attribute to communication. Cultural differences exist not only between persons who speak different languages but between persons who speak the same language as well. Every cultural group has its own rules or preferences for interaction. When these are ignored or unknown, we are likely to misinterpret the meaning of messages received and miscalculate the impact of messages sent.

Communication Is Influenced by Ethics

Every time we communicate, we decide implicitly or explicitly whether we will do so ethically. Ethics are the moral principles, values, and beliefs that the members of society use to guide behavior. Since communication has consequences, it involves judgments of right and wrong. When the agreed-upon standards of behavior are violated, the behavior is judged unethical. For example, most of us expect those with whom we interact to be honest, play fair, respect our rights, and accept responsibility for their actions.

Can you identify an experience in which the understanding or misunderstanding of culture contributed to your communication effectiveness or ineffectiveness?

Can you identify a communication experience in which, looking back, you believe communication between you and another person was effective or ineffective because of the presence or absence of ethical behavior on your part?

Can you cite an example of how improving a specific communication skill enabled you to resolve a problem in your personal, academic, or professional life?

technopoly

a culture in which technology monopolizes the thought-world

Communication Is Competence-Based

According to communication scholar Osmo Wiio, if communication can fail, it will.[8] The problem we face is determining how we can prevent communication from failing. One solution is to make wise choices. In certain situations, some messages are appropriate and okay to say to particular receivers while others are not.

While we all have different communication strengths and weaknesses, we can all benefit from getting better at communicating. When we add to our knowledge and make a commitment to develop the skills to apply that knowledge across an array of communication situations or contexts, we gain communication competence. For example, included among the skills necessary for effective communication is the ability to think critically. When we can think critically, we have the ability to examine ideas reflectively and to decide what we should and should not believe, think, or do, given a specific set of circumstances.[9]

Communication Is Being Transformed by Media and Technology

As media critic Marshall McLuhan cautioned, "The medium is the message."[10] In McLuhan's view, different channels of communication affect the way a sender encodes a message and the way a receiver responds to a message. The same words delivered face-to-face, on paper, or via radio or television do not constitute the same message. The channel of communication changes things. For example, terminating a relationship via an answering machine or e-mail is very different from delivering such news in person. What channel would you use, for example, to say "good-bye"? Which channel would you use to tell someone "I'm sorry"? What about "I love you"?

Not just the medium, but also its content, changes communication. The content of books, newspapers, radio, television, and film, for example, also influence our cultural values, often reinforcing the stereotypes we have of gender, race, and ethnicity and contributing to the perceptions we have of various people and groups in society, including ourselves.

New forms of communication also alter our communication experiences. According to media scholar Neil Postman, a new technology does not merely add or subtract something; it changes everything. Postman contends that our culture is now a **technopoly**—a culture in which technology monopolizes the thought-world.[11] Technology continues to speed up communication as it brings the world into our living rooms and bedrooms, offices and cars. Instead of valuing sequential understanding and careful logic, we now value immediate gratification and emotional involvement. Technology has also given us the ability to interact in more ways, more quickly, and with more people than ever before. For example, we experienced the cyclone in Myanmar and the terrorist strike in India as these events occurred. E-mail and digital cameras make it possible for us to see, interact with, and visit with people across the country and around the world.

We are evolving new ways of discovering ideas and information; new ways of relating with friends and strangers; and new ways of learning about our world, our identities, and our futures. As we expand our real and virtual communication repertoires, as we live not only our real life but a second life, we need to ask and try to answer a number of questions: What changes are digital media creating in us? How are they influencing our social and emotional lives and

Work It Out

Work with others to share your thoughts and answer the following questions: Is technology increasing or undermining social contact? As Postman fears, are we becoming tools of our tools? Are technological innovations overwhelming us with information or underwhelming us with a lack of credibility? Are they freeing us or complicating our lives? Are they bringing us closer together or keeping us apart?

cultural sensibilities? How are they altering our desire to relate to others—that is, our desire to communicate? What does it mean to be a communicator in a digital age?

For one thing, whether you are e-mailing, instant messaging, visiting a chat room, or blogging, online messages tend to be more permanent. Ethically challenged individuals can access your files, private messages may be made public, or messages you send may be used against you or forwarded to someone you had no intention of communicating with. On the other hand, when online it is easier to find people who share your interests. In addition, you can choose to remain anonymous. You decide what aspects of yourself to reveal to others or whether you wish to remain disguised. Also, unless you post your picture, you are more likely to be evaluated on the basis of what you write, rather than how you look.

Like television in the 1950s, the Internet and digital media are society-altering devices affecting personal interaction. The Internet is taking up more and more of our time.[12] Although e-mail and text messaging have increased some forms of human interaction, they may be limiting others. Internet use affects person-to-person interaction and sociability. Some observers believe that Internet use advances sociability by creating another medium of communication with colleagues, friends, and family as well as by providing opportunities to forge new relationships. Others counter that it is socially isolating and a poor substitute for social activities and face-to-face interaction. Critics contend the more we use the Internet, the less time we are likely to spend face-to-face with friends and family members.[12]

Cell phones and personal digital assistants keep us connected. In your opinion, are they facilitating or impeding human interaction?

What do your Internet experiences reveal? In what ways does the time you spend online contribute to social or antisocial activity? Do you find that Internet use is isolating, adding to the time you spend alone? Do you find it promotes active engagement with others, facilitating more social time? Does online time complement or displace the time you spend face-to-face? Compare your answers with these research findings: For every minute that individuals spend on the Internet, the time they spend alone increases by 35 to 40 seconds.[13] It is harder to be engaged with others while Internet engaged (see Figure 1.5).[14] Some 33 percent of college students spend over 10 hours each week online, and almost 20 percent spend over 20 hours a week on the Internet. That's more time than college students spend using television and radio (see Figure 1.6).[15] Internet users also spend less time talking on the phone with friends and family. In addition, for every extra hour of Web-time, Internet users report spending less time with traditional media.

The most common Internet communication endeavors are e-mail and instant messaging, with some 90 percent of Internet users reporting themselves to be e-mailers. A little over 30 percent of users engage in entertainment online, participating in computer games and the like. Over 25 percent of users enter chat rooms—frequently interacting with anonymous, rather than known, others. Internet users also multitask. Approximately 50 percent of college students use the Internet while watching television, and a little less than half are online while listening to the radio.

> **How would you describe the role that online interaction plays in your life? Do you think it plays different roles in the lives of males as compared with females?**

Work It Out

Describe the ways that online interaction is affecting offline communication activities. Work with others to identify how you believe the Internet is affecting society for better or for worse. For example, to what extent, if any, has Internet use affected the time you have for family or friends?

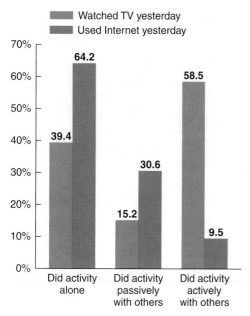

FIGURE 1.5 Sociability of the Internet versus Television.

Note: For those who spent time watching Television, $N = 3,304$. For those who spent time online, $N = 757$. Percentages can sum to greater than 100% because categories are not mutually exclusive.
Source: Reprinted by permission of BurstMedia.

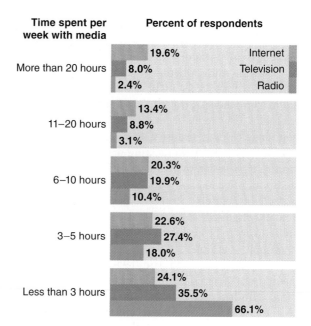

FIGURE 1.6 College Students Are Online, Even When Watching Television.

Note: Respondents were 18- to 24-year-old college students.
Source: Reprinted by permission of BurstMedia.

Table 1.1 Percentage of College Students Who Actively Participate in Online Activity

	Female College Students	Male College Students
Instant messaging	57.2%	62.3%
Downloading music/MP3 files/online concerts	51.2%	55.0%
Pursuing school/work activities	60.2%	44.9%
Playing online games	49.3%	46.4%
Reading entertainment news/gossip	47.8%	44.9%
Listen to Internet radio	45.8%	43.5%
Reading local/national/international news	46.3%	42.5%
Viewing streaming video	34.3%	49.3%
Shopping	41.8%	35.3%
Researching health/medical information	32.8%	21.7%
Reading sports scores and news	10.4%	34.8%
Searching local restaurant/club listings	16.9%	23.6%
Reading news on fashion/trends	23.9%	17.4%
Reading horoscope	22.9%	9.1%
Looking up weather info	5.5%	6.8%

Note: Participants were college students aged 18–24 years old.
Source: Reprinted by permission of BurstMedia.

NON SEQUITUR © 2004 Wiley Miller. Dist. By UNIVERSAL PRESS SYNDICATE. Reprinted with permission. All Rights Reserved.

(See Table 1.1 for an overview of online activities in which college students participate.)[16] Where do you fit into these findings?

A question to consider is this: Does what happens online stay online, or do our online experiences affect our offline realities?[17] The cell phone, for example, is no longer just a means of social interaction, it is also a source of news and public information, as well as a medium through which we express our social identity.[18] In addition, cell phone texting has changed the way we communicate. We may be reluctant to make a telephone call to deliver certain kinds of messages, but we are willing to send those messages via text. Are there messages that you prefer to send by texting rather than by talking face-to-face with another person? The more socially anxious you are, the more you may prefer "to play it safe," and the greater the likelihood that you will use text messaging as a preferred means of forming and managing close personal relationships.[19] New media give us new communication options.

hyper-competitive culture
the contention that one needs to defeat another to achieve one's goals

Media Wise

Does Reality TV Reflect Reality?

In reality-type television programs, such as *Survivor, American Idol, The Bachelor, America's Next Top Model,* and *Big Brother,* people are thrown together, filmed continuously, and frequently isolated from or permitted to have only limited contact with the outside world as they compete against each other in an effort to win money, fame, and/or love. A pop-culture trend, these shows have ratings that prove huge numbers of people view them. Critics ask whether shows like these, which emphasize wealth, beauty, and popularity, are "in reality" promoting the worst in human behavior. What is more, they ask, do programs that place people in unusual situations—situations that exist in a setup environment and deviate from most of the everyday experiences that the vast majority of us have—reflect reality at all?[20]

What do you think? Does reality television reflect reality? What values do your most and least favorite reality television shows promote? What do your most and least favorite shows suggest about human nature? What do they reveal about our competitiveness and the role competition plays in our lives? In your opinion, are shows like these symptomatic of **hyper-competitive culture,** the belief that one needs to defeat another in order to achieve one's goals? And what do they reveal about our communication ethics? Will people do anything to win? Do these shows encourage us to live in the here and now? Do they fuel our materialistic greed and our desires for what is superficial by making us eager to sacrifice privacy, relationships, common sense, and morality in the drive to acquire great wealth, fame, and beauty? And what do they suggest about us as viewers? Have we become, as author Clay Calvert suggests, a "voyeur nation"?

FUNCTIONS OF COMMUNICATION: WHAT CAN IT DO FOR YOU?

As we see, every communication experience serves one or more functions. For example, communication can help us discover who we are, help us establish meaningful relationships, or prompt us to examine and try to change either our own attitudes and behaviors or the attitudes and behaviors of others.

Understanding and Insight

One key function of communication is self-other understanding: insight into ourselves and others. When you get to know another person, you also get to know yourself; and when you get to know yourself, you learn how others affect you. We depend on communication to develop self-awareness.

We need feedback from others all the time, and others are constantly in need of feedback from us. Interpersonal, small-group, public, and media communications offer us numerous opportunities for self-other discovery. Through communication encounters we are able to learn why we are trusting or untrusting, whether we can make our thoughts and feelings clear, under what conditions we have the power to influence others, and whether we can effectively make decisions and resolve conflicts and problems.

Work It Out

Compile a list of the communication activities you engaged in yesterday, together with the function(s) served by each one.

Meaningful Relationships

In building relationships, we cannot be overly concerned with ourselves but must consider the needs and wants of others. It is through effective communication that our basic physical and social needs are met.

Psychologists tell us that we need other people just as we need water, food, and shelter. When we are cut off from human contact, we become disoriented and maladjusted, and our life itself may be placed in jeopardy. People who are isolated from others—people who lack satisfying social relationships—are more likely to experience health problems and to die early than people who have an abundance of satisfying relationships.

Communication offers each of us the chance to satisfy what psychologist William Schutz calls our "needs for inclusion, control, and affection."[21] The **need for inclusion** is our need to be with others, our need for social contact. We like to feel that others accept and value us, and we want to feel like a full partner in a relationship. The **need for control** is our need to feel that we are capable and responsible, that we are able to deal with and manage our environment. We also like to feel that we can influence others. The **need for affection** is our need to express and receive love. Since communication allows each of these needs to be met, we are less likely to feel unwanted, unloved, or incapable if we are able to communicate meaningfully with others.

Today, it is a given that we will need to interact with persons who are culturally different from us. To attempt to insulate ourselves from such intercultural contacts is virtually impossible, nor is it desirable. It is through communication that we can reveal to others what is important to us and what we stand for, as well as learn what is important to them and what they stand for.

Communication also gives us the chance to share our personal reality with people from our own culture, as well as people from different cultures. Whether we live in an East Coast urban area, a southern city, a desert community, a home in sunny California, a village in Asia, a plain in Africa, or a town in the Middle East, we all engage in similar activities when we communicate. We may use different symbols, rely on different strategies, and desire different outcomes, but the

need for inclusion
the need for social contact

need for control
the need to feel we are capable and responsible

need for affection
the need to express and receive love

"I Hate Him"

Over 24 years ago, researcher Gordon Allport wrote the following in his now-classic *The Nature of Prejudice*:

> *See that man over there?*
> *Yes.*
> *Well, I hate him.*
> > *But you don't know him.*
> *That's why I hate him.*

Why does lack of knowledge or familiarity breed hate? Why might we experience hate when encountering people from a new or unfamiliar culture or group? Although Allport was writing over two decades ago, his comments remain true today. Why? To what extent do you believe that enhanced self–other understanding can help resolve this predicament? Explain.

processes we use and the motivations we have are strikingly alike. Equally significant is the fact that insensitivity to another's needs and preferred ways of interacting can hamper our ability to relate effectively.

Influence and Persuasion

During interpersonal, small-group, public, mediated, and online communication, people have ample opportunities to influence each other subtly or overtly. We spend much time trying to persuade one another to think as we think, do what we do, like what we like. Sometimes our efforts meet with success, and sometimes they do not. In any case, our experiences with persuasion afford each of us the chance to influence others so that we may try to realize our own goals.

Career Development

There is a positive relationship between the ability to communicate and career success. Employers seek to hire people who know how to make communication work. If you develop the abilities to speak so that others listen, listen when others speak, critically evaluate what you read and hear, adapt to differences in cultural perspectives, handle conflicts and solve problems, and make sound decisions, then you will exhibit skills valued by employers.[22]

How could the attitude by the employer or employee affect their relationship and ability to work together?

cyberbole
exaggerated claims about the effects new technologies have on society

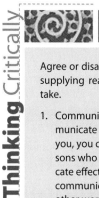

Reflect and Respond

Agree or disagree with each of the following statements, supplying reasons and examples for each position you take.

1. Communication is communication. If you can communicate effectively with persons who are similar to you, you can also communicate effectively with persons who are different from you. If you can communicate effectively with others when face-to-face, you can communicate equally well with them when online. In other words, neither the gender nor the nationality of the communicators, nor the means used to interact

with others, should influence the satisfactions derived from or the outcomes of a communication experience.

2. Too many observers of our new, technologically wired society spout **cyberbole**—exaggerated claims about the effect the new technology has on society. In reality, the problems of social division in our society far outweigh what the Internet can bring to us. In the end, according to skeptic Steve Woolgar, the Internet will probably be like the telephone—"this huge new revolution that didn't make much difference to existing social structures."[23]

COMMUNICATION SKILLS IN PRACTICE

GUIDELINES FOR IMPROVING YOUR EFFECTIVENESS AS A COMMUNICATOR

The major purpose of this book is to help you gain an understanding of communication and to assist you in developing your skills at interpersonal, small-group, public, mass, and online communication. To achieve these goals, you will need to do the following:

✓ Become Actively Involved in the Study of Communication

The materials in this book will benefit you only if you make a commitment to try out and experience the principles discussed. First, each chapter opening lists targets, or objectives, that specify what you should have learned after completing your study of the chapter. Use these lists to clarify your personal communication objectives as you make your way through the book. Next, a plethora of boxes—Skill Builder, Exploring Diversity, Ethics & Communication, Media Wise, and Thinking Critically—are included to help you explore communication and become aware of what you must know and do to become a more effective communicator. A number of these features contain self-analysis and assessment scales. Together, they give you an opportunity to process and apply your new knowledge to actual communication experiences. If you use them as directed, you will increase your opportunities to grow, because you will be actively using your own learning and diagnosing your own needs for self-improvement.

Focus on Service Learning

Develop a two- to three-minute presentation promoting the importance of communication for delivery to a class of elementary, junior high, or senior high school students and/or the parents and teachers. In addition to reviewing the value of communication and the reasons it is fundamental to our lives, the tasks required include confirming a school's participation, securing a date and time, developing the content of your presentation, and delivering it. For online help in completing this assignment, you may want to visit the Web site of the National Communication Association at www.natcom.org.

✓ Set and Track Personal Goals

To increase your communication effectiveness, you should work to maintain or master a number of skills and work to eliminate a number of ineffective behaviors. To function effectively in interpersonal, small-group, public, mass, or online communication, you will need the following:

–The ability to understand and communicate with yourself

–An appreciation of the extent to which gender, culture, media, and new technologies affect communication

–The capacity to listen to and process information

–Sensitivity to silent messages that you and others send

–Knowledge of how words affect you and those with whom you relate

–An understanding of how relationships develop

–An understanding of how feelings and emotions affect relationships

–The ability to handle conflict by learning how to disagree without being disagreeable

–An understanding of how beliefs, values, and attitudes affect the formulation and receptions of messages and the development of speaker-audience relationships

–The desire to apply all these skills and perceptions to each communication experience and arena

☑ Believe in Yourself

Above all else, you need to believe that you are worth the time and effort required to develop your communication skills. You also need to believe that developing these skills will immeasurably improve the quality of your life. We think you are worth it. Now, you need to believe you are worth it, because communication works!

Revisiting Chapter Objectives

1. **Define *communication*.**   Communication is the deliberate or accidental transfer of meaning. Human communication takes place interpersonally (one to one), in small groups (one to a few), in public forums (one to many), via the media, or online.

2. **List the essential elements of communication and explain their interaction using representative communication models.**   The essential elements of communication are people, messages, channels, noise, context, feedback, and effect. Models of communication illustrate the communication process in action.

3. **Describe the core principles of communication.**   Communication reflects a number of general principles. First, since communication is a dynamic process, each interaction is part of a series of interconnected communication events. Second, every communication experience is unique, unrepeatable, and irreversible. Third, communication has no opposition. Fourth, culture influences communication. Fifth, it is influenced by ethics. Sixth, it is competence-based.

4. **Discuss how digital media are transforming communication.**   New forms of communication are altering the nature of our communication experiences. We use more ways of relating to others than ever before. As we expand our virtual communication repertoires, including the use of e-mail and instant messaging, we increase some forms of communication and limit others.

5. **Explain what being a good communicator can do for you.**   Communication serves a number of essential functions in our lives. It promotes self-other understanding, helps us establish meaningful relationships, enables us to examine and attempt to change the attitudes and behavior of others, and enhances career development. Developing communication skills is a life-long process. This book explains the strategies you can use to assess your own communication abilities, improve the effectiveness of your communication relationships, and enhance the quality of your life.

6. **Identify guidelines for improving your effectiveness as a communicator.**   Once you become actively involved in the study of communication, commit to setting and tracking personal goals, and believe in yourself, you are on the road to mastering communication skills to last a lifetime.

Resources for Further Inquiry and Reflection

To apply your understanding of how the principles in Chapter 1 are at work in our daily lives, consult the following resources for further inquiry and reflection. Or, if you prefer,

THE WRAP-UP

choose any other appropriate resource. Then connect the ideas expressed in your chosen selection with the communication concepts and issues you are learning about both in and out of class.

Listen to Me

"Stan" (Eminem)
"You Oughta Know" (Alanis Morrisette)
"Bohemian Rhapsody" (Queen)
"Dance with My Father" (Luther Vandross)
"Disposable Heroes" (Metallica)
"Communication Breakdown" (Led Zeppelin)

What message is the speaker sending regarding both the functions and the effects of communication?

View Me

The Day after Tomorrow   *Spider-Man 3*
Traffic   *When a Man Loves a Woman*
Cast Away   *The Truth about Cats and Dogs*
An Inconvenient Truth   *Sideways*

What do the main characters or narrator in the selected film reveal about the nature of communication and how it has an impact on others?

Read Me

Edmond Rostand. Anthony Burgess, trans. *Cyrano de Bergerac*. New York: Applause Books, 1998.

Toni Morrison. *Beloved*. New York: Knopf, 1998.

Garth Stein. *The Art of Racing in the Rain*. New York: Harper, 2008.

Randy Pausch with Jeffrey Zaslow. *The Last Lecture*. New York: Hyperion, 2008.

These authors identify certain understandings we must internalize if we are to be successful communicators. Identify and discuss the understandings conveyed by your selected author.

Tell Me

Share with the class the insights you gained from your chosen Listen to Me, View Me, or Read Me selection.

React to the following statement with reasons justifying your stance: *More communication does not always make things better*.

www.mhhe.com/gamble10e

Key Chapter Terminology

Use the Online Learning Center at www.mhhe.com/gamble10e to further your knowledge of the following terminology.

channels 6
communication 4
context 7
cyberbole 17
effect 8
essentials of communication 5
external feedback 8
feedback 7
group communication 5
hyper-competitive culture 15
internal feedback 8

interpersonal communication 4
intrapersonal communication 4
mass communication 5
message 6
need for affection 16
need for control 16
need for inclusion 16
negative feedback 7
noise 7
online, or machine-assisted, communication 5

positive feedback 7
public communication 5
receivers 5

senders 5
social capital 3
technopoly 12

Idioms in Translation

ascend the professional and personal ladders of success — achieve professional and personal goals

blow this up — exaggerate

e-culture — online culture

human capital — what we know

tied up — detained

Culture Cue

Whereas Asians tend to bow on first meeting, people from the United States are likely to shake hands. In China, as in America, punctuality is emphasized. The Chinese view lateness as a serious affront.

Test Your Understanding

Go to the *Self Quizzes* on the book's Online Learning Center at www.mhhe.com/gamble10e.

www.mhhe.com/gamble10e

CHAPTER 2

After finishing this chapter, you should be able to

1. Define *intercultural communication.*

2. Compare and contrast culture and co-culture, ethnocentrism and cultural relativism, melting-pot philosophy and cultural pluralism.

3. Compare and contrast the following: individualism and collectivism, high-context communication cultures and low-context communication cultures, high-power-distance cultures and low-power-distance cultures, masculine and feminine cultures.

4. Identify the various groups that influence our cultural identity.

5. Discuss how technology is bringing diversity into our lives.

6. Identify techniques you can use to reduce the strangeness of strangers.

Communicating in a Multicultural Society and World

Have you ever drawn a conclusion about or ascribed positive or negative characteristics to someone without really knowing him or her? Do you believe another person ever formed an opinion of you or judged you without really knowing you? If you answer yes to either of these questions, it is likely that stereotypes played a role.

Stereotypes express the knowledge, beliefs, and expectancies we have for the members of a particular group.[1] While some of the stereotypes we hold of any cultural group are positive, others are astoundingly negative and overly generalized. While some contain kernels of truth, others keep us from identifying misconceptions. For which groups of people do you have positive and negative stereotypes? And what do the members of these groups think of you? How does each of your evaluations influence whether or not you interact with one another? For example, many Muslims in the United States are asking that others view them more objectively and stop treating them with suspicion. They want stereotypes of them abandoned, saying that individuals should be able to distinguish between mainstream Muslims and those belonging to the radical fringe.[2]

It's not just relationships with Muslims that are suffering. Relations between African Americans, Hispanics, and Asian Americans are also complicated by the stereotypes we hold of one another. Yet all these groups share a common desire and need—to get along better with each other.[3] Stereotyping is just one of the topics we address in this chapter as we explore a host of factors that influence our ability to communicate in a multicultural society and world.

GLOBALIZATION, DIVERSITY, AND GLOCALIZATION

In the *age of globalization*, the likelihood of working and living with people from all over the world increases daily. **Globalization** is the increasing economic, political, and cultural integration and interdependence of diverse cultures—the worldwide integration of humanity. Globalization is related to two other concepts—*diversity* and *glocalization*. **Diversity** is the recognition and valuing of difference, encompassing such factors as age, gender, race, ethnicity, ability, religion, education, marital status, sexual orientation, and income. **Glocalization** is a newer concept describing how globalization affects and merges with local interests and environments. All three forces affect communication. Because it is now critical to learn about other cultures and to refrain from stereotyping them, embracing diversity is becoming more important than ever.[4]

Digital technology is helping to erase the notion of territorial boundaries between countries, gradually eroding the idea of the term *nation*. People we once considered strangers are now friends and co-workers, creating the need for us to be

globalization
the increasing economic, political, and cultural integration and interdependence of diverse cultures

diversity
the recognition and valuing of difference

glocalization
how globalization affects and merges with local interests and environments

What does this cartoon suggest about the propensity to stereotype? Can you supply an example from your own experience that demonstrates why identifying people belonging to a group in fixed, limited, and simplistic ways impedes communication?

multiculturalists

persons respectful of and engaged with people from distinctly different cultures

> How does the world in which you are growing up differ from the one in which your parents or caregivers grew up?

Work It Out

What does the following quote featured on a wall at the Holocaust Museum in Washington, D.C., suggest about the importance of understanding and accepting diversity?

In Germany, the Nazis first came for the communists, and I didn't speak up because I wasn't a communist. Then they came for the Jews, and I didn't speak up because I wasn't a Jew. Then they came for the trade unionists, and I didn't speak up because I wasn't a trade unionist. Then they came for the Catholics, but I didn't speak up because I was a Protestant. Then they came for me, and by that time there was no one left to speak for me.

multiculturalists—persons respectful of and engaged with people from distinctly different cultures. An early observer of how the mass media affect behavior and thinking, Marshall McLuhan predicted many years ago that our world would become a global village.[5] He was right. We are now linked physically and electronically to people around the globe. In addition to using the Internet with increasing frequency, many of us move—for personal or professional reasons—a number of times during our lives.[6] We also travel regularly to other countries, some of us to visit relatives (one in five Americans was born abroad or has at least one parent who was), others to represent an employer, and still others to vacation.

We differ, however, in our willingness to embrace diversity. In the book *Bowling Alone*, written at the turn of this millennium, author Robert Putnam reported that reciprocal and trustworthy social networks were on the decline, a fact he attributed, at least in part, to racial diversity. Putnam reported that we were doing more and more things alone, but why? After studying 30,000 people across the United States, Putnam discovered a correlation between ethnically mixed environments and the withdrawal from public life. He found that people living in diverse communities tended to "hunker down." Sadly, they were more likely to distrust their neighbors— whether they shared the same or a different race, a similar or different background.[7] Do you think this is still true? Are the "gay community" and the "African-American community" communities even though they lack diversity? The world of work reveals a different story. In organizations, people with *identity diversity* (people who come from different races and religions) and *cognitive diversity* (people who have different outlooks and training) come together to do the organization's work. Thus, the challenge we face is to follow the lead of diverse organizations and create a new and broader sense of "we," that is, to harness diversity to build community.[8]

The remainder of this chapter will sensitize you to the ways cultural values and habits influence interaction. Learning about such differences will help you (1) appropriately respond to varied communication styles, (2) recognize the need to expand your choices as a communicator, and (3) increase the effectiveness of your interactions with persons of different cultures.

DEFINING INTERCULTURAL COMMUNICATION

Whenever cultural variability influences the nature and the effects of communication, **intercultural communication** is at work. Thus, when we speak about intercultural communication, we are concerning ourselves with the process of interpreting and sharing meanings with individuals from different cultures.[9] In actuality, intercultural communication comprises a number of forms. Among its many variations are **interracial communication** (which occurs when interactants are of different races), **interethnic communication** (which occurs when the communicating parties have different ethnic origins), **international communication** (which occurs between persons representing political structures), and **intracultural communication** (which includes all forms of communication among members of the same racial, ethnic, or other co-culture groups).[10]

Cultures and Co-Cultures

To become more adept at communicating with persons who are culturally different from ourselves, we need to learn not only about their cultures but also about our own. A **culture** is the system of knowledge, beliefs, values, customs, behaviors, and artifacts that are acquired, shared, and used by its members during daily living.[11] Within a culture as a whole are **co-cultures;** these are composed of members of the same general culture who differ in some ethnic or sociological way from the parent culture. In our society, African Americans, Hispanic Americans, Japanese Americans, the disabled, gays and lesbians, cyberpunks, and the elderly are just some of the co-cultures belonging to the same general culture.[12] (See Figure 2.1.)

Have you ever felt like an outsider? Persons who believe they belong to a *marginalized group*—that is, a group whose members feel like outsiders—have a number of options to choose from regarding how they want to interact with members of the dominant culture or even if they want to interact with them at all. Have you or has anyone you know used any of the following strategies?

Co-culture members who use the strategy of **assimilation** attempt to fit in, or join, with members of the dominant culture. They converse about subjects that members of the dominant group talk about, such as cars or sports, or they dress as members of the dominant culture dress. They give up their own ways in an effort to assume the modes of behavior of the dominant culture. In comparison, co-culture members who use the strategy of **accommodation** attempt to maintain their cultural identity even while they strive to establish relationships with members of the dominant culture. A gay or lesbian who takes his or her partner to an occasion in which members of the dominant culture will be present, such as a company or

intercultural communication
interaction with individuals from different cultures

interracial communication
the interpreting and sharing of meanings with individuals from different races

interethnic communication
interaction with individuals of different ethnic origins

international communication
communication between persons representing different nations

intracultural communication
interaction with members of the same racial or ethnic group or co-culture as yours

culture
a system of knowledge, beliefs, values, customs, behaviors, and artifacts that are acquired, shared, and used by members during daily living

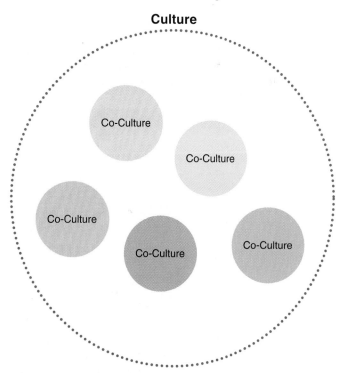

FIGURE 2.1   A Culture and Its Co-Cultures.

The term *co-culture* is preferred over *subculture* because the prefix *sub* denotes inferior status. A co-culture is a culture within a culture.

co-cultures
groups of persons who differ in some ethnic or sociological way from the parent culture

assimilation
the means by which co-culture members attempt to fit in with members of the dominant culture

accommodation
the means by which co-culture members maintain their cultural identity while striving to establish relationships with members of the dominant culture

separation
the means co-culture members use to resist interacting with members of the dominant culture

Were you ever the only person of your age, race, ethnicity, or sexual preference in a group? How did the experience make you feel?

family celebration, is using the strategy of accommodation. On the other hand, when members of a co-culture resist interacting with members of the dominant culture, they employ the strategy of resistance, or **separation.** Because these persons, such as Hassidic Jews, prefer to interact with each other rather than have contact with persons they perceive to be outsiders, they tend to keep to themselves.

Members of co-cultures can practice *passive, assertive, aggressive,* or *confrontational* communication approaches in their efforts to accomplish their objectives relative to the dominant culture. Co-culture members who practice a *passive* communication approach seek to avoid the limelight; they accept their position in the cultural hierarchy. Rather than defend their ways and oppose others, they embrace the cultural beliefs and practices of the dominant culture. Recent immigrants to the United States who desire to attain citizenship may choose this path, hoping to blend in so that they do not disturb the status quo. Co-culture members who employ an *assertive* communication approach may seek to communicate a shared cultural identity with members of the dominant group; they want others to accommodate their diversity. They are receptive to rethinking a number of their ideas, give up or modify some, and hold strong with regard to others. After the September 11, 2001, terrorist attacks, for example, many Arab Americans spoke openly of their patriotism, their support for the war against terror, and their desire for others to allow them to live according to their values and beliefs. Co-culture members who opt to display a more *aggressive* communication approach defend their own beliefs and traditions with intensity and may find themselves perceived by members of the dominant culture as "hurtfully expressive" or "self-promoting." They make it difficult for members of the dominant culture to ignore their presence or pretend they do not exist.[13] They adopt this strategy to de-marginalize themselves and actively participate in the world known to members of the dominant culture. In their early years as a group, the members of Act Up, a gay rights organization employed this approach. (See Table 2.1.)

Many theorists believe that understanding both the general culture and its co-cultures is essential for effective communication. Merely knowing another's language, jargon, or argot or sharing some but not all of a group's values does not necessarily

Using more than one language on a sign fosters communication with the members of a co-culture.

Table 2.1 Preferred Strategies and Communication Approaches
of Marginalized Groups

Strategy	Communication Approach	Example
Separation	Passive	Lunching alone, living in an area with similar people
Accommodation	Assertive	Wearing a yarmulke to work, wearing a sari to a party
Assimilation	Aggressive, confrontational	Staging a protest

ensure understanding. It is also necessary to become aware of the norms and rules of the culture or co-cultures that might influence the nature of interactions you have with its members, whether those interactions occur in public or in private.

Thus, when you and the individuals with whom you are interacting belong to different cultures, for you to understand each other, you each need to consider the role culture plays in shaping your communication. According to cultural anthropologist Edward T. Hall, culture is communication and communication is culture.[14] Culture teaches you how to think and what to think about. Culture teaches you what is beautiful or ugly, helpful or harmful, appropriate or out of place. Culture is the lens through which you view the world; it is the mirror you use to reflect and interpret reality.[15]

Culture Guides Communication

Among the lessons taught by culture are how to say "hello" and "good-bye," when to speak or remain silent, how to act when you're angry or upset, where to focus your eyes when functioning as a source or receiver, how much to gesture during speech, how close to stand to another, and how to display happiness or rage at another's actions. By teaching you lessons like these, culture guides behavior and communication. It tells you who you are, how to act, how to think, how to talk, and how to listen.[16]

When cultures meet, when we interact with persons whose values are different from ours or whose behavioral norms differ from our own, we must first recognize and acknowledge our differences. We must come to accept diversity if we are to be able to process other cultures' influences and communicate with each other in a meaningful way. **Ethnocentrism,** the tendency to see your own culture as superior to all others, is a key characteristic of failed intercultural communication efforts. Persons who are ethnocentric experience great anxiety when interacting with persons from different cultures. Quick to utter statements like "They take our jobs," "They're everywhere," and "They're just not like us," those who embrace ethnocentrism lack cultural flexibility and are particularly unprepared to meet the challenges posed by our society and our world today.[17] The more ethnocentric you are, the greater your tendency

> **Compare and contrast the lessons taught you by your culture with the lessons taught peers by other cultures.**

ethnocentrism
the tendency to see one's own culture as superior to all others

Culture is the lens through which we see the world. Can you provide an example of how your culture has influenced your view of events?

Ethnocentrism versus Cultural Relativism

Evaluate the extent to which you display culturally ethno-centric or culturally relativistic tendencies by labeling the following statements true or false. For each statement, provide an example of behaviors you used when interacting with or attempting to avoid interacting with a member of another culture. Be specific.

1. I would rather communicate with someone like me than with someone unlike me.

2. I can cooperate with people like me, but I find it difficult to cooperate with people unlike me.

3. I trust those who are like me more freely than I trust those who are different from me.

4. I am less fearful when I am around people like me than when I am around people unlike me.

5. I go out of my way to be with people like me.

6. I go out of my way to maintain my distance from people unlike me.

7. I am much more apt to blame people unlike me for causing trouble than I am to blame people like me.

8. I use my frame of reference to assess the rightness of the behaviors of people like and unlike me.

9. I believe that people unlike me threaten my ability to succeed.

10. I believe that people unlike me should make an effort to become more like me.

What do your answers and examples tell you about the extent to which you and others practice ethnocentrism or cultural relativism? Are there some cultures different from your own that you are more comfortable with than others? Why do you think that is so? Are you content with your responses? Why or why not? What steps are you willing to take, if any, to minimize the potentially negative effects of ethnocentrism?

---

is to view groups other than your own as inferior. As a result, you tend to blame others for problems and seek to maintain your distance from them.[18]

Cultural relativism is the opposite of ethnocentrism. When you practice cultural relativism, instead of viewing the group to which you belong as superior to all others, you work to try to understand the behavior of other groups on the basis of the context in which the behavior occurs rather than from your own frame of reference.

Two other factors, stereotypes and prejudice, also influence how we react to persons from cultures different from our own. As we noted at the opening of this chapter, **stereotypes** are mental images or pictures we carry around in our heads; they are shortcuts, whether positive or negative, that guide our reactions to others.[19] When attached to the way we view the world, stereotypes generate unrealistic pictures of others and prevent us from distinguishing an individual from a group. Racial profiling is just one example of how stereotyping affects worldview.

Prejudice describes how we feel about a group of people whom, more likely than not, we do not know personally. A negative or positive prejudgment, prejudice arises either because we want to feel more positively about our own group or because we feel others present a threat, real or not.[20] Prejudice leads to the creation of in-groups and out-groups, with out-group members becoming easy targets for discrimination. Because of the negative expectations that stereotypes and prejudice produce, we may try not to interact with people who are the objects of our prejudice. (We discuss stereotypes and prejudice again in Chapter 4.)

cultural relativism
the acceptance of other cultural groups as equal in value to one's own

stereotypes
mental images or pictures that guide our reactions to others

prejudice
a positive or negative prejudgment

Identify the extent to which ethnocentrism and/or cultural relativism affects you or those you know.

TAKING THE DEMOGRAPHIC PICTURE: DIVERSITY IN FOCUS

To what extent has the amount of contact you have with persons of diverse cultural backgrounds changed since you were a child? When you were younger, you were more apt to interact with persons just like yourself. Your experience today most likely is different. Continuing developments in technology and changes in demography are influencing the nature of our interactions.

Intercultural communication is now the norm. In fact, living in the United States gives you an incredible opportunity to interact interculturally without having to pay for international travel. But it hasn't always been that way. Years ago, the United States embraced a **melting-pot philosophy.** According to that theory, when individuals from other countries came here, they lost or gave up their original heritage and became Americans. The national motto, *E pluribus unum*—a Latin phrase meaning "one out of many"—reflected this way of thinking. It was believed that diverse cultural groups should be assimilated into the parent, or dominant, culture.

Over time, this philosophy was replaced by one that stresses **cultural pluralism.** Cultural pluralists advocate respect for uniqueness, tolerance for difference, and adherence to the principle of cultural relativity. In a multicultural society, every group, it is believed, will do things differently, and that's OK.

Demographers tell us that diversity will shape our country's future. According to U.S. Census Bureau statistics, the five largest ethnic groups are composed of people who identify themselves as White (207.7 million), African American (36.6 million), Hispanic (38.8 million), Asian American (12.7 million), and Native American (3.5 million). Hispanics are now the largest minority group, followed by African Americans, Native Americans, and Hawaiian Pacific Islanders.[21] In one generation, minorities may become the majority. (See Figure 2.2.)

melting-pot philosophy
the view that different cultures should be assimilated into the dominant culture

cultural pluralism
adherence to the principle of cultural relativism

FIGURE 2.2

Source: New York Times, August 14, 2008, p. A18.

Majority minorities

The Census Bureau projects that the share of ethnic and racial minorities will reach 54 percent of the total United States population and surpass that of non-Hispanic whites by 2042.

*Hispanics can be of any race
Source: Census Bureau

Population projections

250 million
200 million — Non-Hispanic White
150 million
100 million — Other
50 million
0
2010   2020   2030   2040   2050

Racial and ethnic breakdown

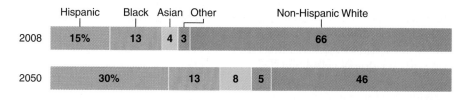

Hispanic   Black   Asian   Other   Non-Hispanic White

2008 | 15% | 13 | 4 | 3 | 66

2050 | 30% | 13 | 8 | 5 | 46

Percent minority by age group

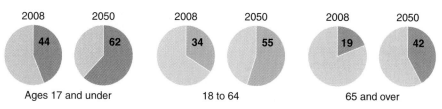

2008   2050   2008   2050   2008   2050
44   62   34   55   19   42

Ages 17 and under   18 to 64   65 and over

The United States is the most demographically diverse country in the world. Because of this and because of advances in communications and transportation, we will continue to experience an increasing number of contacts with members of other cultures. This alone makes it especially important for us to be able to understand and interact with persons of different backgrounds, nationalities, and lifestyles. We are truly interconnected with all of humanity.

THE INTERCULTURAL COMMUNICATION IMPERATIVE: REDUCE THE STRANGENESS OF STRANGERS

> **What steps have you taken to reduce the strangeness of strangers?**

While intercultural communication is inevitable, we are neither as effective nor as successful at it as we could be. The reason is clear: Not all of us work hard enough to understand or to be understood by those with whom we differ.

According to intercultural communication theorists Larry A. Samovar and Richard E. Porter, there are too many of "us" who do not work as hard as we should at intercultural communication simply because we do not wish to live or interact with "them."[22] Too many of us have adopted an "us versus them" mentality, which prevents us from effectively meeting the challenges cultural diversity presents. To counter this, we need to conduct ourselves in a manner designed to reduce the strangeness of strangers; that is, we need to open ourselves to differences by adding to our storehouse of knowledge, by learning to cope with uncertainty, and by developing an appreciation of how increasing our cultural sensitivity will positively affect our communication competence.

> **Have you ever considered your culture superior to another culture? How did your feelings influence your relationship with members of that culture?**

We take a giant step toward improving intercultural communication by accepting the fact that our culture is not superior to others. Nor should we base our behavioral expectations for the members of other cultures on our own culture's norms. To do so would cause us to label the responses of those who belong to other cultures as foreign or strange. To the extent that we are able to use our understanding of another's culture to reduce the number of misunderstandings between us, to the extent that we do not interpret the behavior of others on the basis of our own frames of reference, we take further steps toward reducing the strangeness of strangers.

Exploring Cultural Dialectics

> **Indicate where you fall on each of the cultural dialectics described in this section. Are your preferences different from those displayed by your parents? Are they different from those practiced by your grandparents? If so, how?**

Let's continue by focusing on four variables used to distinguish cultures: (1) individualism versus collectivism, (2) high-context versus low-context communication, (3) high power distance versus low power distance, and (4) masculine or feminine culture. Identified by Hofstede, Kluckhohn and Strodtbeck, and Hall, these dialectics reveal a culture's values and help us make comparisons across cultures.[23]

Individualism versus Collectivism

individualistic cultures
cultures in which individual goals are stressed

collectivistic cultures
cultures in which group goals are stressed

The cultural dimension of individualism versus collectivism reveals how people define themselves in their relationships with others. **Individualistic cultures,** such as those of Great Britain, the United States, Canada, France, and Germany, stress individual goals, whereas **collectivistic cultures,** represented by many Arab, African, Asian, and Latin American countries, give precedence to group goals. Individualistic cultures cultivate individual initiative and achievement, while collectivistic cultures tend to nurture group influences. This means that, while the "I" may be most important in individualistic cultures, the "we" is the dominant force in collectivistic

Exploring Diversity

Understanding Other Cultures

Make a list of individuals whose cultural backgrounds differ from your own and with whom you have recently communicated. How many of the following questions can you answer with respect to each person on your list?

1. How do the individual's feelings about socialization differ from your own?
2. How does the individual's concept of self compare with yours?
3. To what extent do the individual's values and attitudes differ from yours?
4. Which of your behaviors did the individual have difficulty understanding or accepting? Which of his or her behaviors did you have difficulty with?
5. Which of the individuals you interacted with did you find most like you? Most unlike you? Can you identify your points of similarity and difference?

6. To what extent was the individual more cooperative or competitive than you?
7. In what ways did the individual's use of verbal language differ from your own?
8. In what ways did the individual's nonverbal behavior differ from your own?
9. How did the individual's treatment of time and space differ from your own?
10. In what ways did the individual's thinking processes differ from yours?

For those questions you cannot answer, take the time to conduct research; then answer them.

ones. In collectivistic cultures the individual is expected to fit into the group; in individualistic cultures emphasis is placed on developing a sense of self.

High Context versus Low Context

A second way cultures vary in communication style is in their preference for high-context or low-context communication. Cultures with **high-context communication** systems are tradition-bound; their cultural traditions shape the behavior and lifestyle of group members, causing them to appear to be overly polite and indirect in relating to others. In contrast, cultures with **low-context communication** systems generally encourage members to exhibit a more direct communication style. Members of low-context cultures tend to gather background information when meeting someone for the first time. Thus, they will ask people they have just met where they went to college, where they live, and who they work for. Persons from high-context cultures are much less likely to ask such questions.[24] In addition, persons from low-context cultures are apt to feel that they have to explain everything rather than rely on nonverbal, contextual information as demonstrated by those who display a preference for high-context communication. In contrast, persons who believe that most messages can be understood without direct verbal interaction reveal their preference for high-context communication. Asian cultures typically emphasize high-context communication, whereas Western cultures typically represent low-context communication systems. For example, the Japanese have traditionally valued silence, believing that a person of few words is thoughtful, trustworthy, and respectable. Thus, the Japanese spend considerably less time talking than do people in the United States. This orientation also helps explain why the Japanese often perceive self-disclosures during interaction as socially inappropriate.

High Power Distance versus Low Power Distance

Power distance measures the extent to which individuals are willing to accept power differences. Individuals from **high-power-distance cultures,** such as Saudi Arabia,

---

What roles or rituals are used to celebrate the achievements of persons belonging to an individualistic culture? To a collectivistic culture? Which culture would feature a "salesperson of the year" award? Which would reward the achievements of the team?

high-context communication
a tradition-bound communication system which depends on indirectness

low-context communication
a system that encourages directness in communication

high-power-distance cultures
cultures based on power differences in which subordinates defer to superiors

India, and Malaysia, view power as a fact of life and are apt to stress its coercive or referent nature. Superiors and subordinates in these countries are likely to view each other differently; subordinates are quick to defer to superiors. In contrast, individuals from **low-power-distance cultures,** such as Israel, Sweden, and the United States, believe power should be used only when it is legitimate; thus, they are apt to employ expert or legitimate power. Superiors and subordinates from low-power-distance countries emphasize their interdependence by displaying a preference for consultation; subordinates will even contradict their bosses when necessary.[25]

Masculine versus Feminine Culture

Cultures differ in their attitudes toward gender roles.[26] In highly masculine cultures, members value male aggressiveness, strength, and material symbols of success. In highly feminine cultures, members value relationships, tenderness in members of both sexes, and a high quality of life. Among highly **masculine cultures** are Japan, Italy, Germany, Mexico, and Great Britain. Among highly feminine cultures are Sweden, Norway, the Netherlands, Thailand, and Chile. Masculine cultures socialize members to be dominant and competitive. They tend to confront conflicts head-on and are likely to use a win-lose conflict strategy. In contrast, the members of **feminine cultures** are more apt to compromise and negotiate to resolve conflicts, seeking win-win solutions.

Interpreting Cultural Differences

Where a culture falls on the individualistic-collectivistic, low-context–high-context communication, and power distance scales affects the interactional preferences of its members. In Japanese and Chinese societies, for example, individuals tend to understate their own accomplishments and successes, while members of North American cultures typically are taught to be assertive and take credit for their personal achievements. It appears that individualistic cultures tend to use low-context communication, while high-context communication tends to predominate in collectivistic cultures. Thus, whereas members of low-context communication cultures interact in a direct way with each other, members of high-context communication cultures interact indirectly. For example, North Americans tend to speak directly on an issue, whereas individuals from Japan, Korea, and China prefer to avoid confrontation, to preserve a sense of harmony, and to make it possible for the individuals with whom they are speaking to save face, or maintain self-esteem. Similarly, rarely will one Saudi Arabian publicly criticize another; to do so would label the individual as disloyal and disrespectful.[27] When persons from diverse power-distance cultures interact, unless these differences in orientation are acknowledged, interactions may well result in misunderstandings.

THE COST OF CULTURAL IGNORANCE

Communicators who fail to realize that persons from different cultures may not look, think, or act as they themselves do run the risk of having those with whom they interact judge them to be insensitive, ignorant, or **culturally confused.** The culturally confused pay a high price. Cultural misunderstandings often lead to lost opportunities and increased levels of tension between people. The following examples demonstrate the extent to which cultural ignorance affects communication:

- Showing the sole of a shoe means nothing to observers in the United States or Europe. As a result, when visiting Saudi Arabia, the American and European

---

low-power-distance cultures
cultures that believe that power should be used only when legitimate

masculine cultures
cultures that value aggressiveness, strength, and material symbols of success

feminine cultures
cultures that value tenderness and relationships

What assumptions do the following proverbs lead you to make about the identified culture's members? How can understanding the proverbs a culture embraces help enhance communication with that culture's members?

God helps those who help themselves.

The squeaky wheel gets the grease.
— *(American)*

When spiderwebs unite, they can trap a lion.

It takes a whole village to raise a child.
— *(African)*

No need to know the person, only the family.
— *(Chinese)*

It's the nail that sticks out that is hammered.
— *(Japanese)*

culturally confused
lacking an understanding of cultural difference

delegates to a conference thought nothing about crossing their legs and pointing their shoes toward the speaker while listening to his presentation. The speaker, however, was horrified. In Muslim cultures, the gesture is perceived as insulting.[28] Similarly, while crossing your legs in the United States indicates you are relaxed, in Korea it is a social faux pas.

- John, who represented the interests of an American multinational corporation, and Yu-Chen, his Taiwanese counterpart, had difficulty establishing a working relationship. John's eyeblink rate increased as he became more and more nervous, fearing that his efforts to resolve their misunderstanding had reached an impasse. This only made things worse. Blinking while another person talks is considered normal to North Americans; to Taiwanese it is considered impolite.[29]

- McDonald's fast-food chain unintentionally offended thousands of Muslims when it printed an excerpt from the Koran on its throwaway hamburger bags.[30] Muslims saw this as sacrilegious. The mistake could have been avoided if McDonald's had displayed greater sensitivity and awareness.

- The Japanese view the business card as an extension of a person, while Americans view it as a business formality and a convenience. Consequently, while the Japanese handle business cards with great care, making certain to put them in safe places, Americans are quick to put them away and thus often end up insulting the Japanese.[31]

- Arabs typically adopt a direct body orientation when communicating. Americans employ a stance that is somewhat less direct and thus often find the communication of Arabs aggressive and unnerving. Arabs and South Americans also tend to gesture vigorously when speaking to others, causing the less physical Americans to construe their behavior as inappropriate and unmannerly. It is common in Middle Eastern cultures for both males and females to physically exaggerate responses, while in the United States emotions are more likely to be suppressed. In Japan, individuals may try to hide or mask certain emotions. It is common among Asian cultures to exhibit reserve and emotional restraint.

- Eye contact preferences also differ across cultures. Americans place a high value on eye-to-eye communication and tend to distrust those who fail to look at them directly. The Japanese, in contrast, believe eye contact over a sustained period of time shows disrespect. Among Asian cultures, too much eye contact is deemed intrusive. Arabs, on the other hand, maintain direct eye contact with those they interact with for prolonged periods.

- Americans tend to value personal achievement and individualism. In contrast, Asian and Native American cultures stress group cohesion and loyalty, placing greater emphasis on group rather than individual achievement.

Failing to develop insights into cultural nuances and differences can be costly. Recognizing and responding to differences among cultures allows for more meaningful relationships. At the same time, we need to be mindful that not everyone from a particular culture exhibits the same characteristics and communication traits.

Being unaware of how others outside a culture view that culture's members can also be costly: Communication researchers Melvin and Margaret DeFleur surveyed

Work It Out

In Japan, the word for "different" is the same as the word for "wrong." Compare and contrast a culture in which the goal is to become as much like others as possible with a culture in which the goal is to distinguish oneself from others. Which cultural attitude are you most comfortable with?

Imagine you are given the task to create a metaphor for the United States, one that accurately describes the way immigrants are assimilated into U.S. society. How do you think your parents would depict this situation? Why might a person not identify fully with members of his or her own culture until becoming an immigrant in another country?

How do you adapt when in the company of people who are more at home with an alternative cultural convention?

Work It Out

Research and supply examples of how a failure to understand the customs or language of persons from a different country and culture contributed to a communication breakdown or embarrassed one of the parties.

Describe a cultural misunderstanding in which you or someone you know was involved. Was it resolved?

Ethics and Communication

Through Others' Eyes

Imagine you arrive in the United States from a foreign country. Though perhaps unlikely, also imagine that you are totally unfamiliar with what life in the U.S. is like and totally unknowledgeable when it comes to American pop culture. In fact, you have never viewed American television, watched American films, or listened to American CDs. You do, however, read English fluently. You find a current issue of *TV Guide* and start reading it. Based on your perusal of prime-time programming, what characteristics would you attribute to Americans? How many of your listed characteristics would you consider positive? Negative?

If asked to summarize your discoveries, what conclusions would you draw about what Americans value? What subjects would you identify as of great interest to them? How would you assess their attitudes toward persons from other cultures? Finally, what suggestions would you like to offer them?

Do you believe any of the following cultural practices are unethical?

- *cockfighting*
- *the withholding of medical intervention, such as a blood transfusion*
- *female circumcision*
- *the stoning of a rape victim*

If you answer yes to any, explain why. If you answer no to any, explain why not. To what extent do your answers support or negate the belief that every culture has a right to its own customs and beliefs?

cultural imperialism
the expansion of dominion of one culture over another culture

1,259 teenagers from twelve countries whose main contact with Americans was through popular culture including television programs and movies they watched and the music they listened to. Based on these vicarious experiences, in their judgment, Americans were violent, materialistic, sexually loose, disrespectful of people unlike them, unconcerned about the poor, and prone to criminal activity. The DeFleurs concluded that the exporting of American commercialized popular culture contributes to cultural imperialism and helps foster feelings of anti-Americanism.[32]

If imperialism is the expansion of dominion of one country over another country, then **cultural imperialism** is the expansion of dominion of one culture over another culture. Cultural imperialism's critics assert that the news, entertainment, and products of an industrialized country such as the United States overwhelm the national cultures of other countries. They contend that our ethnocentricity leads us to promote our way of life as superior.

There are signs, however, that the reign of American pop culture is beginning to erode. Foreign film successes such as Stephen Chow's *Kung Fu Hustle*, Zhang Yimou's *House of Flying Daggers*, and Ang Lee's *Crouching Tiger, Hidden Dragon* have been successes in the United States. U.S. music charts also regularly feature vocalists from other countries who speak in Spanish or another language, and foreign news services such as Al Jazeera and the BBC are influencing news coverage. Cross-fertilization of ideas inevitably leads to more diversity. Increasingly, we are finding ourselves exposed to mediated and real-life situations involving persons culturally different from ourselves. This exposure contributes to our learning about ourselves and diverse others. According to researchers, the effectiveness of the United States in the global arena depends on our ability to communicate competently with people from other cultures.[33]

IDENTIFYING INFLUENCES ON CULTURAL IDENTITY

We all belong to a number of groups, including those defined by gender, age, racial and ethnic, religious, socioeconomic, and national identities. Our cultural identity is based on these group memberships.

How we define *gender roles*, for example, affects the way males and females present themselves, socialize, work, perceive their futures, and communicate. U.S. men tend to adopt a problem-solving orientation, while women tend to be relationship oriented.[34] We also have ideas regarding the meaning and significance of *age*, including how persons our age should look and behave. In the United States, large numbers of people place great value on looking youthful and appearing to be younger than they are. In contrast, in Muslim, Asian, and Latin American cultures, people respect, rather than deny, aging. Our *racial and ethnic identities* are similarly socially constructed. Some racial and ethnic groups, for example, share experiences of oppression. Their attitudes and behaviors may reflect their struggles, influencing their attitudes toward contemporary issues such as affirmative action. *Religious identity* is at the root of countless contemporary conflicts occurring in the Middle East, India, and Pakistan. Similarly, *socioeconomic identity* frames how we respond to issues of our day. The significant gap between the ultrawealthy and the middle and working classes in the United States is contributing to their developing different attitudes on a wide array of issues. *National identity* refers to our legal status or citizenship. People from different countries have been U.S. citizens for generations, yet some still perceive them as foreigners. Do you?

In addition to recognizing how gender, racial and ethnic, religious, socioeconomic, and national differences affect cultural identity, we also need to acknowledge the role generational differences play in our communication with one another. Demographers usually classify people into four generations: matures, boomers, gen X, and gen Y. Called "the greatest generation," matures were born between 1900 and 1945. World War II and the Cold War were two of their key defining experiences. Matures are known for respecting authority, following the rules, being loyal

Media Wise

The Cultural Storyteller

What stories about other cultures do film and television tell? Over the years, media producers have delivered a mixed message, both using and removing stereotypes from films and television programs. Disney, for example, changed the voice of the original Big Bad Wolf in the *Three Little Pigs* from having a heavy Jewish accent to a falsetto. Similarly, writers revised the lyrics to the opening song in *Aladdin* after complaints by the American-Arab Anti-Discrimination Committee. In the film, however, both Jasmine and her father, though Arabian, speak unaccented, standard American English, while the speech of the "Arabic bad guys" includes foreign accents. How might associating a foreign accent with being evil affect viewers? Like Arabs, who often are presented as sheiks or terrorists, threatening or cunning, Latinos also have been stereotyped in media. Too often, the parts Latinos play are demeaning and reminiscent of pre-civil-rights-era portrayals of African Americans. Latinos are often cast as the criminal, the maid, the crime victim, the harlot, or the male or female buffoon. Imagine seeing yourself portrayed as a victim, or as subservient to the dominant Anglo society. How might such a portrayal affect your perception of yourself and the options you have? How might they affect your view of your culture?

Both film and television are agents of norms and values. What stories are television and film currently telling? To answer this question, watch a week's worth of prime-time programming on a particular station or view a week's worth of highly ranked DVDs. Count the number of characters in each program or DVD that are from another culture. What did you learn from each character about his or her culture? In your opinion, were cultural stereotypes used to develop each of these characters? If so, describe them. To what extent, if any, did what you view reinforce or alter your existing attitudes toward members of that culture? What emotional reactions, if any, did each character trigger in you? Would you say that the shows or DVDs contributed to your having predominantly positive or negative attitudes toward the members of another culture? Finally, using one or two words, identify the key value of each viewed show or DVD. For example, the message of one show or DVD might focus on materialism, the message of another on force and violence.

to their employing organizations, and respecting timeliness. Boomers, born between 1946 and 1964, came of age during the space race, the civil rights movement, Vietnam, and Watergate. They are famous for questioning authority, displaying a "can-do" attitude, and focusing on how to get their way. The first TV generation, boomers actually had to get off the couch to change channels. Gen Xers, who were born between 1965 and 1982, saw traditional gender roles bend and flex. The Web emerged during their formative years. They are known for seeking a work-life balance, and being loyal to people, not organizations. Gen Y members, born after 1982, are referred to as the millennial generation or digital natives. They are known for being technologically savvy (they podcast, send text messages, blog, and seek a second life). They also have exceedingly high expectations, are proficient multitaskers, and are interested in "whatever they're interested in." They are apt to spend more time with the Internet and media than they do face-to-face with others. One out of three gen Y members is a minority.

TECHNOLOGY AND INTERCULTURAL COMMUNICATION

The Internet permeates national boundaries and erodes the connection between location and experience. It enables us to interact more easily with people who have different worldviews than we do.[35]

Technology and computer networks are also changing the traditional definition of a community. When we speak of a communication community today, no longer are we limited to real neighborhoods. Our concept of community has widened. **Virtual neighborhoods and communities** such as Second Life now also populate the communication landscape. Second Life is a virtual world, a social networking site in which users create avatars—alternative selves or images of characters they use to travel around and interact with other users. Why are people seeking a second life? Perhaps the neighborhoods in which they live are not delivering the person-to-person contact they seek. Seeking surrogate neighborhoods and relationships, millions of people communicate online. However, some critics contend that, rather than

virtual neighborhoods and communities

online, surrogate communities

In your opinion, to what extent, if any, does participating in a virtual neighborhood or community increase opportunities for learning about diverse cultures?

bringing us together, computer networks are isolating us. What online communities are missing, they assert, is the essence of a real neighborhood, including a sense of location and a feeling of permanence and belonging. Critics also believe that the culture of computing, especially when it comes to the Internet's newsgroups, attracts extreme political positions and contributes to long-standing international conflicts. Advocates, in contrast, assert that it facilitates international dialogue.[36]

Being able to reach so many different people who live in so many different places so quickly gives a new sense of communication power. Wherever we live, we can use the Internet to help bring diversity and new cultures into our lives. Over time, the Internet may change our social and business lives. Through it, we may meet a wider array of people. Sites such as MySpace and Facebook introduce us to new friends and contacts as well as reacquaint us with old friends. The question is whether we will commit ourselves emotionally to our online relationships and alliances or keep them superficial? What kinds of relationships will we develop by meeting online with diverse individuals in distant lands without actually meeting them? Will all voices really be heard? Will we be more or less tolerant of each other? Will we be aware that words posted to global online groups have consequences, just as they do when delivered in person?

We also need to face the fact that, in some places, technology is considered an evil and governments censor the Web in the effort to control what their people see on the Internet. For example, a court order in Turkey blocked people in the country from accessing YouTube after clips were posted on the site that the government believed insulted the memory of that nation's founder. Turkish visitors to the site saw a message in Turkish and English reading, "Access to www.youtube.com site has been suspended. . . ."[37] Despite this and the fact that some bloggers in countries such as Iran are required to register their sites, the numbers of people going online continues to grow.

Increased access to the Internet provided via libraries and schools is helping to shrink the **digital divide** (information gap) in this country. More minorities, elderly, and poor people now go online, democratizing access and decreasing the chances of what some civil rights leaders worried would be a *technological apartheid*. However, gaining access to computers remains a problem in many places around the world because of the lack of or the unreliability of electricity or because of high poverty levels. Reaching and wiring all the world's people is a mammoth challenge. The Internet, however, is one key to preserving the world's languages and cultures.

digital divide
information gap

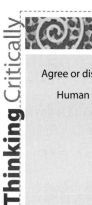

Thinking Critically

Reflect and Respond

Agree or disagree with the following statement; supply reasons and examples that support your position.

Human beings draw close to one another by their common nature, but habits and customs keep them apart.

—*Confucius*

COMMUNICATION SKILLS IN PRACTICE

GUIDELINES FOR IMPROVING YOUR ABILITY TO COMMUNICATE INTERCULTURALLY

Having the desire to relate more effectively with persons of different cultures is critical to improving your ability to communicate interculturally. Also important is limiting your reliance on stereotypes that can diminish your success when you interact with others. In addition, you need to be able to reduce your uncertainty levels regarding the persons of different cultures with whom you communicate. Since you do not necessarily share the same communication rules, the degree of ambiguity you feel when interacting with them increases as your ability to predict their responses decreases. The following guidelines should help you increase your tolerance for ambiguity, enhance your ability to handle new situations, and better prepare yourself to meet the communication challenges of today and tomorrow:

☑ Refrain from Formulating Expectations Based Solely on Your Own Culture

When those you interact with have diverse communication styles, it is critical that you acknowledge the differences and accept their validity. By not isolating yourself within your own group or culture, you allow yourself to be more fully a part of a multicultural society and thus a better communicator.

☑ Recognize How Faulty Education Can Impede Understanding

It is important to identify and work to eliminate any personal biases and prejudices you have developed over the years. Determine, for example, the extent to which your family and friends have influenced your feelings about persons from other cultural groups. Do those you have grown up with appear comfortable or uncomfortable relating to persons of different cultural origins? To what extent have their attitudes affected your intercultural communication competence?

☑ Make a Commitment to Develop Communication Skills and Abilities Appropriate to Life in a Multicultural World

While culture is a tie that binds, the creation of the global village makes it essential that you leave the comfort of your cultural niche, become more knowledgeable of other cultures, and strive to be culturally aware.

It is important to familiarize yourself with the communication rules and preferences of members of different cultures so that you can increase the effectiveness of your communication encounters. Your ability to develop intercultural communication skills depends in large part on how many of the following promises you are willing to make:

I will make a commitment to seek information from persons whose cultures are different from my own.

I will try to understand how the experiences of persons from different cultures leads them to develop perspectives that differ from mine.

I will pay attention to the situation and the context when I communicate with persons from different cultures.

I will make every effort to become a more flexible communicator.

I will not insist that persons from other cultures communicate with me on my terms.

Intercultural communication will become increasingly important in the coming years. We hope you feel better prepared to meet your future.

Revisiting Chapter Objectives

1. **Define *intercultural communication*.** Intercultural communication is the process of interpreting and sharing meanings with individuals from different cultures.

2. **Compare and contrast culture and co-culture, ethnocentrism and cultural relativism, melting-pot philosophy and cultural pluralism.** A culture is a system of knowledge, beliefs, values, customs, behaviors, and artifacts that are acquired, shared, and used by members. A co-culture is a group of persons who differ in some ethnic or sociological way from the parent culture. Ethnocentrism is the tendency to see one's own culture as superior to all others. Cultural relativism is the acceptance of other cultural groups as equal in value to one's own. The melting-pot philosophy advocates the assimilation of different cultures into the dominant culture. Cultural pluralism acknowledges that other cultural groups are equal in value to one's own.

3. **Compare and contrast the following: individualism and collectivism, high-context communication cultures and low-context communication cultures, high-power-distance cultures and low-power-distance cultures, and masculine and feminine cultures.** Individualistic cultures stress individual goals. Collectivistic cultures stress group goals. High-context communication cultures are tradition-bound, valuing indirectness. Low-context communication cultures encourage directness in communication. High-power-distance cultures view power as a fact of life with subordinates deferring to superiors. Low-power-distance cultures believe power should only be used if legitimate. Masculine cultures value aggressiveness, strength, and material success. Feminine cultures value relationships, tenderness, and a high quality of life.

4. **Identify the various groups that influence our cultural identity.** Among the groups that influence cultural identity, and on which cultural identity is based, are those defined by gender, age, racial and ethnic, religious, socioeconomic, national, and generational identities.

5. **Discuss how technology is bringing diversity into our lives.** For many of us, the Internet facilitates this task. Enabling us to join a wide range of online communities and interact with people who have different worldviews, the Internet enhances our ability to bring diversity and culture into our lives.

6. **Identify techniques you can use to reduce the strangeness of strangers.** Although the lessons taught by culture influence our communication style

THE WRAP-UP

THE WRAP-UP

preferences, there are techniques we can use to reduce the strangeness of strangers, adding to the storehouse of knowledge that underscores our communication competence and, as a result, increasing our ability to handle the communication challenges of today and tomorrow.

Resources for Further Inquiry and Reflection

To apply your understanding of how the principles in Chapter 2 are at work in our daily lives, consult the following resources for further inquiry and reflection. Or, if you prefer, choose any other appropriate resource. Then connect the ideas expressed in your chosen selection with the communication concepts and issues you are learning about both in and out of class.

 Listen to Me

"Square Dance" (Eminem)
"Born in the U.S.A." (Bruce Springsteen)
"Land Down Under" (Men at Work)
"My Woman from Tokyo" (Deep Purple)
"Colors of the Wind" (Vanessa Williams)
"Al Otro Lado del Rio" (Antonio Banderas)
"Imagine" (John Lennon)
"War" (Bob Marley)
"American Idiot" (Green Day)

What do the views of the song's speaker or speakers suggest about the ability they have to meet diversity's challenges?

 View Me

Borat	Dances with Wolves
Bend It Like Beckham	The Joy Luck Club
Boys Don't Cry	Brüno
Mississippi Burning	Milk
Gran Torino	American History X
The Terminal	Remember the Titans

How does culture influence the interaction of the characters in the film? What lessons about the effects of culture can be taught through the film?

 Read Me

Thomas L. Friedman. *The World Is Flat: A Brief History of the Twenty-First Century.* New York: Farrar, Straus, & Groux, 2005.
Harper Lee. *To Kill a Mockingbird.* Philadelphia: Lippincott, 1960.
Wen Ho Lee. *My Country versus Me: The First-Hand Account by the Los Alamos Scientist Who Was Falsely Accused.* New York: Hyperion, 2002.
Khaled Hosseini. *The Kite Runner.* New York: Riverhead, 2003.
Khaled Hosseini. *A Thousand Splendid Suns.* New York: Riverhead, 2007.
Sherman Alexie. *Reservation Blues.* New York: Atlantic Monthly, 1995.
Eric Weiner. *Geography of Bliss: One Grump's Search for the Happiest Places in the World.* New York: Twelve, 2008.

Discuss how age, gender, ethnic affiliation, family ties, education, beliefs and religion, and/or nationality influence and shape attitudes.

 Tell Me

Share with the class the insights you gained from your chosen Listen to Me, View Me, or Read Me selection.

Choose a side and discuss the arguments for or against using English as a universal language.

Key Chapter Terminology

Use the Online Learning Center at www.mhhe.com/gamble10e to further your knowledge of the following terminology.

www.mhhe.com/gamble10e

accommodation 26

assimilation 26

co-cultures 26

collectivistic cultures 30

cultural imperialism 34

cultural pluralism 29

cultural relativism 28

culturally confused 32

culture 25

digital divide 37

diversity 23

ethnocentrism 27

feminine cultures 32

globalization 23

glocalization 23

high-context communication 31

high-power-distance cultures 31

individualistic cultures 30

intercultural communication 25

interethnic communication 25

international communication 25

interracial communication 25

intracultural communication 25

low-context communication 31

low-power-distance cultures 32

masculine cultures 32

melting-pot philosophy 29

multiculturalists 24

prejudice 28

separation 26

stereotypes 28

virtual neighborhoods and
   communities 36

Idioms in Translation

get connected — communicate digitally or via the Internet

save face — maintain self-esteem

storehouse of knowledge — information

Culture Cue

In Arabic cultures and other cultures with collectivist mindsets, the individual is subordinate to the collective. In the United States, the individual is still paramount.

Test Your Understanding

Go to the *Self Quizzes* on the book's Online Learning Center at www.mhhe.com/gamble10e.

www.mhhe.com/gamble10e

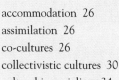

CHAPTER 3

After finishing this chapter, you should be able to

1. Define *self-concept*.

2. Explain the nature of the self-concept.

3. Identify how different factors, including the self-fulfilling prophecy, popular culture, gender, and culture influence self-concept formation and behavior.

4. Discuss the relationships among the Johari window, impression management, and self-awareness.

5. Explore the relationship between technology and the self-concept.

6. Identify guidelines for improving self-awareness and understanding.

Communication and the Self-Concept: Who Are You?

Shows like *American Idol, So You Think You Can Dance,* and *America's Got Talent* present people who believe they can sing, dance, or do something special. The individuals who appear tell themselves they have what it takes "to make it." Do you think you're good enough to be on such shows? Whether you are in the classroom, the board room, or your home, you carry your self-concept with you. As you interact with others, your self-concept affects the relationships you develop, even influencing whether you develop lasting relationships at all. Do you talk to yourself? Of course you do! Who am I? is a question you likely ask yourself often. Intrapersonal communication, as we learned in Chapter 1, is thinking, or self-talk; it is the communicating we do with ourselves, the basis for all other communication, and communication's most important element. How we see and talk to ourselves today is a result of all our communication experiences. It also expresses our relationship with ourselves. What words would you use to describe the relationship you have with yourself? Do the words you chose suggest that you feel good about yourself? If so, to what do you attribute your feeling good about yourself? If you do not feel good about yourself, what is it that keeps you from doing so? Let's find out.

> There are three things extremely hard, Steel, a Diamond, and to know one's self.
> —*Benjamin Franklin*

> . . . the self is not something that one finds. It is something that one creates.
> —*Thomas Szasz*

WHAT IS THE SELF-CONCEPT?

How we communicate with ourselves and how others communicate with us builds in us a sense of self. Our sense of self evolves as we interact with different people, find ourselves in new situations, and form new relationships. It is important that you spend some time considering who you are and what you intend to do with the rest of your life. The question, Who am I? is a serious one. How you answer it is extremely significant, since who you think you are to a large extent determines what you choose to do, how you choose to act, whom you choose to communicate with, and even whether you desire to communicate. If someone were to ask you on 10 separate occasions, "Who are you?"—and if each time you had to supply a different answer—what types of responses would you offer? Would you be able to group your responses into categories? For example, you might see yourself in reference to your sex (male or female), your gender (masculine or feminine), your religion (Buddhist, Jewish, Muslim, Christian), your race (African, Hispanic, Caucasian, Asian), your nationality (U.S. citizen, Turkish, German), your physical attributes (fat, thin), your roles (wife, son, student, employee), your attitudes and emotions (hopeful, pessimistic, personable), your mental abilities (smart, slow), and your talents (musically or artistically gifted). The words you use to describe yourself reveal both to yourself and to others what you think you are like.

"I don't want to be defined by who I am."

How do you explain the cartoon character's dilemma? Why might the character not want to be defined in this way?

self-awareness

the ability to reflect on and monitor one's own behavior

self-concept

everything one thinks and feels about oneself

self-image

the sort of person one perceives oneself to be

self-esteem

how well one likes and values oneself

Work It Out

In your opinion, is it society's role to help raise your self-esteem? Provide reasons in support of your position.

The self is a social product—a composite of who we think we are, who other people think we are, and who we think others think we are. Some of us are more self-aware than others; this developed **self-awareness** (the ability to reflect on and monitor one's own behavior) facilitates a fuller understanding of the self, including the attitudes, beliefs, and values we hold as well as the strengths and weaknesses we have.[1]

How we think about ourselves, the **self-concept** (your self-identity—your perceived self—the rather consistent and organized image you form of yourself) is composed of two parts—self-image and self-esteem. **Self-image** is your mental picture of yourself; it is the kind of person you perceive yourself to be. Self-image includes the roles you see yourself performing, the categories you place yourself within, the words you use to describe or identify yourself, and your understanding of how others see you. **Self-esteem,** on the other hand, is your self-assessment; it is your evaluation of your ability and worth and indicates how well you like and value yourself. Self-esteem usually derives from your successes and failures and colors your self-image with a predominantly positive or negative hue. According to researcher Chris Mruk, self-esteem has five dimensions, which affect your feelings about yourself and your communication with others:

- competence (your beliefs about your ability to be effective)
- worthiness (your beliefs about the degree to which others value you)
- cognition (your beliefs about your character and personality)
- affect (how you evaluate yourself and the feelings generated by your evaluation)
- stability or change[2]

Our self-concepts significantly affect our behavior, including what we think is possible. How the self-concept affects communication is the focus of the remainder of this chapter.

EXPLORING THE SELF-CONCEPT AND BEHAVIOR CONNECTION

Self-concept concerns us all. One sports coach, for example, notes, "If I single some out for praise, I would kill the others' self-esteem." One person praises another for a job that wasn't very well done, observing that "I didn't want to hurt his self-esteem."[3] Some school systems even believe that the promotion of self-esteem should be a central goal of education.[4] Others challenge the merit of a

Ethics and Communication

Self-Concern and Concern for Others

In her book *The New Peoplemaking,* Virginia Satir notes:

> Every person has a feeling of worth, positive or negative; the question is, Which is it?
>
> Every person communicates; the question is, How, and what happens as a result?
>
> Every person follows rules; the question is, What kind, and how well do they work for her or him?

Every person is linked to society; the question is, In what way, and what are the results?[5]

How would you answer each of these questions with regard to yourself? Your parents? Your friends? The people you work with? What does each set of answers reveal about self-concern and concern for others? How is this an ethical issue?

"feel-good curriculum" and disdain the fact that we walk around on eggshells to avoid hurting another person's self-esteem.[6] Why is self-esteem considered so critical? What impact does it have?

Some believe that an overemphasis on reinforcing self-esteem, especially in persons whose self-esteem is already high, has precipitated bullying in some segments of our culture. Why do people tease or bully others? What motivates one person to want to belittle another person? What is bullying? Who is a bully? Bullying is persistent teasing, name-calling, or social exclusion. Too often a bully is likely to be among the most popular people, admired by others, and high among those persons others want to "hang" with.[7] Some researchers say the behavior of a person who bullies can be attributed to a self-appraisal that is unrealistically inflated.[8] A prime contributor to aggression in person-to-person interaction appears to be unusually high self-esteem combined with a sense of arrogance and narcissistic tendencies.[9] Consider the adulation in our society that is accorded our icons of popular culture, including professional athletes, and music and movie stars. Our behavior helps precipitate the self-centered, egomaniacal characteristics they too often exhibit. Balance is needed in how much praise we give people, lest we help create in them a perception of their own self-importance that is out of whack with reality.

People with very low self-esteem define themselves primarily by their limitations and tend to be negative about a lot of things. In

> Who in your opinion has better self-esteem, males or females?

> Have you ever been teased or bullied? How did it affect your sense of self?

Our self-concept is shaped by our experiences.

Describe Yourself

Is it possible to define yourself in just a single word? Try it.

Generally, respondents resist labeling themselves as members of a special interest group or easily identifiable minority group.

For example, in a *New York Times*/CBS News poll none of the 97 Black respondents said "Black," and none of the 967 Whites said that being White was the defining fact of their lives. Instead, the word given most often in the survey was *American*.

For those who answered, it was certainly a challenge. "You cannot reduce yourself to one word. It is too compli-

cated," said Suzanne Keller, a sociologist at Princeton University. "People really feel multiple. They have multiple poses and attitudes and roles and one is no more important than the next."

Author Margaret Atwood seemed to feel the same way when asked to define herself in one word. She picked *indescribable*, warning that "one must always resist the tyranny of adjectives."

Now ask 10 people to describe themselves in one word. How do their responses compare with the ones in the study?

---

comparison, people with high self-esteem tend to be significantly happier than their low–self-esteem counterparts.[10] If their self-esteem is undeservedly high, they also are likely to ignore their own weaknesses. People in this category suffer from an inflated sense of their worth, displaying an inappropriate overconfidence in their abilities. This may be because they were overpraised by those around them and told that they did "a great job" whether that was true or not. These people are unprepared for the criticism of supervisors; they quickly fall apart if told that they are wrong or lacking in some ability.[11] People in both the extremely high and extremely low self-esteem groups also have something in common: They tend to be self-absorbed. In contrast, people with healthy self-esteem do not have an inflated sense of their abilities and are not awash in "unwarranted self-regard."[12] Instead, they are in touch with both their strengths and their weaknesses, and are able to tolerate feelings of frustration. Expecting a positive outcome, they persist when at first they fail. They are both confident and resilient, traits necessary for success.[13] Researchers now believe that high self-esteem, rather than causing good performance, is its result. According to J. D. Hawkins, president of the National Self-Esteem Association (NSEA), "self-esteem is more than just feeling good about yourself. It's about being socially and individually responsible."[14]

HOW IS YOUR SELF-CONCEPT FORMED?

How did your self-concept develop? The day you recognized yourself as separate from your surroundings, life began to change as you strove to fit into the world as you saw it. Your concept of self—that relatively stable set of perceptions you attribute to yourself—became your most important possession.

While you are not born with a self-concept, you certainly do play a key role in building one.[15] Even though you are constantly undergoing change, once built, the theory or picture you have of yourself is fairly stable and difficult to alter. For example, have you ever tried to revise your parents' or friends' opinions about themselves? Did you have much luck? Our opinions about ourselves grow more and more resistant to change as we become older and presumably wiser. The statements we make are more or less accurate maps of the territory that is ourselves, but some of us map ourselves better than others do—that is, some of us have a

---

Work It Out

Define and devise suggestions for handling the problem of bullying.

In your opinion, is self-control more important than self-esteem?

Part of knowing who we are is knowing we are not someone else.
—Arthur Miller,
Incident at Vichy

Of all the people in your life, who has had the most influence on the development of your self-concept?

more accurate mental picture of our personal strengths, weaknesses, and needs than others do.[16]

A number of forces converge to help create your self-concept. Among them are the image that other people have of you, which helps guide the way they relate to you; the way you experience and evaluate yourself; the roles you perform; the media messages you absorb; the expectations you and others have for you; and the gender, cultural, and technological messages you internalize.

To a large extent, your self-concept is shaped by your environment and by the people around you, including your parents, relatives, teachers, supervisors, friends, and co-workers. If people who are important to you have a good image of you, they probably make you feel accepted, valued, worthwhile, lovable, and significant, and you are likely to develop a positive self-concept as a result. On the other hand, if those who are important to you have a poor image of you, more than likely they make you feel left out, small, worthless, unloved, or insignificant, and you probably develop a negative self-concept as a consequence.

It is not difficult to see how people you value influence the picture you have of yourself and help determine the ways you behave. Nineteenth-century poet Walt Whitman recognized this:

> There was a child went forth every day,
> And the first object he look'd upon, that object he became,
> And that object became part of him for the day or a certain part of the day,
> Or for many years or stretching cycles of years.

Roles, Self-Evaluations, Behavior, and the Self-Concept

Self-concept, besides being your own theory of who and what you are, is a mental picture you have of yourself. This mental image is easily translated into the faces or masks you wear, the roles you play, and the ways you behave. If you feel you have little worth, you probably expect to be taken advantage of. When you expect the worst, you usually get the worst. Similarly, if you feel you have significant worth, you probably expect to be treated fairly, supported, and otherwise held in esteem by others. When you expect to succeed, you usually find success.

The nature of the self at any given moment is a composite of all the factors that interact in a particular environment. Thus, how you look at yourself is affected by how you look at other people, how other people actually look at you, and how you imagine or perceive that other people look at you. We might say that self-concept is derived from experience and projected into future behavior. Of course, your self-concept may be realistic or unrealistic. Unfortunately, we never really come to know all there is to know about ourselves, so we keep searching for clues.

The language we use, the attitudes we display, and the appearances we present also change as we vary the masks we wear and the roles we perform. We become different selves as we move from one set of conditions to another. The more we attempt to be ourselves, the more selves we find. Conditions and circumstances affect the nature of the self.

Developmental psychologist Jean Piaget notes that the construction of the self occurs as a person acts on his or her environment and figures out what he or she can and cannot do.[17]

Work It Out

Devise a list of activities that you believe are instrumental in shaping self-concept.

Work It Out

Imagine how your self-concept will change as you age. In your opinion, will it become more or less positive? What do you believe will account for the change?

How do your employer and your friends picture you?

Pessimism is self-fulfilling. Pessimists don't persist in the face of challenges, and therefore fail more frequently—even when success is attainable.
—Martin P. Seligman

Ethics and Communication

Age, Physical Challenges, and Self-Esteem

We live in both an age-conscious (people classify us and treat us certain ways because of how old or young we appear to be) and an age-obsessed society (because of ageism, large numbers of people, with media encouragement, fixate on looking and acting youthful). Because youth is revered in the United States, we use hair dyes and sometimes plastic surgery to attempt to look more youthful.

In some other societies, including China and Arab countries, age rather than youth is revered and respected. Thus, while a person in the United States might refer to an older citizen as "an old codger," in these cultures endearing, not deprecating, words are used to refer to older persons. The Chinese respect age. For example, the Chinese sent experienced scholars who were in their fifties and sixties to the United States in a cultural exchange program and expressed offense when the United States sent young adults to China in return.[18] In Arab cultures the belief about aging is expressed through this proverb: "A house without an elderly person is like an orchard without a well." Contrast this with the practice in the United States of "segregating the elderly from the rest of society" by encouraging them to live in retirement communities and nursing homes.[19] Unfortunately, large numbers of elderly people, prone to assimilating society's devalued appraisals, suffer from lower self-esteem."[20]

How do you feel about aging? What messages have you received from parents and older friends and relatives regarding their sense of self as they age? Do you agree with Ann E. Gerike, author of *Old Is Not a Four-Letter Word: A Midlife Guide,* that aging brings with it a more reliable inner voice, an acceptance that life is not always fair, and a willingness to shoulder responsibility instead of blaming others for what happens? Or, in your world, does youth rule?[21] What messages do you send older people with whom you relate regarding your estimations of their worth and abilities?

Just as we stereotype the aged, we also are prone to stereotyping people with disabilities. Because we tend to categorize people on the basis of physical appearance, we predict more negative outcomes when relating to people we perceive as disabled and whom we believe to be more dependent, unstable, and easily offended than the able bodied. The question is: are attitudes toward the disabled more disabling than the disability they have? Log on to AbilityOnline.org. Describe how sites such as this one can facilitate the strengthening of self-esteem by helping reduce the effect of a person's disability on his or her self-concept.

What steps do you think we should take to improve the effects that aging and disability have on self-concept?

Work It Out

Complete a chart that contains adjectives describing how you picture yourself in relation to those with whom you communicated yesterday. Explain what the chart reveals about your self-image. Who made you feel more positive or negative about yourself and why?

When it comes to thinking about the self and who we want to be today, some of us categorize ourselves as optimists. If we suffer a defeat, we view it as a temporary setback brought about by circumstances, bad luck, or other people. Optimists are resilient; they do not view defeat as their own fault. Psychologist Albert Bandura tells us that an optimistic belief in our own possibilities and competence endows us with feelings of **self-efficacy.** (Note: We are talking about optimism, not unrealistic optimism based on overconfidence.) When we have strong feelings of self-efficacy, we are more persistent, less anxious, and less depressed. We don't dwell on our inadequacy when something goes wrong; instead, we seek a solution. Those of us who are persistent are apt to accomplish more. As we do so, our belief in ourselves grows.[22] Some of us categorize ourselves as pessimists. Unlike optimists, pessimists lack resilience and believe that bad events are their own fault, will last, and will undermine whatever they do. Instead of believing they can control their own destiny, pessimists believe that outside forces determine their fate. In effect, they "can't because they think they can't," in contrast to optimists, who "can because they think they can." Psychologist Martin Seligman tells this story:

> We tested the swim team at the University of California at Berkeley to find out which swimmers were optimists and which were pessimists. To test the effects of attitude, we had the coach "defeat" each one: After a swimmer finished a heat, the coach told him his time—but it wasn't his real time. The coach had falsified it, making it significantly slower. The optimists responded by swimming their next heat faster; the pessimists went slower on their next heat.[23]

Clues to self-understanding come to you continually as you interact with others and with your real-world or online environments. To understand yourself, you need to be open to information that other people give you. Just as we tend to categorize ourselves and others, so others tend to categorize themselves and us. For better or worse, the categorization process is a basic part of interpersonal communication. We classify people according to their roles, their status, their material possessions, their personality traits, their physical and vocal qualities, and their skills and accomplishments. Which of these categories are most important to you? Which do you think are most important to the people who are significant in your life? How do others help shape your image of yourself? How do they enhance or belittle your sense of self?

Popular Media and Technology: Seeing Ourselves in the Electronic or Online Looking Glass

Thus far we have established that your self-image is made up partly of information and feelings drawn from past experiences and partly from your interactions with others. At least five other important sources affect your opinion of who you are: television, film, radio and music, the print media (especially advertisements), and the Internet. We are all influenced by media images, including the personalities and characters that populate the media, to a greater extent than we may realize. Subtly but effectively, these visual and aural media shape our views of ourselves and our relationship to our world. For example, Fred Rogers, the personality behind the children's television program *Mr. Rogers' Neighborhood*, repeatedly reminded his young viewers (Were you one of them?), "You've made this day a special day just by being you. You are the only person like you in this whole world. And people can like you just because you're you." Similarly, advertisements help convince us that we're the most important person in the world. Is helping individuals think the most about themselves, whether or not they've accomplished anything, a good thing? Could it be

self-efficacy
an optimistic belief in one's own competence

> According to the psychologist Martin P. Seligman, pessimists can learn to be optimists. How do you think optimism would enhance the self-concept? Describe how you handle defeat.

> Are you the person you think you are, the person someone else thinks you are, or the person you think someone else thinks you are? Why?

HOW TO TELL IT'S GOING TO BE A LOW SELF-ESTEEM DAY...

Work It Out

What cultural values does advertising convey? Who is highlighted in the ads? How many ads focus on how people look and the lifestyles they have? Are there differences between the advertising messages aimed at women and those aimed at men? Are the messages different for members of cultural groups different from the one to which you belong?

Work It Out

If you could trade places with any television or film star or character, who would you be? What does this person, real or fictional, "do" for you? Do you have a more positive image of this person than you have of yourself? Why? Would you like to be more like the media image, or would you like the image to be more like you?

dangerous for individuals to possess so much "unalloyed self-regard" that they become "black holes of self-esteem"?[24]

Let's continue by considering how popular media and the experience of growing up digitally affect your picture of yourself. First, many media and Internet offerings expose us to a standard of living few of us can expect to achieve. Thus, our evaluation of ourselves as providers—or even as successful—may be seriously colored by what we see. Shows like *My Super Sweet 16, Nip/Tuck, America's Next Top Model, Make Me a Supermodel,* and *Bridezillas* feature and encourage egocentricity, fueling extremely high self-expectations that prove unattainable for most.[25] Second, media and online offerings may affect the ways parents and children perceive themselves and each other. After all, both parents and children are exposed to a steady succession of media counterparts who appear either so perfect that even their mistakes become the raw material of a closer relationship or so absurd that their foibles can only constitute charming comedy. Third, the visual media fill our need for a bigger, better, smarter, prettier, stronger personal image. When we were younger, it was easy and fun to try on television and film images. For example, we could become Harry Potter, a Power Ranger, Iron Man, Daredevil, Lara Croft, a Hobbit, Triple X, or Xena. As we mature, however, this process becomes more subtle. As adolescents, we attempt to become like popular idols or heroes by imitating their fashions, adopting their speech mannerisms, and copying their movements and gestures. Thus, we communicate the picture we have of ourselves, or the picture we would like to have, through the way we dress, move, speak, and so on. When you put on a certain outfit, comb your hair in a new style, walk or speak in a particular way, or choose to wear a certain artifact, you are telling other people something about who you think you are, whom you would like to resemble, and how you would like to be treated. Fourth, today's teenagers and young adults are often smarter on cyber issues and have more digital expertise than those for whom they work or learn. You are users and creators of content, not just viewers or listeners, as were your parents. You have new, powerful tools for self-expression, including Facebook, MySpace, and YouTube. Members of generations X and Y do not appear to have the same filters for censoring or limiting the release of personal information that members of older generations have.[26] Instead, they are comfortable focusing on themselves, even if others see it as self-absorption.

Media Wise

My Media Life

1. Divide your life into three approximately equal stages. (For example, if you are 18 years old, your life would be divided into these segments: ages 1 to 6, ages 7 to 12, and ages 13 to 18. If you are 24, it would be divided into these segments: ages 1 to 8, ages 9 to 16, and ages 17 to 24.) From each life period, select a media offering (broadcast or online) that you believe exerted some influence on the way you thought and felt about yourself, your daily existence, or the people with whom you interacted. Give specific examples.

2. Compare and contrast the image you have of each of the following with the image portrayed in the broadcast or online media. Which image do you prefer and why?

a doctor	the police
a teacher	the poor
a family	Latinos
a teenager	the rich
marriage	business executives
the elderly	African Americans
gays and lesbians	Muslims

Media and online offerings can support us or deflate us. They can cause us to feel good, adequate, or inferior. For example, the way society perceives and the media depict the physically challenged affects their self-concept and the way persons without disabilities relate to them. People without disabilities stereotype the physically challenged as helpless so frequently that the physically challenged become motivated to serve as public educators in the effort to have others redefine their perceptions. Sometimes, they even refer to the nondisabled as "TABs" (temporarily able-bodied).[27] We are more alike than we commonly acknowledge.

Expectations: The Self-Fulfilling Prophecy and the Pygmalion Effect

Consider the following excerpt from *The People, Yes*, by poet Carl Sandburg:

> Drove up a newcomer in a covered wagon. "What kind of folks live around here?" "Well, stranger, what kind of folks was there in the country you come from?" "Well, they was mostly a lowdown, lying, gossiping, backbiting lot of people." "Well, I guess, stranger, that's about the kind of folks you'll find around here." And the dusty grey stranger had just about blended into the dusty grey cottonwoods in a clump on the horizon when another newcomer drove up. "What kind of folks live around here?" "Well, stranger, what kind of folks was there in the country you come from?" "Well, they was mostly a decent, hardworking, law-abiding, friendly lot of people." "Well, I guess, stranger, that's about the kind of people you'll find around here." And the second wagon moved off and blended with the dusty grey.[28]

The speaker in this passage understands the significance of the self-fulfilling prophecy. A **self-fulfilling prophecy** occurs when an individual's expectation of an event helps create the very conditions that permit that event to happen (see Figure 3.1).

self-fulfilling prophecy
a prediction or an expectation that comes true simply because one acts as if it were true

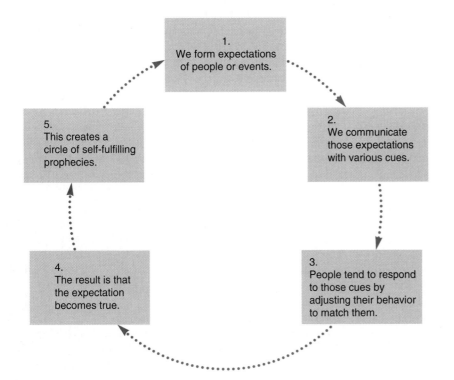

FIGURE 3.1

The Self-Fulfilling Prophecy in Action.

Source: From "Self-Fulfilling Prophecy: Better Management by Magic" by Len Sandler in *Training: The Human Side Of Business,* February 1986. Copyright 1986 by VNU Business Publications USA. Reproduced by permission of VNU Business Publications via the Copyright Clearance Center.

Work It Out

Describe what an instructor needs to do to become a positive Pygmalion.

Pygmalion effect

the principle that we fulfill the expectations of others

Do you have any beliefs that cause you to function in ways that are self-defeating? What are they? What can you do to eliminate them?

Work It Out

Identify people who have functioned as positive or negative "Pygmalions" in your life. Then complete these sentences: I work best for people who . . . ; I work least for people who . . .

Many colleges now admit and graduate more women than men. Some observers place the blame for this new gender gap on "feminized pedagogy" that emphasizes collaboration not competition. In their eyes, boys and men are becoming the new "victims." What do you think?

In other words, your predictions can cause you and others to behave in ways that increase the likelihood of an initially unlikely occurrence. For example, have you ever anticipated botching a presentation and then did so? Have you ever assumed you wouldn't like someone and you turned out to be correct? Did it occur to you that you might have acted in a way that caused your prediction to come true?

Perhaps the most widely known example of the self-fulfilling prophecy is the **Pygmalion effect.** The term comes from the Greek myth of Pygmalion, a sculptor, who falls in love with a beautiful statue of his own creation. The goddess Aphrodite, moved by Pygmalion's obsession with the statue, comes to his rescue and brings it to life. George Bernard Shaw adapted the story to a more modern setting, and Shaw's version in turn served as the basis for the stage and film musical *My Fair Lady.* In this version, Henry Higgins (Pygmalion) seeks to transform a flower seller, Eliza Doolittle, into a refined, well-spoken lady of the upper class. The play illustrates the principle that we live up to labels. We, like Eliza Doolittle, learn to act like the sorts of people others perceive us to be.

A real-life example of the startling effects of self-fulfilling prophecies is a classroom experiment described by psychologist Robert Rosenthal.[29] In the experiment, teachers were notified that certain of their students were expected to bloom—that is, to do exceptionally well—during the course of the school year.

What the teachers did not know was that there was no real basis for this determination. The experimenters had simply selected the names of the "bloomers" at random. Do you think the selected students actually bloomed? If you said yes, you are quite right. Those students did perform at a higher level than would otherwise have been expected and did improve their IQ scores.

Why did this happen? First, the teachers' expectations apparently influenced the way they treated the selected children. The teachers gave those students extra positive verbal and nonverbal reinforcement, waited patiently for them to respond if they hesitated, and did not react negatively when they offered faulty answers. Second, the way the teachers treated the students had a marked impact on the way the students perceived themselves and their own abilities. The bloomers responded to the prophecy that had apparently been made about them by fulfilling it.[30]

Gender bias in education also contributes to self-fulfilling prophecies. The former president of Harvard University, Lawrence H. Summers, gave a speech some years ago in which he attributed the underrepresentation of women in the top ranks of science and mathematics to possible inborn differences in their ability when compared to men. When academic administrators, teachers, and peers act on the belief that women are unable to perform as well as men in science and math, they create a self-fulfilling prophecy. Women remain underrepresented in the sciences and math.[31] Expectations, gender bias, and self-fulfilling prophecies feed off each other. However, if you change the expectation, and communicate it to others, often you can change the result.

The self-fulfilling prophecy has important implications, not only for education but also for our personal lives. Have you ever joined a group of people you were convinced would not like you? What happened? Very likely you were proved right. What you probably did was act in a way that encouraged them to dislike you. The self-fulfilling prophecy also plays itself out in families. If a parent tells a child that he or she cannot do anything right, the child will soon incorporate this idea into his or her self-concept and fail at most of the tasks he or she attempts. In contrast, if a parent repeatedly demonstrates to a child that he or she is lovable or capable, the child will probably live up to that expectation as well.[32]

The Pygmalion effect is also at the root of many business problems.[33] Apparently, some managers treat employees in ways that precipitate superior performance, while many others unconsciously treat workers in ways that precipitate inferior performance. High expectations tend to result in increased productivity, whereas low expectations result in decreased productivity. Thus, subordinates more often than not confirm the expectations of their superiors. For this reason, when you assume a leadership role, you have the potential to function as both a positive and a negative Pygmalion. Which would be more effective?

What about the messages you send yourself? A variation of the Pygmalion effect is the **Galatea effect.** (Galatea is the name Pygmalion gave his statue once it was brought to life.) The Galatea effect refers to the expectations we have for ourselves rather than the expectations others have for us. We tend to realize the expectations we have for ourselves. We react to the internal messages we continuously send ourselves. Our feelings about our own competence and ability can exert an influence on our behavior in much the same way that our performance can be influenced by others' high or low expectations for us. Thus, how we and others answer the question, Who are you? affects how we behave.

> Biologists have determined that, technically speaking, the bumblebee cannot fly. Fortunately, the bumblebee doesn't know this. Remember: People rise no higher than their expectations.

Galatea effect
the principle that we fulfill our own expectations

Gender: Do Males and Females See Themselves Differently?

Do you think you would feel differently about yourself if you were of the opposite sex? If you answered yes, is it because you believe that others would treat you differently? Would they encourage you to exhibit certain behaviors while at the same time discouraging you from exhibiting others?

> How does being male or female affect the nature of your self-concept?

Research tells us that others do treat us differently because of our gender. For example, we dress male and female babies in different colors and styles. For the most part, our prevalent conceptions of masculinity and femininity are reinforced in the television shows we view, the films we watch, the books we read, the toys we play with, and the online sites we frequent. For instance, some years back, young girls were given Barbies that said, "Let's go shopping," while young boys were given G.I. Joes that said, "Attack." A group calling itself the Barbie Liberation Organization attempted to call attention to such sexual stereotyping and make a statement about the way toys influenced behavior by switching G.I. Joe voice boxes with Barbie voice boxes, thereby altering the dolls to say the unexpected. The result? "A mutant colony of Barbies-on-Steroids who roar of things like 'Attack!' 'Vengeance is mine!' and 'Eat lead, Cobra!' The emasculated G.I. Joes meanwhile giggled, 'Will we ever have enough clothes?'"[34] The experiences we have during our formative years influence our later views of masculinity and femininity, thus affecting our identities.

Others may treat us differently because of our gender.

In one of his columns, aptly titled "Beauty and the Beast," *Miami Herald* columnist and humorist Dave Barry reported that, for men, being considered average-looking is just fine; for women, being average is not good enough.[37] To what extent, if any, do your experiences support such findings and observations?

No one can make you feel inferior without your consent.
—*Eleanor Roosevelt*

As girls age, their play often becomes less stereotypical. Instead of opting to play with dolls or stuffed animals, they become more likely to choose sports and computer games. Boys, however, tend to remain stereotypically masculine in their choices—that is, unless no one is watching, in which case the boys choose "feminine" toys as frequently as "masculine" ones.[35] This freedom is curtailed when others, especially their fathers, are observing. The experiences we have during our formative years influence our later views of masculinity and femininity, thus affecting our identities. Our perceptions of self are affected by what we have come to believe about our gender. For example, when asked to describe their characteristics, males mention qualities such as initiative, control, and ambition. Females, in contrast, lead with qualities such as sensitivity, concern for others, and consideration. Generally, U.S. males derive their self-esteem from their achievements, status, and income, while females derive theirs based on appearance and relationships.[36] Although appearance has traditionally played little role in the self-image of men, that is changing. A new emphasis is being placed on the looks and builds of men, with extreme muscularity or thinness as the goal. In your opinion, is being physically attractive too important to both females and males?

Many women develop a less positive self-concept than men do. Our society expects those who are feminine to be nurturing, unaggressive, deferential, and emotionally expressive. Because of this expectation, young women are rewarded for having a pleasing appearance, revealing their feelings, being forgiving, and being helpful to others. While women of all ages appear to value relationships, adolescent girls become so preoccupied with pleasing others that they metaphorically "bend themselves into pretzels."[38] Do you find this still true today? Girls are more likely to be self-critical and self-doubting than are boys. Men are more apt to develop an independent sense of self. Since men are expected to be strong, resilient, ambitious, in control of their emotions, and successful, qualities highly valued by U.S. society, they are reinforced for displaying them. Independence is central to their lives and often leads to their feeling better about themselves than do women.[39] Women, however, are better at organizing and multitasking.[40] This was expressed humorously some years back by stand-up comic Carol Leifer: "I just had a baby an hour ago and I'm back at work already. While I was delivering, I took a course in tax-shelter options."

Culture and the Self-Concept: How Important Is the "I"?

Identity does not develop in the same way in every society.[41] Who we are, at least in part, emerges from participation in a culture.

In North American and Western European cultures, the self is considered paramount. People from these cultures tend to reflect the importance placed on individuals as they set and work toward the realization of personal goals. In contrast, people from Asia, Africa, and Central and South America, places where collectivistic cultures are dominant, are more likely to downplay their own goals, emphasizing instead goals set or valued by the group as a whole.[42] Japanese parents, for example, do not lavish praise on their children because they are concerned that, if they do, the children will end up thinking too much about themselves and not enough about the group.[43] In Western cultures, the assumption is that your life will be enriched if you are able to define who you are—all your possible selves. Stress is placed on the power of personal control. There is an intra-individual focus.[44] Even in popular culture, the focus is on self-reliance ("I Did It My Way"), self-realization ("I Gotta Be Me"), and self-love ("The Greatest Love of All"). In the United States, for example, we emphasize self-determination. In contrast to the independence emphasized in Western cultures, the emphasis in collectivistic cultures is on the interdependent self. Identity is not defined individually, but rather, in relation to others. Thus, the focus is extra-individual.[45]

For members of collectivistic cultures, the self is not of prime importance. In their view, the group, not the individual, is the primary social unit. Thus, whereas individualistic cultures link success with personal achievement, collectivistic cultures link it to group cohesion and loyalty. This basic difference is symbolized by the fact that the "I" in the Chinese written language looks very much like the word for *selfish*.[46] While Western cultures emphasize self-promotion, Asian cultures decry self-importance and reward cooperation with the group. No one is singled out; members share credit and blame. Members of collectivistic cultures gain a sense of identity via their group memberships, not by stressing their self-importance, as members of Western cultures tend to do.[47] Loyalties in collectivistic cultures are directed at others instead of the self. For members of those cultures, the "we" takes precedence over the "I"; the self is not developed at the expense of the group. For members of African, Asian, and Latino cultures, family is a priority, even guiding the culture's members when it comes to career and life-relationship choices. Thus, culture influences our whole notion of self.

Researchers use the terms **idiocentric** to refer to an individualistic point of view and **allocentric** to mean a primarily collectivistic way of thinking and behaving.[48] Which term would you use to describe your standpoint?

As you can see, your self-concept—how you define yourself—is influenced by your unique personal experiences as well as by your membership in a group or groups. Together with culture, these influences play integral parts in helping you formulate a sense of self. According to **distinctiveness theory,** a person's own distinctive traits (red-headed, minority group member, left-handed) are more salient to him or her than are the more prevalent traits (Caucasian, brunette, right-handed) possessed by other people in the immediate environment. For example, persons who are members of groups that are a numeric minority in the United States are more mindful of their ethnicity. For this reason, a White person is much less apt than a minority group member to mention his or her ethnicity when asked to define himself or herself. As a result, an African-American woman in a large group of Caucasian women will probably be well aware of her race. When the same woman is with a large group of African-American men, she is more conscious of her gender and less conscious of her race.[49]

Your culture also feeds your self-concept. For example, African-American girls tend to have higher overall self-esteem during their adolescent years than do Caucasian or Latina girls. According to Peggy Orenstein, Latina girls experience the most serious self-esteem crisis. She notes that between the ages of 9 and 15, the number of Latina girls who are happy with the way they are plunges by 38 percentage points.[50] Despite basic differences in orientation, however, young people throughout the world still share many attitudes regarding the self. Most are concerned about developing and maintaining social relationships, especially with their peers, and most are confident in their ability to assume responsibility for themselves in the future. However, despite this apparent optimism, about 25 percent of the teenagers described themselves as sad and lonely, emotionally empty, and overwhelmed by life's problems; these youngsters are burdened with the weight of poor self-images.

Online Learning Center

Go to the Online Learning Center at www.mhhe.com/gamble10e and answer the questions in the *Self Inventory* to evaluate your understanding of individualistic and collectivistic orientation.

idiocentric
exhibiting an individualistic orientation

allocentric
exhibiting a collectivistic orientation

distinctiveness theory
the theory stating that a person's own distinctive traits are more salient to him or her than are the more prevalent traits possessed by others in the immediate environment

Idiocentric versus Allocentric

Assess the extent to which you exhibit an individualistic (idiocentric) or collectivistic (allocentric) orientation by evaluating the following statements. If the statement is very important to you, rate it a 5; somewhat important, a 4; neither important nor unimportant, a 3; somewhat unimportant, a 2; and very unimportant, a 1.

I Matter

_____ 1. I desire to prove my personal competency.

_____ 2. I've got to be me.

_____ 3. I want others to perceive me as having stature.

_____ 4. I need to achieve personal fulfillment.

_____ TOTAL

We Matter

_____ 1. If I hurt you, I hurt myself.

_____ 2. I desire harmony at all costs in my relations with others.

_____ 3. My goal is to preserve the welfare of others, even if it is at my expense.

_____ 4. I am loyal to tradition.

_____ TOTAL

To determine your score, total the numbers you entered for each category. Which score is higher? A higher "I Matter" score indicates greater idiocentric tendencies. A higher "We Matter" score indicates greater allocentric tendencies.

Young people are not the only group that describes themselves as lonely. The 2000 U.S. Census found that 27 million Americans live by themselves—more than twice the number of single-person households reported in 1970. Singles, including seniors, now constitute the largest census group. An editorial in the *New York Times* noted that although solitary living cannot be equated with loneliness, it may certainly involve some loneliness:

> If [individuals are] elderly, they may take great pleasure in having the wherewithal to live on their own, especially if they remember when the old depended on relatives for meals and a bedroom off the hall. If they're young, they may rejoice that the pressure's off, that marriage is no longer regarded as the ceremony that separates the desirable from the unwanted. On the other hand, they may not. To some of them, a home empty of companions may be synonymous with an empty life.[51]

In fact, even though we network on MySpace, send excessive numbers of text messages, and blog, more and more people are reporting that they experience transitory, if not persistent, bouts of loneliness.[52]

If men define situations as real, they are real in their consequences.
—W. I. Thomas

DEVELOPING SELF-AWARENESS

To enhance our ability to communicate with others, we need to use ourselves as a resource. By focusing on and acknowledging ourselves, we become more aware of ourselves and more sensitive to our own thoughts and feelings.

Viewing Ourselves and Others: The Johari Window

Self-understanding is the basis of self-concept. To understand yourself, you must understand your own way of looking at the world. To understand others, you must understand how they look at the world.

Psychiatrist Eric Berne believes that we enact identity scripts—the rules for living we learned growing up that spell out our roles and how to play them.[53] He finds that we sometimes pattern our transactions in such a way that we repeatedly enact the same script with a different set of players. In other words, it is not uncommon for us to attempt to "stage" dramas with casts of characters drawn from different phases of our lives. We might, for example, repeatedly enact life scenes in which we express the belief that others are out to get us or that they are jealous of us. This urge to repeat transactions can become a problem if it leads us to failure rather than to success. The remedy is to become aware of the scripts we enact, identify those that are not productive, and rewrite them. Once we are in control of the scripts we use, taking part as an active and not a passive player, we put ourselves in position to script our own lives.

At one time or another, we all wish that we knew ourselves or others better. The concept of self-awareness, basic to all functions and forms of communication, can be explored through a psychological testing device known as the **Johari window.** Joseph Luft and Harrington Ingham developed an illustration of a paned window to help us examine both how we view ourselves and how others view us.[54] Before proceeding further, let's look at the window (see Figure 3.2).

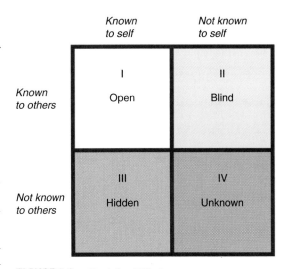

FIGURE 3.2   **The Johari Window**

Source: From *Group Processes: An Introduction to Group Dynamics* by Joseph Luft. Copyright ©1984, 1970, 1963 by Joseph Luft. Reprinted by permission of The McGraw-Hill Companies.

Pane I, the **open area,** represents information about yourself that is known to you and another. For example, your name, age, religious affiliation, and food preferences might all be found in this pane. The size and contents of the quadrant vary from one relationship to another, depending on the degree of closeness you share with that other person. Do you allow some people to know more about you than others?

Pane II, the **blind area,** contains information about you that others, but not you, are aware of. Some people have a very large blind area and are oblivious to their own faults and virtues. At times, people may feel compelled to seek outside help, such as therapy, to reduce the size of their blind area. Do you know something about a friend that he or she does not know? Do you feel free to reveal this information to your friend? Why? What effect do you think your revelation would have on your friend's self-image?

Pane III, the **hidden area,** represents your hidden self. It contains information you know about yourself but do not want others to find out for fear they will reject you. John Powell, author of *Why Am I Afraid to Tell You Who I Am?* expresses the fear of rejection this way: "If I tell you who I am, you may not like who I am, and it is all that I have."[55] Sometimes it takes a great deal of effort to avoid becoming known, but at one time or another each of us feels a need to have people important to us know us well and accept us for what we are.

When we move information from Pane III to Pane I, we engage in the process of **self-disclosure.** Self-disclosure occurs when we purposely reveal to another person information about ourselves that he or she would not otherwise know. None of this is to suggest that the hidden area should not be allowed to exist within each of us. It is up to you to decide when it is appropriate for you to share your innermost thoughts, feelings, and intentions with others; it is also up to you to decide when complete openness is not in your best interest.

Many of us choose to upload to sites such as Facebook and YouTube photos featuring ourselves and our friends engaged in various activities. Some of us keep diaries on blogs for anyone to read. Keeping certain information about ourselves from

Johari window

a model containing four panes that is used to explain the roles that self-awareness and self-disclosure play in relationships

open area

the part of the self containing information known to both the self and others

blind area

the part of the self known to others but not known to oneself

hidden area

the part of the self that contains information about the self known to oneself but that is hidden from others

self-disclosure

the process of revealing to another person information about the self that this person would not otherwise know

FIGURE 3.3

Interpersonal Styles, in
Terms of the Johari Window.

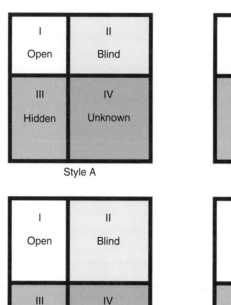

Style A

Style B

Style C

Style D

unknown area

the part of the self that is unknown
to oneself and others

others doesn't seem to be as prevalent as it used to be. Instead, some of us appear to derive power from revealing secrets.[56]

While self-disclosure is a process we normally control, what happens when this process is taken out of our control? What happens when another party, without our permission, takes information from our hidden area and reveals it in public? While anyone who knows us well can do this, some media practitioners have made a business out of forced disclosures. The late tennis star Arthur Ashe, for example, was forced to reveal he had AIDS, although he and his family preferred to keep it private, because otherwise the story of his condition would have appeared in a well-known tabloid. Similarly, because New York governor David Paterson feared that the media would expose that he and his wife had both had past affairs, he held a press conference to reveal it.

Pane IV of the Johari window is the **unknown area** in your makeup. It contains information about which neither you nor others are aware. Eventually, education and life experience may help bring some of the mysteries contained in this pane to the surface. Only then will its content be available for examination. Have you ever done something that surprised both you and the people close to you? Did you and a friend ever exclaim together, "Wow! I didn't know I could do that!" "I didn't know you could do that!"

People commonly develop a style that is a consistent and preferred way of behaving interpersonally. Figure 3.3 illustrates four representative styles. Style A is characteristic of people who adopt a fairly impersonal approach to interpersonal relationships. Dominated by their unknown areas, these people usually withdraw from contacts, avoid personal disclosures or involvements, and thus

Skill Builder

Symbolizing the Self

Take four objects to class. The first object should reveal something about the way you see yourself, something you believe everyone recognizes about you. In other words, it should represent an aspect of your open area. The second object should reveal something about you that up until this point you believe resided in your hidden area. This second object could symbolize an attitude, feeling, desire, or fear that you had hoped to keep from others but are now willing to move into the open pane. The third object you bring to class should represent how you believe another person sees you. For example, do you believe that a friend or relative sees you as you see yourself?

How do you think your perceptions are similar? How are they different?

Finally, after selecting these three objects, ask someone else to choose an object that represents his or her perception of you. Take this fourth object to class along with the other three. Be prepared to discuss how your perceptions of yourself and the other person's perception of you conflict or coincide. For example, did the object selected by the other person help you move information from the blind area to the open area? To what extent has each phase of the experience altered the appearance of your Johari window?

---

project an image that is rigid, aloof, and uncommunicative. In Style B, the hidden area, or facade, is the dominant window. Here we find people who desire relationships but also greatly fear exposure and generally mistrust others. Once others become aware of the facade, they are likely to lose trust in these people. Style C is dominated by the blind area. People who are characterized by this style are overly confident of their own opinions and painfully unaware of how they affect others or are perceived by others. Those who communicate with such people often feel that their own ideas or insights are of little concern. In Style D, the open area, or area of free activity, is dominant. Relationships involve candor, openness, and sensitivity to the needs and insights of others.

Communication of any depth or significance is difficult if the people involved have little open area in common. In any relationship you hope to sustain, your goal should be to increase the size of the open area while decreasing the size of the hidden, blind, and unknown areas. As human beings we are thinking about others and what they think about us. The question is whether we are able and willing to share what we are thinking.

> Which style appears to be most characteristic of you and the people you interact with?

> You are going for a job interview. What information will you share with the interviewer? What will you keep hidden? How can what you are blind to about yourself hurt your chances of getting the position?

Managing Impressions

It is normal for us to want to present ourselves to others in desirable ways. However, this leads us to ask some questions: When we say something publicly, do we always feel it privately? Do we present a different self than we feel?

When we create a positive image of ourselves to influence what others think of us and how they view us, we are practicing **impression management.** Among the strategies we use to manage the impressions others have of us are *self-enhancement* (we bolster our own image) and *other-enhancement* (we bolster the image of others).

While the **perceived self** is the self we believe ourselves to really be, according to sociologist Erving Goffman, we use **facework** to present a public image, our *presenting self,* that is as favorable as possible to others. Oftentimes, we show different sides of ourselves to different people. Sometimes this choice is conscious and our communication is strategic—designed to accomplish a specific purpose. Other times, this choice is unconscious—in effect, we are on automatic pilot. What matters

impression management
the creation of a positive image designed to influence others

Work It Out

How do you imagine that your best friend would draw your Johari window? How would a close relative draw it? How would you draw it?

perceived self

the self we believe ourselves to be

facework

the means used to present a public image

high self-monitors

people highly attuned to impression management efforts

low self-monitors

people who pay little attention to responses others have to them

most is if the side we show is authentic, that is, a true reflection of our self-concept. If it is not, then as Goffman suggests, our front-stage behavior may contrast with our back-stage behavior or the behavior we exhibit when we are alone.[57] Do your experiences support this?

Human beings are unique in being able to observe their own behavior. **High self-monitors** are people who are highly attuned to their impression management efforts. **Low self-monitors** pay little attention to the responses others have to their messages. Still others believe that it is unethical to attempt to artificially control a communication by trying to present to others a version of you that is idealized; they believe it is disingenuous to treat relating to others like a performance. To which, if any, of these groups do you belong?

SELF-CONCEPT AND TECHNOLOGY

If you're interested in improving the impression you make on others, computer-mediated communication might give you an advantage. After all, the computer gives you more control over the information you choose to reveal to others as well as the information you choose to keep hidden. For example, e-mail enables you to edit the messages you send until you create one that will succeed in communicating the impression you desire. It gives you the ability to correct what you say and take back a message by not sending it. "Some communicators just do better when they can push the delete key."[58] Online you can also deliver messages that it might be too difficult to deliver, were you face-to-face, especially if you are shy. For some, instant messaging is a means of avoiding an "OMG" ("omigod" or cringe-inducing) face-to-face interaction moment. According to an Associated Press-AOL poll, 43 percent of those surveyed report using instant messaging to communicate things they wouldn't say in person. Others use it because they fear rejection; it is a lot easier to close the window and disappear if someone rejects you online than if you are in their physical presence.[59] Similarly, if the receiver doesn't like your message, he or she can ignore it rather than having to walk away or insult you to your face.

The Internet may also be a factor in influencing the way we think of ourselves. If we have a positive self-concept, we are probably better able to adapt to both the rapid changes and the technological innovations of our world. Some use the Internet to see themselves differently. Do you? The Internet makes it possible for us to inhabit virtual worlds, participate in simulations, and assume different personae. If you don't like how you are characterized or treated online, you can change, even reinventing yourself by morphing into different identities. This type of transformation is far different from being a student part of the day, an athlete another part of the day, an employee during some hours, and a child at home. In cyberspace you can have parallel identities or parallel selves and use them to develop relationships and manage the many selves within you.[60] A Pew Internet and American Life Project survey revealed, for example, that teenagers in the United States typically have more than one e-mail address or screen name. Many adopt multiple personae to hide their real identity from friends or strangers. A large number of people experiment online by pretending to be those whom they are not. They provide fake personal data in their e-mails or instant messages. In effect, they use the Internet to try out new identities.[61] By

Work It Out

Kenneth Gergen believes that we have more than "one true self." According to Gergen's *The Saturated Self: Dilemmas of Identity in Contemporary Life*, we use different personas in different social situations. Have you ever surprised yourself or someone else by using an inappropriate persona? What identity dilemma did you expose in the process?

Work It Out

What if you were to design a personal Web site with the function of communicating you to all who access the site? The persons who visit your site might be friends you already know or faceless, anonymous strangers. What aspects of yourself would you highlight? What facts would you downplay or ignore? How much would you reveal about yourself? What pictures would you include? How does having a personal site or being on one like MySpace enhance or diminish your ability to manage the identity you present to others?

"On the Internet, nobody knows you're a dog."

constructing a number of imaginary selves and experimenting with different kinds of social relationships, they are able to explore unexplored aspects of themselves. They might, for example, pretend to be the opposite sex, conceal their culture or where they live, and gloat as they hide any number of physical or psychological characteristics. Who we are online can simply be who we want to be for the moment. Psychologist Sherry Turkle notes that, in an online world, "The obese can be slender, the beautiful plain, the 'nerdy' sophisticated."[62] Thus, for some people, communicating online gives them an opportunity to feel more positive about themselves.[63] In addition, some researchers believe that online interaction can affect psychological health. While some researchers believe Internet use correlates positively with depression and loneliness, others contend that it decreases them and actually enhances self-esteem.[64] In your opinion, is an online persona an extension of who you are in real life? Is it part of the real you or completely separate and distinct from your real-life self? Consider the following comment by a woman who is about to come face-to-face with a man whom she met online:

> I didn't exactly lie to him about anything specific, but I feel very different online. I am a lot more outgoing, less inhibited. I would say I feel more like myself. But that's a contradiction. I feel more like who I wish I was. I'm just hoping that face-to-face I can find a way to spend some time being the online me.[65]

Blogs are another way people are using technology by creating online journals (virtual diaries) that define and reveal to others how they see themselves and their world. Visit the blogs of both someone you know and someone who is a relative stranger to you. What does each person's blog reveal to you about his or her self-concept and willingness to reveal him- or herself to others? What clues did you use to make your judgments?

Do you feel freer to be yourself on or off-line? Why?

The following line is from T. S. Eliot's poem "The Love Song of J. Alfred Prufrock":
Prepare a face to meet the faces that you meet.
To what extent, if any, do you behave as the line advises?

Do you ever find yourself doing things in private, such as making faces at yourself in a mirror, that you would never think about doing in front of other people?

Have you ever been anyone but yourself online? If so, what prompted you to adopt an alternative identity? If you spoke with people online who you later discovered were not who they represented themselves to be, how did you feel? What did you do?

Thinking Critically

Reflect and Respond

First, agree or disagree with the following statement; state the reasons for your response.

I may not be what I think I am. I may not be what you think I am. I may well be what I think you think I am.

Then, consider this: Each of your friends, relatives, and co-workers probably sees you as a somewhat different person. Write a paragraph that describes your perception of how one person from each of these groups sees you. Who has the most positive view of you? Whose view, in your opinion, is most accurate? Why?

COMMUNICATION SKILLS IN PRACTICE

GUIDELINES FOR IMPROVING SELF-AWARENESS AND AWARENESS OF OTHERS

Focus on Service Learning

Choose an organization such as the American Cancer Society or a homeless shelter. Do some preliminary research about the organization, including but not limited to visiting its Web site before approaching it. Identify issues related to the purposes of the agency that could adversely affect the self-concept of the agency's clients. What strategies can you suggest the organization use to ameliorate harm to the clients' self-image?

Throughout this chapter, we have stressed that we all carry figurative pictures of ourselves and others with us wherever we go. Together, these pictures form a mental collage of past, present, and future images of ourselves—alone or interacting with other people. If you closely examine your various images, you probably will discern that how you look in each is related to when the picture was taken, what environment you were in, and with whom you were communicating. Each picture reveals a somewhat different you, because you change and grow from moment to moment, situation to situation, and year to year.

We sometimes forget that our self-image and our images of others can change. Keeping "self-pictures" updated and current is a challenge. Sharpening a fuzzy image, refocusing an old image, and developing a new image can help you discard worn-out perceptions of yourself and others. Use the following guidelines to improve the "picture-taking" skills you have gained while working your way through this chapter.

✓ Watch Yourself in Action

You can increase your self-awareness by continuing to examine your self-image and your relationship to others. Developing a clear sense of who you are is one of the most worthwhile goals you can set for yourself. Be willing to watch yourself in action. Periodically examine your own self-perceptions—and your self-misconceptions.

Study the composite picture that emerges from your reflections. How close are you to becoming the person you would like to be?

✓ Ask How Others Perceive You

How others perceive you may be very different from how you perceive yourself. Obtaining information from others can help you assess how realistic your self-concept is. Others who come to know you may observe strengths you have overlooked, traits you undervalue, or weaknesses you choose to ignore. However, you do not have to accept all the pictures other people take of you.

No one can prevent you from adhering to your own beliefs and rejecting the opinions of others. Looking at other people's pictures of you does mean, however, that you are at least opening yourself to the possibility of change by attempting to see yourself as others see you.

☑ Commit to Self-Growth

Carl Sandburg wrote, "Life is like an onion; you peel off one layer at a time." As you move from yesterday through today and into tomorrow, your self is in constant transition. Try not to let your view of yourself today prevent you from adapting to meet the demands of changing circumstances and conditions. Continually formulating new answers to the question, Who am I? will allow you to discover the vibrant, flexible, and dynamic qualities of your self.

Revisiting Chapter Objectives

1. **Define *self-concept*.** Self-concept is the entire collection of attitudes and beliefs you hold about who and what you are. It is the mental picture you have of you.

2. **Explain the nature of the self-concept.** Self-concept can be positive or negative, accurate or inaccurate. Your self-concept influences all aspects of your communicative behavior—with whom, where, why, and how you choose to communicate.

3. **Identify how different factors including the self-fulfilling prophecy, popular culture, gender, and culture influence self-concept formation and behavior.** You are not born with a self-concept. Rather, your self-concept is shaped by your environment, by its technology, and by those around you, including your parents, relatives, instructors, supervisors, friends, and co-workers. A self-fulfilling prophecy occurs when prior expectations of an event help create the very conditions that permit the event to exist. The prediction leads to the behavior. The media, as well as other people, help determine which self-fulfilling prophecies you experience. Similarly, once we learn the attributes of maleness and femaleness, what we believe about gender affects our self-perceptions as well. Culture is another factor influencing how we look at the self, the expectations we set for ourselves and others, and our behavior.

4. **Discuss the relationships among the Johari window, impression management, and self-awareness.** You can change and improve your self-concept by developing great self-awareness and understanding. The Johari window can help you identify the open, blind, hidden, and unknown areas of your self. When we create a positive image of ourselves to influence what others think of us and how they view us, we are practicing impression management.

5. **Explore the relationship between technology and self-concept.** The Internet is influencing how we conceive of ourselves. We use it to control aspects of our communication and explore ourselves, sometimes experimenting with or assuming different personae.

6. Identify guidelines for improving self-awareness and understanding.   By consistently watching yourself in action, learning how others perceive you, and committing to self-growth, you keep your self-awareness and understanding updated and current.

Resources for Further Inquiry and Reflection

To apply your understanding of how the principles in Chapter 3 are at work in our daily lives, consult the following resources for further inquiry and reflection. Or, if you prefer, choose any other appropriate resource. Then connect the ideas in your chosen selection with the communication concepts and issues you are learning about in and out of class.

Listen to Me

"Beautiful" (Christina Aguilera)
"I'm a Loser" (Beck)
"Breakaway" (Kelly Clarkson)
"Eleanor Rigby" (The Beatles)
"Hands" (Jewel)
"Kim" (Eminem)
"Unpretty" (TLC)
"Unwritten" (Natasha Benningfield)

The speaker or speakers in these songs express beliefs about how communication affects the self. Choose a song, and use it to explain the interaction between communication and self-concept.

View Me

Beautiful
Girl Fight
Hoop Dreams
Bee Movie
Monster
The Truth about Cats and Dogs
American Beauty
Shrek

How do the incidents described in the film enhance your understanding of self-concept and its influence on person-to-person interaction?

Read Me

What do these two cartoons suggest about the self-concepts of males and females? Which do you believe is more accurate? Why?

"I know I'm wrong, but I'm sure you can make me more wrong."

Tell Me

Share with the class the insights you gained from your chosen Listen to Me, View Me, or Read Me selection.

Women and men spend more cosmetics and body alterations today than was spent in 1970, yet the number of women and men unhappy with their appearance has increased and will probably continue to do so. In a brief presentation, agree or disagree with this statement, and state the reasons for your position.

Key Chapter Terminology

Use the Online Learning Center at www.mhhe.com/gamble10e to further your knowledge of the following terminology.

www.mhhe.com/gamble10e

allocentric 55	open area 57
blind area 57	perceived self 60
distinctiveness theory 55	Pygmalion effect 52
facework 60	self-awareness 44
Galatea effect 53	self-concept 44
hidden area 57	self-disclosure 57
high self-monitors 60	self-efficacy 49
idiocentric 55	self-esteem 44
impression management 59	self-fulfilling prophecy 51
Johari window 57	self-image 44
low self-monitors 60	unknown area 58

Idioms in Translation

growing up digitally — maturing in the Internet age

kill another person's self-esteem — cause his or her self-esteem to decrease

on automatic pilot — acting without deliberate effort or awareness

walk around on eggshells — be extraordinarily careful

Culture Cue

Members of collectivist cultures, including the Chinese, believe that humility is a virtue. They exhibit a high frequency of deference behaviors, including gaze avoidance and the suppression of emotional displays that might offend others. Members of individualist cultures, such as North Americans, do not usually practice humility, nor do they display such deference behaviors with any frequency. Instead they stress individual initiative and achievement.

Test Your Understanding

Go to the *Self Quizzes* on the book's Online Learning Center at www.mhhe.com/gamble10e.

www.mhhe.com/gamble10e

After finishing this chapter, you should be able to

1. Define *perception* and explain its stages.

2. Identify barriers to perception, including perceptual sets, selectivities, first impressions, stereotypes, allness, blindering, and fact-inference confusions.

3. Discuss how culture and gender affect perception.

4. Explore how media and technology influence perception.

5. Use guidelines for increasing perceptual accuracy.

Communication and Perception: I Am More Than a Camera

Why is it that we develop different meanings for the same experience? How can we account for perceptual gulfs? Do we ever experience or see the same things? How do we decide which recounting of experience is true? What do different versions of the same event tell us about perception? And if we cannot agree on what we see or on what happened, how are we able to communicate with one another? These are some of the questions we address and try to answer in this chapter.

All people do not perceive you similarly. For example, when one consultant asked a group of college students how they believed employers perceived them, she told the students that the word she was looking for began with the letter "e." Students, believing that employers viewed them positively, suggested answers such as "enthusiastic" and "energetic"; the correct answer was "entitled."[1]

What is the relationship between perception and communication? As we will see, perception and communication are connected to, interact with, and influence each other. Perception influences how we understand situations, other people, and ourselves. For example, we do not perceive our friends and strangers the same way. In fact, communication influences all our perceptions. The meanings we form and the messages we send to others about what we see and how we think shape their understanding of events and us. People living in different countries, the members of different generations, and the members of different genders, races, religions, or classes (just to name a few groups) are likely to perceive things differently. No matter what we're talking about, interpretation mirrors ideology. By exploring the "I" behind the eye, we will come to better understand why we think and act differently, why we are more than a camera, and why "where we stand depends on where we sit."[2]

If, to people, crickets appear to hear with their legs, it is possible that to crickets, people appear to walk on their ears.
—*Anonymous*

As I am, so I see.
—*Ralph Waldo Emerson*

Online Learning Center

Go to the Online Learning Center at www.mhhe.com/gamble10e and answer the questions in the *Self Inventory* to evaluate your understanding of perceptual differences.

WHAT IS PERCEPTION?

Perception is a complex process. Certainly we use our senses to perceive, but perception includes more than just the eye alone, the ear alone, the nose alone, the skin alone, and the tongue alone. What occurs in the "real world" may be quite different from what we perceive to occur. During perception, we make experience our own. We define **perception** as the process of selecting, organizing, and subjectively interpreting sensory data in a way that enables us to make sense of our world.

perception
the process by which we make sense out of experience

Perceiving Stimuli: The "Eye" and the "I"

Consider whether geography influences perceptions. That is, to what extent, if any, do you believe that people living in the East as compared with the West, or the North as compared with the South, think and perceive life differently?

We all inhabit different worlds. We view reality from different angles, or vantage points. Our physical location, interests, personal desires, attitudes, values, personal experiences, physical condition, and psychological states interact to influence our judgments or perceptions.

How do you absorb information from the world around you? Do you look and listen? Do you touch, taste, and smell your environment and those who interact in it? Certainly. Your senses function as perceptual antennae and gather information all the time.

However, it is impossible for you to process all the stimuli available to you. Without realizing it, you take steps to select or limit what you perceive. You will see this for yourself if you try the following test:

1. For the next 60 seconds, attempt to internalize everything that exists in the room you now inhabit. Make an effort to react to each sound, sight, smell, touch, and taste that is present in your environment.
2. Were you able to focus simultaneously on each stimulus or sensory experience, or did you find yourself skipping from one stimulus to another and back again?

What if you woke up tomorrow as a person of a race or an ethnicity different from your own? How do you imagine your view of your life and the world would change? Would a change in age affect you the same way? What about a change in gender?[3]

Most probably, you found yourself switching between stimuli; thus, you are aware that you simply cannot effectively handle, or process, all the sensory experiences that compete for your attention. Information theorists tell us that the eye can process about 5 million bits of data per second; they also tell us that the brain can utilize only some 500 bits per second. We are therefore forced to identify or select those stimuli we will attend to or experience. We combat data overload by simply not assimilating large amounts of data. Instead, we decide what to focus on, selecting only the data we want for more close and careful viewing. In effect, we shift our searchlight of attention from one potential person, place, or thing to another, until one catches our interest, bringing our flickering searchlight into focus and to a stop[4]. Thus, when you exhibit **selective perception**—an aspect of the perceptual process that includes both selective exposure and selective attention—you expose yourself to and attend to particular stimuli while ignoring others. Selective perception enables you to create a more limited but more coherent and meaningful picture of the world, one that conforms to the beliefs, expectations, and convictions you hold.

selective perception
the means of interpreting experience in a way that conforms to one's beliefs, expectations, and convictions

Perceptual processes are not only highly selective but also personally based. For this reason, different people experience the same cues in very different ways. Thus, we never really come into direct contact with reality.[5] Instead, everything we experience is manufactured by the nervous system.

How do you imagine your perception would change were it necessary for you to move around in a wheelchair? Besides making you feel shorter, how would your new height affect what you would be able to see and access easily?

Age also appears to influence perception. According to researchers, in contrast to the brain of a college-aged student, the aging brain takes in and processes more data, sifting through large amounts of information, to the perceiver's benefit. Thus, college students are more likely to ignore distractions, while older people, because of their reduced ability to filter, are more apt to exhibit broader attention spans. As a result, they tend not to make snap judgments regarding what is or could become important. This frees them to learn more about situations and people—giving them a potential perceptual advantage.[6]

"Wernock, here, sees your suit as half empty, but I see it as half full."

Do different people perceive you differently? Why?

Organizing Stimuli: The "I" of the Beholder

We have said that perception provides each of us with a unique view of the world—a view sometimes related to, but not necessarily identical with, that held by others. Since we cannot actually become one with the world out there, we are forced to use our senses to help create a personal picture of the people and objects that surround us. How do we make sense of our world? How do we process the stimuli that compete for our attention?

During the perception process, we are active, not passive, participants. We do not simply relax and absorb stimuli available to us, the way a sponge absorbs liquid. We select, we organize, and we evaluate the multitude of stimuli that bombard us, so that what we focus on becomes figure and the rest of what we experience becomes ground.[7] This is how the **figure-ground principle** functions.

To experience the concept of figure and ground, examine Figure 4.1. What do you see? At first glance, you probably see a vase—or you may see two people facing each other. When stimuli compete for your attention, you can focus on only one, because it is simply impossible to perceive something in two ways at once. Although you may be able to switch your focus rapidly, you will still perceive only one stimulus at any given time.

In addition to using the figure-ground principle as an organizing strategy, we also use **closure**—the tendency to fill in missing perceptual pieces. Look at the stimuli pictured in Figure 4.2. What do you see? Most see a dog rather than a collection of inkblots and a rectangle, triangle, and circle rather than some lines and an arc. Because we seek to fill in gaps, we mentally complete the incomplete figures. We fill them in on the basis of our previous experiences and our needs. We make sense of relationships and events in much the same way. We fill in what

Work It Out

Why does moving up in a job or life make it harder to see what goes on below? Identify steps you can take to discover differences in perception before they create problems.

figure-ground principle
a strategy that facilitates the organization of stimuli by enabling us to focus on different stimuli alternately

closure
the tendency to fill in missing perceptual pieces to perceive a complete world

FIGURE 4.1

Figure and Ground. Do you see a vase or two people?

FIGURE 4.2

Test for Closure.

is not there by making assumptions, or inferences—some of which are more accurate and valid than others.

Think of an example of an event or occurrence that you misremembered. Why do you believe the erroneous memory occurred?

Processing Stimuli: The "I's" Memories

As we see, perception involves a series of stages: (1) the selecting stage, during which we attend to only some stimuli from all those to which we are exposed; (2) the organizing stage, during which we give order to the selected stimuli; and (3) the interpreting/evaluating stage, during which we make sense of or give meaning to the stimuli we have selected and organized based on our life experiences (see Figure 4.3). Perception also involves a fourth stage, the responding stage, during which we decide what to think, say, or do as a result of what we have perceived. How we interpret and respond to selected stimuli also determines whether or not a particular person or experience enters our memory. If a perception does enter our memory, we can retrieve it at another point in time. Whether or not our memory is reliable, however, depends on whether our reconstruction of experience is accurate and clear. Our perceptual abilities influence how we interpret and remember events. For example, many Americans still have vivid memories of September 11, 2001. In interviews, when asked to recall those memories, people spoke of having watched television all morning, riveted to the TV by images of the two planes striking the twin towers. Their memory of what they think they witnessed is false. There was no video that day of the first plane hitting the North Tower of the World Trade Center. Despite this, 76 percent of New Yorkers surveyed said they saw it on September 11, as did 73 percent of people nationwide. What is more, they were confident about their memories. Memories of events that did not actually happen the way we remember them are at the root of countless disputes; they are reminiscent of these lines from an old Lerner and Lowe song: "We met at nine," "We met

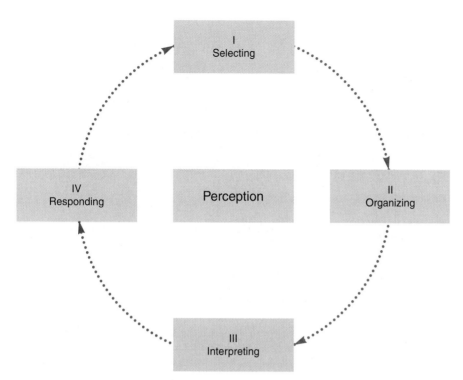

FIGURE 4.3

Stages of Perception.

at eight," "I was on time," "No, you were late." "Ah yes, I remember it well!"* What we remember depends on what we believe, even if what we believe never happened or is based on misinformation that subsequently was retracted.[8] Memory is a human construct, an amalgam of what we experience, read, piece together, and want to be true. A number of reasons account for our misremembering events: (1) Memories are transient and tend to fade over time; (2) we remember aspects

Managing Memories

Because we seek to remember more than can possibly be managed by our brains, our brains plays favorites with our memories. To recollect some memories more accurately, we block out distracting memories. We don't recall some names, numbers, or details, not because we necessarily have faulty memory, but because those memories have been crowded out by memories of people, places, or events we judged to be more important. Thus, one key to remembering is to make good decisions about what to forget![9] Learning how to develop a more efficient and clutter-free memory will facilitate both deliberate and spontaneous information retrieval.

Think back over the past week. Distinguish between people, places, and events you encountered or experienced that you believe are important to remember and those that you would do well to ignore or forget. Identify the specific criteria you used to make your decisions. For example, did you choose to remember something because you thought you might need it or be able to use it at a later point in time, because it reflected your attitudes, beliefs, or values, or because it was related to your goals? To what extent were you able to make bias-free choices? That is, did you choose to remember information that agreed or disagreed with your views, was pleasant as well as unpleasant?

---

*"I Remember It Well." Words and Music by Alan Jay Lerner and Frederick Loewe © 1957, 1958 Chappell & Co. Copyrights renewed. All Rights Reserved. Used by permission.

How do you decide which version of an event is true?

"Are you going to trust your father's selective memory over mine?"

of an event but are likely to misattribute them; and (3) our biases distort our recollections. In other words, our memories are fallible.[10] When it comes to memory, there is little correlation between confidence and accuracy.

BARRIERS TO PERCEPTION

Many variables affect us during the perceptual process, interacting to guide us in making our perceptual selections. Some of these constitute barriers to perception.

Perceptual Sets: Is Your Past Following You?

perceptual sets

expectations that produce a readiness to process experience in a predetermined way

Past experiences often provide us with expectations, or **perceptual sets,** that affect how we process our world. To better understand the concept of a perceptual set, quickly read the statements written in the triangles in Figure 4.4. Then examine the words more carefully. During your first reading, did you miss anything that you now perceive? Many people fail to see the second *the* or *a* in the statements on

FIGURE 4.4

Test for Perceptual Sets.

Barefoot
in the
the park

Snake
in the
the grass

Busy
as a
a beaver

Exploring Diversity

What Do You See? What Do You Think?

1. Patricia Williams, the author of *Seeing a Color-Blind Future*, asks: "How can it be that so many well-meaning white people have never thought about race when so few blacks pass a single day without being reminded of it?" How would you answer her? In your opinion, is color blindness a legitimate hope for the future? Why or why not?

2. If education influences perception, do you think that Congress should pass an Academic Bill of Rights to ensure that a diversity of dissenting viewpoints are heard in all your classes? Why or why not?

the first reading. Did you? Why? We are so accustomed to seeing words in familiar groups, or clusters, that often we simply fail to perceive a number of single words when we see them in such phrases. Faster, more accomplished readers make this mistake more readily than slower, less skillful readers.

Past experiences create perceptual sets in numerous ways. Sometimes culture is a factor. In Saudi Arabia, for example, the way women are raised influences how people both within that culture and outside it perceive them. In Saudi Arabia, women have few legal rights, are usually not permitted to drive a car, and need a man's permission to obtain a passport; clearly, the Saudis and Americans perceive women very differently.[11]

Motivation is another variable affecting our perceptual sets and thus our perception. Both hunger and poverty, for instance, can alter the way we interpret experience. In one study, researchers showed sailors some ambiguous pictures and asked them to describe what they saw. Sailors who were hungry "saw with the stomach"—to them, an elongated smudge looked like a fork, and a swirl looked like a fried onion. In a second study, rich and poor children were shown circles of various sizes and were asked which ones were the same size as certain coins. The poor children consistently chose circles that were much too large. Why? A quarter looks bigger to the poor than to the rich.[12]

Obviously, education is also an important part of our past experience. How much education and what kind of education we have had affect the way we process and perceive information.[13] At times, education can become a barrier rather than a facilitator of or aid to perception. When asked to interpret a stimulus as simple as a nursery rhyme or as complex as a world event, a sociologist, an economist, a political scientist, or a biologist might bring her or his specific professional bias to the assignment, which could blind each person to other possible interpretations.

As is apparent, perceptual sets are the result of unique experiences. The lessons life has taught you necessarily differ from those life has taught others. As a result, people can perceive the same stimulus differently.

Exploring Selectivities: Are You Open or Closed? Are You a Distorter?

selective exposure

the tendency to expose oneself to information that reaffirms existing attitudes, beliefs, and values

selective attention

the tendency to focus on certain cues and ignore others

selective retention

the tendency to remember those things that reinforce one's way of thinking and forget those that oppose one's way of thinking

Four types of selectivity concern us: (1) **selective exposure**—the tendency to expose ourselves to information that reaffirms existing attitudes, beliefs, and values; the tendency to close oneself to new experiences; (2) **selective attention**—the tendency to focus on certain cues and ignore others; (3) *selective perception*—the tendency to see, hear, and believe only what we want to; and (4) **selective retention**—the tendency to remember those things that reinforce our way of thinking and forget those that oppose our way of thinking.

A key factor in how we view our world is the extent to which we open ourselves to experiences. Although numerous sensory stimuli compete for our attention, we tend to practice selective exposure; we select only those experiences that reaffirm our existing attitudes, beliefs, and values. We likewise tend to ignore or diminish the significance of those experiences that are incongruent with our existing attitudes, beliefs, and values. Just as children sometimes place their hands over their ears to avoid hearing what a parent is saying, so we select what we will perceive by deciding whether to expose ourselves to a variety of types and sources of information. When driving through poverty-stricken areas, for example, people often roll up their automobile windows. They tell themselves that they are doing this for self-protection, but rolling up the windows is also a means of self-deception that helps them avoid contact with some of the depressing sights and sounds of their society. How difficult is it for you to expose yourself to certain new ideas, places, or experiences?

As for selective attention, you are more apt to overhear someone seated near you speak of wanting to buy a home if you are a real estate agent than if you are in computer sales. Think of the last time you were in a setting where background or ambient noise was very loud. Perhaps you were at a football game, concert, or party, or on a jam-packed train. When in a crowd, most people actively filter out what they are not interested in and respond selectively to only their preferred conversation, exhibiting what psychologists call "the cocktail party effect," a form of selective attention. Selective attention, as we see, help us adapt to our environment.[14] Selective perception is a related concept. When it comes to selective perception, we tend to overlook negative qualities in persons we like, just as we tend to deemphasize the negative policies of institutions we support. We see what we want to see and hear what we want to hear. As a result of selective perception, different people may interpret the same message or event differently.

Finally, our memories aid us in this process by enabling us to engage in selective retention—we recall better the positive qualities of persons we like and the negative qualities of persons we dislike. Perception is subjective. What we think about as well as what we think about one another are powerful forces. The reality

Work It Out

View the same news broadcast with others whose political views differ sharply from your own and with others who share your views. Compare and contrast your interpretations of the delivered information. What did you discover?

is that we can bias the selection process and end up with quite a distorted view of the people in our lives as well as the world. For example, think about a relationship that has soured and that you are planning to terminate. Since making this decision, have you become more aware of qualities the person has that you do not like? Why do you suppose this is so? When we like or love someone, we tend to perceive primarily his or her positive qualities. This is called the **halo effect.** However, when our perception of another changes for the worse, we are more likely to see only his or her negative qualities. This is called the **horn effect.**

First Impressions: Do You Freeze Your Perceptions of Others?

How important are **first impressions?** Do the snap judgments we make about people matter? According to a study by researchers Artemio Ramirez and Mike Sunnafrank, assessments made during the first few minutes of meeting someone strongly influence the nature of a relationship. Ramirez and Sunnafrank randomly paired 164 college freshmen in a communications class, let them chat for 3, 6, or 10 minutes, and then asked them to predict the kind of relationship they would share, ranging from casual acquaintance to close friend. At the end of the course, students were again asked to assess their predictions. Results revealed that students who reported a positive impression were more likely to have developed a friendly relationship even if they were given only 3 minutes to make their assessment. The results support the predicted outcome value theory developed by Sunnafrank, which says that when we first meet another person, we predict the probable outcome of our relationship and try the hardest to develop relationships we expect to be rewarding.[15]

On what basis do you make initial judgments about the people you meet? What makes you decide if you like or dislike someone? Is it his or her economic status? Is it the job he or she holds? Perceiving others and the roles they play is an essential part of the communication process. In this section, we will explore how we form first impressions and why we sometimes stereotype other people. We will attempt to determine why we often feel it is necessary to "freeze" our perceptions of people to conform to our expectations. First impressions can dramatically affect perception. A first impression—or **primacy effect,** as it is sometimes called—can even affect the result of communication efforts. Trial lawyers, for example, depend to some degree on the primacy effect when selecting jurors. The first impression that potential jurors make on attorneys will often determine whether the attorneys accept them or use peremptory challenges to remove them from consideration.

Even if our first impressions are wrong, we tend to hold on to them. Doing this can cause a number of problems. For example, if the opinion we have of someone is erroneous, we can sustain our inaccurate perception by clinging to it and reshaping the conflicting information available to us until it conforms to the image we hold. Thus, we may never come to experience the real person—only our faulty conception of him or her. And it is this faulty conception that will influence the way we respond to that person. Suppose, for instance, you make a new friend, Kevin, at work. You tell an old friend about him. Your old friend tells you, "Yeah. I know that guy. Worked with him two years ago. He's nothing but trouble. Always looking to use people. He'll bleed you of your ideas, pass them off as his own, and leave you far behind as he makes his way to the top. Did it to

halo effect
the perceiving of qualities that are primarily positive

horn effect
the perceiving of qualities that are primarily negative

first impressions
initial judgments about people

> Agree or disagree with the following statement, giving reasons for the position you take: *You never get a second chance to make a good first impression.*

primacy effect
the ability of one's first impression to color subsequent impressions

me. And he'll do it to you. Watch and see." The danger here is that this evaluation may be unfair, biased, or simply wrong. Kevin might have changed during the past two years, or your friend's initial assessment of him might be incorrect. But your friend's words will probably influence the way you interact with Kevin, and you will probably find reasons to substantiate your first impression, whether or not such reasons are actually present. You simply may not be able to avoid a basic stumbling block to accurate perception—closing your mind after forming a first impression.

In a communication interaction, receivers' psychological states can affect their first impressions of senders. Sometimes receivers use cues provided by senders, mix those cues with their own preconceptions, and create perceptions based partly on myth or fiction. When such perceptions involve dividing people into groups, it is called stereotyping.

Stereotypes: Do You Squeeze Others into Niches?

stereotype
a generalization about people, places, or events held by many members of a society

A **stereotype** is a generalization about people, places, or events that many members of a society hold. For example, when we go into a physician's waiting room for the first time, we carry with us a general idea, or stereotype, about what to expect and how to behave in that environment. In other words, we have developed an ability to identify and generalize about what we consider appropriate in a physician's office. While waiting to be examined, we would not expect to find flashing laser lights or people dancing to loud music.

The stereotypes we hold affect how we process stimuli around us. For one thing, while we remember more favorable information about in-groups, we retain more unfavorable information about out-groups. Our stereotypes also cause us to disregard any differences individuals may have that set them apart from the stereotyped group. When we stereotype, instead of responding to the communication or cues of individuals, we create expectations, assume they are valid, and behave as if they had occurred. Thus, when we stereotype, we judge persons on the basis of what we believe about the group in which we have placed them. We emphasize similarities and overlook discrepancies. Stereotyping leads us to oversimplify, overgeneralize, and grossly exaggerate what we observe. Lazy perceivers develop prejudices; **prejudice** involves making a negative prejudgment based on membership in a social category. Lazy perceivers also rely on stereotyping as their key perceptual process. Because it discourages careful observation and encourages pigeonholing, it discourages the noting of differences and encourages categorization.

prejudice
a biased, negative attitude toward a particular group of people; a negative prejudgment based on membership in a social category

Sports reporter Jerry Bembry reports the following incident:

> At a basketball media day at the Naval Academy, a ranking Navy official was greeting the news media. Each journalist received a gracious hello, but when the Navy man got to me, I was asked a question.
>
> "So," the official said, extending his hand. "Where did you play ball at to get this job?"
>
> His assumption: Because I'm an athletic-looking African American male, my education must have come in combination with an athletic scholarship. It's a question I'm often asked, although I've never played collegiate sports.
>
> No matter how many times such instances happen to me, it's unsettling.[16]

Has anyone ever stereotyped you? If so, how did his or her doing so affect your relationship?

Unfortunately, holding racial and ethnic stereotypes is widespread. Among personalities recently exposed for harboring stereotypical perceptions are the Nobel Prize winner James Watson, who made disparaging remarks about the intelligence

Ethics and Communication

Prejudiced Eyes

What we see in other people's faces depends on what we know, or think we know, about people. When researcher Paul Chance showed subjects a set of photographic portraits and asked them to set aside those of Jews, the guesses were not very accurate. He reported that the subjects who were anti-Semitic were not any better at the task than the other subjects, but they set aside more photographs. To their prejudiced eyes, more people looked Jewish.[17]

Why do you think the prejudiced subjects saw more faces as "Jewish"? How might this affect their ability, for example, to hire people to work for them?

Using the images you carry around in your head, list the traits you believe are most characteristic of the members of each of the following groups: Afghans, Pakistanis, North Koreans, Israelis, and the French.

1. Do you believe it is possible to identify characteristics for groups with whom you have had little, if any, personal contact? Why or why not?

2. How do you imagine that your list would influence future communication with members of these groups?

---

of Blacks and Africans, commenting that he was "inherently gloomy about the prospect of Africa" because "all our social policies are based on the fact that their intelligence is the same as ours—whereas all the testing says not really." He then added that while he hoped all races were equal, "people who have to deal with Black employees find this is not true." The radio personality Don Imus called the members of Rutgers University's championship women's basketball team "nappy-headed hos." Duane "Dog the Bounty Hunter" got caught on tape using the N-word.[18]

In your opinion, what accounts for such behavior? Could it be that even when people believe they are prejudice free, they harbor unconscious biases?

Experts believe stereotyping can be as big an issue among groups of minorities as it has been between Whites and minorities. In other words, stereotypes, unfortunately, are everywhere. In fact, a variety of ethnic groups share the same stereotypes as Whites.[19] Commonly held stereotypes about Hispanics include that they are foreign-born, have a lot of children, and speak only Spanish. Existing stereotypes about Asians include that they are inscrutable and disloyal and that they own restaurants and laundries. Americans are likely to be stereotyped as being boisterous and loud. African Americans are stereotyped as being good dancers and good athletes.

Stereotypes are dangerous because, even at best, they are oversimplifications and overgeneralizations; often, they are gross exaggerations and misrepresentations. Stereotypes based on half-truths and derived from invalid premises pose major problems. Ralph Ellison, an African American and author of the book *Invisible Man*, noted:

> I am an invisible man. No, I am not a spook like those who haunted Edgar Allan Poe . . . I am a man of substance, of flesh and bone, fiber and liquid . . . and I might be said to possess a mind. I am invisible, understand, simply because people refuse to see me. Like the bodiless heads you see sometimes in circus sideshows, it is as though I have been surrounded by mirrors of hard, distorting glass. When they approach me they see only my surroundings, or figments of their imagination— indeed, everything and anything except me.[20]

Stereotypes do a special kind of harm when groups believe their own caricatures. If, for example, African Americans believe the stereotype and think that they are good only at sports, music, and dance, then it is entirely possible for some group members to exhibit "internalized oppression," act on the stereotype, and harass achievers in the group who do not fit that stereotype.[21]

Stereotypes also promote racial profiling.[22] For too many years, police have stopped drivers on the basis of their skin color rather than on how they were driving. In a similar situation, Aquil Abdullah, an American rowing champion, was denied permission to board his plane at Newark's Liberty International Airport because he had a common Muslim name.[23] Although most Caucasian Americans perceive themselves to be unbiased, when unconscious stereotypes are measured, approximately 90 percent link African Americans with negative traits. (To examine a test of unconscious stereotyping, go to https://implicit.harvard.edu/implicit/.) If, however, individuals make a conscious attempt to see someone as unique, race-based stereotypes diminish.[24]

The term *stereotype* is derived from a printing practice in which the typesetter repeatedly uses the same type to print text. In effect, when we stereotype, we repeatedly use the same thoughts, or fixed mental images, to "print" the same judgment repeatedly. We use our knowledge, beliefs, and expectancies about a human group to make judgments about people and our potential interaction with them. We apply the judgment to all members of the group, failing to acknowledge the uniqueness of what we are describing. We use the stereotype as a means of rationalizing our behavior in relation to members of that group.

Now, consider this. Earl Kaufmann decided to change his legal name to "Scary Guy." Why? He had so many body piercings and tattoos—even his scalp was covered—that others found his appearance frightening, even shocking. Scary Guy had an objective: to change the world, one stare at a time. He began traveling the world and speaking to students with the goal of using his looks to teach people to reject prejudice. Typically, Scary Guy begins a presentation by walking in and standing in silence, letting the audience sit in fear. "Kids are afraid of me," he said. "They judge me. They don't want to talk to me. Some of them think I'm a wrestler, a biker, a drug dealer. Some think I'm all of those things. They think I've done time." During the presentation, however, the members of Scary Guy's audience learn to see his true colors, talking his message of not prejudging others to heart.[25]

We are all individuals. Whenever we interact with another person, we must realize that we are communicating with a person, not with a stereotype. Furthermore, we need to understand that our stereotype of any group is necessarily based on incomplete information and that, although stereotypes may be partly true, they are never completely true. In fact, when we stereotype, categorize, or pigeonhole others, we are really stereotyping, categorizing, or pigeonholing ourselves.

To improve our perceptual capabilities, we must make an effort to see differences as well as similarities among people. To paraphrase communication expert Irving J. Lee, the more we are able to discriminate among individuals, the less we will actively discriminate against individuals.[26] We can be aware of stereotypes but reject them.

Allness: Do You Assume That's All There Is?

allness

the erroneous belief that any one person can know all there is to know about anything

Knowledge of everything about anything is certainly an impossibility. In his book *Science and Sanity*, Alfred Korzybski coined the term **allness** to refer to the erroneous belief that any one person can possibly know all there is to know about everything.[27] Even if we are wise and do not assume that our favorite newscaster (or even our favorite friend) is telling us all there is to know about a topic, we often persist in believing that he or she is telling us all that is important about the topic. Did you ever ask someone to fill you in on the content of a class session you missed? Did you assume that the person was giving you all the important information? Did a later exam prove you wrong?

How can we avoid allness? We can begin by recognizing that, because we can focus on only a portion of a stimulus or an event, we necessarily neglect other aspects of that stimulus or event. Another safeguard is to refrain from thinking of ourselves as the center of the world.

Allness can impede the development of effective relationships. To counteract allness, try to end every assessment you make with the words *et cetera* ("and others"). You can never know everything there is to know about anything, and these words remind you that you should not pretend to know it all.

FIGURE 4.5

Test for Blindering.

Blindering: Is Your Focus Too Narrow?

We can illustrate the concept of **blindering** as a factor in perception with the following exercise: Attempt to draw four straight lines that will connect each of the dots in Figure 4.5. Do this without lifting your pencil or pen from the page or retracing a line.

blindering

the process by which one unconsciously adds restrictions that limit one's perceptual capabilities

Did you find the exercise difficult or impossible? Most people do. Why? The problem imposes only one restriction—that you connect the dots with four straight lines without lifting your pencil or pen from the page or backtracking over a line. Most of us, however, add another restriction: After examining the dots, we assume that the figure to be formed must be a square. Actually, no such restriction exists, and once you realize this, the solution becomes clear. (Check the answer in the Answer Key at the back of the text.) In effect, the image of a square "blindered" you in your attempts to solve the problem.

Just as we put blinders on a horse to reduce the number of visual stimuli it receives, we can also put blinders on ourselves. Blinders may help a horse, but they can drastically hinder human beings. Because it is a habit that forces us to see only certain things or to see things only in certain ways, blindering can lead to undesirable actions or prevent us from finding solutions. It can also impede needed actions or decisions.

Inferences: Do You Confuse What You Infer with What You Observe?

If you're familiar with *The Colbert Report* on Comedy Central, then you probably know that its host, Stephen Colbert, coined a new word, *truthiness*. Designated as a "Word of the Year" by the *Merriam-Webster Dictionary*, *truthiness* is defined as "truth that comes from the gut, not books" or "the quality of preferring concepts or facts one wishes to be true, rather than concepts or facts known to be true." Thus, another factor affecting our perception and evaluation of people

Work It Out

Watch a day or evening soap opera and detail the number of confusions of facts versus inferences that occur during the program.

Is determining what is true, false, or an inference easy for you? Is that true?

and events is the failure to distinguish what we think or wish to be true, or what we infer, from what we observe. For example, if you plan to leave your home to drive to a friend's house about a mile away, you probably make some inferences: that when you put the key into the ignition, your automobile will start; that you will not have a flat tire; and that no construction will block your approach to the friend's home. Likewise, when a traffic light turns green, you usually infer that it is safe to cross the street.

It is important to distinguish facts from inferences. A **fact** is something that you know to be true on the basis of observation. You see a woman walking down the street, carrying a briefcase. The statement "That woman is carrying a briefcase" is a fact. If the woman with the briefcase has a frown on her face, you may state, "That woman is unhappy." This second statement is an **inference**, since it cannot be verified by observation. Facts are not always easy to come by, and sometimes we mistakenly believe we have facts when we actually have inferences. Failing to recognize this distinction can be embarrassing or dangerous. For example, when actor and concert pianist Dudley Moore began flubbing lines, walking unevenly, and having difficulty playing the piano, he was mistakenly accused by entertainment industry insiders of being drunk, when in reality he was suffering from an incurable neurological disease.[28]

Acting as if an assumption is a certainty is risky. When we confuse facts with inferences, we are likely to jump to conclusions. Test your ability to distinguish facts and inferences by completing the Skill Builder on page 81, "The Detective." How did you do? (Check your answers against the Answer Key at the back of the text.) This test is not designed to discourage you from making inferences. Of necessity, we live our lives on an inferential level. It is designed, however, to discourage you from making inferences without being aware of doing so. It is also designed to help you stop operating as if your inferences were facts.

Are you aware of the inferences you make? As semanticist S. I. Hayakawa noted, the real question is not whether we make inferences but whether we are cognizant of the inferences we make. One of the key characteristics of a mature relationship is that neither party to it jumps to conclusions or acts on inferences as if they were facts.

fact

that which is known to be true based on observation

inference

an assumption with varying degrees of accuracy

He laughed because he thought that they could not hit him; he didn't imagine that they were practicing how to miss him.

—Bertolt Brecht

The Detective

Read the following story. Assume that the information contained in it is true and accurate. Then assess each statement that follows the story. On a sheet of paper, indicate whether you think the statement is definitely true by writing *T,* definitely false by writing *F,* or questionable by writing a question mark. (Note: A question mark indicates that you think the statement could be true or false, but on the basis of the information in the story, you cannot be certain.) Respond to the statements in the order given. Do not go back to change any of your responses.

A tired executive had just turned off the lights in the store when an individual approached and demanded money. The owner opened the safe. The contents of the safe were emptied, and the person ran away. The alarm was triggered, notifying the police of the occurrence.

1. An individual appeared after the owner had turned off the store's lights.
2. The robber was a man.
3. The person who appeared did not demand any money.
4. The man who opened the safe was the owner.
5. The owner emptied the safe and ran away.
6. Someone opened the safe.
7. After the individual who demanded the money emptied the safe, he sped away.
8. Although the safe contained money, the story does not reveal how much.
9. The robber opened the safe.
10. The robber did not take the money.
11. In this story, only three persons are referred to.

The following lists summarize the essential differences between facts and inferences:

Facts	Inferences
1. may be made only after observation or experience	1. may be made at any time
2. are limited to what has been observed	2. extend beyond observation
3. can be offered by the observer only	3. can be offered by anyone
4. may refer to the past or to the present	4. may refer to any time—past, present, or future
5. approach certainty	5. represent varying degrees of probability

CULTURE, GENDER, AND PERCEPTION: INTERPRETING THROUGH DIFFERENT "I"S

There is more to perception than meets the eye. We see the world not necessarily as we are but as we have been conditioned to see it. Our culture, our gender, and our past experiences precipitate in us a preference for **perceptual constancy**—the desire to see exactly as we have seen in the past. Thus, many of our perceptions are learned. The more similar our life experiences, the more similarly we will perceive the world. The more dissimilar our life experiences, the wider the gap between us and others with respect to the way we view things.[29] Not everyone perceives things the same way we do. Cultural habits or selectivities see to that.

perceptual constancy
the desire to perceive experience exactly as we have perceived it in the past

Have you ever considered why the United States almost always appears in the center in our maps of the world? Is there any geographical reason for this? Or could it be an example of ethnocentrism on the part of mapmakers and users?

Work It Out

Provide examples of how culture and gender influence perception. Then, compile a list of reasons why a diverse problem-solving group might outperform a homogeneous one.

cultural nearsightedness

the failure to understand that we do not all attribute the same meanings to similar behavioral clues

I would hope that a wise Latina woman with the richness of her experience would more often than not reach a better conclusion than a White male who hasn't lived that life.

—*Judge Sonia Sotomayor*

Do you agree? Why or why not?

Culture and Perception

Culture teaches us how to perceive. For example, when looking at configurations created by the craters on the moon, North Americans see a man, while Native Americans report a rabbit, the Chinese a lady fleeing her spouse, and Samoans a woman weaving.[30] Whether we are judging beauty, describing snow, or evaluating a child's behavior, our culture influences our assessment of reality. Individuals from different cultures are simply trained to regard the same cues differently; they interpret what they perceive through a cultural lens. Some years ago, researchers used a binocular-like apparatus to compare the perceptual preferences of Native Americans and Mexicans. Each subject was shown 10 pairs of photographs—in each pair, one photo displayed a picture from U.S. culture and the other photo, a picture from Mexican culture. After viewing the paired images through the binocular-like device, the subjects reported their observations. Results showed that both the Native Americans and the Mexicans were more likely to report having seen a picture from their own culture.[31] Similarly, most of us find it easier to interpret the emotions communicated via the verbal and nonverbal facial expressions of members of our own culture than those expressed by members of other cultures. We also tend to be more perceptually accurate in recognizing and interpreting the expressions of emotion sent by members of our own culture.[32]

In an effort to blunt "the culture effect," educators in some conflict-ridden societies have adopted a textbook that requires students to synthesize rather than choose one of two conflicting versions. The Peace Research Institute in the Middle East publishes a booklet that divide pages into three columns, one for the Israeli version of history, one for the Palestinian version, and one left blank for the student to fill in.[33]

Additionally, culture teaches us to expect others to behave in certain ways when faced with specific conditions. Misunderstandings can result, however, when each party in an interaction is operating according to different assumptions and rules. For North Americans, talk is desirable and is perceived as a tool used to achieve goals or to complete tasks. They view the opposite of talk, silence, more negatively. Because North Americans tend to value directness and honesty, they are likely to perceive someone who fails to "tell it like it is" as either vague or cowardly. In contrast, members of Asian cultures value silence, believing that one who understands need not speak. From the Asian perspective, a person who states the obvious is merely showing off. Can you see how not understanding the perceptions of the members of both cultures could lead to difficulties in communicating?

We have not all experienced the same lessons, and thus we do not attribute the same meanings to similar behavioral cues. When we fail to understand this concept, we exhibit **cultural nearsightedness.** We misread cues and miss opportunities to use the differences between us as a means to help ourselves perceive each other more clearly.

Gender and Perception

Like ethnicity, gender influences the interpretation of experience. Men and women have different standpoints, perceive different realities, have different expectations set for them, and exhibit different communication styles. Beliefs

regarding gender-appropriate behavior not only influence how men and women see each other but also
affect how they relate to each other. From childhood
on, both men and women are conditioned to use
behaviors that conform to their gender: While men are
rewarded for displaying strength and independence,
women are reinforced for expressing their feelings and
being nice to others. While women are categorized as
emotional, men are classified as rational.[34]

Through interaction with parents, teachers, peers,
and others, we internalize the lessons of appropriate
male and female behavior. These lessons frame our
perceptions and teach us how society expects us to
behave. These constructs, however, can limit the way
each gender is perceived and may lead to males' and
females' being judged on the basis of gender expectations rather than observed cues. Perceived differences
between male and female behavior develop as a result
of others' expectations, the behavior role models
exhibit, the traditional educational institutions that
promote stereotyped notions of sex roles, and the
media that send repeated confirmation of male and
female stereotypes.[35] If we want to change the perception of the kinds of behavior appropriate for males and
females, then we need to change the way society categorizes them.

As we perceive, we sort stimuli, selecting some
and rejecting others. What we select and store in our
internal database determines our view of reality and
gives our lives a sense of stability. If, for example, we conclude that men are
more dominant than women, then we feel we can more readily predict their
actions and thus recategorize them as such. When expectations lead to misper-
ceptions, undesirable consequences can result. All too frequently, rigid categorizing creates communication problems. For example, during the war in Iraq,
we witnessed an evolution in the Pentagon's and the public's perception regarding the types of positions in which women in the military could serve. Some
20 percent of U.S. forces in Iraq were women, with over 150,000 women having served there as of 2007. Though technically "not in combat," but serving
in support roles for troops, women often find themselves in combat situations
since there is no definitive "front line" in modern warfare. Like their male
counterparts, women soldiers came under attack, with some being injured or
killed.[36] Some observers are able to reconcile the role of women as central
figures in their families with that of soldiers in combat, others are unwilling to
juxtapose both perceptions. Where do you stand? Are you perceptually ready
for women to serve regularly in combat zones? Should we ungender combat?
Why or why not?

Similarly, criticisms of mass media productions often include a discussion of
how women and minorities are systematically relegated to roles that are consistent
with traditional stereotypes. These portrayals reinforce perceptions that perpetuate
racism and sexism.[37]

Is this woman redefining a gender prescription? Will her
behavior change how others perceive women?

Recent research reveals
that bylines of men ap-
pear significantly more
frequently on newspa-
per and magazine
opinion pages than do
bylines of women (see
www.womenTK.com,
for example). How do
you believe this byline
imbalance is affecting
coverage, if at all?

Are there any gender-
based definitions that
you or any one you
know have helped
redefine?

THE MEDIA AND PERCEPTION

The media also play a role in determining how we perceive experience. According to the book *Glued to the Set: The 60 Television Shows and Events That Made Us Who We Are Today*, we are defined by and, thus, become like what we watch.[38] More and more ads on television contain examples of multicultural socializing, showing Americans playing and living together regardless of race. In an effort to reach a diverse range of consumers, the ads present racially mixed scenarios in which ethnic communities in the United States mesh effortlessly. But do these ads represent reality? Unfortunately, according to researchers, they do not. Most neighborhoods are still racially segregated with a strong tendency to swing disproportionately toward either a White population or an ethnic group. The average White person's neighborhood is 83 percent White, the average Black person's neighborhood is 54 percent Black, and the average Hispanic lives in a neighborhood that is 42 percent Hispanic.[39] Despite this, marketing professor Sonya Grier believes that in suggesting "multiculturalism is socially desirable," the ads reflect aspirations of what life could be, not what life is.[40] Such ads play a part in determining how we perceive experience.

Television programs face similar challenges. For example, the Council on American-Islamic Relations expressed concern that Muslims are the media's new "bad guys." In television and cable offerings, Muslim extremists are no longer portrayed as antisocial fanatics hiding in seedy places; the new stereotype presents Muslims as neighbors who are terrorists.[41] If most viewers get their knowledge of Muslims from the media, what messages do such portrayals send? Muslims are not alone in protesting stereotypical depictions. Representatives of Italian Americans, African Americans, Mexican Americans, older Americans, and women, just to name a few, also have protested offensive depictions of the members of their groups. Why? Because the more television people watch, the more accepting they become of social stereotypes, and the more likely they are to help perpetuate the unrealistic and limiting perceptions shown them. According to **cultivation theory**, a theory propounded by George Gerbner and colleagues focusing on the mass media's ability to influence users' attitudes and perceptions of reality, television is the primary means through which we form perceptions of society and people. The theory proposes that heavy television viewers develop perceptions that are inconsistent with facts.[42]

What are some of the specific perceptual lessons we learn from the media? Are they affecting the way we look at politicians and our political system, older

cultivation theory

a theory propounded by George Gerbner and colleagues focusing on the mass media's ability to influence users' attitudes and perceptions of reality

How are films redefining qualities desired in men?

people, men and women, and minorities? According to the Pew Research Center for the People and the Press, almost a quarter of people aged 18–29 get their political information from late-night comedy programs.[43] Author Russell Peterson believes that the cumulative effect of the relentless ribbing given politicians on programs such as those hosted by personalities Bill Maher, Jon Stewart, and Stephen Colbert has the effect of making us perceive politicians as corrupt, laughable, and egomaniacal. According to Peterson, this could lead to our perceiving democracy as a joke.[44] When it comes to how we think of seniors, because of their under-representation in media, we may think of them as invisible or unimportant. Media may also limit our perceptions of men and women.

Whereas the media often present men as active, independent, powerful, and virile, they portray women as passive, dependent, and incompetent, and as the objects of male sexual desires. Whereas men are shown taking care of business, women are more typically shown taking care of their looks and other people, especially family members. From the point of view of the media, then, males dominate and females are subservient.[45] Males are providers. Females are caregivers.

For similar reasons, we might also come to perceive minorities inappropriately. Although the statistics are improving, minorities still occupy more supporting than leading roles and instead of being depicted in complimentary ways, they are sometimes depicted stereotypically. As a result of media depictions, our perceptions of Native Americans also may be inaccurate. For example, the print media too frequently present an image of them that is negative and degrading, suggesting that "all American Indians are poor, greedy, corrupt alcoholics, who just cannot seem to succeed in American society."[46] Representing Native Americans in this way undermines their ability to act effectively or be taken seriously.

Media Wise — Frames of Reference

1. Intermittent reports of terrorist threats distort perceptions of risk, inducing an experience of fear that is out of proportion with actual danger. The more attention the media pay to a particular risk factor, the worse we assume the risk to be. For example, Dr. Baruch Fischoll, a psychologist at Carnegie Mellon University and a leader in the study of risk perception, reports: "If scientists are studying it and the news reports it, people assume it must be worth their attention."[47] Another risk researcher, Dr. Paul Slovic, reports that adding to this effect is the finding "that people put more stock in reports of bad news than in reports that might increase their trust."[48]

   Give an example of a media report that caused you to perceive a risk as greater than it was in reality. Did it involve weather? Traffic? Crime? Environmental issues? Political issues?

   Films perpetuate inaccurate perceptions that induce fear in viewers. View one of the following films: *Collateral Damage, Syriana, True Lies, Rules of Engagement, Executive Decision,* or *Not Without My Daughter.* In what ways, if any, does the film perpetuate bias against Arabs? In your opinion, is the "Arab as terrorist" stereotype responsible for increasing our fear and arousing our suspicion regarding who may or may not be a potential terrorist?

2. The popular media are also reflecting a crossing of cultures. An increasing number of films, such as *Hancock, Monster's Ball,* and *The Matrix Reloaded,* feature a rainbow cast, that is, a cast of all colors. Leon Wynter, author of *American Skin: Pop Culture, Big Business, and the End of White America,* suggests that commercial transracial representations sell because they "present a vision of the American dream in which we are liberated from the politics of race to openly embrace any style, cultural trope or image of beauty that attracts us regardless of its origin."[49] Others suggest such films sell because of the disproportionate representation of minorities in the audience; for example, market studies reveal that Black people buy movie tickets at higher rates than those of other ethnic groups.[50] To what extent, if any, do you find that rainbow casting is helping change perceptions of who in society is fit to occupy positions of power? Explain.

On the other hand, Leon E. Wynter, author of the book *American Skin: Pop Culture, Big Business and the End of White America,* notes that we are now witnessing the browning of mainstream commercial culture. In addition to superstars like Oprah Winfrey and Tiger Woods, we also have actor Dennis Haysbert as an insurance pitchman and ads like the Budweiser "Whassup?!" commercial that feature basically anonymous Black men talking Black street talk. It appears that American pop culture is becoming increasingly transracial. Products that aspire to be perceived as "all-American" depict a racially diverse image. According to Wynter, America wants to perceive itself as a unified multiracial society.[51] To this end, Hollywood has been using more of a color-blind approach to casting actors, giving audiences multiracial casts with the implied message that differences in skin color amount to "no big deal."[52] This is in line with the new "postethnic" "ObamAmerica" reality that reveals ethnic labels are becoming less important to large numbers of people whose personal identity is shaped more by cultural preferences than by skin color or ethnic heritage.

TECHNOLOGY AND PERCEPTION

According to social psychologist Kenneth Gergen, as new communication technologies continue to spread our relationships across the globe and as our knowledge of other cultures continues to revitalize our attitudes, depriving us of firm behavioral norms, we tend to exist in a state of flux, in which perceptions are partial and negotiated rather than complete and fixed.[53] As a result, perceptions derived from information received over the Internet may be both accurate and inaccurate, depending on whether the goal of the information provider is clarity or distortion. As with other media, the information we receive via the Internet is only as reliable as the source.

Computer-mediated communication raises a variety of perception-based issues involving the nature of communication and identity. We tend to perceive and interact with people differently when we relate to them online than when we talk to them face-to-face. A number of researchers even refer to communication that occurs in the world of cyberspace as unreal in order to differentiate it from communication that occurs in real life, also known as IRL, and without the aid of computer mediation.[54] Fantasy and playfulness play significant roles in online interactions, allowing people to experiment in ways that may be uncomfortable for them in real life. Thus, the Internet is precipitating perceptual revisions of the self and others.[55]

The Internet inspires some of us to feel larger than ourselves. In addition, the availability of the computer and **virtual reality** allows many of us to spend more time in our dreams. As sociologist Sherry Turkle reminds us, "In film and photography, realistic-looking images depict scenes that never took place between people who never met."[56] Anyone can create an image, import sections of pictures, and blend them into a new whole. Image processing and synthesis enable us to create illusions of reality. In effect, with digital media you never know what is real, what is the truth. As a result, Web users must develop the ability to look critically at what they perceive rather than simply accept what is on the screen as a given; it is imperative for them to analyze, weigh, probe, and take stock

Work It Out

Devise a list of new rules for processing information received over the Internet.

virtual reality

an environment that exists as data in a computer system

Work It Out

In *Against the Machine: Being Human in the Age of the Electronic Mob,* author Lee Siegel asserts the Web is creating a nation of laptop-addicted Internet zombies who are losing the capacity for human interaction. In addition, Siegel asserts that the blogosphere abounds with anonymous or false accusations that ruin reputations or heap undeserved praise. Visit a Starbucks and surf the blogosphere. To what extent do your own perceptions support or contradict Siegel's claims?

Ethics and Communication

Image Making

Before digital photography, people perceived photos as truthful. In fact, a decision by *Jet Magazine*'s publisher John H. Johnson to print the gruesome photograph of the brutally murdered and mutilated African-American teenager Emmett Till, revealing to the nation the level of brutality and inhumanity that led to his death, is credited with having sparked the civil rights movement.[57] Today, however, what you see in photographs or in the media is not necessarily what is really there. Digital manipulation lets users tinker with reality, changing the "taking" of a photo to the "making" of a photo. Today, products can be digitally inserted into the background of films postproduction without viewer knowledge. Separate pictures can be combined to make it appear as if people who were never actually together are standing or seated next to each other. The appearance of people can also be altered, making them more or less attractive, slimmer or heavier than they actually are. Type the words "fake pictures" into an Internet search engine and you'll find people willing to alter any photo.

In your opinion, should the Federal Communications Commission require disclaimers when counterfeit images are shown on TV? What measures, if any, should be taken to protect consumers from "phony reality"? What measures should consumers take to protect themselves?

of what they perceive. This practice differs from the experiences of the members of earlier generations, who would rarely perceive a picture and feel it was a fake. Back then, it was felt that a fact was a fact. Today, we all know better. We now see a photograph and realize that it could be a total fabrication.[58]

For example, although more than a decade has passed since *Time* magazine was accused of darkening a cover photo of O. J. Simpson in order to make him look more sinister, magazines are still being accused of cover doctoring. Tennis player Andy Roddick believed his biceps had been so conspicuously enlarged in the photograph of himself on the cover of *Men's Fitness* that he wrote in his blog that he was "pretty sure I'm not as fit as the Men's Fitness cover suggests," adding that the cover refinishers had also erased a prominent birthmark on his right arm.[59] Are accuracy and truthful representation in danger of disappearing? Today, it is all too common to find magazines picturing fuller-figure models as slimmer and

Do you think this picture of former president George W. Bush kissing Venezuela's president, Hugo Chavez, is a fabrication?

retouching the images of celebrities or public figures to conceal visible flaws in ways that complement their appearances. Both French president Nicolas Sarkozy and Russia's former president Vladimir Putin had their physical appearances "improved" by capable users of image-editing software such as Photoshop.[60] Malicious retouching also occurs—such as a convincing fake photo that surfaced during John Kerry's run for president of the United States in 2004. The photo showed him sharing the stage with Jane Fonda at an antiwar rally during the Vietnam War. This had never occurred. By contrast, when the war in Iraq began, the U.S. government attempted to manage images of the war by altogether banning photographs of soldiers' coffins returning to the United States.[61] In your opinion, is there a difference between *manipulating* and *filtering* the way we perceive reality? Which do you believe is more dangerous: digital manipulation or the filtering that occurs when a newspaper editor, for example, chooses whether to include a photograph, selects which photo or quotation to use, or makes the decision to report a story or remain silent?

We also need to understand how other factors, such as race, influence our attention to Web sites. For example, research reveals that African Americans are more attentive when visiting a Black-targeted site, while Caucasians are equally attentive to White- and Black-targeted sites. It appears that race or ethnicity may be of more interest to people whose racial or ethnic group is in the minority of their social environment than to people of the majority group. Since they are in the majority, Caucasians may be less mindful of their race when browsing a Web site.[62]

We are also faced with a number of questions: Will emerging technologies help us become more flexible and resilient? Or will they cause us to think strictly logically and constrain us to prescribed, more conventional thought channels? Will they facilitate our ability to use our virtual experiences to enrich our real experiences? Or will they contribute to our losing our sense of reality by enabling us to lose ourselves in a virtual world that disappears when we disconnect our modems?

COMMUNICATION SKILLS IN PRACTICE
GUIDELINES FOR INCREASING THE ACCURACY OF YOUR PERCEPTIONS

Focus on Service Learning

Visit a Web site on teaching the dangers of stereotyping, such as http://school.discovery.com/lessonplans/programs/stereotypes. Then, on the basis of information you find there, other research you conduct, and the knowledge you now have, prepare to conduct a workshop for an audience of your own choosing (young children, parents, members of the police force, physicians, lawyers) that uses a series of case studies you create to help the audience members avoid drawing the wrong conclusions from perceptions.

Although our effectiveness as communicators is determined in part by our perceptual abilities, we rarely consider ways to increase our perceptual accuracy. Let's examine some suggestions for improving perceptual skills.

☑ Be Aware That Your Perceptual Processes Are Personally Biased

By becoming aware of your role in perception, by recognizing that you have biases, by acknowledging that you do not have a corner on the truth market, you can increase the probability that your perceptions will provide you with accurate information about the world around you and the people who are a part of it.

☑ Take Your Time

Effective communicators are not in a hurry; they take the time they need to process information fairly and objectively. When we act too quickly, we often

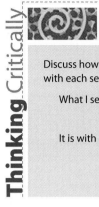

Reflect and Respond

Discuss how the excerpts that follow help amplify our understanding of the nature of perception. Then agree or disagree with each selection; supply reasons and examples that support your position.

What I set down here is true until someone else passes that way and rearranges the world in his own style.

—*John Steinbeck*

It is with our judgments as with our watches; no two go just alike, yet each believes his own.

—*Alexander Pope*

make careless decisions that reveal poor judgment. In our haste, we overlook important clues, make inappropriate or unjustified inferences, and jump to conclusions. Delaying a response instead of acting impulsively gives us an opportunity to check or verify our perceptions.

☑ Try to Be More Open

Frequently, we act like robots or computers that have been programmed to look at the world in a set way. But a person is neither a robot nor a computer. We can take steps to become more observant and broaden our expectations. We need to become willing to expect the unexpected and to expand the size of our perceptual window. This will happen if we recognize that our reality is subjective, incomplete, and unique. Thus, if we want to cultivate a fuller, more valid perception of our world, we must be willing to review, revise, and update our view of the world.

☑ Develop Your Ability to Empathize

Differing perceptions lie at the heart of an array of interpersonal and global communication challenges. If we can experience the world from a perspective other than our own—in effect, recreating it from the other party's perspective—we can help facilitate mutual understanding. Both cognitive and emotional behaviors are integral components of empathy. The cognitive component, perspective taking (the ability to assume the viewpoint of another person), requires that we take on the opinions of another, setting our own opinions away until we understand theirs. The second component of empathy, emotional understanding, requires that we step into the shoes of the other person and feel what they are feeling. The third component, caring, is "the icing on the cake." When you genuinely care about the welfare of another person and you combine this with the personal realization of what their situation is like, that is, you have made their experience your own, thinking and feeling as they do, at least temporarily, you gain a greater appreciation of what the world looks like through their eyes. This reflection or mirroring response reveals that we have the capacity to

Ethics and Communication

Through the Eyes of the Beholder

The defendant, 12-year-old Raymond Thomas, had shot 16-year-old Reggie Haines. How do you teach a 12-year-old defendant a lesson he will never forget? One judge devised a novel sentence in an effort to accomplish that objective. Circuit Judge Lynn Tepper imposed a sentence that required 12-year-old Thomas to get a feel for what life was now like for his gunshot victim. As punishment for shooting Haines point-blank in the forehead, Judge Tepper ordered that Thomas first serve time in a wheelchair, then that he use a walker, and finally that he walk with a cane. The judge told Thomas:

"You're going to be moving around in Reggie's world, which you created. You will go to the bathroom in a

wheelchair. You will get in and out of bed, eat, try to drink from the water fountain in a wheelchair." The judge continued, "Perhaps you will appreciate what Reggie had to go through to get where he is today, which is a miracle." [63]

What message is the judge's sentence designed to communicate? In your opinion, is the punishment ethical? Why or why not? Do you believe that Raymond Thomas will perceive the judge's message as intended? In addition, will the sentence enable Raymond Thomas to perceive what Reggie is really going through?

take action, feel emotions, and perceive objects that facilitate our more fully understanding what other people are doing, feeling, and saying. For example, what makes you think that someone who wears a broad smile is happy? You activate parts of your brain that are at work when you're happy and when you experience happiness, perhaps even mimicking, in part, the person's expression by mirroring it with your own unconscious muscle movements.[64] In effect, empathizing frees us to share the emotions and experiences of others. The ability to empathize can make a difference in life.

THE WRAP-UP

Revisiting Chapter Objectives

1. **Define *perception* and explain its stages.**   Perception is the process of selecting, organizing, and subjectively interpreting sensory data in a way that enables us to make sense of our world.

2. **Identify barriers to perception, including perceptual sets, selectivities, first impressions, stereotypes, allness, blindering, and fact-inference confusions.**   By becoming aware of your role in perception, by recognizing that you have biases, and by acknowledging the limiting effects of first impressions and stereotypes, you increase the accuracy of your perceptions. Effective communicators try not to take perceptual shortcuts, stereotyping others in ways that promote prejudice and preventing them from seeing the uniqueness inherent in every individual. They also do their best not to act with too much certainty or too quickly on what they perceive, lest they erroneously think they know it all, place too many restrictions on problem solving, or make inappropriate unjustified inferences by jumping to conclusions.

3. **Discuss how culture and gender affect perception.** Culture and gender, in addition to precipitating in us the desire for perceptual constancy, also teach us how to perceive, thereby influencing our assessments of reality. Both culture and gender cause us to expect others to behave in certain ways and often lead to the development of different standpoints. In effect, we see life through cultural and gendered lenses.

4. **Explore how media and technology influence perception.** Both the media and technology play roles in determining how we perceive experience. When it comes to media offerings, critics contend that, too frequently, we become what we watch, effectively learning the stereotypes and skewed images of reality the media present to us. Technology similarly raises a host of perception-based issues revolving around the nature of identity and virtual reality.

5. **Use guidelines for increasing perceptual accuracy.** We increase our perceptual ability when we recognize that perceptual processes are personally biased, take the time we need to process information fairly and objectively, try to become more open, and work to develop the ability to empathize.

Resources for Further Inquiry and Reflection

To apply your understanding of how the principles in Chapter 4 are at work in our daily lives, consult the following resources for further inquiry and reflection. Or, if you prefer, choose any other appropriate resource. Then connect the ideas expressed in your chosen selection with the communication concepts and issues you are learning about both in and out of class.

 Listen to Me

"Perception of Life" (Brainstorm)
"Theme From the Bottom" (Phish)
"The Way I Am" (Eminem)
"I've Seen It All" (Bjork)
"Suspicious Minds" (Elvis Presley)
"Jenny from the Block" (Jennifer Lopez)
"Wonderful World" (Louis Armstrong)
"One Day at a Time" (Jonas Brothers)

These songs explore one or more aspects of perception. Choose a song and discuss how the speaker's perception affects his or her relationship with one or more other people.

 View Me

Oleanna	*The Constant Gardener*
Big	*American History X*
Dancer in the Dark	*Girl Interrupted*
Penelope	*The Cider-House Rules*
Groundhog Day	*Remember the Titans*
Life Is Beautiful	*A Beautiful Mind*
Rashomon	*Crash*
A History of Violence	*Freaky Friday*

In each of these films, perception plays a key role in the plot. Choose one film and identify the lessons we learn regarding how perception can alter one's reality and life experiences.

THE WRAP-UP

Read Me

Toni Morrison, *The Bluest Eye*. New York: Plume, 2005.

Mark Medoff. *Children of a Lesser God*. New York: Dramatists Play Service, 1980.

Ralph Ellison. *The Invisible Man*. New York: Random House, 1989.

Laura Z. Hobson. *Gentleman's Agreement*. New York: Simon & Schuster, 1947.

Stephen Colbert. *I Am American (And So Can You!)*. New York: Grand Central, 2007.

How does the perception of the main character or characters in the work affect both their experiences and their interaction with others? To what extent, if any, does stereotyping play a role in limiting perception?

Tell Me

Share with the class the insights you gained from your chosen Listen to Me, View Me, or Read Me selection.

Find examples that enable you to support or negate the following: Once you have a belief, it influences your perception of all other relevant information. Once you call a country hostile, you will interpret ambiguous actions on the part of its leaders as indicative of that hostility.

Key Chapter Terminology

www.mhhe.com/gamble10e

Use the Online Learning Center at www.mhhe.com/gamble10e to further your knowledge of the following terminology.

allness 78	perception 67
blindering 79	perceptual constancy 81
closure 69	perceptual sets 72
cultivation theory 84	prejudice 76
cultural nearsightedness 82	primacy effect 75
fact 80	selective attention 74
figure-ground principle 69	selective exposure 74
first impressions 75	selective perception 68
halo effect 75	selective retention 74
horn effect 75	stereotype 76
inference 80	virtual reality 86

Idioms in Translation

absorb stimuli — take in information

pigeonholing — categorizing based on stereotypes

saw with the stomach — let hunger guide interpretation

Culture Cue

The question How are you? should not be interpreted as an inquiry about your health. When it is asked, the expected response is, "Fine. Thank you."

Test Your Understanding

Go to the *Self Quizzes* on the book's Online Learning Center at www.mhhe.com/gamble10e.

www.mhhe.com/gamble10e

After finishing this chapter, you should be able to

1. Define *language,* and explain the relationships among words, things, and thoughts.

2. Identify factors at work in the communication of meaning.

3. Identify problems with meaning, including patterns of miscommunication.

4. Discuss the relationship between culture and language.

5. Discuss the relationship between gender and language.

6. Explain how power and incivility affect language use.

7. Explain how technology is affecting language use.

8. Identify guidelines for developing language skills.

Language and Meaning: Helping Minds Meet

You want to communicate your thoughts to others. What do you do? You translate your thoughts into a code you believe others will understand. Often, your chosen code is composed of words. But what if you were not permitted to use words to make yourself understood? The words that constitute language—whether we are text messaging or talking to someone face-to-face—are so much a part of our lives that many of us would feel totally ineffective as communicators if prohibited from using them. Too frequently, we appreciate the ability to communicate only when it is threatened or lost. We depend on the words of our language to help us share meaning with others. By understanding how language works, we become better able to use words to do just that.

In this chapter, we define language and explore the roots of miscommunication. We consider how aspects of our society affect language use and conclude with guidelines for developing language skills.

Whatever we call a thing, whatever we say it is, it is not. For whatever we say is words, and words are words and not things. The words are maps, and the map is not the territory.
—Harry L. Weinberg, "Some Limitations of Language"

Tact is . . . a kind of mind reading.
—Sara Orne Jewett

Online Learning Center

Go to the Online Learning Center at www.mhhe.com/gramble10e and answer the questions in the *Self Inventory* to evaluate your understanding of communication terms.

language
a unified system of symbols that permits the sharing of meaning

symbol
that which represents something else

triangle of meaning
a model that explains the relationship which exists among words, things, and thoughts

LANGUAGE: WORDS, THINGS, AND THOUGHTS

Language is a unified system of symbols that permits the sharing of meaning. A **symbol** stands for, or represents, something else. Words are symbols, and thus words represent things. Notice the words *represent* and *stand for* rather than *are*. This is a very important distinction. Words stand for, or represent, things but are not the things they stand for. Words are spoken sounds or the written representations of sounds that we have agreed will stand for something else. Thus, by mutual consent, we can make anything stand for anything.

The process of communication involves using words to help create meanings and expectations. However, as important as words are in representing and describing objects and ideas, meaning is not stamped on them. Meanings are in people, not in words. Your goal in communicating with another person is to have your meanings overlap, so that you can each make sense out of the other's messages and understand each other.

Language fulfills its potential only if we use it correctly. The **triangle of meaning,** developed by two communication theorists—C. K. Ogden and I. A. Richards—helps explain how language works (see Figure 5.1).[1] In Ogden and Richards' triangle of meaning, the three points are *thought, word,* and *thing.* The broken line connecting *word* (a symbol) and *thing* (a referent, or stimulus) indicates that *the word is not the*

Ethics and Communication

Looking at Language

1. There is a joke among language scholars:

   Q: What do you call a person who speaks three languages?
   A: *A trilingual.*

   Q: What do you call a person who speaks two languages?
   A: *A bilingual.*

   Q: What do you call a person who speaks one language?
   A: *An American.*

   In his book *Language Shock*, Michael Agar notes that a commonly held stereotype is that Americans find it particularly difficult to enter into the world that goes with another language because it requires them to adopt another point of view, another way of perceiving.[2] To combat this stereotype and change the way Americans look at the world and at themselves, should they have to learn another language? Why or why not? And if they should, which one(s) should they study?

2. According to Steven Pinker, a linguist and author of *The Stuff of Thought: Language as a Window into Human Nature,* whatever language we do speak is the joint creation of millions. Pinker tells us language works because it reflects the world as we jointly experience it. Language does not just convey reality; it also has social functions. Words do not mean what they mean, but we are what we say. Pinker explains that because of our concern for our relationships, we frequently fail to say what we mean, opting to use indirect or ambiguous speech instead.[3]

   In your opinion, is it ever ethical to conceal words under veils of politeness and innuendo? Is it ever ethical to be calculatingly ambiguous? Would you, for example, use indirect speech to help another person save face? Would you use it to negotiate an agreement or treaty? Are some things better left unsaid?

Thought

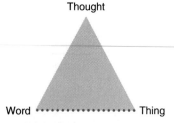

Word ························· Thing

FIGURE 5.1

Triangle of Meaning.

thing and that there is no direct connection between the two. Thus, when you use words, you need to remind yourself that the only relationships between the words you use and the things they represent are those that exist in people's thoughts (including, of course, your own). Frequently, even the existence of an image (a physical object) does not establish meaning. Some time ago, a public service commercial depicting a rat and a child living in a tenement was shown on television. The child was seen beckoning to the rat as she repeated, "Here, kitty, kitty! Here, kitty, kitty!" Although this example may seem somewhat bizarre, its meaning is really quite clear: It is possible for two of us to look at the same object but give it different meanings, because the meaning of anything is inside each person who experiences it.[4] If you are to be a successful communicator, you should understand the relationships that exist between words and people's thoughts and reactions.[5]

THE COMMUNICATION OF MEANING

The communication of meaning from one person to another is a key function of language. The factors identified in this section relate to problems in the sharing of meaning.

Work It Out

Working in groups, provide examples of difficulties you have had sharing meaning with others. Then answer the following questions: How can words create walls between people? Who should be "in charge" of meaning: the speaker or the receiver? What should both the speaker and the receiver do to help avoid a word-wall?

Word Barriers

In talking to others, we often assume too quickly that they understand what we mean. There are many reasons, however, we may not be understood as we want

The Triangle of Meaning at Work

Situation 1. "Congratulations. You've just given birth to a 3.5 kilogram baby." How do you respond? Your joy is momentarily muted if you don't know what a kilogram is. There is no information in bare facts; information comes from what you do with the facts and what you bring to them. If you've never stored a mental image of a kilogram, you can't generate a mental image of the baby's weight from the data.[6]

Situation 2. Imagine that you're at an old Western Union telegraph office. The telegraph operator hears a message on the wire and bursts into tears. You hear the same dots and dashes but have no reaction at all. Why not? If you don't know Morse code, the information means nothing, even if you hear it loud and clear. The same type of scenario might occur today when it comes to the under-

standing and interpretation of text messages. For example, one AT&T advertisement reads: "mnE Ps dnt bleev der is a gNR8N d/c b/t em n thr teen." It then asks: "Do you speak teen?" Meaning is found not in the cues reaching our senses but rather in the associations we attach to them. Meaning is not in the cues reaching our senses, but in the associations we attach to them.

Situation 3. What difference does it make if U.S. officials refer to North Korea as "the imperialist aggressor," a member of the "axis of evil," or as a "superpower of concern."[7] Could the term used to describe a country influence how we perceive and behave toward the people living in that country?

Situation 4. Provide your own example of the triangle of meaning at work.

---

to be and why the words we use can create barriers. In Lewis Carroll's *Through the Looking Glass*, Humpty Dumpty and Alice have the following conversation:

"I don't know what you mean by 'glory,'" Alice said.
Humpty Dumpty smiled contemptuously, "Of course you don't—till I tell you. I meant, 'There's a nice knock-down argument for you!'"
"But 'glory' doesn't mean 'A nice knock-down argument,'" Alice objected.
"When I use a word," Humpty Dumpty said in a rather scornful tone, "it means just what I choose it to mean—neither more nor less."

Words, like eyeglasses, blur everything that they do not make more clear.
—Joseph Jourbert

We can make words mean whatever we want them to mean. Nothing stops us—except our desire to share meaning with others.

Meanings Are Both Denotative and Connotative

We may experience a problem in communication if we consider only our own meaning for a word. Although *we* know what we mean, the crucial question is,

What does this cartoon reveal about the kinds of problems we may encounter when attempting to share meaning? Why do others sometimes misunderstand or misread the intentions behind our words? What recourse do we have when this happens?

What does our word bring to mind for those with whom we are communicating? When we think about what language means, we must think in terms of both **denotative** (objective, or dictionary) **meaning** and **connotative** (subjective, or personal) **meaning.**

denotative meaning

dictionary meaning; the objective or descriptive meaning of a word

connotative meaning

subjective meaning; one's personal meaning for a word

Meaning and Time

Every noteworthy event, particularly catastrophes, catapult words into everyday speech and dictionaries. September 11, 2001, is no exception. When the American Dialect Society met to decide the top or newly reconditioned words of the previous year, *9/11* was voted the expression most likely to last.

Words come and go from dictionaries. For example, the words *carbon footprint* (the amount of greenhouse gas emissions an individual is responsible for), *green audit* (an inspection of a company to define its impact on the environment), *carbon-neutral* (achieving a zero level of carbon dioxide emissions), *Chelsea tractor* (a gas-guzzling sport utility vehicle), *manbag* (a male handbag), and *tataki* (Japanese raw or slightly seared meat or fish) are among the 2,500 new words being added to the sixth edition of the Oxford English Dictionary.[8]

What personal meanings do you have for the word "waxing"? How is the word defined in the dictionary?

By Isabella Bannerman, www.CartoonStock.com. Used with permission.

John and Judy spent their Saturday waxing.

Skill Builder

A Time Capsule for Words

1. Briefly define each of the following terms:

   Net _____

   Hooking up _____

   Cougar _____

   Previvor _____

   Colbert bump _____

   Freegan _____

   McJob _____

   Straight _____

   Cookies _____

2. Show the list, without definitions, to your parents, older relatives, or older friends, and ask them to write their definitions for the words.

3. Compare your meaning for each term with the meanings given by others. Why do you suppose their meanings differed from yours?

4. Pretend it is now the year 2030. On a separate sheet of paper, create a new meaning for each word listed.

(To get a good sense of how time affects meaning, try the Skill Builder "A Time Capsule for Words" above.)

Many "old" words acquire vivid new meanings every decade or so. Viruses today are not just germs spread from person to person, but malicious programs that can spread instantaneously from one computer to computers globally.[9] Consequently, when we use a word that referred to a particular object at a particular time, we should attempt to determine if it still means the same thing now.

Meaning and Place

Words change meaning not only over time, but also from one region of the country to another. For example, what would you envision having if you were to stop for a soda? For an egg cream? What each word brings to mind probably depends on the region of the country you grew up in. In some parts of the United States, *soda* refers to a soft drink, but in others it refers to a concoction of ice cream and a soft drink. In some sections of the country, *egg cream* refers to a mixture of seltzer, syrup, and milk, but elsewhere it conjures up the image of an egg mixed with cream.

Work It Out

What do you think? Do different generations and different regions of the country have different meanings for the same words or different words for the same things?

Meaning and Experience

The meanings we assign to words are based on our past experiences with the words and with the things they represent. Consider the word *cancer*, for example. If you were dealing with three people in a hospital—a surgeon, a patient, and a statistician—how do you imagine each would react to this word? The surgeon might think about operating procedures or diagnostic techniques, or about how to tell a patient that he or she has cancer. The patient might think about the odds for recovery and might well be frightened. The statistician might see cancer as an important factor in life expectancy tables.

Unlike denotative (dictionary) meanings—which are generally agreed to and are objective, abstract, and general—connotative (personal) meanings are individual, subjective, and emotional. Thus, your own experiences influence the meanings you assign to words; that is, your connotative meanings vary according to your own feelings for the object or concept you are considering.

Whether Language Is Concrete or Abstract Influences Meaning

The language we use varies in its specificity. Consider this family pet. We could call it:

> dog
> domesticated canine
> small, domesticated canine
> a standard Poodle
> Lucy

In each instance, our description becomes somewhat more specific. Alfred Korzybski and S. I. Hayakawa devised an abstraction ladder to describe this process.[10] The ladder is composed of a number of descriptions of the same thing. Lower items focus specifically on the person, object, or event, while higher items are generalizations that include the subject as part of a larger class. As the words we use move from abstract (less specific) to concrete (more specific), they become more precise in meaning and are more likely to appeal to our senses and conjure up a picture. Specific words, like *Lucy*, clarify meaning by narrowing the number of possible images a person pictures.

Using high-level abstractions serves a number of functions. First, because high-level abstractions function as a kind of verbal shorthand, they enable us to generalize, and our communication becomes easier and faster. Second, because they also enable us to be deliberately unclear, high-level abstractions allow us to limit understanding and avoid confrontations when we believe it is necessary. When, for example, a friend asks you what you think of a new outfit or your boss asks you what you think of a new corporate strategy, if telling the truth appears too risky to you, you can offer an abstract answer to the question and avoid being put on the line. On the other hand, relying on high-level abstractions can also cause meaning to become fuzzy—primarily because the words you use can be misunderstood. The goal is to use the level of abstraction that meets the needs of your communication objectives and the situation.

> **Who do you imagine finds it easier to speak concretely, men or women?**

Lucy is a poodle with personality.

PROBLEMS WITH MEANING: PATTERNS OF MISCOMMUNICATION

If we do not make an attempt to analyze how people's backgrounds influence them in assigning meaning, we may have trouble communicating with them. For most of us, words have more than a single meaning. In fact, a commonly used word can frequently have more than 20 definitions. We know that a strike in bowling is different from a strike in baseball. We know that striking a match is not the same as striking up the band. For this reason, we must pay careful attention to the context of a message. Unfortunately, we frequently forget that words are rarely used in one and only one sense, and we assume when we speak to others that our words are being understood in only the way we intend them to be understood. Our receivers, however, may assume that their interpretation of our words is the meaning we intended. Let's explore what happens when this occurs.

If you cry "Forward" you must be sure to make clear the direction in which to go. Don't you see that if you fail to do that and simply call out the word to a monk and a revolutionary they will go in precisely opposite directions?
—Anton Chekhov

Bypassing: Confusing Meanings

> All someone said was "Hi, Jack!" but at a suburban Detroit airport, those two words precipitated a crisis.
>
> A microphone happened to be open when an individual abroad a corporate jet greeted the co-pilot. Air traffic controllers in the airport's control tower equated those words with "hijack." The police, the SWAT team, and the FBI were alerted. The plane was ordered to return to the tower.[11]

Sometimes people think they understand each other, when, in fact, they are really missing each other's meaning. This pattern of miscommunication is called **bypassing,** because the interactants' meanings simply pass by one another.

We can identify two main kinds of bypassing.[12] The first occurs when people use different words or phrases to represent the same thing but are unaware that they are both talking about the same thing. For example, two urban politicians once argued vehemently over welfare policies. One held that the city's welfare program should be "overhauled," whereas the other believed that "minor changes" should be made. Far too much time passed before it was realized that the first politician's overhaul was actually equivalent to the second politician's minor changes.

The second, and more common, type of bypassing occurs when people use the same word or phrase but give it different meanings. In such cases, people appear to be in agreement when they substantially disagree. Sometimes this type of bypassing is harmless. Semanticists tell a tall, but otherwise useful, story about a man who was driving on a parkway when his engine stalled. He managed to flag down another driver, who, after hearing his story, consented to push the stalled car to get it started. "My car has an automatic transmission," the first man explained, "so you'll have to get up to 30 or 35 miles an hour to get me moving." The other driver nodded in understanding, and the stalled motorist then climbed back into his own car and waited for the other car to line up behind him. After much more waiting, he turned around—to see the other driver coming at him at 30 miles per hour.

Developing an awareness that bypassing can occur when you communicate is a first step in preventing it from interfering with or needlessly complicating your relationships. If you believe it is possible for your listener to misunderstand you, then be willing to take the time needed to ensure that your meanings for words

bypassing
miscommunication that occurs when individuals think they understand each other but actually miss each other's meaning

Work It Out
Provide an example of how each type of bypassing caused a problem for you or someone you know. Then think of instances when being "word-minded" rather than "person-minded" caused problems for you.

What type of behavior would you exhibit around vats labeled "Gasoline Drums"? You would probably be careful not to light any matches, and you would likely counsel anyone who smoked not to toss away any cigarette butts. Would you change your behavior if the labels on the containers read "Empty Gasoline Drums"? Chances are, you might relax a bit and give less thought to the possibility of starting a fire—although empty drums are actually more dangerous because they contain explosive vapor.

overlap. To avoid bypassing, you must be "person-minded" instead of "word-minded." Remind yourself that your words may generate unpredictable or unexpected reactions in others. Trying to anticipate those reactions will help you forestall communication problems.

Labeling: Confusing Words and Things

Sometimes we forget that it is people, not words, who make meanings. When this happens, we pay far too much attention to labels and far too little attention to reality. We can approach this phase of our study of meaning by considering the problem of labels and how strongly they can influence us.

How important are labels in our culture? A judge ruled that an individual could not change his name to a number because a number was totalitarian and an offense to human dignity. What does a number, as opposed to a name, signify? Would we change if our names were changed?[13] In *Romeo and Juliet*, Shakespeare offered some thoughts on the significance of names when he had Juliet, of the Capulet family, say these words to Romeo, a Montague:

> 'Tis but thy name that is my enemy;
> Thou art thyself, though not a Montague.
> What's Montague? It is nor hand, nor foot,
> Nor arm, nor face, nor any other part
> Belonging to a man. O! be some other name;
> What's in a name? that which we call a rose
> By any other name would smell as sweet;
> So Romeo would, were he not Romeo call'd.

Our name-brand society is a testament to the power of labels to alter perceptions of value. Recent tests, demonstrating how advertising can trick the taste buds of young children, revealed that anything made by McDonald's tastes better to them—even carrots, milk, and apple juice—if wrapped in paper with the McDonald's label. Labeling, known in marketing jargon as *branding*, also appears to have the ability to physically alter perceptions of taste.[14] As we noted earlier, the word is not the thing. Words are symbols, and when we let them blind us to what they represent, we give them "magic" powers.

Did McDonald's use of the word McCafé change your perception of its coffee? Why or why not?

Evasive and Emotive Language

Frequently, our reaction to a person or event is totally changed by words. If we are not vigilant, we can easily be manipulated or conned by language.

Analyze the following sets of words to see how your reactions may change as the words used change:

1. coffin   casket   slumber chamber
2. girl   woman   broad
3. backward   developing   underdeveloped
4. the corpse   the deceased the loved one

Thus, if we like an old piece of furniture, we might refer to it as an antique. If we don't like it, we're likely to call it a piece of junk. Words broadcast attitude. For example, a few years ago, PETA (People for the Ethical Treatment of Animals) asked the Federal Trade Commission to revise the fur label term "animal producing the fur" to read "animal slaughtered for the fur."[15] The word **euphemism** is derived from the Greek term meaning "to use words of good omen." When we use a euphemism, we substitute a pleasant term for a less pleasant one. Euphemisms can help conceal a communicator's meaning by making the message delivered appear more congenial than it actually is. Employees who lose their jobs are "dehired," undergo a "vocational relocation," are left "indefinitely idling," or experience a "realignment" or "constructive dismissal" or are "freed up for the future." It seems that only on *The Apprentice* does someone actually utter the words, "You're fired!" When the environment became a political campaign issue, strategist Frank Luntz advised candidates to use the term *climate change* in place of *global warming* because "while global warming has catastrophic communications attached to it, climate change sounds a more controllable and less emotional challenge."[16] He also suggested they use *conservationist* instead of *environmentalist* because the former conveys a "moderate, reasoned, common sense position," while the latter has the "connotation of extremism."[17] William Lutz, the coiner of the term *doublespeak*, equates the evasive use of language with linguistic fraud and deception.[18] Lutz believes the following are prime examples of doublespeak: calling the invasion of another country a "predawn vertical insertion," naming a missile the "Peacemaker," and referring to taxes as "revenue enhancement." Because the thinking is that everybody fears the word *cloning*, people who oppose cloning research tend to use the word, while people who support it call it somatic cell nuclear transfer or something else. Should people use words to disguise reality? For example, in an effort to blunt criticism of the nearsighted cartoon figure Mr. Magoo by the National Federation of the Blind, a Disney spokesperson said that Mr. Magoo isn't blind but, rather, "visually limited."[19]

Politically Correct Language

The following definitions appear in Henry Beard and Christopher Cerf's tongue-in-cheek guide, *The Official Politically Correct Dictionary and Handbook*:

lazy: motivationally deficient
wrong: differently logical
ugly: cosmetically different
prostitute: sex-care provider
fat: horizontally challenged[20]

What is politically correct language? Is it sensitive speech or censored speech? In what ways, if any, does its use sustain, or violate, our right of free speech? According to Diane Ravitch, author of *The Language Police*, words that might offend feminists, religious conservatives, multiculturalists, ethnic activists, or members of other groups are routinely deleted from the textbooks read in U.S. schools because they are believed to be politically incorrect. For example, one textbook author rewrote Bob Dylan's folk song "Blowin' in the Wind," which had asked, "How many roads must a man walk down before you call him a man?," to

What's in a name? Is who you are affected by what you are called? Do the names of your friends affect your opinions of them? Would you mind if your instructor called you a number, or a nick-number, rather than your name? Does changing your name change your identity?

euphemism
a pleasant word that is substituted for a less pleasant one

Work It Out

When we are preoccupied with or blinded by labels, we display an *intensional* orientation. When we focus on what lies behind the label—the world of experience—we display an *extensional* orientation and refuse to let labels fool us. Provide examples of how advertisers and politicians use labels to their advantage. For each example offered, identify what the consumer or public needs to do to look beyond the label and display extensional orientation. Advertisers count on consumer's acting as if words and things were the same. While such behavior benefits advertisers, it usually harms consumers.

Each of us has learned to see the world not as it is, but through the distorting glass of our words. It is through words that we are made human, and it is through words that we are dehumanized.

—*Ashley Montagu, "The Language of Self-Deception"*

read "How many roads must an individual walk down before you can call them [sic] an adult?"[21]

Like so many other words, politically correct language means different things to different people. For some of us, being politically correct means making the effort not to offend by selecting words that demonstrate our respect for and sensitivity to the needs and interests of others. Politically correct language can help take the sting out of confrontations by blunting the sharpness of the words we use. For example, in the United States, over a period of time, the word *slow* was replaced by the word *retarded*, which was changed to *challenged* and then to *special*. Similarly, over a half century, the defining term for persons of African ancestry has shifted from *colored* to *Negro* to *Black* to *Afro-American* to *people of color* to *African American*.[22] When we use politically correct language, we adapt our language to reveal our sensitivity to the preferences of those with whom we are conversing.

For others, however, political correctness means that we feel compelled by societal pressures not to use some words—oftentimes referred to as taboo words—because we believe that doing so could cause others to label us as racist, sexist, homophobic, or ageist. For example, some years ago, a student at one Ivy League university was thought to be racist when he yelled, "Shut up, you water buffalo!" out a window at a noisy group of African-American women. Still others view political correctness and sensitivity training as a danger to free speech. Which of these three positions comes closest to the one you hold?

CULTURE AND LANGUAGE

Since culture influences language use, communication between members of diverse cultures can be challenging.

Culture Influences the Words Used

dominant culture
the culture in power; the mainstream culture

Both the **dominant culture** (the culture in power, the mainstream culture composed of people who share the same values, beliefs, and ways of behaving and communicating and who pass them on from one generation to another) and co-cultures (groups of people such as African Americans, Hispanics, Asians, musicians, athletes, environmentalists, and drug users, who have a culture of their own outside the dominant culture) have different languages. Hence, usages vary from culture to culture. If a concept is important to a culture, there will be a large number of terms to describe it. For example, in our culture, the word *money* is very important and we have many words to describe it: *Wealth, capital, assets, backing, resources*, and *finance* are just a few. Inuktitut, the Inuit language,

Culture influences communication, including our choice of words.

has different words for snow that is falling (*quanniq*), snow on the ground (*aput*), snow that is blowing (*pirsiriug*), snow that is drifting (*natiruvaaq*), wet snow (*masak*), wet and compact snow (*kinirtaq*), fresh and wet, soggy snow (*aquilluqaaq*), the first snowfall of autumn (*apigiannagaut*), encrusted snow that gives way underfoot (*katakarktariaq*), and snow causing crunchy sounds when you walk (*qeqergranaartoq*), to name just a few.[23] In contrast to the Inuit, Arabs have only one word for snow—*talg*—and it refers to either ice or snow. Similarly, there are at least 19 Chinese words for silk and 8 for rice. And because the Chinese care deeply for their families, there is a plethora of words for relations. The Chinese have five words they can use for uncle, depending on whose brother he is.[24]

The world we experience helps shape the language we speak, and the language we speak helps sustain our perception of reality and our view of our world. This idea is contained in the **Sapir-Whorf hypothesis.** According to the Sapir-Whorf hypothesis, people from different cultures perceive stimuli and communicate differently, at least in part, because of their language differences. The Sapir-Whorf hypothesis has two threads: linguistic determinism and linguistic relativity. **Linguistic determinism** suggests that our language influences how we interpret the world. **Linguistic relativity** suggests that, since language affects thought, persons who speak different languages will perceive the world differently. In *When Cultures Collide*, Richard Lewis explains why the Zulu language has 39 words for green, while English has but 1. According to a Zulu chief, before their national highway system existed, the Zulu were required to make long trips across the savannah, or grasslands. Since no signposts or maps existed to facilitate their journeys, they had to rely on the descriptions of those who traveled the road before. Thus, the Zulu devised different words for tree leaves, bush leaves, leaves vibrating with the wind, river greens, pool greens, tree trunk greens, crocodile greens, and so on. The different greens functioned much as a map would in alerting the travelers to important route signposts.[25]

> Some cultures encourage minimal verbal communication. A Japanese proverb says, "By your mouth you shall perish." What do you think this proverb means?

Sapir-Whorf hypothesis
the belief that the labels we use help shape the way we think, our worldview, and our behavior

linguistic determinism
the belief that language influences how we interpret the world

linguistic relativity
the belief that persons who speak different languages perceive the world differently

Cultural Differences Can Lead to Confused Translations

Translating ideas from one language to another can lead to problems. Sometimes the situation produced by a bungled translation, while costly, is still amusing. For example, an English-speaking representative of an American soft drink company could not understand why Mexican customers laughed when she offered them free samples of Fresca soda. In Mexican slang, the word *fresca* can be translated as "lesbian." Similarly, Beck's beer has been translated into Chinese as *Bei Ke*, which means "shellfish overcome."[26] Along the same lines, Dr Pepper no longer runs its "I'm a Pepper" ads in the United Kingdom, because *pepper* in British slang means "prostitute."

Other times, however, a poor translation can insult and confuse recipients. For example, one Spanish-language letter sent to welfare recipients about changes in New Jersey's welfare program contained numerous grammatical errors, suggesting a lack of multicultural competency. Referring to the recipient's ability to support himself or herself, the letter uses the word *soportarse*. But the common translation of the verb *support* in Spanish is *sostener* or *mantener*. In Spanish, *soportarse* means "to tolerate oneself." Another section translated *parole violator* as "rapist under oath."[27]

Work It Out
Research instances when the use of a word caused problems for a corporation or the government. Discuss how the word problem was or could be solved.

Poorly translated reports have economic and political repercussions. For example, one badly translated version of a Chinese tourism reporter's speculative musings on how an appreciation of the Chinese currency might play itself out triggered a trading panic and the potential reevaluation of world currencies. Who was to blame? While the reporter blamed the translator's garbled English, the translator blamed the reporter for putting too many vague sentences in the story, thereby causing the mistranslation. What can be done to avoid such problems?

linguistic prejudice
the use of prejudiced language

prejudiced language
sexist, ageist, or racist language; language disparaging to the members of a co-culture

racial code words
words that are discriminatory but not literally racist

Culture Influences Communication Style

Because members of Asian cultures practice the principles of *omoiyari* (listeners need to understand the speaker without the speaker's being specific or direct) and *sassuru* (listeners need to use subtle cues to infer a speaker's meaning), they are apt to keep their feelings to themselves and use language more sparingly and carefully than do Westerners.[28] Because Westerners value straight talk, prefer to speak explicitly, and use inductive and deductive reasoning to make points, they may interpret the round-about expressions of Asians as evasive, manipulative, or misleading.

The way parents in both Western and Asian cultures handle a request from a child to whom they do not want to accede provides a prime example of the cultural differences in directness. When confronted with such a situation, most U.S. parents would simply say no. In Japan, however, the parent would give reasons for denying the child's request but will not say no directly.[29] Every culture teaches its members its preferred style. Whereas in the United States we prefer to be up-front and tell it like it is, many Asian cultures stand by the value of indirectness because it helps people save face and avoid being criticized or contradicted in public.

As we see, in some cultures, symbolism and vagueness are embedded in language and users intuitively understand that words do not necessarily mean "what they mean." For example, according to social scientist Kian Tajbakhsh, whereas in the West, 80 percent of language is denotative, in countries such as Iran, 80 percent is connotative. In the West, "yes" generally means yes; in Iran, "yes" can mean yes, but it often means maybe or no. In Iran, people use a social principle called *taarof* (insincerity) to avoid conflict. According to this principle people will tell you what they think you want to hear, for example, praising you, but they won't necessarily mean it.[30] What kinds of problems result when people from different cultures use words differently?

Do you believe your culture would influence your response to this child?

Exploring Diversity

Walk in My Moccasins

Those who fought for eliminating the use of Indian names, mascots, and rituals in sports and society did so because they believed such portraitures were caricatures and objectified Indians. Those who wanted to continue their use criticized those opposed as overly sensitive and humorless. What do you think?

How would you react if the name of your college's sports team was the "Fighting Whites" and chose for its mascot a White man in a suit? To protest the use of the name "Fighting Reds" by one of their opposing teams, one multiracial Colorado sports team did just that!

What about the U.S. military's use of equipment such as the Apache, Chinook, and Black Hawk helicopters? What about the names of popular cars such as Jeep Cherokee and Pontiac? How would you respond if automakers marketed a car named the "Wandering Jew"? Do you believe that when it comes to the contemporary use of racial slurs, products, and mascots, we have a double standard? If so, what action, if any, should we take?

Prejudiced Talk

Sometimes members of a dominant culture use derogatory terms or racist language to label members of a co-culture, disparage them as inferior or undesirable, and set them apart from the mainstream group. **Linguistic prejudice** or the use of **prejudiced language** reflects the dominant group's desire to exert its power over other groups. Such language stresses the differences between people of different groups, downplays any similarities, claims that the persons who are different do not make an effort to adapt, and notes that they are involved in negative acts and that they threaten the interests of in-group members.[31]

The courts have ruled that managers who use **racial code words** (words that are discriminatory but are not literally racist), such as "you people" and "one of them," help create a racially hostile environment. As a result of this ruling, many businesses are banning the use of such phrases.[32] Additionally, corporate advertisers and educational institutions have long used Native American names such as "redskins," "braves," "Seminoles," along with logos and images including severed heads and tomahawk chops to "play Indian" and sell products and events.[33] In your opinion, were these representations racist? The National Collegiate Athletic Association (NCAA) has banned such exploitative practices unless the named American Indian tribe explicitly approves the use, as the Seminole tribe of Florida has for Florida State University.

Globalization Influences Language Use

Because of free trade, and the popularity of Hollywood and the Internet, the use of English around the world is growing. With globalization, more and more companies use English as their internal language.[34] This side effect of globalization does

Do you support or oppose the use of Native American mascots or rituals in sports? Why?

Work It Out

Culture talks. People from different cultures often need to relate to and negotiate with one another. However, their negotiations sometimes fail because they fail to understand how the members of other cultures perceive and use verbal communication. Such lack of understanding leads to the creation of a cultural wall, keeping them from adapting their communication style as needed.

Using a series of role plays, demonstrate the cultural wall concept by showing what could happen if people from the United States or Western Europe who lacked knowledge about the culture of their counterparts needed to interact or negotiate with (1) Eastern Europeans, (2) Latin Americans, (3) individuals from the Middle East or North Africa, and (4) Asians. Repeat the role-plays, this time showing how knowledge of another culture can prevent a cultural wall from causing a breakdown in communication.

not please everyone. The fear among non-English-speaking nations is that, if their citizens use English, the use of their native languages will disappear, threatening national identity. For example, so many young Germans mix their language with English so freely that their speech is called Denglish, a blend of *Deutsch* (meaning "German") and *English*.[35]

The adoption of English or English-sounding words is common for persons within the United States for whom English is not their first language. When people from different groups converge, they begin to straddle cultural worlds, with language acting as the bridge. For example, the influence of English on New York Spanish produced Spanglish, a blend of Spanish and English. Spanglish is now used in television programs and in Hallmark greeting cards. Recognizing the largest minority group in the United States, advertisers also run Spanish-language ads, sometimes with English taglines to reach the growing Hispanic and Latino audience.

Hip-Hop and Rap Talk

Hip-hop is a social community that uses rap, a special language, to help express its culture.[36] Rap is a celebration of language that speaks to both the body and the brain. The rapper's words arrive in syncopated speech, peppered with both rapid-fire rhymed boasts and taunts. The subjects of rap range from sex, money, and guns to love, politics, the minutiae of our lives, and the American social experience. Rappers redefine the meanings of words. When someone attuned to the hip-hop culture says, "I'm keeping it ghetto," he or she means "I'm keeping it real." Since its introduction about a quarter of a century ago, critics have maligned and praised rap. Some critics blame rap for

What do you think of the NCAA's decision? Can you imagine a team today being called the "Cleveland Africans," the "Cleveland Asians," or the "Cleveland Hispanics"? Why or why not?

Rap is a language that speaks to both the body and the brain. Some critics malign it while others praise it. What do you think of it?

promoting violence and misogyny. Testifying before Congress, Master P, whose real name is Percy Miller, apologized to women for past songs he sang that demeaned them. However, rapper and record producer Levell Crump, also known as David Banner, defiantly told legislators, "I'm like Stephen King. Horror music is what I do. . . . Change the situation in my neighborhood and maybe I'll get better."[37] Edgar Bronfman, Jr., the chairman of Warner Music Group, added that tasteless language "is in the eye of the beholder."[38] Others praise rap for promoting peace and minority influence. For some, rap is the defining pulse for the Iraq war, enabling soldiers to express and relieve their fears, aggression, and exhaustion, as well as share with others what it is like there.[39] For the United States, rap is a key to winning over Arab youth; the United States broadcasts raps to Arab audiences on Radio Sawa.[40]

Work It Out

Some observers say that the ambiguous nature of rap reveals that rappers are using a coded language so that they can better juggle multiple constituencies. What do you think? Can you provide examples of how rappers redefine words?

GENDER AND LANGUAGE

Language influences the attitudes we hold about males and females, as well as the way that males and females perceive each other.

Sexism in Language

Too many people persist in sex-role stereotyping. For example, if you refer to a surgeon as a "he" and a nurse as a "she" when you have no knowledge of the person's sex, or if you highlight the sex of a professional by alluding to a "male nurse" or a "female lawyer" instead of keeping language gender-free, sexism is present.

Sexist language perpetuates negative stereotypes and negatively affects communication. Past use of male generics, such as *mankind, chairman, spokesman, manpower,* and *Man of the Year,* share blame for causing men to be perceived as more important or significant than women. To counter this perception, many companies and individuals stopped using male generics, or other kinds of sexist language, and use gender-neutral language instead.

Another way that language use may be sexist is the way words are used to address women. "Women, much more than men, are addressed through terms of endearment such as honey, cutie, and sweetie, which function to devalue women by depriving them of their name while renaming them with trivial terms."[41]

Additionally, while the English language has more masculine terms than feminine terms, it has more negative feminine terms than masculine ones.[42]

Finally, psychologist Albert Mehrabian has studied reactions to unisex names. He notes that when a boy's name catches on with girls, it usually loses favor as a name for boys. Historically, U.S. parents have felt free to choose androgynous names for girls. In contrast, some countries, like Finland, have official lists of boys' and girls' names that parents must select from.[43] Names often reflect fashion, taste, and culture. In Venezuela, for example, legislators introduced a bill that prohibited Venezuelan parents from giving their children names that exposed them to ridicule or were hard to pronounce in Spanish.[44] In Thailand, children are given English nicknames like Pig, Money, Fat, and Seven because they are easier for foreigners to pronounce.[45] In southern Africa, parents choose the names of children to convey a specific meaning, and not to convey the latest fad, as is common in the West.

Names such as Godknows, Enough, Wind, and Rain are common in southern Africa.[46] Mehrabian, author of *Baby Name Report Card*, reports that people in the United States respond differently to different names, exhibiting more positive reactions to more common names.[47]

Gender and Speech Style

Sometimes the sex of communicators affects not only the meaning we give to their utterances but also the very structure of those utterances. Women, for example, tend to use more tentative phrases, or **qualifiers,** in their speech than men do. Phrases like "I guess," "I think," and "I wonder if" abound in the speech patterns of women but not in those of men. This pattern is also passed on to the very young through their favorite cartoon characters. Past studies revealed that female cartoon characters, more than male characters, used verbs that indicated lack of certainty ("I suppose") and words judged to be polite.[48] When students were shown cartoon characters and asked to identify a character's sex based on the words the character spoke, students assigned the logical, concise, and controlling captions to male characters and the emotional, vague, and verbose captions to female characters.[49] Do cartoon characters continue to perpetuate such stereotypes?

Men and women rely on different conversational strategies. Women, for example, tend to turn statements into questions more than men do, saying something like "Don't you think it would be better to send them that report first?" Men, in contrast,

qualifiers
tentative phrases

pop language
words and phrases used to sell oneself as hip or cool

Media Wise

What Words Do We Remember? What Words Do We Use?

1. In *Words That Work: It's Not What You Say, It's What People Hear,* author, pollster, and media commentator Frank Luntz makes the following observation: "Great movie quotes become part of our cultural vocabulary."[50] For example, though they are from films made years ago, many of us still use phrases such as "I'll be back," from *The Terminator;* "What we've got here is a failure to communicate," from *Cool Hand Luke;* "You talking to me?" from *Taxi Driver;* and "I'm mad as hell and I'm not going to take it any more," from *Network.* Interestingly, a male uttered each of these lines. Similarly, ad slogans such as "You deserve a break today" (McDonald's) and "I am stuck on Band-Aids . . . " (Band-Aids) are equally remembered and stick in our brains, to be remembered forever. What quotes from recent films do you think we will still be using in years to come? Why? How many were spoken by men? How many by women?

2. In the book *Slam Dunks and No-Brainers: Language in Your Life, the Media, Business, Politics, and, Like, Whatever,* media critic Leslie Savan laments the growing use of **pop language,** words and phrases used to sell oneself as "with it." She says that phrases such as "Don't go there," "Get over it," "You've got that right," "duh," and

"bling" constitute a new subdivision of English, projecting an attitude and a vocabulary derived from television and advertising, and virtually clicking into place without their users needing to think, effectively turning them into corporate pawns. Do you think she's right? Is pop language use displacing more complex thinking? Keep count of the number of pop phrases that you and others use during a typical day. What words could have been spoken in their place that might have been more expressive of personal thoughts? Who uses pop language more, men or women?

3. The study "Sex Bias in the Newspaper Treatment of Male-Centered and Female-Centered News Stories" by K. G. Foreit and colleagues, published in the journal *Sex Roles* over 30 years ago, revealed that a woman's marital status was mentioned in 64 percent of the stories examined, while a male's marital status was mentioned in only 12 percent. Have things changed today? Pick up a copy of a current English-language newspaper or magazine. Identify and count the number of male-centered and female-centered news stories in it. Also count the number of times the marital status of each person is referred to in each story. Have we made any progress?

typically respond with a more definitive "Yes, it would be better to send them that report first." According to Robin Lakoff, a researcher on language and gender, women do not "lay claim to" their statements as frequently as men do. In addition, women use more **tag questions** than men do. A tag is midway between an outright statement and a yes-no question. For instance, women often make queries like these: "Joan is here, isn't she?" "It's hot in here, isn't it?" By seeking verbal confirmation for their perceptions, women acquire a reputation for tentativeness. Similarly, women use more **disclaimers** than men do, prefacing their remarks with statements like "This probably isn't important, but. . . ." While male speech tends to be dominant, straightforward, and attention-commanding, female speech tends to be gentle, friendly, and accommodating.[51] Such practices weaken the messages women send to others.

According to communications researcher Patricia Hayes Bradley, even if men use tag questions, the perceptual damage done to them by this weaker verbal form is not as great as the damage done to women. Bradley found that when women used tag questions and disclaimers or failed to support their arguments, they were judged to be less intelligent and knowledgeable—but men were not. Simply talking "like a woman" causes a woman to be judged negatively.[52] Researchers Nancy Henley and Cheris Kramarae believe that females face a disadvantage when interacting with males: "Females are required to develop special sensitivity to interpret males' silence, lack of emotional expression, or brutality, and to help men express themselves. Yet it is women's communication style that is often labeled as inadequate and maladaptive."[53] Do you agree?

Gender-Lects

Gender affects how men and women use and process language in a number of other ways as well. According to linguist Deborah Tannen, men and women speak different **gender-lects.** While women speak and hear a language of connection and intimacy, Tannen finds that men speak and hear a language of status and independence.[54] As a result, when conversing with men, women tend to listen attentively rather than interrupt or challenge what a man is saying. Why? Tannen holds that it is because challenging the man could damage the established connection that most women believe must be preserved at all costs.

In addition, men and women tend to speak about different topics. Monica Hiller and Fern Johnson conducted a topic analysis of conversations held in two coffee shops, one frequented by young adults and the other by middle-aged and older customers. Their research revealed that, whereas men and women both talked about work and social issues, women talked about personal issues and the older men virtually never discussed personal issues.[55] Although men and women frequently talk to each other, their cross-gender talk differs topically from man-to-man or woman-to-woman talk. Women talk about their doubts and fears, personal and family problems, and intimate relationships, while, in general, men talk more about work and sports.

tag questions
questions that are midway between outright statements and yes-no questions

disclaimers
remarks that diminish a statement's importance

gender-lects
Deborah Tannen's term for language differences attributed to gender

What topics do you talk about with same-sex friends?

Which, if any, of these cartoons do you believe to be true? why?

LANGUAGE AND POWER

Some people seem to announce their powerlessness through their language. Because they speak indirectly, people perceive that they lack self-confidence and power. In contrast, persons perceived to be "powertalkers" make definite statements, such as "Let's go out to dinner tonight." Powertalkers direct the action; they assume control.

Typically, powertalkers hesitate less in their speech. Instead of filling statements with nonfluencies, such as "I wish you wouldn't, uh, keep me waiting so long," powertalkers enhance their sense of self-worth by projecting their opinions with more confidence. They eliminate fillers, such as "er," "um," "you know," "like," and "well," which serve as verbal hiccups and make a speaker appear weak.

Powerful talk is talk that comes directly to the point. It does not contain disclaimers ("I probably shouldn't mention this, but . . .") or tag questions like those described in the section "Gender and Speech Style." If you speak powertalk, your credibility and your ability to influence others will increase. Changing the power balance may be as simple as changing the words you use.

Talking powerfully is also less risky. According to Deborah Tannen, speaking indirectly in some situations actually causes problems. She cites the following conversation about de-icing between a pilot and a copilot as an example of its dangers:

> *Copilot:* Look how the ice is just hanging on his, ah, back, back there, see that? . . .
>
> *Copilot:* See all those icicles on the back there and everything?
>
> *Captain:* Yeah . . .
>
> *Copilot:* Boy, this is a, this is a losing battle here on trying to de-ice those things . . .
>
> *Copilot:* Let's check these tops again since we've been here a while.
>
> *Captain:* I think we get to go here in a minute.[56]

Has indirectness ever caused problems for you? What prevented you or the person you were speaking with from being more direct?

Less than a minute later, the plane crashed. While the copilot, probably because of his lower status, had tried to warn the pilot indirectly, the pilot failed to act on the cues. Indirectness, it seems, is easier for higher-status persons to ignore. As a result, flight crews today are trained to express themselves in more direct ways, and pilots are taught to pick up on indirect hints.

Flight crews are trained to express themselves in direct ways.

PROFANITY AND OBSCENITY: INCIVILITY AND THE COARSENING OF LANGUAGE

When accepting an award on live television, rock singer Bono commented, "This is really, really f___k-ing brilliant." An NBC news broadcaster, not realizing they were still on the air, yelled at the cohost: "What the f___k are you doing?" Students at one college screamed obscenities at a recent college basketball game, targeting a player who had chosen not to play for their school, yelling vulgarities at him and calling his relatives whores. *Sports Illustrated*, in an article on student boorishness, called the 2007–2008 basketball season the ugliest one in years.[57] Has it become acceptable to utter obscenities in public, including in the media? The use of insults, vulgar expressions, and speech that degrades and encourages hostility in others is on the rise.

According to Timothy Jay, a leading scholar on cursing in the United States, contemporary teenagers are more likely to use expletives casually—uttering swear words some 80 to 90 times each day. Because the lines between public and private language are blurred, today's teens have more difficulty than teens in previous generations adjusting their conversation to fit their audience.[58] The same appears to be true in the workplace. A female employee of a major construction company felt compelled to complain to the director of human resources about the cursing used in the company's facilities. The company responded by publishing "A Language Code of Ethics." It defined inappropriate language as "unwanted, deliberate, repeated, unsolicited profanity, cussing, swearing, vulgar, insulting, abusive or crude language." The company is now a cuss-free workplace, and workers who violate the policy can be disciplined.[59]

Profanity has become common, especially in high-stress jobs. Some policies differentiate between "casual" and "causal" swearing. Casual swearing is bad language we use for the fun of it, because we are too lazy to use other words and we think we can get away with it. Causal swearing is profanity produced by the inability to control an aroused emotion, such as anger, frustration, or impatience.[60]

Why are we so comfortable using profanity? Might it be because profanity and speech that degrades have become so much a part of our mediated language

What kind of language do you find personally offensive? How does your language use change from person to person? Would you feel comfortable using obscenities with any of the following people: your best friend, your instructor, your employer? Why or why not?

What do you think? Can profanity ever be funny? Has profanity become an acceptable part of life, or should we develop the skill and discipline not to swear but to interact in a more civil manner?

Work It Out

Provide examples of the use of the n-word in song lyrics. Discuss if you believe the n-word is a WMD—a word of mass destruction. How does the use of the word affect you? Determine who, if anyone, in your opinion can use it, when if at all, and under what circumstances.

landscape, used in virtually every crime-adventure television or cable program or film? Commonplace profanities now function as fillers—they slide off the tongue much as the words *you know* and *like*.

Profanity-laced speech has become normative, identifying users as a member of a group. In addition, according to linguist Steven Pinker, swear words have emotional power because they capture our attention and force us to consider their unpleasant connotations. Were it not for the taboos associated with using them, Pinker contends, they would lose their emotional edge.[61]

Sometimes pejorative words that are used to stigmatize or degrade the members of a group are reclaimed by the group and redefined by group members as positive in nature. For example, gays and lesbians now use the term *queer* to make positive statements about who they are. Some women proudly refer to themselves as girls. And some African Americans, in an effort to invalidate the meaning that bigots attached to it, now use the racial epithet *nigger* among themselves.[62] Thus, the word, once strictly taboo, is now common in popular culture. The "n-word" was coined by slave traders over 400 years ago to degrade blacks. Recently, Web sites like abolishthenword.com and college and public forums have been exploring the n-word's usage, with some critics attempting to encourage the elimination of the word's casual use. Lawmakers have even sponsored resolutions to ban the word's use. On the other hand, proponents of the Web site niggaspace.com, modeled after the social networking site MySpace, draw a distinction between differently spelled versions of the n-word. For example, according to the site's founder, "nigga" embodies brotherhood and fraternity, not ignorance and hate.[63] In your opinion, can you solve the problem of racism by banning or respelling a word?

Some observers believe that the popularity of text messaging is due to people's longing for private conversations. The ability to send silent text messages in public spaces is appealing. Many people text-message during movies and sports events or on subways. Are you one of the many? Educators believe that we should know where to draw the line between formal and conversational writing. "Generation text" members, however, commonly mix rapid-fire Internet English and schoolwork. Do you ever do this?

TECHNOLOGY AND LANGUAGE USE

Is text messaging causing us to speak in extremely short sentences? Because we can reread the instant or text messages we receive before deciding how to respond, are we in danger of forgetting how to make instantaneous or improvisational conversation? We now chat so often without talking that some observers believe we are in danger of wiping out spoken conversation.

Internet user Andrew Walker sometimes lapses into **onlinespeak** when writing offline: In one school paper, he wrote, "Surplus is an excess. But surplus can also mean 2 much," His instructor deducted 10 points. The protocol of informality that marks digital communication for Andrew and millions of others has set off a debate regarding whether the Internet invigorates language or strips it of its expressive power.[64]

When linguists talk of dialects, by tradition, they are referring to the spoken word. The Internet and texting, however, have spawned a new written dialect, one in between speech and writing, in which punctuation is abandoned, capital letters are used primarily if you are "shouting," and an array of acronyms substitute for phrases. Knowing and using the dialect allows us to develop a sense of belonging to the group—a group that exists in cyberspace. BTW stands for "by the way," TTFN for "ta-ta for now," and IMHO for "in my humble opinion." RUOK stands for "Are you okay?" CUL8R translates as "See you later," while TAH means "Take a hint," A3 means "anytime, anywhere, anyplace," and YTLKIN2ME asks, "You talking to me?"

onlinespeak

the informal communication style that marks electronic communication

It is not uncommon to find friends in the same room texting rather than talking to each other. Why? They want to share but don't want others to hear what they're saying! Have you ever been a part of or privy to such behavior, perhaps when in a car, a classroom, or your own living room? In between calling and sending e-mail, some people use texting as a means of creating a social circle apart from others. Like other technologies, texting has its own private language. AT&T has even developed a tutorial that decodes texting acronyms meant to keep parents from being privy to the conversations of their children. POS, for example, means "parent over shoulder," PRW means "parents are watching," p911 means "parent alert," and KPC means "keeping parents clueless." Some acronyms become obsolete soon after becoming widely known.[65]

Communication on the Internet continues to evolve. For example, on Second Life, begun back in 2003, users enter an Internet-based virtual world complete with its own vocabulary and sets of abbreviations. In SL (Second Life), an *adfarm* is a land parcel containing deliberately ugly advertising images, while a *griefer* is a SL resident who harasses other residents by using offensive language or otherwise disrupting their in-world experience. A user-defined world, Second Life offers its residents a place to play, conduct business, and converse using one or more personal avatars. Users can also instant message with other avatars in private chat rooms. Second Life has two main methods of text-based communication: local chat and global instant messaging. The latter method is used for private conversations between two avatars, among the members of a group, or even between objects and avatars. Avatars can also send each other e-mail. And instant messages can be rolled over to "real life" if the user sets up their profile that way. The question is, Does Second Life help us improve or limit our abilities to make ourselves understood? Does it provide us with virtual practice that transfers to our first life, or does it offer us the opportunity to escape from the demands of real-world face-to-face interaction?

> Technological developments are leaving their mark on language. Being *uninstalled* means being fired. *Doing a bit flip* means experiencing a disturbing personality alteration. *Engaging in nonlinear behavior* (NLB) means acting irrationally. *Taking a bio-break* means taking a trip to the bathroom. Can you offer other examples of technology's impact on language?

COMMUNICATION SKILLS IN PRACTICE

GUIDELINES FOR USING AND THINKING CRITICALLY ABOUT LANGUAGE

Throughout this chapter, we have stressed that mastery of certain language skills will improve your ability to communicate effectively with others. Use the following guidelines to ensure that your words work *for* you rather than *against* you.

☑ Identify How Labels Affect Your Behavior

Words are not the things they represent. Always remember that words are nothing more than symbols. No connection necessarily exists between a symbol and what people have agreed that symbol represents. In other words, symbols and their representations are independent of each other.

All of us at times respond as if words and things were one and the same. Think of how often you buy a product such as Intimate, Brut, Bold, Caress, Secret, or Angel because of what the label seems to promise. How many times have you turned against a person because he or she is called liberal, conservative, feminist, chauvinist, intellectual, or brainless? Examine your behavior with

Thinking Critically

Reflect and Respond

Language expert Wendell Johnson was fond of noting that the language we use puts not only words in our mouths but also notions in our heads.

On the basis of your personal understanding of language use and misuse, discuss the kinds of notions that language may promote.

Focus on Service Learning

First, use the Web to investigate the kinds of language problems that a local health clinic or another local service organization of your own choosing confront daily. Next, visit the local health clinic or service organization. Then, using the knowledge you have gained from researching the subject and reading this chapter, meet with representatives of the clinic or service organization. Share with them how an understanding of differences in language and meaning could benefit the clinic's or organization's staff by enabling them to avoid creating or compounding a language-based barrier.

> Count the number of times you use purr words and snarl words each day. What do they reveal about your likes and dislikes? How do your words give you away?

others. Make certain that you react to people, not to the categories in which you or others have placed them.

☑ Identify How the Words You Use Affect Your Feelings and Attitudes

Few of the words you select to describe things are neutral. As S. I. Hayakawa and Alan R. Hayakawa, authors of *Language in Thought and Action*, note:

> We are a little too dignified, perhaps, to growl like dogs, but we do the next best thing and substitute series of words, such as "You dirty double-crosser!" "The filthy scum!" Similarly, if we are pleasurably agitated, we may, instead of purring or wagging the tail, say things like "She's the sweetest girl in all the world."[66]

We all use *snarl words* (words with highly negative connotations) and *purr words* (words with highly positive connotations). These words do not describe the people or things we are talking about; rather, they describe our personal feelings and attitudes. When we make statements like "He's a great American," "She's a dirty politician," "He's a bore," "She's a radical," we should not delude ourselves into thinking that we are talking about anything but our own preferences.

It is also important to realize that a word that does not function as a snarl or purr word for you may function that way for someone else, even if you do not intend it to be given such an interpretation. Therefore, become conscious of how others react to the words you use. Listen to people around you, and attempt to read their responses to your words. Which words that incite them would not incite you? Which words do you find unacceptable or offensive? Why?

☑ Identify How Experience Can Affect Meaning

Since we assign meaning on the basis of our experience, and since no two people have had exactly the same set of experiences, it follows that no two people have exactly the same meanings for the same word.

Too frequently, we let our words lead us away from where we want to go; we unwittingly antagonize our families, friends, or co-workers. We are infuriated, for example, when an important business deal collapses because our position has not been understood, or we are terrified when the leaders of government miscommunicate and put their countries on a collision course.[67] To avoid such problems, we must remember that meanings can change as the people who use words change.

☑ Be Sure That Meanings Are Shared

Since intended meanings are not necessarily the same as perceived meanings, you may need to ask people with whom you are speaking such questions as "What do you think about what I've just said?" and "What do my words mean to you?" Their answers serve two important purposes: They help you determine whether you have been understood, and they permit the other people to become involved in the encounter by expressing their interpretations of your message. If differences in the assignment of meaning surface during this feedback process, you will be able immediately to clarify your meanings by substituting different symbols or by relating your thoughts more closely to the background, state of knowledge, and experiences of your receivers.

☑ Avoid Slang

Slang is a style of language used by special groups but not considered proper by society at large. Although we may use slang when conversing with our friends, it is inappropriate and unwise to use it when speaking to an instructor or when delivering a speech to the town council.

☑ Avoid Jargon

A good rule to follow to achieve clarity is to keep jargon to a minimum unless your receiver is schooled in the jargon. In other words, speak the same language as your listener. Many jurors, for example, are not familiar with "legalese." Thus, to ensure understanding, it is far clearer for a prosecutor to say the defendant "lied" instead of using the phrase "willfully falsified" to describe the behavior of the accused.

> As John Condon, author of *Semantics and Communication*, advises, "Learning to use language intelligently begins by learning not to be used by language."

Revisiting Chapter Objectives

1. **Define *language*, and explain the relationships among words, things, and thoughts.** Language is a unified system of symbols that permits a sharing of meaning. Language allows minds to meet, merge, and mesh. When we make sense out of people's messages, we learn to understand people. As Ogden and Richards' triangle of meaning illustrates, there is no direct relationship between words and things. Words do not "mean"; people give meaning to words.

2. **Identify factors at work in the communication of meaning.** Among factors influencing the communication of meaning are word barriers; the difference between denotative and connotative meaning; the relationships between meaning and time, meaning and place, and meaning and experience; and whether language is concrete or abstract.

THE WRAP-UP

THE WRAP-UP

3. **Identify problems with meaning, including patterns of miscommunication.** Among factors contributing to confusion are the propensity for bypassing, labeling, evasive and emotive language use, and disagreements over politically correct language.

4. **Discuss the relationship between culture and language.** Culture influences how we experience, process, and use language. In part because language and perception are intertwined, language use varies from culture to culture. We see this in how culture influences the words we use, contributes to confused translations, and affects communication style.

5. **Discuss the relationship between gender and culture.** Gender also influences the experiencing, processing, and use of language. Language also influences the attitudes we hold about males and females, as well as how males and females perceive each other.

6. **Explain how power and incivility affect language use.** Some people talk more powerfully than others, coming directly to the point, projecting opinions with confidence, and eliminating nonfluencies and fillers from their speech. Although many of us have learned to adjust our language use to fit our audience, incivility in language use is on the rise.

7. **Explain how technology is affecting language use.** How we communicate online frequently differs from how we communicate in person. Some people believe the Internet is invigorating language, while others believe it is stripping language of its expressiveness.

8. **Identify guidelines for developing language skills.** We need to use common sense to recognize that certain styles of language are appropriate at certain times and in certain places. We also need to make ourselves as clear as possible by selecting words with meaning for our listeners and by taking into account their education level and the sublanguages they understand.

Resources for Further Inquiry and Reflection

To apply your understanding of how the principles in Chapter 5 are at work in our daily lives, consult the following resources for further inquiry and reflection. Or, if you prefer, choose any other appropriate resource. Then connect the ideas expressed in your chosen selection with the communication concepts and issues you are learning about both in and out of class.

 Listen to Me

"Shut Up" (The Black Eyed Peas)
"Woman Is the Nigger of the World" (John Lennon)
"Because of You" (Kelly Clarkson)
"Speak My Language" (Cure)
"Snoop Dogg" (Snoop Dogg)
"Meaning" (Gavin DeGraw)

Discuss the extent to which word choice influences listener attitudes toward the song or the extent to which it influences the nature of a relationship described in the song.

 View Me

In Her Shoes	*Bulworth*
Kingdom of Heaven	*The Interpreter*
The Stepford Wives	*What Women Want*
Clueless	*Windtalkers*

In each of these films, the use of words either interferes with or facilitates a character's objective. Choose one film and discuss the role language plays in it to advance or impede the character's goals.

Read Me

Frank Luntz. *Words That Work: It's Not What You Say, It's What People Hear.* New York: Hyperion, 2007.

Amy Tan. *Saving Fish from Drowning.* New York: Putnam's, 2005.

William Gibson. *The Miracle Worker.* New York: Bantam Books, 1975.

Steven Pinker. *The Stuff of Thought: Language as a Window into Human Nature.* New York: Viking, 2007.

Leslie Savan. *Slam Dunks and No-Brainers: Language in Your Life, the Media, Business, Politics, and, Like, Whatever.* New York: Vintage, 2006.

Discuss how one of the preceding works illustrates the concept "meaning is in people, not in words."

 Tell Me

Share with the class the insights you gained from your chosen Listen to Me, View Me, or Read Me selection.

Consider the following two statements made by one person: "I value freedom of speech." "I find hate speech and racist, sexist, and ageist speech objectionable." How do you reconcile the two positions? In your opinion, should any of the objectionable kinds of speech have First Amendment protection? In a brief presentation, explain why or why not.

Key Chapter Terminology

Use the Online Learning Center at www.mhhe.com/gamble10e to further your knowledge of the following terminology.

bypassing 101

connotative meaning 98

denotative meaning 98

disclaimers 111

dominant culture 104

euphemism 103

gender-lects 111

language 95

linguistic determinism 105

linguistic prejudice 106

linguistic relativity 105

onlinespeak 114

pop language 110

prejudiced language 106

qualifiers 110

racial code words 106

Sapir-Whorf hypothesis 105

symbol 95

tag questions 111

triangle of meaning 95

www.mhhe.com/gamble10e

Idioms in Translation

collision course — dangerous path

inspect the territory — look closely at what is in front of your eyes

macho — very masculine

save face — avoid being the object of criticism or embarrassment

transfer meaning — communicate meaning

Culture Cue

While the closest expression to "no" for a Japanese is "It is very difficult," an American will say "no" and mean no. Similarly, a Japanese "yes" only means "I heard you." In contrast, people in the United States pride themselves on saying what they want to say as directly and unambiguously as possible.

Test Your Understanding

Go to the *Self Quizzes* on the book's Online Learning Center at www.mhhe.com/gamble10e.

www.mhhe.com/gamble10e

After finishing this chapter, you should be able to

1. Define *nonverbal communication,* and explain its functions.

2. List aspects of nonverbal messages.

3. Explain why the face is an important source of information.

4. Explain how artifactual communication can affect interaction.

5. Distinguish among the following terms: *intimate distance, personal distance, social distance,* and *public distance;* and *informal space, semi-fixed-feature space,* and *fixed-feature space.*

6. Identify the ways gender, diversity, and technology influence nonverbal behavior.

7. Identify how you can improve your nonverbal communication effectiveness.

Nonverbal Communication: Silent Language Speaks

Because we believe that learning to interpret and send nonverbal messages effectively will benefit you, our focus in this chapter is on nonverbal communication. Frequently more powerful than words, one person's nonverbal communication often provides reasons for how others respond. Can you think of examples of how you have used the nonverbal communication of others to guide your reaction to and interaction with them?

Recently, customs inspectors at John F. Kennedy Airport carefully watched hundreds of passengers get off a flight from South America. As people moved past them, they looked for telltale body language indicative of exceptional nervousness. One man caught their attention. His lips were so chapped and dry they appeared white and "his carotid artery was jumping out of his neck." They took the man aside and discovered that he had paid cash for a business-class ticket, even though he was a low-paid service worker. X-rays revealed that the man had swallowed several bags of heroin pellets.

Since 9/11, the science of spotting nervous or threatening behavior has gained respect. According to one security consultant, "well-trained body language profilers might have spotted and questioned some of the September 11th hijackers" using basic behavior pattern recognition work. In fact, security personnel positioned at airports and in office buildings are now trained to watch for darting eyes and hand tremors in addition to identifying other cues of suspicious behavior. For example, they are being taught that our lips get thinner when we become angry, and our blink rate increases when we become nervous. They now know that our nostrils flare when we are aroused, and our blood flow increases, reddening our skin when we prepare for a physical or mental fight.[1]

What you are speaks so loudly that I cannot hear what you say.
—Ralph Waldo Emerson

It is easy to be wise after the event.
—Arthur Conan Doyle's Sherlock Homes

Online Learning Center

Go to the Online Learning Center at www.mhhe.com/gamble10e and answer the questions in the *Self Inventory* to evaluate your understanding of nonverbal communication.

COMMUNICATING WITHOUT WORDS

Do you know people who have had trouble establishing and maintaining good relationships at work and in their personal lives, but neither they nor you can figure out why? The answer may be that they lack the nonverbal communication skills essential for social success.[2] Some of us, it appears, have trouble picking up on social cues that others of us use regularly and take for granted. The nonverbally skill-less are, for all practical purposes, communication clueless. The founder of psychoanalysis, Sigmund Freud, once wrote: "He that has eyes to see and ears to hear may convince himself that no mortal can keep a secret. If his lips are silent, he chatters with his fingertips; betrayal oozes out of him at every pore."

Do nonverbal cues make it possible for you to read a person like a book? Do they make it possible for others to read you like a book?

Exploring Diversity

The Magic of Sign Language

Marilyn Daniels's book *Dancing with Words*[3] is an exploration of the dynamics of language acquisition through a special form of nonverbal communication. Daniels contends that the use of sign language not only makes hearing students bilingual but also increases the vocabulary learning, reading, and spelling skills of students in all subjects. She also believes that signing positively influences the self-assurance of hearing students, enhancing their ability to interpret and express ideas as well. According to Daniels, sign language is a natural language that, while strongly rooted in deaf communities throughout the world, also fulfills the diverse communicative needs of daily life, including facilitating communication in the home by allowing babies and young children to express their needs without becoming frustrated.

Should we all be required to take a course in sign language? If so, why? If not, why not? Can you think of how the use of sign language might enhance your communication with hearing persons?

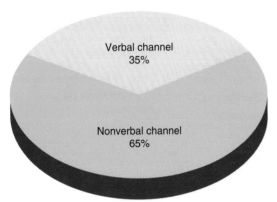

Verbal channel
35%

Nonverbal channel
65%

We all communicate nonverbally. In a normal two-person conversation, the verbal channel carries less than 35 percent of the social meaning of a message; this means that more than 65 percent of the meaning is communicated nonverbally (see Figure 6.1).[4] By analyzing nonverbal cues, we can enhance our understanding of what is really being said when people talk. The nonverbal level can also help us define the nature of each relationship we share. With practice, we can learn to use the nonverbal mode to provide us with "ways of knowing" that would not otherwise be available to us.[5]

FIGURE 6.1

Communication of Social Meaning.

CHARACTERISTICS OF NONVERBAL COMMUNICATION: CUES AND CONTEXTS

What is nonverbal communication? The term **nonverbal communication** designates all the kinds of human messages and responses not expressed in words.

The twinkle in his eye, the edge in her voice, the knowing look of his smile, the rigidity of her posture, the confidence in his walk, her dress, his hairstyle, where she sits, how closely he stands in relation to another, her eagerness to arrive early—each of these cues contains clues regarding the attitudes, feelings, and personality of the displayer. Often, however, we are virtually unaware of what we do with our body, our voice, or the space around us when we interact with others. We simply act and react without considering how the way we act and the way we react modifies, reinforces, or distorts the messages we are communicating.

Sometimes we consciously use nonverbal cues to send specific messages. Our use of nonverbal cues is then purposeful. For example, we may smile when meeting someone for the first time, shake hands firmly when we meet the person who is interviewing us for a job, or wear a flag lapel pin as a sign of our patriotism.

If, at this very moment, someone were to photograph you, what could others surmise by examining the photograph? How are you sitting? Where are you sitting? How are you dressed? What would your facial expression reveal about your reaction to this chapter?

Like verbal communication, nonverbal communication is ambiguous. (Think about the example we just gave—the photograph of you reading this chapter. Would different people interpret the photograph the same way?) Like words, nonverbal

Work It Out
Brainstorm all the ways we communicate nonverbally.

nonverbal communication
the kinds of human messages and responses not expressed in words

Toni Smith, the basketball player with her back to the flag, used her nonverbal behavior to express her attitude toward U.S. foreign policy.

> For the next two minutes, face another person and try not to communicate anything to him or her. What happened? Did you look at each other? Look away? Giggle? Smile? Fidget?

messages may not mean what we think they do. Thus, we have to be careful not to misinterpret them. Don't be surprised if you find that the real reason a person glanced at a clock, left a meeting early, or arrived late for class is quite different from what you assumed. All nonverbal communication must be evaluated or interpreted within the context in which it occurs.

Furthermore, verbal and nonverbal messages can be—and often are—contradictory. When we say one thing but do another, we send an incongruent, or **mixed message.** As you become aware of the nonverbal cues you and others send, you will begin to recognize contradictory messages that impede communication. Whenever you detect an incongruity between nonverbal and verbal (word-level) messages, you will probably benefit by paying greater attention to the nonverbal messages. Researchers in communication believe that nonverbal cues are more difficult to fake than verbal cues—hence the importance of examining the nonverbal dimension.

Work It Out

Role-play a communication scenario that involves the use of a mixed message. Ask your audience which message they believe and why.

mixed message
message that occurs when words and actions contradict each other

FUNCTIONS OF NONVERBAL COMMUNICATION

Nonverbal communication serves an array of communicative functions that can work both independently of and in conjunction with verbal messages to clarify meaning. Knapp and Hall identify a number of these functions.[6]

> Say to a partner, "I am really glad to be here," but meanwhile do everything you can to indicate the opposite.

Message Reinforcement or Complementation

Nonverbal cues reinforce the verbal message by adding redundancy. The woman who says, "I love you," to her fiancé and covers her partner's face with kisses. When an instructor asks, "Did you complete the assignment?" and you reply, "Sure did!" and make an OK sign with your fingers. Message reinforcement occurs when the nonverbal and verbal messages complement each other.

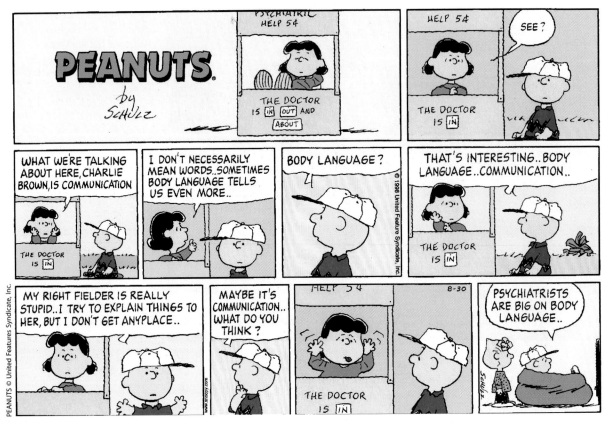

What does this cartoon suggest regarding the importance of nonverbal communication? How have you used another person's body language to enhance communication?

Message Negation

Nonverbal cues can also contradict or negate a verbal message—such as a man who says to his lover, "I need us to spend more time apart," as he moves closer with each word spoken. Such a message is contradicted or canceled by the communicator's nonverbal cues. The interaction represents a double message—the nonverbal cues and the words spoken are at odds with each other. Remember, the nonverbal message is usually the more accurate reflection of meaning.

Message Substitution

Nonverbal cues can replace or substitute for verbal cues. A hand gesture lets everyone know you're OK. A shrug of the shoulders lets others know when someone doesn't care about something. Placing your finger over your lips can indicate that you'd like everyone in the room to stop talking. In each case, instead of words being spoken, an action is performed.

Message Accentuation or Intensification

Nonverbal cues also can be used to underscore or intensify parts of a verbal message. Slowing down speech to stress the meaning and importance of key words, smiling when you say, "It's nice to meet you," and clutching your hair when you say, "I'm so angry I could pull my hair out!" are nonverbal cues that accent or emphasize the verbal messages sent.

Message Regulation

Finally, nonverbal cues help regulate the back-and-forth flow of person-to-person interaction. We direct conversational turn taking with nonverbal cues. With eye contact, posture, gestures, and voice, we signal that we have finished speaking or indicate who should talk next. Nonverbal cues help us manage and control communication. They provide the traffic signals for verbal exchanges.

If we are going to use nonverbal cues effectively, we must understand them. The following section considers the important features of nonverbal communication.

ASPECTS OF NONVERBAL COMMUNICATION

Whereas we use language to communicate explicit information and message content, we use nonverbal communication to convey relational messages, including how we feel about another person, as well as status, power, and deception.[7] To arrive at a better understanding of communication and develop skills that will permit us to both send and receive cues more accurately, we will examine the following areas: body language (kinesics), clothing and artifacts, voice (paralanguage), space and distance (proxemic and environmental factors), colors (meanings and associations), time (communicative value of chronemics), touch (haptics), and smell (olfactics). The types of messages that fall within these categories do not occur in isolation; they interact, sometimes supporting and sometimes contradicting one another.

Body Language: Kinesics

Kinesics is the study of the relationship between body motion, or body language, and communication. Body language includes facial expression (particularly eyebrows, forehead, eyes, and mouth), posture, and gestures. Thus, hand movements, a surprised stare, drooping shoulders, a knowing smile, and a tilt of the head are all part of kinesics. The role of signing and gestures in learning garnered attention when it was reported that infants and toddlers who learn to use and read gestures may learn to read faster and do better on future IQ tests than children who do not.[8] Consciously using multiple channels facilitates communication.

Facial Expressions

How well do you read faces? Research has shown that many people are able to decipher facial cues with great accuracy, but others lack this ability. Unpopularity, poor grades, and a variety of other problems that plague schoolchildren may be attributed to an inability to read the nonverbal messages of teachers and peers. According to psychologist Stephen Norwicki, "Because they are unaware of the messages they are sending, or misinterpret how other children are feeling, unpopular children may not even realize that they are initiating many of the negative reactions they receive from their peers."[9] Your ability to read someone's face increases when you know the person, understand the context of the interaction, and are able to compare and contrast the person's facial expressions with others you have seen him or her make.

kinesics
the study of the relationship between human body motion, or body language, and communication

---

Did you know that the 80 muscles in the face can create more than 7,000 expressions?

The face is the single most important broadcaster of emotions. What message is your face sending right now?

facial management techniques
the means we use to control the expressions we reveal to others

How can you use facial cues to determine if others—including your boss, co-workers, and friends—are being honest with you?

Of all the nonverbal channels, the face is the single most important broadcaster of emotions. Since we cannot put the face away, we take great pains to control the expressions we reveal to others.

How do we do this? We use the following **facial management techniques:** intensifying, deintensifying, neutralizing, and masking. When we intensify an emotion, we exaggerate our facial responses to meet what we believe to be the expectations of others who are watching us. Have you ever pretended you loved a gift so as not to disappoint the giver, when in reality you couldn't stand it? When we deintensify an emotion, we deemphasize our facial expressions so that others will judge our reactions to be more appropriate. Were you ever very angry with a professor but were compelled to restrain yourself because you feared the professor's response if you let your anger show? When we neutralize an emotion, we avoid displaying it at all. Sometimes neutralization is an attempt to display strength, as when we are saddened by the death of a relative but want to appear brave. In U.S. culture, men neutralize fear and sadness more frequently than women do. Finally, when we mask an emotion, we replace it with another to which we believe others will respond more favorably. Thus, we sometimes conceal feelings of jealousy, disappointment, or rage.

Your facial appearance also influences judgments of your attractiveness.[10] In addition, it affects others' assessment of you as being dominant or submissive.[11] Thus, we speak of a baby face, a face as cold as ice, a face as strong as a bulldog's, and so on. What words would you use to describe your own face?

By now you are probably beginning to realize the importance of observing facial expressions. But what should you watch for? For purposes of analysis, a person's face can be divided into three general areas: (1) the eyebrows and forehead, (2) the eyes, and (3) the mouth. Let us focus on each area separately.

Eyebrows and Forehead If you raise your eyebrows, what emotion are you showing? Surprise is probably most common, but fear may also be expressed by raised eyebrows; when you are experiencing fear, the duration of the movement will probably be longer.

The brows help express other emotions as well. Right now, move your brows into as many configurations as you can. With each movement, analyze your emotional response. What do the brows communicate?

The forehead also helps communicate your physical and emotional state. A furrowed brow suggests tension, worry, or deep thought. A sweating forehead suggests nervousness or great effort.

Work It Out
How does eye contact or its lack affect your interactions with others? Use the following experimental conditions when talking to others to find out: (1) Keep your eyes on the floor. (2) Glance around continually. (3) Stare at the other person's face. (4) Look at the other person's waist. (5) Maintain comfortable eye contact. Compare and contrast your results.

Eyes The second of the three areas is the eyes. Ralph Waldo Emerson noted, perceptively, "The eyes of men converse at least as much as their tongues." What do your eyes reveal to others?

Many expressions refer to the eyes—"shifty eyes," "the look of love," "the evil eye," "look me in the eye." Various eye movements are associated with emotional expressions: A downward glance suggests modesty; staring suggests coldness; wide eyes suggest wonder, naivete, honesty, or fright; and excessive blinking suggests nervousness and insecurity. Researchers have also shown that as we begin to take an interest in something, our blinking rate decreases and our pupils dilate.

The direction of eye gaze also provides interesting insights. For example, have you considered in what direction people look when they are not looking directly at you—and what that might signify? Richard Bandler and John Grinder, two of the founders of neurolinguistic programming, have developed a number of interesting theories. They suggest that people look in one direction when they try to remember something seen or heard and in another direction when they try to invent something. To test their hypothesis, try this with a partner. Face each other. One person asks the following series of questions; the other person thinks of a response to each. When asking the questions, watch for any patterns in the direction your partner looks while thinking of a response.

Questions That Evoke Visually Remembered Images
What color are the carpets in your car?
What color are your mother's eyes?
What color is your instructor's hair?

Questions That Evoke Visually Invented Images
How would you look from my point of view?
How would you look in purple and green hair?
What would your home look like after it had been ravaged by fire?

Questions That Evoke Auditorily Remembered Images
Can you hear your favorite music?
Can you hear music you dislike?
What are the first four notes of Beethoven's Fifth Symphony?

Questions That Evoke Auditorily Invented Images
How would your dog sound singing "Mary Had a Little Lamb"?
What would King Kong sound like tiptoeing through the tulips?

Bandler and Grinder suggest that a right-handed person will look in the directions shown in Figure 6.2. Do your experiences confirm their findings? Could a lawyer or negotiator ask questions and then use these findings to determine whether the person answering had invented the reply? Could a CIA agent use the technique to determine if an informant was telling the truth? If the findings are valid, presumably the answer is yes. The agent, for example, could inquire about where hostages were being held: "What does the house look like? Did you see terrorist members there?" If the informant looked up and to the right, he or she might be creating images rather than actually remembering; in other words, the informant might be lying.

Whatever your conclusions about the direction of eye gaze, it is important to maintain eye contact with others to recognize not only when others are not looking at you but where they are looking. Because these cues are not consciously controlled, they will seldom mislead us.

civil inattention
the polite ignoring of others so as not to infringe on their privacy

How long we look or gaze at a person or thing also communicates a message. In our culture, it is deemed acceptable to stare at animals and inanimate objects, such as paintings or sculptures, but rude to stare at people. Instead of staring at others, we are supposed to practice **civil inattention,** avoiding sustained eye contact and letting our eyes rest only momentarily on people (in other words, keeping our eyes to ourselves).

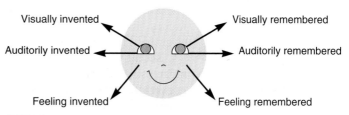

FIGURE 6.2 **How Direction of Gaze Varies According to the Nature of the Item under Consideration.**

The presence or absence of eye contact indicates whether a communication channel is open or closed. What does the eye contact of these people suggest about their relationship?

Although it is permissible to look at someone we do not know for one or two seconds, after that we are expected to move our eyes along.

Despite civil inattention, in any gathering, the first thing most people do is eye one another. Eye contact gives us feedback on how we are coming across to others in interpersonal and public situations. It can indicate whether the communication channel is open. It is much easier to avoid talking or listening to people if we have not made eye contact with them. Eye contact between people also offers clues to the kind of relationship they share. For one thing, it can signal a need for inclusion or affiliation. People who have a high need for affiliation will frequently return the glances of others. There is a high degree of eye contact between people who like each other. We also increase eye contact when communicating with others if the physical distance between us is increased.

Of course, we must keep in mind that eye contact is influenced by culture. Some cultures use eye contact more than we do; other cultures use it less. Arabs engage in more direct eye contact and the Japanese in less eye contact than is typical of Americans. The Japanese, in fact, believe that prolonged eye contact is a sign of disrespect. Japanese children learn at an early age to avoid direct eye contact and to direct their gaze to the area of the Adam's apple instead.[12]

The fact is, the eyes have much to tell us.

What is communicated if eye contact is missing? Lack of eye contact can cause others to think that we are trying to hide something or that we do not like them. It can also suggest that two people are in competition with each other. Others may interpret its absence as signifying either boredom or simply a desire to end an interaction. How do you rate your own eye contact? When are you a looker and when are you a nonlooker?

Mouth   People who do not smile are perceived to be unfriendly, uninterested in others, or bored. People respond more favorably to those who smile.[13]

Like the eyes, the lower facial area has much to communicate. For example, some people smile with just the mouth and lips. For others, the smile appears to consume the entire face. As a child, were you ever told to "wipe that smile off your face"? Why? Besides happiness, what can a smile communicate?

How does your face look when you are not smiling—when it is at rest? Some faces have a neutral expression; others have a frown, snarl, or habitual smile—that is, the corners of the mouth seem to turn up naturally.

When you choose to smile, how do people react to your smile? People often find that others will return a smile to those who smile at them but will look away from, or avoid stopping to speak to, a person whose lips are pursed in a frown. To what extent do your experiences confirm this?

Both men and women tend to smile when seeking approval, but in general, women smile more frequently than men do. Women tend to smile even when given negative messages.[14] Why do you think this is so?

Recently, marketers for products such as Yahoo and cappuccino machines began using the images of women sticking out their tongues in ads. According to nonverbal communication researcher Maureen O'Sullivan, "the mouth is a sexual orifice," and the gesture of "sticking out one's tongue can have multiple meanings. It can be an act of rudeness, disgust, playfulness, or outright sexual provocation." She believes we are seeing more tongues in ads because marketers are running out of body parts to expose.[15] What do you think?

Posture

How many times have you heard the following admonitions?

"Stand up straight!"

"Why are you hunched over that desk?"

What kinds of nonverbal messages does your posture send to others? The way we hold ourselves when sitting or standing is a nonverbal broadcast, giving others information that they use to assess our thoughts and feelings.

Research provides enough information for us to draw some general conclusions about how others are likely to interpret our posture. Nancy Henley, in her book *Body Politics,* suggests that "the bearing with which one presents oneself proclaims one's position in life."[16] Television and film support this premise by frequently contrasting the upright bearing of a wealthy person with the submissive shuffle of a servant or the slumped demeanor of a nobody. In line with this, researcher Albert Mehrabian notes that when people assume inferior roles, they reflect this by lowering their heads. In contrast, when they assume superior roles, people often raise their heads.

> Even though women in general smile more than men do, young children think that the smile of a male is friendlier than the smile of a female. Do you agree? Explain.

> Recall an instance when posture affected your perception of someone else.

Ethics and Communication

Nonverbal Cues and Status

Do you think if you were taller, spoke louder, and were perceived by others as more dominant, it would help you advance in your career? One female chief executive officer persists in wearing stiletto heels even though she is five feet, nine inches tall. She believes they make her appear more intimidating.[17] Another male CEO, six feet, three inches tall, in the midst of heated negotiations, puts his hand on the shoulder of those shorter than him, crowding into their personal space, attempting to demonstrate decisiveness and dominance. Another CEO says that he would rather be bald than short.[18] In fact, in *Blink,* author Malcolm Gladwell notes that 30 percent of Fortune 500 CEOs are at least six feet, two inches tall, versus just 4 percent of all men.[19] According to Stanford University professor Lara Tiedens, business people acquire status by looking directly at others, using an open stance and vigorous gestures, speaking loudly in a deep voice, interrupting at will, and leaning in close to reduce the space of others while expanding their own. Thus, she recommends that, to advance, you try to be seen as taller and louder, even borderline rude.[20] Others counter that chest beating and shouting matches are passé, akin to bullying, and a waste of time. Where do you stand?

Each of us has certain expectations regarding the postures we expect others to display. For instance, we might expect a high-ranking military officer to adopt an extremely straight and somewhat official posture. Henley suggests that standing tall, in and of itself, helps a person achieve dominance.

Another aspect of posture to consider is how we lean, or orient ourselves, when we communicate. If you were speaking to someone who suddenly turned or leaned away from you, would you consider that a positive sign? Probably not. We usually associate liking and other positive attitudes with leaning forward, not withdrawing. When you are communicating with others, a slight forward tilt of your upper body may indicate that you are interested in what they have to say. Mehrabian found that we lean either left or right when communicating with a person of lower status than ourselves. This right or left leaning is a part of our more relaxed demeanor.[21]

Gestures

The movements of our arms, legs, hands, and feet constitute important nonverbal data. For instance, the way you position your arms transmits information about your attitudes. Cross your arms in front of you. Do you feel closed off from the world? Stand up and put your hands on your hips. How does this stance make you feel? (You may remind yourself of the old stereotype of an army sergeant.) Next, clasp your arms behind your back in a self-assured manner. Then, hold your arms stiffly at your sides, as if you were a nervous speaker or a wooden soldier. Finally, dangle your arms at your sides in a relaxed fashion. Become aware of the arm positions that you habitually use. What message does each of these positions communicate?

Our legs also convey information about us. Try standing as a model would stand. Next, sit down and put your feet up on a desk or table. Then stand with your feet wide apart. Does this last stance make you feel more powerful? Why? The distribution of body weight and the placement of legs and feet can broadcast stability, femininity, masculinity, anger, happiness, or any number of other qualities. For a communication encounter, choose the stance that most accurately reflects your goals. Keep in mind that crossing one's legs does not necessarily play well from country to country. In fact, it is perceived as highly offensive in Turkey and Ghana.

Gestures, however, do not have universal meanings. Consider, for example, our "OK" gesture made by forming a circle with the thumb and forefinger. In Japan, the thumb and forefinger making a circle is used as a symbol for money. To most Americans, this joining of thumb and forefinger signifies that all is positive; the French and Belgians, in contrast, would interpret the gesture as meaning "you're worth zero."[22]

A lack of universality in gesturing can create problems for global advertisers. For years, in its advertisements for insurance, Allstate implied that it offers consumers security and protection by using the image of a person holding out his or her hands while a voice-over intones, "You're in good hands with Allstate." The ad failed in Germany, however, because in that country hands held out symbolize begging rather than security and protection.[23]

Attractiveness

Do you notice how people look? Do their looks influence your perception of them? Appearance communicates—making general attractiveness an important aspect of

---

Try on various postures and see what you feel like in each. How does each posture affect your emotional state?

Leaning forward communicates liking and interest. Are you aware when you do this? Is it always a conscious move?

The filmmaker Michael Britto has documented hundreds of different handshakes that New Yorkers use to say hello. He discovered that the kind used sometimes depends on where someone lives. For example, the 1-4-5 is a three-part greeting consisting of a finger to the nose, four placed on the chest near the heart, and a five-finger slap. Another has greeters clasping wrists, and another, touching the knuckles of their clenched fists (like the Obamas'"bump"). What kind of handshake do you use? What does it suggest to others?

Media Wise

Clothes Talk

Television shows such as *Desperate Housewives* and *Dirt* featured characters prone to parading around in their underwear. Similarly, celebrities, such as fashion icons Victoria Beckham and Ashley Olsen, often sport visible underwear. Wearing such clothing has become as much a gesture (and is as acceptable) as matching pumps to a handbag.

In addition to serving as statements that counter images of uptightness, articles of clothing have become billboards or picket signs, advertising positions on or interest in issues. For example, T-shirts that picture Jesus and the message "Put Down the Drugs and Come Get a Hug" reveal an attitude about religion or spirituality, whereas those that feature sayings such as "War Is Not the Answer" reveal the wearer's position on political matters. Again, celebrities have popularized the practice.

Inventory your clothing and accessories. Do you wear clothing that resembles or shows your underwear? Do any of your garments advertise a message? To what extent do you support or find each practice objectionable?

body communication. When it comes to height, for example, tall people tend to "come out on top" whether in elections or job interviews.[24] When it comes to weight, a cold shoulder and brusque treatment are routinely given to people who are perceived as obese.[25] People judged to be attractive date more, earn higher grades, and are rated as more persuasive and likable than others.[26] Obsessing on being attractive may cause men to engage in bodybuilding, women to diet, and both men and women to turn to plastic surgery as a solution to feeling unattractive.[27]

Judgments of race are also based on clues the face and body provide. For marketers, ethnic ambiguity—the multiracial face of youth—is becoming the new American beauty. Advertisers judge a face whose heritage is hard to determine as most desirable. Ethnic mixing is changing the face of attractiveness—and influencing casting choices in advertisements and films.[28]

Clothing and Artifacts

Since people make inferences about our age, social and economic status, educational level, group membership, athletic ability, personality, and relationships to others by the way we dress, our use of **artifactual communication** (the use of personal adornments, such as clothing, jewelry, makeup, hairstyles, and beards) provides important nonverbal cues.

We use artifacts to create an image or a first impression. For example, some of us wear glasses even though our eyes are perfectly normal or we could wear contact lenses instead, believing, rightly or wrongly, that glasses make us appear more intelligent, interesting, or mysterious.[29]

How we dress influences how we behave. Consider singer Rihanna. Does Rihanna's dress support her behavior? Given the kind of music she sings, could she just as easily wear more prim and proper attire? Why or why not? While Rihanna purposefully wears such clothing to her job, could you wear the same or similar clothing to yours? Unless you are a singer or dancer, you probably answered this question with "Are you kidding?" or "No way." The clothing we wear to work should support the job roles and functions we perform.

It is clear that we react to people on the basis of their clothing. In the early stages of a relationship, clothing and appearance affect first impressions and exert influences that lead to acceptance or rejection. In addition, judgments regarding our success, character, dominance, and competence are made on the basis of the type of clothing and jewelry we wear.[30]

artifactual communication
the use of personal adornments

Does Rihanna's outfit support her image?

paralanguage

vocal cues that accompany spoken language

Typically, we respond more positively to those we perceive to be well dressed than we do to those whose attire we find questionable or unacceptable. We are also more likely to respond to requests from or follow the lead of well-dressed individuals, including persons in uniform, than we are to listen to or emulate those whose dress suggests lower status or lack of authority.[31]

Voice: Paralanguage

Your friend asks you a question, and you matter-of-factly reply, "Mm-hmm." Another person shares a revealing piece of gossip with you, and you shout, "Huh!" Reading about the ethical lapses of some politicians, you click your tongue: "Tsk, tsk, tsk." These elements of speech that are not standard words are a part of **paralanguage.** How good you are at using paralanguage determines whether or not you will be able to do your part to convey the meaning of a message to others.[32]

In many ways, you either play your voice—like a musical instrument—or are a victim of your voice. Would you ever advise someone to get a new voice? What about yourself? Are you happy with the sound of yours? Have you ever heard how you sound on a tape of a meeting or on your answering machine? Does your tone

"You're right. It does send a powerful message."

go up and down, or do you speak in a monotone? Can you tell a good story, or do your words fall flat? If a new hairstyle and a new outfit are part of the job search, why aren't we similarly concerned with the sound of our voice? According to voice expert Thomas Murry, depth of knowledge and impact of voice are equally important in who gets hired and who succeeds in business.[33] Albert Mehrabian estimates that 38 percent of the meaning of a message delivered during face-to-face conversation is transmitted by voice or vocal cues.[34] Frequently, *how* something is said is *what* is said.

Among the elements of paralanguage are pitch, volume, rate, and pauses. Let us examine these elements of paralanguage more closely.

Pitch is the highness or lowness of the voice; it is the counterpart of pitch on a musical scale. We tend to associate higher pitches with female voices and lower pitches with male voices. We also develop vocal stereotypes. We associate low-pitched voices with strength, sexiness, and maturity and high-pitched voices with helplessness, tenseness, and nervousness. Although we all have what is termed a characteristic, or **habitual, pitch,** we have also learned to vary our pitch to reflect our mood and generate listeners' interest.

Some people tend to overuse one tone to the exclusion of others. These people have monotonous voices characterized by too little variety of pitch. Other people speak at or

Yawning can help you discover your optimum pitch

near the upper end of their pitch scale, producing very fragile, unsupported tones. One way to discover a pitch that is not overly high is simply to yawn. Try it now. Permit yourself to experience a good stretch; extend your arms to shoulder level and let out a vocalized yawn. Do it again. Now count to 10 out loud. To what extent does the pitch of your voice appear to have changed? Is it more resonant? It should be. If you indulge yourself and yawn once or twice before stressful meetings or occasions, you will be able to pitch your voice at a more pleasing level.

Volume, or degree of loudness, is a second paralinguistic factor that affects perceived meaning. Some people cannot seem to muster enough energy to be heard by others. Others blast through encounters. Have you ever sat in a restaurant and heard more of the conversation at a table several feet away than you could hear at your own table? Volume frequently reflects emotional intensity. Loud people are often perceived as aggressive or overbearing. Soft-spoken people are often perceived as timid or polite.

The **rate,** or speed at which we speak, is also important. Do you, for example, expect high-pressure salespeople to talk rapidly or slowly? Most often, they speak very quickly. Similarly, those who are selling gadgets in department stores or on television also speak at a quick clip to retain the audience's interest and involvement. With regard to persons from other cultures, increased rate enhances judgments of credibility.[35]

Of course, more stately or formal occasions require slower speaking rates broken by planned pauses or silences. (Politicians at rallies typically punctuate their speeches with pauses that function almost as applause signs.) Frieda Goldman-Eisler, a communications researcher, has concluded that two-thirds of spoken language comes to us in chunks of fewer than six words.[36] Therefore, knowing when to pause is

pitch
the highness or lowness of the voice

habitual pitch
the characteristic pitch one uses

volume
the degree of loudness of the voice

rate
speaking speed

How do the voices of 4-year-olds and teenagers differ? The voices of college-aged men and retired men? Are there differences in vocal characteristics between, say, a corporate executive and a construction worker?

"I think I've finally found my own voice."

an essential skill. Pauses slow the rate of speech and give both sender and receiver a chance to gather their thoughts. Unfortunately, many people feel that all pauses must be filled and consciously or unconsciously seek ways to fill them. Frequently, we fill a pause with meaningless sounds or phrases: "Er—huh—uh—"; "You know? You know?" "Right! Right!" "OK! OK!" Such **nonfluencies** disrupt the natural flow of speech. Since pauses are a natural part of communication, we should stop trying to eliminate them. Instead, we should give pauses a chance to function.

Silence, the absence of both paralinguistic and verbal cues, also serves important communicative functions.[37] Silence, for example, can allow you time to organize your thoughts. It can also be used to alert receivers that the words you are about to share are important. In addition, choosing not to speak to someone at all can be a forceful demonstration of the indifference one person feels toward another and can be a very powerful message of disconfirmation. Silence can also be used as a form of punishment after an argument or as a conflict to indicate that one person is still angry with the other. Silence, as we see, can communicate a number of meanings. It can indicate that two people are so comfortable with each other that they do not feel a need to talk, or in a different context, it can reveal a person's shyness, by suggesting discomfort or the inability to keep a conversation moving. On the other hand, silence may simply indicate that you, at the moment, agree with what is being said or simply have nothing to say.

Besides communicating emotional content, the voice also communicates personal characteristics. Listening to a voice can sometimes help you identify the speaker's individual characteristics. For instance, on the telephone we are frequently able to determine a speaker's sex, age, vocation, and place of origin even though we have never met him or her. We also tend to associate particular voice types with particular body or personality types. For example, what type of appearance would

nonfluencies

meaningless sounds or phrases that disrupt the flow of speech

silence

the absence of both paralinguistic and verbal cues

Work It Out

Ask a group of friends to try to guess which of the following emotions you are expressing while you recite the first seven letters of the alphabet: happiness, sadness, anger, jealousy, fear, love, nervousness, pride, satisfaction, sympathy.

Silence can indicate how comfortable two people are in each other's presence.

you expect in a person who has a breathy, high-pitched voice? How do you think a person who has a throaty, raspy voice would look? As a communicator, you should be aware that your voice suggests certain things about you.

Space and Distance: Proxemic and Environmental Factors

How much of the space on our planet do you call your own? How much space do you carry around with you? Are there times when people encroach on your space? In his book *The Hidden Dimension,* Edward Hall uses the term **proxemics** for human beings' "use of space."[38] *Proxemics* is the study of the space that exists between us as we talk and relate to each other, as well as the way we organize the space around us in our homes, offices, and communities. Architects and interior designers, for example, are using proxemics to humanize hospitals. In hospitals with soft lighting, single rooms, relaxing gardens, and artwork, patients heal more quickly, nurses remain more loyal to employers, and doctors perform better. By adding therapeutic touches to a typically sterile environment, such as providing patients with views of trees from their windows and more accessibility for family and friends to visit, patients have speedier and fuller recoveries.[39] Seating patterns, for example, influence our communicative behavior. How might another environment, such as a school, use an understanding of proxemics to encourage learning?

proxemics
the study of the use of space

Distances—Intimate, Personal, Social, Public

Hall identified four distances that we keep between ourselves and other people, depending on the type of encounter and the nature of the relationship:

> intimate distance: 0 to 18 inches
>
> personal distance: 18 inches to 4 feet
>
> social distance: 4 to 12 feet
>
> public distance: 12 feet to limit of sight

Intimate distance ranges from the point of touch to 18 inches from the other person. At this distance, physical contact is natural. We can wrestle, and we can

intimate distance
a distance ranging from the point of touch to 18 inches from a person

The amount of distance between us depends on the nature of our encounter and our relationship to each other. What do the distances between each of these interactants communicate to you about the relationships?

make love. Our senses are in full operation. They are easily stimulated but also easily offended if we find ourselves in an uncomfortable situation. Have you ever had someone come too close to you and wanted that person to back off? Did you yourself back away? Sometimes we are forced to endure intimate distance between ourselves and strangers in crowded buses, trains, and elevators. How do you feel and respond in such situations?

personal distance

a distance ranging from 18 inches to 4 feet from a person

Hall's **personal distance** ranges from 18 inches to 4 feet. When communicating at this distance, you can still hold hands or shake hands with another person. This is the most common distance between people talking informally in class, at work, or at parties, and we are apt to conduct most of our conversations within this range. If you reduce personal distance to intimate distance, you are likely to make the other person feel uncomfortable. If you increase it, the other person is likely to begin to feel rejected.

social distance

a distance ranging from 4 feet to 12 feet from a person

Hall's **social distance** ranges from 4 feet to 12 feet. At the social distance—in contrast to the personal distance—we are not likely to share personal concerns. By using social distance, we can keep people at more than arm's length. Thus, this is a safer distance, one at which we would communicate information and feelings that are not particularly private or revealing. Many of our conversations at meals and at business conferences or meetings occur within this space. In business, the primary protector of social space is the desk. Of course, the greater the distance between people, the more formal their encounters. (At a social gathering, you can normally tell how well people know one another by examining how close they stand to each other.)

Public distance (12 feet and farther) is commonly reserved for strangers with whom we do not wish to have an interaction. Distances at the farther end of the range are well beyond the area of personal involvement and make interpersonal communication very unlikely. People waiting in an uncrowded lobby for an elevator frequently use public distance. It can be assumed that if a person opts for public distance when he or she could have chosen otherwise, that person does not care to converse.

What happens when we violate distance norms? Researchers tell us that the outcomes of such violations can be positive. For example, if the approaching person is perceived to be attractive or is viewed as a high-reward source, our evaluation of the approacher may become more favorable, especially if the distance violation is accompanied by other behaviors, such as compliments.[40]

Spaces—Informal, Semi-Fixed-Feature, and Fixed-Feature

The nature of our environment affects the amount of distance we are able to maintain between ourselves and others. Researchers in nonverbal communication divide environmental spaces into three classifications: informal, semi-fixed-feature, and fixed-feature. These categories are based on the perceived permanence of any physical space.

Informal space is a highly mobile, quickly changing space that ranges from intimate to public (from no space between us and others to 25 feet or more). Informal space functions as a personal bubble that we can enlarge to keep people at a distance or decrease to permit them to get closer.

In contrast to the high mobility of informal space, **semi-fixed-feature space** uses objects to create distance. Semi-fixed features include chairs, benches, sofas, plants, and other movable items. (Some office walls and partitions can be classified as semi-fixed features, since they are designed to be relocated as spatial requirements change.) Researchers find that barriers such as desks reduce interaction. One study of doctor-patient relationships found that patients were more at ease speaking with a physician seated in a chair across from them than they were when the physician was sitting behind a desk.[41] Why do you think this was so? In many public places, if interaction is desired, the space will usually contain chairs facing each other. Such arrangements are found in bars, restaurants, and lounges. In contrast, the chairs in waiting rooms at airports and bus terminals are often bolted together in long parallel rows.

Fixed-feature space contains relatively permanent objects that define the environment around us. Fixed features include immovable walls, doors, trees, sidewalks, roads, and highways. Such features help guide and control our actions. For example, most classrooms are rectangular, with windows along one side, usually to the students' left. The window location also determines the front of the room. Shopping malls and department stores rely on fixed features to help route pedestrian traffic in certain directions that will increase sales. The next time you shop in a carefully designed store, examine its fixed features. Can you walk, unimpeded, to any department, or are you carefully "directed" through the perfumes, lingerie, and knickknacks? Why?

Territoriality and Personal Space

Another aspect of proxemics is our need for a defined territory. Some animals mark their territory by urinating around its perimeter and will defend their area

public distance
a distance of 12 feet and farther from a person

Can you tell how interested people are in you by where they stand in relation to you? Explain. Think of an instance when you unconsciously expressed an interest in someone else by where you stood in relation to him or her.

informal space
space that is highly mobile and can be quickly changed

semi-fixed-feature space
space in which objects are used to create distance

fixed-feature space
space that contains relatively permanent objects

Work It Out
Compare and contrast the way men and women use space. For example, determine whether men use space as a means of asserting dominance over women.

Work It Out
Examine the arrangement of your classroom. How are the chairs arranged? Does the professor use a lectern or desk or speak from a raised platform? Come up with an alternative classroom design that you believe will promote more interaction. Then, redesign it to inhibit interaction. Do the same for an office.

Ethics and Communication

Guarded Territory and the New Need for Security

A majority of persons living in the United States would like to live in a gated community.[42] Gated communities require that someone allows you to enter or that you have a permit that affords you the right of entry. They are typically protected by armed guards, gates, walls, or fences. As in Robert Frost's poetic line "Good fences make good neighbors," security devices and details in gated communities keep their members feeling safe by keeping out those whom the community does not want let in. Sometimes tire-piercing or other antiterrorist devices are used to guard against false entry into the community.

The prime motivator for living in a gated community is the desire for personal safety. On the other hand, because gated communities signal that outsiders should stay out, critics contend that social fragmentation is the cost society pays to allow those living inside them to feel secure. Thus, the fear is that gated communities precipitate in-groups and out-groups who compete for rights to use the same space.

Where do you stand? Are gated communities a good idea? Are there other kinds of living arrangements that could produce security without closing off a community to the outside world?

---

territoriality
the need to demonstrate a possessive or ownership relationship to space

markers
items that reserve one's space

Why do you think people would rather stand than occupy the middle seat in a train? What does the behavior of people in elevators reveal about the need for personal space? Most people stare at the floor. Many contemplate their feet or stare at the buttons or at the ceiling. Diverting eye contact decreases feelings of involvement.

against invaders. Human beings also stake out space, or territory, and territoriality is an important variable in interpersonal communication. What examples of **territoriality**—the need to demonstrate a possessive or ownership relationship to space—can you remember encountering? Are you familiar with "Dad's chair"? "Mom's bureau"? How do you feel when someone invades your room—your territory? What happens when someone stands too close to you? How are you treated when you enter another person's territory?

To establish territory, we use **markers**, items that reserve our space, set boundaries that help distinguish space, or identify a space as ours. At the library, for instance, you may spread your things out, over, and across the table, so that others will not find it easy to enter your territory. In large corporations, a person's status is often reflected by the size of his or her space. Thus, the president may be accorded a large top-floor territory, while a clerk is given a desk in a second-floor room amid a number of other desks and office machines. Regardless of the size of our location, however, we identify with it and frequently act as if we own it.

Colors: Meanings and Associations

Do you currently have a favorite color? A few years ago, one color authority, the Pantone Color Institute, named blue iris as its color of the year, noting: "Blue Iris brings together the dependable aspects of blue, underscored by a strong, soul-searching purple cast. Emotionally, it is anchoring and meditative with a touch of magic."[43] Acknowledging this, the advertising and marketing company JWT noted that "blue is the new green," particularly as it denotes ecological concerns.[44] One year earlier, the favored color had been chili pepper red. The leader of the Color Association, Margaret Welch, said bamboo, a yellow-green, was her personal color of the year, adding that it "just has a power. You know, these are very insecure times."[45]

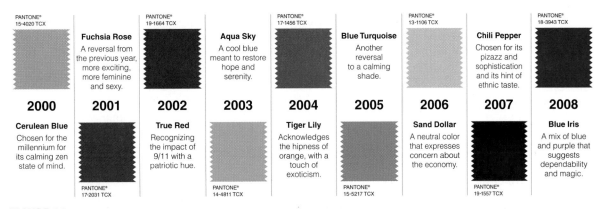

FIGURE 6.3   **Favored colors**

Source: "A New Year, A New Color. But Are We Blue?" by Cathy Horyn, New York Times. Dec 20, 2007, p. C1, C11.

Color affects us emotionally and physiologically. Look at the color palette representing favored colors for the past decade in Figure 6.3. Do you agree with their descriptors?

Colors seem to have more than a passing effect on us. It has been found that color affects us emotionally and physiologically.

Max Luscher, in his book *The Luscher Color Test*, claims that, when people look at pure red for a long time, their blood pressure, respiration rate, and heartbeat all increase.[46] This is because red tends to excite the nervous system. In contrast, when researchers examined the effect of dark blue, they found just the opposite: Blood pressure, respiration rate, and heartbeat decreased, and people tended to become calmer.

In the past decade, an increasing number of U.S. companies have chosen to be associated with the color blue: "Big Blue" (IBM), JetBlue (an airline), BlueKite (a wireless technology company), Blue Martini (a software company), and Blue Nile, to name just a few. According to the executive director of the Pantone Color Institute, "Blue is invariably connected with sky and water. The sky has never fallen and water has never gone away. It has dependability and constancy."[47]

Time: Communicative Value of Chronemics

Chronemics is the study of how we use time to communicate. The meaning of time differs not only around the United States but also around the world.[48] While some people are preoccupied with time, others regularly waste it. While some are typically early, others are chronically late. While some travel through life with a sense of urgency, others amble through it at a more leisurely pace. Some people function best in the morning (the early birds), while others perform best at night (the night owls). Chronemics expert Robert Levine notes that clock addiction is difficult to break. Because the West is becoming more devoted to the clock by the minute, altering the pace of your life poses numerous challenges.

Do you have enough time for most of your activities? Are you usually prepared for exams or assignments? Do you arrive for appointments on time, early, or late?

Work It Out

View an array of cable and television programs on home design. Identify the messages you believe the material possessions and furnishings featured in the program communicate to viewers. Do the same for prime-time sitcoms or dramatic offerings.

Work It Out

Bring in examples of the kinds of messages the colors on packaged goods communicate to consumers. Consider this: market research reveals that when choosing which detergent to purchase, women believe that detergents packaged in blue boxes may be too weak, those packaged in yellow boxes may be too strong, but those packaged in blue boxes with splashes of yellow are probably just right.

chronemics
the study of the use of time

Some students are habitually 15 minutes late to class—even when their previous class was just down the hall. What cues does such habitual lateness transmit to an instructor? Should the instructor conclude that the student is not interested in the class? That the student does not like the instructor? That the student is unable to organize activities to accomplish even the simplest goal?

Recent surveys reveal that tardiness is a chronic problem among chief executive officers of corporations, who arrive late for 6 in 10 meetings.[49] Edward Hall says that "time talks."[50] What does your use or misuse of time say about you? To what extent do others communicate with you by their use of time?

Would you make real estate tycoon Donald Trump wait for a meeting with you, or would you arrive on time or even early? When negotiating a real estate transaction, a group of Chinese millionaires once made Trump wait for them—close to an hour. Do you feel that they were sending a message?

How long we wait for something or someone is related, first, to the value we place on whatever it is we are waiting for and, second, to our own status. We are taught to value what we wait for. In fact, if something is too readily available, we may decide we do not want it after all. Status determines who waits. If we are "important," others usually have access to us only by appointment; thus, it is easier for us to make others wait—and difficult or impossible for others to make us wait.

How well do you structure your time? In his book *The Time Trap*, Alex MacKenzie lists several barriers to the effective use of time:

attempting too much (taking on too many projects at once)

estimating time unrealistically (not realizing how long a project will take)

procrastinating (putting it off, and off, and off . . .)

allowing too many interruptions (letting yourself be distracted by telephone calls, friends, and so on)[51]

Do any of these apply to you? How might you go about improving your use of time?

Our sense of time is even reflected in how we use technology. For example, in text messages and e-mails, commas now appear rarely. Some observers believe that the disappearing comma is a metaphor for the frenetic pace of life today.[52] The comma, after all, signals a pause—the need to slow down before moving on, and slowing down is not what we seem to be doing. Instead, we multitask, as noted in this description of one student:

> Over the next half an hour, Megan will send about a dozen instant messages discussing the potential for a midweek snow day. She'll take at least one cellphone call, fire off a couple of text messages, scan Weather.com, volunteer to help with a campus cleanup . . . , post some comments on a friend's Facebook page and check out the new pom squad pictures another friend has posted on hers.[53]

Does this sound familiar? It is not restricted to students. Wherever we go, we find people feverishly using PDAs and cell phones even when dining at a restaurant or in meetings with others.

Touch: Haptics

haptics
the study of the use of touch

You cannot shake hands with a clenched fist.
—*Golda Meir*

Another category of nonverbal communication is touch, also referred to as **haptics**. According to researchers, touch is "one of the most provocative, yet least well understood" of nonverbal behaviors.[54] Yet all humans need to touch and be touched.[55] Research reveals that a hug and 10 minutes of hand-holding with a romantic partner greatly reduce the harmful physical effects of stress. It appears that, because touch lowers stress hormones, such loving contact protects us throughout the day.[56] Especially for women, hugs, by buffering them from stress, do their hearts good.[57]

How accessible are you to touch?

The amount of touching we do or find acceptable is, at least in part, culturally conditioned. Where do you touch your father? Your mother? Your brother? Your sister? A friend of the same sex? A friend of the opposite sex? In general, women are more accessible to touch than are men. Touch also correlates positively with openness, comfort with relationships, and the ability to express feelings.[58] Both men and women will often kiss women in greeting; men who meet usually shake hands. Usually, men touch women more than women touch men.[59] Physical contact between males is often limited to contact sports, such as football and soccer.

The kind of touch believed appropriate depends upon the kind of relationships individuals share and the situation they find themselves in. One system of analysis identifies the following touch categories: functional-professional (touch that is impersonal or businesslike, such as the kind of touch that occurs when a doctor examines a patient); social-polite (touch used to acknowledge another person, such as a handshake); friendship-warmth (touch that expresses appreciation or warm feelings for another person, such as a pat on the back); love-intimacy (touch occurring in romantic relationships, such as a hug or kiss); and sexual arousal (the most intimate kind of personal contact used to express physical attraction).[60]

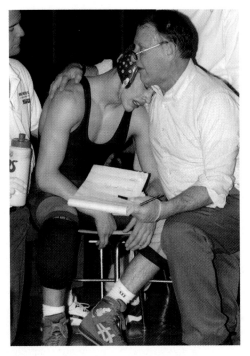

Touch facilitates the expression of feelings.

Touch can also reflect status. High-status people touch others and invade their space more than do people with lower status.[61] The person who initiates touch is usually the one with the higher status. Nancy Henley points out that we are unlikely to go up to our boss and pat him or her on the shoulder.[62] Would you put your arm around the president of your college or university? Why? Would your behavior change if you met the president at a party? Probably not. The president, however, might well put an arm around you or another student. The person who initiates touching usually also controls the interaction.

Touch, of course, functions importantly in sexual communication. If people hold hands, we assume they have a romantic interest in one another. Are we right? Most American women use a variety of lotions to keep their hands soft to the touch.

How we use touch sends many messages about us. It reveals our perceptions of status, our attitudes, and even our needs. In his book *The Broken Heart*, psychologist James L. Lynch establishes a correlation between many diseases—particularly heart disease—and loneliness.[63] Lynch tells the story of one man, hooked up to heart-monitoring devices, who was in a coma and near death. When a nurse would walk into his room and hold his hand for a few moments, his heartbeat would change from fast and erratic to slow and smooth.

Smell: Olfactics

What do happiness and contentment smell like? **Olfactics,** the study of the sense of smell, could help us find the answer. Industries are based around our preoccupation with smells and odors. We put on perfumes or colognes and deodorants, clean

olfactics
the study of the sense of smell

Work It Out

Marasmus, a Greek word meaning "wasting away," was the term used in the nineteenth and early twentieth centuries to describe a disease babies placed in orphanages or hospitals died from. These infants suffered from a lack of physical contact. Today, in part because of the threat of sexual harassment, teachers refrain from touching students, and employers refrain from touching people with whom they work. Is such a lack of touch contributing to people's thinking that the corporations they work for are cold and uncaring? Should warm and healing, as opposed to sexual, touching be put back into our schools and workplaces? What should be the rules of touch?

ourselves with scented soaps, freshen our breath with mouthwash, spray our homes with scented sprays, and burn scented candles in an effort to increase perceptions of attractiveness by enhancing our smell as well as the smell of our home or surroundings.

What kinds of messages does smell send? While some cultures consider the natural smells of both people and the environment to be normal, large numbers of Americans are obsessed with masking natural odors and substituting what they perceive to be more pleasant ones.

Smells are associated with attraction, often triggering our emotions or romantic feelings. What smell triggers what emotion depends on our associations, memories, and to some degree, culture. For example, in the United Kingdom, the smell of root beer is reviled whereas people in the United States think it smells good. In England, sarsaparilla and wintergreen, ingredients in root beer, are also used in medicine.[64] Researchers have also studied how smell, specifically pheromones, chemicals emitted by one individual to evoke behavior in another individual, contributes to sexual arousal. Women, research reveals, prefer men whose smell resembles their own.[65] Recently, researchers have also shown that homosexual and heterosexual men respond differently to two odors that may play a part in sexual arousal, with gay men responding similar to women.[66]

Interestingly, smell aids memory recall—both good and bad. In fact, our sense of smell sharpens when something bad happens, alerting us to the odor, and helping us steer clear of impending danger.[67] Give examples of how smell has triggered good and bad memories for you.

TRUTH, DECEPTION, AND NONVERBAL COMMUNICATION

Actors and actresses use nonverbal cues to encourage us to suspend our disbelief and accept them as persons whom they are not. They carefully rehearse the parts they play, down to the smallest gestures and artifacts. As a result, they are able to control the nonverbal cues they exhibit, so that they present the characters being performed in exactly the way they desire.

What about the rest of us? We, too, may use nonverbal cues to create false impressions in others. While the aim of some deceptive communication is to help receivers save face (we try to appear calm when we are nervous) or to protect oneself from the embarrassment that bluntness can cause ("Yes, I love your new hairstyle," we say when we hate it), the goal of too many deceivers is to take advantage of those with whom they are interacting. Most of us, however, do not rehearse for every one of our person-to-person encounters. Our lives are not that plotted or planned. We do not map out the nonverbal cues we will use during our continuing interactions with others. But what if we could, and what if we did? Would others be able to discern our intentions? Would they be able to tell that we were not really feeling what we were expressing?

In general, people tend to pay closer attention to the nonverbal cues of persons whom they do not trust or whom they suspect may be lying than they do to the rest of the people with whom they interact.[68] Those who plan and rehearse the deceptive messages they are sending tend to be self-confident and experience no guilt about their deception. They are least likely to be suspected by others and, therefore, least likely to be uncovered as liars. This, to be certain, is not necessarily a good thing for those of us trying to detect deceptiveness in others.

Some of us are better at nonverbal deception than others. For example, persons whose occupations require that they sometimes act differently than they feel are most successful at deception. Included in this group are lawyers, diplomats, and salespersons.[69] Researchers also tell us that, as we age, most of us become better liars.[70] Those among us who are high self-monitors are also usually better dissemblers than those of us who possess less self-awareness.

Those of us who are better at nonverbal detection than others are more watchful. Unsuccessful liars are vulnerable to leakage, deception clues that careful observers pick up. Sometimes, it is a change in expression on the face, a movement of the body, a vocal inflection, a deep or shallow breath, a long pause, a slip of the tongue, a microfacial expression, or an ill-timed or inappropriate gesture.[71] How do you protect yourself from being lied to? While there are no specific nonverbal clues that indicate someone is lying, one book went so far as to provide readers with 46 clues to deception.[72] Although the context of the behavior must always be considered, among the nonverbal behaviors typically exhibited by deceivers are increased eye blinking, hand fidgeting, posture shifts, the making of speech errors, rising pitch, and hesitations.[73]

Who do you believe is better at nonverbal deception, a child or an adult? Why?

GENDER AND NONVERBAL BEHAVIOR: MASCULINE AND FEMININE STYLES

The ways men and women use nonverbal communication often reflect societal practices. While men, for example, are expected to exhibit assertive behaviors that demonstrate their power and authority, women are expected to exhibit more reactive and responsive behaviors. Thus, men often talk more than women and interrupt women more frequently than they are interrupted by women.[74]

During interactions, while both men and women gaze primarily at each other's face, men tend to be more visually dominant than women. **Visual dominance** is measured by comparing the percentage of looking while speaking with the percentage of looking while listening. When compared with women, men display higher levels of looking while speaking and lower levels when listening. Thus, the visual dominance ratio of men is usually higher than that of women and, again, reflects the use of nonverbal cues to reinforce perceptions of social power.[75]

Men can use space and touch to assert their dominance over women. They are much more likely to touch women than women are to touch them. Again, women are more typically the recipients of touching actions, rather than the initiators. Men also tend to claim more personal space than women usually do, and they more frequently walk in front of women than behind them. Thus, in general, males are the touchers, not the touchees, the leaders rather than the followers.

What kinds of nonverbal cues do women display more than men? According to body language experts, whereas power posture was in vogue in the 1990s, women now do more slouching, using it to express rebelliousness, boredom, and wealth. In

visual dominance

a measure calculated by comparing the percentage of looking while speaking with the percentage of looking while listening

How might a crowded train affect persons from contact and non-contact cultures?

fact, what has come to be known as "the sultry slouch" remains a virtual fashion accessory for women.[76] In contrast to their posture of noninvolvement, women tend to smile and show emotion more often than men do. In general, they are more expressive than men are and exhibit higher levels of involvement when engaged in person-to-person interaction than men do. Women stand closer to one another than men do. Women also use nonverbal signals to draw others into conversations to a greater extent than men do. While women demonstrate an interest in affiliation, men generally are more interested in establishing the strength of their own ideas and agendas.[77] In addition, when tests are given to assess nonverbal decoding ability, including the ability to read another person's feelings by relying on vocal or facial cues, females usually outperform males.[78]

CULTURE AND NONVERBAL BEHAVIOR

contact cultures
cultures that promote interaction and encourage displays of warmth, closeness, and availability

low-contact cultures
cultures that maintain more distance when interacting

People throughout the world use nonverbal cues to help them express themselves. In large measure, the culture of a people modifies their use of such cues. People who belong to **contact cultures**—that is, cultures that promote interaction and encourage displays of warmth, closeness, and availability—tend to stand close to each other when conversing, seek maximum sensory experiences, and touch each other frequently. This is not the case, however, among members of **low-contact cultures,** where such behaviors are discouraged. Saudi Arabia, France, and Italy are countries with contact cultures; their members relish the intimacy of contact when conversing. In contrast, Scandinavia, Germany, England, and Japan are low- or lower-contact cultures, whose members value privacy and maintain more distance from each other when interacting.[79]

In similar fashion, people from different cultures may not display emotion or express intimacy in the same ways. Among the members of Mediterranean cultures, for example, it is normal for emotive reactions to be uninhibited. Thus, it is common for the cultures' members to express a feeling like grief or happiness

Do you think you can teach nonverbal communication, the way you can teach a foreign language? Why or why not?

together with open facial displays, magnified gestures, and vocal cues that support the feeling. On the other hand, neither the Chinese nor the Japanese readily reveal their inner feelings in public, preferring to display less emotion, maintain more self-control, and keep their feelings to themselves; for these reasons, they often appear to remain expressionless.[80] In contrast, persons in the United States are likely to be emotionally expressive and to smile freely.

The cultural background of the individuals communicating also affects their use of personal space and touch. Americans stand farther apart when conversing than do persons from Middle Eastern cultures. Whereas Americans expect persons who live next door to them to be friendly and to interact with them, this expectation is not shared by the Japanese. Consequently, whereas the Japanese may view Americans as overly friendly, Americans may conclude that the Japanese are unfriendly, cold, and distant. Middle Easterners are apt to do a significant amount of touching; they walk with their arms around each other and are apt to touch each other during conversations a lot more than are persons from noncontact cultures.

Even when the nonverbal cues displayed in different cultures are the same, they do not necessarily convey the same meaning. In the United States, for example, a head nod symbolizes agreement or consent, while in Japan it means only that a message was received. Hand signals can be confusing to those not tuned in to the culture. For example, people in the United States use their hand pointing at their chest when they talk about themselves. The Japanese use their forefinger pointed at their nose. Similarly, diverse cultures feel differently about silence. Whereas in the United States we are apt to perceive another person's silence as a negative and to infer that he or she is too self-absorbed, is not listening, is not interested, or has nothing of value to add to a conversation, other cultures interpret silence in a more favorable light. In Japan, for example, silence is frequently preferred to speech.

Culture also affects the treatment of space. In an effort to enhance the relationships between the external environment and the inner self, the Chinese,

What kind of statement does a tattoo or a tongue or belly button ring make? Do you believe such artifacts signal defiance, independence, or something else? What inferences are persons who do not use such personal adornments likely to make about those who do?

The U.S. military provides soldiers serving in Iraq "smart cards" with facts like these: In Iraq it is considered unclean to use your left hand for contact with others. It is similarly considered rude to back away from someone during conversation. Why is knowing such facts key to winning the hearts and minds of the people?

Focus on Service Learning

Apply the knowledge you have gained from this chapter, together with research you conduct online using the resources of your college library, and other sources, such as www.csupomona.edu/~tassi/gestures.htm, to develop a presentation on cultural norms of nonverbal communication in the United States. Arrange to share your presentation with at least one of the following: an instructor who teaches English as a second language (ESL) at a local community school to recent immigrants, the ESL teacher and his or her students at a local high school, or specialists in ESL and those they teach at your own college.

Etiquette

If interactions speak louder than words, then it is important to be aware of how the local customs of different countries can guide communication. A lack of knowledge can cause perceptions in natives of an assault on traditional values. In contrast, exhibiting cultural intelligence, the ability to engage in cross-cultural code switching, can facilitate the establishment of effective relationships with people from diverse countries and cultures. Consider the lessons inherent in the following two situations:

1. Refusing a drink when in Russia on business can cause a problem because drinking is a social tradition that Russian business people use to gauge whom they are dealing with, and to see if they can trust you.[81]

2. When the Middle Eastern version of the reality program *Big Brother* aired in the Arab world, one segment had a handsome Saudi kiss a Tunisian beauty. The kiss led to protests and accusations of moral depravity among viewers who already objected to unrelated men and women sharing a house. The show was taken off the air.[82]

Nonverbal behavior and interaction etiquette do not necessarily transfer from one culture to another. Imagine that you are preparing to do business with the people of another country of your choosing. What nonverbal understandings would you need to facilitate success?

and now others, use feng shui (pronounced "fung-SHWAY"), the ancient Chinese art of placement, to add harmony and balance to living spaces. Feng shui introduces the five elements in nature into design: earth, fire, water, wood, and metal. For example, it uses green plants to bring the outdoors inside, and red candles and fabrics to increase energy.[83] The goal is to arrange space, furniture, walls, colors, and objects to promote blessings and to harness the life force (chi).

For us to experience more effective interaction with people from different cultures, we must make the effort to identify and understand the many ways each culture shapes nonverbal communication. We need to acknowledge that our communication style is not intrinsically better than others, that awareness will contribute to more successful multicultural exchanges.

emoticons

symbols that replace nonverbal cues during machine-assisted communication

Work It Out

Carnegie Mellon University professor, Scott E. Fahlman, believes he was the first to use three keystrokes—a colon followed by a hyphen and a parenthesis—as a horizontal "smiley face" in a computer message, paving the way for emoticoms to express sentiments that might otherwise be misinterpreted online. To mark a quarter century of use, he and colleagues began an annual student contest for innovation in technology-assisted person-to-person communication. Work with others to create a new emoticon, explain its make-up, and discuss the need it meets.

TECHNOLOGY AND NONVERBAL COMMUNICATION

Nonverbal communication is alive and well in cyberspace. Just as those who communicate in cyberspace rely on established netiquette guidelines for the standards of behavior acceptable during their online interactions, so they have also evolved a system of written symbols to help reinforce those standards. These symbols, called **emoticons,** replace physical gestures and facial expressions, substitute for nonverbal cues, and help those engaged in online dialogues convey action, emotion, and emphasis.[84]

Emoticons, or relational icons, help add personalization and more expressive emotional exchanges to computer-mediated communication as a way to approximate the warmth and intimacy of face-to-face interactions. Thus, emoticons, are used also at times to indicate subtle mood changes.[85] For example, a symbol called the smiley face looks like :-) and indicates the humorous intent of the sender. It may wink mischievously, ;-), or frown, :-(, depending on whether the online comment is to be interpreted humorously or sarcastically. Similarly, capitalizations and asterisks, such as GREAT and ***, convey a user's emphasis and enthusiasm.

The following list contains other emoticons that can be used to describe a communicator's physical or emotional condition or to depict feelings and actions that straight text alone could not depict. These symbols are commonly understood by online users.

:-P	someone sticking out the tongue
= :-O	someone screaming in fright, their hair standing on end
:-&	someone whose lips are sealed
!#!^*&:-	a schizophrenic[86]

Of course, persons unfamiliar with online culture would more than likely be confused by the use of emoticons. Lacking more conventional social context cues, they would not be able to use the symbols to achieve understanding.

Since online communicators probably are not able to hear each other, they have also created a shorthand to describe their reactions. For instance, they may describe themselves as "rolling on the floor laughing" with the abbreviation ROFL.

Technological changes are affecting our nonverbal communication in other ways as well. According to Nelson Thall, the president and chief executive officer of the Marshall McLuhan Center on Global Communication, the current variety in fashion is an outgrowth of the electronic technological revolution. According to Thall, "Our clothing is an extension of our skin, just like a hammer is a technological extension of our hand."[87] Thall contends that since computers and the Internet allow people to be nationless, sexless, and ageless, fashion now reflects that option. We now dress similarly across borders and wear clothing that is technologically friendly, with room for cell phones, beepers, PDAs, and so on. We even have a wearable computer, also known as a personal optical mobile appliance or personal multimedia appliance. An increasing percentage of the U.S. population ages 15 to 50 now also carry or wear a wireless computing and communications device.

In addition, in our security-conscious age, technology is also being called into play to aid in person identification and behavior analysis by helping with the reading of nonverbal cues. The CIA, for example, has commissioned two research centers, the Salk Institute and Carnegie-Mellon University's Robotics Institute, to try to teach computers to watch for detailed facial-language clues. Hidden computers are also used to pick up stress in the speech patterns of travelers when they check in at airports.[88]

> Do you think jokes play as well online as they do when delivered by someone in person? How does the loss of nonverbal cues influence the impact of a joke? How could you use emoticons to compensate for the loss of such cues?

Has technology become an accessory? Is it now a regular part of your wardrobe? Does wearing it help enhance your credibility?

COMMUNICATION SKILLS IN PRACTICE
GUIDELINES FOR EFFECTIVE NONVERBAL COMMUNICATION

The following guidelines should prove helpful as you continue to develop your ability to make valid judgments and decisions on the basis of nonverbal communication.

☑ Observe the Communicators

Ask yourself if the sex, age, or status of the communicators will exert an influence on their relationship. Assess to what extent, if any, attractiveness, clothing, or physical appearance should affect the interaction. Determine if, in your own mind, the communicators' dress is appropriate to the environment. Decide if the communicators appear to like each other and to have similar goals.

☑ Observe Body Language

What does each communicator's facial expression reveal? Are his or her facial expressions relatively consistent or fleeting? Do these expressions tend to fluctuate drastically? Assess the extent to which you believe the facial expressions are genuine.

Analyze significant bodily cues. Attempt to decide if hand or foot movements suggest honesty or deception. Decide if either of the interactants moves too much or too little. Ask yourself if both are equally involved in the exchange. Is one more eager to continue the communication than the other? Would one prefer to terminate the communication? How do you know?

Assess the extent to which the interactants mirror each other's posture. Ask yourself how posture supports or contradicts their status relationship. Do the interactants appear to be relaxed or tense? Why? Determine if they have used their bodies to include or exclude others from their conversation. Analyze when and why the communicators alter their postures.

Watch the eye behavior of the participants. Determine if one looks away more than the other. Determine if one stares at the other. To what extent, if any, does excessive blinking occur? When is eye contact most pronounced? How does the eye contact of one participant appear to affect the other?

☑ Listen for Vocal Cues

Assess whether the communicators are using appropriate vocal volumes and rates of speaking, given their situation. Determine if and how the way something that is said verbally supports or contradicts what is being said nonverbally. Analyze how and when silence is used. Be responsive to signals of nervousness and changes in pitch.

☑ Observe Touching

Watch to see if the participants touch each other at all. Determine, if you can, why they touched. How did touching or being touched affect the interactants? Was the contact appropriate or inappropriate to the situation? Why?

Thinking Critically

Reflect and Respond

Agree or disagree with the following statement; supply reasons and examples that support your position.

Because of the important implications of nonverbal cues—in interviews, in advertising, and in interactions in general—the impressions we form are due more to the nonverbal signals displayed than to the words spoken by the communicators.

☑ Examine the Environment

For any nonverbal interaction, ask yourself if any environmental stimuli are likely to affect it. Determine if other people present could influence the communicators. Attempt to determine whether colors and decor will have an impact on the nature and tone of the communication. Analyze the amount of space available to the interactants. Determine whether architectural factors might alter the outcome. Where are chairs, tables, passageways, and desks situated? Why did the interactants situate themselves as they did? What type of behavior would we expect to see in this environment?

Revisiting Chapter Objectives

1. **Define** *nonverbal communication,* **and explain its functions.**   Nonverbal communication includes all the human responses that are not expressed in words. Over 65 percent of the social meaning of the messages we send to others is communicated nonverbally. Perceiving and analyzing nonverbal cues can help us understand what is really happening during a conversation.

2. **List aspects of nonverbal messages.**   Nonverbal messages fall into eight main categories: (1) body language, or kinesics (facial expressions, posture, eye gaze and eye contact, and gestures); (2) clothing and artifactual communication; (3) voice, or paralanguage (including pitch, volume, rate, and pauses); (4) space and distance, or proxemic factors (including both the space that exists between us when we talk to each other and the way we organize space in our homes, offices, and communities); (5) colors; (6) time, or chronemics; (7) touch, or haptics; and (8) smell, or olfactics.

3. **Explain why the face is an important source of information.**   Since the face cannot be easily hidden, it is an important source of nonverbal information and communicates a variety of emotions. In addition, eye contact, pupil size, and the smile provide additional cues to informed observers.

4. **Explain how artifactual communication can affect interaction.**   Artifactual communication, another category of nonverbal cues, is an integral part of the nonverbal package. It includes the use of personal adornments, such as clothing, jewelry, makeup, hairstyles, and beards. People are apt to make inferences about us based on the way we dress.

5. **Distinguish among the following terms:** *intimate distance, personal distance, social distance,* **and** *public distance;* **and** *informal space, semi-fixed-feature space,* **and** *fixed-feature space.*   Proxemic cues, including the treatment of space and territory, influence interaction and help define the communication experience. According to Edward Hall, there are four distances that we keep between ourselves and other people: intimate distance—0 to 18 inches; personal distance—18 inches to 4 feet; social distance—4 to 12 feet; and public distance—12 feet to the limit of sight. In addition, researchers divide environmental spaces into three categories—informal, semi-fixed-feature, and fixed-feature—based on the perceived permanence of the physical space.

THE WRAP-UP

6. **Identify the ways gender, diversity, and technology influence nonverbal behavior.** The use of nonverbal cues is affected by variables such as gender, culture, and technology. The ways men and women use nonverbal cues reflects societal practices. To a large degree, people modify their use of nonverbal cues depending on the culture they belong to or identify with. Nonverbal communication is also affected by whether communication is occurring online or offline.

7. **Identify how you can improve your nonverbal communication effectiveness.** You can improve your effectiveness as a nonverbal communicator by observing and analyzing body language (facial expressions, gestures, posture, and so on), vocal cues, and touching behavior, together with the impact of the physical environment.

Resources for Further Inquiry and Reflection

To apply your understanding of how the principles in Chapter 6 are at work in our daily lives, consult the following resources for further inquiry and reflection. Or, if you prefer, choose any other appropriate resource. Then connect the ideas expressed in your chosen selection with the communication concepts and issues you are learning about both in and out of class.

 Listen to Me

"When You're Mad" (NeYo)
"Green Eyes" (Coldplay)
"Your Body Is a Wonderland" (John Mayer)
"Superman" (Eminem)
"The Sound of Silence" (Simon and Garfunkel)
"You've Lost That Lovin' Feeling" (The Righteous Brothers)
"Pocketful of Sunshine" (Natasha Bedingfield)

Each song describes the effects of one or more nonverbal cues on an individual and/or a relationship. Identify and discuss the cue or cues emphasized, being certain to explain the impact on communication.

 View Me

Mother-in-Law	The Break Up
The Mask	Look Who's Talking
Edward Scissorhands	The Terminal
Hitch	

The characters in these films have a prime nonverbal channel either masked or unmasked. Discuss the extent to which the character is affected by his or her ability or inability to use a nonverbal cue effectively.

 Read Me

Joan Didion. *The Year of Magical Thinking.* New York: Knopf, 2005.
Arthur Conan Doyle. *Sherlock Holmes.* New York: Knopf, 1996.
Sister Souljah. *The Coldest Winter Ever.* New York: Pocket Books, 2000.
Mark Haddon. *The Curious Incident of the Dog in the Night.* New York: Doubleday, 2003.

On the basis of your reading of one of these books, discuss how nonverbal cues can be used to help identify someone who is guilty, identify a real friend, or otherwise function as a critical source of information.

 Tell Me

Share with the class the insights you gained from your chosen Listen to Me, View Me, or Read Me selection.

According to baseball legend Yogi Berra, "Sometimes you can observe a lot by watching." Give an example of what you think Yogi meant.

Key Chapter Terminology

Use the Online Learning Center at www.mhhe.com/gamble10e to further your knowledge of the following terminology:

artifactual communication 131	nonfluencies 134
chronemics 139	nonverbal communication 122
civil inattention 127	olfactics 141
contact cultures 144	paralanguage 132
emoticons 146	personal distance 136
facial management techniques 126	pitch 133
fixed-feature space 137	proxemics 135
habitual pitch 133	public distance 137
haptics 140	rate 133
informal space 137	semi-fixed-feature space 137
intimate distance 135	silence 135
kinesics 125	social distance 136
low-contact cultures 144	territoriality 138
markers 138	visual dominance 143
mixed message 124	volume 133

Idioms in Translation

adam's apple — larynx

baby face — young-looking face

bling — ostentatious jewelry

clock addiction — obsession with time

give a cold shoulder to — ignore

have no backbone — act cowardly

jumping out of his neck — pulsating

keep your chin up — stay optimistic

read a face — search for nonverbal clues

shoulder a burden — be burdened by a problem

shrug off a problem — ignore a problem

stare down — confront, challenge

turn back the clock — return to an earlier time

Culture Cue

The standard greeting in the United States is a smile and a handshake. People from Middle Eastern countries stand more closely together and touch much more often than do people in the United States. Although touch may be somewhat more common in the United States than it used to be, touching frequency remains significantly less than in the Middle East. On the other hand, the amount of physical contact in the United States is twice that practiced by Asians.

Test Your Understanding

Go to the *Self Quizzes* on the book's Online Learning Center at www.mhhe.com/gamble10e.

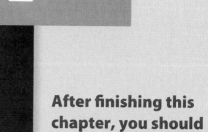
After finishing this chapter, you should be able to

1. Define *hearing, listening,* and *critical thinking.*

2. Compare and contrast helpful and harmful listening and thinking habits.

3. Explain and use the HURIER model.

4. Define *feedback,* distinguish among and use different types of feedback, and explain how each type affects communication.

5. Set appropriate listening goals.

6. Explain how gender, culture, and media and technology influence listening.

7. Use guidelines for effective listening.

Listening, Feedback, and Critical Thinking

Do you know someone who never seems to pay attention when you speak to him or her? How do you feel when your words fall on deaf ears? How frustrated do you become when the person you are talking to either ignores you or tells you that she or he is listening but is actively engaged in something else? Can someone really listen to you while looking at another person or pursuing another activity? By contrast, do you know someone whose attention never wavers when talking with you, whose eyes lock on yours, whose facial expressions announce interest in you, and whose questions and ability to paraphrase demonstrate an understanding of you? If you do, then you know a person who knows what it means to be an effective listener.[1]

To get what you want in your career, stop talking and start listening.
—Anonymous

Listening is not just hearing what someone tells you word for word. You have to listen with a heart.
—Anna Deavere Smith

The Chinese character for "listening" (see Figure 7.1) combines a number of symbols representing the ears, the eyes, and the heart, suggesting that when we listen, we need to give our undivided attention and should not rely on our ears alone but should use our eyes and our hearts as well. In your opinion, do most of the people you know accomplish this goal? Do you?

LISTENING AND COMMUNICATION

Famed American author Ernest Hemingway is said to have spoken the following words: "I like to listen. I have learned a great deal from listening. Most people never listen." On the basis of your personal experiences, do you think Hemingway's conclusion is right? Do most people never listen?

One college student, Brett Banfe, convinced that he had failed miserably in listening to others, vowed to correct his failing by remaining silent for a year: "I noticed I wasn't really listening to people. I was just waiting for people to stop talking so I could chime in," Banfe said.[2] "I'd wait for them to stop talking, then I'd start talking. Because . . . my opinion was the right one anyway. It was like, 'Thanks a lot for your input, but here's how it really happened.'"[3] While you may think that the

Ear

Eyes

Undivided Attention

Heart

FIGURE 7.1 We Do Not Listen with Our Ears Alone, as the Chinese Character for Listening Reveals.

Online Learning Center

Go to the Online Learning Center at www.mhhe.com/gamble10e and answer the questions in the *Self Inventory* to evaluate your understanding of critical thinking.

Work It Out

Make a list of everyone and everything you listened to yesterday. Categorize by function or purpose the kinds of listening in which you engaged.

action taken by Brett Banfe seems extreme, far too often listening is something we take for granted. However, listening is a difficult, intricate skill, and like other skills, it requires training and practice.

Listening affects all kinds of communication. From the time the alarm clock rings until the late news winds up, we are inundated with things to listen to. As we proceed through our day and as we move from person to person, from class to lunch, from formal discussions to casual conversations, we are constantly called on to listen. We are expected to listen to others whenever we interact face-to-face with friends and acquaintances, use the telephone, attend meetings, participate in interviews, take part in arguments, give or receive instructions, make decisions based on information received orally, and generate and receive feedback.

Listening versus Hearing

Listening and hearing are not the same thing. Most people are born with the ability to hear. **Hearing** is a process that occurs automatically and requires no conscious effort on your part. If the physiological elements within your ears are functioning properly, your brain will process the electrochemical impulses received, and you will hear. However, what you do with the impulses after receiving them belongs to the realm of listening.

Have you ever felt like Lucy does in this cartoon—angry because the person you were talking to was focused on something other than your words? What did you do?

What is listening? **Listening** is a deliberate process through which we seek to understand and retain aural (heard) stimuli. Unlike hearing, listening depends on a complex set of skills that must be acquired. Thus, whereas hearing simply happens to us and cannot be manipulated, listening requires us to make an active, conscious effort to comprehend and remember what we hear. Furthermore, who we are affects what we listen to. In your environment, from minute to minute, far too many sounds bombard you for you to be able to pay attention to each one. Thus, in listening, you process the external sounds of your environment to select those that are relevant to you, your activities, and your interests. This is not to say that listening is just an external process. It is also an internal process. We listen to the sounds we hear, and we listen to what others say, but we also listen to what we say aloud and what we say to ourselves in response. (Do you ever talk to yourself? Are you your own best listener? Most of us are.)

The Ethics of Listening

While all of us continually engage in activities that require us to listen, some of us fail to pay enough attention to the role listening plays in these activities. The tragic shootings at educational institutions such as Columbine High School in Littleton, Colorado, should put us on notice that we need to listen to each other. Listening, as well as the failure to listen, has an impact on our relationships.

How Responsive a Listener Are You?

Although we expect others to listen to us, we sometimes ignore our ethical responsibility to listen to them. We fake listening or do not listen as carefully as we could. Consequently, problems due to ineffective listening occur.

At one time, a poll of American teenagers indicated that as many as half of them believed that communication between themselves and their parents was poor—and that a primary cause was poor listening. Parents, too, often feel that communication is failing. One woman was convinced that her daughter must have

> Do you think it is possible to listen with more than your ears? Can you listen with your heart?

hearing
the involuntary, physiological process by which we perceive sound

listening
the deliberate, psychological process by which we receive, understand, and retain aural stimuli

> Self-talk—listening to what you say to yourself—can help you make sense of the way you listen to and react to the people in your life.

> Effective listeners focus their attention. What difficulties do you have when attempting to focus?

> How does one listen ethically? What distinguishes the ethical listeners from an unethical listener?

MANKOFF

"I'm sorry, dear, I wasn't listening. Could you repeat what you've said since we've been married?"

> When we are mindful, we fully engage ourselves in the moment, paying careful attention to the here and now. We focus completely on what another person says and does. We do not judge the other, but demonstrate our interest in understanding his or her ideas. If we fail at listening, does it mean we are mindless?

mindfulness

emptying one's mind of personal concerns and interfering emotions, and choosing to focus on the person and the here and now

Work It Out
Describe what you do to prepare to listen.

a severe hearing problem and took her to an audiologist. The audiologist tested both ears and reported back to the distraught parent: "There's nothing wrong with her hearing. She's just tuning you out."

A leading cause of the high divorce rate (approximately half of all marriages in the United States end in divorce) is the failure of husbands and wives to interact effectively. They don't listen to each other or respond to each other's messages. Presidents of major companies also identify listening as one of their major communication problems.[4] One nationwide survey revealed that 14 percent of each workweek is wasted as a result of poor listening. That amounts to about seven weeks of work per year.[5] A survey of personnel managers also identified listening as the skill most needed at work if work teams are to succeed.[6]

When we make the ethical commitment to listen to others, we focus and attend fully to them without allowing competing thoughts or stimuli to divert our attention. In effect, we practice **mindfulness**—by emptying our minds of personal concerns and interfering emotions, and choosing to focus on the person and what is happening in the here and now—a skill many of us find difficult to master.[7]

Effective listeners—people who not only know how to listen but also want to listen—make better employers and employees, doctors and patients, friends and significant others.[8] Many people enroll in professional courses focused on how to improve listening skills,[9] but you have that opportunity now.

Are You Prepared to Listen?

Think back over the years you have spent as a student. Did you receive training in writing? Reading? Speaking? The answer to each of these questions is probably yes. In fact, many children now learn to read and write before they start school, and reading and writing skills are taught and emphasized throughout our educational careers. But what about listening? Of the four communication skills—reading, writing, speaking, and listening—listening has received the least attention from educators, yet listening is the fundamental process through which we initiate and maintain relationships, and it is the primary process through which we take in information.

How Well Do You Use Your Listening Time?

A recent study revealed that college students like you spend as much time listening to media as engaged in interpersonal communication. Some 55.4 percent of a college student's day is now spent listening, while only 17.1 percent of it is spent reading, 16.1 percent speaking, and 11.4 percent writing.[10] These figures are in line with earlier studies showing that, on average, college students devoted 42 to 53 percent of the time spent communicating to listening, 16 to 32 percent speaking, 15 to 17 percent reading, and 9 to 14 percent writing.[11] We spend more time listening than engaging in other forms of communication. These results hold true on the job, where listening is an integral element in creating relationships with others at work.[12] In fact, employees of Fortune 500 companies spend the majority of their day—approximately 60 percent of it—listening.[13]

Take a moment to review your personal listening situation. Think of interactions you have had that were complicated because you or someone else failed to listen effectively. For example, when was the last time you jumped to a wrong conclusion? Missed an important word?

Do you make an active, conscious effort to comprehend and remember what you hear?

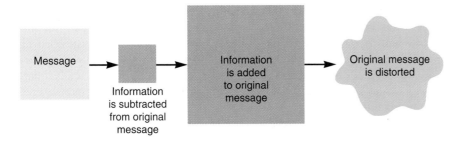

FIGURE 7.2

Serial Communication.

Source: William Haney. *Communication and Organizational Behavior.* Homewood, IL: Irwin, 1973.

Failed to realize you were not being understood? Reacted emotionally or let yourself become distracted? Far too often, instead of listening, we daydream our way through our daily contacts—we take side trips or otherwise tune out what is said to us. In other words, we adopt destructive "unlistening" behaviors.

Most people estimate that they listen with 70 to 80 percent accuracy. This means they believe that they can listen to others and accurately retain 70 to 80 percent of what is said. However, researchers like Ralph Nichols tell us that most of us actually listen at only 25 percent efficiency—that is, instead of retaining 75 percent of what we hear, we lose 75 percent.[14]

> According to sociologist Deborah Tannen, "Boys learn to hold center stage by talking; girls learn to listen." Do you agree or disagree? Why?

How Much of a Role Do You Play in Ensuring the Integrity of a Message?

Although most of us have supposedly had many years of practice in listening, errors are extremely common. According to communication theorist William Haney, we frequently run into problems when we use **serial communication,** or chain-of-command transmissions, to relay messages (see Figure 7.2). In serial communication, person 1 sends a message to person 2; person 2 then communicates his or her perception of person 1's message (not person 1's message itself) to person 3, who continues the process.

serial communication
a chain-of-command transmission

Whenever one person speaks or delivers a message to a second person, the message occurs in at least four different forms:[15]

1. message as it exists in the mind of the speaker (his or her thoughts)
2. message as it is spoken (actually encoded by the speaker)
3. message as it is interpreted (decoded by the listener)
4. message as it is ultimately remembered by the listener (affected by the listener's personal selectivity and rejection)

Gossip is a form of serial communication.

In traveling down this unwieldy chain of command from person to person, ideas can become distorted by as much as 80 percent. Several factors are responsible. First, because passing along complex, confusing information poses many problems, we generally like to simplify messages. As a result, we unconsciously (and consciously) delete information from the messages we receive before transmitting these messages to others. Second, we like to think the messages we pass along to others make sense. (We feel foolish if we convey a message we ourselves do not understand or deliver a message that appears illogical.) Thus, we try to make sense of a message before communicating it to someone else. We do this by adding to, subtracting from, or otherwise altering what we have heard. Unfortunately, as we see in Figure 7.2, once we make sense of the message, it may no longer correspond to the message originally sent. Such errors occur even though we have had years of practice in listening. Estimates are that a 20-year-old person has practiced listening for at least 10,000 hours; a 30-year-old, at least 15,000 hours; and a typical 40-year-old, 20,000 or more hours.[16] These figures are mind-boggling, but have we in reality been practicing listening or unlistening? Research suggests that we have been practicing unlistening.

By listening accurately and ethically, you help avoid communication difficulties and breakdowns and increase your chances of being well liked and appreciated by others.[17] Who has the primary responsibility for clear and effective communication—the speaker or the listener? An old proverb says, "Nature gave us two ears and one mouth so that we can listen twice as much as we speak." Actually, since everyone functions as both sender and receiver, everyone must assume 51 percent of the responsibility for communication. This practice might not be mathematically sound, but it would certainly increase the effectiveness of our interpersonal, small-group, public, and mediated communication.[18]

Are You Ready to Collaborate with the Speaker?

There is a relationship between a speaker's acts and a listener's responses. Typically, speaker gaze coordinates this relationship. While listeners usually look more at the speaker than the reverse, at key points a speaker will look directly at the listener, signaling that the speaker is seeking a response. If the listener is attentive, this creates a period of mutual gaze known as "the gaze window." When this occurs, the listener responds with a nod, a "mhm," or another verbal or nonverbal reaction that lets the speaker know she or he is listening and collaborating in the dialogue or conversation.[19]

Audience members demonstrate readiness to listen to a speaker by using their eyes and bodies to communicate their receptivity, some more expressively than

> Comedian George Burns once said, "I can't help hearing, but I don't always listen." Describe an occasion when this statement might have been applied to your own behavior. What happened as a result?

> In what ways is listening a collaborative experience?

How do you use your body and eyes to demonstrate readiness to listen?

others. For example, when you are a member of an audience, do you ever find yourself leaning forward, fixing your eyes on the speaker, or signaling your agreement or disagreement with the speaker by using facial expression and head nods?

TYPES OF LISTENING

Do you spend time listening to music on your iPod, on your CD player, or at concerts? Why? Is it because you enjoy it? When our primary motivation for listening is pleasure or relaxation—to unwind, to escape, or to be entertained—we listen appreciatively. Listening to music, a movie, or a comedy routine are just a few examples of the kinds of **appreciative listening** we engage in. Courses in music or film appreciation teach us how to listen appreciatively. Unlike the next three types of listening we define, appreciative listening usually does not require us to focus on organizing or remembering what we have listened to. In contrast to appreciative listening, when we listen to gain knowledge, we listen comprehensively. Examples of **comprehensive listening** include listening to directions, a lecture, a job description, or a person's position on an issue of concern, such as whether abortion should be legal. Often, however, we seek not only to gain knowledge, but also to evaluate the worth of what we have listened to. When we listen critically, we listen to determine the usefulness, soundness, and accuracy of messages. During **critical listening** our critical thinking skills also come into play as we decide whether to accept or reject a message. We talk more about comprehensive and critical listening later in this chapter.

The last type of listening, and the focus of this section, is **empathic listening.** The goal when we listen empathically is to understand the feelings and point of view of another person. Perhaps you serve as a relative's sounding board, listen to the troubles of a friend, or help a co-worker talk through problems. You also help restore that person's sense of emotional balance because you understand him or her as he or she desires to be understood, interpreting the situation he or she is facing as if it were your own. Thus, imagining yourself in another's place is essential in empathic listening.[20]

According to author Daniel Goleman, empathic listeners are effective at *decentering*—placing the focus on others rather than on themselves. They listen from the speaker's point of view, using three different skills to accomplish this: *empathic responsiveness* (the experiencing of an emotional response that corresponds to the emotions of another person),[21] *perspective taking* (placing yourself in another person's shoes)[22] and *sympathetic responsiveness* (feeling concern and compassion for the situation the other person faces). If you use only sympathetic responsiveness, however, your listening will fall short of empathic listening. If you only *feel for* a person, without using perspective taking and empathic responsiveness, you cannot succeed in *feeling with* the person.[23]

Empathic listeners rely heavily on two communication skills: the ability to read the nonverbal cues of others, including their eye contact, physical contact (touching), and facial expressions; and the ability to use the active listening tool—*the paraphrase*—to let those they listen to know that they care enough to listen, understand what is said, and respond to the expressed feelings. When you paraphrase, you engage in listening actively, which means you put yourself in the speaker's place in an effort to understand the speaker's feelings and send back to the speaker what you believe the speaker communicated when delivering his or her total message; that is, you internalize and reflect the message's verbal content as well as the speaker's feelings.

> How do you establish listening goals? How do you determine whether you have realized your objectives?

appreciative listening
listening for enjoyment or relaxation

comprehensive listening
listening to gain knowledge

critical listening
listening to evaluate the worth of a message

empathic listening
listening to help others

paraphrasing

restating in your own words what another person has said

How do you paraphrase? **Paraphrasing** is a three-step process in which you do the following:

1. make a tentative statement that invites correction—for example, "If I'm not mistaken . . ."
2. repeat the basic idea or ideas in your own words.
3. check your interpretation with the other person, saying something like, "Is that correct?"

For example:

Person 1: I am so mad at my professor. He's making me rework my entire paper. I worked forever on it.

Person 2: If I'm not mistaken, your professor is asking you to rewrite the paper you turned in. You're feeling frustrated because you worked hard. Is that right?

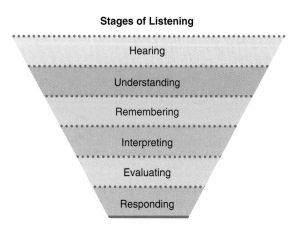

Work It Out

Discuss and describe listening situations during which you believe you functioned as an empathic listener. Identify the behaviors you exhibited that justify your use of that title.

Empathic communication and paraphrasing have roles to play in both our personal and our professional lives. Research reveals that listening to family stories and reminiscing about the past may be both physically and emotionally healing for both the teller and the listener, contributing to their sense of overall well-being.[24] Findings from medical research also underscore the importance of effective listening. Medical school curricula now include courses that teach medical students how to listen, ask open-ended questions, and establish productive, caring, and empathic relationships with patients.[25] Doctors who do not practice empathic listening frequently interrupt their patients. This keeps them from eliciting relevant background on the patient's life circumstances and symptoms. The result? Costly mistakes.[26] Far too often doctors fail to paraphrase what a patient says, cutting off the patient's words after allowing only a scant 18 seconds for the patient to reveal what is troubling him or her.[27]

HURIER model

a model of listening focusing on six skill areas or stages

As we make our way through this chapter, we will see that, in addition to being a tool used in empathic communication, the paraphrase is of value in other listening venues as well.

THE STAGES OF LISTENING: MORE THAN MEETS THE EAR

Stages of Listening

Hearing

Understanding

Remembering

Interpreting

Evaluating

Responding

FIGURE 7.3 The HURIER Model (Stages of Listening).

A model of listening developed by listening researcher Judi Brownell, called the **HURIER model,** takes a behavioral approach to listening, suggesting that listening is composed of both mental processes and observable behaviors.[28] The model focuses on six skill areas, or listening stages: *h*earing, *u*nderstanding, *r*emembering, *i*nterpreting, *e*valuating, and *r*esponding (see Figure 7.3).

The Hearing Stage

As the model indicates, the first stage of the listening process is *hearing*. Sounds fill our world and compete to be noticed. Usually, however, we hear what we listen for, meaning that we choose to attend to some aspects of what we hear while ignoring the rest. Once we *attend* to a message—demonstrate our willingness to organize and focus on what we are hearing—if the message holds our attention, we will also seek to understand it.

The Understanding Stage

During stage two, *understanding*, or listening comprehensively, we relate what we have listened to, to what we already know. We do not judge the message until we are certain we comprehend it. We might, for example, ask questions about or paraphrase what we believe another person said during the understanding stage.

According to Ralph Nichols and Leonard Stevens, the authors of *Are You Listening?*, words that cause listeners to react emotionally interfere with understanding. Nichols calls these red-flag words. **Red-flag words** produce emotional deafness, sending listening efficiency down to zero.[29] Among the words known to function as red flags for some listeners are *AIDS*, *spastic*, and *income tax*.

Other factors that interfere with understanding are the environment (for example, it could be too hot, too cold, too messy) and people themselves (speaking too fast, too slow, too loudly, or too softly). We also think faster than others speak. This is called the **speech-thought differential.** A person usually speaks at a rate of 125 to 150 words per minute. We think, however, at over 500 words per minute, meaning that we have time left over to take mental excursions and to daydream. To use the speech-thought differential to enhance understanding, we need to internally summarize, question, and paraphrase what is being said.

red-flag words
words that trigger emotional deafness, dropping listening efficiency to zero

speech-thought differential
the difference between speaking and thinking rates

The Remembering Stage

Once our brain assigns meaning to a message, the next stage is *remembering*, in which we try to retain what we have listened to for future use. We personally decide how much of what we have listened to is worth storing in memory and how much we can forget. Intense feelings or the reinforcement of a message increases our chances of remembering. Once we remember a message, we should be able to recall it when necessary. However, we cannot possibly remember everything. Some forgetting is necessary for mental health.

We have two kinds of memory, short-term memory and long-term memory. Most of what we listen to we store briefly in our short-term memory. Unless we use and apply what is stored in short-term memory, we forget it before being able to transfer it into long-term memory. This helps explain why we remember only 50 percent of a message immediately after listening to it, and approximately 25 percent after a period of time has passed. Long-term memory, our more permanent memory bank, plays a key listening role by connecting new experiences to past ones.

We use three key tools to enhance recall. The first is *repetition*. The more we repeat an idea, the more likely we are to recall it later. The second tool is the now-familiar three-step *paraphrase*. By restating in your own words what a person just told you, you not only check on your understanding of what was said, but also help yourself recall it. The third tool is *visualization*. By picturing what someone has said to you—connecting a visual image to a name, a place, or numbers—you can help improve your recall. For example, you might picture a person named John Sanderson as standing atop a large sand pile. Many memory problems are due not to faulty memory, but rather to people's losing their ability to pay attention. Attention and focus build memory.[30]

The Interpreting Stage

During the fourth stage, *interpreting*, we make sense of a message, using *dual perspective taking*—considering the message from the sender's perspective as well as our perspective. If we are successful, we do not impose our personal meaning onto another person's message.

The Evaluating Stage

During stage five, *evaluating*, we weigh the worth of a message and critically analyze it. (Evaluating is a type of listening referred to earlier in this chapter as critical listening.) During the evaluating stage we distinguish facts from inferences, weigh the evidence provided, and identify any prejudices or faulty arguments that could slant meaning. We stay mindful rather than mindless, listening between the lines and being careful not to jump to conclusions.

The Responding Stage

During the last stage, *responding*, we react to what we have listened to and offer feedback to let the speaker know our thoughts and feelings about the message. We become the speaker's radar. (We cover feedback in more depth later in this chapter.)

The HURIER model provides a foundation for us to consider key aspects of the listening process and our own listening behavior.

Listening versus Unlistening: Exploring the Unethical Behaviors of Ineffective Listeners

Of course, we do not—probably, we cannot—listen at full capacity all the time. But we should be aware of our ineffective listening behaviors if they prevent us from understanding what could be important to us or to someone else. Many factors contribute to ineffective listening, and the following kinds of ineffective listeners are certainly not the only ineffective listeners we can identify. However, we have probably interacted with most of those identified here at some point in the past.

- **Fraudulent listeners.**   Fraudulent listeners are pseudolisteners; they are also nodders. Persons who practice fraudulent listening and engage in nodding pretend that they are listening. They look at the speaker, nod their heads appropriately in agreement or disagreement, and utter remarks such as "mm" or "uh-huh" that imply they are paying attention. In actuality, the words are falling on deaf ears.

- **Monopolistic listeners.**   Monopolistic listeners want you to listen to them, but they have neither the time nor the desire to listen to you. Frequently egocentric, and as a result, intrigued and obsessed with their own thoughts and ideas, monopolizers deny your right to be listened to while defending their right to express themselves, no matter what the cost.[31]

    According to researcher Alfie Kohn, men are more likely than women to be monopolistic listeners, or "ear hogs." Kohn finds that men interrupt

> How many of the ineffective listener categories are you familiar with? Would you ever place yourself in any of the groups?

women's statements more frequently than women interrupt men's statements; in fact, in his research 96 percent of the interruptions in male-female interactions were initiated by men.[32] Do you believe this finding is still valid?

- **Completers.** Completers are gap fillers; they never quite get the whole story when they listen. To make up for what they have missed or misinterpreted, they manufacture information to fill in the gaps. While the impression is that they got it all, nothing could be farther from the truth.

- **Selective listeners.** Selective listeners are like bees going after the honey in a flower; they zero in on only those portions of a speaker's remarks that interest them or have particular importance to them. Everything else the speaker says is considered irrelevant or inconsequential and thus is rejected. Selective listeners, in their search for just the honey, often miss the flower.

- **Avoiders.** Avoiders figuratively wear earmuffs; they close their ears to information they would rather not deal with. Sometimes they pretend not to understand what you tell them or act as if they did not hear you at all. Sometimes they simply forget, in short order, what you have told them.

- **Defensive listeners.** Defensive listeners tend to perceive the remarks of other persons as personal affronts or attacks. Usually insecure, they are apt to pounce when another person asks a simple question, or they are likely to perceive a threat in the comments of another, when none actually exists. When we listen defensively, we assume others are going to criticize or belittle us; we assume that they do not like, trust, or respect us. As a result, an innocent question, such as, "Did you file your expense account?" may be interpreted as criticism for having spent too much on a business trip.

- **Attackers.** Attackers wait for you to make a mistake, so that they can undercut and challenge what

Work It Out

Describe your experiences with the kinds of faulty listeners depicted in this section. What would have to happen for each situation to be replayed more successfully?

We wear earmuffs when we close our ears to information we would rather not listen to.

Media Wise

Talk, Talk, Talk

Talk radio, a mediated form of interpersonal communication that is growing in influence, allows callers a higher level of psychological comfort than does face-to-face interaction, because they can remain relatively anonymous while interacting with another person. Programs featuring argumentative hosts, such as Guardian Angels founder Curtis Slewa and pundits Rush Limbaugh, Al Franken, and Bill O'Reilly, often become either yelling matches between the host and a caller who openly disagrees with an espoused position the host has taken or love fests between the host and a caller who support each other's views.

Why is this? In her book *The First Word: The Search for the Origins of Language,* Christine Kenneally offers a rationale for such poor listening behavior. She describes an experiment in which two apes, skilled in sign language, were thrown together and encouraged to interact. Rather than engaging in meaningful communication, however, they had an arm-waving, sign-shouting match, with neither ape willing to listen to the other.[33] Is there a lesson in there for us? Are we hardwired to prefer listening to ourselves rather than others?

you have to say. They lie in wait, hoping to gather ammunition they can use to diminish your effectiveness. They also are not above distorting your words to advance their personal goals. Attacking listeners are apt to precipitate defensiveness in the person they are listening to. Rather than working to understand your meaning and conducting a discussion with you that is open and fair, they compete with you in an effort to outdo you.

Feedback: A Prerequisite for Effective Listening

The feedback process is intimately connected with the listening process. Developing an understanding and appreciation of the way feedback works is essential to improving your listening skills.

What Is Feedback?

The term *feedback* implies that we are feeding someone by giving something back to him or her. Feedback consists of all the verbal and nonverbal messages that a person consciously or unconsciously sends out in response to another person's communication. As students, you continually provide your instructors with feedback. Many of you, however, are probably not completely honest when you send feedback. At times when you are confused or bored, you may nevertheless put on an "I'm interested" face and nod smilingly, indicating that you understand and agree with everything your instructor is saying. Unfortunately, such behavior tends to encourage the sending of unclear messages.

Types of Feedback

We constantly provide others with feedback, whether we intend to or not. Everything we do or fail to do in a relationship or interaction with others can be considered feedback. Sometimes we send feedback consciously, intending to evoke a particular response. For example, if you laugh or chuckle at a speaker's joke or story, you may be doing so because you want the speaker to feel that you enjoyed the story and hope he or she will tell more jokes. In contrast, some of the feedback we transmit is sent unconsciously and evokes unintended or unexpected responses. Often, when our words or behaviors prompt a reaction that we never intended, we respond with useless phrases such as "That's not what I meant!" or "I didn't mean it that way!" or "What I meant was . . ."

What we intend to convey by feedback, then, may not be what others perceive. Sometimes others intentionally choose not to perceive our messages. At other times, confusion results because feedback that we mean to be nonevaluative in tone is interpreted as evaluative. Distinguishing between these two categories of feedback will help us use both types effectively and appropriately.

Evaluative Feedback When we provide another person with **evaluative feedback**—that is, an evaluative response—we state our opinion about a matter being discussed. For example, "How did you like my speech?" will almost always evoke a response that will be perceived as evaluative. A slight hesitation before the words "I loved it" might be perceived as a negative response. When we give evaluative feedback, we make judgments—either positive or negative—based on our own system of values. As we go about the business of daily life, judgments about the relative worth of ideas, the importance of projects, and the classification of abilities are a necessity. By its very nature, the

---

In *The Argument Culture: Moving from Debate to Dialogue,* linguist Deborah Tannen discusses how the mind-sets of people living in the United States predispose them to attack rather than listen effectively to others.[34] Do you find this is true when it comes to relationships you share in your social and career life?

Imagine someone who writes 50 love letters but receives no answer. Has this person received feedback?

evaluative feedback
a positive or negative judgment

Work It Out
Provide examples of the most helpful and the least helpful feedback you ever received. What, in your view, makes some feedback more valuable than other feedback?

effect of evaluative feedback is either positive and rewarding or negative and punishing.

Positive Evaluative Feedback   Positive evaluative feedback tends to keep communication and its resulting behaviors moving in the direction they are already heading. If a company places an advertisement and achieves a tremendous growth in sales, the company will tend to place the same or a very similar ad in the same or very similar media in the future. If a person wearing a new hairstyle is complimented, he or she will tend to keep that hairstyle. If you are speaking to an instructor who appears receptive to your ideas and suggestions, you will tend to continue offering ideas and suggestions in the future. Thus, positive evaluative feedback makes us continue behaving as we are already behaving and enhances or reinforces existing conditions or actions.

Negative Evaluative Feedback   Negative evaluative feedback serves a corrective function in that it helps extinguish undesirable communicative behaviors. When we perceive feedback as negative, we tend to change our performance accordingly. For example, if you were to tell a number of off-color stories that your listeners found in bad taste, they might send you negative responses. They might turn away, attempt to change the subject, or simply maintain a cold, lengthy silence. Each cue would indicate that your message had overstepped the bounds of propriety; as a result, you would probably discontinue your anecdotes.

Formative Feedback   **Formative feedback** is timed negative feedback. Don Tosti, an industrial psychologist, used timed negative feedback with some interesting results.[35] Tosti discovered that, in a learning situation, it is best to provide positive feedback immediately after someone has displayed a desired behavior. Thus, comments such as, "You did a good job" and "Keep up the good work" should be offered immediately, because these responses give people a sense of pride and pleasure in themselves and their work. However, Tosti suggests that what he calls "formative negative" feedback should be given only just before an undesired behavior (or a similar behavior)

formative feedback
timed negative feedback

Work It Out

Test the theory behind formative feedback. Whenever you send evaluative feedback messages, preface your statements so as to make it clear that you are offering an opinion. Use phrases like "It seems to me," "In my opinion," and "I think" to show your awareness that other interpretations are possible. Avoid using phrases like "You must" or "That's stupid" because such comments tend to make others defensive.

Feedback in Japan

Are you culturally sensitive when giving feedback? For example, many Japanese—unlike Americans—use an indirect style of communication. Thus, when interacting with someone from Japan, if you give feedback directly (for example, telling someone outright, "You are not working hard enough"), the feedback, instead of being viewed as helpful, might be viewed as a threat. And if it is perceived as a threat, it could well be ineffective. An American giving feedback to another American, however, can give feedback more directly.

Do you believe we ought to change the way we provide feedback to conform to the preferences of another culture? Explain.

is about to be repeated. Tosti believes that withholding negative feedback until the person can use it constructively makes the feedback seem more like coaching than criticism. Comments such as "OK, team, let's eliminate the errors we made last time" and "When you go out there today, try to . . ." reduce the extent to which negative feedback is perceived as harmful rather than helpful. Thus, giving formative feedback just before an activity is to be performed again can help eliminate the feelings of rejection that sometimes accompany negative feedback. (In contrast, it should be remembered that immediate positive feedback can do wonders for people's self-image and morale.)

nonevaluative feedback
nondirective feedback

Nonevaluative Feedback   In contrast to evaluative feedback, **nonevaluative feedback,** or nondirective feedback, makes no overt attempt to direct the actions of a communicator. Thus, we use nonevaluative feedback when we want to learn more about a person's feelings or when we want to help another person formulate thoughts about a particular subject. When we offer nonevaluative feedback, we make no reference to our own opinions or judgments. Instead, we simply describe, question, or indicate an interest in what the other person is communicating to us.

Despite its nonjudgmental nature, nonevaluative feedback is often construed as being positive. That is, other people's behaviors may be reinforced when we probe, interpret their messages, and offer support as they attempt to work through a problem. Nonevaluative feedback reaches beyond positive feedback, however, by providing others with an opportunity to examine their own problems and arrive at their own solutions. For this reason, carefully phrased nonevaluative feedback can be enormously helpful and sustaining to people who are going through a difficult period.

We consider four kinds of nonevaluative feedback here. Three—probing, understanding, and supporting—were identified by David Johnson. The fourth—"I" messages—was identified by Thomas Gordon.[36]

probing
a nonevaluative technique in which we ask for additional information

Probing   **Probing** is a nonevaluative technique in which we ask people for additional information to draw them out and to demonstrate our willingness to listen to their problems.[37] Suppose that a student is concerned about his or her grades in a particular course and says to you, "I'm really upset. All my friends are doing better in geology than I am." If you use probing, you might ask, "Why does this situation bother you?" or "What do you suppose caused this to happen?" Responding in this way gives the other person the chance to think through the overall nature of the problem while providing him or her with an opportunity for emotional release. In contrast, comments like "So what? Who cares about that dumb class?" or "You really were dumb when you stopped studying" would tend to stop the student from thinking through and discussing the problem and, instead, would probably create defensiveness.

Understanding   A second kind of nonevaluative response is what Johnson calls **understanding.** When we offer understanding, we seek to comprehend what the other person is saying to us, and we check ourselves by restating what we believe we have heard. Doing this shows that we care about other people and the problems they face.

Examine the following paraphrases to develop a feel for the nature of this kind of response:

Person 1: I don't think I have the skill to be picked for the team.

Person 2: You believe you're not good enough to make the team this year?

Person 1: I envy those guys so much.

Person 2: You mean you're jealous of the people in that group?

If we use understanding early in a relationship, in effect, we communicate that we care enough about the interaction to want to be certain we comprehend what the other person is saying to us. Such a response strengthens the relationship because it encourages the other person to describe and detail his or her feelings.

Supportive Feedback   A third kind of nonevaluative feedback is what Johnson calls **supportive feedback.** This response indicates that a problem the other person deems important and significant is also viewed by the listener as important and significant.

Suppose a friend comes to you with a problem she feels is extremely serious. Perhaps your friend has worked herself into a state of extreme agitation and implies that you cannot possibly understand the situation. In offering supportive feedback, you would attempt to calm your friend down by assuring her that the world has not ended and that you do understand the problem.

Offering supportive feedback is difficult. We have to be able to reduce the intensity of other people's feelings while letting them know that we consider their problems real and serious. Such comments as "It's stupid to worry about that" and "Is that all that's worrying you?" are certainly not supportive. A better approach might be to say, "I can see you are upset. Let's talk about it. I'm sure you can find a way to solve the problem." A friend who is upset because he or she has just failed an exam needs supportive feedback: "I can see you are worried. I don't blame you for being upset." This is certainly not the time to suggest that there is no valid reason for being upset or that your friend's feelings are inappropriate. When we use supportive feedback, we judge the problems to be important, but we do not attempt to solve them ourselves; instead, we encourage people to discover their own solutions.

According to Doris Iarovici, a medical student at Yale, "One of the best things you can do for any patient is to listen and show that you care."[38] This, in a nutshell, is supportive feedback.

"I" Messages   Certain nonevaluative feedback messages are called **"I" messages,** a term coined by Thomas Gordon. When we deliver an "I" message, we do not pass judgment on the other person's actions but simply convey our own feelings about the nature of the situation.

understanding
a nonevaluative response that uses restatement to check comprehension

supportive feedback
a nonevaluative response indicating that the receiver perceives a problem as important

"I" messages
nonevaluative responses that convey our feelings about the nature of a situation

According to Gordon, when people interact with us, they are often unaware of how their actions affect us. We have the option of providing these people with either evaluative or nonevaluative feedback. Neither type is inherently good nor bad. However, far too often, the way we formulate our evaluative feedback adversely affects the nature of our interactions and the growth of our relationships. For example, do any of these statements sound familiar? "You made me angry!" "You're no good!" "You're in my way!" "You're a slob!" What do these statements have in common? As you have probably noticed, each one contains the word *you*. Each also places the blame for something on another person. When relationships experience difficulties, people tend to resort more and more to name-calling and to blaming others. Such feedback messages create schisms that are difficult and sometimes even impossible to bridge.

"you" messages

responses that place blame on another person

To avoid this situation, Gordon suggests that we replace **"you" messages** with "I" messages. If, for example, a parent tells a child, "You're pestering me," the child's interpretation will probably be "I am bad," and this interpretation will evoke a certain amount of defensiveness or hostility toward the parent ("I am not bad!"). But if the parent tells the child, "I'm really very tired and I don't feel like playing right now," the child's reaction is more likely to be "Mom is tired." Such an approach is more likely to elicit the type of behavior the parent desires than would name-calling and blaming ("You are a pest"). Using "I" messages as feedback will not always evoke the behavior you want from the other person, but it will help prevent the defensive, self-serving behaviors that "you" messages frequently elicit.

"I" messages have one other aspect you should be aware of. It is quite common to say "I am angry" to another person. Anger, however, is a secondary emotion. We are angry because of a stimulus or stimuli. In actuality, we develop anger. For example, if your child or a child you are watching ran into the street, your first response would probably be fear. Only after the child was safe would you develop anger, and then you would probably share your anger—rather than your fear—with the child. When formulating an angry "I" message, be certain to look beyond or beneath your anger and ask yourself why you are angry. Try to identify the forces that precipitated your anger—these are the feelings that should be expressed. Thus, if someone says something that hurts you, find ways to express the initial hurt rather than the resulting anger.

Effects of Feedback

How do you think feedback affects communication? Suppose that someone is telling you a funny story. What would happen if you should consciously decide to treat this person politely but neither smile nor laugh at the story? Such a reaction—polite but somber—can cause the best of storytellers to stop communicating. Sometimes in the middle of a story, the teller will notice that the listener is not amused. At this point, in an attempt to determine if the receiver has heard what was said, the sender will repeat or rephrase key parts of the story: "Don't you understand? What happened was . . ." or "You see, what this means is . . ." The feedback given by the respondent in any encounter strongly influences the direction and outcome of the interaction.[39] You might want to try the "no laugh" procedure the next time someone begins to relate a humorous incident or tale to you. If you do, note how not laughing affects the sender's ability to formulate a message.

The Skill Builder on the next page, adapted from an experiment designed by Harold Leavitt and Ronald Mueller, demonstrates how feedback affects the development of our relationships.[40] Feedback usually increases the accuracy with which

Focus on Service Learning

Choose one of the following activities:

Research the work conducted by on-site personnel at a local crisis center. Visit the center's Web site as well as Web sites such as www.suicidehotline.com or www.rapecrisiscenter.org. Then visit the local crisis center itself. Observe and listen to the persons who answer the phones at the site. On the basis of your knowledge and research, develop a workshop designed to enhance the skills of current phone personnel.

or

Visit a nursing home and research the special needs of the elder people who live there. This experience can help you more fully understand the importance of listening and of empathy. Familiarizing yourself with Web sites such as www.paservicelearning.org/Reach/Reach7.htm can add to your knowledge. Once you have completed your information gathering, volunteer to visit with, listen to, and read to residents at a local nursing home.

Skill Builder

Now You Have It; Now You Don't

Choose a partner. You and your partner should each draw on a card or slip of paper three designs consisting of a random series of straight, interconnecting lines (like the sample below). Do not show the diagrams to each other. The purpose of the exercise is to give verbal instructions that will enable your partner to reproduce your diagrams.

Deliver your instructions under three conditions:

1. *Zero feedback.* When you explain your first design, turn your back to your partner and neither watch nor comment on his or her efforts. Your partner is not allowed to speak to you or look at you during this phase. This situation approximates a zero feedback (no feedback) condition.

2. *Limited feedback.* When you describe the second design, you may turn and watch your partner work. You may comment on what he or she is drawing, but your partner may not speak to you or look at you. This approximates a limited feedback condition.

3. *Free feedback.* Finally, when you describe your third design to your partner, you may interact openly with each other. You may observe and comment on your partner's efforts, and your partner may interact with you by facing you and asking you questions to check on the accuracy of his or her drawing. This approximates a free feedback condition.

Next, if time permits, you and your partner should reverse roles and repeat the three steps.

Which condition produced the fastest replication? Why? Which condition produced the most accurate replication? Why? During which phase of the experience were you most confident? Least confident? Why? How did functioning as sender or receiver alter your feelings during each phase of the experience?

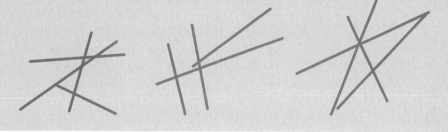

information is passed from person to person. However, it also increases the amount of time required to transmit information. Under the "zero feedback" condition (phase 1 of the exercise), the speaker requires less time to transmit the information to the receiver than he or she would under either the "limited feedback" condition (phase 2) or the "free feedback" condition (phase 3). Still, most communicators feel that the added time is more than compensated for by the increased accuracy of the replications. In other words, under the free feedback condition, time is not wasted.

THE ROLE OF CRITICAL THINKING: ASSESSING THE CREDIBILITY OF WHAT YOU LISTEN TO

While you listen to information, you interpret and assign meaning to the spoken words. Your primary focus is on gaining and retaining information. When you go the next step and engage in **critical thinking,** you think carefully about what another person has said to you, and you evaluate the believability of the spoken message. Just as speakers can get carried away with their message's urgency and importance, so listeners can end up believing false or dangerous ideas that have been made to appear reasonable. Consequently, it is essential for you as a listener to stay alert, so that you are ready to challenge and raise questions about what

critical thinking
the careful and deliberate process of message evaluation

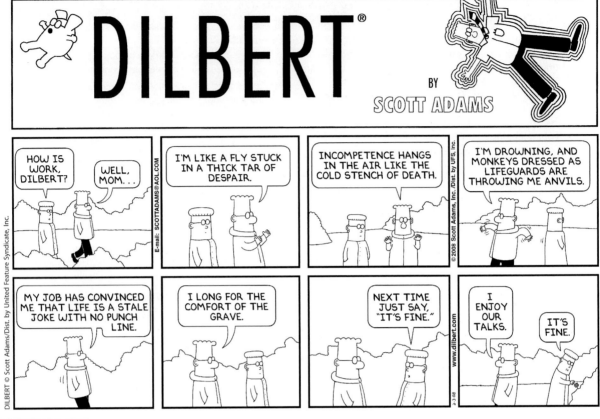

What advice would you give Dilbert?

you are listening to. When functioning as a critical thinker, you make a commitment to think for yourself. Thus, your primary goal is no longer only to understand information, but also to evaluate the person you are listening to and his or her ideas, deciding whether that individual is credible and ethical and whether he or she is drawing a reasonable conclusion.

What Critical Thinkers Think About

What do critical thinkers think about? As a critical thinker, you determine if there is a logical connection between ideas and feelings. Rather than falling prey to strong emotional appeals, you examine the evidence on which conclusions are based and establish if they are valid or contain weaknesses and inconsistencies. Critical thinkers listen carefully in an effort to determine if what they are listening to makes sense and is worth retaining or acting upon.[41]

Work It Out

Identify the dangers of uncritical thinking by providing examples from your own life of complications that ensued because you or others failed to think critically.

The Critical versus the Uncritical Thinker

The following characteristics differentiate a critical thinker from an uncritical one.

The Critical Thinker

1. knows what he or she does not know
2. is open-minded and takes time to reflect on ideas

3. pays attention to those who agree and disagree with him or her

4. looks for good reasons to accept or reject expert opinion

5. is concerned with unstated assumptions and what is not said, in addition to what is stated outright

6. insists on getting the best evidence

7. reflects on how well conclusions fit premises and vice versa

The Uncritical Thinker

1. thinks he or she knows everything

2. is closed-minded and impulsive; jumps to unwarranted conclusions

3. pays attention only to those who agree with him or her

4. disregards evidence as to who is speaking with legitimate authority

5. is concerned only with what is stated, not with what is implied

6. ignores sources of evidence

7. disregards the connection or lack of connection between evidence and conclusions[42]

Critical thinkers do not rush to judge another's words. Instead of prejudging or evaluating the words of another prematurely, they exhibit a willingness to reexamine ideas. Thus, they withhold their evaluation until they have had sufficient opportunity to assess the information being given to them.

Questions to Facilitate Critical Thinking

You can ask yourself a number of questions to facilitate the critical-thinking process:

1. Is the speaker's message plausible? Could it have reasonably occurred? Does it have a high probability of being true?

2. Does the support provided by the person speaking back up his or her claims? Are the claims he or she makes verifiable?

3. What do I know of the speaker's credibility or authority? Is the speaker reliable; that is, is she or he someone I should trust?

4. Is the speaker's message free of inconsistencies or contradictions?

When you think critically about what other people say to you, you do much more than merely hear their words.

GENDER AND LISTENING STYLE

Women and men are likely to exhibit different listening styles. Women tend to search for relationships among message parts; they rely more on their feelings and intuition. They listen to enhance their understanding as well as to establish personal relationships. Women also demonstrate a greater ability to switch between competing messages; unlike men, who tend to focus on their reactions to only one speaker at a time, women appear able to split their focus. They are more receptive, in general, than are men to what is happening around them. Thus, women are more likely than men to be engaged in conversation with one person and still pick up on the words of another person

Work It Out

Do you think the descriptions of male and female listening styles contained in this section are valid? Provide examples that support your response.

who is conversing with someone else nearby. In contrast to men, women listen to confirm the relationship as well as the person.[43] They also use head nodding and facial expressions to indicate their interest in a conversation. Because they view talk as a relationship developer, women also provide more vocal and verbal feedback when speaking with others. Women consider it important that others perceive them as receptive and open.[44] Thus, they use more listening cues than men and excel at empathizing and at identifying moods.

Men, in comparison, are more at home with comprehensive listening and less at home with the emotional content of messages. Men are more likely to focus on a message's structure or pattern. Their tendency is to direct their listening efforts toward a goal. Men listen to solve problems.[45] As a result, they listen primarily to get the facts; they want to get to the bottom line. Men will also play up their expertise and use it to control or dominate conversations. Their goal is to have others respect them. In addition, in contrast to women, who exhibit more eye contact when listening than men do, men are more likely than women to survey the environment and direct their gaze away from the person they are conversing with.[46] While past research reported that men did not listen to provide emotional support, more recent research finds that men and women alike place a value on this listening style.[47]

Of course, gender differences continue to be redefined. In your experience, have the observations made above changed? Which do you believe are still valid?

Would You Ask for and Listen to Directions?

Research reveals sex differences when it comes to navigation ability. Women prefer directions containing landmarks to guide them in getting from one place to the next (start at Grove Street and then go until you see a bookstore), whereas men typically prefer receiving Euclidean information, instructions that tell them where to start and how far to go (start at Grove Street and go east for three blocks).[48] But which sex finds it easier to ease into the listening mode and ask for directions? Before answering, consider this:

Is it possible that men do not like to put themselves into a listening mode? Can it be that the male need for independence and control actually makes it harder for men to listen? What are the chances that women, used to seeking help from others, are better than men at listening to advice?

According to Deborah Tannen, author of *You Just Don't Understand: Women and Men in Conversation*, men desire dominance so strongly that they would prefer to drive right past a police officer than to stop and ask for directions. For men, listening to directions implies inferiority. But, according to Tannen, American women are so used to asking for help that they tend to ask strangers for directions even when they are well aware of where they are going.

What do you think? Do men and women listen differently? Should they? Explain.

SIX CHIX © 2006 Isabella Bannerman.
King Feature Syndicate.

INFLUENCE OF CULTURE ON LISTENING

As the psychological distance between people who live in different countries shrinks, our need to listen to others who neither live in the country we live in nor have the same native language increases. The globalization of business and our personal thirst for traveling to diverse geographical locations demands that we become more aware of cultural differences in listening styles and behavior.

According to C. Y. Cheng, the Chinese place greater emphasis on the receiving process and less emphasis on the sending process, reflecting the East Asian concern for interpretation and anticipation.[49] In Japan anticipatory communication is the norm. Speakers rarely tell or ask directly for something they want, leaving receivers to guess and accommodate speakers' needs. This communication style helps speakers and receivers save face in case what the speaker wants done cannot be accomplished.[50] In comparison, Germans practice action-oriented listening. They are inquisitive and exhibit a direct style. Israelis, who carefully analyze information, prefer the content style of listening. Collective in orientation, they tend to de-emphasize the personal aspects of interactions. The individually oriented Americans, on the other hand, exhibit a people-oriented style, focusing more on the feelings and concerns of the people involved in an interaction and emphasizing the interaction's social aspects. At the same time, however, they are focused on the time that interaction consumes—a time-oriented style.[51]

Dialogic listening focuses on what happens between people as they respond to each other, work toward shared understanding, and build a relationship.[52] Too frequently, life's pressures keep us from adopting open-ended, tentative approaches to conversation. We seem to prefer certainty, closure, and control. Whereas persons from Eastern cultures practice more speculative, metaphoric thinking, believing that people should listen more than they talk, members of Western cultures are less open and tentative in their listening behaviors, preferring specifically focused and concrete thinking instead.[53]

Within the United States, listening rules vary depending on the racial group to which you belong. African Americans, in general, display a more participative listening style than do European Americans. When listening to a speaker, African Americans are likely to shout out responses as a means of demonstrating their interest and involvement. By acknowledging that people from different regions and countries differ in both how they listen and respond, you are less apt to misinterpret someone's words or actions.[54]

> In what ways, if any, do you adjust your listening style to take cultural differences into account?

dialogic listening
listening that focuses on what happens to people as they respond to each other

Work It Out

Role-play a conversation in which at least one participant engages in dialogic listening.

INFLUENCE OF MEDIA AND TECHNOLOGY ON LISTENING AND THINKING

How are media and technology changing the listening landscape? What roles are they playing in challenging our abilities to listen?

Media Influences

Is television viewing shortening attention spans? If young children watch more than an hour of television each day, research reveals they are at risk for developing attention deficit problems, as compared with children who watch less TV. Blame is placed on television's quickly changing visual images, which researchers believe may overstimulate and permanently rewire a brain in the process of developing.[55]

Television and radio together account for significant amounts of what we listen to. Increasingly, segments on both television and radio programs are being shortened for fear we will not pay attention to them if they are long, discuss complicated information, or contain descriptions of complex feelings. In the place of complex information, television substitutes more and more graphics. Radio fills in with music and talk shows with guests who, too often, shout over each other, unwilling to listen to another person's point of view, and denying the show's listeners the opportunity to listen to and/or participate in a meaningful discussion.

Do people listen differently when viewing others on television, listening to them on radio, or interacting online than they do when face to face?

Technology Influences

Although they have been working on it for about two decades, scientists have yet to devise a computer that functions as a virtual best friend—one that is able to listen sensitively and empathically to a user.[56] Diametrically opposed to the efforts of these scientists are people who believe that our connections to computers, e-mail, and the Internet are impeding our ability to listen. Focusing our attention on the visual rather than the aural, critics contend, causes us to emphasize the eye over the ear. Despite this perceived failure of the scientists (we wonder if not succeeding is really a benefit) and the objections of critics, our technological listening landscape continues to evolve rapidly.

Media Wise

Listening Gains and Losses

New technologies are changing our listening landscape. Online users spend less time listening to the radio, for example, than do nononline users. They also spend less time watching television. Consider this: How much more reading do you do today than in years past? Are you now reading more and listening less than you used to? In your opinion, what are the chances that e-mail use ultimately will wipe out voice contact?

On the other hand, we can now listen to radio over the Internet or via podcasts. We can now personalize our listening stimuli. In effect, we direct our own listening experiences. Is being able to control what you listen to a good thing? Or did having your listening experience determined for you by others make it impossible for you to filter out what you didn't want to listen to and enable you to develop skills that will now deteriorate? Explain your responses.

Today, in addition to technology providing us with perpetual linkages to others, we also have an expanding listening environment, tuning in and listening globally—using radio, television, CDs, cell phones, personal message systems, podcasts, blogs, and other computer-assisted means of communicating.[57] Indeed, our appetite for traditional media as well as for the computer and the Internet is eating into time spent listening to other people in face-to-face settings. In fact, even when we are face-to-face with another person, perhaps when at lunch, on a walk, or out for a drive, one of us may be conversing with a third person on a cell phone. Interpersonal etiquette appears to be at an all-time low. The world has become our phone booth. Perhaps we need cell-free zones, so that we can listen more attentively to the person we are with.[58] Perhaps we need cell-free zones for other reasons as well. More and more state legislatures have passed bills restricting car cell-phone use to handsfree rather than handheld models. However, merely listening on a phone has been shown to distract drivers. Listening while driving decreases driver accuracy by causing drops in function in the parts of the brain associated with visual and spatial processing, leading to more accidents.[59] Thus, although multitasking has become a way of life, driving and cell-phone use probably should not be part of our multitasking repertoire. Perhaps, listening is too complex an activity for us to multitask at all, if we want to do it well.

In addition to being surrounded by cell-phone users, according to David Shenk, author of *Data Smog,* we are being inundated with information: e-mail, net-to-phone, cell phones, pagers operating virtually nonstop, enveloping us within a toxic environment of continuous overstimulation.[60] Media theorist Todd Gitlin refers to the "media torrent" directed at us—that continual flow of information with which the media supersaturate our minds.[61] It is probable that one outcome of this overload is a decrease in listening effectiveness.

Advances in technology will continue to add listening wrinkles. For example, in the past when we listened, we were generally face-to-face with the speaker; we engaged in real-time, synchronous listening. Then came the telephone, and we had the option of not having to share the same space when we exchanged a real-time conversation. Finally, we are in the era of voice mail; we can now have serial conversations (asynchronous listening) with a person who is in a different location and does not hear our words as we speak them. More and more of our conversations are occurring asynchronously.[62] Continuing advances add to the listening challenge. We can now be more selective about our willingness to listen at all. Caller ID allows us to see who is calling and thus to decide who we want to listen to, while call waiting makes it possible for us not to miss a call from someone important to us. We can now line up our listeners.

We now even have gadgets that listen and obey our commands. For example, we can ask our phones to play songs, direct us to a local bakery, or convert voice mail into e-mail. Maybe one day we will be able to yell out the name of our favorite program at the television set, and it will appear on the screen.[63] How might being able to speak our minds to our machines and have them obey alter the expectations we have when people and not machines are listening to us?

With the exception of films shown in theaters, media or computer-generated messages are usually processed by individuals viewing or listening to them alone or in small groups. Because we now process messages, CDs, and videos from around the world, our ears, habitually crossing national boundaries and opening wider and wider, are helping to erase cultural, informational, and personal barriers.

Work It Out

Describe how technology is enhancing or limiting your opportunities and abilities to listen.

Exploring Diversity

Online Listeners

Is having someone listen to you online the same as having someone listen to you in person? Even when cybercommunicators are using the same online language, because of the Internet's global reach, that language may not be their native language. As a result, the meanings given to the words used may differ drastically. As in face-to-face interaction, not all online listeners receive the same message. As you interact with persons from different cultures in cyberspace, ask yourself these questions:

1. Do they favor a direct or indirect style?
   While some cultures, including those in the United States, tend to exhibit a direct style in communicating—communicators tell it like it is—many Asian cultures use an indirect style, preferring to emphasize politeness and face-saving strategies rather than truth telling. Which style do you prefer?

2. Do they offer hard evidence or tell stories?
   In the United States, our decision making is influenced by logical reasons and credible testimony. In contrast, members of other cultures tend to be influenced by stories other sources tell convincingly. What kind of substantiation do you tend to offer? Receive?*

3. What kind of feedback do they offer?
   In the United States, we expect to receive honest feedback that reveals the feelings of those with whom we communicate. In Asian cultures, however, communicators believe it is more important to offer positive reactions than truthful ones. Not every culture perceives feedback the same way. What kind of feedback do you prefer?

4. How do opportunities for anonymity influence online listening behavior?
   Because we may remain anonymous, some of us tend to exhibit less ego involvement when listening online than when interacting face-to-face. How does the change in ego involvement affect you?

The real-time transmission of voice is possible over the Internet. Internet phones enable you to use your computer as a telephone. You can talk with another person anywhere in the world for as long as you want without the cost of a long-distance phone call. It is also possible to chat across the Internet using videoconferencing programs. Such programs make it possible for individuals to both hear and see each other.[64]

Thus, we have to ask the following questions: While we may be listening more to the sounds of new media, are we listening less to each other? How actively can we listen to another human being in our immediate environment when technological advances are absorbing our attention and propelling us across national boundaries and into settings far removed from the ones with which we are most familiar?

COMMUNICATION SKILLS IN PRACTICE
GUIDELINES FOR IMPROVING LISTENING

☑ Use Your Listening Time Wisely

Rather than assume you know what another person is going to say so that you allow yourself to tune out, fully tune in and listen attentively to understand what the other person says. By stopping yourself from taking listening sidetrips or daydreams, you free yourself to focus on and comprehend the other's message. Summarize and ask yourself questions about the substance and meaning of what you are hearing. Use thinking time to identify the other person's major points and reasons given to justify or support them.

Thinking Critically

Reflect and Respond

Agree or disagree with the father's thinking in the following excerpt from Steven R. Covey's *The 7 Habits of Highly Effective People*. Be sure to supply reasons and examples that support your stance.

> A father once told me, "I can't understand my kid. He just won't listen to me at all."
>
> "Let me restate what you just said," I replied. "You don't understand your son because he won't listen to you?"
>
> "That's right," he replied.

> "Let me try again," I said. "You don't understand your son because he won't listen to you?"
>
> "That's what I said," he impatiently replied.
>
> "I thought that to understand another person, you needed to listen to him," I suggested.
>
> "Oh!" he said. There was a long pause. "Oh!" he said again, as the light began to dawn. "Oh, yeah! But I do understand him. I know what he's going through. I went through the same thing myself. I guess what I don't understand is why he won't listen to me."[65]

☑ Give Real, Not Pseudo, Attention

You can't half-listen. Too many of us fake attention when listening. Although our external cues—we look at the other person, smile, nod our heads—say that we are listening, we are only pretending to listen. Instead of feigning attention, perhaps because of boredom or disinterest, focus on interpreting the meaning contained in the other person's words.

☑ Withhold Judgment

When we prejudge a person or his or her message, we uncritically accept or reject both the person and his or her ideas. Understanding needs to precede evaluation.

☑ Maintain Emotional Control

Sometimes we distort the ideas of others merely because we do not like or agree with them. Listening involves processing, not manufacturing information. Rather than allow an emotional eruption to cause a listening disruption, we need to work harder when our emotions cause us to feel overly aroused, defensive, alienated, elated, or outraged. Feelings of rapture and hero-worship can limit understanding as much as can anger or hostility.

☑ Be Willing to See from Behind Another Person's Eyes

A willingness to look at a situation from another's perspective increases the likelihood that you will be able to see and feel what the other person is experiencing. You do not have to agree with another individual, but it helps to understand where thoughts and feelings come from.

☑ Listen with Your Whole Body

Listening is an active, not passive process. By displaying an attentive posture and making meaningful eye contact, your body helps your mind increase its readiness to listen.

THE WRAP-UP

Revisiting Chapter Objectives

1. **Define *hearing, listening,* and *critical thinking.*** Listening is a deliberate process through which we seek to understand and retain aural (heard) stimuli. Unlike hearing, which occurs automatically, listening depends on a complex set of acquired skills, including critical thinking. When you engage in critical thinking, you think carefully about what another person is telling you, and you evaluate the believability of the message. You also seek to determine if there is a logical connection between ideas and feelings.

2. **Compare and contrast helpful and harmful listening and thinking habits.** The average person listens at only 25 percent efficiency, losing 75 percent of what is heard. A graphic illustration of the results of inefficient listening is distortion of a message in serial communication (when a message is passed from one person to another in a series). A principal reason for poor listening is failure to determine the involvement level appropriate in a particular situation. Various behaviors we adopt cause us to unlisten—that is, they impede true understanding and critical reflection.

3. **Explain and use the HURIER Model.** The HURIER model takes a behavioral approach to listening. Using it can help you to develop listening skills. The model focuses on the six key areas or stages of listening: hearing, understanding, remembering, interpreting, evaluating, and responding.

4. **Define *feedback,* distinguish among and use different types of feedback, and explain how each type affects communication.** A prerequisite of effective listening is effective feedback. Feedback consists of all the verbal and nonverbal messages that a person consciously or unconsciously sends out in response to another person's communication. Through feedback, you either confirm or correct the impressions others have of you and your attitudes. There are two main types of feedback. (1) Evaluative feedback gives an opinion, positive or negative, and attempts to influence the behavior of others. (2) Nonevaluative feedback gives emotional support. Probing, understanding (or paraphrasing), supportive feedback, and "I" messages are all forms of nonevaluative feedback that help sustain interpersonal relationships. When listening and giving feedback to people from other cultures, you must be extremely sensitive to cultural norms.

5. **Set appropriate listening goals.** You can improve your listening skills by learning to focus your attention while listening and by setting appropriate listening goals. Listening to understand ideas, to retain information, to analyze and evaluate, and to empathize require skills different from those used for listening appreciatively.

6. **Explain how gender, culture, and media and technology influence listening.** Recognizing how gender, culture, and media and technology influence listening skills may further enhance your ability to develop more effective listening practices. New technological advances, while giving you the ability to listen globally, also compete for your listening time.

7. **Use guidelines for effective listening.** By using your listening time wisely, offering real attention, being willing to withhold judgment, controlling your emotions, displaying a willingness to see from another's perspective, and listening with your whole body, you increase your listening effectiveness.

Resources for Further Inquiry and Reflection

To apply your understanding of how the principles in Chapter 7 are at work in our daily lives, consult the following resources for further inquiry and reflection. Or, if you prefer, choose any other appropriate resource. Then connect the ideas expressed in your chosen selection with the communication concepts and issues you are learning about both in and out of class.

 Listen to Me

"Wake Me Up When September Ends" (Green Day)
"Teary Eyed" (Missy Eliot)
"Bridge over Troubled Water" (Simon and Garfunkel)
"Speak My Language" (The Cure)
"Janie's Got a Gun" (Aerosmith)
"Hey Joe" (Jimi Hendrix)
"She's Leaving Home" (The Beatles)
"The Sound of Silence" (Simon and Garfunkel)

Each of these songs describes a listening problem or skill. Choose one and use it to explain the role deficient or helpful listening plays in life.

 View Me

In Her Shoes	*Away We Go*
Elizabethtown	*Analyze This*
Flightplan	*First Wives Club*
Disturbia	*Good Will Hunting*
The Negotiator	*Jerry McGuire*

Listening, effective and/or ineffective, plays a central role in each of these films. Choose one, and discuss how the ability or inability to listen complicates or facilitates the life of one or more of the film's characters.

 Read Me

Ashley Smith. *Unlikely Angel*. New York: Morrow, 2005.
Jennifer Weiner. *In Her Shoes*. New York: Pocket Books, 2002.
Edward Albee. *Who's Afraid of Virginia Woolf?* New York: Pocket Books, 1975.
Christopher Durang. *The Marriage of Bette & Boo*. New York: Grove Press, 1994.
Jeanette Walls. *The Glass Castle*. New York: Simon & Schuster, 2005.

Discuss how the work contributes to our understanding of the role of listening in relationships and in other life experiences.

 Tell Me

Share with the class the insights you gained from your chosen Listen to Me, View Me, or Read Me selection.

Who is your best listener? Explain what this person has done to earn this title.

Key Chapter Terminology

Use the Online Learning Center at www.mhhe.com/gamble10e to further your knowledge of the following terminology.

appreciative listening 159
comprehensive listening 159
critical listening 159
critical thinking 169
dialogic listening 173
empathic listening 159
evaluative feedback 164
formative feedback 165
hearing 155
HURIER model 160
"I" messages 167

listening 155
mindfulness 156
nonevaluative feedback 166
paraphrasing 160
probing 166
red-flag words 161
serial communication 157
speech-thought differential 161
supportive feedback 167
understanding 167
"you" messages 168

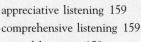

www.mhhe.com/gamble10e

THE WRAP-UP

Idioms in Translation

at home with — comfortable with

be out of touch — fail to understand

listening wrinkle — listening problem

multitasking — engaging in more than one task at a time

play up — emphasize

tuning you out — not listening to you

zero in on — focus on

Culture Cue

While nodding, smiling, and making polite noises is characteristic of how Asians listen, Americans are likely to misinterpret such cues as signifying agreement.

www.mhhe.com/gamble10e

Test Your Understanding

Go to the *Self Quizzes* on the book's Online Learning Center at www.mhhe.com/gamble10e.

LOOKING BACK AND AHEAD

Consider This Case: First Impressions

Stacey couldn't believe her luck. She'd been offered the summer internship of her dreams, working for Ángel de la Música, a new, independent record label with offices downtown. The company was small but growing, and Rick Sanchez, the founder and president, hadn't wasted any time setting up a company Web site in Spanish and English and contacting music distributors in Latin America. Rick had told Stacey that one of her assignments as a summer intern would be to help him and the marketing manager choose a list of 10 U.S. cities in which to hold promotional events over the next year, such as contests sponsored by local radio stations, music store appearances by the label's newest artists, and even a couple of free concerts. It all sounded exciting, and Stacey couldn't wait to begin.

"*Hola*, Stacey!" Rick greeted her cheerfully on her first day. "I was hoping I could introduce you to everyone, but I'm going to be gone most of the day meeting with some agents and promoters. There's a couple of new bands I want to sign, and I've got to get to them before anyone else does." He grinned at Stacey as he grabbed his jacket and headed for the door. "Listen, can you take a tour of the office, meet everybody, and then check in with me around four? I'll be back by then and we'll talk, OK?"

"Sure," said Stacey, hiding her surprise. "Perfect!"

"Great—thanks!" said Rick, and he was gone.

Stacey stood in the middle of Rick's office for a minute, thinking. Finally, she flung her coat over a chair and headed back to the reception area.

"*¿Puedo ayudarle?*" the receptionist asked.

"Hi," Stacey replied. "I don't speak Spanish very well; I'm sorry. I'm Stacey and I'm the new summer intern." She held out her hand. "How do you do?"

The young man at the desk shook hands. "I'm Luis," he said. "Rick run out on you already?"

"Oh!" said Stacey. "No, not really. That is, he had a meeting to go to, and . . ."

"Yeah," said Luis. "But you're still wondering what to do with yourself today, aren't you?"

"Well," said Stacey, "I'm not, actually. I want to meet everyone, introduce myself." She tried to smile.

"OK," said Luis, smiling back. "Maybe I can help you with that. Here's the company telephone list. This will tell you who everybody is. See how it's organized by department, with everybody's title next to their name?"

"Hey, thanks! This looks great," said Stacey in relief. She studied the list for a minute while Luis took a phone message in Spanish for Rick. "Where would I find María Lopez? She's the head of marketing."

"Down the hall to the left," said Luis as the phone rang again. Stacey waved her thanks and set off to find the marketing manager. Given her assignment for the summer, she figured María was someone it would be important to meet. She was already imagining herself giving Rick a brief but impressive account of her day when she felt herself bump hard into someone coming quickly around a corner.

"Oh! I'm so sorry!" Stacey cried. The middle-aged woman she'd walked into sighed, adjusted her glasses, and walked away without a word. As Stacey turned the corner to the left, she heard Luis greet the woman in Spanish. Stacey understood only one word, the woman's name. *María*.

Red-faced, Stacey scurried around the corner and buried herself in the phone list, looking for someone else she could meet.

By four that afternoon she was exhausted but pleased. Sitting in Rick's office waiting for him to return, she mentally reviewed her day. She'd met Lourdes, who managed the contracts department; Joe, the head designer for the label; Tina, Rick's part-time assistant; and Timotéo, who was Ángel de la Música's tech expert and Webmaster. Stacey had expected the company's tech people to be young, but Tim had pictures on his desk that he proudly pointed out were of his grandchildren. Tim had shown her the company's Web site for music downloads and asked her opinion about the pricing strategy the company was considering. Victoria, the financial officer, had found Stacey in Tim's office and offered to take her to lunch, where she teased Stacey for not knowing much Spanish and then talked endlessly about her boyfriend.

Stacey hadn't seen María again, but she had met Greg, the advertising manager, and the heads of manufacturing and the warehouse, who had both been expecting to find Rick in the office. All in all, thought Stacey, smoothing out her crumpled phone list, it had been a day well spent. Suddenly she heard voices speaking Spanish outside Rick's office.

"Sorry, María," Luis, the receptionist, was saying. "Rick's not back yet. I haven't heard from him all day."

"That son of mine!" María exclaimed. "Late again! I'll wait for him in his office."

DISCUSSION QUESTIONS

1. How do you think Stacey's self-concept changed throughout the day? Why?
2. Do you think Stacey's poor Spanish skills will be a handicap during her internship? What does she have to offer Ángel de la Música?
3. Did Stacey make any prejudgments about the staff of Ángel de la Música? How well do you think she dealt with them on her first day?
4. Are there any potential self-fulfilling prophecies at work in this case? How can Stacey avoid them?
5. How can Stacey use communication skills to ensure that her internship is a success for her and for Ángel de la Música?

LET'S GO TO THE DVD

Investigating *Crash*

The film *Crash* represents the complexity of human communication. While putting the spotlight on race and social divisions, it demonstrates the interconnectivity of humanity. After viewing the film, respond to the following questions:

1. Using a communication model featured in the text or one of your own creation, analyze a *Crash* scenario.
2. What message does the film send regarding race relations and social life?
3. What role does self-concept play in a viewer's interpretation of the film? What role do you imagine it plays in the actions of any two characters in the film?
4. Use your knowledge regarding the processes of perception and listening to analyze what happens in *Crash*.
5. Based on your understanding of verbal and nonverbal codes, give examples from the film of how words and nonverbal cues impede or foster communication.

CHAPTER 8

After finishing this chapter, you should be able to

1. Explain why we need interpersonal relationships.

2. Define and discuss the following terms: *inclusion, control,* and *affection.*

3. Explain and distinguish among social penetration, cost-benefit/social exchange theory, and relational dialectics theory.

4. Identify and describe the 10 stages of relationships.

5. Discuss how deception, gender, and technology affect interpersonal communication.

6. Identify ways to enhance your satisfaction with your relationships.

Understanding Relationships

Reality-type television offerings such as *Real World, Shot at Love with Tila Tequila,* and *The Bachelor* or *The Bachelorette* present us with men and women who, for fame, money, or the hope of finding that special someone, allow us to watch them in action as they decide whether to develop, work to sustain, or end a relationship with each potential partner. Why do shows like these attract so many viewers? Is it because we like the voyeur experience, watching and eavesdropping as people begin relationships, negotiate their ground rules, share conversations with or about each other, and then select the level at which their relationship stabilizes or terminates? Or is it that relationships are the primary content of our social lives, and we hope that by watching and vicariously experiencing the relationships of others we will learn from them, grow, and get better at developing our own relationships? However you answer these questions, for many people, nothing is more important than interpersonal relationships.

People meet and separate. But funny things happen in between.
—Mark L. Knapp

. . . when you start out with someone, you're essentially driving a strange car for the first time and none of the controls are labeled.
—Jerry Seinfeld

An **interpersonal relationship** is a meaningful, dyadic, person-to-person connection in which two interdependent people engage in communication of a personal nature, develop a shared history, and try to meet each other's social needs. By definition, a dyad is indivisible. During our life span, we share a variety of social connections, some more complicated, meaningful, and/or important to us than others. A number of our relationships succeed and will last for years, perhaps even a lifetime. Others fail or are short-lived. According to Virginia Satir, author of both *Peoplemaking* and *The New Peoplemaking,* communication is the largest single factor determining the kinds of relationships people have with each other.[1] This chapter explores the nature of our relationships, our satisfaction or dissatisfaction with them, and the steps we can take to improve them.

interpersonal relationship
a meaningful connection, such as friendship, between two persons

Online Learning Center

Go to the Online Learning Center at www.mhhe.com/gamble10e and answer the questions in the *Self Inventory* to evaluate your understanding of relationship building.

THE ROLE OF RELATIONSHIPS

How important to you are your relationships? As society places more and more emphasis on technology, some fear we will place less and less emphasis on personal relationships. Linguist John L. Locke, for example, argues that modern technology is robbing us of the inclination to speak meaningfully to one another. He believes that our social voices are disappearing, leaving us isolated. He argues that, while technologies such as e-mail increase the amount of functional information we have access to, they lack the capacity for intimate talking. From his point of view, we

Why do you believe reality-based television programs are so popular?

Skill Builder

One Relationship, Indivisible

Make two lists of relationships. The first list should contain all the interpersonal relationships in which you have participated during the past month that you consider successful and likely to endure for at least another five years. The second list should contain the interpersonal relationships you experienced during the same time period that you expect will not continue much longer. Identify the differences that led you to draw your conclusions about each relationship's future. What do these differences tell you about the qualities necessary to sustain a relationship?

autistic society

a society at home with computers but disadvantaged when it comes to establishing human intimacy

high-tech–high-touch society

a technologically advanced society that values interpersonal relationships

Work It Out

Develop an original definition of interpersonal communication.

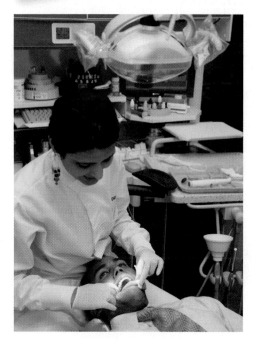

Do you consider the doctor-patient relationship personal or impersonal? Why?

live in an **autistic society,** a society that is at home with computers but disadvantaged when it comes to establishing human intimacy.[2] Locke's critics, however, note that his fears may be unfounded. They believe that, while e-mail may strip away some of the intimacy of face-to-face conversation, it also strips away some of the fear, guilt, anger, and self-consciousness.[3] Other theorists reason that, to compensate for the alienation machine-made barriers foster, we internalize a greater need to develop warm, personal relationships. As a result, a major theme of our time is the desire for closer, more personal ties. It appears that forecaster John Naisbitt was right: Our high-tech society has precipitated in us an increasingly prevalent desire for "high-touch" contacts.[4] Technology is not eliminating our need for relationships but is helping foster friendships, even love. Thus, critics contend that we do not live in an autistic society but, rather, in a **high-tech–high-touch society.**[5] In our society, traditional barriers of time and space no longer exist. Relationships begin across time zones and international borders.[6] Instant and text messages vie with phone calls as social glue.[7] In our technologically advanced world, meaningful relationships, while more difficult to maintain, become even more precious.[8] Indeed, social contacts have a positive effect on mortality.[9]

In fact, according to one study, people who never married were 58 percent more likely than married couples to die during an eight-year period.[10] People devoid of relationships are more likely to become ill and die, at least in part because social isolation compromises their immune systems.[11]

Each of our dyadic relationships fulfills different ends. For example, when we are in a doctor-patient, professor-student, or husband-wife relationship, the relationship makes different demands on us and will come to be characterized by unique communication patterns that differentiate it from others. Some of the relationships we share, such as therapist-patient or employer-employee, depend on our being able to coordinate action with another person so that we are able to complete a task or project. Others are social, helping us avoid isolation or loneliness by providing us intimacy or friendship. Some relationships are impersonal and short lived, as when we encounter a clerk in a store or chat with another person when in line for a movie. Such brief relationships have little, if any, history, and demand little personal involvement. Other relationships are more personal and less ephemeral, as are the relationships we have with some family members and friends, or they could be romantic, as are relationships with significant others. Some relationships we keep purely professional, much like the ones we probably have with our doctors. We invest most in our longer-term relationships—the ones we share with friends, family, and significant others.

Functions of Relationships: Three Basic Needs

A vast body of research spurred by the work of William Schutz demonstrates that we attempt to meet our needs for inclusion, control, and affection through friendships, work, and romantic relationships.[12]

Inclusion has to do with the varying degrees to which we all need to establish and maintain a feeling of mutual interest with other people—a sense that we can take an interest in others and that others can take an interest in us. We want others to pay attention to us, to take the time to understand us. Wanting to be included is normal. We all remember how it feels to be left out—to be the last person asked to join a team, to not be invited to an important party, or to be ignored during a mealtime conversation. When our need for inclusion is met, we tend to feel worthwhile and fulfilled. If it goes unmet, we tend to feel lonely, and our health may even suffer.

Loneliness is an all too common affliction of our age.[13] Research reveals, for example, that men aged 50 and older who have no close friends or relatives are three times as likely to die after suffering high levels of emotional stress than are persons whose lives are less lonely.[14] What exactly is **loneliness?** Loneliness begins with a recognition that the interpersonal relationships we have are not the kinds we would like to have.[15] Thus, loneliness results from a perceived discrepancy between desired and achieved social relationships.[16]

Control deals with our need to establish and maintain satisfactory levels of influence and power in our relationships. To varying degrees, we need to feel that we can take charge of a situation, whereas at other times we need to feel comfortable assuming a more submissive role. When our control need goes unmet, we may conclude that others do not respect or value our abilities and that we are viewed as incapable of making a sound decision or of directing others' or our own future.

Finally, **affection** involves our need to give and receive love and to experience emotionally close relationships. If our need for affection goes unfulfilled, we are likely to conclude that we are unlovable and that therefore people will remain emotionally detached from us (that is, they will try to avoid establishing close ties with us). In contrast, if our experiences with affection have been more pleasant, we are probably comfortable handling both close and distant relationships, and most likely we recognize that not everyone we come into contact with will necessarily care for us in the same way.

These three basic needs differ from each other in a significant way. Inclusion comes first; that is, it is our need for inclusion that impels us to establish a relationship in the first place. By comparison, our needs for control and affection are met through the relationships we have already established. Thus, as psychologist William Schutz notes, "Generally speaking, inclusion is concerned with the problem of in or out, control is concerned with top or bottom, and affection with close or far."[17]

Which one of your relationships do you currently consider the most important? Why do you value this relationship more than others?

inclusion
the need for social contact

loneliness
the perceived discrepancy between desired and achieved social relationships

control
the need to feel we are capable and responsible and are able to exert power and influence in our relationships

affection
the need to experience emotionally close relationships

Feelings of inclusion or loneliness can affect our health and the way we view ourselves.

We need to get close to each other to have a sense of community, to feel we're not alone in the world. But we need to keep our distance from each other to preserve our independence, so others don't impose on or engulf us.
—Deborah Tannen, That's Not What I Meant

How do you navigate this duality in your own life? That is, how do you balance your need for individuality with your need for social contact?

phatic communication

communication designed to open the channels of communication

Work It Out

Provide examples of conversations that changed the nature of any of your relationships.

Building Relationships Using Verbal and Nonverbal Conversations

In a news article on flirting, the author observes: "Woman spots man. Man spots woman. Woman smiles. Man looks away. Woman looks away. Man looks back." Will they speak to each other?"[18] According to Robert E. Nofsinger, author of *Everyday Conversation*, "Almost everything we do that concerns other people involves us in conversation."[19] We talk to relate; we converse our way through our lives. Talking is fundamental to every relationship—whether it is beginning, ending, or continuing.[20]

Typically, the more time we spend speaking with our relationship partners about our day, the healthier is the relationship we share.[21] Nofsinger also reminds us, "Our family life is created and enacted each day through conversation. And, in large part, we find employment (or fail to) through our everyday talk."

Most conversations follow a five-step pattern (though they may not divide neatly into five steps): (1) open, (2) provide feedforward, (3) elaborate on your goal, (4) reflect back on what you have said, and (5) close. The opening typically involves a verbal greeting—for example, "hi there"—and/or a nonverbal greeting—perhaps a knuckle bump. You might introduce yourself, ask a question, or make an interesting statement. (If conversing online, you might open with a greeting line containing an emoticon.) During the feedforward section, you might widen the conversational opening by engaging in **phatic communication,** offering surface clichés designed to keep the channels of communication open. For example, you might say, "What's up! How are you doing?" or perhaps discuss the weather—and then provide a preview of the conversation's purpose—"You need to know about this." In the next step, goal elaboration, you explain your goal or purpose, making statements of fact such as "I really support PETA," or statements of feeling such as "I think Juana really is into Joe and I'm jealous." During the fourth step, you reflect back on what you have discussed and seek common ground, for example, by saying, "Isn't that ridiculous?" or "So, what do you think should be our next step?" In the last phase of a conversation, you close and say your good-byes—called *leave-taking*, again using verbal and/or nonverbal cues.

The expectation in conversation is that both parties take turns speaking and listening. By taking turns or refusing to take turns—that is, either through or because of the absence of *reciprocal turn taking*—we influence both the direction of our conversations and our relationships. By offering *turn-yielding cues*, we let the other person know that we have finished commenting and are now prepared to listen. On the other hand, if we ignore *turn-requesting cues*—messages that signal the other party's desire to speak, opting to continue our domination of the conversation, this may not bode well for the relationship's future.

The better we are at keeping a conversation going, perhaps using self-disclosure techniques to draw others into conversation with us, the greater is the likelihood that such conversations help us develop friendships.[22] As a result, although some of the ineffective conversations we have are likely to lead to relationships that go nowhere, others will be particularly effective because we work at making them that way.

Following are two special conversational environments we want to explore: the grapevine and the gossip mill.

The Grapevine

When people perceive a threat or feel insecure at work, and no formal communications from management are forthcoming to guide them or ease their minds, they may use the **grapevine** (a type of informal, conversational network existing in organizations) to communicate key messages that relate to personal or professional matters of importance. Whenever you pass a message to someone in the organizational network, it is wise to assume that what you pass along will be repeated to others. Although research reveals the grapevine to be uncannily speedy and accurate, the messages carried over it are not necessarily delivered unscathed, but often emerge distorted or incomplete.[23] By tapping into the grapevine, however, you may discover clues regarding what is happening in organizational or social circles that could affect you. People report that the grapevine is especially active during times of crisis or change. Do your experiences confirm this?

Where does most of the gossiping you do occur?

The Gossip Mill

The **gossip mill** is the network through which unverified information is spread. When we converse with one person about another person who is not present, though we may believe we are only making small talk, we are actually spreading gossip. Why do humans spend so much time gossiping? Perhaps gossip is so prevalent in society because we have become addicted to it. Social researchers estimate that gossip consumes two-thirds of all conversation, functioning as a form of social glue—getting us into inner circles and providing us with even more valued information to pass on. Sharing gossip also signals our trust that the individual we are talking to will not use the information to harm us.[24]

What do men and women who gossip talk about? Men tend to gossip about the people they work with, work-related issues, or politics and sports. Women tend to gossip about their social relationships and neighbors. A percentage of what both men and women gossip about involves more than perception checking or the harmless announcement of an event such as a marriage or a birth. In the spirit of *Desperate Housewives*, their gossip also contains conjectures about what friends, politicians, movie stars, famed athletes, or family members are up to. The gossiper frequently hypothesizes about the behavior of an absent party, spreads malicious rumors or false information about the person, and muses about topics such as whether the person is cheating on a significant other or is about to be fired. Thus, though gossip may endow people who gossip with transient feelings of importance, it is also likely that gossiping contributes to others' perceiving those who gossip more negatively.[25] As a result, gossiping can be a risky business.

grapevine
a type of informal, conversational network existing in organizations

gossip mill
the network through which unverified information is spread

DIMENSIONS OF RELATIONSHIPS: BREADTH AND DEPTH

We can describe every relationship—whether with a friend, a family member, a lover, or a co-worker—in terms of two concepts: breadth and depth. **Breadth** has to do with how many topics you discuss with the other person. **Depth** has to do

breadth
the number of topics you discuss with another person

depth
a measure of how central the topics you discuss with another person are to your self-concept

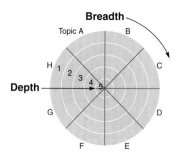

Sample Topics (breadth of topics)

A. Leisure
B. Career goals
C. Relationship with friends
D. Family relations
E. Health
F. Romance
G. Secrets
H. Self-concept

FIGURE 8.1   Breadth and Depth in Relationships.

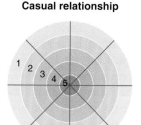

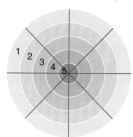

Layers (depth)

1. Most superficial layer
   (food, clothing, likes, dislikes)
2. Impersonal layer
   (job, education information)
3. Middle layer
   (political leanings, social views)
4. More personal layer
   (goals, values, beliefs, fears, secrets, dreams)
5. Most personal layer—the inner core—
   self-concept

FIGURE 8.2   Casual and Intimate Relationships.

Use arrows to show the contrast in depth and breadth between one of your casual relationships and one of your more intimate relationships.

Work It Out

Bring in the juiciest example of gossip you are able to find about a well-known personality. Discuss why you believe the public has an interest in such information. What do you and people you know gossip about? What kinds of messages have you sent or received via the gossip mill? Does gossip function as a form of social glue, cementing relationships, or does it function as a type of interpersonal toxin, ruining relationships instead? To what extent, if any, do the attitudes and examples that men and women offer differ?

with how central the topics are to your self-concept and how much you reveal.

The relationship theory of social psychologists Irwin Altman and Dalmas Taylor can be schematized as shown in Figure 8.1.[26] Central to their **social penetration theory** is the idea that relationships begin with relatively narrow breadth (few topics are spoken about) and shallow depth (the inner circles are not penetrated) and progress over time in intensity and intimacy as both breadth and depth increase. Thus, our relationships develop incrementally as we move from discussing few to many topics, and from superficial topics (the periphery of the circle) to intensely personal topics (the center of the circle). Figure 8.2 is an exercise using these concepts.

The social penetration model is useful for a number of reasons. First, it helps us visualize the nature of our relationships by indicating the range of topics we communicate about and the extent to which we reveal ourselves through our discussions. Second, the model helps explain why certain relationships seem stronger than others.

social penetration theory
the theory that states that our relationships begin with relatively narrow breadth and shallow depth and develop over time

Self-Disclosure

Together, the nature and the amount of information we share with another person affect the strength and the quality of our interpersonal relationship. When we deliberately reveal information about ourselves to another person, information that we consider significant and that would otherwise not be known to the person were it not for our purposeful intervention, we take steps to increase both the breadth of information people have about us and the depth of understanding they have for what makes us tick. **Self-disclosure** is the voluntary, purposeful revealing of confidential personal information about us that others would not otherwise have access to. The amount of disclosing we do with another person usually is a gauge of how close we feel to the person or how close we desire to become. On the other hand, when a relationship begins to wane, usually there are decreases in the breadth as well as the depth of our disclosures. We refrain from talking about some topics, and we discuss the topics we do talk about in less depth. Such changes signal that we are becoming less personal or intimate and have begun the depenetration, or pulling-away, process. Thus, self-disclosure reflects the health of a relationship. When disclosure between relationship partners is reciprocal and honest, partners feel more secure in the relationship. They become comfortable sharing their humanness.

Privacy and Relationships

Although social penetration theory reveals the breadth and depth of the information we are willing to share in our various relationships, it is **communication privacy management theory** that describes the establishment of the boundaries

self-disclosure
the process of revealing to another person information about the self that he or she would not otherwise know

communication privacy management theory
theory that describes the establishment of the boundaries and borders that we decide others may or may not cross

How do you feel when someone reveals more to you than you are ready for? Have you ever made anyone feel uncomfortable by revealing too much too quickly? What prompted you to do it? How did the other person react?

© The New Yorker Collection 1994 Robert Weber from cartoonbank.com. All Rights Reserved.

"Let's go someplace where I can talk."

and borders that we decide others may or may not cross. For each of our relationships, we compute a "mental calculus" to guide us in deciding whether to share information with another person or keep it private, avoiding disclosure by engaging in the deliberate withholding of information.[27] At times, you may want to conceal what your partner wants you to reveal. Such a disagreement can precipitate *boundary turbulence,* the tension created when the parties to a relationship are unable to agree on the boundaries of self-disclosure. What might cause you to strengthen a boundary or shorten a border? Should we discover a partner gossiping, spying, or otherwise violating our confidence, the likelihood that we will keep personal information private increases and so does the likelihood that the curtain will drop on that relationship.

DEVELOPMENT AND ANALYSIS OF RELATIONSHIPS

Relationships can be analyzed with reference to their stages, costs and benefits, or dialectical perspectives. As you read about each stage, consider how it applies to a close relationship of yours. (See Figure 8.3.)

> Which of these relationship stages do you find the most and least challenging?

Stages of Relationships: From Beginning to Ending to Beginning . . .

All relationships we share are complex (each of us is a unique bundle of experiences, thoughts, fears, and needs) and ever-changing (as we change, our relationships change—they grow stronger or weaker over time). Relationships pass through a number of stages as they strengthen, stabilize, or dissolve.[28] We will explore them now.

Stage 1: Initiating

initiating
the relationship stage during which contact is first made

Initiating involves the things that happen when we first make contact and look for signals that either lead us to begin a conversation or tell us that we have nothing to gain by conversing. If we decide to converse, we search for an appropriate conversation opener—for example, "Nice to meet you" or "What's happening?"

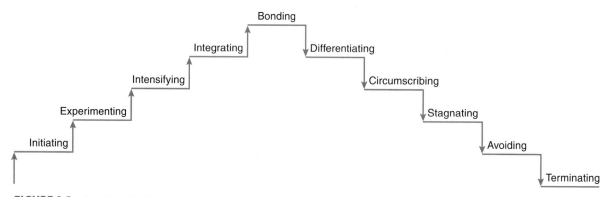

FIGURE 8.3   Relationship Stages.

What happens when we can't find an appropriate opener? The following passage from *Conversationally Speaking* by Alan Garner describes one such possibility:

> I decided to marry her. Courtship would be a mere formality. But what to say to begin the courtship? "Would you like some of my gum?" sounded too low-class. "Hello," was too trite a greeting for my future bride. "I love you! I am hot with passion!" was too forward. "I want to make you the mother of my children," seemed a bit premature.
>
> Nothing. That's right, I said nothing. And after a while, the bus reached her stop, she got off, and I never saw her again.
>
> End of story.[29]

Relationships typically begin with small talk. What do you say to initiate communication with someone you'd like to get to know?

Stage 2: Experimenting

Once we initiate contact, we try to find out more about the other person; we begin to probe the unknown. This is the stage of **experimenting.** In an effort to get acquainted, we exchange small talk, such as telling the other where we're from and whom we know. Although many of us may hate small talk, or cocktail party chatter, according to Mark Knapp it serves several useful functions:

experimenting
the relationship stage during which we begin to probe the unknown, often through the exchange of small talk

1. It provides a process for uncovering integrating topics and openings for more penetrating conversations.
2. It can serve as an audition for a future friendship or a way to increase the scope of a current friendship.
3. It provides a safe procedure for indicating who we are and how the other person can come to know us better (reduction of uncertainty).
4. It allows us to maintain a sense of community with our fellow human beings.[30]

In an article on small talk, Michael Korda notes: "The aim of small talk is to make people comfortable—to put them at their ease—not to teach, preach, or impress. It's a game, like tennis, in which the object is to keep the ball in the air for as long as possible."[31]

Flirting often occurs during this stage. When conversing, you may exhibit contact readiness cues, leaning forward toward the person you are talking to, raising your eyebrow, tilting your head to the side if you are a woman, or keeping your body position open if you are a man.

At this stage, relationships lack depth; they are quite casual and superficial. The vast majority of them never progress beyond this point.

Have you had some relationships that did not pass beyond the experimentation phase but that you now wish had gone further? What kept them from progressing?

Stage 3: Intensifying

When a relationship progresses beyond experimenting, it enters the third stage, **intensifying.** During this stage, people become good friends—they begin to share things, disclose more, become better at predicting each other's behavior, and may even adopt nicknames for each other or exhibit similar postural or clothing cues. In a sense, they are beginning to be transformed from an "I" and an "I" into a "we."

intensifying
the relationship stage during which two people become good friends

Stage 4: Integrating

The fusion of "I" and "I" really takes place in stage 4, **integrating.** We now identify two individuals as a team, a pair, a couple, or "a package." Interpersonal synchrony is heightened; the two people may dress, act, and speak more and more alike or share a song ("our song"), a savings account, or a project.

integrating
the relationship stage in which two people are identified as a couple

A wedding signifies the formal bonding of a couple.

Stage 5: Bonding

In stage 5, **bonding,** two people announce that they are formalizing their commitment to each other. They institutionalize their relationship with a formal contract—a wedding license or a business contract, for example. The relationship takes on a new character. It is now guided by specified rules and regulations. Sometimes this alteration initially causes discomfort or rebellion as the two people attempt to adjust to the change.

Stage 6: Differentiating

In stage 6, **differentiating,** instead of continuing to emphasize "we," the two people involved attempt to reestablish an "I" orientation, to regain a unique identity. They ask, "How are we different?" "How can I distinguish me from you?" During this phase, previously designated joint possessions take on a more individualized character; "our friends" become "my friends," "our bedroom" becomes "my bedroom," "our child" becomes "your son" (especially when he misbehaves). Although an urge to differentiate the self from the other is not uncommon (we need to be individuals as well as members of a relationship), if it persists, it can signal that the relationship is in trouble or that the process of uncoupling has begun.

Stage 7: Circumscribing

In stage 7, **circumscribing,** both the quality and the quantity of communication between relationship partners decreases. Sometimes a careful effort is made to limit areas open for discussion to those considered safe. Other times there is no actual decrease in breadth of topics, but the topics are no longer discussed with any depth. In other words, fewer and less intimate disclosures are made, signaling that one or both partners desires to withdraw mentally or physically from the relationship.[32] Dynamic communication has all but ceased. A lack of energy, shrinking interest, and a general feeling of exhaustion characterize the relationship.

Stage 8: Stagnating

When circumscribing continues, the relationship stagnates. In stage 8, **stagnating,** the two parties feel that they no longer need to relate to each other because they know how the interaction will proceed; they conclude that it is better to say nothing. Communication is at a standstill. Only the shadow of a relationship remains: The two mark time by going through the motions while feeling nothing. In reality, they are like strangers inhabiting the hollow shell of what once was a thriving relationship. They still live in the same environment, but they share little else.

Stage 9: Avoiding

During the stage of **avoiding,** the participants actually go out of their way to be apart; they avoid contact with each other. Relating face-to-face or voice-to-voice has simply become so unpleasant that one or both can no longer continue the act.

bonding
the relationship stage in which two people make a formal commitment to each other

differentiating
the relationship stage in which two people identified as a couple seek to regain unique identities

circumscribing
the relationship stage in which both the quality and the quantity of communication between two people decrease

stagnating
the relationship stage during which communication is at a standstill

avoiding
the relationship stage during which the participants intentionally avoid contact

How did your last relationship end?

Although communicated more directly at some times than at others (sometimes the "symptom" is used as a form of communication; at other times an effort is made to disconfirm the other person), the dominant message is "I don't want to see you anymore; I don't want to continue this relationship." At this point, the end of the relationship is in sight.

Stage 10: Termination

At stage 10, **termination,** the bonds that used to hold the relationship together are severed; the relationship ends. Depending on how the participants feel (whether or not they agree on termination), this stage can be short or drawn out over time and can end cordially (in person, over the telephone, with an e-mail or legal document) or bitterly. All relationships eventually terminate (by the death of one participant if not before), but this does not mean that saying good-bye is easy or pleasant.[33]

"Would you mind waiting in the hall for a bit while I clean up the remnants of my last relationship?"

termination

the relationship stage during which the relationship ends

Do you find breaking up hard to do? Some breakups are harder than others. According to communication researcher Steve Duck, when undergoing a relationship breakup, we typically pass through four stages: (1) *the self-talk stage,* in which we place our focus on relationship negatives, consider withdrawing totally from the relationship, and explore the potential positives of entering into an alternative relationship; (2) *the interpersonal communication stage,* in which we and our partner decide to confront, negotiate, and discuss possibilities for relationship repair and reconciliation, assess the ramifications of withdrawing from the relationship, and

Work It Out

Using the 10 stages discussed here, chart and describe an imaginary relationship between two people—Joan and Jane Doe.

ultimately decide to separate; (3) *the group and social communication stage*, during which we explore how to relate after breaking up (we may gossip about the other, telling stories and placing blame as a means of saving face); and (4) *the grave dressing and public stage*, during which we each offer a relationship postmortem—providing our respective publics with our own version of the breakup.[34] Today, many couples who break up use the Web to tell their version of the relationship split, offering a continuing stream of postings, some very angry, some sad. While usually mortifying or anger producing for the attacked partner, the postings are therapeutic for the blogger.[35]

Steve Duck and Julia Wood recently revisited Duck's approach to relationship dissolution, now conceptualizing the breakup as an event composed of five distinct processes: (1) *intrapsychic processes*, in which partners brood about problems and their dissatisfaction with the relationship; (2) *dyadic processes*, in which the rules and established patterns governing the relationship break down ("You don't send me flowers any more"); (3) *social support processes*, in which the parties air their relationship's dirty laundry for others outside the relationship, expecting those they know to choose sides; (4) *grave-dressing processes*, during which they figure out what explanation for the breakup they will give to friends, children, co-workers, and others; and (5) *resurrection processes*, during which they enter and move forward in a future, minus their former partner.[36]

Summary

Work It Out

Identify relationships in your own life that have stabilized at one or more of Knapp's "coming together" stages: initiating, experimenting, intensifying, integrating, bonding.

A relationship may stabilize at any one of the stages. Many relationships never proceed beyond the experimenting stage; others stabilize at the intensifying stage, the bonding stage, and so on. When the participants disagree about the point of stabilization, difficulties can arise. Movement through the stages may be forward or backward. For instance, we may advance and then retreat, deciding that a more superficial relationship is what we really desire. Additionally, we proceed through the stages at our own pace. Some relationships, especially those in which time is perceived to be limited, develop more quickly than others; the rate at which the participants grow together or apart, however, usually depends on their individual needs. What is important to remember is that many relationships do not arrive at a stage and simply stay there. Rather, they can be recursive. Relationships may even terminate and then begin anew.

A Special Case: Relationship Termination Caused by Death

grief process

a mourning process composed of five stages: denial, anger, guilt, depression, and acceptance

What happens when death takes a loved one or a relationship partner away? When this occurs, many of us experience feelings of loneliness and social isolation. Actually, the **grief process** (see Figure 8.4) entails a number of stages: The first stage is denial—we deny what has happened. Denial diminishes as we acknowledge the impact of our loss and the feelings that accompany it. The second stage is anger—feeling helpless and powerless, we strike out and rail against the loss. The third stage is guilt—we turn our anger against ourselves. We feel bad about things we have said or done to hurt the person who has died. We find ourselves left with a sense of unfinished business. In the fourth stage, depression, we feel that nothing will be right again. Looking forward feels impossible.

We feel lonely, empty, and isolated. The fifth stage is acceptance—while things will not be the same, we believe that we will make it through and be able to go on with life.[37] The question is, How do we get to stage 5?

The tendency in those who are closest to someone who has suffered a loss is to try to protect the person and shield him or her from sadness. Instead of trying to suppress and walk around sadness, however, we should work to help mourners experience it. For example, even though the death of a family member might make a family turn inward, for the person(s) grieving, expressing feelings to friends who are not directly affected by the loss can help.

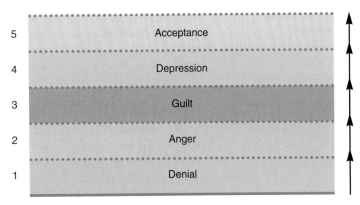

FIGURE 8.4 The Grief Process.

Before arriving at acceptance, a grieving person experiences a series of emotions.

Even very young children grieve, although their grief may be different from the grief experienced by adolescents and adults. With help and support, however, people of all ages can handle rather than submerge grief and, as a result, recover from grief's effects and go on with their lives. Part of the process involves constructing an image of the deceased loved one that the bereaved can take with them into their continuing lives.[38] It is the processing of feelings that appears to be key.

Research reveals that we do not simply replace a former partner but, rather, remain loyal to the deceased partner in almost all new relationships that we form, whether the relationship takes the form of a consummate partner, less intimate steady companion, or service provider. Still, reengagement in consummate partnerships and steady companionship is effective in reducing loneliness and helping us fulfill our relational needs.[39]

Cost-Benefit/Social Exchange Theory and Relationship Development

Though relationships may proceed through stages, they are not always predictable. No relationship is foreordained in heaven or hell for success or failure. Rather, our relationships develop as a consequence of the energy we commit to them and as a result of what we do with and for one another.

Unless the people who share a relationship continue to grow together and adapt to their continually changing environment, the relationship may begin to deteriorate at any point. According to **cost-benefit/social exchange theory,** we work to maintain a relationship only as long as the benefits we perceive for ourselves outweigh the costs.[40] These benefits include feelings of self-worth, a sense of personal growth, a greater sense of security, additional resources for accomplishing tasks, and an increased ability to cope with problems. In comparison, costs include the time spent trying to make the relationship work, psychological and physical stress, and a damaged self-image. We enter our relationships with a **comparison level** in mind; we have a general idea, standard, or expectation of the kinds of rewards and profits that we believe we ought to get out of the relationship. When the rewards we receive equal or surpass our comparison level, we

Personalization has hit the casket industry. You can now purchase a casket adorned with scenes of the last supper, your favorite flag, or your favorite musical group. Some critics see these "art caskets" as an expression of self-absorption and narcissism, while others see it as a meaningful way to have the last word in self-expression. What do you think?

cost-benefit/social exchange theory

the theory that we work to maintain a relationship as long as the benefits we receive outweigh the costs

comparison level

an expectation of the kinds of rewards and profits we believe we ought to derive from a relationship

comparison level for alternatives

the comparing of rewards derived from a current relationship with ones we expect to get from an alternative relationship

usually feel satisfied with the relationship. However, we also have a **comparison level for alternatives;** we compare the rewards we get from a current relationship with the ones we think we are able to get from an alternative relationship. If we believe that present relationship rewards are below those we could receive from an alternative relationship, then we might decide to exit our present relationship and enter a new one.

In general, however, when we think of a relationship in economic terms, the greater our rewards or profits and the lower our costs, the more satisfying a relationship will be. Each relationship partner acts out of a self-oriented goal of profit taking.[41] When costs begin to outweigh benefits, we are more and more likely to decide to terminate the relationship. In contrast, when benefits outweigh costs, the relationship will probably continue to develop. Cost-benefit/social exchange theory predicts that the worth of a relationship influences its outcome. Positive relationships will probably endure, whereas negative relationships will probably terminate.

Relational Dialectics Theory

dialectical tensions

tensions that occur when opposing goals meet

According to relational dialectics theorists, relationships are not linear but, rather, consist of the oscillation between contradictory goals or desires. During relationship development, communicators seek to meet important goals, some of which may be incompatible. When opposing goals meet, they create **dialectical tensions.** Three central relational dialectical tensions exist between connection and autonomy, predictability and novelty, and openness and privacy.[42] Let us explore each in turn.

Connection versus Autonomy

We desire to be independent of our significant others and to find intimacy with them. We want to be close as well as separate. Perhaps you have found yourself saying the following about a partner. "He barely spent any time with me." "I have no time for myself." "She made me feel trapped." "He just wouldn't commit to being an 'us.'" "I need my freedom." If any of these statements sound familiar, then you and a partner had conflicting desires for connection and independence. Since we want to establish more intimate connections with others we care about, we cherish the sharing of experiences. At the same time, however, we need to preserve an independent identity. We do not want our relationships to destroy our individuality. Some relationships do not survive the connection-autonomy negotiations; instead of working out an acceptable balance that preserves individuality while creating intimacy, partners break up. On the other hand, as a result of resolving their connection-autonomy disagreements, relationship partners can redefine their relationship and become even closer.[43]

Predictability versus Novelty

We desire the excitement of change and the comfort of stability. We want both a routine and spontaneity. Too much routine becomes boring. Perhaps these words sound familiar: "We always do the same things." "I want to do something different." "I know everything there is to know about her." Variety adds spice to normal routines. The challenge for relationship partners is to find the right mix between the desire for predictability and the need to keep the relationship fresh and interesting.

Openness versus Privacy

We wrestle with tensions between dislosure and silence or concealment. For many of us, complete openness is intolerable to contemplate. While we want to share our inner selves with people we care deeply about, there are times when we do not feel like sharing and desire the preservation of privacy instead. Desiring privacy some of the time does not mean a relationship is on the rocks. Our desires for openness and closedness wax and wane. We go through periods of disclosing and periods of withholding.[44] During every stage of our relationship, our desires for openness and privacy can fluctuate.

Work It Out
Using the relational dialectics described here, describe an imaginary relationship between a couple—John and Jane Doe.

Resolving Dialectical Tensions

When a relationship is successful, partners are able to manage the dialectical tensions by using a number of different strategies. First, they can negotiate a balance between connection and autonomy, predictability and novelty, and openness and closedness. Second, they can choose to favor one dialectic and ignore the other. Third, they can segment each of the dialectics by compartmentalizing different areas of their relationship and assigning each dialectic to different times or spheres. Fourth, they can reframe the dialectics by defining them as not contradictory at all.[45] One ineffective way of handing dialectical tensions is to deny that they exist. Instead of confronting the challenges that face the relationship, the partners ignore them.

> While most of us would condemn lying, during the course of a typical week, nearly every one of us lies. How do you explain this?

DECEPTION AND RELATIONSHIPS

Are we living in the age of deception?[46] Over the past few years, photos have been digitally altered to influence or mislead readers or viewers; major corporations, such as Enron, Global Crossing, and Arthur Andersen, have been charged with deceiving stockholders and the public; news reporters have staged stories; and the entertainment industry has based the outcomes of a number of new programs on the ability of participants to lie.

But it's not just in the public sector that lies are told. We also, all too commonly, lie in our daily conversations—with people admitting to having lied to their parents, teachers, spouse, friends, family members, and themselves. *Telling the truth* and *lying and deception* are each ways of relating, and we appear to use one or the other in the effort to obtain a result we desire.[47] In your opinion, is it harmful, unethical, or immoral to consciously lie, deceiving others or yourself? Would you ever *want* someone to lie to you? What would you *never* be willing to lie about to another person or yourself?

> Consider your feelings about lying. How do you define the word *lie*? To whom would you lie? What kinds of situations call for a lie? How many times in the past month have you lied to someone with whom you share a relationship? How many times were you caught? What happened as a result?

Lying and Relationship Development

A lie is the deliberate presentation of information you know not to be true. You can lie by omission or commission. When you lie by omission, you deliberately withhold relevant information, thereby causing people to draw an erroneous conclusion. When you lie by commission, you make a statement you know to be false.

Why do people lie? According to some researchers, we lie to continue to satisfy the basic needs fulfilled by our relationships, to increase or decrease desired

Why are you lying to me who are my friend?
—Moroccan proverb

equivocate

use purposefully vague language to finesse a response

In Tennessee Williams's play *A Streetcar Named Desire,* one of the characters—Blanche DuBois—says, "I don't tell the truth. I tell what ought to be truth." Does this practice help or hinder the development of relationships? Why?

How is a liar like a counterfeiter?

Focus on Service Learning

Speak at a local meeting of parents and teachers about the importance of honesty in relationships. You can limit your topic by focusing on the role of honesty in online interaction, parent-child interaction, teacher-child interaction, parent-teacher interaction, or friendship. For help in completing this assignment, in addition to consulting research articles and books, you may want to visit Web sites such as www.coping.org.

Trust gives us the ability to rise above our doubts.

—*John K. Rempel,*
John G. Holmes

tolerance of vulnerability

the degree of trust you place in another person to accept information you disclose without hurting you or the relationship

and undesired affiliations, to protect our self-esteem, and to achieve personal satisfaction.[48] Most often, when we lie, we benefit ourselves, although a percentage of our lies are designed to protect the person or persons we are lying to, and an even smaller percentage benefit a third party.

In fact, sometimes we **equivocate** (use purposefully vague language to finesse a response) in an effort to avoid having to tell the unvarnished and unpleasant truth. Being deliberately vague helps us spare another's feelings and/or relieves us of having to confront our anger. For example, if asked how we like a gift given to us, we might reply, "It's really special," when what we really think is that it is tasteless. Or if asked how we like someone's hairstyle, we might say, "It's really you," when we believe it detracts from the person's appearance. Equivocating takes the teller off the hot seat. It also helps the receiver save face. While people believe equivocating is better than lying, when asked, they still say that they prefer to be told the truth.[49] Do you believe them?

Studies of deception reveal that the act usually strains the liar psychologically and physically. Just the act of information suppression causes thoughts to flood the consciousness, which contributes to liars looking and sounding tenser than usual.[50]

How does a lie affect our relationships once it is uncovered? Imagine sharing a relationship, no matter how ideal in other aspects, in which you could never rely on the words or gestures of the other person. Information exchanged in that relationship would be virtually worthless, and the feelings expressed would be practically meaningless. As Sissela Bok, the author of *Lying,* observed, people who discover they have been lied to "are resentful, disappointed and suspicious. They feel wronged; they are wary of new overtures." Further, Bok notes, people "look back on their past beliefs and actions in the new light of the discovered lies."[51] While bending the truth to sustain a relationship may be a common practice, unless trust and truthfulness are present, it is only a matter of time before the relationship will die. Lying is likely to precipitate a relationship crisis. Many relationship breakups are attributed directly to the discovery of a major deception.

Trust and Relationship Development

There is potential for trouble in any relationship. As we saw in the previous section, one cause of trouble is lying. Another, equally important, cause is the undermining of trust. Trust is an outgrowth of interpersonal communication. It is a reflection of how secure we are that a person will act in a predicted and desirable way. When we trust another person, we have confidence that he or she will behave as we expect and that the person will not use whatever personal information we have confided to him or her to harm us. Some of us are more trusting than others. How trusting are you? Whether or not you trust another person depends on whether prior relationships have reinforced trusting behavior or consolidated your fears about the risks of exhibiting trusting behavior. Trust creates a paradox: To be able to trust, we must be willing to take the risk of trusting. When we take the risk, we risk being wrong. If we fail to take the risk, however, we can never be right.[52] The degree of trust you place in another person to accept information you disclose to him or her without hurting you or the relationship is your **tolerance of vulnerability.** Your tolerance of vulnerability varies from person to person, topic to topic, and situation to situation.

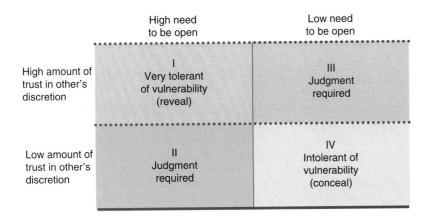

FIGURE 8.5

Rawlins's Trust Matrix.

Who would you place in each category? Why?

Source: Matrix created by William K. Rawlins from "Openness as Problematic in Ongoing Friendships: Two Conversational Dilemmas," by W. K. Rawlins, *Communication Monographs* 50 (March 1983), p.11. Reproduced by permission of Taylor & Francis Group, LLC, www.taylorandfrancis.com.

Researcher William Rawlins designed a matrix, shown in Figure 8.5, that we can use to analyze the amount of trust we place in different people at different times in a relationship's development. We can also use this matrix to determine which of our relationships have more stability or staying power than others. A relationship in which the partners have difficulty trusting one another is a troubled relationship.

Troubled relationships often involve the sending of **hurtful messages** (messages designed to upset or to cause emotional pain that further hampers trust). If the hurtful messages are intense, making it difficult for their target to ignore or forget them, they poison the relationship, making it impossible to sustain closeness in or derive satisfaction from it.

hurtful messages

messages designed to upset or to cause emotional pain that further hampers trust

How do you respond when you are the target of a hurtful message? According to researchers Vangelisti and Crumley, the more emotional pain hurtful messages cause, the greater is the likelihood that we will respond by acquiescing. The less they hurt us, the more probable it becomes that we will seek to communicate our invulnerability instead. The healthier and more satisfying a relationship, the more likely it becomes that we will respond actively when we are the target of hurtful messages.[53]

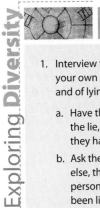

Exploring Diversity

Does the Truth Lie?

1. Interview three people from cultures different from your own regarding their experiences of being lied to and of lying to someone else.

   a. Have them identify who lied to them, the nature of the lie, and their reactions upon discovering that they had been lied to.

   b. Ask them the nature of the lie they told to someone else, their reason for telling the lie, and the other person's reaction upon discovering he or she had been lied to.

   c. Whether they were the ones lying or being lied to, ask them the specific effect the lie had on their relationship with the other person.

2. People belonging to Asian cultures are likely to value social harmony more than telling the truth. In these cultures a person is expected to tell another person what that person wants or needs to hear. Compare and contrast that orientation with the desire that members of Western European cultures have to determine the truth. Could the differences in orientation be reflective of one culture's emphasis on collectivism and the other culture's preference for individualism? Which orientation do you believe helps preserve relationships? Which do you believe is more sociable?

3. Could telling someone the truth ever undermine trust the way lying does? Explain your answer.

Does The Truth Hurt?

1. A television program, *The Moment of Truth,* left behind a trail of damaged relationships. In exchange for the opportunity to win a lot of money, contestants agreed to answer a series of personal questions truthfully in front of family members, friends, and their significant other. Contestants could call it quits at any time—keeping whatever money they had earned up until that point—if they chose not to answer a question for fear it would harm a relationship. However, if a lie-detector test indicated the contestant was lying when answering a question, he or she was eliminated—winning nothing. In their efforts to collect the money, contestants have admitted to cheating on a spouse, wishing they had married someone else, not wanting to have children with their current mate, and keeping a spreadsheet of sexual conquests, just to name a few.

   What do you see as the upside and downside of a show like this? What happens when the truth really hurts?

2. On shows such as *What Not to Wear, Trading Spouses,* and *Clean House,* people "put it all out there," parading their flaws before millions of viewers just to have the opportunity to have personal and family problems solved for free. In effect, they literally and figuratively air their dirty laundry for all to see.

   Are we a nation of exhibitionists, unafraid to speak about things or behave in ways that at one time would have caused us to be ashamed? Do we like to watch others who behave or live in ways we consider shameful so that we can tell ourselves that we would not do or say what they do? To what extent do you believe that shows like these desensitize us to the problems they expose, even normalizing some of the coarser behaviors featured?[54]

LAUGHTER AS AN INTERPERSONAL TOOL

Like trust, laughter is an interpersonal tool. Every day we give and receive social laughter while interacting with friends, co-workers, and lovers. Laughter punctuates our conversations so regularly that we are apt not to think about or notice it. However, if laughter disappeared from any of our important relationships, we would miss it.

In the section "A Special Case: Relationship Termination Caused by Death," we discussed the grief that accompanies the death of someone we love. Even in grief, however, humor can play a part. Humor can help us cope with anything. Once you are able to laugh again, you know that you are regaining control. Laughter helps reduce our stress by releasing our excess energy. Like other interpersonal competencies, it also helps us develop fresh perspectives on events large and small by freeing us of anxious feelings or frustrations.

According to Dr. Robert R. Provine, laughs are rhythmic bursts of social glue.[55] He reports that much of what we laugh at in life is predominantly the stuff of social banter, not necessarily particularly funny or clever. Laughter, however, is contagious. When we hear laughter, we usually start

Laughter is a relationship tool. What role does it play in the relationship you share?

laughing ourselves. Its infectious nature can have dramatic effects on our relationships. We, not just our relationship partners, laugh at what we say; in fact, the average speaker laughs 46 percent more frequently than do those listening to him or her. While laughter does not intrude on speech, it does provide its punctuation. It helps us synchronize our moods and perhaps our actions. As such, it may also help solidify our relationships.

Like any relationship tool, laughter has a downside too. The opposite of joyful laughter is jeering, malicious laughter, laughter that is designed to punish, belittle, or exclude rather than include another. In this case, laughter, rather than expressing our sociability, signals our disdain for and power over another person.

> Research shows that a male speaker with a female listener laughs less often than does the woman. However, when a woman speaks to a man, she laughs much more than her male partner.[56] Why do you think that is so?

GENDER, CULTURE, AND RELATIONSHIPS

Both gender and culture influence how we form and maintain relationships.

Gender and Relationships

How do young men and women view the relationships they are likely to share in the future when it comes to intimacy? When polled regarding their reasons for desiring intimacy in relationships, 20 of the top 25 reasons given by men and women were the same, with attraction, showing affection, and expressing love included among them.[57] Whereas in some studies men and women agreed that romance depended on the men being allowed to be in charge, more recent studies revealed that, for both women and men, having a feminist partner was perceived to be a benefit. In fact, feminist women were the most likely to be in romantic relationships characterized as healthier in terms of perceived relationship quality, equality, stability, and intimacy.[58]

Males and females may differ in their behavior during the preliminary stages of a romantic relationship—for instance, when flirting. According to one educator, flirting is "a verbal power struggle between men and women."[59] For men "it is a form of foreplay," while for women it is more often "a way of making a connection."[60]

Because of the way they are socialized, men and women may share their feelings differently.

Work It Out

Identify the expectations that men and women have for same-sex friendships. Give examples of the extent to which the expectations of men and women are similar and different.

Women also are more perceptive than men in describing their relationships; women are less apt than men to project their own feelings onto their partner.[61] Women tend to self-disclose more than men, but when men do self-disclose, they reveal more negative information than women typically reveal.

Things change in cyberspace, where women tend to be more honest when it comes to the disclosure of personal information.[62] Although men post more videos, women, more than men, tend to post provocative pictures of themselves on social networking sites, much like celebrities do. For members of generation X and Y, privacy does not appear to be the priority it once was.[63] In addition, women are dominating content creation in blogs or MySpace, perhaps because, as one gender researcher speculates, they have been trained to be social, communal, and make stories about themselves whereas men have been taught not to engage in confessional or emotional communication.[64]

In addition, women focus on the maintenance of relationships more than men do. Women are eager to acquire personal information about their relational partners. They desire a partner who demonstrates care and concern and who is empathetic. As a result, they use more maintenance strategies than do men.[65]

In your opinion, is the male or the female partner more likely to end a heterosexual relationship? How would you feel if you had no right to terminate a relationship that made you unhappy?

This is not to imply that men and women do not share any commonalities in their views regarding relationships, because they do. Both men and women value same-sex friends and desire friends they can trust, who accept them and help them. In fact, people who have fulfilling same-sex friendships report high levels of personal well-being. So do people who share effective relationships with siblings.[66]

Researchers do affirm that women place a higher value on emotionally close relationships than do men, whose friendships frequently seem to lack emotional depth.[67] Because of the ways men are socialized, they often feel uncomfortable expressing their feelings directly with words, preferring instead to express them through shared activities such as sports.[68] Thus, women use personal and disclosive talk to develop and sustain their relationships to a greater extent than do men. While women bond through talk, men bond through doing things together.[69]

Culture and Relationships

Attitudes toward self and others influence the effectiveness of the relationships persons from different cultures share. Acceptance, for instance, is one necessary factor for relationship satisfaction. Sometimes what happens in society can have a big impact on what happens in our relationships. For example, when Barack Obama won the presidency of the United States, African Americans reported feeling a newfound pride in themselves, acknowledging that they also felt like they had earned society's approval. They believed that with Obama's election it had become more feasible for them "to live the American dream." They were not alone. By claiming the top prize in politics, Barack Obama had swept away a racial barrier, astonishing, inspiring, and giving new hope to people who previously had viewed their non-White racial identities as defining and limiting their future. While the election of Barack Obama may not have erased or even healed all racial divisions or tensions, it did bridge skin-color, age, gender, and class divides, giving new hope, not only for global relationships, but also for interpersonal, multigenerational, and multicultural relationships as well.

What do persons from different cultures want in their relationships? Researchers report that, to be satisfied in their relationships with Whites, both African

Americans and Mexican Americans need to feel that Whites respect, confirm, and accept them.[70] What preferences do persons from different cultures reveal during their interactions? Asians, for example, practice the positive exchange of ideas, demonstrating care for the other person during the exchange. They value harmony as a means of relationship nurturance. Conformity and group well-being are especially important to them. Generally, they do not reach out to strangers, and they make great efforts to conceal unfavorable information about members of the group to which they belong from those whom they perceive to be outsiders.[71] Latinos, in contrast, tend to focus on relational support.[72]

While some cultures emphasize social relationships and instruct individuals to give preference to the interests of others over their own private interests, other cultures, including American culture, stress individualism. While Americans find it natural to begin and end relationships, Asian cultures believe that relationships should be long-lasting, characterized by loyalty and the fulfillment of obligations.

Not all cultures treat all relationships similarly. Some cultures, for example, have different rules for heterosexual relationships and same-sex relationships, while others have men and women performing different roles in relationships, While Western culture values heterosexual marriage, in the United States some states have given legal status to domestic partnerships enabling gays and lesbians and unmarried heterosexuals to have the same rights as married heterosexuals. Many Scandinavian countries have done the same. In some countries, however, same-sex couples face ostracism or severe consequences—including being arrested or put to death. When it comes to the roles men and women perform in relationships, in the United States, both men and women can begin and end their romantic relationships. In other cultures, parents select relationship partners for their children. Sometimes their goal is to bring two families together; other times, it is to reap a financial reward. In the United States, we typically believe that any person has the right and ability to dissolve a relationship that makes him or her unhappy.

TECHNOLOGY AND OUR RELATIONSHIPS

Technology and the Internet enable men and women alike to initiate, sustain, and end relationships in new ways. In fact, while many still frequent the bar scene or read personal ads, large numbers of people start and build personal relationships online, with many having online romances.[73] The popularity of love connection sites such as Match.com, E-Harmony, and J-Date, just to name a few, shows that online services are redefining how increasingly busy people choose to approach romantic relationships.[74]

Work It Out

Identify how communicating with a friend online compares and contrasts with communicating face-to-face.

Differences between face-to-face and online communications may influence relationship development, regardless of whether the relationship is a romance or a friendship. First, until we meet face-to-face, unless we post photos or use a Webcam, the person in cyberspace remains invisible to us. Second, since we cannot see most of the nonverbal behavior that accompanies the person's words, we may misinterpret the intended meaning of a message. Third, because we control the pace of online interaction, some of the spontaneity as well as the immediate feedback that characterize face-to-face communication and make it interesting are missing. Fourth, because we do not have access to as much information (verbal and nonverbal) as face-to-face interaction provides, it may be harder for us to decide whether to trust the person we are relating to online. Fifth, simply

distance relating

relating with persons via e-mail, chat rooms, and instant messages

because of the inelasticity of time, online interaction may substantially reduce face-to-face interpersonal interaction. As the online world becomes an active social scene, users may scale back or cut off traditional interactions. Sixth, fakers may click their way into online relationships. For example, teenagers may present themselves as adults, and some adults who want to have relationships with children or teens may present themselves as members of these groups. Because persons met online may be concealing their true identities, it is wise to proceed cautiously, being careful not to reveal personal information that could compromise personal security. Thus, although online relationships may form quickly, they also are likely to involve greater deception, if one or more of the parties to the relationship manipulates or deliberately conceals their true self or nature. What is more, rather than fostering accurate perceptions of one another, the parties are more likely to perceive each other based on their wants or needs.[75]

Despite such drawbacks, both researchers and users see benefits in **distance relating** and developing relationships online. Researcher Sherry Turkle, author of *Life on the Screen: Identity in the Age of the Internet*, finds that when people form new online relationships, they express different aspects of themselves and come to see themselves as the sum of their distributed presence on the windows they open on their screens.[76] And a user notes: "It's easier to talk to girls on the Internet than in school. Sometimes I can't talk well in person. It doesn't come out like I want it."[77] Also, since anonymity is a characteristic of significant online interactions, gender, race, and appearance are easier for users to disregard. At least until they share photos or meet face-to-face, online users are more likely to place looks on the back burner. Instead, whether or not an online relationship continues depends more on the ability of users to build rapport.

Social networking online also may help the homebound overcome conditions that make them feel isolated and lonely. While the homebound may not be able to meet in person with others because of their situation, they are now able to initiate and sustain surrogate online contacts. One recent user reported the following: "There was a guy we met in Second Life who was really great: affable, funny, smart and fun—we really connected. Months later, we were shocked to find out he was completely disabled by cerebral palsy, to the point he could only work one finger on one hand and couldn't talk. In that moment, the power of virtual worlds to enhance people's lives really crashed down on us."[78]

Blogging is also having an impact on relationship development. While many believe that blogging strengthens connections between friends, romantic partners, and family members (users post photos, stories, and links they like on their personal sites), some ask whether using blogs to disclose or expose innermost secrets is a benefit. One blogger's site, PostSecret.com, contains a plethora of secrets for millions of others to read. For some users, the site offers opportunities for self-clarification and the opportunity for catharsis—to get something off their chest. For others it offers one more voyeurism opportunity and the chance to identify with the poster of the secret.[79] Thus, conscious decisions about how to manage privacy are also being played out online, especially on social networking sites such as MySpace or Facebook. Although privacy gives us the right to keep our personal feelings secret, many people decide to post "secrets" for all to read.

Users rely on text messaging to augment their online interactions. When it comes to maintaining a connection with someone whom we consider either a romantic partner or a friend, text messaging has supplanted e-mail as our preferred means of "talking."[80] Large numbers of people send text messages to flirt, arrange dates, break up, or even ask for a divorce. Its use is so prevalent that critics are asking if excessive reliance on the medium encourages mindlessness. Some Web sites even offer users ready-to-use text messages in the spirit of greeting cards, enabling them to bridge the relationship spectrum, perhaps asking for a date or breaking up without even speaking to the other person.[81] What do you think? Is it possible to establish a meaningful connection with someone by sending an original or ready-to-use text message, or is texting merely a means of avoiding real contact or intimacy?

"You can access me by saying simply 'Agnes.' It is not necessary to add 'dot com.'"

COMMUNICATION SKILLS IN PRACTICE
GUIDLINES FOR IMPROVING YOUR RELATIONSHIP SATISFACTION

Our relationships contribute to feelings of happiness or unhappiness, elation or depression. While they can enrich and stimulate us, they can also limit and harm us. To enhance your ability to develop relationships that satisfy, follow these guidelines.

☑ Actively Seek Information from Others and Reinforce Others Attempting to Seek Information from You

People who fail to initiate contacts or fail to reinforce the conversational attempts of others are less likely to build stable foundations for effective relationships. Passive, restrained communicators are simply more likely to remain

Thinking Critically

Reflect and Respond

Using yourself or someone you know as an example, agree or disagree with the following statement by interpersonal communication theorist Steve Duck. Supply reasons and examples that support your stance.

Unfortunately, the evidence is that some people are not good at this basic human activity [conducting close personal relationships]. . . . Relationships do not conduct themselves in the ways that common sense often supposes.[82]

chronically lonely. Although we all experience short-term loneliness from time to time, sustained chronic loneliness leads to social apathy, which in turn increases loneliness.

☑ Recognize the Characteristics of Friendship

friendships

relationships characterized by enjoyment, acceptance, trust, respect, mutual assistance, confidences, understanding, and spontaneity

People who share effective **friendships** report that the following qualities are present: enjoyment (they enjoy each other's company most of the time), acceptance (they accept each other as they are), trust (both assume that one will act in the other's best interest), respect (each assumes that the other will exercise good judgment in making life choices), mutual assistance (they are willing to assist and support each other), confidences (they share experiences and feelings with each other), understanding (they have a sense of what the other thinks is important and why the other behaves as he or she does), and spontaneity (they feel free to be themselves).[83]

☑ Recognize That Relationships Evolve

Ours is a mobile and increasingly technological society in which each change we experience has the potential to bring us different relationships. Be prepared for changes in relationships; recognize that in your life you are likely to experience a certain amount of turnover and change. As you grow and develop, so will your relationships.

☑ Know When to Sever a Relationship

While one party to a relationship may desire to sustain it, not all relationships or connections are meant to continue. When a relationship is draining your energies and confidence, or when it becomes unhealthy, you need to extricate yourself from it before it destroys you.

☑ Recognize That Communication Is the Lifeblood of a Relationship

Without communication, relationships shrivel and die. Any relationship that is worth your time and energy depends on effective communication to sustain and nourish it. Your desire and motivation to communicate are key ingredients in the establishment and growth of a relationship.[84]

Revisiting Chapter Objectives

1. **Explain why we need interpersonal relationships.** Communication is one variable common to all relationships. As a result of communication, we establish and nurture or withdraw from and end our relationships. Relationships play many roles in our lives. They fulfill our needs for inclusion, control, and affection.

2. **Define and discuss the following terms: *inclusion, control,* and *affection.*** We need to feel that others take an interest in us, that they view us as capable of exerting control over our lives, and that we are lovable. It is through conversation that we establish, maintain, and end our relationships.

3. **Explain and distinguish among social penetration theory, cost-benefit/social exchange theory, and relational dialectics theory.** Every relationship we share is unique and varies in breadth (how many topics we discuss with the other person) and depth (how much we are willing to reveal to the other person about our feelings). Most relationships develop according to a social penetration model, beginning with narrow breadth and shallow depth; over time, some relationships increase in breadth and depth, becoming wider, more intimate, or both. Cost-benefit/social exchange theory holds that we work to maintain those relationships that yield the greatest personal profits and fewest costs. Relational dialectics explores the oscillation that occurs between conflicting relationship goals.

4. **Identify and describe the 10 stages of relationships.** Researchers have identified a number of stages our relationships may pass through: initiating, experimenting, intensifying, integrating, bonding, differentiating, circumscribing, stagnating, avoiding, and termination. Note that a relationship may stabilize at any stage. When the participants disagree about the point of stabilization, problems are likely to arise.

5. **Discuss how deception, gender, and technology affect interpersonal communication.** Relationships are also affected by gender and cultural preferences, lies or deception, vulnerability and trust, and even technological innovations.

6. **Identify ways to enhance your satisfaction with your relationships.** It is important to recognize that how we communicate plays a key part in determining whether our relationships are as effective and rewarding for us as they could be.

Resources for Further Inquiry and Reflection

To apply your understanding of how the principles in Chapter 8 are at work in our daily lives, consult the following resources for further inquiry and reflection. Or, if you prefer, choose any other appropriate resource. Then connect the ideas expressed in your chosen selection with the communication concepts and issues you are learning about both in and out of class.

THE WRAP-UP

Listen to Me

"You'll Think of Me" (Keith Urban)
"Crash into Me" (The Dave Matthews Band)
"Don't Know Why" (Norah Jones)
"She's Leaving Home" (The Beatles)
"Irreplaceable" (Beyoncé)
"You've Got a Friend" (James Taylor)
"Fifty Ways to Leave Your Lover" (Paul Simon)

These songs explore close relationships. Choose one and discuss the speaker's beliefs about his or her role in the relationship.

Read Me

Candace Bushnell. *Lipstick Jungle*. New York: Hyperion, 2005.
Lauren Weisberger. *Chasing Harry Winston*. New York: Broadway Books, 2008.
Edward Albee. *Who's Afraid of Virginia Woolf?* New York: Dramatist Play Service, 1962.
Robert Harling. *Steel Magnolias*. New York: Dramatist Play Service, 1998.
William Shakespeare. *The Taming of the Shrew*. Edited by Robert Heilman. New York: Penguin Books, 1998.
Tennessee Williams. *A Streetcar Named Desire*. New York: New American Library, 1947.
Kate Jacobs. *The Friday Night Knitting Club*. New York: Berkley, 2008.

These works explore the nature of friendships and/or intimate relationships. Choose one and use it to describe how the nature of the communication shared by people contributes to the health or toxicity of their relationship.

View Me

Elizabethtown   *The Bucket List*
The Proposal   *Sweet November*
Prime   *Secrets and Lies*
The Boiler Room   *When Harry Met Sally*
Wall Street   *My Sister's Keeper*

These films explore the stages of relationships and why we maintain or end a relationship, as well as the role honesty and deception play in relationship building or termination. Choose one film and use it to discuss the factors just identified.

Tell Me

Share with the class the insights you gained from your chosen Listen to Me, View Me, or Read Me selection.

In a brief presentation, respond to the following questions: What do you consider the most acceptable rationale for lying? Do you think it is more acceptable to lie if the lie will benefit you or if the lie will save others from hurt?

Key Chapter Terminology

www.mhhe.com/gamble10e

Use the Online Learning Center at www.mhhe.com/gamble10e to further your knowledge of the following terminology.

affection 185
autistic society 184
avoiding 192
bonding 192
breadth 187
circumscribing 192
communication privacy management theory 189
comparison level 195

comparison level for alternatives 196
control 185
cost-benefit/social exchange theory 195
depth 187
dialectical tensions 196
differentiating 192
distance relating 204
equivocate 198

Idioms in Translation

adds spice — adds interest

bond — connection

breadth of topics — number of topics

break up or sever the bonds of a relationship — end a relationship

connect with — communicate with

depth of topics — how much you reveal

dissolve a relationship — end a relationship

small talk — superficial conversation

what makes us tick — what makes us who we are

Culture Cue

Members of Asian and Arab cultures may continue to hold hands when their handshake ends. In Saudi Arabia, for example, handholding between two men is a sign of respect. In the United States, Americans typically release hands after a handshake. Compared to Latino, U.S., and European couples, Asian couples are less likely to have their arms around each other when walking in public.

Test Your Understanding

Go to the *Self Quizzes* on the book's Online Learning Center at www.mhhe.com/gamble10e.

www.mhhe.com/gamble10e

THE WRAP-UP

After finishing this chapter, you should be able to

1. Identify and distinguish among the following relationship life contexts: acquaintanceship, friendship, and romantic, family, and work relationships.

2. Define *emotional intelligence*.

3. Explain how attraction, proximity, reinforcement, similarity, and complementarity affect the development of relationships.

4. Discuss the sharing of feelings, including how the suppression or disclosure of feelings affects relationships.

5. Define *assertiveness, nonassertiveness,* and *aggressiveness,* and explain how feelings can be handled effectively during conflicts.

6. Build skills to effectively handle feelings in relationships.

Person to Person: Relationships in Context

For years, many of us have watched reality-type shows such as *The Hills,* in which a camera follows the characters' every move as they enter into and disengage from relationships. Some of the characters are in real friendships. Some date, end up as lovers, or marry. Others find themselves embroiled in conflict and then perceive one-time friends as enemies. We observe as Heidi, Spencer, and their cohorts share rather raw, emotionally intense interactions. We imagine what it would be like to be them. Can you see yourself sharing your life and personal relationships with millions of viewers? The people in *The Hills* did just that, displaying their lives and personal relationships, conflicts and emotions, for us to judge.

There are no empty people, only people who have deadened their feelings and feel empty.
—Theodore Isaac Rubin

Over time, some participants demonstrate that they can handle their emotions, while others act more like very young children, revealing an inability to control their emotions and a general lack of emotional intelligence. **Emotional intelligence,** a relatively recent concept, includes the ability to motivate oneself, to control impulses, to recognize and regulate one's moods, to empathize, and to hope.[1] Our success in our relationships depends to a great degree on how emotionally intelligent or mature we are. If, for example, we can understand and manage our emotions, such as anger and jealousy, and be sensitive to others' feelings as well, then we can also improve our ability to get along with a broad array of people in diverse contexts.

emotional intelligence
the ability to motivate oneself, to control impulses, to recognize and regulate one's moods, to empathize, and to hope

Thus, while this chapter explores relationships in context, it is also about emotions and feelings—your emotions and feelings and the emotions and feelings of people with whom you share relationships.

In successful relationships we communicate clearly and effectively about our feelings.[2] Relationships involve a huge amount of emotional work.

RELATIONSHIP CONTEXTS: FROM FRIENDSHIP TO ROMANCE TO FAMILY TO WORK

Relationships are colored by the life contexts in which they occur. By exploring the different kinds of relationships we share, we can learn how to strike a balance between intimacy and distance with the people we interact with regularly, whether that interaction occurs with friends, lovers, family members, or persons with whom we work. We will see how we have been socialized to express or limit our expression of emotions about relationships, depending on the relational context we find ourselves in.

Which reality programs do you watch, if any? Would you ever agree to work on your relationships on television or the Internet for strangers to observe?

Think of the most emotionally intelligent person you know. What behaviors distinguish this person from the least emotionally intelligent person you know?

Work It Out

Complete these two tasks: (1) identify the specific steps you would take to reduce uncertainty about someone you do not know well, and (2) explain the basis for then deciding whether a relationship with this person would or would not be rewarding.

Relationships, Uncertainty Reduction, and Predicted Outcomes

No matter how close we eventually become with another person, we start out as strangers. What is your goal when you meet someone for the first time? According to uncertainty reduction theory, when we initially meet someone, uncertainty characterizes our relationship.[3] Because we prefer the known to the unknown, our communication goal is to reduce the uncertainty we have about that person.[4] To create understanding, we need to gain knowledge. We desire to find out what the other person is like, and we want to figure out how to act. Do you agree? If so, how do you accomplish your objectives?

We rely on three key strategies to reduce uncertainty and increase predictability during an interpersonal relationship: (1) passive strategies, during which we unobtrusively observe the other person while he or she is engaged in doing something, preferably interacting with others; (2) interactive strategies, during which we communicate directly with the other person, asking probing questions that encourage the person to talk about himself or herself; and (3) active strategies, during which we get information about this person from a third party, manipulate a situation that enables us to observe another person, or set up a situation in which we can have someone else observe us as we talk with the other person. The more we interact with and converse with another person, the more our uncertainty decreases. The more we discover that we and the other person share things, the more our uncertainty wanes. The more we and the other person share a communication network—that is, interact with the same people—the more uncertainty is reduced. Since interpersonal ignorance is uncomfortable, the urge to reduce uncertainty motivates communication. If we are able to reduce uncertainty to the point that we become comfortable in the situation, our interaction will increase and the relationship may continue. Just as reducing uncertainty acts as a bridge to relational development, so it can also be used to bridge some culture gaps.[5]

Another factor that affects relationship development is the predicted outcome value of the potential relationship. Researchers believe that we formulate a personal hypothesis regarding whether or not a given relationship will be rewarding. Because we typically have limited information at the outset of a relationship, our initial judgment may be based on a person's physical appearance, the behaviors we observe, or the information we obtain from others.[6] As we reduce our uncertainty, our ability to make accurate predictions about a relationship's future increases. How accurate have you been at predicting the success of relationships at a first meeting?

Acquaintanceships

acquaintanceships

relationships with persons we know by name and with whom we converse when the chance arises

We have **acquaintanceships** with people we know by name, with whom we converse when the chance arises, but with whom our interaction is usually limited in scope and quality. Unless we want to turn an acquaintance into a friend, we rarely go out of our way to see that person, preferring instead to leave our meeting each other to chance.

Friendships

What is a Friend? I will tell you. It is a person with whom you dare to be yourself.

—Frank Crane

A number of our acquaintanceships develop into friendships. Friends accept each other, confide in each other, trust each other to keep confidential any disclosed

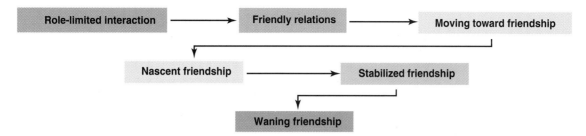

FIGURE 9.1   Rawlins's Six-Stage Model of Friendship.

role-limited interaction
the beginning stage of friendship

friendly relations
the friendship stage in which we explore whether we have enough in common to continue building a relationship

moving toward friendship
the friendship stage in which we make small personal disclosures demonstrating the desire to expand our relationship

confidences, provide each other with emotional support, share interests, and expect their relationship to last.[7]

Of course, we might grow closer to some friends than others. It is to our very closest friends that we usually confide our most private thoughts and feelings.

What competencies do we rely on to keep our friends? First, we become proactive in making time to spend with our friends. We initiate opportunities to be together whether in person or online. Second, we focus on and are responsive to our friends, refraining from selfishly placing the focus on ourselves. Third, we are willing to self-disclose. As friends, we share our feelings with one another. Fourth, we offer each other emotional support, especially when either of us feels emotionally or psychologically vulnerable. The expectation is that friends help each other. For example, researchers have found that friendships affect a person's ability and willingness to quit smoking.[8] And fifth, we manage any conflicts in ways that meet each person's needs.[9]

As friendships develop and become closer, we begin to increase our knowledge of and trust in each other, and both the breadth and depth of our relationship are enhanced. Bill Rawlins's six-stage model explains how friendships develop.[10] (See Figure 9.1.)

According to Rawlins, friendship begins with **role-limited interaction,** during which two individuals make initial contact in some context. At this point, we are unclear whether our relationship will develop, and we act tentatively in relating to each other. The next interaction stage, **friendly relations,** finds us exploring whether we have enough in common to continue building a relationship. During the **moving toward friendship** stage, we step beyond conventional social rules and role playing and make small personal disclosures as a means of indicating that we'd like to expand our friendship. We invite the other person to interact with us in a context outside those that happen serendipitously.

Friends often build relationships while dining together.

As the other person echoes our moves toward friendship, we enter the **nascent friendship** stage and begin to consider each other friends. We substitute our own rules in place of the social stereotypes and standards that regulated our interactions to this point. We plan the activities we will share together. Our interactions become more regular. We enter the **stabilized friendship** stage once we decide that our friendship is secure and will continue. We trust each other and respond to each other in ways that display our trustworthiness. When friends begin to drift apart, they enter the **waning friendship** stage. Sometimes this happens when friends take their friendship for granted. Other times, one or both make less of a personal effort to keep the friendship going. Perhaps career, personal, or family obligations get in the way. Perhaps a trust is violated or one person develops new interests that the other person does not share. Since friendships do not maintain themselves, when one or more of the preceding situations occur, the friendship may dissolve.

Romantic Relationships

Romantic love is different from the kind of love we feel for our friends or family members. Although statistics reveal that over half of all marriages in the United States ultimately fail, when we enter into marriage or a civil union, we expect it to last. In fact, it is the expectation of permanence that helps distinguish a romantic relationship from other kinds of relationships.

Three additional characteristics unique to romantic relationships are commitment (the intention to remain in the relationship even if trouble occurs), passion (intensely positive feelings of attraction that make you want to be with the other person), and intimacy (sustained feelings of closeness and connection). Although any one of these can exist without the others, all three are essential to a romantic relationship.[11] So is a context of trust. Trust frees partners to share their feelings and innermost thoughts.

Romantic relationships, like friendships, develop in stages that reflect each party's perception of

During the nascent friendship stage, friends may run together. What kinds of activities do you get together with your friends for?

nascent friendship

the friendship stage that finds us considering each other friends

stabilized friendship

the friendship stage in which we decide that our friendship is secure and will continue

waning friendship

the friendship stage during which friends begin to drift apart

Romantic relationships have an expectation of permanence.

the amount of self-disclosing that is occurring and the kind of intimacy shared.

Not all romantic relationships are healthy. Some turn dark and become destructive. When a romantic relationship becomes dysfunctional, it is characterized by **toxic communication,** which includes the consistent use of verbal abuse and/or physical or sexual aggression or violence. Although spousal abuse is all too common, the highest incidence of violence occurs among unmarried cohabiting couples.[12] Relationship well-being is higher if a relationship we share develops in the way we think it should.[13]

Like romantic relationships, dysfunctional relationships move through a series of stages. During the first stage, relational tensions build in the abuser, who blames a partner for problems and seeks an excuse to vent anger. In the second stage, the tensions erupt into violence. In the third stage, the abuser apologizes and promises to make it up to the victim, assuring the victim that it will never happen again. In the fourth stage, there is a lull in violent activity, during which the victim again feels loved. Ultimately, however, relational tensions again build, and the cycle of abuse continues.[14] (See Figure 9.2.)

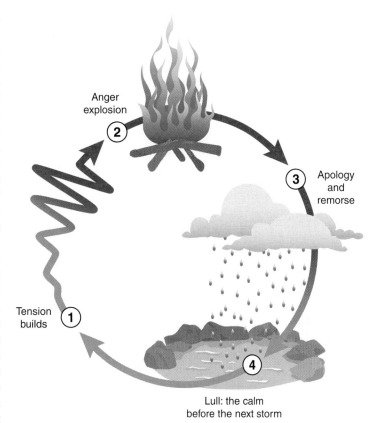

FIGURE 9.2   The Abuse Cycle.

toxic communication
the consistent use of verbal abuse and/or physical or sexual aggression or violence

Family Relationships

Most of our earliest relationships occurred within our family. Family members mutually influence each other as they work out the nature of their relationships. They are also expected to play certain roles in relation to each other and to the family as a whole. Among the roles family members perform are wage earner, homemaker, financial manager, and child care provider. These roles may be shared or may be the prime responsibility of a single family member. In healthy families, role relationships evolve as family members grow, develop, and enter different life stages.

Family members also have expectations for each other. They expect to receive emotional support from one another. They expect members to pull together to preserve the family unit. The rules that guide family interaction help regulate the behavior of family members. They reveal how family members divide tasks—who is in charge of what and the like. To thrive in a family, you need either to follow or to successfully renegotiate the rules that prescribe member behavior.

When a family practices healthy communication, members offer emotional and physical support to each other, reveal their feelings and thoughts to each other, meet each other's needs, and display flexibility and a willingness to adapt

TV, the Internet, and the Family

First, consider this. In what ways, if at all, are television and the Internet influencing the following: (1) how we organize the space in our home, (2) meal scheduling, (3) the nature of our conversations, and (4) our conception of social reality including family life? Do you find that media and technology are creating new, shared spaces, or are they fostering feelings of loneliness and separateness?

Next, consider this question: How do media images of family influence the image you have of your own family and the kind of family you would like to be able to create, were you free to do so? Select a television family and contrast it with your own. Describe the members of each family, their roles and relationships to each other, the factors that appear to hold the family together, the subjects family members discuss, the conflicts they handle, and the ways they resolve them. To what extent, if any, does your analysis of the television family contribute to your evaluating your own family as more or less positive? Explain.

to change. On the other hand, when a family's communication practices become dysfunctional—that is, when they prohibit members from adequately expressing their feelings or needs or contain messages that are physically, sexually, or emotionally abusive—then family relationships suffer and deteriorate.[15]

The composition of families in the United States continues to evolve. The once-dominant nuclear family comprising a wife, a husband, and biological children is no longer the norm.[16] The United States is now a composite of an array of family types, including (1) *the single-parent family* (now over 12 million strong), in which an adult lives with one or more children; (2) *couples,* in which two adults live together with no children; (3) *the stepfamily,* in which two adults live with children who are not the biological offspring of both parents; (4) *the unmarried-with-children family;* (5) *the adopted family,* in which one or both adults adopt one or more children; (6) *the gay or lesbian family,* in which two adults of the same gender live together with or without adopted or biological children; and (7) *the extended family,* in which related intergenerational adults live together.

Unlike the young people of generations past, young people today are marrying later. Approximately three-quarters of men and some two-thirds of women in their 20s have not married yet. The decline in married couple households is reflected in an increasing number of cohabiting couples. For the first time, unmarried adults represent more than half of American households.[17]

Work Relationships

Friendships affect the well-being of both individuals and organizations. Even at work, we develop friendship networks that benefit us both in and out of the office.[18] In fact, the office has replaced college as the top marital hunting ground. Only 14 percent of people who are married or in a relationship say they met their partners in school; 18 percent say they met at work. When we work in an organization, we share interdependent relationships with the other people who work in the organization. When we are knowledgeable about how to build person-to-person on-the-job relationships, we put ourselves in a better position to nurture both our personal growth and the organization's growth. The notion of the rugged individual in the organization appears to be passé; replacing the rugged individual is the team player—a person who is effective working with one or more other employees both within and between groups. Team players realize

It is becoming more and more common to meet a "significant other" at work.

the potential to work together to develop meaningful partnerships with many others in the organization.[19]

The relationship level is where most of the work of the organization gets done; it is also where many of the organization's difficulties are encountered. These aspects of communication are discussed in greater depth in Part Three of this book.

EMOTIONS IN RELATIONSHIPS: FACTORING IN FEELINGS

Emotions play a role in all relationships. When a relationship is healthy, relational partners understand how their emotions affect their relationship and how the relationship affects their emotions. How well are you able to read and express feelings in the relationships you share? For example, can you tell and react appropriately when a friend, family member, or co-worker is feeling happy, grows sad, becomes angry, or experiences jealousy? Can your relational partners do the same for you?

The Range of Emotions

Most of us experience a normal range of emotions. We typically attain our highest levels of happiness when we are in a stable, long-lasting, and contented relationship. That contentment may last until something happens, like a partner passes away or falls out of love with us, breaking our heart. Then, happiness's emotional counterpart, sadness, disturbs our happy state. Because we need both negative and positive emotions, unless it persists for an extended period of time, sadness is neither a disease nor an emotion to stigmatize or silence, but rather it is quite the normal reaction when a hope, dream, or relationship fails.[20] After all, we recognize happiness because we have suffered the blues, and vice versa.[21] By suffering through emotional pain, we may appreciate the happiness we had, become more resilient, or make a better choice down the line.[22]

Not everyone experiences an emotion or expresses their feelings in the same way. Your ability to accept the reactions of other people indicates your awareness that they may experience responses to events and situations that are separate and distinct from your own. As Carroll Izard observes, "The joyful person is more apt to see the world through 'rose colored glasses,' the distressed or sad individual is more apt to construe the remarks of others as critical, and the fearful person is inclined only to see the frightening object (tunnel vision)."[23] Feelings are our reaction to what we perceive; they define and color our relationships and image of the world. Whether we are at work or at home, with a friend or significant other; whether we want to create liking, build trust, engage in self-disclosure, influence others, resolve conflicts, or handle anger, we need to be in touch with and communicate feelings.

WORKING THROUGH FEELINGS IN RELATIONSHIPS

Feelings are at the heart of our relationships. A key step in the study of how feelings affect and color relationships is to recognize what causes us to seek out some people, but not others, as relational partners.

Factors in Attraction

> Think of a person who you believe is attracted to you. To what personal qualities do you attribute his or her attraction?

Why are we attracted to one person and not to another? Why do we develop a positive attitude toward one person and a negative attitude toward another? A number of researchers have identified variables that influence how attracted people feel toward one another.[24] Attractiveness (not surprisingly), proximity, similarity, reinforcement, and complementarity are named consistently as determinants of attraction.

Attractiveness

The first kind of information we process when we interact with someone is that person's outward attractiveness. We tend to like physically attractive people more than physically unattractive people, and we tend to like people who exhibit pleasant personalities more than those who exhibit unpleasant personalities. Of course, judgments of what is physically attractive and what constitutes a pleasant personality are subjective.[25]

Work It Out
Describe how attractiveness, proximity, similarity, reinforcement, and complementarity play a role in whether or not you are attracted to another person. Rank these attractors in terms of their importance to you.

Proximity

Proximity is the second factor influencing attraction. Living physically close to another person or working near another person gives us ample opportunity to interact, talk, share similar activities, and thus form an attachment. For these reasons, the closer two people of the opposite sex are geographically, the more likely it is that they will be attracted to each other and marry. In all fairness, however, we should examine an opposite effect of proximity. According to Ellen Berscheid and Elaine Walster, the authors of *Interpersonal*

Attraction, the closer people are located, the more likely it is that they can come to dislike each other. Berscheid and Walster note: "While propinquity may be a necessary condition for attraction, it probably is also a necessary condition for hatred."[26] What do you think?

Reinforcement

Reinforcement is the third factor appearing in practically all theories of interpersonal attraction. We will feel positive about people who reward us or who are associated with our experiences of being rewarded, and we will feel animosity or dislike for people who punish us or are associated with our experiences of punishment. Thus, we are likely to like people who praise us, like us, and cooperate with us more than people who criticize us, dislike us, and oppose or compete with us. Of course, reinforcement can backfire: If people become overzealous in their praise and fawn over us too much, we question their sincerity and motivation. But in general, as social psychologist Eliot Aronson notes, "We like people whose behavior provides us with a maximum reward at minimum cost."[27]

Similarity

Similarity also affects our attraction to others. We are attracted to people whose attitudes and interests are similar to our own and who like and dislike the things we like and dislike. We usually like people who agree with us more than we like those who disagree with us, especially when we are discussing issues we consider salient or significant. In effect, similarity helps provide us with social validation.

Complementarity

Not all the evidence suggests that we seek to relate only to carbon copies of ourselves, however. In fact, **complementarity**—the last of the factors influencing interpersonal attraction—suggests just the opposite. Instead of being attracted to

complementarity
the attraction principle which states that opposites attract

Proximity is a factor influencing both attraction and dislike. How has it affected your relationships?

people who are similar to us, we frequently find ourselves attracted to people who are dissimilar in one or more ways. Both psychologist Theodore Reik and sociologist Robert Winch note that we often tend to fall in love with people who possess characteristics that we admire but do not ourselves possess. Thus, a dominant woman might seek a submissive man, and a socially awkward man might seek a socially poised woman.

Can You Feel What I Feel?

Our relationships with most of the people we contact in the course of a lifetime will be transitory and will not amount to much. At times, however, we find that our interchanges continue; then it becomes quite important to be able to determine what the person with whom we are communicating is feeling. At that point, it is just as necessary for us to understand the world of the other person as it is for us to understand ourselves.

Feelings by themselves are not inherently good or bad. Feelings as such do not disrupt relationships, build walls, or add problems to your life. Rather, it is what you think and how you act when experiencing feelings that can affect a relationship for better or worse. For example, anger and fear are not necessarily harmful. As Izard notes, "Anger is sometimes positively correlated with survival, and more often with the defense and maintenance of personal integrity and the correction of social injustice."[28] Fear may also be associated with survival and at times helps us regulate destructive aggressive urges. Thus, it is not any emotion itself that is an issue but, rather, how you deal with the emotion and the effect it has on you and on those who are important to you.

Anger's Effects

Why do you become angry with another person? Most typically, anger results from interference with the pursuit of a goal. Being either physically or psychologically restrained from doing what you would like to do can produce anger. So can being personally insulted or rejected. Thus an action that shows someone's disregard for our feelings and needs may anger us.

Anger, like its close cousin, hostility, is a potentially damaging state. According to psychiatry professor Redford Williams, strong evidence indicates that hostility alone damages the heart: "It isn't the impatience, the ambition or the work drive. It's the anger. It sends your blood pressure skyrocketing. It provokes your body to create unhealthy chemicals. For some hostile people, anger is poison."[29] Research suggests that genes may account for 27 to 40 percent of a person's tendency toward anger.[30] Some people have free-floating hostility, meaning that they are usually angry, often without real cause. These people are the most at risk.

Learning to express anger constructively is a valuable skill.

Media Wise

Rants and Revelations

On radio and television talk shows, on MTV, in blogs, in political and self-help columns, and in books, we find people ranting, engaging in name-calling, venting, delivering tirades, and also revealing their innermost secrets. Listening and reacting to extremely angry or confessional human beings are new entertainment forms.[31]

Song lyrics, Internet sites, and blogs contain frequent references to anger and/or the private thoughts of their authors or creators. Talk show hosts and guests spew hate across the airwaves and cable, probe for and reveal new depths of intimacy, and confess to having dark thoughts or desires. Is cacophony in media driving out reason? Are public, personal confessions making personal disclosures less meaningful?

Consider these questions:

1. What functions do you think mediated rants serve? Do we need to take steps to restore civility into the common discussion of social problems? If you think no steps are necessary, why not? If you think they are, what are they?

2. With respect to public disclosures of private matters, are we creating a new type of online intimacy? And if we are, are we making intimacy in the real world less important?

This is not to suggest that all expression of anger is unhealthy. Indeed, for people who express some anger, versus a lot of anger, the risks of disease may be lower than for persons who express little or no anger. In fact, moderate expressions of anger, when compared with low expressions of anger, decrease the risk for heart attack and stroke by about 50 percent.[32] Unexpressed anger can lead to passive-aggressive behavior and the development of a negative and hostile personality. Consequently, demonstrating anger management—that is, learning to express anger constructively by expressing angry feelings in an assertive, not aggressive, way, redirecting anger, and calming oneself down—is a valuable skill.

Emotional Creation and Contagion

Have you ever put on a happy face? What happened? Did you discover that smiling actually made you feel happy? What effect did your smile have on people

We unconsciously mirror and imitate the moods and emotions of individuals with whom we interact.

Ethics and Communication

Emotional Contagion

Emotional Intelligence author Daniel Goleman, psychoanalyst Carl Jung, and psychologist Elaine Hatfield each contend that our moods can be contagious. In fact, the more emotionally expressive people are, the more likely they are to transmit their moods when they talk with another person. The transmission of emotion appears to occur both instantaneously and unconsciously.

If we assume this phenomenon is true, should a person who is experiencing a bout of sadness or a similar depressive emotion be kept isolated from others so as not to "infect" them with the same feeling? What do you think? Would we be better off if we were exposed only to people who were in good moods? Why or why not?

Work It Out

Describe the last time someone caught your mood and the last time you caught another person's mood. Was the mood caught a relationship enhancer or detractor? Why?

emotional contagion

the catching of another person's mood

around you? Putting on a sad, happy, or frightened face can produce the feeling that the expression represents. Facial expressions in and of themselves elicit feelings; they are not simply the visible sign of an emotion.[33] Thus, while emotions may influence facial expressions, facial expressions may similarly influence emotions.

Our moods may also be contagious. If you have ever started your day in a great mood, gone to class, and then ended up in a bad mood, you may want to consider that someone gave you that nasty mood. The more empathetic we are, the more apt we are to be susceptible to **emotional contagion** and to catch someone else's mood. According to psychologist Elaine Hatfield, we do this by unconsciously mirroring and/or imitating the moods and emotions of those with whom we interact.[34]

SHARING FEELINGS IN RELATIONSHIPS

Our feelings tell us about our needs and about the state of our relationships.[35] People who share healthy relationships are able to pay direct attention to the emotional reactions that occur during their interactions. They take time to become aware of these emotions by periodically asking themselves, "What am I feeling?" Once the feeling has been identified, their next step is to estimate its strength: "How strong is this feeling?" Next, they ask, "How did I get to feel this way?" "Where did the feeling come from?" "How did I contribute?" In healthy relationships, an emotion is reported as experienced—for instance, "I'm getting angry, and I'm beginning to say things I really don't mean."

Healthy relationships do not consist totally of positive feelings. Other feelings are also important. Unfortunately, many of us lack the commitment, courage, and skill needed to express our own feelings—particularly when those feelings are not positive—or to allow other people to express their feelings to us. Many people are reluctant to work their feelings through; instead, they ignore or deny a feeling until it eventually becomes unmanageable.

Thus, we often keep our feelings too much in check or, when we do express them, we express them ineptly and incompletely. Did you know that the majority of people who are fired from their jobs are asked to leave not because of incompetence but because of personality conflicts? Many of the problems we have with friends, parents, or employers are due to the inability to express or accept messages about feelings. Efforts to sacrifice or disregard feelings inevitably lead to problems with relationships or failures of relationships. In the next section we examine how this happens.

Suppression and Disclosure of Feelings

Sometimes the way we handle feelings impedes our relationships with others.[36] For example, in any relational context, we may bury our real feelings, hesitate to express them, or unleash them uncontrollably.

Censoring Your Feelings

Feelings are not the enemy of healthy human relationships, yet at times we are taught to act as if they were. As a result, many of us grow up afraid of feelings.

Have important people in your life ever expressed sentiments similar to the following to you?

"You shouldn't feel depressed about what happened."

"If you can't tell me you're pleased with the way it looks, then don't say anything."

"Don't you scream at me! You have no right to get angry with me!"

"There's nothing to be afraid of! Why are you such a baby?"

As these examples imply, feelings and emotions are frequently perceived as dangerous, harmful, and shameful. When this is the case, we censor our feelings and become overly hesitant to express them to others or to let others express their feelings to us. We exhibit only socially approved feelings for fear of being considered irrational or emotionally volatile. This leads to communication that is shallow, contrived, and frequently inappropriate.

Often, so as not to make waves or alienate others, both males and females act the part of the nice guy. At times people desperately want others to like them and so are willing to pretend to feel, or not feel, a particular emotion. People may also become what Theodore Isaac Rubin calls **emotional isolationists**.[37] That is, they may try to protect themselves from any exchange of feelings by minding their own business and avoiding entanglements or involvements. Or they may overintellectualize every experience in an attempt to render their emotions impotent. Each of these techniques is counterproductive and can ultimately cause problems with relationships.

Display Rules

Various types of unwritten laws, or display rules, guide us in deciding when or when not to show our emotions. For instance, when we are young, we may be told not to cry at school, not to yell in front of strangers, or not to kiss in public. As adults, we may be advised not to flirt at office parties, not to display anger when disciplined, or not to be too outspoken during a meeting.

> When was the last time you censored your feelings from another person? What was it about the relationship you shared that contributed to the decision?

emotional isolationists
persons who seek to avoid situations that may require the exchange of feelings

"Do you know how masculine it is to risk crying?"

One determinant of display rules is gender. Although feelings do not discriminate between the sexes, and although members of both sexes obviously are equally capable of emotions of all kinds, our society for some reason deems it appropriate for men and women to behave differently with regard to their emotions. Theodore Isaac Rubin, author of *The Angry Book,* observes, "members of both sexes get equally angry" and "are equally expressive"; nevertheless, different rules and taboos regarding the expression of anger, and other emotions, have been internalized by males and females.[38] While men and women are equally likely to experience anger, women are far more likely to suppress, repress, and deny it.[39] Only 9 percent of women report that they deal with anger by directly confronting the person who caused it, and 25 percent insist that they wouldn't express anger to a family member.[40] Instead, they keep it bottled up by enacting a "no anger" script.

Gender also influences how we react when someone tears up or cries. Although in serious situations, such as a significant other's death, crying is accepted as perfectly normal, if you tear up or cry in the workplace, some people view it as a manipulative ploy or a sign of instability. Approximately three decades ago, studies revealed that men's tears were looked at negatively. Now, however, many perceive tearing up to humanize men. In fact, crying on the job does more damage to a woman's career than to a man's, and both women and men react more favorable to men who tear up. However, both men and women are perceived more positively when merely tearing up, as opposed to crying outright, at work.[41]

In our society, men are generally viewed as more rational, objective, and independent than women. Women are perceived to be more emotional, subjective, and dependent than men. Women are also supposed to do more disclosing than men. When asked, people typically indicate that the "male" traits are more desirable than the "female" traits. But Kay Deaux notes in *The Behavior of Women and Men* that the supposedly female characteristics are not all seen as bad:

There is a cluster of positively valued traits that people see as more typical of women than men; these traits generally reflect warmth and expressiveness. Women are described as tactful, gentle, aware of the feelings of others, and able to express tender feelings easily. Men in contrast are viewed as blunt, rough, unaware of the feelings of others, and unable to express their own feelings.[42]

The second important determinant of display rules is culture. For example, in some African societies, people will assume that you are friendly until you prove to them that you are not. When they smile, it means that they like you; if they don't smile, it means that they distrust you. The Japanese, on the other hand, often laugh and smile to mask anger, sorrow, or disgust. People from Mediterranean countries often intensify emotions such as grief, sadness, and happiness, whereas the British deintensify, or understate, these emotions.

The third determinant of display rules is personal values. In effect, we decide for ourselves under what conditions and with whom we will freely share or inhibit our emotional expressions. You might, for instance, feel it inappropriate to show anger before a parent, but you might readily reveal it to a boyfriend, girlfriend, or spouse. You might hesitate to express your innermost fears to an instructor or employer, but you might readily disclose them to a close friend.

> To whom do you feel free to say, "I'm frightened of that," or "What you just did disappointed me," or "I really care about you"?

Our personal display rules might also cause us to develop a characteristic style of emotional expression.[43] We might become *withholders* and try never to show how we feel, or we might become *revealers* and try always to show how we feel. Or we might become what Paul Ekman and Wallace Friesen call unwitting expressors, blanked expressors, or substitute expressors.[44] *Unwitting expressors* reveal their feelings without being aware that they have done so. (They then wonder how someone could read their emotions.) *Blanked expressors* are certain that they are communicating feelings to others but, in fact, are not. (They are then confused or upset when people fail to pick up on their cues.) *Substitute expressors* substitute the appearance of one emotion for another emotion without realizing they have done so. (They then cannot understand why people react in unexpected ways.) Thus, personal display rules sometimes work to impede interpersonal relationships.

Exploring Diversity

Culture, Gender, and Emotional Displays

When it comes to the display of emotion, our culture and our gender appear to compel us to act in accordance with societal norms. For example, Asians are less likely than Americans to express negative emotions publicly, and men generally tend to be more reticent in expressing emotions such as sympathy, sadness, and distress, while women are more inhibited when it comes to expressing anger and sexuality.

How are these cultural and gender expression differences sustained? Parents and society, in general, reinforce them. For example, recent studies reveal that, in the United States, we still treat boys and girls differently when it comes to their emotional lives. According to psychologist Virginia O'Leary, "The stereotypes of emotionality for men and women are as strong as ever, in spite of two decades of efforts to break them down." Some of the most compelling laboratory research shows, for instance, that when provoked, men and women have equivalent reactions in terms of heart rate and other physiological responses, but, when questioned, men usually say they are angry, while women usually say they are hurt or sad.

In another study, men and women viewed scenes of accidents and their victims. Although physiological measures indicated that both the men and women were equally affected by the scenes, the men's faces showed no expression, while the women's faces expressed sympathy.

Consider the following questions:

1. To what extent does your own behavior confirm or contradict the preceding observations? Explain.

2. How might the different messages that men and women send about their emotions affect their ability to communicate honestly and effectively with each other?

Effects of Suppressed Feelings on Relationships

As Jerry Gillies, the author of *Friendship*, writes, "You are not making contact if you are not putting out what you really are."[45] Interpersonal communication theorist Sidney Jourard noted that dissembling, concealing, and being hesitant to reveal feelings are "lethal" habits for men.[46] Jourard believed that men, because they are not as apt to express their feelings as are women, encounter stresses that cause them to have a shorter life span than women. Now that women are assuming what were traditionally male roles, will they, too, feel more compelled to keep their feelings to themselves? Whatever the answer, it is acknowledged that all people are likely to experience personal and interpersonal difficulties when they try to repress or disguise their feelings.

Effects of Disclosed Feelings on Relationships

Certainly, there are people to whom you may not choose to reveal your feelings, and there are situations in which you decide that disclosure of your feelings would be inappropriate. Nevertheless, when you take the risk of revealing your feelings to others, your relationship is likely to reap definite benefits.

First, by honestly revealing your feelings, you make it less threatening for the other person to reveal his or her feelings. You demonstrate that you care enough to share your feelings; thus, risk taking becomes a reciprocal process. Second, you acknowledge that emotions are acceptable. You do not censor the feelings the other person experiences, nor do you decide which feelings he or she may and may not feel. You express an interest in the whole person; instead of using emotions as weapons, you show that you are willing to use them as tools. Third, by describing your feelings and by sharing your perceptions with others, you become more aware of what it is you are actually feeling. Fourth, you give yourself the opportunity to resolve difficulties and conflicts in a productive way. Fifth, by revealing your feelings, you can indicate to others how you want to be treated. In contrast, by keeping quiet—by saying nothing—you encourage others to continue behavior of which you may disapprove. Feelings, when respected, are friendly, not dangerous.

CONFLICTS AND RELATIONSHIPS

conflict
perceived disagreement

Conflict, or perceived disagreement about views, interests, and goals, is a part of every relationship. It is not so much the conflict or disagreement that creates problems in our relationships but the way we approach and handle it. Thus, while disagreements are normal and their presence does not signal relationship trouble, how we choose to manage conflict with another is an indicator of a relationship's health.

Managing Conflict: Handling Feelings during Conflict

One of our objectives in this chapter is to investigate conflict to see how we can learn to handle it effectively. You have been, and will continue to be, faced with conflicts all your life. Observing your own conflicts and giving more thought to them can be a positive experience.

Conflict develops for a multitude of reasons and takes a multitude of forms. It can arise from people's different needs, attitudes, or beliefs. Conflict tests each relationship we share with another person and in so doing helps us assess the health or effectiveness of the relationship. Handled well, conflict can help each participant develop a clearer picture of the other; thus, it can strengthen and cement a relationship. Handled poorly, conflict can create schisms, inflict psychological scars, inflame hostilities, and cause lasting resentments. Thus, conflicts can produce highly constructive or highly destructive consequences.[47]

Every relationship worth maintaining, every relationship worth working at, is certain to experience moments of conflict. As David Johnson notes, "A conflict-free relationship is a sign that you really have no relationship at all, not that you have a good relationship."[48] To say there should be no conflict amounts to saying that we should have no relationships. If a relationship is healthy, conflicts will occur regularly. If a relationship is healthy, conflicts will also be handled effectively.

How we approach conflict can create problems. Handled poorly, conflict can destroy relationships and inflame hostilities.

Research also indicates that how your parents handled conflict may have influenced your early academic achievement and emotional well-being.[49] There is evidently a link between the emotional lives of your parents and your own emotional health.[50]

Poor conflict management and poor communication skills include one or more of the following behaviors:

■ Attacking a partner by making accusations or displaying passive aggression. Once negativity characterizes the tone of a relationship, sarcasm, inflicting guilt, and displays of inconsiderate behavior become all too common.

■ Acting defensively. Once people feel threatened or attacked, they tend to adopt a defensive posture—retaliating in inappropriate ways, backtracking on agreements, or whining incessantly to signal displeasure.

■ Stonewalling. When the parties to a relationship ignore problems or refuse to talk about differences calmly, they build a relationship wall that is virtually impossible to hurdle.

■ Communicating contempt. Once partners display contempt for one another, the relationship enters dangerous territory, otherwise known as relationship badlands.[51]

Managing conflict is a skill. We manage conflict skillfully when we engage each other in a dialogue in lieu of practicing a monologue. Instead of criticizing or attacking another person's behavior, we choose to speak respectfully in language absent of threats. Rather than trying to win the conflict and setting up a win-lose situation, we converse to be understood. You have your perspective; the other person has his or her perspective. But there are usually many perspectives, not only the two you hold.

Reexamine your personal conflict inventory or identify your style of managing conflict. Do you feel a need to deny that a conflict exists, withdraw, surrender, placate, or distract by introducing irrelevancies? Do you intellectualize, blame, find

Work It Out

Share a conflict you were party to that was settled responsibly and one that escalated out of control. Create a list of rules for handling conflict effectively.

What conflicts have you been involved in recently—in class, at work, or at home? Why did you define each situation as a conflict?

fault, or force the other person to accept your ideas by physically or emotionally overpowering him or her? Why? What elements of your relationship elicit irrational responses instead of a rational discussion of the disputed issues?

Gender, Culture, and the Handling of Conflict

When women and men, and individuals from diverse cultures, communicate, they carry their assumptions, beliefs, and perceptions of each other with them. What soon becomes apparent is that the sexes, and different cultures, approach conflict in different ways.

From childhood on, males are typically more competitive and aggressive, while females adopt more cooperative behaviors. Since most males are more concerned with power, they tend to make demands, while most females, more concerned with relationship maintenance, tend to make proposals. Males often fail to provide rationales for positions, while females freely offer reasons.

Women and men may also have different notions of friendship. Women share their feelings more intensely with each other than do men, whose friendships are built less around talk and more around activities. When it comes to loyalty, however, the same behavioral code applies to both sexes. Both men and women are capable of betraying confidences or being selfless and extremely generous. But when do you tell on a friend who has done something wrong? When do you step in to stop a friend from harming someone? And when do you protect your friend? According to sociologist Michael S. Kimmel, two conflicting values are tied to masculinity: Always do the right thing, and never betray your friends.[52] Men tend to decide on a case-by-case basis whether friendship is more valuable than money or personal fulfillment, often setting up conflict-fraught situations to test each other's loyalty. Do you find that women tend to act similarly?

Sexual orientation plays a role in conflict management. According to researchers, gays and lesbians tend to be nicer than straight people during relationship conflicts. Less fearful, belligerent, or domineering, they also are more likely to use humor to diffuse conflict.[53] Gays, however, when compared to lesbians and heterosexuals, have more difficulty making up or repairing their relationships once a conflict is over.[54] No matter what your sexual preference, conflict, if handled well, creates the opportunity to explore possibilities rather than just fight for your position.

For example, if one party to a conflict is uncomfortable engaging in conflict, while the other withdraws from conflict, both are likely to be left feeling unhappy. In fact, negative marital interactions that include name-calling and disdain-signaling nonverbal cues like eye-rolling can have an adverse effect on health, particularly in women. One researcher notes, "How often someone rolls their eyes at you can predict how often you need to go to the doctor."[55] Instead of making either yourself or a partner sick, by choosing to face and handle a conflict with sensitivity, you allow for the clarification of situational boundaries and norms, the expression of feelings, the identification of needs, the establishment of a workable power balance, and the building of a foundation for handling future problems.

As with men and women, different cultures socialize their members to behave in different ways when faced with conflict. Whereas members of individualistic cultures, such as exists in the United States, are likely to exhibit a direct approach that emanates from the belief that individuals have a right to defend themselves, members of collectivistic cultures believe that such behavior is out of place or rude. Instead, they tend to value harmony, restraint, and nonconfrontation.[56]

My idea of an agreeable person is a person who agrees with me.
—Benjamin Disraeli

Hesitant to refuse a request directly, the members of a collectivistic culture might say, "Let me think about that" in place of "No."

The members of collectivist cultures place significant value on face by seeking to create or preserve a positive image. As a result, they are less likely to overtly express their disagreement and tend not to engage in or condone personal attacks on one another. Rather, they value their relationships and display their respect for them by not saying what they think if it might hurt others.[57]

By becoming sensitive to such differences, and recognizing the assumptions on which they are based, we can work toward developing a clearer understanding of how conflicts can be resolved.[58]

We see that, in any situation, problems can develop if we fail to deal with conflict appropriately. We can also see that there are certain definite benefits to be derived from handling conflict effectively. Alan Filley, in the book *Interpersonal Conflict Resolution,* identifies four major values arising from conflict. First, many conflict situations can reduce or even eliminate the probability of more serious conflict in the future. Second, conflict can foster innovation by helping us acquire new ways of looking at things, new ways of thinking, and new behaviors. Third, conflict can develop our sense of cohesiveness and togetherness by increasing closeness and trust. Fourth, it can provide us with an invaluable opportunity to measure the strength or viability of our relationships.[59] Conflict, after all, is a natural result of diversity.

> **Can you think of situations in your own life that illustrate the four values of conflict discussed here?**

How Conflict Arises: Categorizing Conflicts

We have examined what conflict is and how we feel about it. Now let us explore how and why it arises. Conflict is likely to occur wherever human differences meet. As we have seen, conflict is a clash of opposing beliefs, opinions, values, needs, assumptions, and goals. It can result from honest differences, from misunderstandings, from anger, or from expecting either too much or too little from people and situations. Note that conflict does not always require two or more people; you can sometimes be in conflict with yourself. **Self-conflict** occurs when we find ourselves having to choose between two or more mutually exclusive options—two cars, two classes, two potential spouses, two activities; the internal struggle in such a situation is called **intrapersonal conflict.** In contrast, **interpersonal conflict** is the same type of struggle between two or more people. Interpersonal conflict can be prompted by differences in perceptions and interests; by a scarcity of resources or rewards, such as money, time, and position; or by rivalry—situations in which we find ourselves competing with someone else. Those involved in an intrapersonal or interpersonal conflict usually feel pulled in different directions at the same time.

We can categorize conflict in different ways. First, we can classify the goal or objective about which a conflict revolves. Goals or objectives can be nonshareable (for example, two teams cannot win the same basketball game) or shareable (your team can win some games and the other team can win some). Or they can be fully claimed and possessed by each party to the conflict. (You can each win everything—members of the rival Teamsters and Independent Truckers unions all get raises.)

Second, conflicts can be categorized according to their level of intensity. In a **low-intensity conflict,** the persons involved do not want to destroy each other; they devise an acceptable procedure to help control their communications and

self-conflict
the type of conflict that occurs when a person has to choose between two or more mutually exclusive options

intrapersonal conflict
internal conflict

interpersonal conflict
conflict between two or more people

low-intensity conflict
a conflict in which the persons involved work to discover a solution beneficial to all parties

Skill Builder

Tied in Knots

This exercise was suggested by an experience included in Virginia Satir's book *Peoplemaking*.

1. Think of some idea, belief, value, need, or goal that has involved you in a conflict situation.

2. Identify the relevant aspects of yourself or the other person or persons involved. Briefly summarize each position.

3. Choose class members to play the parts of those you perceived yourself to be in conflict with.

4. Cut heavy twine or rope into 10-foot lengths, one for each player. Also cut a number of 3-foot lengths to tie

around each player's waist, including your own. Next, tie your 10-foot lead rope to the rope around your waist. Then, hand your rope to the person with whom you perceive yourself to be in conflict, who will also hand his or her rope to you.

5. While tied to each other, begin to talk about the issue that is the cause of conflict.

_____

Source: Virginia Satir. *Peoplemaking.* Palo Alto, CA: Science and Behavior Books, 1988.

---

medium-intensity conflict

a conflict in which each person feels committed to win, but winning is seen as sufficient

permit them to discover a solution that is beneficial to each. In a **medium-intensity conflict,** each person feels committed to win, but winning is seen as sufficient. No one feels that the opposition must be destroyed. In a **high-intensity conflict,** one person intends to destroy or at least seriously hurt the other. In high-intensity conflicts, winning as such is not necessarily sufficient; to mean anything, victory must be total.

Are you able to disagree without becoming disagreeable? What steps would you take to resolve a value conflict?

A conflict can also be classified as a pseudoconflict, a content conflict, a value conflict, or an ego conflict. A **pseudoconflict** (as the term implies) is not really a conflict but gives the appearance of a conflict. It occurs when a person mistakenly believes that two or more goals cannot be achieved simultaneously. Pseudoconflicts frequently revolve around false either-or judgments ("Either I win or you win") or around simple misunderstandings (failing to realize that you really agree with the other person). A pseudoconflict is resolved when the people realize that no conflict actually exists.

A **content conflict** occurs when people disagree over matters of fact: the accuracy or implications of information, the definition of a term, or the solution to a problem. If the interactants realize that facts can be verified, inferences tested, definitions checked, and solutions evaluated against criteria, they can be shown that a content conflict can be settled rationally.

A **value conflict** arises when people hold different views on a particular issue. As an example, consider the American welfare system. A person who values individual independence and self-assertiveness will have opinions about public welfare that differ greatly from those of someone who believes that we are ultimately responsible for the well-being of others. The realistic outcome of such a conflict would be that the interactants would disagree without becoming disagreeable—that is, they would discuss the issue and learn something from one another, even though they might continue to disagree. In effect, they would agree that it is acceptable to disagree.

Ego conflicts have the greatest potential to destroy a relationship. An **ego conflict** occurs when the interactants believe that winning or losing is a reflection of their own self-worth, prestige, or competence. When this happens, the issue itself is no longer important because each person perceives himself or herself to be on the line. Thus, it becomes almost impossible to deal with the situation rationally.

At this point, you should understand that conflict can develop for a number of different reasons, and you should be aware of the types of disagreements and problems that can arise during intrapersonal and interpersonal conflict. Particular conflict-generating behaviors affect each of us differently.

Some of us perceive ourselves to be involved in a conflict if we are deprived of a need; others do not. Some of us perceive ourselves to be involved in a conflict if someone impinges on our territory or disagrees with us about the way we define a role; others do not. Take some time to discover your own sources of conflict. Making such observations will help you understand the types of issues that draw you into disharmony with yourself and others. It will also let you see how you tend to respond when faced with a conflict situation. We will now examine constructive and destructive ways of handling conflict in greater detail.

Resolving Conflict: Styles of Expression

As we have seen, our emotions and how we handle them can make or break the relationships we enter into. In other words, we can make our feelings work for or against us. There are three basic ways of handling emotionally charged or conflict-producing situations: nonassertively, aggressively, and assertively.

Nonassertiveness

Have there been moments in your life when you believed you had to suppress your feelings to avoid rejection or conflict, or when you felt unable to state your feelings clearly? Are you ever afraid to let others know how you feel? If you have ever felt hesitant to express your feelings to others, intimidated by another person, or reluctant to speak up when you believed you were being treated unfairly, then you know what it is to exhibit **nonassertiveness.** When you behave nonassertively, you force yourself to keep your real feelings inside. Frequently, you function as a weather vane or change colors as a chameleon does in order to fit the situation in which you find yourself. You become an echo of the feelings around you. Unfortunately, nonassertive people rarely take the steps needed to improve a relationship that is causing problems; as a result, they frequently end up with something they don't really want. With so much at stake, why do people refrain from asserting themselves?

---

high-intensity conflict
a conflict in which one person intends to destroy or seriously hurt the other

pseudoconflict
the situation that results when persons mistakenly believe that two or more goals cannot be achieved simultaneously

content conflict
a disagreement over matters of fact

value conflict
a disagreement that arises when persons hold different views on an issue

ego conflict
a disagreement in which persons believe that winning or losing is tied to their self-worth, prestige, or competence

Work It Out

When evaluating a conflict, Americans tend to see one side as right and the other as wrong. In contrast, the Chinese are more likely to see the validity of both sides. What do you see as the benefits and drawbacks of each orientation?

nonassertiveness
the hesitation to display one's feelings and thoughts

Why might you hesitate to protect your rights; that is, why would you be reluctant to assert yourself? Under what circumstances would nonassertiveness be most likely to occur? Under what circumstances, if any, might it be the appropriate decision?

Experience shows that we hesitate to assert ourselves in our relationships for a number of reasons. Sometimes inertia or laziness is a factor; the easiest response is simply no response at all. (After all, assertion can be hard work.) At other times, apathy leads us to be nonassertive; we simply do not care enough to become actively involved. Frequently, fear can lead to nonassertiveness. In particular, we may fear that rejection might result from active self-assertion. (We become convinced that speaking up may make someone angry.) Or we may simply feel we lack the interpersonal skills needed for assertiveness.

Another important cause of nonassertiveness is shyness. Each of us feels inadequate from time to time. We may feel exploited, stifled, or imposed upon. These feelings manifest themselves in a variety of ways—as depression, as weakness, as loneliness—but most of all, according to psychologist Philip G. Zimbardo, as shyness. Shyness is embarrassment in advance. It is created by the fear that our real self will not match up with the image we want to project.[60]

According to Zimbardo and Shirley L. Radl, coauthors of *The Shyness Workbook*, few shy people consider their shyness a positive trait; they see it as evidence that something is wrong with them. Zimbardo and Radl note: "Shyness is not a permanent trait but rather is a response to other people evoked by certain situations. The unpleasant feelings of shyness come from having low self-esteem and worrying about what other people will think of you."[61]

According to Lynn Z. Bloom, Karen Coburn, and Joan Pearlman, authors of *The New Assertive Woman*, in our society shyness or nonassertiveness is often considered an asset for women but a liability for men.[62] To what extent do your experiences support this? Do you think women gain more from being nonassertive than men lose? Why?

There are many degrees of shyness. For example, shyness can take the form of mild bashfulness, or it can simply cause you to increase the distance you like to keep between yourself and others. Unfortunately, extreme shyness can make you fear all social relationships and can prevent you from expressing or even acknowledging your emotions. Of course, it is your right not to assert yourself. We discuss this more when we discuss assertion later in this chapter and accommodation in Chapter 11.

Work It Out
Identify individuals with whom you are likely to behave nonassertively, assertively, and aggressively. Identify factors that influence your behavioral choices.

Which situations in your life make you feel shy? What are the consequences of your shyness?

Work It Out
Describe an interpersonal situation in which someone took advantage of you and you permitted it. What do you believe motivated the other person? What motivated you? Describe a situation in which you took advantage of someone else. Why do you believe the other person allowed you to victimize him or her?

Aggressiveness

Unlike nonassertive people, who often permit others to victimize them and are reluctant to express their feelings, persons who display **aggressiveness** insist on standing up for their own rights to the point at which they ignore and violate the rights of others. Although some people deliberately defy pushy people, in general, aggressive people manage to have more of their needs met than nonassertive people do. Unfortunately, they usually accomplish this at someone else's expense. The aggressor always aims to dominate and win in a relationship; breaking even is not enough. The message of the aggressive person is selfish: "This is the way I feel. You're stupid if you feel differently. This is what I want. What you want doesn't count and is of no consequence to me." In contrast to the nonassertive person, who ventures forth in communication hesitantly, the aggressive person begins by attacking, thereby precipitating conflict. It is therefore not surprising that a conversation with an aggressive person will often escalate out of control: The target of the aggressor frequently feels a need to retaliate. In such situations, no one really wins, and the result is a stalemated relationship.

People feel a need to act aggressively for a number of reasons. First, according to two assertiveness counselors, Arthur J. Lange and Patricia Jakubowski, we tend to lash out when we feel ourselves becoming vulnerable; we attempt to protect ourselves from the perceived threat of powerlessness.[63] Second, emotionally volatile experiences that remain unresolved may cause us to overreact when faced with a difficulty in a relationship. Third, we may firmly believe that aggression is the only way to get our ideas and feelings across to the other person. For some reason, we may think that people will neither listen to nor react to what we say if we take a mild-mannered approach. Fourth, we may simply never have learned to channel or handle our aggressive impulses. (In other words, we may not have mastered a number of necessary interpersonal skills.) Fifth, aggression may be related to a pattern of repeated nonassertion in the past; the hurt, disappointment, bewilderment, and sense of personal violation that resulted from nonassertion may have risen to the boiling point. No longer able to keep these feelings inside, we abruptly vent them as aggressiveness.

Damaged or destroyed relationships are a frequent result of aggression. Neither the nonassertive nor the aggressive person has many meaningful relationships. For this reason, we need to find a middle ground, or golden mean, between the extremes of nonassertion and aggression.

Assertiveness

The intent of nonassertive behavior is to avoid conflict of any kind; the intent of aggressive behavior is to dominate. By contrast, the intent of assertive behavior is to communicate honestly, clearly, and directly and to support your beliefs and ideas without either harming others or allowing yourself to be harmed. If we can assume that both nonassertion and aggression are due at least partly to having learned inappropriate ways of reacting in interpersonal encounters, we should be able to improve our interpersonal relationships if we work to develop appropriate ways of reacting. Understanding the nature of assertiveness will help us accomplish this goal.

When you display **assertiveness,** you protect yourself from being victimized; you meet more of your interpersonal needs, make more decisions about your own life, think and say what you believe, and establish closer interpersonal relationships without infringing on the rights of others. To be assertive is to recognize that all people have the same fundamental rights and that neither titles nor roles alter this fact. We all have the right to influence the way others behave toward us; we all have the right to protect ourselves from mistreatment. Furthermore, we all have the right to accomplish these objectives without guilt.

Assertive people have learned how to stop themselves from sending inappropriate nonassertive or aggressive messages. Thus, assertive people announce what they think and feel without apologizing but without dominating. This involves learning to say "no," "yes," "I like," and "I think." In this way, neither oneself nor the other person is demeaned; both are respected.

The focus of assertiveness is negotiation. Assertive people try to balance social power to equalize the relationships they share. Whereas aggressive people often

aggressiveness

the expressing of one's own thoughts and feelings at another's expense

Online Learning Center

Go to the Online Learning Center at www.mhhe.com/gamble10e and answer the questions in the *self inventory* to evaluate your understanding of assertiveness. View clip 4 to see examples of aggressive and assertive communication.

assertiveness

the expressing of one's thoughts and feelings while displaying respect for the thoughts and feelings of others

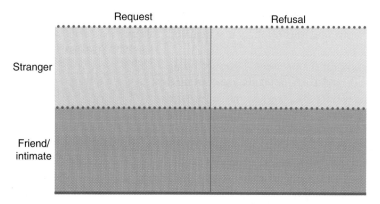

FIGURE 9.3

Relationship Window.

Which quadrant poses the most challenges for you? Which poses the fewest problems? Why?

hurt others and nonassertive people often hurt themselves, assertive people protect themselves as well as those with whom they interact. This means attending to feelings and using specific verbal and nonverbal skills to help solve interpersonal problems.

Remember that being assertive does not mean being insensitive, selfish, stubborn, or pushy. It does mean being willing to defend your rights and communicate your needs, and it does mean being willing to attempt to find mutually satisfactory solutions to interpersonal problems and conflicts. It is up to you to decide whether you would like to redefine some of the ways you relate to others. It is up to you to determine whether you need to shake off any inappropriate and unproductive ways of behaving in favor of assertiveness.

You may, of course, encounter difficulties as you attempt, through assertiveness, to promote more successful and open communication with others. Most assertion situations fall into at least one of four categories: (1) an interaction with a stranger, in which you are requesting something; (2) an interaction with a friend or an intimate, in which you are requesting something; (3) an interaction with a stranger, in which you are refusing something; (4) an interaction with a friend or an intimate, in which you are refusing something.[64] These situations may be represented as a relationship window (see Figure 9.3).

Most people will experience the majority of their difficulties with assertiveness in one or more of the quadrants shown in Figure 9.3. For example, some people may find it easy to refuse a stranger's request but difficult to deny that of a friend. For others, refusing close friends or strangers alike may pose few problems; instead, they may experience great anxiety when making requests of others.

At one time or another, we will all have some difficulty in at least one of the quadrants. Once you have identified your own problem areas, however, you can begin to examine your behavior more closely. You can begin to recognize when you feel a need to fight, when you feel a need to flee, and when you feel a need to assert yourself. Fighting or fleeing makes sense for animals and is therefore characteristic of their behavior. These alternatives do not necessarily make sense for human beings in dealing with one another; still, we sometimes flee from each other, and we sometimes fight with each other. Sometimes we display these behaviors because we want to, sometimes because we feel we must, and sometimes because we don't know what else to do or may think we lack the social skills to do anything else. What we can do, however, is use our problem-solving ability to develop assertive ways to handle interpersonal difficulties. We can learn to be socially adept.

For any relationship to grow, the participants need to demonstrate at least a minimal level of assertiveness in their communication with each other. The important thing is to try to let your actions be dictated by the circumstances and the people. There is no single right way to act in every interpersonal encounter, and the choice of how you act should be your own. In general, however, we can all increase our feelings of self-worth by learning to be more assertive.[65]

TECHNOLOGY, RELATIONSHIPS, AND THE COMMUNICATION OF EMOTION

To what extent does our involvement with persons in cyberspace affect the relationships we already share with friends, significant others, family members, and people at work? Do you feel successful managing multiple interpersonal worlds?

The Internet has given us the potential to expand our relationship reach. The Web, in many ways, is the ultimate *noncontact* person-to-person network. Online social networking sites such as Facebook, MySpace, and Second Life let us "get out" and socialize or "make friends" with people we hardly know by encouraging us to declare our friendships on the basis of the flimsiest of connections. Online we often have not a real connection, but only the appearance of connection. Yet we talk with one another very casually and with a familiarity that belies how weak the ties between us may be.[66] When using Facebook, we repeatedly have to decide whether to accept or reject someone as a friend. Friendship decisions in the real world are rarely so direct. As we discussed, real-world friendships take time to evolve. Participating in sites like Facebook, on the other hand, might be compared to having to decide instantly at a party whether you want someone as a friend.[67] Often, because we do not want to appear rude, we tend to accept more people as friends online—sometimes as many as 5,000 friends, the limit allowed by Facebook, or more than that, since MySpace has no limit—than we otherwise would be likely to do.[68] In real life, people don't usually ask outright if they can be our friend, as they do online. Is it possible that the more time we spend talking online, the less time we spend talking to friends whom we can see physically and touch? By engaging in a net of hyperlinked friendships, are we in danger of devaluing or diluting our real-world friendships? Or are our online friendships helping us fill the need we have to be recognized and valued by others? Is being linked to another person online the same as having that person as a friend?

Some observers believe that because the Internet connects its users by fostering a "put it all out there" orientation, it contributes to emotionally detached people thinking they are going places together or getting somewhere when, because they never leave the confines of their own rooms, they are going and getting nowhere. They are interacting in a social environment that critics contend serves the needs of asocial individuals.[69] It is not necessarily easy to turn virtual relationships into real-world ones while you are sitting in front of your computer screen.[70]

Not all online relationships are pleasant. When interacting online, in addition to interacting pleasantly, individuals can hurl insults, or **flames,** that feed interpersonal conflict. In fact, some people send computer-assisted messages to persons that they would never dare send if they were face-to-face with those individuals. Because there is neither rootedness to place nor danger of physical contact while interacting via computer, but there is the potential for anonymity, certain persons may even allow themselves the freedom to become verbally abusive or aggressive. How

Work It Out

In a cyberaffair, one person carries on an interpersonal relationship that is not necessarily physical or intimate with another person online. In cybersex, which is anonymous and built on fantasy, persons talk about having sex, describing various sexual acts, with an online partner. If your significant other were to have a cyberaffair or engage in cybersex, would you consider him or her to be guilty of infidelity? Why or why not? What relational factors do you believe lead someone to have a cyberaffair or engage in cybersex?

Work It Out

Identify the similarities and differences in your on- and offline relationships with friends. In which environment do you find it easier to self-disclose, be more blunt, and handle conflict?

flames
online insults

"I wish our marriage had a restore point."

you react when you are the target of such flaming or verbal abuse is revealing. Some people who are flamed withdraw, sit on the side, or turn away, while others counter the personal attack by replying immediately to the same audience. As with speech, the tone we imagine other persons to be using as they type their computer-mediated messages to us often becomes more important than what they actually write.[71]

In addition to the surge in online friendships, online matchmaking sites in the United States also are increasing in popularity and now reach around the world. A number of factors are driving online matchmaking, prime among them women working, young people relocating far from their family homes, and the longing for true love. The art of pairing up people has become a lucrative online business, with sites such as Match.com, eHarmony, Perfectmatch.com, and Yahoo Personals profiting.[72]

According to the Pew Internet and American Life Project, of the 92 million unmarried Americans aged 18 and older, about 16 million have tried online dating.

People from diverse cultural backgrounds respond differently to the various online dating sites. For example, U.S. users eagerly post personal profiles and photos of themselves on sites, creating a virtual bar scene. By contrast, in Asian countries, single women feel threatened by the lack of privacy such public posts create. American users find themselves attracted to eHarmony, with its deeply probing questions that assist users in coming to know themselves. Chinese users, in contrast, might be put off by such questionnaires since most have been brought up in a culture that teaches them not to look at themselves, but to look to others for information and guidance.[73]

Computers and cell phones provide us with virtual bulletin boards from which we can tell our virtual contacts about our day. From messages of love, to arguments, to suicide threats, Twitter users post mini-blogs—running diaries focusing on the myriad mundane details of their lives, posting minute-by-minute their every thought and feeling. And when their lives take a dark turn, for example, with the contemplation of suicide or a bad breakup, their network goes along with them, functioning as a life-saving or life-altering safety net, sending off Twitter entries that let the suffering person know that she or he is not alone. Does this mean that programs such as Twitter turn virtual acquaintances into people who suddenly are privy to what, at one time, would have been our innermost secrets? Or is what Twitter creates only artificial intimacy?[74]

Is it possible that cell phones are also influential in determining our friends? Longtime friendships sometimes suffer when one party to the relationship changes

Are blogs appropriate places to make personal disclosures? Do you think it is possible to learn things online about people with whom you share relationships that would be difficult to learn offline? How do you prefer to disclose your thoughts and feelings to others, on- or offline? Why?

cell phone carriers. Carriers' plans encourage talk and text messaging with people in the same network. Thus, cell phone networks have become a reflection of friendship networks.[75] Text messages have even been referred to as "symbolic gestures of friendship."[76] They are also used in romance. People commonly use their cell phones to talk and text message to set up details of dates, leading some observers to question when the date actually begins—with the sending of messages or when the parties are face-to-face. What do you think?

Let us move from friendship and romance to work. New technologies are redefining how and where we work. Greater and greater numbers of us spend significant parts of our day in front of computers (desk or laptop), on cellular telephones, and in general, less tied to the notion of a traditional office. For many of us, the office is a relic. We telecommute, linked with others by a computer network. We have more virtual contact and less and less face-to-face contact. To combat the dearth of face-to-face interaction workers have with each other, some employers go out of their way to arrange opportunities for employees to meet face-to-face for casual exchanges.

New technologies are also changing how the boss delivers both good and bad news to workers. According to one study, people are more honest when using e-mail to communicate bad news than they are with other methods, such as phone or personal delivery. When negative feedback is delivered via e-mail, it contains less sugarcoating. According to managers, e-mail also lets them dole out praise more quickly. Managers now give workers virtual pats on the back.[77]

Can you read the emotions of people you interact with online? What cues do you use?

COMMUNICATION SKILLS IN PRACTICE
GUIDELINES FOR HANDLING FEELINGS EFFECTIVELY IN RELATIONSHIPS

Many of us have trouble expressing our feelings in person and online. Either we behave nonassertively and keep our emotions too much in check, or we behave aggressively and become excessively demanding or belligerent. The result is that our emotions impede the development of healthy relationships and foster the development of unhealthy relationships.

It is sad that we are rarely, if ever, taught to reveal our emotions in ways that will help our relationships. The key to using our feelings to promote effective relationships is learning to express them effectively. The following guidelines should help you communicate feelings in positive ways and thereby enrich the quality of your interpersonal encounters and relationships.

☑ Work on Feelings You Have Difficulty Expressing or Handling

By now you should have a good idea of what feelings you have trouble expressing or responding to. Now concentrate on expressing or responding to these

Reflect and Respond

Agree or disagree with the following quotation. Supply reasons and examples from a number of relationship contexts to support your stance.

In a sense we have two brains, two minds—and two different kinds of intelligence: rational and emotional. How we do in life is determined by both—it is not just IQ, but emotional intelligence that matters.[78]

feelings when they arise. A first step is to let others know what feelings cause problems for you.

☑ Stand Up for Your Emotional Rights

When we sacrifice our rights, we teach others to take advantage of us. When we demand rights that are not ours, we take advantage of others. Not revealing your feelings and thoughts to others can be just as damaging as disregarding the feelings and thoughts of others.

☑ Check Your Perceptions

So far we've discussed *your* feelings, but what about the other person's feelings? Sometimes our interpretations of another person's feelings are determined by our own. Checking your perceptions requires that you express your assessment of others' feelings in a tentative fashion. Sample perception checks include the following: "Were you surprised at what Jim said to you?" "I get the feeling that what I said annoyed you. Am I right?" and "I'm not certain if your behavior means you're confused or embarrassed."

Focus on Service Learning

Run a seminar on emotional intelligence or anger management for a local organization. Design your seminar by using the material contained in this chapter, researching scholarly and popular articles on your selected seminar topic, and visiting Web sites such as www.eiconsortium.org or www.unh.edu/emotional_ intelligence/ or www.apa.org/ pubinfo/anger.html. Before offering your seminar, rehearse it by presenting it to a campus group.

☑ Show Respect for Feelings

Don't try to persuade yourself or others to deny honest feelings. Comments like "Don't feel that way," "Calm down," and "Don't cry over spilt milk" communicate that you believe the other person has no right to a particular feeling. Feelings are potentially constructive and should not be treated as destructive.

☑ Be Willing to Apologize

Apologies, when genuine, work wonders, diffusing tension and hostility, and restoring good will. When apologizing, begin by taking responsibility for your behavior and identifying what you did wrong. Acknowledge how what you did must have affected the other person's feelings. Explain how you could have responded differently by acknowledging one or more alternative ways of behaving. Express your sorrow and regret. Correct your behavior. End by asking for forgiveness.

☑ Practice Four Basic Assertive Behaviors

Practice the following assertive behaviors:

1. Stop automatically asking permission to speak, think, or behave. Instead of saying, "Do you mind if I ask to have this point clarified?" say, "I'd like to know if . . . " In other words, substitute declarative statements for requests for permission.

2. Establish eye contact with people with whom you interact face-to-face. Instead of looking down or to the side (cues that imply uncertainty or insecurity), look into the eyes of the person you are speaking to. This lets people know you have the confidence to relate to them honestly and directly.

3. Eliminate hesitations and fillers ("uh," "you know," "hmm") from your speech. It is better to talk more slowly and deliberately than to broadcast the impression that you are unprepared or lack self-assurance.

4. Say "no" calmly, firmly, and quietly; say "yes" sincerely and honestly; say "I want" without fear or guilt.

Revisiting Chapter Objectives

1. **Identify and distinguish among the following relationship life contexts: acquaintanceship, friendship, and romantic, family, and work relationships.**   Our relationships occur in various life contexts. Among the different kinds of relationships we share are acquaintanceships, friendships, romantic relationships, family relationships, and work relationships. While interaction with acquaintances is usually limited in scope and quality, some do develop into friendships. As friendships become closer, relationship breadth and depth are enhanced. The expectation of permanence distinguishes romantic relationships from other relationship types. We play roles in both family and work relationships. In families that practice healthy communication, family members pull together to preserve the family unit. Members of an organization who are "team players" also recognize their interdependence.

2. **Define *emotional intelligence*.**   We are experiencing some emotion to some degree at any given time. Our emotional intelligence, the ability we have to motivate ourselves, to control our impulses, to recognize and regulate our moods, to empathize, and to hope, determines how effective we are at handling feelings in our relationships.

3. **Explain how attraction, proximity, reinforcement, similarity, and complementarity affect the development of relationships.**   Among the factors that can cause us to establish relationships with some people but not others are attractiveness (we favor people who are physically attractive and who have pleasing

THE WRAP-UP

personalities), proximity (we are more apt to interact with people whom we live near or work with), reinforcement (we like being around people who reward us), similarity (we enjoy being with people whose attitudes and interests are similar to ours), and complementarity (sometimes we find ourselves attracted to people who are dissimilar to us).

4. **Discuss the sharing of feelings, including how the suppression or disclosure of feelings affects relationships.**   Feelings are at the heart of our important interpersonal relationships, and our moods may be contagious. Thus, how we deal with our emotions can influence a relationship's course. When we censor or fail to disclose our feelings, our interactions may become shallow and less fulfilling. Concealing, not expressing feelings honestly, or uncontrollably unleashing them can impede relationships.

5. **Define *assertiveness, nonassertiveness,* and *aggressiveness,* and explain how feelings can be handled effectively during conflicts.**   There are three ways of expressing feelings in emotionally charged or conflict-producing interpersonal situations: assertively (we express our feelings and thoughts honestly without infringing on the rights of others), nonassertively (we fail to express our real feelings), and aggressively (we stand up for our rights by ignoring or violating the rights of others).

6. **Build skills to effectively handle feelings in relationships.**   We need to work on feelings we have difficulty with. Standing up for our emotional rights, checking perceptions, respecting how we and others feel, and apologizing when appropriate facilitates this effort.

Resources for Further Inquiry and Reflection

To apply your understanding of how the principles in Chapter 9 are at work in our daily lives, consult the following resources for further inquiry and reflection. Or, if you prefer, choose any other appropriate resource. Then connect the ideas expressed in your chosen selection with the communication concepts and issues you are learning about both in and out of class.

 ### Listen to Me

"Un-Break My Heart" (Toni Braxton)
"Emotion" (Destiny's Child)
"Emotions" (Mariah Carey)
"Happy Together" (The Turtles)
"Song Sung Blue" (Neil Diamond)
"You Can't Hurry Love" (The Supremes)
"What's Love Got to Do with It?" (Tina Turner)
"Toxic" (Britney Spears)
"50 Ways to Leave Your Lover" (Paul Simon)

Discuss the lessons the selected song teaches about how people's feelings affect their relationships.

 ### View Me

A History of Violence	*Atonement*
Wedding Crashers	*Jungle Fever*
Just Friends	*Parenthood*
The Story of Us	*Anger Management*
A River Runs through It	*No Country for Old Men*

These films explore relationships in a specific context. Choose one film and discuss the relationship's context, what we learn from the film about the effective and/or ineffective handling of emotions, how the suppression or expression of feelings affects relationships, and how conflict can influence a relationship's course.

Read Me

Janet Evanovich. *Metro Girl*. New York: HarperTorch, 2005.
Anita Shreve. *Light on Snow*. Boston: Little, Brown, 2005.
Judith Guest. *Ordinary People*. New York: Viking Press, 1976.
Jacqueline Mitchard. *The Deep End of the Ocean*. New York: Viking Press, 1996.
Jodi Picoult. *The Tenth Circle*. New York: Washington Square, 2008.

These books are about families in crisis. Discuss how a crisis such as the untimely death, disappearance, or rape of a child affects family members. Identify the problems family members face as they try to cope with their emotions. What, if anything, do family members do to improve their communication climate and get in touch with their emotions?

 Tell Me

Share with the class the insights you gained from your chosen Listen to Me, View Me, or Read Me selection.

Discuss your opinion regarding one of the following positions: Computer-mediated communication within virtual communities is a means of widening our social relationships. Computer-mediated communication within virtual communities is a means of diminishing the need for in-person relationships.

Key Chapter Terminology

Use the Online Learning Center at www.mhhe.com/gamble10e to further your knowledge of the following terminology.

acquaintanceships 212
aggressiveness 233
assertiveness 233
complementarity 219
conflict 226
content conflict 231
ego conflict 231
emotional contagion 222
emotional intelligence 211
emotional isolationists 223
flames 235
friendly relations 213
high-intensity conflict 231
interpersonal conflict 229

intrapersonal conflict 229
low-intensity conflict 229
medium-intensity conflict 230
moving toward friendship 213
nascent friendship 214
nonassertiveness 231
pseudoconflict 231
role-limited interaction 213
self-conflict 229
stabilized friendship 214
toxic communication 215
value conflict 231
waning friendship 214

www.mhhe.com/gamble10e

Idioms in Translation

be outspoken — talk bluntly
come out of a shell — emerge from shyness
don't cry over spilt milk — don't worry about what has already been done

echo feelings — replicate emotions
lash out — attack
pouring out — revealing

Culture Cue

Compliments are often used to start conversations in the United States. Typically the person beginning an interaction compliments something the other person is wearing or has done.

LOOKING BACK AND AHEAD

Consider This Case: Breaking Up Is Hard to Do

"Hey, Hiroko, what's up?" Nick slung his backpack to the floor in Starbucks and dragged an empty chair next to his friend. "You look pretty glum."

"Nick! Hey." Hiroko made room on the table for Nick's coffee. "Good to see you. Kathy's here too." He nodded in the direction of the counter where a young woman was collecting her order. "We're both feeling down."

"What's happening?" Nick said, shrugging out of his coat.

"Casey's moving out." Casey was one of Hiroko and Kathy's housemates in their residence near campus.

"Wow, that's too bad. How come?"

"Her mom is pretty sick, so Casey's moving back home to help her dad take care of her two little brothers. She's going to have to commute to school for a while."

Kathy sat down with them and nodded a hello at Nick. "We're pretty bummed," she confirmed. "None of us knew about her mom, and we had no clue anything big like this was coming. We're drowning our sorrows in latte, right, Hiroko?"

"Latte! No way," said Hiroko. "Black coffee for me."

"Well," said Nick, "I'm sorry to hear about Casey's mom. But Casey'll still be around school, right? And all you have to do is advertise for another housemate. How about me?" he grinned.

"Funny, Nick," said Hiroko dourly. Nick had one of the few single dorm rooms on campus and treasured his privacy. "It's not that easy. I'm really worried about what losing Casey is going to mean for us."

Kathy sipped her drink and nodded. "She's so cheerful all the time, Nick. I don't know whether I can explain. When you're sitting there feeling sorry for yourself because you're the only one home on a Friday night, or you're dragging yourself off to an early class or worrying about an exam or something, Casey can just walk into the room and suddenly . . . ," she shrugged,

looking for words, "suddenly, you feel better. She knows how you feel; she knows what to say to you."

Hiroko nodded. "Not only that," he said, "but she's our peacemaker. She hates it when any of us have conflicts." He turned to Kathy. "Remember when Zack and I got into that stupid thing about who was supposed to clean up after his birthday party?" Zack was another housemate of theirs. "Remember how he invited all those extra people? I was furious at him, and he didn't even care, but Casey fixed it up between us," he said with admiration. "I don't know how, but she did it. Zack and I are cool with everything now."

"She makes our household *work*," Kathy sighed. "Everything's different when she's there. We're going to be lost without her." There was silence for a minute while Nick watched Kathy and Hiroko, who were staring into their drinks.

"Hey, come on, you two!" Nick finally said with a laugh. "You shouldn't feel so down about this! I bet you can find another housemate with no problem. Advertise, interview a few candidates, pick the most cheerful one." He reached under the table for his backpack and got ready to get up. "What's so hard about that?"

Kathy and Hiroko stared at him in disbelief.

DISCUSSION QUESTIONS

1. What are some of the interpersonal communication skills that Casey seems to have? Do you think she uses them well? Why or why not?
2. What do you think Kathy and Hiroko are feeling right now? Why?
3. How well have Kathy and Hiroko expressed their feelings to Nick?
4. What are Nick's perceptions about the housemates' situation? Is he accurately interpreting their words, their feelings, both, or neither? Explain your answer.
5. What can the housemates do to ensure that their interpersonal relationships survive Casey's departure?

LET'S GO TO THE DVD

Investigating *Rachel Getting Married*

In *Rachel Getting Married,* Kym returns home from rehab one day before her sister Rachel's marriage to Sidney, a musician. Kym's reintroduction into her dysfunctional family acts as a catalyst causing repressed conflicts to surface, precipitating an examination of interpersonal relationships, old and new. After viewing the film, respond to the following questions:

1. Pick any two characters in the film and analyze what their conversations suggest about their relationship.

2. How is the romantic relationship between Rachel and Sidney portrayed?

3. In what way does the wedding ceremony function as a metaphor for the concepts of family, friendship, and love?

4. How do the characters handle their emotions?

5. How do the characters respond when faced with interpersonal conflict?

6. What does the film reveal about the dark side of relationships?

After finishing this chapter, you should be able to

1. Define *group*, distinguishing a team as a special kind of group.

2. Provide examples of how a group's climate affects its operations.

3. Enumerate the advantages and disadvantages of group decision making and problem solving.

4. Define and distinguish among task, maintenance, and self-serving group roles.

5. Explain and provide examples of how cooperation versus competition and a defensive versus a supportive climate affect the interactions of group members.

6. Compare and contrast various decision-making methods.

7. Describe and use the reflective-thinking framework and brainstorming to increase your effectiveness at problem solving.

8. Understand how to improve group member communication.

Groups and Teams: Strategies for Decision Making and Problem Solving

Have you ever been in a group composed of difficult members? Did the members of your group undermine the group's ability to function, as do the characters in the award-winning comedy series *The Office*? Who among us has not had to interact in a group with people who act foolishly, are self-obsessed, have glaring flaws, or otherwise behave in ways that block the group's progress?

How a group's members interact with one another affects not only the group's success but also whether members want to stay in or leave the group. When it comes to your future, teamwork is one of the most important communication skills to master.[1] Global organizations need people skilled in teamwork, people who are able to work together with others to innovate, solve problems, and make decisions in a variety of settings.

Are you in love with your job? A recent survey revealed that significant numbers of people either never loved their jobs or fell out of love with them after a while.[2] Critics place some of the blame for job dissatisfaction on employers, noting that work is a relationship and needs nurturing. In an effort to improve employee satisfaction, and because of its power to transform work relationships, many contemporary organizations are emphasizing team building as the key to improving the functioning, satisfaction, and productivity of work group members.[3] Teamwork and the ability to collaborate with others are valued abilities on the open market.[4]

A team is a group of people with a strong sense of their collective identity, acting collaboratively. The members agree on their need for each other if they are to accomplish their goals. Unlike other groups, teams by definition are composed of people who have *diverse skills* and bring *different resources* to a problem or task. Teams depend on members' pooling their abilities, knowledge, and insights to solve problems and make better decisions than any single individual in the team could do acting alone. All teams are groups. However, because not every group has members contributing specialized knowledge or different resources, not every group is a team.[5] (See Figure 10.1 for a look at the differences in behavior the members of nominal (in name only) and real (functioning) teams exhibit.)

We profit from working together in groups and teams. Research suggests that teamwork can be its own reward. Researchers note that, just as desserts and money cause many of us to experience delight, so does cooperating with each other to achieve a goal. Using magnetic resonance imaging (MRI) to take portraits of the brain, researchers have shown that humans derive pleasure when they choose to forego immediate personal gain and opt instead to cooperate with others for the long-term common good.[6]

Talented administrators know that they do not know all there is to know.
—Anonymous

Not even computers will replace committees, because committees buy computers.
—Edward Shepherd Mead

FIGURE 10.1   Key Dimensions of Teams.

Groups vary on each dimension from one extreme to the other. How would you describe a group you currently belong to? Is your group a real team?

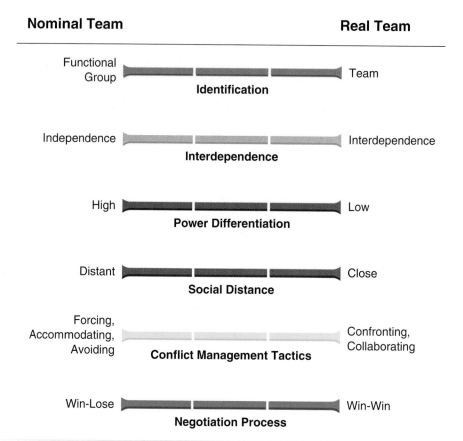

GROUPS, TEAMS, AND YOU

How important are groups and teams in your life? Try to visualize what your personal and professional life would be like if you belonged to no groups or teams. What would you miss? Some of the groups we belong to, such as the group of friends who meet for dinner once a week, are social. Some are more formally organized, such as the Parent-Teacher Association. Some, such as the Rotary Club, serve both public and private purposes. Others exist primarily to meet the needs of the organizations in which we work. Thus, groups provide much of the social fabric of our lives. In addition, they are also the basic building blocks of organizations, and when it comes to the world of work, team management is fast becoming the norm.

Over two-thirds of U.S. companies use formal work teams to accomplish their objectives.[7] Workers now participate in more groups and teams and attend more meetings than ever before. It is commonplace for committees of employees to make the kinds of decisions that "dictatorial" executives once handled. In fact, the majority of a manager's time is spent in meetings of one kind or another. Thus, today's workers and managers are experienced at participating in different kinds of groups. **Quality circles,** for example, are small groups of employees who meet regularly to discuss organizational life and the quality of their work environment. During these meetings, employees make recommendations for improving products and work procedures. **Self-directed teams** are autonomous groups in which

Online Learning Center

Go to the Online Learning Center at www.mhhe.com/gamble10e and answer the questions in the *Self Inventory* to evaluate your understanding of group interactions. View the nominal and real team animations.

quality circles

small groups of employees who meet regularly to discuss organizational life and the quality of their work environment

self-directed teams

autonomous groups of employees empowered to make decisions and supervise themselves

employees possessing an array of skills and talents work together, empowered to make decisions and even supervise themselves. Among the major companies championing such approaches are Xerox, Procter & Gamble, and General Electric.[8] Do you feel prepared to become part of such groups?

You already spend a great deal of time in groups. A large part of your socialization—your adaptation to society—occurred in your family group. Much of your leisure time is spent in the company of groups of friends. If you attend a religious service, you become part of a group. If you participate in student government, a study group, or sports, you are part of a group. As a class member, you belong to a group. Thus, from your earliest days, you have been a member of a variety of groups.

Employees spend extensive amounts of time in meetings.

CHARACTERISTICS AND COMPONENTS OF GROUPS

While defining a group can be tricky business,[9] identifying the characteristics groups have in common will help you understand how to behave more effectively when you are part of one. Although we realize that social groups are important, in these chapters we focus on the work-related decision-making, problem-solving group, also called the task group.

By the time you conclude your study of small-group communication, you will have the information you need to understand the forces that shape and modify group behavior, and the skills you need to improve the quality of interactions in task groups. The knowledge and abilities you gain will be transferable to other areas of your life.

> Our world contains over 6 billion individuals. It also contains hundreds of millions of formal and informal groups. How do the groups you belong to influence you as an individual?

Group Membership

A **group** is a collection of people. But it is not just a random assemblage of independent individuals; rather, it is composed of individuals who interact verbally and nonverbally, occupy certain roles with respect to one another, and cooperate to accomplish a definite goal. The members of a group recognize the other individuals who are part of the activity, have certain kinds of attitudes toward these people, and obtain some degree of satisfaction from belonging to or participating in the group. They acknowledge the do's and don'ts of group life, the norms that specify and regulate the behavior expected of members. Furthermore, communication

group
a collection of individuals who interact verbally and nonverbally, occupy certain roles with respect to one another, and cooperate to accomplish a goal

within a group involves more than the casual banter that occurs between strangers at bus stops or in department stores.

Group Size

What is the optimal size for a group? In task-oriented groups, it is the smallest number of people capable of handling the assigned task.[10] The larger the group, the more difficult it becomes to schedule meetings, share information, and equalize opportunities for participation.

Most group theorists and practitioners set the lower limit of group size at three members. For most tasks, groups of five to seven people work best. This size enables members to communicate directly with each other as they work on a common task or goal, such as solving problems, exchanging information, or improving interpersonal relationships.

Group Goals, Structure, and Climate

Every group establishes its own **group goals** (motivation for existing, the end state desired), **group structure** (member positions and roles), **group patterns of communication** (patterns of message flow), **group norms** (informal rules for interaction), and **group climate** (emotional atmosphere). Every participant in the group usually has a stake in the outcome, develops relationships with the other members of the group, and assumes roles and relationships that relate to group tasks and either foster or impede the group's effectiveness. Thus, the members' styles of interaction have an impact on the kind of atmosphere, or climate, that develops in the group. Conversely, the climate affects what members say to each other and how they say it. For example, have you ever belonged to a group that had too "hot" a climate—one in which members were intolerant of each other and tempers flared? Have you ever belonged to a group that had too "cold" a climate—one in which members were aloof, sarcastic, unconcerned about hurting one another's feelings, or too self-centered to notice that the needs of others were not being adequately met?

A group's climate tends to persist. If the group climate is cold, closed, mistrustful, or uncooperative, individual members frequently react in ways that perpetuate those characteristics. In contrast, if the group climate is warm, open, trusting, and cooperative, members usually react in ways that reinforce those characteristics. In the book *Communication within the Organization*, Charles Redding suggested that an effective climate is characterized by (1) supportiveness, (2) participative decision making, (3) trust among group members, (4) openness and candor, and (5) high performance goals.[11] The healthier the group climate, the more cohesive the group.

Group climate affects group norms—the explicit and implicit rules that members internalize concerning their behavior. In some groups, members exhibit certain behaviors that they would not dare exhibit in others. For example, in which groups that you belong to do you feel free to ask a question that might be considered "dumb," interrupt someone who is talking, express disagreement with another member, openly express support for an unpopular position, point out that someone is not making sense, offer a comment unrelated to the topic, or simply not attend a meeting? In some groups, interaction is formal and stuffy; in others, it is informal and relaxed. Groups invariably create standards that they expect members to live up to. In this way, a group is able to foster a certain degree of uniformity.

In Chapter 11 we take a closer look at leadership behaviors, conflict resolution, and problems that develop in groups. For now, let us recognize that

---

What are your reasons for joining a group or team? Do you or other members ever bring hidden agendas to the group? Who tends to have more hidden agendas, male or female group members?

If given the choice, would you rather work in a group composed of members with homogeneous or diverse backgrounds? Why?

---

group goals
a group's motivation for existing

group structure
group member positions and roles performed

group patterns of communication
patterns of message flow in a group

group norms
informal rules for interaction in a group

group climate
the emotional atmosphere of a group

What norm or principle of group interaction is the one most consistently violated in the groups to which you belong? Who tends to violate that norm most, men or women?

certain attributes facilitate the group process, whereas others work against it. Douglas McGregor, a recognized expert in organizational communication, summarized the characteristics of an effective and well-functioning group as follows:

1. The atmosphere tends to be informal, comfortable, and relaxed.

2. There is a lot of discussion in which virtually everyone participates, but it remains pertinent to the task.

3. The task or objective is well understood and accepted by the members. There will have been free discussion of the objective at some point, until it was formulated in such a way that the group members could commit themselves to it.

4. The members listen to each other. Every idea is given a hearing. People do not appear to be afraid of being foolish; they will offer a creative thought even if it seems fairly extreme.

5. There is disagreement. Disagreements are not suppressed or overridden by premature action. The reasons are carefully examined, and the group seeks to resolve disagreements rather than dominate dissenters.

6. Most decisions are reached by a kind of consensus in which it is clear that everyone is in general agreement and willing to go along. Formal voting is at a minimum; the group does not accept a simple majority as a proper basis for action.

7. Criticism is frequent, frank, and relatively comfortable. There is little evidence of personal attack, either overt or hidden.

8. People are free to express their feelings and their ideas about the problem and the group's operation.

9. When action is taken, clear assignments are made and accepted.

10. The chairperson of the group does not dominate it, nor does the group defer unduly to him or her. In fact, the leadership shifts from time to time, depending on the circumstances. There is little evidence of a struggle for power as the group operates. The issue is not who controls but how to get the job done.

11. The group is self-conscious of its own operation.[12]

random thoughts by archy

i have noticed that when chickens quit quarreling over their food they often find that there is enough for all of them i wonder if it might not be the same way with the human race

—*Don Marquis,* archy's life of mehitabel

© Six Chix Ann Telnaes, King Features Syndicate.

NOW REMEMBER, "JUST BECAUSE EVERYBODY ELSE IS DOING IT" IS A PLENTY GOOD ENOUGH REASON.

Do you agree with the advice given by the sheep?

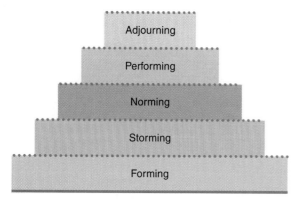

FIGURE 10.2 Stages of Group Development.

The Dynamics of Group Development

Once a group is in place, its development occurs in stages. According to researchers, the key stages that a group moves through are forming, storming, norming, performing, and adjourning.[13] (See Figure 10.2.)

Forming. Upon joining a new group, we may experience some initial confusion or uncertainty, resulting in our experiencing *primary tension*. We are unsure about how to behave or interact with others and are unclear about the roles that we will have in the life of the group. We need to figure out who is in charge and why we were brought together. Thus, in the *forming stage* of a group, our primary objective is to fit in and be perceived as likable. We also make an effort to find out about other group members and the group's task. Once we feel valued and accepted, we begin to identify with the group.

Storming. Invariably, members experience some conflict as they determine how to work together. Typically, groups experience both task and relational conflicts. During the *storming stage*, the group's members experience *secondary tension*—tension that results from members' disagreeing and/or struggling to exert leadership as they work to clarify goals and the roles members will have in the life of the group. During this stage, rather than being concerned with fitting in, members now focus on expressing their ideas and opinions and securing their place in the group power structure.

Norming. Over time, a clear group structure emerges. Members firm up roles, and a leader or leaders emerge. During the *norming stage*, the group solidifies its behavioral norms, especially those relating to conflict management. In addition, the group forms a sense of identity as member awareness of interdependence and the need to cooperate with each other increases.

Performing. The emphasis of the group then switches to task accomplishment. During the *performing stage*, often perceived as the most important stage of group development, members combine their skills, knowledge, and abilities to overcome obstacles and reach the group's goals. Group members focus on problem solving.

Adjourning. Finally, during the *adjourning stage*, members review and reflect on their accomplishments or failures and determine how or whether to end the group and the relationships that have developed. Ending a group can involve having a party or simply saying good-bye to each other, or it can be more complicated and prolonged, with some groups opting to continue working together on a new or different task, and some members choosing to continue relationships that developed during the group's life.[14]

Sometimes a group holds a celebration when its task is completed.

How a group develops through each of these stages determines how effectively it is able to function.

USING GROUPS TO MAKE DECISIONS AND SOLVE PROBLEMS

We form small groups to share information we require, to solve common problems, and to make decisions about achieving certain identified common goals. But why use a small group instead of a single person? Working in groups is both frustrating and rewarding; groups can facilitate or limit problem-solving effectiveness.

Advantages of the Small Group

In many ways, using a group to solve a complex problem is more logical than relying on one individual. Group problem solving offers a number of important advantages.

First, it permits a variety of people with different information and different points of view to contribute to the problem-solving, decision-making process. That is, a small group facilitates the pooling of resources. The broader the array of knowledge that is brought to bear on any problem, the more likely an effective solution becomes. Second, participating in a group apparently increases individual motivation. Group efforts often lead to greater commitment to finding a solution and then to greater commitment to that solution. Third, group functioning makes it easier to identify other people's mistakes and filter out errors before they can become costly or damaging. Groups are frequently better equipped than individuals to foresee difficulties, detect weaknesses, visualize consequences, and explore possibilities. As a result, they tend to produce superior decisions and solutions. Fourth, the decisions or solutions of a group tend to be better received than those of an individual. As the adage says, "There is strength in numbers." The person or persons to whom a group solution is reported will tend to respect the fact that a number of people working together came to one conclusion. Fifth, working as part of a group is generally more pleasant and fulfilling than working alone. The group provides companionship, a chance to affirm ideas and feelings, and an opportunity for self-confirmation. It is rewarding to know that others respect us enough to listen and react to what we have to say. It is even more rewarding to have our thoughts and concerns accepted by others. (These advantages are summarized in Table 10.1.)

> If, as the saying goes, "a camel is a horse designed by a committee," why do we do so much of our work in groups?

> *You know . . . everybody is ignorant, only of different subjects.*
> —Will Rogers

> Should problem solving be a team or an individual activity? Why?

> *There is a tendency to define one's own group positively in order to evaluate oneself positively.*
> —John C. Turner

> Give an example of how you have enacted the above quotation.

> Which of the advantages and disadvantages shown in Table 10.1 have you experienced when part of a group?

Table 10.1 Why Use Teamwork?

Advantages	Disadvantages
Varied resources can be pooled.	Laziness is encouraged.
Motivation and commitment are increased.	Personal goals may conflict with group goals.
Errors are easier to identify.	A few high-status members may dominate.
Decisions are better received.	Stubbornness leads to deadlock.
Rewards of working with others are provided.	Riskier decisions are made.
	Reaching a decision takes longer.

Disadvantages of the Small Group

This is not to suggest that using a group does not have potential drawbacks. Group problem solving has several disadvantages.

First, when we are working with a number of other people, it sometimes becomes very tempting to let someone else handle the duties and responsibilities. A lazy group member can maintain a low profile and simply coast along on the efforts of others. Second, personal goals sometimes conflict with group goals. As a result, people may try to use the group to achieve self-oriented objectives that might interfere with or even sabotage group objectives. Third, the decision-making, problem-solving process may be dominated by a few forceful, persistent members who do not take the time to ensure that all members have a chance to speak and be heard. Actual or perceived status plays a part here. Group members may be hesitant to criticize the comments of high-status people, and low-status people may be reluctant to participate at all. Consequently, position and power can affect whether ideas are offered, listened to, or incorporated into group decisions. Fourth, certain people who are set on having their ideas and only their ideas accepted may be unwilling to compromise. When this happens, the group decision-making machinery breaks down, and frequently no solution can be agreed on. In other words, the group becomes deadlocked. Fifth, the decisions reached and the actions taken after a group discussion are often riskier than the decisions individuals would have made or the actions individuals would have taken. This phenomenon is known as the *risky shift*. Sixth, it often takes longer to reach a group solution than an individual decision. In business and industry, where time is frequently equated with money, the group can be a costly tool. (See Table 10.1 for a summary of these drawbacks.)

> As a new employee, what problems might you experience when interacting with others in a problem-solving group?

> In a group decision, risk is inescapable. How does calculating the risk increase your chances of making a good choice?

When to Use a Group for Decision Making and Problem Solving

Groups can bring out the worst as well as the best in human decision making.
—*Irving Janis*

In view of these pros and cons, we ask: When does it make sense to use a group? At what point do the advantages outweigh the possible disadvantages?

Experience suggests that we use a group rather than an individual to make decisions and solve a problem if the answer to most of the following questions is yes:

1. Is the problem complex rather than simple?
2. Does the problem have many parts, or facets?
3. Would any one person be unlikely to possess all the information needed to solve the problem?
4. Would it be advisable to divide the responsibility for problem solving?
5. Are many potential solutions desired, rather than just one?
6. Would an examination of diverse attitudes be helpful?
7. Are group members more likely to engage in task-related than non-task-related behavior?

In these complex times, it often makes sense for individuals of varied expertise to pool their knowledge and insight to solve problems. Group effort is futile if the members pool only ignorance and obstinacy. The more information the members can gather and share, the more likely they are to rid themselves of bias, and in turn, the more objective their work becomes.[15]

UNDERSTANDING THE ROLES GROUP MEMBERS PLAY

The authors of the book *Tribal Leadership: Leveraging Natural Groups to Build a Thriving Organization* contend that, although the faces in every group are different, members in different groups really perform the same set of roles.[16]

Roles are patterns of behavior. There are roles that we expect group members to play (functional roles) because they contribute to the group's effectiveness, and roles we expect group members to refrain from playing (dysfunctional roles) because of their harmful effects on the group.

Even though their **group role-classification model** was formulated almost a half century ago, the system proposed by Kenneth Benne and Paul Sheats is still commonly used today. It describes the functions participants should seek to assume—and the functions they should avoid—during the life of a group.[17] Benne and Sheats considered goal achievement (completing the task) and group maintenance (building relationships) the two basic objectives of any group. They further reasoned that eliminating self-serving roles (nonfunctional behaviors) is a requirement or condition that must be met if the preceding goals are to be realized. Guided by these assumptions, Benne and Sheats identified three categories of roles:

1. task-oriented roles
2. maintenance-oriented roles
3. self-serving roles

group role-classification model
a model that describes functions participants should seek to assume and to avoid in groups

> What task and maintenance roles do you typically perform in groups? What different roles might you take on to improve your effectiveness as a group member?

task roles
group roles designed to help the group achieve its goals

Task-Oriented Roles

The following are among the **task roles** that help the group realize its goals:

Initiating. The member defines a problem; suggests methods, goals, and procedures; and starts the group moving along new paths or in different directions by offering a plan.

Information seeking. The member asks for facts and opinions and seeks relevant information about the problem.

Opinion seeking. The member solicits expressions of feeling and value to discover the values underlying the group effort.

Information giving. The member provides ideas and suggestions and supplies personal experiences as well as factual data.

Opinion giving. The member supplies opinions, values, and beliefs and reveals his or her feelings about what is being discussed.

Members in a group perform different roles. Which roles do you most enjoy performing? Which roles do you find most challenging?

Clarifying. The member elaborates on the ideas of others, supplies paraphrases, offers examples or illustrations, and tries to eliminate confusion and increase clarity.

Coordinating. The member summarizes ideas and tries to draw various contributions together constructively.

Evaluating. The member evaluates the group's decisions or proposed solutions and helps establish standards for judgment.

Consensus testing. The member checks on the state of group agreement to see if the group is nearing a decision.

Maintenance-Oriented Roles

maintenance roles

group roles designed to ensure the smooth running of a group

The following **maintenance roles** help the group run smoothly:

Encouraging. The member is warm, receptive, and responsive to others and praises others and their ideas.

Gatekeeping. The member attempts to keep communication channels open; he or she helps reticent members contribute to the group and works to keep the discussion from being dominated by one or two members.

Harmonizing. The member mediates differences between participants and attempts to reconcile misunderstandings or disagreements; he or she also tries to reduce tension by using humor or other forms of relief at appropriate junctures.

Compromising. The member is willing to compromise his or her position to maintain group cohesion; he or she is willing to admit error and modify beliefs to achieve group growth.

Standard setting. The member assesses whether group members are satisfied with the procedures being used and indicates that criteria have been set for evaluating group functioning.

Self-Serving Roles

self-serving roles

group roles that impede the functioning of a group by preventing members from working together effectively

Self-serving roles prevent the group from working effectively:

Blocking. The member is disagreeable and digresses in an effort to ensure that nothing is accomplished.

Aggression. The member criticizes or blames others and works to deflate the egos of other group members in an effort to enhance his or her own status.

Recognition seeking. The member attempts to become the focus of attention by boasting about his or her own accomplishments rather than dealing with the group task; he or she may speak loudly and exhibit behavior that is unusual.

Withdrawing. The member appears indifferent, daydreams, is lost in thought, or sulks.

Dominating. The member insists on getting his or her own way, interrupts others, and gives directions in an effort to run or control the group.

The Social Loafer

A common complaint expressed by students who have to work in groups is that some members end up having to do the work of other members who do not share a comparable level of commitment to the group or its task. Upon joining a group, members who function as social loafers reduce their work effort, miss meetings, or engage in otherwise dysfunctional behavior.

Why do you think that social loafers tend to be more prevalent in groups in individualistic cultures than in collectivist cultures? What steps should a group take to reduce the impact a social loafer has on other members and the group?

Joking. The member appears cynical or engages in horseplay or other inappropriate or irrelevant behaviors.

Self-confessing. The member uses other group members as an audience and reveals personal feelings or insights that are not oriented toward group concerns.

Help seeking. The member tries to elicit sympathy or pity from other members.

> What roles do you find yourself performing most frequently? What conditions in the group, or what personal needs, do you think precipitate such behavior on your part?

UNDERSTANDING GROUP MEMBER RELATIONSHIPS AND INTERACTION

In addition to the various roles played by group members, the nature of the relationships shared by the members is also highly significant in determining whether the group will operate effectively. For this reason, the following questions deserve our attention: To what extent do members of a group cooperate or compete with one another? To what extent do the members foster a defensive or a supportive environment?[18]

Cooperation versus Competition

Obviously, the personal goals of each member have an impact on the operation of a group. If individual members view their goals as congruent or coinciding, an atmosphere of cooperation can be fostered. However, if individual members see their goals as contradictory, a competitive atmosphere will develop. Too frequently, group members attempt to compete with one another when cooperating would be more beneficial to the group. Psychologists Linden L. Nelson and Spencer Kagen believe that it is irrational and self-defeating to compete if cooperating makes better sense.[19] When a group experience develops into a dog-eat-dog situation, all the members may go hungry.

> How do you act in a group when facing situations you define as cooperative? When facing situations you define as competitive? To what extent does the sex of the other group members appear to make a difference?

Few factors do more to damage a group's ability to maintain itself and complete a task than competition among members, yet highly competitive individuals do belong to groups and do, in fact, affect the group's communication climate and emergent goal structure. The term *goal structure* describes the way members relate to each other. Under a **cooperative goal structure,** the members of a group work together to achieve their objectives, and the goals of each person are perceived as compatible with or complementary to those of the others. Group members readily pool resources and coordinate their efforts to obtain what they consider common aims. In contrast, when a group develops a **competitive goal structure,** members do not share resources or coordinate efforts. Consciously or unconsciously, individuals work to hinder one another's efforts to obtain the goal. According to psychologist Morton Deutsch, group members who have a competitive orientation believe that they can achieve their goals only if other members fail to do so.[20]

cooperative goal structure

a goal structure in which the members of a group work together to achieve their objectives

competitive goal structure

a goal structure in which members hinder one another's efforts to obtain a goal

Supportiveness versus Defensiveness

Defensive behavior occurs when a group member perceives or anticipates a threat. When you feel yourself becoming defensive, you may experience one or more of the following symptoms: a change in voice tone (as you become nervous, your throat and vocal mechanism grow tense and your vocal pitch tends to rise), a tightening of your muscles and some degree of rigidity throughout your body, and a rush of adrenaline accompanied by an urge to fight or flee. Now let us examine the behaviors that can precipitate such reactions.

In general, we tend to become defensive when we perceive others as attacking our self-concept. In fact, when we behave defensively, we devote a great amount of energy to defending the self. We become preoccupied with thinking about how the self appears to others, and we become obsessed with discovering ways to make others see us more favorably. When a member of a group becomes overly

defensive behavior

behavior that occurs when one perceives a threat

When did you last behave defensively in a group? What precipitated such a response from you? How did your response affect others?

Supportiveness enhances group relationships.

Table 10.2 Behaviors Characteristic of Defensive and Supportive Climates

Defensive Climate	Supportive Climate
1. Evaluation	1. Description
2. Control	2. Problem orientation
3. Strategy	3. Spontaneity
4. Neutrality	4. Empathy
5. Superiority	5. Equality
6. Certainty	6. Provisionalism

concerned with self-protection, he or she may compensate either by withdrawing or by attacking the other members. When this happens, the conditions necessary for the maintenance of the group begin to deteriorate. In short, defensive behavior on the part of one group member gives rise to defensive listening in others. The postural, facial, and vocal cues that accompany words can also raise the defense level. Once the defensiveness of a group member is aroused, that person no longer feels free to concentrate on the actual meaning of messages others are trying to send. Instead, the defensive member feels compelled to distort messages. Thus, as group members become more and more defensive, they become less and less able to process each other's emotions, values, and intentions accurately. For this reason, the consequences of defensiveness include destroyed or badly damaged individual relationships, continuing conflicts and increased personal anxiety within the group, wounded egos, and hurt feelings.

Before we can work to eliminate or even reduce defensiveness in our group relationships, we must understand the stimuli that can cause us to become defensive in the first place. Sociological researcher Jack R. Gibb identified six behaviors that cause defensiveness and six contrasting behaviors that allay or reduce the perceived level of threat (see Table 10.2).[21]

Online Learning Center

Go to the Online Learning Center at www.mhhe.com/gamble10e to view the clip that shows examples of defensive and supportive communication.

Evaluation versus description. Group relationships can run into trouble if a member makes judgmental or evaluative statements. As Gibb notes in the article "Defensive Communication," "If by expression, manner of speech, tone of voice, or verbal content the sender seems to be evaluating or judging the listener, then the receiver goes on guard."[22] Although it is true that some people do not mind having their actions praised, it is also true that most of us do mind having our actions condemned; moreover, whether judgment is positive or negative, the anticipation of judgment can hinder the creation of an open communication climate. In contrast to evaluative statements, descriptive statements recount particular observable actions without labeling those behaviors as good or bad, right or wrong. Instead, you simply report or question what you saw, heard, or felt.

Control versus problem orientation. Communication that group members see as seeking to control them can arouse defensiveness. In other words, if your intent is to control other group members, to get them to do something or change their beliefs, you are likely to evoke resistance. How much resistance you meet depends on how openly you approach these people and on whether your behavior causes them to question or doubt your motives. When we conclude that someone is trying to control us, we also tend to conclude that he or she considers us ignorant or unable to make our own decisions. A problem orientation, however, promotes the opposite response. When senders communicate that they have not already formulated solutions and will not force their opinions on us, we feel free to cooperate in solving the problems at hand.

Strategy versus spontaneity. Our defensiveness increases if we feel that another group member is using a strategy or is trying to put something over on us. No one likes to be conned or to be the victim of a hidden plan. We are suspicious of strategies that are concealed or tricky. We do not want others to make decisions for us and then try to persuade us that we made the decisions ourselves. Thus, when we perceive ourselves as being manipulated, we become defensive and self-protective. In contrast, spontaneous behavior that is honest and free of deception reduces defensiveness. Under such conditions, the receiver feels no need to question the motivations of the sender, and trust is engendered.

Neutrality versus empathy. Neutrality is another behavior that increases defensiveness in group members. We need to feel that others empathize with us, like us, and see us as worthwhile and valued. We need to feel that others care about us and will take the time to establish a meaningful relationship with us. If, instead of communicating empathy, warmth, and concern, a group member communicates neutrality or indifference, we may well see this as worse than rejection.

Superiority versus equality. Our defensiveness is aroused if another group member communicates feelings of superiority about social position, power, wealth, intelligence, appearance, or other characteristics. When we receive such a message, we tend to react by attempting to compete with the sender, by feeling frustrated or jealous, or by disregarding or forgetting the sender's message altogether. On the other hand, a sender who communicates equality decreases our defensive behavior. We perceive him or her as willing to develop a shared problem-solving relationship with us, as willing to trust us, and as feeling that any differences between us are unimportant.

Certainty versus provisionalism. The expression of absolute certainty or dogmatism on the part of a group member will probably succeed in making us defensive. We are suspicious of those who believe they have all the answers, view themselves as our guides rather than our fellow travelers, and reject all information that we attempt to offer. In contrast, an attitude of provisionalism or open-mindedness encourages the development of trust. We perceive people who communicate a spirit of provisionalism—instead of attempting to win arguments, to be right, and to defend their ideas to the bitter end—as flexible and open.

DECISION MAKING IN GROUPS: REACHING GOALS

Thus far, we have established what a group is, the stages groups pass through during their development, and when and why it makes sense to use a group. In the process, we noted that every group member performs roles, and every group has a goal—a reason for existing. We turn now to examining how groups reach their goals.

In our society, we usually relegate critical decisions to groups. Depending on the group, a wide variety of decision-making strategies or approaches may be used. In this section, we investigate the diverse methods members can adopt to arrive at a decision, as well as the advantages and disadvantages of each approach. Let's start by considering these questions: How do the groups to which you belong make decisions? Do different groups use different strategies? Why? Does the method any one group uses change from time to time? Why? Are you happy with each group's approach?

Strategies: Methods of Decision Making

Before we examine the different methods that groups use in making decisions, consider the following list to decide which decision-making strategy or strategies a group you belong to would employ most often if you had your way. Do this by ranking the possibilities from 1 (your first choice) to 8 (your last choice).

_____ Ask an expert to decide.

_____ Flip a coin.

_____ Let the majority rule.

_____ Let the group leader decide.

_____ Stall until a decision no longer needs to be made.

_____ Let the minority rule, because that is sometimes fair.

_____ Determine the average position, since this is least likely to be offensive to anyone.

_____ Reach a **decision by consensus;** that is, be certain all have had input into the discussion, understand the decision, can rephrase it, and will publicly support it.

Then consider the implications of your ranking.

An effective group bases its decision-making strategy on a number of variables, including (1) the nature of the problem, (2) the time available to solve the problem, and (3) the kind of climate in which the group is operating or would prefer to operate.

Experience reveals that methods of group decision making vary considerably in their effectiveness. Majority vote is the method used most frequently. Most elections are decided and many laws are passed using this approach, and a large

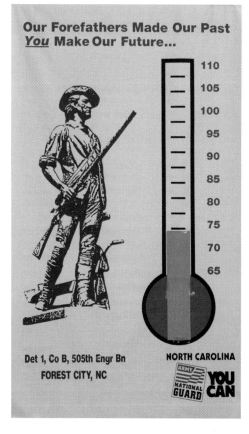

Our Forefathers Made Our Past *You* Make Our Future...

Det 1, Co B, 505th Engr Bn
FOREST CITY, NC

NORTH CAROLINA
ARMY NATIONAL GUARD
YOU CAN

decision by consensus
a decision that all members understand and will support, reached as a result of members' voicing feelings and airing differences

> Identify the methods of decision making that are used most often in your class, at home, and at work. Are you satisfied with them? Why?

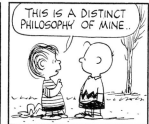

Ethics and Communication

Group Polarization

There is a tendency in decision making that involves a movement toward *group polarization,* in which discussion is found to strengthen the average inclination of group members. For example, when business students were asked to imagine themselves having to decide whether to invest more money in the hope of preventing losses in various failing projects, individually 72 percent chose to reinvest money, while in groups 94 percent came to that decision.[23] Discussion with like-minded people strengthens existing views. How might such a trend influence the beliefs of prejudiced and unprejudiced persons when it comes to issues involving racial profiling, affirmative action, and those responsible for increases in crime? How might it influence the thinking of like-minded terrorist groups?

According to Malcolm Gladwell, the author of *Blink,* snap decisions (rapid cognitions) can be valid, useful, and often better than those based on prolonged, rational analyses. In your opinion, do snap decisions help or impede group problem solving?

---

number of other decisions are made on the basis of the vote of at least 51 percent of a group's members. Lest we overlook the importance of the minority, however, we should note that it, too, can carry weight. Think of how often committees subdivide responsibilities, with the result that subgroups actually end up making the key recommendations and thus the key decisions.

Another popular decision-making strategy is averaging, by which the most popular decision becomes the group's decision.

Letting the expert member decide what the group should do is also fairly common. In this case, the group simply defers its decision-making power to its most knowledgeable member.

In many groups the leader retains all the decision-making power. Sometimes this is done after consultation with group members; at other times it is done without consultation.

Although each of these methods has been used successfully by a variety of groups, the most effective decision-making strategy is decision by consensus. When a group achieves consensus, all members agree on the decision. Even more important, all of them help formulate the decision by voicing their feelings and airing their differences of opinion. Thus, they all understand the decision and will support it.

The greater the involvement of members in the decision-making process, the more effective the decision will be. Of course, decisions by a leader, by an expert, or by a majority or minority vote all take less time than consensus; however, it is the group that will usually be responsible for implementing the decision. If members disagree with a decision or do not understand it, they may not work very hard to make it succeed. A leader may make routine decisions or may be called on to make decisions when little time is available for a real discussion of the issues; under most circumstances, however, one person cannot be the best resource for all decisions. A drawback of the decision-by-expert method is that it is sometimes difficult to determine who the expert is. Also, decision by an expert—like decision by a leader—fails to involve other group members. Decision by averaging, on the whole, is superior to either decision by a leader or decision by an expert. With averaging, all members can be consulted and individual errors will cancel each other out, and an average position will usually not dissatisfy anyone too much. On the other hand, an average position usually does not satisfy anyone very much; thus, commitment to the decision tends to be rather low.

Under most circumstances, the quality of decision making and the satisfaction of the participants are higher when a group seeks consensus. Consensus puts the resources of the entire group to effective use, permits discussion of all issues and alternatives, and ensures the commitment of all members. It is not the decision alone that is important in group interaction; also of concern are the reactions and feelings of group members.

Questions for Decision Makers: Facts, Values, and Policies

The actual content of decision making is based on three key kinds of questions: questions of fact, questions of value, and questions of policy.

Questions of fact focus on the truth or falsity of a statement. Existing information may be inconsistent or contradictory, and group members try to ferret out the truth. For example, a group might seek to determine whether evidence proved beyond a doubt that Scott Peterson was involved in the murder of his wife, Laci, or that former vice president Dick Cheney was implicit in exposing the identity of CIA agent Valerie Plame. In contrast, **questions of value** are not factual; they involve subjective judgments. "Who was the best president to serve in the past 100 years?" and "How desirable are physical fitness programs?" are questions of value. **Questions of policy** help us determine what future actions, if any, we should take. In fact, the key word in a question of policy is the word *should:* "What should colleges do to prevent student suicides?" "What should the United States do to discourage terrorism?"

questions of fact
questions involving the truth or falsity of a statement

questions of value
questions involving subjective judgments

questions of policy
questions designed to help determine future actions

A Framework for Decision Making: Reflective Thinking

The quality of a group's decisions depends at least partly on the nature of its decision-making system. There is a generally agreed-upon structure, consisting of several stages, which, if used properly, can increase the problem-solving effectiveness of most groups. This is called the **reflective-thinking framework.** It was first proposed by John Dewey in 1910. It is probably still the sequence most groups commonly use.[24]

reflective-thinking framework
a system for decision making and problem solving that is designed to encourage critical inquiry

The reflective-thinking framework has six basic components:

1. What is the problem? Is it clearly defined? Do we understand the general situation in which it is occurring? Is it stated so as not to arouse defensiveness? Is it phrased so as not to permit a simple yes or no answer? (For example, "What should the college's policy be toward final exams for seniors?" instead of "Should the college stop wasting the time of its seniors and eliminate final exams?" and "What should the government's policy be toward gun control?" instead of "Should the government restrain trigger-happy hunters?")

2. What are the facts of the situation? What are its causes? What is its history? Why is it important? Whom does it affect, and how?

3. What criteria must an acceptable solution meet? By which and whose standards must a solution be evaluated? What are the principal requirements of the solution? How important is each criterion?

4. What are the possible solutions? How would each remedy the problem? How well does each satisfy the criteria? What are the advantages and disadvantages of each?

5. Which is the best solution? How would you rank the solutions? Which offers the greatest number of advantages and the smallest number of disadvantages? Would some combination of solutions be beneficial?

6. How can the solution be implemented? What steps need to be taken to put the solution into effect?

To make this framework function, every member of the group must suspend judgment. Group members must be open to all available ideas, facts, and opinions. They must guard against early concurrence, which could force them to conclude the discussion prematurely. All data and alternative courses of action must be appraised thoroughly. Instead of insisting on your own position and closing yourself to new information, you need to explore all the major variables that contributed to the problem and investigate all the major issues that may be involved in producing a workable solution.

As you make your way through the framework, ask yourself if (1) the resources of all the group members are being well used, (2) the group is using its time to advantage, (3) the group is emphasizing fact-finding and inquiry, (4) members are listening to and respecting one another's opinions and feelings, (5) pressure to conform is being kept to a minimum while an honest search for diverse ideas is made, and (6) the atmosphere is supportive (noncritical), trusting (nonthreatening), and cooperative (noncompetitive). Remember, if group members are afraid to speak up, closed-minded, reluctant to search for information, or unmotivated, they will not perform effectively.

The Search for Better Ideas: Brainstorming

Life is the sum of all your choices.

—Albert Camus

According to Jay Cocks, a business theorist and writer, "In an era of global competition, fresh ideas have become the most precious raw materials."[25] Where do fresh ideas come from? Betty Edwards, author of *Drawing on the Right Side of the Brain*, believes that fresh ideas come from developing creative problem-solving skills, as well as from encouraging creativity in the workplace.[26] To prepare students to meet the demands of the twenty-first century, colleges and universities across the country are offering entire courses on creativity and creative problem solving.

In his now classic book on idea generation, *A Technique for Producing Ideas*, advertising copywriter James Webb Young suggested that any new idea owed its birth to the ability of others to see new relationships between known facts. In other words, we create new ideas by combining old elements in new ways. First published in 1939, but reissued and still referred to, Young's book offers a guide to jump-starting idea generation, a skill much needed in an age of increased global competition.[27] Why is this important to you? If you can come up with new creative solutions, you may find yourself of greater value to the companies and corporations of today and tomorrow. James Webb Young was not alone in searching for creative ways to develop new ideas. Following on Young's contributions, management consultants introduced **brainstorming,** a key technique we rely on to thaw frozen patterns of thinking and encourage creativity. What is brainstorming?

brainstorming
a technique designed to generate ideas

A number of researchers suggest that the best way to have a good idea is to have lots of ideas. Frequently, however, instead of suspending judgment and permitting ideas to develop freely, problem solvers tend to grasp at the first solution that comes to mind. Recognizing that this practice inhibits the search for new avenues of thought, Alex Osborn devised a technique called brainstorming.[28] This method is used primarily to promote a free flow of ideas and can be incorporated into the problem-solving process. For instance, although groups use brainstorming most frequently when members are attempting to identify a solution, it can also be used to help identify the factors causing a problem, the criteria that a solution should meet, and ways to implement the solution.

Work It Out

In a group, brainstorm how to improve some aspect of college life. Compare and contrast the system you developed with the system currently in operation. Ask others outside your group to identify the extent to which your proposed new system simplifies or complicates the system currently in use.

While today most people know what brainstorming means, too few have been taught to do it correctly.[29] To ensure your group brainstorming sessions are effective, group members need to follow these guidelines:

1. Temporarily suspend judgment. That is, do not evaluate or criticize ideas. Instead, adopt a "try anything" attitude. This will encourage rather than stifle the flow of ideas.

2. Encourage freewheeling. The wilder the ideas that are offered, the better. It is easier to tame a wild idea later than it is to replace or invigorate an inert idea. At this point, the practicality of an idea is not of primary importance.

3. Think of as many ideas as you can. At this stage, it is the quantity—not the quality—of ideas that is important. The greater the number of ideas, the better the chance of finding a good one. Thus, in a brainstorming session, no self-censorship or group censorship is permitted. All ideas should be expressed.

4. Build on and improve or modify the ideas of others. Work to mix ideas until they form interesting combinations. Remember, brainstorming is a group effort.

5. Record all ideas. This ensures that the group will have available all the ideas that have been generated during the session.

6. Only after the brainstorming session is finished should group members evaluate the ideas for usefulness and applicability.

I had an immense advantage over many others dealing with the problem inasmuch as I had no fixed ideas derived from long-established practice to control and bias my mind, and did not suffer from the general belief that whatever is, is right.
—*Henry Bessemer (discoverer of a new way of making steel)*

Brainstorming is effective because it lessens the inhibitions of members and makes it easier for them to get their ideas heard; it promotes a warmer, more playful, enthusiastic, and cooperative atmosphere; and it encourages each individual's potential for creativity. But the unique aspect of brainstorming—and perhaps its most important benefit—is suspended judgment.

Too often, one or two group members stifle the creative-thinking effort of a brainstorming group. Despite the lip service they may pay to suspending judgment, they have come to the problem-solving experience with an evaluative mind-set. According to consultant Sidney Parnes, who studies creative thinking and coined

killer phrases

comments that stop the flow of ideas

killer looks

looks that discourage or inhibit the generation of ideas

the term **killer phrases,** this attitude pops up in responses like: "That won't work," "We tried that idea before," "You've got to be joking!" Such comments stop the flow of ideas.[30]

This practice strikes at the heart and nature of brainstorming. It replaces the green light of brainstorming not so much with a yellow light of criticism or thoughtful evaluation as with a red light of frozen judgment. Killer phrases are often accompanied (or replaced) by **killer looks**—looks that discourage or inhibit the generation of ideas. (How often do killer phrases or looks intrude upon your group experiences?) By gaining insight into these types of killers and their effects, you can increase your ability to analyze your own behavior and change it if necessary.

The following classic example describes how to foster creativity in the workplace:

> Pamela Webb Moore, director of naming services (she helps companies figure out good names for their products at Synectics, a creativity consulting firm), uses a number of techniques to encourage creativity.
>
> One technique she uses to limber up the minds of tightly focused corporate managers is "sleight of head." While working on a particular problem, she'll ask clients to pretend to work on something else. In one real-life example, a Synectics-trained facilitator took a group of product development and marketing managers from the Etonic shoe corporation on an "excursion," a conscious walk away from the problem—in this case, to come up with a new kind of tennis shoe.
>
> The facilitator asked the Etonic people to imagine they were at their favorite vacation spot. "One guy," Moore says, "was on a tropical island, walking on the beach in his bare feet. He described how wonderful the water and sand felt on his feet, and he said, 'I wish I could play tennis barefoot.' The whole thing would have stopped right there if somebody had complained that while his colleague was wandering around barefoot, they were supposed to come up with a shoe. Instead, one of the marketing people there was intrigued, and the whole group decided to go off to play tennis barefoot on a rented court at 10 at night."
>
> While the Etonic people played tennis, the facilitator listed everything they said about how it felt. The next morning, the group looked at her assembled list of comments, and they realized that what they liked about playing barefoot was the lightness of being without shoes, and the ability to pivot easily on both the ball of the foot and the heel. Nine months later, the company produced an extremely light shoe called the Catalyst, which featured an innovative two-piece sole that made it easier for players to pivot.[31]

> Do you see a problem as a game or as work? According to organizational behavior teacher Mary Ann Glyn, people who see problems as games come up with more creative solutions than those who consider the same problems work.

Skill Builder

Problem Solving in Organizations

While work groups use a variety of problem-solving methods, including reflective thinking, three other frequently employed techniques include the nominal group technique, the Delphi method, and quality circles. How might your college use each of the following methods to solve a particular problem it faces? Be specific. Which method do you think you would find the most satisfying?

The nominal group technique uses limited discussion, reaching a group decision by secret vote. Especially valuable when group members are reluctant to voice their opinions, perhaps because the issue under discussion is extremely controversial and they do not want their idea attacked, this method enables each group member to contribute equally. The system involves a series of steps that alternates individual work and discussion. (1) The problem is defined for group members. (2) Without having any discussion, every group member writes down ideas for possible solutions to the problem. (3) Going in round-robin sequence, each member, in turn, offers one idea on his or list. The offered ideas are recorded in order on a flip chart or an overhead, so that everyone can see them, until all ideas are exhausted. Duplicate ideas on the list are eliminated. Overlapping ideas on the list are combined. (4) Members clarify ideas. (5) Privately and in writing, every member ranks the listed suggestions. (6) Member rankings are combined to produce a group ranking. (7) Discussion, clarification, and reordering, if necessary, ensue. (8) The ideas with the highest rankings are put into practice.

The Delphi method depends for its effectiveness on a selected group of experts, who do not communicate directly with each other but, instead, respond to a series of questionnaires. It is especially useful when you want to involve all members in finding a solution, when you want to prevent a dominant member from unduly influencing other members, and/or if it would be inconvenient or impossible to get participants physically together in the same location. It, too, contains a series of steps. (1) The problem is defined and the contribution needed from each member is specified. (2) Each member contributes ideas in writing. (3) The ideas provided by all members are combined and redistributed to the members. (4) Members choose the three or four best ideas. (5) Another list is created, using these contributions, and is distributed to members. (6) Members select and submit one or two ideas from the new list. (7) Using these responses, another list is created and distributed to members. (8) The solutions are identified and shared with all members.

A quality circle is a group of employees, often with different areas of expertise and from different levels in an organization's hierarchy, whose task it is to explore and make recommendations for improving the quality and usually the profitability of an organizational function. They use any problem-solving technique they desire to achieve their goal. At the same time, by becoming involved in the decision-making process, workers feel more empowered, bond to the organization, and develop better morale. The goal of any organization should be continual improvement.

Brainstorming is also related to what researcher Rosabeth Moss Kanter calls **kaleidoscope thinking.** According to Kanter,

> A kaleidoscope takes a set of fragments and forms them into a pattern. But when the kaleidoscope is twisted or approached from a new angle, the same fragments form a different pattern. Kaleidoscope thinking, then, involves taking existing data and twisting it or looking at it from another angle in order to see and analyze the new patterns that appear.[32]

kaleidoscope thinking
the taking of existing data and twisting it or looking at it from another angle

Fishboning is a structured brainstorming technique groups use to aid the search for solutions to problems such as poor gas mileage. When using this technique, group members first create a diagram that resembles a fishbone. Two other names for fishbone diagrams are *cause-and-effect diagrams* and *Ishikawa diagrams* (after Kaoru Ishikawa, who created the system). As shown in Figure 10.3, the problem or effect is placed at the fishbone's head, or right side of the diagram, and the problem's possible cause or effects in their order of probable occurrence or significance are positioned as if growing out the fishbone's spine. Subcauses are also shown as contributors to the primary causes.

FIGURE 10.3

Fishbone Technique.

Groups use the fishbone technique to identify the possible causes of a problem however remote they may seem. How can such brainstorming help in the search for an effective solution?

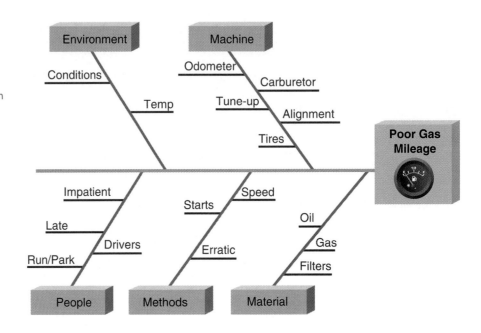

GENDER, CULTURE, AND GROUP INTERACTION

The gender and the cultural backgrounds of a group's members provide a set of unstated assumptions and rules that guide their behavior and affect the group.[33]

Gender and Group Member Behavior

Although 52 percent of all middle managers in corporations are now women, there has been a leveling off in the number of women serving on the prime decision-making and control group in corporations, the board of directors. Women currently hold approximately 14.8 percent of seats on the boards of Fortune 500 companies.[34] However, according to Catalyst, an organization focused on women in the workplace, companies with more female directors not only outperform their rivals financially, but also end up having more female managers serving in them. Female directors help diffuse stereotypes about women in the workplace and serve as powerful role models for more junior colleagues.[35]

Whether serving on boards or working in other kinds of work groups, on average, men and women are likely to focus on different aspects of a group's life and use power differently. Whereas men tend to be more goal oriented, concentrating on the group's task-related matters, women tend to pay more attention to the relationships among group members, displaying more signs of liking or immediacy toward each other. In addition, in contrast to men, who display more signs of power or potency, women tend to be more patient, offering positive responses to one another. Men also are more likely to offer comments that are more objective, compared with women, who tend to be more comfortable sharing subjective opinions.[36]

When it comes to the exercise of power in groups, in contrast to most men, who perceive power as finite, something to be guarded for oneself and used to enhance personal status, most women perceive power as unlimited, as something to share, and as a resource for empowering others.[37]

As to problem analysis, women tend to analyze problems holistically, whereas men analyze problems in a more linear fashion, looking for cause-and-effect relationships. Studies of mixed-sex groups indicate that because men and women contribute in unique ways to a group, having them work together enhances group productivity.[38]

Culture and Group Member Behavior

The cultural backgrounds of group members similarly affect the nature of communication in the work group or team. The good news is that increasing group member diversity leads to more effective problem solving and also enhances the satisfaction of members.[39]

When working in a diverse group, members need to understand how cultural factors influence behavior. For example, since African-American culture in the United States is an oral culture, both verbal inventiveness and playfulness are highly valued. As a result, African Americans rely on back-channel responses (saying things such as "That's right" or "Go on" to indicate their interest and involvement in the discussion). Because European Americans do not tend to use back-channel responses as frequently, African Americans may perceive them as underreactive in the group's communication. In contrast, European Americans may perceive the African Americans as overreactive.

Based on their cultural background, which group member do you imagine would find it more problematic or frustrating to work in a group—a person from an individualistic or a collectivist culture? Because they may experience difficulty focusing on the goals of the group, as opposed to their personal goals, in general, members from cultures that emphasize individual perspectives find working in groups more challenging.[40]

Persons from collectivistic cultures, such as those of Japan, China, and Pakistan, tend to be more conforming in groups than do persons from individualistic cultures, such as those of the United States, Great Britain, Australia, and Canada, who place a greater value on competition and dissent. In Japan, for instance, an organization's members have been taught to feel a sense of obligation to those who provide them with security, care, and support. When paired with the sense of dependency, a force called *on* results. *On* links persons in the group forever because the Japanese believe obligation continues throughout life. Hence, because nothing can be decided without a consideration of how the outcomes will influence everyone involved, consensus seeking, although not time efficient, becomes a priority.[41] Since collectivists use group norms rather than individual goals to guide their participation, they are also likely to be group players, and stress harmony and cooperation.[42] Individualists, on the other hand, are more apt to dominate group discussions and more prone to want to win in decision making. They are more likely to voice their disagreement, unlike collectivists, who prefer to slowly assess the feelings and moods of group members without verbalizing their objections or doubts. Consensus seeking does not come as easy to individualists as it does to collectivists.[43]

Globalization has led to a plethora of culturally mixed work groups with managers from Western countries having to interact with peers from diverse cultures. For example, it is becoming more common to have French, American, German, and Japanese workers on the same project team. Group members from Western cultures soon discover that persons from collectivist cultures find it more difficult than they do to be free and open in their expression of opinion. More commonly, members of collectivist cultures refrain from bringing issues they question into the open because of the difficulty they have expressing their views directly. Faced with this practice, in order to ensure effective discussion and decision making, some Western corporations are encouraging the use of a number of "foreign inspired decision making style" practices among their collectivist partners including (1) the coaxing of group members to speak up and challenge each other, and (2) advocating for consensus decision-making in place of the sometimes-required unanimous consent. With practice, group members are also finding that common goals help overcome cultural differences.[44]

The makeup of a group also influences the nature of the group's goals and whether they will be short- or long-term in nature. Members of Western cultures tend to focus on short-term goals that deliver more immediate payoffs whereas members of East Asian cultures are more patient and willing to defer gratification and thus more likely to seek long-range goals. Group members need to work out their differences in goal orientation to work together harmoniously.

Another variant of culture, age or generational diversity, is also leading companies to grapple with how generational differences affect teamwork. In contemporary workplaces, it is not uncommon to have members from three postwar generations working together on a single project. Age-diverse, multigenerational groups present different kinds of challenges, as is evidenced by a new book called *4genR8tns*.[45] For example, a group's more mature members may become irritated by the impatience exhibited by their group's younger members who think that group meetings take too long to plan and once planned consume too much of their time. Members from earlier generations soon realize that their group's younger members want the time they spend working in groups to be not only meaningful but also enjoyable. In addition, while members from the boomer generation may prefer to display their group's work via a PowerPoint presentation, younger members might well favor report methods that are more interactive. Because younger members also seek regular feedback on the contributions they make toward their

Workplaces are multi-generational. How do the members of your generation approach group work?

group's goal, the group's more mature members can improve group effectiveness by remembering to offer such input regularly.[46]

It is not advisable to follow blanket stereotypes, but, on average, each generation has different preferences regarding group work: (1) Boomers tend to be competitive, to be driven to succeed, and like being singled out for praise, (2) gen Xers tend to be skeptical and independent minded, dislike bureaucracy and formality, and prefer casual meetings, and (3) gen Ys tend to favor teamwork, feedback, and the use of technology. As a result, participating in multigenerational work teams requires each generation to adjust and shift attitudes as they work out their differences. The development of an inclusive workplace culture facilitates this process.

TECHNOLOGY AND GROUPS: GROUPS IN CYBERSPACE

When interacting via the Web, the best way to solve a problem is to rely on an extensive network. In the online world, the person who provides needed information, advice, or an answer to a problem may be on the periphery of a group, as compared to the face-to-face world, when group members share extremely strong links and typically know each other better. Groups now link with others using social networks that have weaved themselves into the fabric of group life by putting workers and others in touch with one another, giving users access to larger, more interrelated pools of information.[47] In effect, online social networks have moved group communication into alternative meeting environments. When online, highly creative teams interact via a "pulsing star" pattern, in which they fan out to gather information and then regroup to share what they discover.[48]

LinkedIn is a social network for professionals who join it primarily to network and connect with other professionals who they use to help them solve daily business problems. One LinkedIn product, Company Groups, automatically gathers all the employees from a company who use LinkedIn into a single, private Web forum. Once in the forum, employees can ask and answer questions, share and discuss information about themselves and their responsibilities, and collaborate on projects. Similar to LinkedIn are Townsquare and SharePoint, which enable a company's employees to follow one another's activities.[49] Connectbeam is a consultancy that sets up secure social networks for the corporate intranets of Fortune 500 companies that do not want workers putting information on social networking sites such as Facebook, which use servers beyond the company's control.

Other sites such as Second Life allow group members to create avatars (digital representations of themselves) that facilitate lifelike collaboration. Group members who use virtual sites report feeling more comfortable talking and expressing ideas or calling things into question even though they would not display such behavior in real-world meetings because of feelings of intimidation.[50] Social networking gets employees talking, brainstorming, and cooperating across the organization, fostering the sharing of information and the collection of ideas.

Group members can also use Twitter—a kind of hyper-grapevine news resource that makes members available to each other—openly texting or instant messaging one another, resolving issues, and getting instant feedback on what they're thinking of doing or on individual contributions to a project. Because "twitterers" need to say what they have to say in 140 characters or less, the medium encourages conciseness.[51]

COMMUNICATION SKILLS IN PRACTICE
HOW TO IMPROVE GROUP MEMBER COMMUNICATION

If a problem-solving group is to be effective in a real or an online setting, certain characteristics need to be present, and concerned members must work to develop these qualities. By becoming aware of the difference between optimal problem-solving behaviors and the actual behaviors you and your fellow group members exhibit, you can begin to improve your group's method and style of operation.

An effective group exhibits the following characteristics:

☑ Group Goals Are Clearly Understood and Cooperatively Formulated by the Members

As theorists Bobby R. Patton and Kim Giffin stressed, "If we aim at nothing, we are pretty apt to hit it."[53]

☑ All Members of the Group Are Encouraged to Communicate Their Ideas and Feelings Freely

Keynote phrases are "I think," "I see," and "I feel." These phrases reveal a personal point of view and indicate that you recognize that someone else may feel, think, or see differently than you do.

☑ Group Members Seek to Reach a Consensus When the Decision Is Important

Input from all members is sought. Each member's involvement is considered critical. Thus, the decision is not left to an authority to make on the basis of little or no discussion.

☑ Consideration Is Given to Both the Task and Maintenance Dimensions of the Problem-solving Effort

Both the quality of the decision and the well-being of the group members are considered important.

☑ Group Members Do Not Set about Problem Solving Haphazardly

A problem-solving framework is used, and an outline is followed that aids the group in its search for relevant information.

☑ Motivation Is High

Group members are eager to search for information, speak up, listen to others, and engage in an active and honest search for a better solution.

☑ An Effort Is Made to Assess the Group's Problem-solving Style

Group members identify and alleviate factors that impede the group's effectiveness as well as identify and foster factors that enhance its effectiveness.

☑ The Environment Is Open and Supportive

Group members feel free to contribute ideas and feelings. They also believe that others will listen to their ideas.

☑ The Climate Is Cooperative

To guard against destructive competition and foster a cooperative orientation, members need to work to demonstrate mutual trust and respect. Participative planning is essential. Coordination, not manipulation, is key.

☑ The Group Encourages Continual Improvement

Group members pay careful attention to how their behavior affects others and how the behavior of others affects them. They continually make the effort to improve and facilitate effective group interaction.

Focus on Service Learning

To apply what you now know about problem solving and working in groups, select a worthy project such as First Night, which protests the prevalence of alcohol at events and designs programs to keep young people alcohol free, or Take Back the Night, which protests the prevalence of sexual violence. After selecting your project and identifying and visiting relevant Web sites, such as www. alcoholpolicysolutions .net or www.redbankfirstnight .com for First Night, or www .campusoutreachservices.com or www.womentakebackthenight . org for Take Back the Night, develop strategies to successfully attract media attention, help raise funds, or raise awareness on campus for the project.

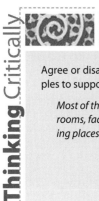

Thinking Critically

Reflect and Respond

Agree or disagree with the following statement attributed to businessperson Arthur Jensen. Supply reasons and examples to support the position you take.

Most of the decisions that affect our lives are not made by individuals, but by small groups of people in executive boardrooms, faculty meetings, town councils, quality circles, dormitory rooms, kitchens, locker rooms, and a host of other meeting places.

THE WRAP-UP

Revisiting Chapter Objectives

1. **Define *group*, distinguishing a team as a special kind of group.**   In communication theory, a group is defined as a collection of people who interact verbally and nonverbally, occupy certain roles with respect to one another, and cooperate with each other to accomplish a definite goal. Some of our most important communication experiences take place in small groups. Today, groups are used, both online and offline, to solve common problems and make decisions by sharing information. A team, a special kind of group, contains people who have diverse skills and bring different resources to a problem or task.

2. **Provide examples of how a group's climate affects its operations.**   To operate effectively, group members need to be supportive; exercise participative decision making; show trust, openness, and candor; and set high performance goals. The healthier the group climate, the more cohesive the group.

3. **Enumerate the advantages and disadvantages of group decision making and problem solving.**   The advantages of using a group instead of an individual are that resources can be pooled, motivation is increased, errors are more likely to be detected, decisions are more readily accepted by those outside the group, and group members can enjoy the companionship and rewards of working with others. There are, however, potential disadvantages to group problem solving: It may encourage laziness among some members; conflict may arise between personal and group goals; the group may be dominated by a few; one or two stubborn members may create a deadlock; the group may make an excessively risky decision; and the decision itself usually takes longer to reach.

4. **Distinguish among task, maintenance, and self-serving roles.**   Group members perform specific group roles. We contribute to the group's objective when we assume a task-oriented role (behaving in a way that promotes the accomplishment of the task) or a maintenance-oriented role (helping maintain the relationships among group members). However, we can undercut the group's effectiveness by playing a self-serving role—seeking to satisfy only our own needs or goals.

5. **Explain how cooperation versus competition and a defensive versus a supportive climate manifest themselves in a group's interaction.**   A group benefits from cooperation and a lack of defensiveness among members. Sharing resources and working together to achieve objectives help the group maintain itself while competition and power plays hinder group functioning and promote defensiveness in members.

6. **Compare and contrast various decision-making methods.**   Groups use a number of methods to make decisions—decision by an expert, by chance, by majority, by the leader, by the minority, by the average of individual decisions, and

THE WRAP-UP

by consensus—or the group can defer a decision entirely. Making decisions by consensus is considered the most effective strategy. When a group achieves consensus, all members have helped formulate the decision, all have agreed on it, and all will support it.

7. **Describe and use the reflective-thinking framework and brainstorming to increase your effectiveness at problem solving.**   Most groups can improve their problem-solving effectiveness by using the reflective-thinking framework, a systematic six-step approach to decision making. Additionally, brainstorming is a useful problem-solving technique because it encourages each member's potential for creativity, releases stuck patterns of thinking, and enhances the discovery of new solutions.

8. **Understand how to improve group member communication.**   Whether your group is meeting face-to-face or online, the following behaviors will contribute to the group's effectiveness: understand and state the goals of the group clearly, encourage members to communicate ideas and feelings freely, pay attention to both task and maintenance needs, keep motivation high, honestly assess the group's problem-solving style, foster an open and supportive climate, and build a cooperative member orientation.

Resources for Further Inquiry and Reflection

To apply your understanding of how the principles in Chapter 10 are at work in our daily lives, consult the following resources for further inquiry and reflection. Or, if you prefer, choose any other appropriate resource. Then connect the ideas expressed in your chosen selection with the communication concepts and issues you are learning about both in and out of class.

 Listen to Me

"Where Is the Love" (Black Eyed Peas)
"We Can Work It Out" (The Beatles)
"We Are the World" (Stevie Wonder)
"Peace on Earth" (U2)
"Burnin' Up" (Jonas Brothers)

How can problem-solving skills be put to work to resolve the problems identified in one of these songs?

 View Me

Munich	*March of the Penguins*
ANTZ	*The Full Monty*
The Italian Job	*12 Angry Men*
Charlie Wilson's War	*Lions for Lambs*

All of these films focus on the role of the group in problem solving. Identify the decision-making and problem-solving lessons you learned from viewing any one of them.

THE WRAP-UP

 Read Me

Jim Collins. *Good to Great*. New York: HarperCollins, 2001.

John Grisham. *Playing for Pizza: A Novel*. New York: Doubleday, 2007.

Patrick Lencioni. *The Five Dysfunctions of a Team*. San Francisco: Jossey-Bass, 2002.

George Orwell. *Animal Farm*. New York: Harcourt Brace, 1954.

Robert D. Putnam. *Bowling Alone: The Collapse and Revival of American Community*. New York: Simon & Schuster, 2000.

How do groups contribute to the establishment of a sense of community? What happens when the sense of community is stifled or disappears? What factors lead a group to destruction? Choose one of these books to use when answering these questions.

 Tell Me

Share with the class the insights you gained from your chosen Listen to Me, View Me, or Read Me selection.

Agree or disagree with this statement, with reasons: The major difference between a group meeting and a funeral is that the purpose of a funeral is perfectly clear.

www.mhhe.com/gamble10e

Key Chapter Terminology

Use the Online Learning Center at www.mhhe.com/gamble10e to further your knowledge of the following terminology.

brainstorming 263	kaleidoscope thinking 265
competitive goal structure 256	killer looks 264
cooperative goal structure 256	killer phrases 264
decision by consensus 259	maintenance roles 254
defensive behavior 256	quality circles 246
group 247	questions of fact 261
group climate 248	questions of policy 261
group goals 248	questions of value 261
group norms 248	reflective-thinking framework 261
group patterns of communication 248	self-directed teams 246
group role-classification model 253	self-serving roles 254
group structure 248	task roles 253

Idioms in Translation

decision-making machinery — decision-making methods

gaining an edge — gaining an advantage

horseplay — rowdy behavior

pooling their abilities — combining their abilities

pros and cons — benefits and drawbacks

round-robin sequence — one-after-another sequence

Culture Cue

Whereas members of collectivist cultures have a strong need for group consensus, people in the United States are more analytical, basing their decision making on objective facts rather than on feelings or faith.

Test Your Understanding

Go to the *Self Quizzes* on the book's Online Learning Center at www.mhhe.com/gamble10e.

www.mhhe.com/gamble10e

CHAPTER 11

After finishing this chapter, you should be able to

1. Define *leadership* and distinguish among various leadership styles: type X, type Y, autocratic, laissez-faire, and democratic.

2. Describe how trait theory, situational theory, functional theory, and transformational leadership contribute to our understanding of leadership.

3. Define *conflict* and explain how you feel when involved in a group conflict.

4. Define *groupthink* and explain its consequences.

5. Distinguish between competitive and cooperative conflict orientations.

6. Identify how to use the conflict grid and describe the benefits and problems that can result from effective and ineffective handling of group conflict.

7. Identify behaviors that can be used to resolve conflicts effectively.

Leading Others and Resolving Conflict

As it neared its end, the race to determine who would become the 2008 Democratic candidate for president came down to a choice between two contenders—Barack Obama and Hillary Clinton—respectively, the first African American and the first female candidates to win large numbers of primary contests and delegates. In becoming serious contenders for the presidency of the United States, both Obama and Clinton had to diffuse the conflicts created by their candidacies as well as overcome prevailing biases. Obama successfully challenged the erroneous belief that an African American would not be taken seriously as a presidential candidate, while Clinton broke through a glass ceiling, shattering long-held assumptions that a woman could not be a serious contender for the White House.

Man is the only animal that can remain on friendly terms with the victims he intends to eat until he eats them.
—Samuel Butler

You can't eat your friends and have them too.
—Budd Schulberg

Interestingly, racism proved to be less of an initial hurdle for Obama than sexism was for Clinton. Critics argued that sexism played the greater role in media coverage, accounting, at least in part, for Clinton's subsequent defeat and Obama's triumph as the Democratic standard bearer. According to CBS News anchor Katie Couric: "Like her or not, one of the great lessons of that campaign is the continued—and accepted—role of sexism in American life, particularly in the media."[1] For example, during one media segment, a commentator critical of Clinton said: "When Barack Obama speaks, men hear, 'Take off for the future.' And when Hillary Clinton speaks, men hear, 'Take out the garbage.'"[2] But Hillary's defeat wasn't just a male thing. Clinton captured just over a majority of women's votes. Why didn't more women vote for her? To what extent did internal conflict and gender play roles in restricting voters' perceptions of who should lead the United States? Despite Hillary Clinton's loss, it was said that "by showing that she has the 'cojones' to rule, she has made the path to the White House smoother for those who will follow."[3]

We have a dual focus in this chapter as we explore the variables of leadership and the management of group conflict. By gaining insight into how both forces affect us, we prepare ourselves to analyze and improve our own leadership and conflict-resolution behavior in groups.

APPROACHES TO LEADERSHIP: THE LEADER IN YOU

What is leadership? What qualities does a good leader possess? Are effective leaders born or made?[4] What sets leaders apart from the pack? Why should anyone be led by you?[5]

What Is Leadership?

leadership
the ability to influence others

Leadership is the ability to influence others. Thus, every person who influences others can be said to exert leadership.[6] Leadership can be either a positive or a negative force. When its influence is positive, leadership facilitates task accomplishment by a group. But if its influence is negative, task accomplishment is inhibited. Every group member is a potential leader.[7] Whether this potential is used wisely or is abused—or whether it is used effectively or ineffectively—depends on individual skills, personal objectives, and commitment to the group.

Groups, especially problem-solving groups, need effective leadership to achieve their goals. Effective leadership can be demonstrated by one or more of the members. Note that there is a difference between being appointed a leader—that is, serving as a designated leader—and exhibiting leadership behaviors. When you function as a **designated leader,** you have been selected to be the leader; this means that an outside force has given you the authority to exert your influence within the group. When you engage in effective leadership behavior without being appointed or directed to do so, you function as an **achieved leader;** that is, you are automatically performing roles that help a group attain task or maintenance objectives.

designated leader
a person given the authority to exert influence within a group

achieved leader
a person who exhibits leadership without being appointed

Recently, in lieu of having one person serve as the leader of a team created to solve a problem, some companies are now requiring team members to share leadership, so that the person in charge at any moment in the group's life is the person who has the key knowledge, skills, and abilities called for at that moment. Teams that have a shared leadership structure tend to be higher performing than teams dominated by one appointed leader are likely to be.[8]

Effective leaders perform combinations of the task and maintenance roles introduced in Chapter 10; they demonstrate role versatility. Such leaders help establish a group climate that encourages and stimulates interaction; they make certain that an agenda is planned for a meeting; they take responsibility for ensuring

Online Learning Center

Go to the Online Learning Center at www.mhhe.com/gamble10e and answer the questions in the *Self Inventory* to evaluate your understanding of conflict.

A scout leader is responsible for the smooth running of the pack. What makes some leaders more successful than others?

that group communication proceeds smoothly. When group members get off track, this type of leader asks relevant questions, offers internal summaries, and keeps the discussion going. This is also the kind of leader who encourages continual evaluation and improvement by group members.

Leadership Styles

Theorists have identified a number of leadership styles. Among them are type X, type Y, autocratic, laissez-faire, and democratic leadership.

Type X and Type Y Leaders

The assumptions we make about how people work together influence the type of leadership style we adopt. The following are eight assumptions that a leader might make about how and why people work. Choose the four with which you are most comfortable.

1. The average group member will avoid working if he or she can.
2. The average group member views work as a natural activity.
3. The typical group member must be forced to work and must be closely supervised.
4. The typical group member is self-directed when it comes to meeting performance standards and realizing group objectives.
5. A group member should be threatened with punishment to get him or her to put forth an adequate effort.
6. A group member's commitment to objectives is related not to punishment but to rewards.
7. The average person prefers to avoid responsibility and would rather be led.
8. The average person not only can learn to accept responsibility but actually seeks responsibility.

If you picked mostly odd-numbered items in the preceding list, you represent what management theorist Douglas McGregor calls a **type X leader.** In contrast, if you checked mostly even-numbered items, you represent what McGregor calls a **type Y leader.**[9] The type Y leader is more of a risk taker than the type X leader. Y leaders are willing to let each group member grow and develop to realize his or her individual potential. X leaders, however, do not readily delegate responsibility; unlike Y leaders, X leaders are not concerned with group members' personal sense of achievement. (Are you satisfied with the set of assumptions you chose? What consequences could they have?)

Autocratic, Laissez-Faire, and Democratic Leaders

In most discussions of leadership styles, three categories in addition to type X and type Y usually come up: the autocratic leader (the "boss"), the democratic leader (the "participator"), and the laissez-faire leader (the "do your own thing" leader).[11] Let's examine each briefly.

Autocratic, or authoritarian, leaders are dominators who view their task as directive. In a group with an autocratic leader, the leader determines all policies and gives orders to the other group members. In other words, this person

---

Work It Out

Explore what leadership means to you by completing these sentences:
A leader is a person who . . .
I like a leader who . . .
I am a leader when . . .
It is essential for a leader to . . .
I possess the following leadership skills: . . .
I lack the following leadership skills: . . .

---

type X leader
a leader who does not trust group members to work and is unconcerned with the personal achievement of group members

type Y leader
a leader who displays trust in group members and is concerned with their sense of personal achievement

autocratic, or authoritarian, leaders
directive leaders

Work It Out

What do you perceive the leader's role to be in situations such as the oil shortage, accusations of torture at Guantanamo, and the controversy resulting from the printing of cartoons featuring the prophet Muhammad?

Work It Out

Develop a list of characteristics that you believe set leaders apart from others.

Media Wise

Shakespeare, Pop Culture, and Leadership

1. A number of the plays of Shakespeare offer insightful explorations of leadership. The lessons contained in them are as relevant in the twenty-first century as they were in the sixteenth century. For example, from the works of Shakespeare, we learn the importance of timing in achieving goals, the value of courage in facing challenges, the value of determination, and the need for establishing a firm, clear vision.[10] While not up to the standard set by Shakespeare's plays, contemporary media offerings such as *The Unit, Generation Kill,* and *Survivor* also explore different types of leaders. As we recognize the types of leaders presented to us, we come to understand them and may even learn to deal with them more effectively.

   Pick a recent film or television show. Identify and discuss one or more leadership lessons you learned from viewing the selected film or program, and explain how one or more of the characters in the film or program deepened your awareness of the people you work with or interact with every day.

2. The 2008 election had both a black male and a white female running for the presidency of the United States. Do you think that Hollywood and the television media helped build unrealistic expectations in the electorate of how the real-life candidates should present themselves and behave as leaders? For example, past plotlines of the hit drama *24* explored the candidacy of the first black presidential contender, the administrations of both the first African American and female presidents, and the travails suffered by both a white male and a white female when serving as the head of a U.S. intelligence agency. Another, shorter-lived series, *Commander in Chief,* explored the trials and tribulations of a female president. Similarly, a Chris Rock comedy, *Head of State*, did the same for an African American commander in chief. Do you believe that pop culture offerings such as these helped prepare the U.S. public and the world for recent social changes? Explain your answer.

   Finally, select either an episode of a television show or a feature film focusing on a white male leader, a minority male leader, a white female leader, or a minority female leader. Describe the depicted leader's strong and weak qualities, problem-solving abilities, conflict-resolution techniques, and preferred decision-making methods. To what extent is the character in your chosen show or movie depicted in stereotypical or nonstereotypical ways?

How do TV and real-life leaders differ?

becomes the sole decision maker. Although such an approach may be effective and efficient during a crisis, the usual outcome of this behavior is low group satisfaction.

The opposite of the autocratic leader is the **laissez-faire leader.** This type of leader adopts a "leave them alone" attitude. In other words, this person diminishes

laissez-faire leader

a nondirective leader

the leadership function to the point where it is almost nonexistent. The result is that group members are free to develop and progress on their own. This style is most effective when a minimum of interference fosters teamwork. Unfortunately, the members of a laissez-faire group often are distracted from the task at hand and lose their sense of direction, with the result that the quality of their work suffers.

The middle leadership position—and the one that has proved most effective—is that of **democratic leaders.** In groups with democratic leadership, members are directly involved in the problem-solving process; the power to make decisions is neither usurped by a boss nor abandoned by a laissez-faire leader. Instead, the leader's behavior represents a reasonable compromise between those two extremes. Democratic leaders do not dominate the group with one point of view, but they do attempt to provide direction to ensure that both task and maintenance functions are carried out. The group is free to identify its own goals, follow its own procedures, and reach its own conclusions. Most people prefer democratic groups. Morale, motivation, group-mindedness, and the desire to communicate all increase under the guidance of a democratic leader.

Though it was only his second day on the job, employees were already getting bad vibes about the new division chief.

Theories of Leadership

Where does leadership ability come from? Why are some people more effective leaders than others? Are some people born to be leaders? Or does every situation create its own leader? Or is leadership a matter of learned abilities and skills? Over the years, theorists have given various answers to these questions.

Trait Theory

The earliest view of leadership was trait theory. According to **trait theory,** leaders are people who are born to lead.[12] Trait theorists also believed there are special built-in, identifiable leadership traits. Accordingly, attempts were made to design a test that could predict whether a person would become a leader.

After many years of research, proof of trait theory is still lacking. Personality traits are not surefire predictors of leadership. For one thing, no one set of characteristics is common to all leaders, and leaders and followers share many of the same characteristics. Also, the situation appears, at least in part, to determine who will come forward to exert leadership. This is not to suggest, however, that trait research did not yield valuable findings. In fact, while the statement "Leaders must possess the following personality traits . . ." is not valid, the research does enable us to note that certain traits are indeed more likely to be found in leaders than in nonleaders.

democratic leaders

leaders who represent a reasonable compromise between authoritarian and laissez-faire leaders

The successful organization has one major attribute that sets it apart from unsuccessful organizations: dynamic and effective leadership.

—P. Hersey and K. Blanchard

trait theory

the theory of leadership asserting that certain people are born to lead

Use the scale in Table 11.1 to assess your leadership traits. For each item, circle the number that best reflects your ability. On which traits did you score highest and lowest?

Table 11.1 **Evaluating Your Leadership Traits**

Trait	Low				High
Dependability	1	2	3	4	5
Cooperativeness	1	2	3	4	5
Desire to win	1	2	3	4	5
Enthusiasm	1	2	3	4	5
Drive	1	2	3	4	5
Persistence	1	2	3	4	5
Responsibility	1	2	3	4	5
Intelligence	1	2	3	4	5
Foresight	1	2	3	4	5
Communication ability	1	2	3	4	5
Popularity	1	2	3	4	5

Work It Out

Create a problem-solving situation and explain how an authoritarian, a laissez-faire, and a democratic leader might handle it. For example, imagine that a corporation needs to purchase data-mining equipment. What behaviors might each type of leader exhibit in a group discussion on this topic? In turn, role-play each leadership style.

situational theory
the theory of leadership asserting that leadership depends on the situation

If you could model yourself after any leader, who would it be and why?

Describe a person who you believe was born to be a leader. What attributes do you believe destined this person to lead?

According to researcher Marvin Shaw, the characteristics identified in Table 11.1 indicate leadership potential. Shaw notes that a person who does not exhibit these traits is unlikely to be a leader.[13] Of course, having leadership potential does not guarantee that you will actually emerge as a leader. A number of group members may have the qualities of leadership, but the final assertion of leadership will depend on more than potential.

Situational Theory

The second theory of leadership is **situational theory.** According to this theory, whether an individual displays leadership skills and behaviors and exercises actual leadership depends on the situation.[14] The development and emergence of leadership can be affected by such factors as the nature of the problem, the social climate, the personalities of the group members, the size of the group, and the time available to accomplish the task. As organizational behavior theorist Keith Davis notes in *Human Relations at Work*, leader and group "interact not in a vacuum, but at a particular time and within a specific set of circumstances."[15] A leader is not necessarily a person "for all seasons."

Fred Fiedler's contingency theory and Paul Hersey and Ken Blanchard's readiness theory are both situational theories. Fiedler's theory contends that predicting a group's leader is contingent upon three situational factors: leader-member relations, task structure, and position power.[16] Hersey and Blanchard's theory contends that the readiness level of a group (the degree that members are willing and skilled enough to perform a task) determines the degree of task or relationship behavior a leader needs to emphasize.[17] Thus, the relationship behavior, task behavior, and maturity of the group members all come into play as a leader determines the style called for. For example, when groups are new, a *telling* style of leadership may be effective. The leader needs to provide direction, training, and instructions. When a group has some confidence in its skills, a *selling* style of leadership, one in which the leader uses both task and relational behavior to persuade members to accomplish tasks, is called for. In contrast, when group members take on more responsibility and become more independent, the leader becomes more equal to other group members. In this case, the leadership style of *participating* is used and decision making is shared. Finally, when the group is ready to provide its own leadership, a *delegating* style is appropriate.

Functional Theory

The third theory of leadership is **functional theory.** In contrast to trait theory and situational theory, which emphasize the emergence of one person as a leader, functional theory suggests that several group members should be ready to lead because various actions are needed to achieve group goals.

Functional theorists believe that any of the task or maintenance activities can be considered leadership functions. In other words, when you perform any needed task or maintenance function, you are exercising leadership. Thus, according to functional theory, leadership shifts from person to person and is shared. Of course, sometimes one or two group members perform more leadership functions than others do. Consequently, one member might become the main task leader, whereas another might become the main socioemotional leader. However, the point is that we can enhance our leadership potential by learning to perform needed group functions more effectively.[18]

From the functional viewpoint, then, leadership is not necessarily a birthright; nor is it simply a matter of being in the right situation at a critical juncture. Instead, we are all capable of leadership, and what is required is that we have enough self-assertion and sensitivity to perform the functions that are needed as they are needed. In effect, this theory is asserting that good membership is good leadership. And the converse is also true: Good leadership is good membership.

functional theory
the leadership theory suggesting that several members of a group should be ready to lead because various actions are needed to achieve group goals

Transformational Leadership

A **transformational leader** transforms a group by giving it a new vision, strengthening its culture or structure. The transformational leader does not merely direct members, elicit contributions from members, or wait for members to catch up with his or her thinking. Instead, the transformational leader helps group members imagine and visualize the future they can build together. Transformational leaders inspire, motivate, and intellectually stimulate group members to become involved in achieving the group's goals. They function as the group's guiding force.[19]

transformational leader
a leader who gives a group a new vision, strengthening its culture or structure

LEADING THE WAY THROUGH CONFLICT MANAGEMENT

How a group handles conflict, which can occur at any point in the group's existence and which can be started by any member of the group, makes a difference in member satisfaction as well as in the decision-making and problem-solving effectiveness of the group. How we feel about conflict and whether we view it positively or negatively reveals how we might act when facing one. The following test will help you assess your personal attitudes toward conflict.

1. State your personal definition of *conflict*, and indicate how you feel when involved in a conflict.
2. Next, use the scale in Table 11.2 to assess the extent to which you consider conflict in a small group positive or negative. For each item, circle the number that best reflects your attitude.
   a. Total your circled numbers. If your score is 10 to 14, you believe that conflict is definitely positive. If your score is 15 to 20, you believe that conflict can be helpful. If your score is 21 to 30, you do not like

Work It Out

Select a group faced with making a significant decision, such as the College of Cardinals, who are responsible for naming a new pope when one dies, or the Federal Drug Administration (FDA), whose responsibility it is to approve new drugs for marketing to the public. Analyze the group dynamics and decision-making pressures the group faces as it approaches its task.

Table 11.2 Conflict: Positive or Negative?

Good	1	2	3	4	5	Bad
Rewarding	1	2	3	4	5	Threatening
Normal	1	2	3	4	5	Abnormal
Constructive	1	2	3	4	5	Destructive
Necessary	1	2	3	4	5	Unnecessary
Challenging	1	2	3	4	5	Overwhelming
Desirable	1	2	3	4	5	Undesirable
Inevitable	1	2	3	4	5	Avoidable
Healthy	1	2	3	4	5	Unhealthy
Clean	1	2	3	4	5	Dirty

> **What high school groups did you belong to? Were you and your group(s) part of the in-group? In your opinion, might the presence of in- and out-groups in high school contribute to the kind of atmosphere that provides the context for school violence, such as the massacre that occurred at Columbine High School?**

to think about conflict; you have very ambivalent feelings. If your score is 31 to 40, you believe that conflict is something to try to avoid. If your score is 41 to 50, you believe that conflict is definitely negative.

b. Determine the average scores for men and for women in the class. How do they compare? If they differ, what do you believe causes the difference? How does your score compare with the average for your sex?

c. Compute the average score for your class as a whole. How does your score compare with the class average?

3. Complete these sentences:

a. The time I felt worst about dealing with conflict in a group was when . . .

b. The time I felt best about dealing with conflict in a group was when . . .

c. I think the most important outcome of group conflict is . . .

d. When I am in conflict with a group member I really care about, I . . .

e. When I am in conflict with a group member I am not close to, I . . .

f. When a group member attempts to avoid entering into a conflict with me, I . . .

g. My greatest difficulty in handling group conflict is . . .

h. My greatest strength in handling group conflict is . . .

conflict
perceived disagreements about views, interests, and goals

The dictionary defines **conflict** as "disagreement, . . . war, battle, and collision." These definitions suggest that conflict is a negative force that of necessity leads to undesirable consequences. To what extent does your score suggest that you support this premise? Somehow, many of us grow up thinking that nice people do not fight, do not make waves. Some believe that if they do not smile and act cheerful, other people will not like them and they will not be accepted or valued as group members.[20]

> **How would being in conflict with others affect your ability to function on the job?**

Avoid Groupthink: A Deterrent to Making Good Decisions

A body of research suggests that "smart people working collectively can be dumber than the sum of their brains."[21] This theory seems to have been at work in the tragedy involving the space shuttle *Columbia*. Investigators questioned the quick analysis by Boeing engineers that NASA used to conclude early in space shuttle *Columbia*'s mission that falling foam did not endanger the shuttle's safety. The conclusion reached by the engineers reveals that the culture of decision making at NASA was indicative of groupthink. This was not the first time NASA was accused of exhibiting a predilection toward groupthink. The agency

> **Agree or disagree, stating your reasons: The group is dumber than its smartest members.**

suffered from the same criticism in 1986 after the loss of space shuttle *Challenger* and its crew on January 28 of that year. The official inquiry into that disaster revealed that the direct cause was a malfunction of the O-ring seal on the solid rocket booster that caused that shuttle to explode 73 seconds after it was launched. It seems that concerns about the O-rings had circulated within the agency for quite a while prior to the accident but that nothing was done about them. Groupthink has also been targeted as a cause of numerous other fiascos, including the sinking of the *Titanic*, the surprise attack on Pearl Harbor, the foiled Bay of Pigs invasion of Cuba, the escalation of the Vietnam War, and the war in Iraq.

What is **groupthink?** How does it come about? According to Irving Janis, author of *Victims of Groupthink*, it occurs when groups let the desire for consensus override careful analysis and reasoned decision making.[22] In effect, then, groupthink is an extreme way of avoiding conflict. While cohesiveness is normally a desirable group characteristic, when carried to an extreme, it can become dysfunctional or even destructive.

Why is dissenting—separating from a herd—not an easy thing for many of us to do? The answer may lie in the following research findings. Researchers have demonstrated that when asked to rate the attractiveness of facial photographs, young men changed their ratings significantly up or down, based on how they believe their peers had rated the same photographs, revealing a decision-making bias fostered by the perceived social pressure to conform. On the other hand, dissenters—those who do distinguish themselves by refusing to conform—become more willing to go the distance in defying the herd when they believe they have allies. If a group member thinks others support him or her, then the dissenter is more likely to stay firm in his or her opinion and make the effort to influence others in the group.[23]

When they engage in sloppy thinking, group members can fall prey to irrationality—behavior that can cause them to make poor decisions. For example,

groupthink
an extreme means of avoiding conflict that occurs when groups let the desire for consensus override careful analysis and reasoned decision making

> In groups characterized by groupthink, members try to maintain harmony by forgoing critical decision making. Did you or anyone you know ever feel a need for self-censorship at a meeting because it seemed dangerous to challenge the leader or boss?

Skill Builder

Are You a Groupthinker?

Are you a groupthinker? To find out, answer yes or no to each of the following questions and explain your answers.

1. Have you ever felt so secure about a group decision that you ignored all warning signs that the decision was wrong? Why?

2. Have you ever been party to a rationalization justifying a group decision? Why?

3. Have you ever defended a group decision by pointing to your group's inherent sense of morality?

4. Have you ever participated in feeding an "us versus them" feeling—that is, in depicting those opposed to you in simplistic, stereotyped ways?

5. Have you ever censored your own comments because you feared destroying the sense of unanimity in your group?

6. Have you ever applied direct pressure to dissenting members in an effort to get them to agree with the will of the group?

7. Have you ever served as a "mind guard"? That is, have you ever attempted to preserve your group's cohesiveness by preventing disturbing outside ideas or opinions from becoming known to other group members?

8. Have you ever assumed that the silence of other group members implied agreement?

Each time you answered yes to one of these questions, you indicated that you have contributed to an illusion of group unanimity. In effect, you let a tendency to agree interfere with your ability to think critically. In so doing, you became a groupthinker. Groupthink impedes effective group functioning; when all group members try to think alike, no one thinks very much.

Can you be both a team player and a non-conformist? Why does resisting the pressure others place on you to be a team player and to go along with what the group wants some-time result in their ridi-culing, bullying, or criticizing you if you refuse?

Why do you think you get less conformity when people are able to respond anonymously?

one professor typically begins a class he teaches on negotiation skills by auction-ing off a $20 bill. Because it is difficult to see a decision-making bias at work, not once in all the years this professor has taught the class has the bidding halted below $20. In fact, it was not uncommon for the bids for the $20 to go as high as several hundred dollars. Getting caught in the raw power of herd behavior can cause group members to swear that black is white or vice versa merely because everyone else says so.[24] They may be decisive in their actions, but they are "deci-sively wrong."[25] Conformity by suppressing conflict acts to impede rational decision making.

Gender, Leadership, and Conflict: Comparing Approaches

Are we shifting away from traditional leadership approaches emphasizing stereo-typical masculine attributes such as competitiveness, aggression, and control to a paradigm reflective of more stereotypically feminine attributes such as collabora-tive problem solving, connectedness, and supportiveness? Observers say we are.[26] Despite the shift, on average, female leaders still score higher than males on people-oriented leadership skills such as being better at empathizing, keeping people informed and providing feedback, sharing responsibility, demonstrating sen-sitivity to the needs of others, and creating environments in which people can learn, grow, think, and achieve together.[27] In contrast, males persist in being per-ceived as better at strategic planning, more in control of emotional expression, and more willing to take the kind of risks that facilitate innovation.[28] The expec-tation is for women to excel at relationship building and participative leadership, and for men to excel at being work-directed and assertive. On the other hand, a man can exhibit a feminine leadership style, just as a woman can display leadership behaviors that are masculine. Indeed, the most effective leadership style may be blended, drawing on both mas-culine and feminine strengths.

Nonetheless, sex-role stereotypes persist in influencing percep-tions of and expectations for male and female leadership styles, with people evaluating the same message differently, depending on whether a male or a female delivered it. Thus, while women deliv-ering some messages are labeled as bossy or overly emotional, men delivering the same message are seen as responsible and as exercis-ing leadership.[29] Too often, when a woman is perceived to be acting like a man, others misinterpret or devalue her leadership efforts. Women such as Hillary Clinton, Condoleezza Rice, and Nancy Pelosi are called on time and time again to enact their "alphaness" whereas it has become somewhat more acceptable for men to shed the "strongman" stereotype.[30]

Women and men also have been socialized to approach con-flict differently. While most males have been socialized to be demanding and competitive, females have been taught to practice cooperativeness, compromise, and accommodation instead. While males tend to become verbally aggressive and adopt a fight mental-ity, women are more likely to engage in protracted negotiation in an attempt to avoid a fight.[31] When asked to describe how their style of handling conflict differed from that of men, women noted that men are overly concerned with power and content issues and

Who would you rather have as the leader of your group or team, a man or a woman? Why?

underconcerned with relational issues. When compared with men, women place more emphasis on preserving their relationships during conflict; instead of focusing on content, they focus on feelings.[32]

Men, however, are more likely to withdraw from a conflict situation than are women. Researchers believe this may occur because men become substantially psychologically and physiologically aroused during conflict and may opt to withdraw from the conflict rather than risk further arousal.[33] Women, in contrast, prefer to talk about conflict in an effort to resolve it.[34] Women, when compared with men, are more likely to reveal their negative feelings and become emotional during conflict. Men, on the other hand, are more apt to keep their negative feelings to themselves and argue logically instead.[35]

> Have you ever observed gender differences during conflict? Do you think you handle conflict more like the typical man or the typical woman? Why?

Culture, Leadership, and Conflict: Comparing Views

Your culture influences the way you communicate when you are part of a group. While cultural variations can enhance a group's operation, at times cultural clashes can impede it. For example, when Corning and the Mexican company Vitro made a cross-border alliance, their communication efforts were hurt by cultural misunderstandings. According to business leaders, problems developed in the relationship because of stereotypes as well as different decision-making and work-style approaches employed by the two companies. While the Americans were accustomed to eating during meetings, the Mexicans were used to going out for leisurely meals. The Mexicans typically put in much longer workdays because of their longer lunches and conducted evening meetings, whereas the Americans wanted to hold business to daytime hours. The Mexicans saw the Americans as too direct, while the Americans viewed the Mexicans as too polite. The decision-making methods of the two companies posed the toughest problem: Because Mexican businesses tend to be much more hierarchical, the decisions were made by the top executives, which slowed down the decision-making process. The Mexicans, unlike the Americans, displayed an unwillingness to criticize. As a result, their conversations were more indirect.[36]

Like the Mexican style, the Japanese decision-making style differs from the American approach. While Americans tend to value openness in groups, the Japanese value harmony. While Americans emphasize individual responsibility, the Japanese stress collective responsibility.[37] Thus, there is a tendency among the Japanese to lose individual identity within the group.[38]

Even though group membership and group identity are highly valued in collectivistic cultures, participating in decision-making groups does not appear to give group members actual decision-making power. In one study of 48 Japanese organizations, while members were encouraged to contribute ideas, the decision-making power remained with the CEO and managers high in the organization hierarchy.[39] Thus, culture influences both membership and leadership style, with the group's cultural makeup affecting the group's potential to develop shared leadership. While the generalizations we are about to make are not true of every person in every country, in general, they are thought to be valid. According to researchers, a large number of countries, including Arab countries, Brazil, Chile, Greece, Mexico, Pakistan, and Peru, tend to accept unequal distribution of power in their institutions and organizations and consequently prefer participating in groups with a centralized decision-making structure. Part of the leader's reluctance to share leadership is because leadership is perceived as the sole prerogative of the appointed leader, who believes others will perceive him or her as weak if he or she attempts to share control. In contrast, countries in which power is distributed more equitably, such as Australia, Canada, Denmark, Israel, and the United States, tend to be more comfortable practicing decentralized or shared decision making.[40]

Cultures also differ along a continuum that ranges from nurturing to aggressive. Group members from societies tending toward the aggressive end of the scale include Arab countries, Hong Kong, Mexico, and the United States. Group members from these countries focus on goal achievement and are likely to be more assertive and competitive even if it comes at others' expense. In general, members from assertive societies tend to vie for control rather than work toward shared leadership, that is, unless sharing leadership is paired with outsmarting or beating the competition. By contrast, group members from more nurturing cultures, such as Finland, Italy, Brazil, and France, tend to emphasize concern for developing the potential of all, preferring to share, rather than compete.

Whether members belong to individualistic cultures, such as Argentina, Austria, Canada, and the United States, or collectivist cultures, such as Greece, Indonesia, Spain, and Turkey, also influences how easy or hard members find it to share leadership. People from individualistic cultures tend to be independent and self-reliant. Enjoyers of personal freedom, they often are not inclined to meet the demands of teamwork. In contrast, people from collectivist cultures are predisposed to helping the team even if it comes at a personal cost.[41]

Like it or not, you are a negotiator. Negotiation is a fact of life. . . . Everyone negotiates something every day.

—Roger Fisher and William Ury,
Getting to Yes

Ethics and Communication

Which Cultural Differences Make a Difference in How a Group Functions?

1. When does culture matter? Which of the following differences do you consider relevant to a group's functioning, and how would you use each one?

   - The Japanese value formality and harmony.
   - The Spanish like to discuss and thrash out issues during an unhurried meal.
   - The British and U.S. Americans like to take short lunch breaks without alcohol.
   - The Chinese are baffled by "brown bag lunch" conferences during which junior staffers rudely dine while a senior executive gives a talk. They see it as rude because it mixes a social event with an official one, something the Chinese rarely do.

   As groups go global, to what extent might the preceding tidbits of knowledge make a big difference to a group that you are in?[42]

2. While gender and ethnicity usually encompass the kinds of diversity groups seek, do you think *personality diversity* in a group, when properly managed, should also be an objective? If so, how might it influence a group's functioning? For example, are highly opinionated, assertive members just as important to the group process as consensus seekers? When forming groups, should we balance creative risk-takers with cautious, detailed thinkers? Would such a diversity of personalities produce conflict? What steps would you need to take to ensure that any resulting conflict expands the group's thinking and problem-solving acumen?[43]

3. In an effort to promote diversity, companies create *affinity interest groups*, groups that bring together workers of specific races, genders, or sexual orientations. But they don't stop there. They are also encouraging persons outside the group or demographic to join the affinity group. The hope is that by having one or more persons from outside the affinity join and work with the members of the affinity group, the company will succeed in (1) avoiding the creation of "us versus them" mind-sets, (2) offering employees opportunities to gain experience with members of different cultures, and (3) providing "epiphany" moments by helping people outside minority groups understand and appreciate minority concerns.[44] Do you agree or disagree with these premises? Offer reasons for your stance.

Win-Win

A new teacher—let's call her Mary—arrived at a Navajo reservation. Each day in her classroom, something like the following would occur. Mary would ask five of her young Navajo students to go to the chalkboard and complete a simple mathematics problem from their homework. All five students would go to the chalkboard, but not one of them would work the problem as requested. Instead, they would all stand, silent and motionless.

Mary, of course, wondered what was going on. She repeatedly asked herself if she might be calling on students who could not do the assigned problems. "No, it couldn't be that," she reasoned. Finally, Mary asked her students what the problem was. Their answer displayed an understanding not many people attain in a lifetime.

Evidently, the students realized that not everyone in the class would be able to complete the problems correctly. But they respected each other's uniqueness, and they understood, even at their young age, the dangers of a win-lose approach. In their opinion, no one would win if anyone was embarrassed or humiliated at the chalkboard, and so they refused to compete publicly with each other. Yes, the Navajo students wanted to learn—but not at the expense of their peers.

Where do you stand? Would typical American schoolchildren behave similarly? Why or why not? Should they behave like the Navajos?

Cooperative versus Competitive Conflict: Win-Win or Win-Lose

A lion used to prowl about a field in which four oxen dwelled. Many a time he tried to attack them; but, whenever he came near, they turned their tails to one another, so that whichever way he approached them he was met by the horns of one of them. At last, however, they fell a-quarreling among themselves, and each went off to the pasture alone in a separate corner of the field. Then the lion attacked them one by one and soon made an end to all four.[45]

How does this story from *Aesop's Fables* apply to our study of conflict? Unlike the oxen, you can learn to handle your conflicts constructively; you can learn to disagree without becoming disagreeable. In general, we can say that people enter a conflict situation with one of two orientations, or perspectives: competition or cooperation. People who have a **competitive set** perceive a conflict situation in all-or-nothing terms and believe that, to attain victory, they must defeat the other participants. They do not believe that their own interests and those of others are compatible. By contrast, people with a **cooperative set** believe that a way to share the rewards of the situation can be discovered.

competitive set
a readiness to perceive a conflict in all-or-nothing terms

cooperative set
a readiness to share rewards to resolve conflicts

Conflict Corner: Can You See It My Way?

Choose a current issue that is significant and controversial (for example, abortion, global warming, capital punishment, nuclear energy). You will be assigned to defend or oppose it. Defenders and opposers will have a chance to meet and prepare their cases. Each defender (A) will be paired with an opposer (B). Person A will have five minutes to present the defense's position to person B. Person B then will have five minutes to present the opposition's position to person A.

Players will then switch roles, so that B presents A's case and A presents B's case.

1. To what extent did reversing roles help you understand and appreciate another point of view?

2. How could such a procedure help a person change from a win–lose orientation to a win–win orientation?

With whom have you had to negotiate recently: friend, spouse, co-worker, boss? Over what: money, goods, services, information, rules, prestige? What was the outcome?

If people bring a competitive orientation to a conflict, they will tend to be ego-involved and will see winning as a test of personal worth and competence. If a conflict is defined as competitive, the participants become combatants: they believe that, to attain victory, they must defeat the other side. In contrast, if people bring a cooperative orientation to a conflict, they tend to look for a mutually beneficial way to resolve the disagreement. For a conflict to be defined as cooperative, each participant must demonstrate a willingness to resolve it in a mutually satisfactory way. If the people involved in a conflict are treated with respect by all the others involved, if they are neither demeaned nor provoked, and if communication is free and open instead of underhanded and closed, the disagreement may be settled amicably.

We can define a conflict as a win-lose situation, or we can define it as a win-win situation. If we define it as win-lose, we will tend to pursue our own goals, misrepresent our needs, attempt to avoid empathizing with or understanding the feelings of others, and use threats or promises to get others to go along with us. If we define a conflict as win-win, we will tend to view it as a common problem, try to pursue common goals, honestly reveal our needs to others, work to understand their position and frame of reference, and make every effort to reduce rather than increase defensiveness.[46]

To transform a conflict from competitive to cooperative, you must use effective communication techniques.[47] You can discover workable strategies and practice them until you can use them for yourself. One strategy is **role reversal**—that is, acting as if you were the person(s) with whom you are in conflict. This strategy can help people involved in a conflict understand each other, find creative ways to integrate their interests and concerns, and work toward a common goal. Reversing roles helps you avoid judging others by enabling you to see things from their perspective. Once you can replace a statement like "You're wrong" or "You're stupid" with one like "What you believe is not what I believe," you will be on your way to developing a cooperative orientation.

Work It Out

Interview a manager. Ask about the nature of a conflict he or she had to resolve and the strategies he or she used to handle it.

role reversal
a strategy in which persons in conflict act as each other in order to understand each other's position

GOALS AND STYLES: A CONFLICT GRID

A number of paradigms, or models, have been proposed to represent the ways we try to resolve conflicts. Among them is Robert Blake and Jane Mouton's **conflict grid** (see Figure 11.1).[48] This grid has two scales. The horizontal scale represents the extent to which a person wants to attain personal goals. The vertical scale represents the extent to which the person is concerned for others. The interface between the two scales indicates how strongly the person feels about these concerns—that is, how his or her concern is apportioned.

Both scales range from 1 (low) to 9 (high), representing increasing importance of personal goals ("concern for production of results") and of other people ("concern for people"). On the basis of this measure, Blake and Mouton identified five main conflict styles. As you consider their grid and the following descriptions of their five styles, try to identify your own conflict style.

A person with a 1.1 conflict style can be described as an **avoider;** the avoider's attitude can be summed up as "lose and walk away." If you have a 1.1 style, your goal is to maintain neutrality at all costs. You probably view conflict as a

conflict grid
a model portraying the styles individuals use to resolve conflicts

avoider
a person who, when faced with a conflict, uses the unproductive strategy of mentally or physically fleeing the situation

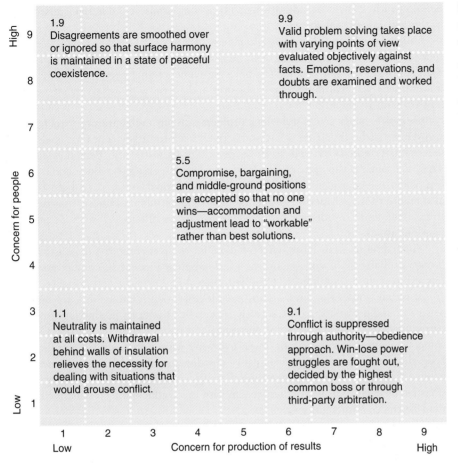

FIGURE 11.1

Blake and Mouton's Conflict Grid.

Source: Reprinted with permission of Grid, International. "The Fifth Achievement" by Robert Blake and Jane Srygley Mouton, *Journal of Applied Behavioral Science* 6, no. 4.

useless and punishing experience, one that you would prefer to do without. Rather than tolerate the frustrations that can accompany conflict, you physically or mentally remove yourself from the conflict situation.

A person with a 1.9 style is an **accommodator,** whose attitude is "give in and lose." If you are a 1.9, your behavior demonstrates that you overvalue the maintenance of relationships and undervalue the achievement of your own goals. Your main concern is to ensure that others accept you, like you, and coexist in peace with you. Although conflicts may exist in your world, you refuse to deal with them. You feel a need to maintain the appearance of harmony at all costs. This discrepancy leads to an uneasy, tense state characterized by a great deal of smiling and nervous laughter.

A person with a 5.5 style is a **compromiser,** whose attitude is "find a middle ground." If you are a 5.5, your guiding principle is compromise. Thus, you work to find a way to permit each participant in a conflict to gain something. Compromise is, of course, a valid strategy in some cases. But it can be a problem if you always settle for a workable solution because you are afraid the conflict may escalate if you try to find the best solution. It is undeniable that "half a loaf is better than none," and this conflict style will leave participants half satisfied, but it can also

accommodator

a person who, when faced with a conflict, overvalues the maintenance of relationships and undervalues the achievement of his or her own goals

> **Why would people who are competitors (9.1) enjoy being surrounded by "yes people" (1.9)? What dangers can such a mix pose?**

compromiser

a person who, when faced with a conflict, tries to find a middle ground

be said to leave them half dissatisfied. Thus, compromise is sometimes referred to as the lose-lose approach.

A person with a 9.1 style is a **competitive forcer,** who takes a win-lose attitude. If you are a 9.1, attaining your personal goals is far more important to you than concern for other people. You have an overwhelming need to win and dominate others; you will defend your position and battle with others, whatever the cost or harm to them.

A person with a 9.9 style is a **problem-solving collaborator,** who takes a win-win attitude. If you are a 9.9, you actively seek to satisfy your own goals (you are results-oriented) as well as those of others (you are also person-oriented). This, of course, is the optimum style when you are seeking to reduce conflict. As a problem solver, you realize that conflicts are normal and can be helpful; you also realize that each person in a conflict holds legitimate opinions that deserve to be aired and considered. You are able to discuss differences without making personal attacks.

According to Alan Filley, effective conflict resolvers rely to a large extent on problem solving (9.9) and smoothing (1.9), whereas ineffective conflict resolvers rely extensively on forcing (9.1) and withdrawal (1.1).[49]

If we are to develop and sustain meaningful group relationships, we need to learn to handle conflicts constructively. A conflict has been productive if all the participants are satisfied with the outcomes and believe they have gained something.[50] In other words, no one loses; everyone wins. In contrast, a conflict has been destructive if all the participants are dissatisfied with the outcomes and believe that they have lost something. Perhaps one of the most important questions facing each of us is whether we can turn our conflicts into productive rather than destructive interactions.

competitive forcer

a person who, when faced with a conflict, adopts a win-lose orientation in which the attaining of personal goals is paramount

problem-solving collaborator

a person who, when faced with a conflict, adopts a win-win orientation, seeking to satisfy his or her own goals as well as those of others

Which conflict-resolving strategies do you use? Why?

LEADING GROUPS AND HANDLING CONFLICT IN CYBERSPACE

In what ways, if any, is online conflict different from face-to-face conflict?

It is quite common for groups to hold virtual meetings—teleconferences, video-conferences, or Web conferences—that link participants in remote locations. Besides facilitating discussion among people in diverse places, these techniques enable corporate, not-for-profit, and government leaders to bring together more people for a meeting than would otherwise be feasible, saving time and money, and increasing productivity.[51] Cyber-teams differ in the degree of virtuality they possess, ranging from hybrid teams that meet both face-to-face and online to those whose members never meet personally. Two variables significantly enhance the online group's success: (1) the extent to which online teams are able to offer members a sense of belonging,[52] and (2) the task orientation and efficiency created by working online.[53] Online groups also have several other advantages. When resolving conflict they tend to be less influenced by member status and less subject to dominance by a single member. Additionally, they often offer participants more flexibility, leaving them free to respond at their own pace and on their own schedules.[54] However, the online groups that members most enjoy are those in which members take active responsibility for their group's progress by adequately preparing for meetings, and ones in which the responsiveness of group members to each other is high, enhancing conflict resolution and promoting collaboration.[55]

Is it easier to hide in a group that meets online than in one that meets face-to-face? Why would you ever want to hide in a group?

COMMUNICATION SKILLS IN PRACTICE

GUIDELINES FOR THE ETHICAL MANAGEMENT OF CONFLICT

Conflict can be resolved productively by applying the principles of effective communication. The following suggestions are a basic guide to conflict resolution:

☑ Recognize That Conflicts Can Be Settled Rationally

Conflicts can be settled rationally if you act like a capable, competent problem solver and adopt a person-to-person orientation.

Recognizing unproductive behaviors is a first step in learning to handle conflicts more effectively. Being willing to express your feelings openly, directly, and constructively without resorting to irrational techniques that destroy trust and respect is a prerequisite for becoming a productive conflict manager. Thus, instead of insulting or attacking others or withdrawing from a conflict, be willing to describe whatever action, behavior, or situation you find upsetting. Do this without evaluating other people negatively or causing them to become defensive. Focus on issues, not personalities. Be willing to listen to and react to what the other person is saying.

☑ Define the Conflict

Once you have recognized that conflicts can be handled rationally, you are ready to ask, "Why are we in conflict? What is the nature of the conflict? Which of us feels more strongly about the issue? What can we do about it?" Here again, it is crucial to send "I" messages ("I think it is unfair for me to do all the work around here"; "I don't like going to the library for everyone else") and to avoid sending blame messages ("You do everything wrong"; "You are a spoiled brat"; "You'll make us fail"). Be very clear that you would like to join with the other group members in discovering a solution that will be acceptable and beneficial for all of you—a solution whereby none of you will lose and each will win.

☑ Check Your Perceptions

A situation is a conflict when it is perceived as a conflict. In conflict-ripe situations, we often distort the behavior, position, or motivations of the other person involved. We prefer to see one set of motivations rather than another because it meets our own needs to interpret the situation that way. When we do this, we deny the legitimacy of any other position. Thus, it is not uncommon for each person in a conflict to believe, mistakenly, that the other person is committing underhanded and even vicious acts. It is not extraordinary for each person to make erroneous assumptions about the other's feelings, nor is it unusual for people to think they disagree with each other simply because they have been unable to communicate their agreement. For these reasons, it is important for each person to take some time to explain his or her assumptions and frame of reference to the others.

After each of you has identified how you feel, it is time to determine whether you understand one another. This calls for active, empathic listening. Along with active listening, role reversal can help people in conflict understand

Reflect and Respond

On the basis of your understanding of leadership and the value of conflict and conflict management, agree or disagree with this excerpt from Deborah Tannen's *Talking from 9 to 5*. Supply reasons and examples from both research and your own life that support the stance you are taking.

When decisions are made by groups, not everyone has equal access to the decision-making process. Those who will take a position and refuse to budge, regardless of the persuasive power or intensity of feeling among others, are far more likely to get their way. Those who feel strongly about a position but are inclined to back off in the face of intransigence or very strong feeling from others are much less likely to get their way.[56]

Focus on Service Learning

Using resources on conflict management and resolution, such as www.campus-adr.org/ or www.conflictresolution.uiuc .edu/mediation/, develop a plan to address a campus conflict such as how to resolve disagreements between dorm and apartment mates. Lead a team in executing your plan, creating press releases for the campus paper, and working with residence hall and student life counselors to develop a workshop based on your plan to present on campus.

one another. Like active listening, role reversal permits you to see things as others in the group see them. If you are willing to listen to and experience another person's point of view, that person will be more likely to listen to and experience yours.

☑ Suggest Possible Solutions

The goal during the "possible solutions" phase is for group members to put their heads together and come up with a variety of solutions. Most important, neither you nor anyone else in the group should evaluate, condemn, or make fun of any of the suggestions. You must suspend judgment and honestly believe that the conflict can be resolved in a variety of ways.

☑ Assess Alternative Solutions and Choose the One That Seems Best

After possible solutions have been generated, it is time to see which solution each person considers best. It is legitimate to try to determine which solutions will let one side win at the other's expense, which will make everyone lose, and which will let everyone win. Your objective is to discover which solutions are totally unacceptable to each side and which are mutually acceptable. (It is crucial to be honest during this stage.) Once all the solutions have been assessed, you are in a position to determine if one of the mutually acceptable solutions is clearly superior to all the others—that is, if it has the most advantages and the fewest disadvantages. Also, be sure to explore whether it is the most constructive solution.

☑ Try Your Solution and Evaluate It

During the "tryout" stage, you see how well the chosen solution is working. You try to ascertain who is doing what, when, where, and under what conditions, and you ask how all this is affecting each person in the group. You want to know if the people involved were able to carry out the job as planned, whether the solution adopted has solved the problem, and whether the outcome has been rewarding to everyone. If not, it is time to begin the conflict resolution process again.

Revisiting Chapter Objectives

1. **Define** *leadership* **and distinguish among various leadership styles: type X, type Y, autocratic, laissez-faire, and democratic.**   To achieve their objectives, groups need effective leadership. Leadership is simply the ability to influence others, and there are many leadership styles. A type X leader believes group members need to be closely controlled and coerced to work. A type Y leader believes members are self-directed and seek responsibility as well as opportunities for personal achievement. The autocratic leader dominates and directs all the other members of the group, whereas the laissez-faire leader lets them do their own thing. In most situations, the democratic leader, who encourages all the members to be involved constructively in decision making and problem solving, is preferred.

2. **Describe how trait theory, situational theory, functional theory, and transformational leadership contribute to our understanding of leadership.**   There are four principal explanations of how people become leaders. Trait theory holds that some men and women are simply born to lead. Situational theory holds that the situation itself—the nature of the problem and the characteristics of the group—determines who assumes leadership. Functional theory holds that a number of group members can and should share the various leadership functions that need to be performed if the group is to achieve its goals. A transformational leader helps group members imagine and visualize the future group members can build together, strengthening the group's culture.

3. **Define** *conflict* **and explain how you feel when involved in a group conflict.**   Conflict is an inevitable part of the life of any group. A group experiences conflict whenever a member's thoughts or acts limit, prevent, or interfere with his or her own thoughts or acts or with those of another member.

4. **Define** *groupthink* **and explain its consequences.**   Conflict is not always a negative force. In fact, the absence or avoidance of conflict can result in groupthink, a problem that occurs when a group allows the desire for consensus to override careful analysis and reasoned decision making.

5. **Distinguish between competitive and cooperative conflict orientations.**   When a conflict is handled constructively, no one loses and everyone wins. A conflict can be destructive if all the participants are dissatisfied with its outcomes and believe they have lost something. The use of cooperative problem-solving methods instead of competitive orientations, which create win-lose encounters, facilitates constructive conflict resolution.

6. **Identify how to use the conflict grid and describe the benefits and problems that can result from effective and ineffective handling of group conflict.**   Whether a conflict helps or hinders a group's operation depends on how the members react to it. If they resort to strategies such as blaming, withdrawing, intellectualizing, distracting, and forcing, their effectiveness will be impaired. However, if they discuss the issues calmly, they can break impasses and solve difficulties. Various styles of handling conflict can be plotted on Blake and Mouton's conflict grid. The most effective style is that of the problem-solving collaborator, who takes a win-win approach and has high concern both for results and for the feelings of other people. It is essential to take into account the various cultures that people may reflect in their approaches to conflict and conflict resolution.

THE WRAP-UP

7. **Identify behaviors that can be used to resolve conflicts effectively.**   A number of communication techniques can help us resolve conflicts that occur both online and offline. The first step is simply to recognize that conflicts can be settled rationally—by focusing on the issues, not on personalities. Next, we should define the conflict and check the accuracy of our perceptions, using "I" messages, empathic listening, and role reversal, as appropriate. Then, we should suggest and assess a variety of solutions to the conflict, choose the best one that is mutually acceptable, and try it.

Resources for Further Inquiry and Reflection

To apply your understanding of how the principles in Chapter 11 are at work in our daily lives, consult the following resources for further inquiry and reflection. Or, if you prefer, choose any other appropriate resource. Then connect the ideas expressed in your chosen selection with the communication concepts and issues you are learning about both in and out of class.

 Listen to Me

"Believe" (Staind)
"Sometimes You Can't Make It on Your Own" (U2)
"The In Crowd" (Ramsey Lewis Trio)
"Leader of the Pack" (The Shangri-Las)
"Rise Above This" (Seether)

Each of these songs explores the nature of a hero or a leader. What leadership and conflict-resolution concepts does any one of these songs illustrate?

 View Me

Apollo 13	*Glory Road*
Titanic	*Lord of the Flies*
Mutiny on the Bounty	*Hotel Rwanda*
Michael Clayton	*The Dark Knight*

These films explore how leadership can impede or foster group effectiveness, including the handling of group conflict. Choose one film and use it to discuss the nature of leadership, dangers of groupthink, or effective conflict management techniques.

 Read Me

Tom Wolfe. *The Right Stuff*. New York: Bantam Books, 1983.
David Halberstam. *The Education of a Coach*. New York: Hyperion, 2006.
Herb Cohen. *Negotiate This!* New York: Warner Business Books, 2003.
Rudolph Giuliani. *Leadership*. New York: Hyperion, 2002.
William Golding. *Lord of the Flies*. New York: Penguin Books, 1999. (Original work published 1954.)
Irving Janis. *Victims of Groupthink: A Psychological Study of Foreign Policy Decisions and Fiascos*. Boston: Houghton Mifflin, 1972.
Barack Obama. *The Audacity of Hope*. New York: Crown, 2006.
Scott McClellan. *What Happened: Inside the Bush White House and Washington's Culture of Deception*. New York: Public Affairs, 2008.

These books explore the nature of leadership or conflict resolution. Choose one and discuss the leadership and/or conflict management lessons contained in it that you consider the most important.

 Tell Me

Share with the class the insights you gained from your chosen Listen to Me, View Me, or Read Me selection.

Agree or disagree with the following statement, with reasons: Truth springs from conflict.

Key Chapter Terminology

Use the Online Learning Center at www.mhhe.com/gamble10e to further your knowledge of the following terminology.

www.mhhe.com/gamble10e

accommodator 291
achieved leader 278
autocratic, or authoritarian, leaders 279
avoider 290
competitive forcer 292
competitive set 289
compromiser 291
conflict 285
conflict grid 290
cooperative set 289
democratic leaders 281
designated leader 278

functional theory 283
groupthink 285
laissez-faire leader 280
leadership 278
problem-solving collaborator 292
role reversal 290
situational theory 282
trait theory 281
transformational leader 283
type X leader 279
type Y leader 279

Idioms in Translation

a body of research — numerous research studies

a host of — numerous

alien to them — unknown to them

deepened your awareness — increased your awareness

devil's advocate — person who argues against what others believe

for all seasons — for all time

never made it up the chain of command — never got to the person in charge

Culture Cue

In the United States, recognition of one's work is a great reward. In Russia, compromise is viewed as a weakness. The Chinese expect a strong relationship before reaching an agreement.

Test Your Understanding

Go to the *Self Quizzes* on the book's Online Learning Center at www.mhhe.com/gamble10e.

www.mhhe.com/gamble10e

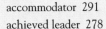

LOOKING BACK AND AHEAD

Consider This Case: Sorry, Wrong Number

"Your participant code has been accepted," said the automated voice on the phone. "The conference has begun; please hold while we connect you."

Relieved, Sam heard a couple of clicks and the familiar musical tone, and then the voice of his boss, Karen, saying, "Hello?" Karen, customer relations manager for a small manufacturer of healthy snack foods, including veggie chips and salt-free dip, worked at company headquarters about 100 miles away. Sayid and Jennifer, two of his co-workers, were located at a branch office about halfway between Sam and Karen. Asher, the fifth member of the department, worked at headquarters and was Karen's assistant.

Sam, the newest employee, worked from his home office, traveling to headquarters once a month. Sayid and Jennifer visited headquarters once a month as well, and the three of them and Asher usually spent the day working with Karen, bringing her up to date on their progress and getting feedback from her about their job performance. Sam's responsibility was to answer the company's toll-free number and respond to customer e-mails sent to the corporate Web site. Customer communications that called for refunds or replacement products, or that required any kind of investigation, were passed along to Sayid and Jennifer for resolution.

"Hi, Karen, it's me, Sam," he said.

"Sam! I've been waiting for you to call in!" Karen's annoyance came through clearly over the phone.

Sam checked his watch. "Am I late?" he asked anxiously. This week had been his turn to send everyone an e-mail confirming their regular weekly conference call, and he was sure that when he set it up, he'd accounted for the fact that Karen's location was in a different time zone from everyone else's. He'd sent the agenda, too, he remembered—the agenda items were their weekly status reports, the new customer complaint form that headquarters wanted them to fill out, and their vacation schedules.

"No, you're not late," Karen snapped. "Asher's late. But I think there's been a mix-up with the

conference call. Sayid just sent me an IM—he and Jennifer are already waiting for us on a different line, wondering where we are. Why are they calling in on a different number?"

"I don't know," said Sam nervously. "Hang on a minute." He clicked open the e-mail he'd gotten from the phone company and checked the call-in number he'd sent everyone. Sure enough, it was a different number from the one they usually used.

"Um, I'm sorry, Karen. It looks like the phone company did give us a different number this week for some reason, and that's what I put in the e-mail—that's the number you and I are talking on now. But I guess Sayid and Jennifer dialed the old one by mistake, and that's why we've got two conference calls going on instead of one. What do you think we should do? Should we hang up and call the other number?"

"Sayid and Jennifer should hang up and call back so they can join us here," said Karen. "You contact the two of them, and I'll keep this line open while I go try to find out where Asher is."

"OK," said Sam. "Again, I'm sorry about the mix-up."

"Well, don't worry about it now," said Karen with a sigh. "Sayid and Jennifer should have read your memo more carefully. The thing is, we're losing time here, and I need to talk to all of you about our department's new goals before I leave for the airport. So let's get everyone on the same page right away, all right?"

"Sure," said Sam, torn between embarrassment at his own error and irritation at Sayid and Jennifer. It was their failure to read his memo carefully that had made him look bad in front of his boss, he reasoned. Even Karen thought so. Why couldn't those two pay more attention?

Cradling the receiver between his ear and his shoulder, he started typing a message to Sayid and Jennifer. Suddenly he took in what Karen had just said. She wanted to talk about goals—why hadn't he put that on the agenda? Desperately, he tried to remember whether Karen had sent him any input about the agenda. Had he remembered to ask her for it? Would Asher, Sayid, and Jennifer blame him if they were caught unprepared for that part of the call?

Suddenly, Sam heard the musical tone that signaled another party joining the call. "Hey, Sam!" said Asher. "Where's Karen? How come you're not in the conference call with Jenn and Sayid?"

DISCUSSION QUESTIONS

1. How could Sam have prevented the problems in this phone call?

2. What can you deduce about Karen's leadership style in this situation?

3. What difference do you think it made to Karen and Sam's conversation that there was no nonverbal component for either of them to interpret?

4. What conflict-resolution style is Sam using? Do you think it's the most effective one to use in this situation? Why or why not?

5. What are some of the advantages and disadvantages of online communication that Sam's experience with Sayid, Asher, and Jennifer reveals?

LET'S GO TO THE DVD

Investigating *The Office*

Using as a resource the organization depicted in the television series *The Office*, write an analysis of the group communication of people who work there. Be sure to answer these questions:

1. How do ethics and culture affect the group?
2. What decision-making and problem-solving techniques does the group use?

3. What kinds of roles do group members enact?
4. How would you describe the group's leadership?
5. How does the group react to conflict? How does it react when facing a crisis?
6. What are the group's strengths and weaknesses?
7. What suggestions can you make to improve the group's functioning?

CHAPTER 12

After finishing this chapter, you should be able to

1. Approach public speaking systematically.

2. Conduct a thorough self-analysis in order to choose the best topic.

3. Understand your audience so that you can tailor your speech directly to them.

4. Explain how the nature of the occasion influences a speech.

5. Choose an effective topic.

6. Clarify your topic and formulate your thesis statement.

The Speaker and the Audience: The Occasion and the Subject

Our technologically rich environment depends on user-generated content. Today, we create, send, and receive countless messages using blogs, Podcasts, YouTube, or Facebook. We e-mail, beam messages, and text others, sharing our thoughts and feelings. The chapters in this part of the text call on you to apply your skill at developing user-generated content and your understanding of and familiarity with technology to a different communication venue: the public speech—another means of opening minds, sharing information, and advocating for ideas.

In our age of abundant electronic connections, public speakers are in demand, and the number of platforms open to them is increasing. In fact, many venues seek speakers these days. From corporate meetings to trade shows, from educational conferences to political rallies, from town meetings to your classroom, speakers play important roles. Public speaking is like a form of currency, only instead of providing access to the marketplace of goods and services, it provides access to the marketplace of ideas. From Bill Gates to Steve Jobs, from the local school superintendent to a concerned parent, from Oprah to Obama, from us to you and your peers, we share the responsibility to make our voices heard. And there is no shortage of advice on how to improve the ability to speak so that others listen. From blogs to self-help books, from DVDs to this text, resources exist to help you become more effective and at ease speaking in public. Are you able to stand before an audience without fear? Can you personalize a message so that others believe your words are meant for them? Do you know how to organize your ideas and stay on course without derailing your objective? Can you deliver your message and not become unnerved, so that audience members leave the experience richer for having listened to you? And can you have fun doing it?

No matter your age, sex, or ethnic or racial background, becoming effective at speaking in public is an important skill to develop. Since public speaking is likely to play an important role in your future, let's prepare to meet that challenge.

In the United States there are more than twenty thousand different ways of earning a living, and effective speech is essential to every one.
—Andrew Weaver

Public speaking can be a horror for the shy person, but it can also be the ultimate act of liberation.
—Susan Faludi

Violence is, essentially, a confession of ultimate inarticulateness.
—Time *magazine*

PUBLIC SPEAKING DEFINED

Public speaking—these are two seemingly harmless words. **Public speaking** is the act of preparing, staging, and delivering a presentation to an audience. We speak every day. Under ordinary circumstances, we rarely give speaking, or our skills in speaking, a second thought—that is, until we are asked to deliver a speech or simply to speak in public. Once

public speaking
the act of preparing, staging, and delivering a presentation to an audience

Online Learning Center

Go to the Online Learning Center at www.mhhe.com/gamble10e and answer the questions in the *Self Inventory* to evaluate your understanding of public speaking.

we know that is what we are going to have to do, if we are like most Americans, we fear it more than we fear bee stings, accidents, heights, or our own death.[1]

Just as we can learn to handle ourselves more effectively in our interpersonal and group relationships, if we take the time that is needed to analyze and practice successful behaviors, we can also learn to handle ourselves more effectively as public speakers. With practice, we can develop the understanding and master the skills that will make us articulate speakers who are organized, confident, and competent, and can communicate ideas in such a way that others will be interested in them and persuaded by them.

We start our examination of public speaking by putting the entire speech-making process into a logical format that you can examine and follow in detail. The process serves as a road map—one you can use to prepare every public presentation you will ever make. In this chapter, as well as Chapters 13 and 14, we explore factors involved in preparing a speech. In Chapter 15 we shift our focus from preparation to presentation and analysis. Then, once we have a handle on how the process works, in Chapters 16 and 17 we investigate two essential speech-making models: the informative speech and the persuasive speech.

> What comes to mind when you hear the words *public speaking?* What do you think? What do you feel?

APPROACHING SPEECH MAKING SYSTEMATICALLY

People respond to the challenge of public speaking in a variety of ways. Some believe that speech making is an inborn skill: "I talk a lot, so this public speaking business poses no difficulty for me." Others view it as torture: "I'm scared stiff! This will be traumatic!" These attitudes represent two extremes, and both can cause problems.

Overconfident people run the risk of being inadequate speakers because they conduct little research and thus are ill prepared. People who are overly anxious or fearful may find it terribly trying and nerve-racking to stand before an audience and deliver a talk. The most effective speakers are those who display a healthy respect for the challenges involved in speaking before others and who work systematically to create, prepare, and deliver an admirable presentation.

Most likely, you will be assigned a speech before you have had the chance to finish reading and applying all the relevant information contained in subsequent chapters, so here we offer a preview of the speech preparation you need as you get ready to speak before your class for the first time.

> *Work It Out*
>
> Identify your favorite talk show hosts. Which host do you believe would make the best speaker? Why?

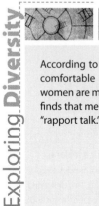

Exploring **Diversity**

Report Talk and Rapport Talk

According to researcher Deborah Tannen, men are more comfortable speaking in public than women are, while women are more comfortable speaking in private. Tannen finds that men excel at "report talk," while women excel at "rapport talk."

Do your experiences confirm or contradict this finding? If this disparity exists, what, if anything, do you think should be done to change it? Men, she believes, are more focused on status, jockeying for position, while women like to refer one thing to another in an effort to reinforce relationships.

The staircaselike chart in Figure 12.1 reveals a systematic, step-by-step approach. As you make your way up the staircase, you move from one speech-making phase into another. There is a logical order to speech making that reduces the process to four landings: (1) topic selection and audience analysis; (2) speech development, support, and organization; (3) presentation practice and delivery; and (4) postpresentation analysis. Although this chapter focuses only on the steps leading to the first landing of the speech-making staircase, we briefly review each of the tasks you need to accomplish as you climb to the top of the staircase, successfully completing and evaluating a speech. Before we look at these tasks, let us remind you that the staircase is only as strong as its foundation. Each time you speak, ask yourself: Are you handling your topic as *ethically* as possible? Are you applying principles of *critical thinking?* Are you as sensitive as you can be to the challenges posed by the *diversity* inherent in receivers?

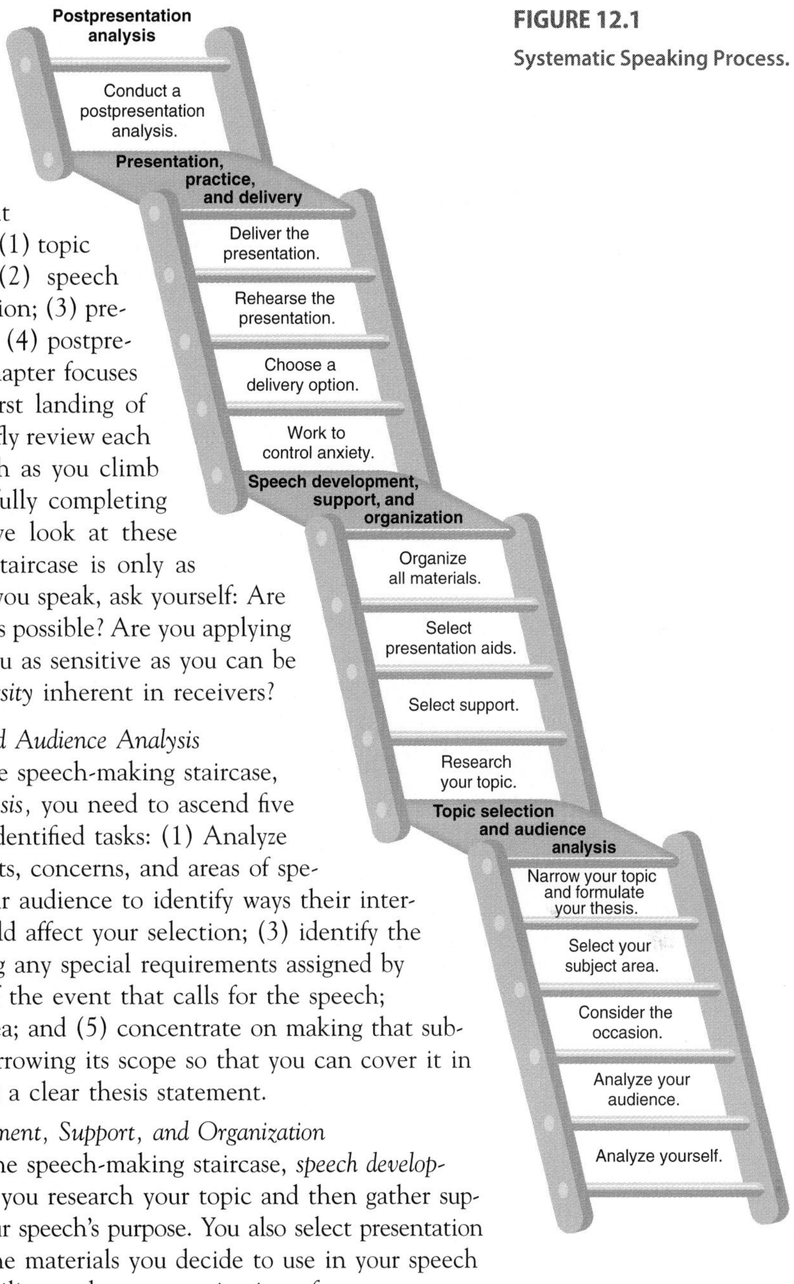

First Landing: Topic Selection and Audience Analysis
To reach the first landing of the speech-making staircase, *topic selection and audience analysis,* you need to ascend five steps, completing each of the identified tasks: (1) Analyze yourself to identify your interests, concerns, and areas of special knowledge; (2) analyze your audience to identify ways their interests, needs, and knowledge could affect your selection; (3) identify the occasion for speaking, including any special requirements assigned by your instructor or the nature of the event that calls for the speech; (4) choose a general subject area; and (5) concentrate on making that subject increasingly specific, by narrowing its scope so that you can cover it in the allotted time and preparing a clear thesis statement.

Second Landing: Speech Development, Support, and Organization
To reach the next landing of the speech-making staircase, *speech development, support, and organization,* you research your topic and then gather supporting materials that clarify your speech's purpose. You also select presentation aids. Finally, you organize all the materials you decide to use in your speech into a logical sequence that facilitates the communication of your message.

Third Landing: Presentation Practice and Delivery
You complete a series of tasks to reach the third landing of the speech-making staircase. Each task helps you to deliver your speech as effectively as possible. First, you work to control anxiety. Then you rehearse your presentation, taking pains to revise it during the rehearsal process as needed. Your ultimate goal is to deliver a presentation that flows, has maximum impact, and is readily comprehensible. You should also anticipate and prepare for questions audience members may ask and reactions they may have. You can then focus the energy produced by any anxiety you

FIGURE 12.1

Systematic Speaking Process.

Postpresentation analysis
Conduct a postpresentation analysis.

Presentation, practice, and delivery
Deliver the presentation.
Rehearse the presentation.
Choose a delivery option.
Work to control anxiety.

Speech development, support, and organization
Organize all materials.
Select presentation aids.
Select support.
Research your topic.

Topic selection and audience analysis
Narrow your topic and formulate your thesis.
Select your subject area.
Consider the occasion.
Analyze your audience.
Analyze yourself.

Work It Out
Brainstorm the criteria you would use to judge a speaker's effectiveness.

There is just no way around it—you have to do your homework. A speaker may be very well informed, but if he hasn't thought out exactly what he wants to say today, to this audience, he has no business taking up other people's valuable time.

— Lee Iacocca, Iacocca: An Autobiography

may be experiencing and put it to work for you during the actual delivery of your speech.

Fourth Landing: Postpresentation Analysis

After delivering your speech, compare and contrast your expectations with what you actually experienced during the delivery of your speech.

Effective speakers critique their performances. They know that they and their receivers will be changed in some way by every speech event; they know that their words, once spoken, leave an indelible impression, and they want to be certain that they learn as much as possible from the experience so that they can apply the lessons learned to the next speech.

The speech-making staircase is one you will climb again and again, working your way from one speech experience to the next. In time, you will master the ins and outs of public speaking. Answering questions such as the following can help prepare you to work your way systematically through the speech-making process:

What kind of presentation are you going to make? _____

What will be its central message? _____

Why are you giving it? _____

Where and when will you deliver it? _____

How much time will you have? _____

Who and how many people will be in your audience? _____

How much do audience members know about your topic? _____

What do you want your audience to think, do, feel, or remember? _____

What are your speech-making goals? _____

What will you do to capture the audience's attention? _____

What will you include in the presentation's body? _____

How will you close? _____

Let us continue our climb up the ladder together.

For the remainder of this chapter, we look more specifically at the steps involved in ascending to the first landing, topic selection and audience analysis, beginning with your need to analyze yourself.

ANALYZE YOURSELF

Speech . . . preserves contact—it is silence which isolates.

—Thomas Mann

Thorough self-analysis is a prerequisite for effective speech making. Although at times topics may be assigned, under many circumstances the choice will be left to you, the speaker. Even when a topic is specified, it is recommended that you conduct a self-analysis to help you uncover aspects that you may find particularly interesting or appealing. Such an analysis can also become the basis for personal stories or anecdotes that can eventually be integrated into your presentation.

There are more topics for speeches than you could possibly exhaust in a lifetime. According to Elie Wiesel, holocaust survivor and Nobel Prize winner, "I don't know what to say," is an all-too-familiar lament:

> But where was I to start? The world is so vast, I shall start with the country I know best, my own. But my country is so very large. I had better start with my town. But my town, too, is large, I had best start with my street. No: my home. No: my family. Never mind, I shall start with myself.[2]

From the Listener's Point of View

1. Describe the behaviors exhibited by the most effective speaker you have had the good fortune to hear.

2. Contrast that description with a description of the most ineffective speaker you ever had the misfortune to hear.

At the outset of your preparation, you should take some time for what corporate trainers call a front-end analysis—a preliminary examination of possibilities. The following sections describe five useful forms that a front-end analysis can take.

Review Your Life: Your Autobiography

You can begin by reviewing your life in terms of potential topics:

1. Divide your life (thus far) into thirds: early, middle, more recent. Compose one sentence to sum up what your life consisted of during each segment (for example, "I lived in Gary, Indiana, with my two brothers and mother, and went to elementary school").

2. Under each summary statement, identify your main interests and concerns at that time of your life.

3. Examine the interests and concerns you listed. Which of them recur? Which have you left behind? Which have you developed only recently?

Consider the Moment: This Moment

A second approach is to consider this very moment as a source of potential topics:

1. On the left side of a sheet of paper, list sensory experiences; that is, list everything you are able to see, hear, taste, smell, or touch from your present vantage point.

2. When you have listed 10 to 15 items, go back over the list and note topics that might be suggested by each observation or experience. Arrange these in a corresponding list on the right side of the paper. For example, if you list "passing train" in the left column, you might enter "mass transportation" in the right column. Note: If you are not satisfied with the topics you have identified, move to another location and begin the process again.

Search the News: Newspapers, Nightly News, and Newsmagazine Shows

A third approach is to work with a newspaper to find potential topics:

1. Take today's newspaper and, beginning with the front page, read a story and compile a list of topics suggested by it.

2. Do not prejudge your ideas. Simply work your way through the paper, looking for possibilities. For example, the July 20, 2008, issue of the *New York Times* devoted space to the growing debt of Americans. What potential topics does such a subject suggest to you? A speech on how people get into debt? The tactics of collection agencies? The problems presented by easy credit? The pressures to consume? The relationship between age, class, race, and debt?[3]

A variation on this approach calls on you to view a nightly local or national news broadcast or newsmagazine program with pen and paper in hand. Divide the paper into two columns. Label the first column "Stories Presented." Label the second column "Ideas Generated by This News Story." Work your way through the program, looking for possibilities. The same methodology will work for newsmagazine programs such as *60 Minutes, 20/20,* and *Nightline.*

Use an Online Topic Generator

A number of Web sites can help with topic generation. Try using the following topic generators:

> www.yukoncollege.yk.ca/~agraham/guides/tpgen.htm
>
> www.speech-topics-help.com

ANALYZE YOUR AUDIENCE

Having conducted a search of yourself, it is now time to determine where your audience fits in. A pitfall for many speakers is speaking to please themselves—approaching speech making with only their own interests and their own points of view in mind and neglecting the needs and interests of their audience. These

Poor preparation may cause audience members to stop paying attention—a direct result of MYGLO—"my eyes glaze over."

speakers will often choose an inappropriate topic, dress improperly, or deliver a presentation that is either too simple or too technical for the audience. We have all heard medical experts address general audiences using such complex language that their listeners were baffled and bored. We have also heard speakers address highly educated groups in such simple language and about such mundane topics that everyone was not only bored but insulted. There is a catchy acronym for describing speeches that bore or confuse audience members; it is **MYGLO,** for "my eyes glaze over"—which is exactly what happens when you lose the audience's attention.[4]

Your focus during the initial stages of speech preparation should not, therefore, be solely on yourself. Be prepared to consider a potential topic from the point of view of your audience. Just as you bring your own background and experiences to a presentation, the audience members will bring theirs. Thus, it is important to consider what your listeners are thinking about, what their needs and hopes are.

To pay proper attention to your audience, you must know something about it. For example, how familiar are the audience members with what you are going to talk about? What is their attitude toward your topic? What are they anxious about? What would they like to know? What are their expectations? If you do not find out the answers to questions like these, you run the risk of having your words fall on deaf ears. Unfortunately, of all the steps in the process of public speaking, audience analysis is most often overlooked.

Beginning Your Audience Analysis: Who Are They?

How can you know, or how can you try to determine, precisely who will attend your presentation? For example, can you expect certain interested groups or individuals to come? Will others whom you do not expect surprise you by showing up?

Information about your audience should come from two key sources: (1) your personal experience with the group and (2) original research.

Work It Out
Make a list of 10 subjects you believe would be inappropriate for delivery to your class. Discuss how each topic might be approached to make it appropriate.

MYGLO
an acronym for "my eyes glaze over"

Work It Out
Explain how you would go about customizing a presentation for delivery before the class. Identify how the presentation would or should differ if it were to be presented to an audience of potential employers instead of peers.

Ethics and Communication

The Magic Bullet of Speech Making

What is the magic bullet of speech making? Practitioners and consultants offer varied answers to this question. One analyst says that to deduce the answer, listen to and view masters of speech-making such as Winston Churchill and Martin Luther King Jr. on YouTube.[5] Another believes the answer lies in embodying both style and substance, that leadership and communication go hand-in-hand.[6] A third, Roger Ailes, president of Fox News, writes that the magic bullet of communication is being likable: "With it, your audience will forgive just about everything else you do wrong. Without it, you can hit every bull's eye in the room, and no one will be impressed."[7]

What do you think the magic bullet is? Is it being emotionally involving, likable, or something else? Is being able to emotionally arouse receivers more or less important than having something significant to say? Should it be? Is being likable more or less important than giving receivers information they need to have but may not enjoy hearing? Should it be? What happens when you have something significant or necessary to say but you fall short when it comes to involving receivers or motivating them to like you? What hurdles does a speaker whom you dislike have to overcome or who fails to involve you emotionally have to overcome?

Speakers sometimes access the Internet to discover how to reach an audience.

Personal Experience

The best source of information about your audience is your personal experience with the group—either as a speaker or as an audience member. If you have attended several functions or are a member of the class or organization you are expected to address, you have personal knowledge of the audience members. Thus, you will probably be able to formulate reasonably accurate predictions about the appropriateness of your material for that group.

Research

What if you have had no previous contact with the group you are to address? If that is the case, you might ask the program planner to provide you with relevant information. For instance, if you have been asked to speak at a professional convention, you would be concerned with specific information about the makeup of the audience: How many will attend the lecture? Will there be students present? These and other factors would have to be taken into account in preparing and customizing the presentation.

Another way to gather information about a group is to obtain copies of public relations material. Recent news releases highlighting the organization may help put you on the same track as your audience. Corporate newsletters and Web sites can also be valuable, as can a trip to the local library for information describing the organization.

The library and the Internet also hold clues to the backgrounds and interests of potential audience members. You can use these resources to discover what local, regional, and national opinion polls reveal about the views potential audience members might have on a variety of social and political issues.

To further enhance your knowledge, you might also directly survey potential receivers. You can use the results of a well-thought-out questionnaire to help estimate how much your listeners already know about your subject and their attitudes toward it. Questionnaires usually contain the following types of questions: closed ended, scaled, and open ended. Closed-ended questions are highly structured, requiring respondents only to indicate which of the provided responses most accurately reflects their own. The following are examples of closed-ended questions:

Please indicate your marital status:

❏ married   ❏ single   ❏ divorced   ❏ widowed   ❏ separated

Do you think prayer should be permitted in public schools?

❏ yes   ❏ no   ❏ undecided

In contrast, scaled questions allow respondents to indicate their views along a continuum ranging by degree from polar extremes such as strongly agree to strongly disagree. The following is a scaled question:

To what extent do you agree or disagree with the following statement? Condoms should be dispensed in public high schools.

Strongly agree   Agree   Neutral   Disagree   Strongly disagree

Open-ended questions allow respondents even more answering freedom. For example:

Respond to this statement: A politician's private life is not the public's business.

Original research also takes the form of direct discussions with members of the potential audience.

Robert Orben, a speech consultant and writer for former president Gerald Ford, tells the following story.[8] A presidential address had been planned for a college campus in Minnesota. The speechwriters knew that many of the students were not supporters of the president. They therefore spent a great deal of time on the telephone with students and school officials in an effort to obtain specific bits of information that could be included in the speech to help create a bond between the president and his audience. Finally, a somewhat disgruntled student provided the writers with the "gem" they felt they needed. They completed the speech, confident that they had done their job well—and they had. Ford began his address by saying, "Washington may have the new subway, Montreal may have the monorail, but this campus has the Quickie!" The students in the audience laughed and applauded warmly. Why? The drinking age was 21 in Minnesota but 18 in a neighboring state. And the 15-mile trip students often took to get to the first bar across the state line was known as "the Quickie." In this instance, talking at length to potential members of the audience provided information that helped establish an atmosphere in which the listeners, although not necessarily in agreement with the speaker, were at least rendered friendly enough to listen to his views.

Demographics of Audiences: What Are They Like?

Since the background and composition of your audience are important factors to consider in planning a speech, every effort must be made to determine audience demographics: age, gender, family orientation, religion, cultural background, occupation, socioeconomic status, educational level, and additional factors (such as membership in organizations). Despite the fact that no one audience will be entirely uniform in all these categories, you should consider each one during your initial planning sessions.

Age

Would you give precisely the same presentation to a group of children that you would give to your class? Almost certainly not. How might your presentations differ? Could you even deal with the same subject? The adult students would bring many more years of experience to your presentation than the children would. Adults may have been through economic hassles and even a war, for instance—experiences that children probably have not yet faced. Of course, the maturity of the two audiences would also differ. These contrasts may seem obvious, but age is a factor often overlooked in planning speeches. You might choose to speak on abortion or birth control to a college audience, but you might fail to realize that the same material would probably have less intrinsic appeal to an audience of senior citizens.

Work It Out

Choose a topic of current interest. How would you approach the topic for a presentation to people your own age? How would you change your approach to appeal to an older or a younger audience?

The background and composition of the audience need to be taken into account when planning a speech.

It's also wise to consider how your own age will affect your presentation. How close are you to the mean, or average, age of your anticipated listeners? If you are about the same age as the audience members, your job may be a little easier. If you are much older or much younger than the audience members, you will need to attempt to see your topic through their eyes and adjust it accordingly.

Your goal is to be sensitive to the references you employ, the language you use, and the rate at which you speak so that you shrink rather than enlarge the age gap that may exist between you and your receivers. Only if the receivers are able to comprehend your words, identify with your examples and illustrations, and recognize the persons and events you refer to will they be in a position to respond as you hope. When you close whatever age gap exists, you increase the likelihood of audience understanding. The point is that the average age of your audience matters. Research shows that, while younger listeners are more open to new ideas, older ones are less receptive to change. You can use information like this to judge how difficult it will be for you to attain your speech-making goal.[9]

Gender

Gender can also influence an audience's reaction to your speech. There are, admittedly, some myths and misconceptions about the effects of gender. (For example, in the past, researchers believed that women could be more easily persuaded than men.[10] Do you think this is a valid viewpoint today?) Still, you need to consider gender differences, especially if you speak to an audience composed entirely or mainly of one sex. Study your potential audience before drawing any conclusions. Although the same topics may appeal to both men and women, gender may affect the ways male and female audience members respond. For example, a discussion of rape may elicit a stronger emotional reaction from the women in your class, whereas a discussion of vasectomy may elicit a stronger

Do you believe that to appeal to the diverse backgrounds and interests of receivers, the speaker should "bounce around" rather than spend too much time catering to the interests and concerns of any one segment of the audience? In your opinion, if a speaker spends too much time attempting to involve only one audience member type, will he or she lose the interest of all the others in the audience? On the other hand, do you see any potential danger in bouncing around?

response from the men. Be aware, though, that the so-called traditional roles of men and women are changing and that stereotypes once attributed to both groups are crumbling.

Family Orientation

Are most of the members of your audience single? Married? Divorced? Widowed? From one-parent or two-parent homes? These factors might influence your audience's reactions to your presentation. The concerns of one group are not necessarily the concerns of another.

Religion

If you are speaking to a religious group with which you have little familiarity, make a point of discussing your topic in advance with some group members. Some groups have formulated very clear guidelines regarding issues such as divorce, birth control, and abortion. It is important for you to understand the audience and its feelings if you are to be able to relate effectively to its members.

Cultural Background

Use your knowledge of an audience's culture and mind-set to bond with listeners. Because our society is increasingly multicultural, it is very important that you attune yourself to beliefs audience members hold, perhaps seeking sources and interviewing experts with different cultural orientations to ensure your speech accurately reflects a diversity of thinking rather than one knowledge system.[11] Your analysis of receivers will also influence your speech's style. For example, receivers from low-context cultures expect a speaker to explicitly explain his or her message, while persons from high-context cultures prefer more indirection. So, as you plan your speech, keep cultural preferences in mind. By identifying racial, ethnic, religious, or cultural differences, you can prevent potential misunderstandings. Being aware of audience makeup helps you predict how audience members will respond to your topic or the position you are advocating. Take time to consider how the presence or absence of receiver diversity might influence how receivers react to you and your speech.

Occupation

People are interested in issues that relate to their own work and the work of those important to them. Consequently, if possible, relate your subject to the occupational concerns of your audience. Also, if you are speaking before an audience whose members belong to a particular occupational group, you must attempt to find or create examples and illustrations that reflect their concerns.

Socioeconomic Status

Researchers have found that there are psychological as well as economic differences among different socioeconomic classes. Having or lacking discretionary income, power, and prestige evidently influences our attitudes and beliefs. Since our society is socially mobile, with a "move-up" philosophy, as a speaker, you can usually assume that your audience members want to get ahead and improve their position in life, and you can adjust your presentation to appeal to that desire.

Educational Level

Although it is important to determine your listeners' educational level, you cannot let your findings trap you into making unwarranted assumptions—either positive or negative—regarding their intellectual ability. Still, in general, you will probably find that the higher people's level of education, the more general their knowledge and the more insightful their questions. In addition, the more knowledgeable members of your audience may have specific data to dispute your stand on controversial issues. An educated and sophisticated audience may be far more aware of the impact of various political and social programs than, say, a group of high school dropouts. A less educated audience may need background information that a more educated audience may consider superfluous.

Whatever the educational level of your listeners, the following are three precepts to keep in mind:

1. Don't underestimate the intelligence of your listeners; don't speak down to them.
2. Don't overestimate their need for information; don't try to do too much in the time that is available to you.
3. Don't use jargon if there's a chance that your listeners are unfamiliar with it; listeners will quickly tune out what they don't understand.

Additional Factors

You may find that you need to consider several additional variables as you prepare your presentation. For example, if your audience is your class, do class members belong to a particular campus organization? Do members of the class involve themselves in any particular types of projects? Do the interests of the class relate in any way to your speech? Do class members have any identifiable goals, fears, frustrations, loves, or hates that could be tied in? How has their environment influenced their perception of key issues?

Which of the audience demographic categories do you consider the most and the least relevant for you as a speaker and as a receiver?

When delivering a toast, what should you know about receivers?

Summary

If used wisely, your knowledge of audience demographics can help you achieve your purpose as a speech maker. It can permit you to draw inferences about the predispositions of audience members and their probable responses to your presentation.

Attitudes of Audiences: What Do They Care About?

Once you have considered audience demographics, your next step is to try to predict the attitudes your listeners will have toward you and toward your presentation. You should consider whether or not the audience members are required to attend, whether the audience is homogeneous or heterogeneous, and whether the audience members favor your stand or are actively opposed to it.[12]

Motivation: Is Attendance Optional or Required?

People may attend a presentation because they want to (that is, they do so willingly), because they have to (they are required to do so), or simply because they are curious. You might attend a town council meeting because a proposed increase in property taxes is being considered, or you might attend a parents' meeting at school out of a sense of duty or because your spouse insisted that you go.

Try to rate your audience on the following scale with respect to audience members' overall motivation:

Required to attend   1   2   3   4   5   Strongly desire to attend

Since the audience's willingness to attend can affect how your presentation is received, it is important to make an educated guess regarding its probable level of enthusiasm. (Of course, it is also important to remember that audience members will not necessarily agree with what you have to say just because they want to attend your talk.)

Values: Is the Audience Homogeneous or Heterogeneous?

A second factor for consideration is the degree of homogeneity—that is, the extent to which everyone in the audience has similar values and attitudes. Of course, it is easier to address a homogeneous audience than a heterogeneous one. In addressing heterogeneous groups, speakers need to vary their appeals to ensure that all segments of the audience spectrum are considered.

Use the following scale to measure the extent to which the members of your audience share similar characteristics and values:

Homogeneous   1   2   3   4   5   Heterogeneous

Level of Agreement: Does the Audience Agree with Your Position?

Whatever your topic, you must attempt to predict your audience members' reaction to the stance you take. For example, they may oppose you, they may support you, or they may be neutral or uninterested. The accuracy of your prediction will determine to some extent how your presentation is received.

Use the following scale to help you assess your audience's position in terms of its similarity or dissimilarity to your own:

Agrees with me   1   2   3   4   5   Disagrees with me

Your objective when speaking to an audience that agrees with your position is to maintain its support. Your objective when speaking to a neutral audience is to gain your listeners' attention and show them how your presentation can be of value to them. When facing an audience that disagrees with you, you need to be especially careful and diplomatic in your approach. In this case, your objective is to change your listeners' minds—to move the audience closer to the "agrees with me" side of the continuum. This task becomes easier if you establish a common ground with audience members—that is, if you first stress values and interests that you share. Keep in mind that your goal is to increase the likelihood that a voluntary

We like to hear what makes us feel comfortable and self-assured. Yet this is exactly what we have no need of hearing; only those who disturb us can improve us.
—*Sydney J. Harris*

audience will attend to your message and that a captive audience will give you a fair hearing.

Level of Commitment: How Much Do They Care?

Finally, you need to consider how much the audience members care about your topic. Is it very important to them? Do they feel strongly enough to be moved to action? Or are your concerns irrelevant to your listeners?

Use the following scale to represent your audience's commitment:

Passive   1   2   3   4   5   Active

Together, the four attitudinal scales will indicate how much background and motivational material you need to include in your presentation.

Predicting the Audience's Reaction

Once you have completed your audience research, you will be in a position to predict your listeners' reception of any topic you select. Consider the following questions:

1. What do the audience members now know about my topic?
2. To what extent are they interested in my topic?
3. What are their current attitudes toward this topic?

As you develop your presentation, you must keep in mind the audience's knowledge of, interest in, and attitude toward the subject matter. These important factors will help you select and shape material specifically for the audience members. If you have been unsuccessful at gathering information about how your audience feels about your topic, you may find it helpful to take the pulse of public opinion, in general, by familiarizing yourself with the results of several public opinion polls on your chosen subject. Log on to a Web site that features public opinion polls, such as www.gallup.com or www.washingtonpost.com, in an effort to get the information you seek.

In addition to focusing on yourself and your receivers, whenever you give a speech, you should also have a clear idea of the nature of the speech-making occasion and how your topic relates to it. Both the occasion and your subject will affect the way you develop your presentation, stage it, and deliver it. We focus on these considerations next.

CONSIDER THE OCCASION

If asked to speak before a group—including your own class—your first response might well be "Why? What's the occasion?" Identifying the occasion and your role in it is also an essential step in the process of preparing a speech. Fortunately, much, if not all, of what you need to know about the occasion is relatively easy to determine. Essentially, only the following need to be specified:

date and time of the presentation
length of the presentation
location of the presentation
nature of the occasion
size of the audience

Date and Time: When and How Long?

Date and time are the most obvious—and among the most important—bits of information you need to acquire. On some occasions, student speakers and professional speakers have arrived an hour early, an hour late, and even a day early or a day late.

Timing can influence a speaker's effectiveness. For example, one well-known speaker arrived late at a New York college and found a hostile audience that had waited nearly an hour. Some professional speakers schedule their engagements so close together—two or three a day—that they must rush out the door rudely, almost before they have completed their talks. In a situation like that, the audience may react angrily.

The length of the presentation can also influence its effectiveness. For instance, one student speaker was supposed to deliver a 10-minute informative speech, "The History of the Corvette." Although it was suggested that he limit his consideration of the topic to two or three major model changes, he attempted to discuss every minute body and grill alteration in the Chevrolet Corvette from 1954 to the present. The instructor made several attempts to stop him, but 40 minutes into the speech he was still going strong. At this point, the instructor announced a class break. The student responded, "That's fine. I'll just continue." And he did—although the majority of his audience had departed.

Are you able to plan a presentation to ensure that you will not run over or under your time limit?

Work It Out

Identify how the nature of the occasion and the reason(s) audience members are attending affect the type of presentation a speaker delivers. Define and then compare and contrast the following presentation types, noting the type of occasion and audience that call for each one: the information-giving presentation or report, the business plan presentation, the persuasive sales presentation or product demonstration, the motivational or inspirational speech, the panel discussion, the Web conference.

Location and Participants: Where and Who?

Reminding yourself of the location of your presentation and of the people directly connected with it is an important aspect of preparing a speech. This may seem obvious, but it is sometimes neglected, with absurd and embarrassing results. For example, at a speech by a world-famous psychologist whose audience consisted of members of the host college and the surrounding community, early in his speech, the eminent Dr. M_____ mumbled what seemed to be the name of another college, although most of his listeners failed to notice. The second time, however, he clearly announced how happy he was to be at X_____, mentioning the wrong college again. (Doubly unfortunate was the fact that college X was a rival of the host college.) By then, some members of the audience appeared embarrassed for the speaker, and others appeared hostile. The third time, the psychologist mentioned not only the wrong school but the wrong town as well. At this point, there was sufficient commotion in the audience for him to realize his error, and in evident confusion he turned to the college president to ask where he was.

How can you avoid such a problem? The minister who officiated at this book's authors' marriage had a possible solution. During the wedding rehearsal, a page in his Bible was marked with a paper clip that held a slip of paper, and later we asked him about it. The minister showed us that it had our names clearly written on it. He explained that, because he was somewhat nervous when conducting a wedding, he frequently tended to forget the names of the bride and groom, even if they had belonged to the congregation for years. The slip of paper provided an unobtrusive reminder. Taking our cue from this experience, we now attach a slip of paper to the first page of our notes whenever we address a group. The slip bears the name of the organization, its location, the name of the person introducing us, the names of the officers, and other important information. Thus, we have at our disposal the data we need, to be integrated as appropriate. You may also want to adopt this simple procedure to avoid unnecessary embarrassment or loss of credibility.

Type of Occasion: Why and How Many?

Why have you been asked to speak? Although every occasion is unique, you can ask some general questions to clarify the situation in your own mind. For example, is it a class session? Right now it probably is, but in the future it could well be a sales meeting, a management planning session, a convention, or a funeral. Is your presentation part of the observance of a special event? For example, is the occasion in honor of a retirement? A promotion? Is it some other type of recognition? Who else, if anyone, will be sharing the program with you? Factors like these can affect the nature of your presentation. An appropriate topic for a retirement party, for instance, might be considered inappropriate for a more formal occasion.

Determining how many people will show up to listen to any particular presentation is difficult. In a classroom situation, for example, on one day the room may be filled, but on another day a speaker may arrive and find that a number of students are out sick or off on a special project for another course. The same problem confronts the professional speaker. It is a good idea to multiply and divide the sponsor's estimate by 2. Thus, you can be prepared to speak to a small group—that is, possibly 20—if 40 are expected—or to a large group—possibly 100—if 50 is the estimate.

Since you are not likely to have an advance person at your disposal when preparing to deliver your presentation—at least not yet—you must do all the advance thinking for yourself. Make it a habit to complete an analysis of both your audience and the occasion before completing work on any presentation. The predictions you make will serve you well as you continue preparing your speech.

Speakers need to be prepared to address sales meetings and management planning sessions.

SELECT YOUR SUBJECT AREA

Carefully examine the list of possible topics you generated thus far. To continue preparing your speech without having selected a subject—on the basis of self-analysis, audience analysis, and occasion analysis—would be like trying to buy an airline ticket without knowing your destination. During this examination, you evaluate your ideas according to specific criteria: (1) apparent worth, (2) appropriateness, (3) interest, and (4) availability of material. When you keep these criteria in mind, selecting a topic will be easier—if only because few of your choices will meet each of the criteria equally well with regard to the needs of particular audiences.[13]

Is the Topic Worthwhile?

You need to determine if the topic is important to you and to the people who will listen to you. Many speakers—including college students and businesspeople—often fall into the trap of choosing topics that are of little value to the audience. One of the authors recalls a time in a military training institute when he heard one colonel tell another, "After 25 years as an officer, I'm expected to waste my time hearing how to inspect a fork!" To that audience of high-ranking officers, the topic "Fork Inspection Techniques" was clearly trivial. You may also find that some topics chosen by others are trivial from your perspective. They may be so commonplace—how to set a table, for example—that they do not merit the time and energy you must expend in listening to them. Many subjects that are acceptable for interpersonal discourse may be inconsequential when presented in a public setting where the speaker's purpose is to inform or persuade. Which topics do you judge to be worth your time? Which, in your opinion, are unworthy of consideration?

Is the Topic Appropriate?

We have already discussed how important it is to determine if a topic is appropriate to you and your personal interests. Two additional facets of this criterion must also be considered: (1) Is the topic appropriate to the audience? (2) Is it appropriate to the occasion? Let's examine each in turn.

By this time, you should have developed an audience profile. That is, you have either determined precisely or made educated guesses about the age, gender, and educational level of the majority of the people who are going to hear your

Skill Builder

| **Topic Evaluation Time** |

1. Working individually or in groups, develop a list of criteria by which you believe a topic for a class speech should be assessed.

2. Share your criteria with others. Which criteria seem to be most important in the selection process? Which appear to be least important? Why?

3. Compare the criteria you developed with those identified in the text. How are they similar or different?

speech. It then becomes imperative for you to ask which of your possible topics is most appropriate for such a mix of people. Sometimes this determination is easy. For instance, you would not ordinarily give a talk about the evils of television to a group of network representatives. Nor, ordinarily, would you opt to speak on the advantages of a women's college to an audience already attending a women's college. Every subject area must be seen through the eyes of its intended audience. Just as an automobile is customized for a particular owner, so a subject area must be customized to reflect the needs of a particular group of listeners. Just as the automobile is painted, detailed, and upholstered with an owner or a type of owner in mind, so you as a speaker must "outfit" your topic to appeal to the audience members you hope to reach. This takes work, but it can be done.

The appropriateness of the topic to the occasion must also be considered. For example, you can probably think of any number of occasions on which a humorous topic would be ill-conceived. Can you think of occasions when a humorous topic would be an asset?

Is the Topic Interesting?

Speech makers often make the mistake of selecting topics they think they should speak about rather than topics they want to speak about. Student speakers, for instance, will sometimes turn to a newspaper or newsmagazine and, without further thought, select a story at random as the basis for a speech. One student insisted on talking about labor-management relations. Why? He thought it sounded like an important subject. Unfortunately, he had spent little time in the labor force and no time in management. And because he did not care enough to do much—if any—research, the entire subject remained foreign to him. Not surprisingly, the speech he delivered was dull and disjointed.

John Silverstein, a spokesman for General Dynamics, put it this way: "You need to believe in your idea. This is very important. What a listener often gauges is how convinced the speaker is. If he has lived it, breathed it, and is himself really sold on it, it generally is enough to sell the argument."[14] Of course, selecting a topic that is appealing to you is a personal matter and can be relatively simple, but determining what will interest your audience can be somewhat more challenging.

Here, students have an advantage. As a student, you know your fellow students, and you should be able to identify topics that will interest them. When addressing less familiar audiences, however, you should feel free to return to your audience analysis and make some educated guesses. Determining an audience's interests is a never-ending challenge—one that some unadventurous speech makers prefer not to tackle. One corporate executive, for example, once delivered a speech that was gratifyingly well received. Unfortunately, he then delivered essentially the same speech for the next five years, although times and needs kept changing. Needless to say, his current audiences are not interested in his topic. Topics must be updated to match the moods, needs, and concerns of listeners; only by updating can you ensure that your topic treats an issue of interest to your audience.

When considering the interests of your audience members, ask yourself how your subject relates to them. Ask yourself what they stand to gain from listening to you. Create an inventory for each of your possible subjects. If you are unable to identify significant ways your audience will benefit from hearing about a topic, there is good reason for you not to speak on that topic.

Is Sufficient Research Material Available?

Before choosing a topic, be certain that material on the subject exists and that you can find it readily—on the Internet, in a library, or somewhere else. Many speakers fall into the trap of requesting material that is unavailable in a school or local library, only to have it arrive too late or turn out to be unpromising. Such an experience can cause last-minute panic, and the result is an inadequately prepared speech maker and an inadequate presentation. Avoid this pitfall by giving careful attention to your library and other nearby sources during the selection phase of your preparation.

NARROW THE TOPIC AND CLARIFY YOUR PURPOSE

It is essential to consider how much time is available for your speech. For example, an army chaplain more than once demonstrated how adept he was at handling time constraints. The chaplain's job was to address groups of recruits during basic training, and on each occasion he was given only three minutes to get his message across. One day his objective was to persuade soldiers not to use foul language. (It was his belief that such a practice degraded both individuals and the service.) Realizing that he could accomplish only so much in the time permitted, he chose to focus on a single word—the particular word that he found most offensive. During his three-minute talk, he suggested that the troops avoid using just that one term. By doing this, the chaplain demonstrated that he understood how important it is to narrow a topic to manageable proportions and, incidentally, succeeded in realizing his objective. (After his speech, the abused word was heard much less frequently around the base.)

Far too many speakers attempt to give audiences "the world" in five minutes. It is essential to narrow your topic to fit the constraints imposed by the situation. Do not try to take on too much. Five minutes is not sufficient time to discuss the history of Russia, the industrial revolution, or even pedigreed dogs.

There is a strategy you can use to avoid biting off more than you can chew—or talk about. Select a topic and place it at the top of a "ladder." Then subdivide the topic into constituent parts; that is, break it down into smaller and smaller units, as shown in Figure 12.2. The smallest unit should appear on the lowest step of the ladder. This process is like whittling or carving a stick

FIGURE 12.2 Ladder Technique for Narrowing a Topic.

of wood. The more you shave off, the narrower the topic becomes. Like the carver, you decide what shape to give your topic and when to stop shaving.

Let's say that you want to speak on the need to save the rain forest. One way to narrow your topic would be to focus on how indigenous people can save the rain forest. Your topic could be focused even further. You might explore how their harvesting of native plants can stop deforestation or, more specifically, how their harvesting of fruit can help preserve the ecological balance. Here's another example: If you want to talk on the current technology revolution, you might focus on how the use of multimedia has revolutionized education or, more specifically, on how computers are used to teach writing skills.

Work It Out

Develop a topic cone for a subject of your own choosing.

Formulate a Purpose Statement and Behavioral Objectives

Once you have identified a topic and narrowed its scope, reexamine exactly why you are speaking. What is your purpose? What do you hope to accomplish? What kind of response would you like from your audience? What do you want your listeners to think or do as a result of your presentation? What is your ultimate objective?

Most speakers have one of two general objectives when they prepare to deliver a speech: They aim either to inform listeners (to share new information or insights with the audience) or to persuade listeners (to convince audience members to believe in or do something). However, in actual speaking situations, the purpose is not always so clear. Persuasive speeches usually contain informative material, and informative speeches may sometimes include elements of persuasion.

This chapter introduces you to both the informative and the persuasive speech. In Chapters 16 and 17, respectively, we look at each format in greater depth.

Work It Out

Develop a "quick-tip list" for formulating purpose statements, behavioral objectives, and thesis statements.

The Informative Speech

If your purpose is to inform, your primary responsibility is to relay information to your audience in an interesting, well-organized, and professional manner. Informative speakers may explain something, demonstrate how something functions, or describe how something is structured. When speaking informatively, you hope to provide a learning experience for your listeners, sharing information they did not possess before your talk. In other words, if your main goal is to inform an audience, you must be certain that the data you provide will enhance your listeners' understanding, and you must find ways to help the audience remember what you say.

To ensure that your purpose is clear—initially to yourself and ultimately to your listeners—you will find it helpful to develop a purpose statement. What this means is that you commit to writing a summary of what you want to accomplish; you describe what you hope to do with your speech. The purpose statement of an informative speech often contains such words as *show, explain, report, instruct, describe,* and (not surprisingly) *inform.* The following are examples of purpose statements for various kinds of informative speeches:

> To explain how selected Chinese character letters evolved
>
> To describe how a tornado forms
>
> To instruct class members on how to reduce personal debt
>
> To report on efforts to use euthanasia to trim herds of wild horses

Notice that each example takes the form of an infinitive verb phrase; thus, each begins with *to.* Notice also that each statement contains only one idea and that it is written from the speaker's perspective.

Sometimes, in addition to developing a purpose statement, it is helpful to view the speech from the perspective of the listeners. To facilitate this process, you can formulate behavioral objectives. Objectives identify what you want the audience to take away after hearing your presentation; that is, they describe the behavior or response you want the audience to exhibit as a result of listening to your speech. For instance, you may want your listeners to be able to list, explain, summarize, state, or apply certain information. The following are examples of behavioral objectives:

> After listening to this speech, the audience will be able to name three kinds of questions that are unlawful in employment interviews.

After listening to this presentation, the audience will be able to discuss the three main reasons college students fail to graduate.

The Persuasive Speech

The same principles used for an informative speech may be applied in formulating a purpose statement and behavioral objectives for a persuasive speech. In a persuasive speech, your main goal is to reinforce or change an audience's beliefs or to make the audience behave in a certain way. The words *convince*, *persuade*, *motivate*, and *act* commonly turn up in purpose statements for persuasive speeches. The following are some examples:

Online Learning Center

Go to the Online Learning Center at www.mhhe.com/gamble10e and view the clips on informative and persuasive speeches. What skills did the speaker lack in the first presentation that she improved in the second version? How will you use what you have learned when preparing to speak in public?

To motivate listeners to contribute money to the American Cancer Society

To persuade class members to become actively involved in the conservation of global resources

To convince class members that racist speech should be exempt from First Amendment protection

With regard to behavioral objectives, you might want your audience to support a plan or take an overt action. The following are examples of behavioral objectives:

After listening to my presentation, audience members will write their representatives, asking them to seek legislation requiring an increase in automobile mileage standards.

After listening to my presentation, students will sign up to will their eyes to an eye bank.

After listening to my speech, students will boycott stores that sell products made using child labor.

In summary, formulating precise purpose statements and behavioral objectives makes good sense. Both can help you focus your efforts and clarify your goals.

Formulate the Thesis Statement

In recent years, public speaking theorists have begun to look more closely at guidelines for writing. As a result, speakers are now often encouraged to develop theses for their speeches, just as writers do for papers. A thesis simply divides a topic into its major components. Thus, once you have formulated a specific purpose, the next step is to prepare a declarative sentence that summarizes the thesis of your speech. When your speech is an informative one and not intended to persuade, the thesis statement is phrased in a relatively objective and neutral manner and is sometimes referred to as the central idea or topic statement of your speech. Its focus is on what you want audience members to understand or learn—for example, "Nuclear power plants have three major parts: the reactor core, vessel, and control rods." When your speech is persuasive, it is simply called the thesis statement or the claim. A thesis for a persuasive speech expresses an arguable opinion or point of view; for example, a thesis for a persuasive speech against the use of nuclear energy plants might be, "Nuclear power plants should be decommissioned." Whether your speech is informative or persuasive, the thesis statement can be a powerful rhetorical device for setting your agenda as a speaker.

Thinking Critically

Reflect and Respond

Agree or disagree with the following statement; supply reasons and examples that support your stance.

Effective public speaking is nothing more than one side of an extended conversation. With the exception of preparation time, public speaking and conversation demand the same skills.

The thesis statement is the core idea or bottom line of your speech; it is your speech in a nutshell. It is a statement of the overriding concept of your speech that all the facts, quotations, and ideas in your speech are designed to support. In effect, the specific statement is the steering wheel of your speech; it directs the course of your speech and determines the content in it. The thesis helps you derive the main ideas or major propositions your speech will explore. Everything you say should support the thesis. In and of itself, the thesis statement does not present all the information you will offer in your speech; instead, it efficiently focuses that information into a brief summarizing statement.

An effective thesis statement fulfills three guidelines. First, it is a single sentence that conveys the essence of the speech. Second, it focuses the attention of the audience members on what they should know, do, or feel after experiencing your speech. Third, it supports the specific purpose. The following are examples:

Thesis: Sleep deprivation costs business billions of dollars a year in employee accidents and avoidable mistakes.

Thesis: Criminalizing eating when driving will decrease accidents and save lives.

Thesis: Getting a good night's sleep will enhance your personal and professional life in four key ways.

Thesis: Community efforts to censor the books we read are an infringement of our individual right of freedom of expression and will limit our ability to think critically about important issues.

Thesis: Decreases in state funding to colleges will result in cuts in educational programs, extracurricular offerings, and financial aid.

As you can see from these examples, the thesis brings you a step closer to the structure of the speech itself.

COMMUNICATION SKILLS IN PRACTICE
IMPROVING ANALYSIS

Effective speech makers do not approach their task haphazardly. As we have seen, careful thought precedes the actual speech. Every speaker, from novice to professional, can benefit from following these suggestions:

Conduct a Systematic Self-analysis as a Preparation for Speech Making

Take the time you need to survey your own likes, dislikes, and concerns. Effective speakers know themselves well. They know what they care about, and they know what ideas they would like to share with others.

Analyze Your Audience

Effective speakers adapt their ideas to reflect the needs and interests of their listeners. Speeches are delivered with the specific purpose of informing or persuading others—of affecting others in certain specific ways. The degree to which you will succeed is directly related to how well you know your listeners and how accurately you are able to predict their reactions.

Analyze the Occasion

It is essential that you learn why, when, where, and for how long you are expected to speak. Without this information, your preparation will be incomplete and insufficient.

Determine if Your Topic Is Supported by Your Own Interests, Your Audience's Interests, and the Demands of the Occasion

Be certain to evaluate your subject according to the following criteria: Is the topic worthwhile? Is the topic appropriate? Is the topic interesting? Is sufficient research material available?

Narrow and Clarify Your Topic

Ask yourself: Have I sufficiently narrowed my focus? Is my thesis clear?

Focus on Service Learning

Using a variety of research sites, including www.cdc.gov/flu/avian/ or www.cdc.gov/westnile/, explain how you can apply what you have learned in this chapter to help a community group share its understanding of avian (bird) flu, swine flu, or West Nile virus with an audience of senior citizens.

Revisiting Chapter Objectives

1. **Approach public speaking systematically.** There is a logical order to speech making that speakers follow: (1) topic selection and audience analysis; (2) speech development, support, and organization; (3) presentation practice and delivery; and (4) postpresentation analysis.

2. **Conduct a thorough self-analysis in order to choose the best topic.** Self-analysis is a prerequisite for preparing an effective speech. Begin by identifying your interests, strengths, and limitations and how they could affect your selection of a topic.

3. **Understand your audience so that you can tailor your speech directly to them.** You also need to conduct demographic and attitudinal analyses of the

receivers. By keeping in mind the background, needs, and interests of audience members, and by considering potential topics from their point of view, you focus attention and adapt the speech to the people you hope to reach.

4. **Explain how the nature of the occasion influences a speech.** Identifying the occasion and your role in it is another essential step in speech preparation. Once you also determine the date, time limit, and location of the speech, as well as the nature of the occasion, you can continue thinking about a suitable topic.

5. **Choose an effective topic.** Carefully examine the list of possible topics generated during self, audience, and occasion analyses in an effort to identify which topics best reflect the following criteria: apparent worth, appropriateness, interest, and availability of material.

6. **Clarify your topic and formulate your thesis statement.** After you have chosen your topic, you need to reexamine your purpose for speaking. Most speakers have one of two general objectives when they prepare to deliver a speech: to inform listeners (to share new information or insights) or to persuade listeners (to convince audience members that they should believe or do something). To ensure that your purpose is clear, you should formulate a purpose statement—a summary of what you want to accomplish, expressed as an infinitive phrase. For example, you may want to inform your audience about something, to describe something, or to explain how something is done. You can also list behavioral objectives—abilities you want the audience to have internalized after listening to your presentation. The thesis statement is the central idea or claim of your speech. It is your speech in a nutshell. A declarative sentence, the thesis statement directs the course of your speech, helping you determine the main ideas or major propositions your speech will explore.

Resources for Further Inquiry and Reflection

To apply your understanding of how the principles in Chapter 12 are at work in our daily lives, consult the following resources for further inquiry and reflection. Or, if you prefer, choose any other appropriate resource. Then connect the ideas expressed in your chosen selection with the communication concepts and issues you are learning about both in and out of class.

 Listen to Me

"Illegal Search" (LL Cool Jay)
"What's Going On?" (Marvin Gaye)
"We Didn't Start the Fire" (Billy Joel)
"Wake Me Up When September Ends" (Green Day)
"41 Shots" (Bruce Springsteen)
"Know your Rights" (The Clash)
"Disturbia" (Rihanna)

What speech subjects come to mind as you listen to each recording?

 View Me

Doubt   *The Hurt Locker*
Wall-E   *The Yes Men*
Hancock

Using the five steps leading to the first landing in the speech-making staircase, explain how well you think the creator of any of the preceding films, or another film of your choosing, succeeded in (1) selecting an appropriate film subject and (2) targeting a potential audience. In addition, what speech topics can you identify related to your selected film?

Read Me

To what extent, if any, does the cartoon below reflect your feelings about public speaking before reading this chapter? After reading this chapter? Explain.

 Tell Me

Share with the class the insights you gained from your chosen Listen to Me, View Me, or Read Me selection.

The National Opinion Research Center (NORC) and the Gallup Poll are two well-known and respected polling organizations. Both conduct polls on a broad array of topics, from attitudes toward the presidency and government to attitudes toward the trustworthiness of the press and the military. To access NORC, go to www.norc.uchicago.edu/. To access the Gallup Poll, go to www.gallup.com/poll/index/asp. In your opinion, should speakers use public opinion polls such as these solely to find out valuable information about audience attitudes prior to developing their own speeches? Or should they use them to decide what topics to speak on or what opinions to support when preparing to speak before audiences, because that way at least they know they'll receive a favorable hearing?

Key Chapter Terminology

Use the Online Learning Center at www.mhhe.com/gamble10e to further your knowledge of the following terminology.

MYGLO 307

public speaking 301

www.mhhe.com/gamble10e

Idioms in Translation

audience makeup — audience composition

booming — popular

feel the pulse — understand the mood

in the spotlight — onstage

magic bullet — secret

nerve-racking — upsetting

wins the ears of — interests

Culture Cue

People from collectivist cultures are more likely than people in the United States to view feelings as a source of truth.

Test Your Understanding

Go to the *Self Quizzes* on the book's Online Learning Center at www.mhhe.com/gamble10e.

www.mhhe.com/gamble10e

After finishing this chapter, you should be able to

1. Identify and use the various online and offline research resources available to you.

2. Conduct an informal survey and a personal interview.

3. Identify various types of supporting material.

4. Explain how visual and audio aids can enhance a presentation.

5. Evaluate the effectiveness of supporting materials.

Developing Your Speech: Supporting Your Ideas

Now that you have considered your choice of subject from both your point of view and the point of view of your audience, and you have taken the nature of the speech-making occasion into account, it is time for you to focus on researching, selecting support and presentation aids, and organizing the speech, the next steps you take on your way up the speech-making staircase (see Figure 13.1). When engaged in research, you investigate your subject, both online and offline. Your research will lead you to an array of supporting materials, including illustrations, statistical evidence, expert opinions, and quotations, to use in your speech. It will also lead you to an array of presentation aids—visual and audio materials you can use to illustrate your speech. Why are such materials valuable? They answer the questions of audience members. As you deliver your speech, audience members listen, silently asking themselves: What do you mean? Why should I accept what you say? Why should I care? If you develop your speech with care, being certain to research, support, illustrate, and organize your ideas, you will make the answers to these questions clear to receivers. Accordingly, once we complete this chapter, we will have climbed to the halfway point of the ladder—speech development, support, and organization. We will then be ready to ascend to the third landing, presentation practice and delivery, and the fourth landing, the postpresentation analysis. Let's continue climbing.

Research is the process of going up alleys to see if they are blind.
—Marston Bates

The world is already full of speakers who are too busy to prepare their speeches properly; the world would be better off if they were also too busy to give them.
—William Norwood Brigance

Basic research is what I am doing when I don't know what I am doing.
—Wernher von Braun

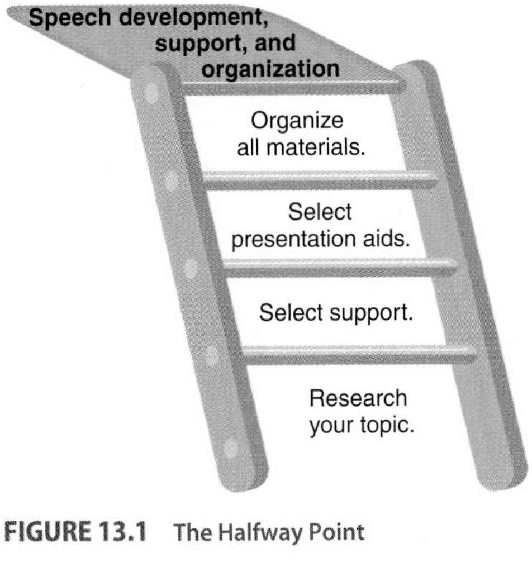

Speech development, support, and organization

Organize all materials.

Select presentation aids.

Select support.

Research your topic.

FIGURE 13.1   The Halfway Point

If you are like many people in America today, you are fascinated with crime scene investigation (CSI) television programs and films that demonstrate the painstaking effort that goes into solving crimes. Like forensic pathologists, whose task it is to take nothing for granted and to leave no stone unturned in the search for clues and the analysis of evidence, so the public speaker also needs to investigate a topic carefully in an effort to discover appropriate supporting material with which to build the substance of a speech.

RESEARCH YOUR TOPIC

Like most people, when you want to see a movie or try a new restaurant, you might start by checking the movie listings of your local newspaper or accessing Fandango online. Or you might decide to drive by the theater to see what films appear on its marquee. When it comes to choosing a new restaurant, you might ask your friends for their advice, peruse a guide such as *Zagat*, or review restaurant home pages on the Internet. What does this have to do with public speaking? The research we do when preparing to speak in public is much like the personal research we conduct daily. However, because a speech is likely to be shared with others in a somewhat more formal setting, we use a more formal research approach.

Research sources available to you include published works, other people, and of course, yourself. If you are discussing some aspect of sports medicine, for instance, you may rely on your experience of being injured when playing a sport. If your topic has to do with business or technology, you may use examples from your work in an industry that relates directly to your topic. Far too often, speakers fail to realize that they can use their personal experiences to establish credibility and add interesting and pertinent examples.

> **What do the investigators of a crime scene and public speakers have in common?**

Conduct Research Online and Offline

Suppose you were going to speak on the role of spin in our society, and you wanted to focus on how both government supporters and dissenters used spin during the waging of the war on terror. Where would you go for information? What sources would you turn to in order to learn what spin is, how it functions, why it is used, what its effects are, and whether it is ethical and/or legal, as well as to find examples of spin in action? For example, both adherents of the Iraqi war effort and those opposed to it spun their stories of the war's successes and failures. Would these stories serve as good examples to use in your speech? Through conducting research, you become able to answer such questions.

Online Learning Center

Go to the Online Learning Center at www.mhhe.com/gamble10e and answer the questions in the *Self Inventory* to evaluate your understanding of investigation.

Libraries contain information storage and retrieval systems—resources that are invaluable for every type of research. The library is one of the few real bargains left in our society. A huge array of material is available free; other materials and services (those available through a variety of photographic and electronic systems) are yours for only a minimal cost. In addition, every academic and public library has on its staff knowledgeable people who have been trained to aid you with your investigative work. In addition to your college library, you can also consult the following Internet libraries: the Internet Public Library (www.ipl.org), the Library Spot (www.libraryspot.com), and the Reference Desk (www.refdesk.com).

Work It Out

Work in groups to research examples of how various groups have used spin to advance their position on national health care.

When you begin library research, consult an array of reference sources to compile a preliminary bibliography. Your first stop may well be the library's electronic catalog. Next, you may move on to a variety of newspaper, magazine, and journal indexes. Depending on your subject, you may also consult bibliographical sources, encyclopedias, and almanacs. And you will almost certainly use online searches.

Use the Library's Online Catalogs

In lieu of the card catalog system, now banished from most libraries, today's libraries usually contain a computerized catalog. Libraries, in increasing numbers, now offer computer or online catalogs that enable you to run more productive Boolean searches. When you run a **Boolean search,** instead of needing to know a specific author or title, you can merely enter two or three keywords into the computer and it will search the library's collection for you. No longer do you need to go from card catalog drawer to card catalog drawer, searching for source materials. The computer makes the search process much more efficient.

Boolean search
a keyword search

Use Reference Works

Since magazines, newspapers, and scholarly periodicals may contain information valuable to you, indexes are critical resources. One of the first indexes you will consult will probably be the *Reader's Guide to Periodical Literature*. It can lead you to a variety of popular, mass-distribution magazines, including *Time, Newsweek,* and *U.S. News & World Report,* all of which may contain information relevant to your subject. The *New York Times Index* and the *Wall Street Journal Index* are also high on the list of indexes you should consider. If your topic warrants it, you may also need to explore issues of *Education Index, Psychological Abstracts,* and *Sociological Abstracts.* These sources will offer you leads to articles that have appeared in a number of scholarly journals.

Work It Out
Have a reference librarian give you a tour of the library and instruction on how to use its resources both on- and offline.

The *World Almanac, Statistical Abstract of the United States,* and *Information Please Almanac* are only three of many such reference works that can provide the speech maker with interesting factual and statistical evidence. Multivolume encyclopedias, such as the *Britannica* and the *Americana,* and one-volume versions, such as the *Random House Encyclopedia* and the *Columbia Encyclopedia,* may also be consulted. Specialized encyclopedias, such as the *McGraw-Hill Encyclopedia of Science and Technology,* may be useful for technologically oriented topics.

Biographical materials can be located in the *Dictionary of National Biography,* the *Dictionary of American Biography,* and even the *New York Times Obituary Index.* Similarly, *Current Biography* can help you research the lives of contemporary public figures.

Use Online Resources

Libraries are user friendly. You can visit yours in person or access it from afar. You also can conduct much of the research for your speech online by using your library's computerized systems when in the library or by using passwords and following logon procedures that give you access when at home or in another more remote location. In preparation for conducting online research, your first step should be to attend a live orientation session in your library or to take an online tutorial. Meet the reference librarian and find out what research databases your college library subscribes to. At the same time, familiarize yourself with the library's electronic catalogs and reference room.

During your research, you will want to consult a variety of online references and databases, including the Reader's Guide to Periodical Literature (www .hwwilson.com), Facts on File (www.fofweb.com), Academic Search Premier (www.ebscohost.com), and LexisNexis (www.lexisnexis.com). Of course, you can also use Google and Google Scholar, popular online databases, or access

FIGURE 13.2

Sample Google Search.

Source: Used by permission of Google.

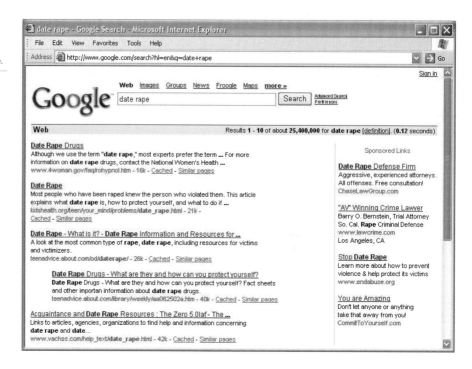

newspapers such as the *New York Times* and the *Wall Street Journal* online (see Figure 13.2).

Among other databases you may want to consult are ERIC, a comprehensive research system that indexes published and unpublished materials on a wide array of educational topics, and American Statistics Index (ASI).

You may want to consult the online encyclopedia Wikipedia, but be wary of using it as a speech source. Wikipedia may offer a quick basic overview of a subject, but because of its penchant for inaccuracy, many instructors question its validity when it comes to students citing it in research. Many people in higher education simply do not view it as a definitive source.

Among the major Internet resources you will want to use when researching your speech are e-mail, newsgroups, and the World Wide Web.

E-Mail You can use e-mail to write to knowledgeable potential sources, a group, or a **listserv,** an e-mail list of several to over hundreds of people who have interest in and knowledge of a particular topic—potentially one that you are researching. Go to Catalist.us, a directory containing information about numerous listservs and whether new members are welcomed, to explore potentially useful listservs.

Before joining a listserv, try to identify the types of messages members send and their usefulness to you. Also read the frequently asked questions (FAQ) file so that you do not ask questions that have already been answered.

Using e-mail, you can also create a listserv for your class. Once you have one in place, you can use it to ask your potential audience members to fill out questionnaires that reveal their attitudes toward your chosen topic. You can also use the class listserv to seek and receive feedback after your speech.

Newsgroups Newsgroups facilitate the exchange of ideas on a broad array of topics through discussion forums. The Internet contains a multitude of newsgroups,

listserv

an e-mail list of people who have interest in and knowledge of a particular topic

Work It Out

Compose a list of potentially relevant listservs and newsgroups for a speech on date rape.

also known as Usenet. In a newsgroup, you can post messages, read the posts of others, and respond to them. Like listservs, newsgroups bring together people interested in sharing ideas about a topic. As with a listserv, before joining a newsgroup, be sure you read through the FAQ file; doing so will ensure you receive maximum benefits from the newsgroup.

You can use binsearch.info or giganews.com to search newsgroups for information on requested topics. Newsgroups that receive news feeds from news services such as the Associated Press are especially useful. You can also use the newsgroup to ask questions and poll people for opinions for a speech.

World Wide Web   Almost any kind of content you can find in print is also available on the World Wide Web. The World Wide Web links all the individual Web sites and contains a vast collection of written, graphic, audio, and video documents. Just as a library offers you books, periodicals, news, and so forth, so does the Web. You can subscribe to various special interest groups or use a search engine to browse for information on your selected topic. A search engine is a program that makes it possible for you to search a database or index of Internet sites for information on topics of interest to you. Popular Internet browsers, such as Firefox and Internet Explorer, include search functions as a part of their home pages, thereby providing ready links to popular search engines and directories. While browsing, you might visit CNN or the Associated Press online, peruse copies of historical documents or the *Congressional Record*. With the Internet, you have easy access to the information that exists on numerous campuses and every continent.[1]

A number of widely used search engines are available, including Google (www.google.com), the most popular search engine; Bing (bing.com), the newest search engine from Microsoft; Yahoo! (www.yahoo.com), the next most popular; followed in popularity by MSN Search (www.msn.com), AOL Search (www.aolsearch.com), and Ask (www.ask.com).[2] Each of these is a search engine as well as a directory. Other Web sites gaining in popularity are Dogpile (www.dogpile.com), Mamma (www.Mamma.com), Vivisimo (www.vivisimo.com), and Go (www.go.com). Among the most useful metasearch engines, these simultaneously search the databases of an array of search engines.

Searching through video available on the Internet is a new challenge facing speech makers. Video search engines such as Google, Blinkx, Truveo, and Every-Zing facilitate this task. Google, for example, uses speech recognition technology to create searchable transcripts of videos.[3]

It is becoming easier to predict the Web site addresses of potential sources. When you know an address, or a uniform resource locator (URL), you are able to access the Web site by simply entering it in your Web browser. Corporate Web sites, for example, usually accessed by www.nameofcorporation.com, will provide you with access to annual reports, copies of speeches, and other information. You can also save your favorite sites as bookmarks, a Web browser feature that allows you to save your favorite links in a file to facilitate future access.

While the information contained in traditional research sources, including books, magazines, and journal articles, is typically reviewed and checked by others before being published, virtually anyone can post information in a Web site or to a newsgroup. Thus, verifying and thinking critically about the quality of the information you find online is a serious responsibility. As you decide what and what not to include in your speech from your Web search, ask yourself who a site's sponsor is. For example, CNN, MSNBC, and Fox are established news

> Which search engine is your personal favorite? Why?

> As you would do with all other research, consider your source when conducting research over the Internet. Check the independence of the information you discover.

organizations, and you can weigh the information you find on their sites in the same way as you would weigh the information you use from their cablecasts. The same goes for major newspapers that also operate Web sites. As you evaluate Web-based information from other sources, it is important to determine if the source has an apparent or hidden bias. Ask yourself if postings are specific or general. Do the claims they make seem justifiable? Do not value a source simply because it is published on the Internet. Seek out confirming sources for what you discover.

Because anyone can publish on the Internet, your college library most likely has criteria for you to use when checking the accuracy and validity of online sources. Compare your library's suggestions with the evaluative criteria we offer:

Work It Out

Work in groups to develop a tip sheet for evaluating information found on the Internet to share with students in grades K–12.

1. Evaluate the author. Who is the author? How credible is she or he to write about your topic?

2. Evaluate the publisher. Who sponsors the site? What does the extension at the end of the site's URL reveal about its sponsor? For example, *.edu* refers to a college or university, *.com* refers to a commercial venture, *.org* tells us the publisher is a nonprofit or trade association, while *.gov* refers to a governmental agency, official, or organization, and *.biz* refers specifically to a business.

3. Evaluate the timeliness of information on the site. When was the site created and last updated?

4. Pursue the links identified on the site. Do they connect you to sources that are credible or questionable? What connections exist between the site and its links?

5. Evaluate the site's purpose. Why does the site exist? Is its primary function to inform, persuade, sell, or entertain? Recall that the end of a site's URL offers clues to its purpose. Sites ending in *.edu* typically having an informational function, *.org*, an advocacy function, and *.com*, a sales function.

6. Determine if the information contained in the site can be confirmed. Compare the site's contents with the contents of other available sources to see if there are any major disagreements or discrepancies.

Conduct Primary Research

You may also want to use primary information to support or flesh out your presentation. Three primary research techniques are (1) personal observation and experience, (2) informal surveys, and (3) interviews.

Personal Observation and Experience

One of the best ways to research a topic is to examine what you know about it. Search your own background and experiences for materials you might want to integrate into your presentation.

If your topic is one for which direct observation of an event, a person, or a stimulus would be appropriate, then by all means go out and observe. An observational excursion might take you to

Informal surveys and formal interviews provide a speaker with statistical information, testimonials, and examples to use in his or her speech.

a biology laboratory, an airport, a supermarket, or a construction site, for example. When conducting a direct observation, be sure to take careful notes. If possible, ask the interviewee's permission to arrive at the location with tape recorder or video recorder in hand. Sit down immediately after the experience and record your thoughts and feelings. File your firsthand notes with the materials gathered during your library research.

Informal Surveys

Developing a reliable scientific survey instrument is complicated. However, informal surveys can provide the speech maker with useful and often entertaining information. Let's say you are investigating the possibility of adding online courses to the curriculum; a survey at your school may produce data you can use. (For instance, you may be able to discover the percentage of students interested in enrolling in such courses.)

Informal surveys normally consist of no more than 5 to 10 questions. To conduct an informal survey with a prospect, you need to identify yourself first and state the purpose of your survey: "Hello, I'm _____. I'm investigating the feasibility of incorporating online courses into the regular curriculum of the college." The survey can be conducted either orally, in writing, or over the Internet. A sample of 25 to 50 people and some simple mathematical calculations should provide adequate statistical information to integrate into your presentation. When you conduct an informal survey, you may gain more than expected. While running the survey or examining the results, you may find interesting off-the-cuff remarks to incorporate in your speech.

Interviews

An interview is similar to a survey except that it is usually more detailed and assumes that the person being interviewed is in some way an expert on the topic under consideration. On your campus, in your community, or in an online Usenet discussion group, you will probably find knowledgeable people to interview about current issues and many other topics. Political, business, and religious leaders, for instance, can often be persuaded to talk to student speakers. And, of course, faculty members of a college are often eager to cooperate.

Be sure to record accurately the information gathered during an interview. Take careful notes and repeat or verify any direct quotations you intend to use in your presentation. Also be certain during the speech to credit the interviewee as your source, unless he or she has asked not to be mentioned by name.

Record Information Derived from Research

The information you gather during your research should be easy for you to retrieve. Either buy a pack of 4- by 6-inch or 6- by 8-inch note cards to record your information or use a laptop computer to compile your notes. When the time comes, either approach will let you move information around to wherever you need it or want to use it in the speech. Try this approach:

- Use a bibliography card or page for each basic article or source you reference.
- Record the title, author, and subject on the top of each card or page.
- Record one bit of information per card.

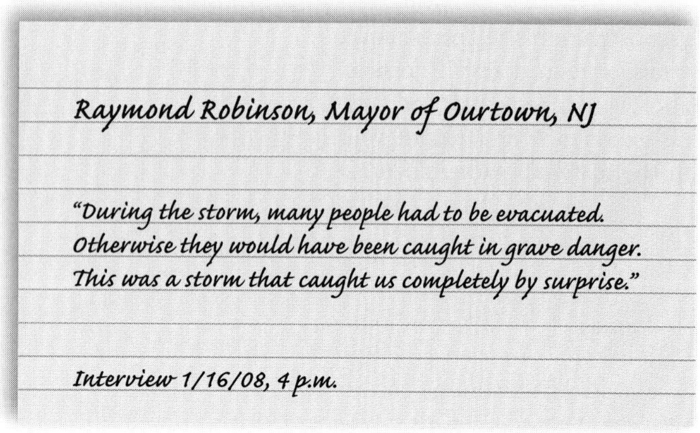

Raymond Robinson, Mayor of Ourtown, NJ

*"During the storm, many people had to be evacuated.
Otherwise they would have been caught in grave danger.
This was a storm that caught us completely by surprise."*

Interview 1/16/08, 4 p.m.

FIGURE 13.3   Notecard Derived from an Interview.

For examples of what note cards and pages look like, see Figures 13.3 and 13.4. Notice how each one contains either a direct quotation from the material or paraphrased information.

Whenever you research, be sure to give each source correct attribution to avoid plagiarizing. The word *plagiarism* derives from the Latin word *plagiarius*, meaning "kidnapper." When you plagiarize, you kidnap or steal the ideas and words of another and claim them as your own. Plagiarism is a growing problem. An increasing percentage of students are guilty of "cut and paste plagiarism," in which the student takes sections from the works of a number of other people and weaves them together into a "new"

FIGURE 13.4

Sample Note Cards.

Using bibliography, direct quotation, and paraphrase cards will increase the speed and accuracy of your information gathering.

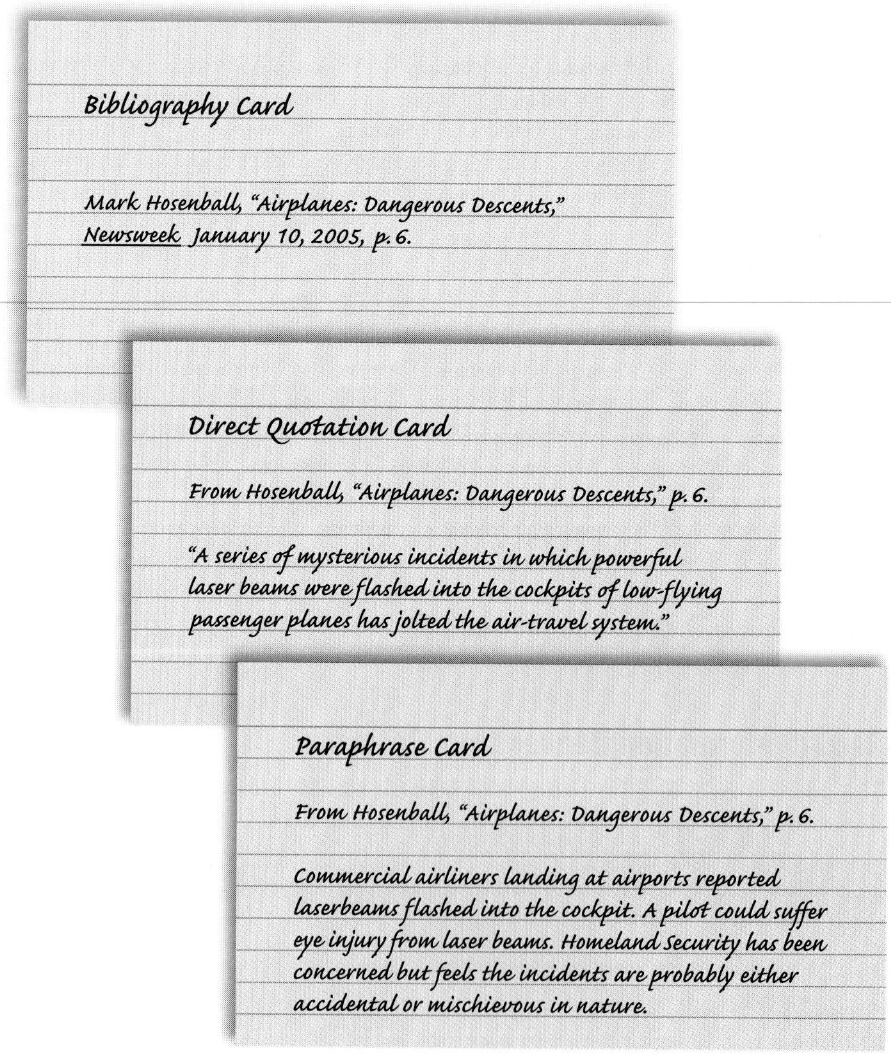

Bibliography Card

Mark Hosenball, "Airplanes: Dangerous Descents,"
Newsweek January 10, 2005, p. 6.

Direct Quotation Card

From Hosenball, "Airplanes: Dangerous Descents," p. 6.

*"A series of mysterious incidents in which powerful
laser beams were flashed into the cockpits of low-flying
passenger planes has jolted the air-travel system."*

Paraphrase Card

From Hosenball, "Airplanes: Dangerous Descents," p. 6.

*Commercial airliners landing at airports reported
laserbeams flashed into the cockpit. A pilot could suffer
eye injury from laser beams. Homeland Security has been
concerned but feels the incidents are probably either
accidental or mischievous in nature.*

work that the student then claims to be his or her own. Here are three simple steps to follow to avoid passing off someone else's ideas or words as your own:

1. Attribute the source of every piece of evidence you cite in your speech. Never borrow the words or thoughts of a source without acknowledging them.
2. Tell receivers when you are quoting a statement, or paraphrase it.
3. Use and credit a variety of sources.

Following these guidelines will demonstrate your respect for the audience and will also help you earn their respect. The unique expression of ideas matters. Giving sources the credit due them not only protects you but also increases your credibility.

Audience members do not expect you to be the sole source of ideas in your speech, but they do expect you to provide oral citations (also known as oral footnotes) when referring to the ideas of others. Such citations are easy to include in your presentation as long as you have done your research and recorded your information carefully. What do you say in an oral citation? If you are citing a speech or article, you might say,

> In his August 23, 2008, speech naming his running mate, presidential candidate Barack Obama told a rally in Springfield, Illinois. . . .

If you are using a direct quotation, state the name of the author and the source:

> In her book *Confidence*, researcher and Harvard Business School Professor Rosabeth Moss Kanter tells readers. . . .

If you are paraphrasing a book or article, you might tell your audience,

> Howard Gardner, author of the best-seller *Changing Minds*, feels that most of us change our minds gradually. The notion that mind change happens suddenly is wrong.

As you build your speech, the experts you bring onto your team give your speech more impact. Be sure to include each source you use in a Works Cited page (for sources actually mentioned during your speech) or in a Works Consulted page (for all the sources you referred to when conducting your research). When preparing your Works Cited or Works Consulted page, use a consistent referencing style. The MLA (Modern Language Association) or APA (American Psychological Association) formats are the most popular. For examples, see the Works Consulted sections of the sample speech outlines included in Chapters 16 and 17, on informative and persuasive speaking.

SELECT SUPPORT: TYPES OF SUPPORTING MATERIAL

Taken together, your research and your experiences should yield a wealth of information to integrate into your presentation. But making your research and experiences come to life for an audience is not an easy task; in fact, it is a key challenge facing the speech maker. Following are some major ways to make research and experience understandable and believable for an audience.[4]

Definitions

It is especially important to use **definitions** when your listeners are unfamiliar with terms you are using or when their associations for words or concepts might differ

definitions
explanations of what a stimulus is or what a word or concept means

from yours. Only if you explain how you are defining a term can you hope to share your meanings with your listeners. Thus, the purpose of a definition is to increase the audience's understanding.

For example, in a speech on the weight loss disorder of exercise anorexia, one student defined the disease as "the obligation or compulsion to continually exercise."[5]

In a speech on post-traumatic stress disorder and soldiers serving in Iraq and Afghanistan, speaker Megan Solan defined *psychological injury* as "that which soldiers suffer when they lose their peace of mind, their ability to function in society and their belief in the existence of human virtues."[6] The student went on to flesh out this definition with specifics: "soldiers learn skills such as the art of deception; the capacity to respond instantly with violent, lethal force; and the suppression of such emotions as compassion, horror, guilt, tenderness, grief, and disgust, all necessary skills for combat, but all skills with dangerous potential within civilian society and severe consequences for the human psyche."[7]

Statistics

statistics

facts expressed in numerical form

Statistics are simply facts expressed in numerical form. They may be cited to explain relationships or to indicate trends. To be used effectively as support, statistics must be honest and credible. If used appropriately, they can make the ideas you are presenting memorable and significant.

In a speech on the dangers of contemporary army recruitment methods, speaker Paula Rawlins of Berry College used statistics to make a key point: "According to *Time* magazine of April 16, 2007, in 2003, fewer than 5,000 recruits were allowed in under waivers, compared to over 8,000 in 2006, nearly a 50 percent increase. That's enough men and women to create an entire infantry division without a single soldier meeting normal recruitment standards."[8]

In a speech on problems with our organ donor system, Amy Solomito of Lafayette College used statistics to emphasize the failure of the current organ donation system: "The Web site of the United Network for Organ Sharing, *unos.org*, reports that as of this morning, 96,201 Americans are waiting for healthy organs. . . . Only 15 percent of these people can expect to receive the organs they need."[9]

Even using the simplest of statistics can prove effective. The following research tidbit was used by a student in a speech on the distraction powers of the Internet: "Last year a joint study of Microsoft and the University of Illinois found that it takes, on average, 16 minutes and 33 seconds for a worker interrupted by an e-mail to get back to what he or she was doing."[10]

Examples and Illustrations

examples

representative cases

illustrations

stories; narrative pictures

Examples are representative cases; as such, they specify particular instances.[11] **Illustrations,** on the other hand, tell stories and thus create more detailed narrative pictures. Both examples and illustrations may be factual or hypothetical. When used effectively, they turn the general into the specific, the unfocused into the focused, and the dull into the interesting, breathing life into a speech.

Solomon D. Trujillo, chairman, president, and CEO of US West, Inc., used a series of examples to demonstrate for audience members that one idea can make a difference:

> We've seen how the idea that all people are created equal can find expression in an African-American woman on a bus in Alabama, or [in] a student on a soda-fountain

Work It Out

Choose a word for which people have different associations—for example, an abstract concept such as honesty, jealousy, freedom, justice, or love. Write your own definition and share it with the class.

stool in North Carolina, or even in a young Hispanic businessman in Cheyenne, Wyoming.

A few weeks back, I was at the University of Colorado talking to a group of business students, and I told them that I would not be in the job I have were it not for Affirmative Action.

When I joined the old Bell system, AT&T had just entered into a consent decree with the government. Before I joined the company, people like me . . . for some reason . . . weren't likely to get hired. Those who were hired . . . for some reason . . . weren't in management jobs.

But people with courage and foresight knew that our nation's promise of freedom and justice for all was an empty one if you had the wrong color of skin, if you were female, if you spoke with an accent, or if your last name ended in a "z" or a vowel.[12]

Illustrations are more detailed than examples. Built like a story, they open, reveal a complication, contain a climax, and describe a resolution. Emotionally compelling, illustrations add a sense of drama to a speech as they focus attention on the issue at hand.

In her speech on the need to put the *care* back in health care, Nancy H. Nielsen, president of the American Medical Association, used the following illustration to make her point:

I was recently in Florida about to speak to the Economic Club. As often happens while on the road, I met a woman who wanted to tell me her story. She was the general manager of the hotel where I was staying, a good job. She told me that her current employer covered all the costs of health care for all employees. A great plan. But her previous employer didn't even offer health insurance. She purchased an individual health policy for six months as she prepared to relocate to Florida to work. The transition took a little longer, so she renewed the policy for another six months. And one week later she found a breast lump.

The insurance company refused to pay, claiming a preexisting condition, despite a normal mammogram one year before and a normal breast exam three months before. When I met her, over four years later, she was paying off the final five thousand dollars of the $50,000 bill for breast cancer treatment.

Who in this room cannot empathize with that woman—and with millions like her across America? She did everything right, and yet the system failed her. She fell in that deep chasm and is working herself to the bone to drag herself out.[13]

Testimony

Whenever you cite someone else's opinions or conclusions, you are using **testimony,** or a testimonial. Testimony gives you an opportunity to connect the ideas in your speech with the thoughts and attitudes of respected and competent people. The testimony you include in a presentation need not be derived exclusively from present-day sources; words of people from the past may also be used to tie today and yesterday together. When using testimonials, be sure to consider whether the people you cite as authorities are credible sources, whether their ideas are understandable, and whether their comments are relevant to your purpose.

In a speech on life after graduation from college, best-selling author and motivational speaker Harvey Mackay used testimony to emphasize the importance of listening, telling his audience,

Bill Marriott, chairman and CEO of Marriott International, the world's largest hotel chain, described the biggest lesson he has learned through the years: "It is to listen to your people. I find that if you have senior managers who really gather their people around them, get their ideas, and listen to their input, they make a lot better decisions."[14]

testimony
someone else's opinions or conclusions

Experts and Cultural Groups

If the testimony of others influences us in making decisions and assessing situations, then an audience's judgments about a public speaker—and about his or her speech—ought to be influenced by people the speaker quotes or refers to, who presumably have special knowledge or experience relevant to the topic.

Does it matter whether a speaker uses experts from the same cultural group as the audience, or would experts from other cultural groups serve just as well in adding strength and impact to the speaker's ideas? Explain your position.

As we see, testimony reinforces a speaker's claims. It may be quoted directly, as in the preceding example, or it may be paraphrased, as illustrated by Theresa McGuiness in her speech advocating that fraternities be abolished:

> Bernice Sandler, executive director of the Project on the Status and Education of Women at the Association of American Colleges, said that 90 percent of the gang rapes reported to her office involved fraternity members. According to Sandler, fraternity members have a word for gang rape: they call it "pulling train." She adds that charts of how many beers it took to seduce sorority women are common in fraternity houses. And if a woman actually does press charges against a fraternity, Sandler says, "Their excuse is, 'she asked for it'—even if she was unconscious."[15]

Use direct quotations when you believe that the language and the length of an expert's remarks are appropriate for your audience. Use a paraphrase when you need to summarize an expert's opinion in fewer words, or when you need to simplify its language.

Comparisons and Contrasts

Comparisons stress similarities between two entities; contrasts stress differences. Both are employed by speakers to help audiences understand something that is unknown, unfamiliar, or unclear.

William L. Laurence combined comparison and contrast when he described the atomic bombing of Nagasaki:

> As the first mushroom floated off into the blue, it changed its shape into a flower-like form, its grand petals curving downward, creamy white outside, rose-colored inside. . . . Much living substance had gone into those rainbows. The quivering top of the pillar was protruding to a great height through the white clouds, giving the appearance of a monstrous prehistoric creature with a ruff around its neck, a fleecy ruff extending in all directions, as far as the eye could see.[16]

Which of the kinds of support mentioned in this chapter appeal most to you? Do you think that men and women are equally attracted to each kind of support? Why?

In a speech on the pollution of U.S. communities, speaker Jillian Collum of the University of Texas at Austin used comparison and contrast to establish the military's role in contaminating the land:

> Our military treats environmental regulations as if they are an unnecessary hassle—because it can get away with ignoring the law. According to the December 20, 2006,

San Diego Union-Tribune, sovereign immunity means that, under federal law, state agencies cannot impose fines on the military. In fact, in November 2006, state regulators discovered that the Navy had piped 14.2 million gallons of sewage into San Diego Bay. If a private company had committed such an offense, they would have been fined $1 million, but, in this case, San Diego was left helpless.[17]

Repetition and Restatement

When a speaker uses repetition, the same words are repeated verbatim. When a speaker uses restatement, an idea is presented again, but in different words. If used sparingly, these devices can add impact to a speech maker's remarks and thereby increase memorability.

One of the most famous examples of successful use of repetition is the speech delivered by Martin Luther King, Jr., in 1963 at the Lincoln Memorial:

> I say to you today, my friends, so even though we face the difficulties of today and tomorrow, I still have a dream. It is a dream deeply rooted in the American dream. I have a dream that one day this nation will rise up . . . live out the true meaning of its creed—we hold these truths to be self-evident, that all men are created equal. . . .
>
> I have a dream that my four little children will one day live in a nation where they will not be judged by the color of their skin but by the content of their character. I have a dream today. . . .
>
> I have a dream that one day every valley shall be exalted, and every hill and mountain shall be made low, the rough places shall be made plain, and the crooked places shall be made straight and the glory of the Lord will be revealed and all flesh shall see it together.[17]

Work It Out

Go to the library and, using recent issues of *Vital Speeches of the Day*, work in groups to locate examples of speakers using each of the supporting materials discussed in this section.

SELECT PRESENTATION AIDS: ILLUSTRATE YOUR SPEECH

The first question to ask yourself about audio and visual aids is, Do I need them? Many speakers make the mistake of not using such aids when the content really demands them. Other speakers use too many audio and visual aids; they clutter the content so much that the presentation becomes confusing and loses momentum. Of late, visual aids have become a weapon of choice of speakers in the public arena. In fact, at congressional hearings, it is common for senators and representatives to use poster board aids that show text in letters large enough to be seen by the cameras.

In this section, we consider (1) how you can determine whether your presentation can be improved by audio and visual aids and (2) how you can select and prepare such aids when they are needed.

Visual aids reinforce a speaker's spoken message. A visual that is tangible can add drama to a presentation.

Why Use Presentation Aids?

Presentation aids have several functions. Ideally, they make it easier for the audience to follow, understand, respond to, and remember your speech. Thus, when deciding whether to use an audio or visual aid, begin by asking yourself if it will serve at least one of those purposes:

- Facilitate the communication of highly technical information, increasing understanding and reducing confusion

- Highlight or add emphasis to one or more points
- Increase listeners' motivation
- Generate more interest
- Enhance recall
- Dramatize data

For example, a three-dimensional model of the molecular structure of a virus might create more interest than words alone can provide. Visuals depicting the damage that cigarette smoke does to human lungs or sound effects that recreate the breathing of lung-cancer victims can similarly add impact. A chart dramatizing the number of infants who fall prey to sudden death syndrome each year, or one symbolizing a decline in real income can also reinforce the spoken message. By providing audience members with an additional channel, audio and visual aids impel them to use their ears and their eyes, pay attention, and care about a speech in ways they otherwise might not.[19]

Selecting and creating materials to help accomplish your speech-making goals is challenging.[20]

Once you decide to use audio or visual aids, you have to make a number of serious decisions. Initially, you will need to identify precise points in your presentation when aids will be effective. One way to prepare yourself to make such judgments is to examine how producers of newscasts select audio and visual aids to complement the work of on-camera reporters. After all, in many ways you are the "producer" of your speech.

Another strategy is brainstorming. Examine the information you have and repeatedly ask yourself the following question: Which specific pieces of information could be improved with audio or visual aids? Keep a record of each idea that comes to mind, being sure to indicate how the audio or visual support would actually be used.

Once you have analyzed your needs for audio and visual reinforcement, it is time to reconsider the possibilities you have identified.

Visual Aids

One of the prime reasons for using visual aids is to increase audience comprehension and retention. Visuals reinforce and help communicate the speaker's spoken message, enabling receivers to understand what words alone cannot transmit.

Types of Visual Aids

Let's now examine a sampling of the types of visual aids at your disposal.

Objects and Models   In your brainstorming session, you may have decided that you would like to use an object to illustrate a certain concept. The object you choose can be the real thing—for example, a set of earphones, a food processor, or a computer.

However, using an actual object is often impractical: Objects like automobiles are obviously too large, and objects like microelectronic chips may be too small. In such cases, it may be necessary to use a model instead. A model can be made of clay, papier-mâché, wood scraps, or other materials. If used creatively, inexpensive materials can serve your purpose very well. Your aim is simply to make a

---

Is it sufficient if all a visual aid does is jog the memory of audience members? Why?

pie, or circle, graph
a circle with the various percentages of the whole indicated by wedges; a means of showing percentage relationships

reasonable facsimile of the object—something that will enable you to share information more meaningfully.

The accompanying photograph shows celebrity spokesperson Sean "P. Diddy" Combs using himself as a model and wearing the message he sought to share with receivers. Do you think a speaker's dress should become part of the speaker's message?

Objects and models make it easier for you to pull your audience into your speech. Since they are tangible, they can make your points more realistic, and they can add drama to your presentation.

Graphs   You can use graphs to make an effective presentation even more successful. The most commonly used graphs are pie, or circle, graphs; bar graphs; line graphs; and pictographs.

A **pie, or circle, graph** is simply a circle with the various percentages of the whole indicated by wedges. By focusing on relationships, pie graphs show how items compare with each other and with the whole. Since the entire circle represents 100 percent, the pie graph is an effective way to show percentage relationships or proportions. In a speech on how to meet the challenges posed by diversity on the job, one student used a pie graph to provide a snapshot of the extent to which employees perceive diversity in the workplace to have changed over the past decade (see Figure 13.5).[21]

If your goal is to show the performance of one variable over time, a **bar graph** might be appropriate. A bar graph is used to compare quantities or magnitude.

In a speech on alcohol abuse, a student used the bar graph in Figure 13.6 to compare and contrast the extent to which members of different gender and ethnic groups suffer from alcohol abuse or alcoholism over the life span.[22] A bar graph can also be used to show the performance of one variable over time. (See Figure 13.7.)

Sean "P. Diddy" Combs is wearing a message he wants others to accept. In your opinion is wearing a message an effective means of communicating? Why or why not?

bar graph

a graph used to show the performance of one variable over time or to contrast various measures at a point in time

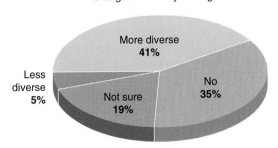

Workplace diversity

Has the level of diversity in your workplace changed from 10 years ago?

- More diverse 41%
- Less diverse 5%
- Not sure 19%
- No 35%

FIGURE 13.5   Pie Graph.

Source: USA Today August 13, 2008. Reprinted with permission.

Who's most at risk?

Rates for alcohol abuse and alcoholism were found to be highest in men and in Native Americans, as reported in a new government study.

Percent of Americans suffering from alcohol abuse or alcoholism in their lifetime

Men	42%
Women	19.5%

Race/Ethnicity

Native American	43%
White	34.1%
Hispanic	21%
Black	20.6%
Asian	11.6%

FIGURE 13.6   Rates for Alcohol Abuse or Alcoholism.

Source: The Record July 3, 2007.

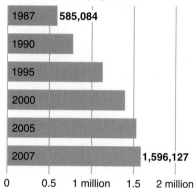

America incarcerated

More than 1 out of every 100 U.S. adults is behind bars, according to a new Pew report. Violent crimes have dropped 25% since 1987, but harsher sentencing for lesser crimes has caused overcrowding and fueled a thriving private-prisons industry. A look at who's doing time in the land of the free:

FIGURE 13.7   Incarceration in America.

Source: Time March 17, 2008.

line graphs

graphs used to illustrate trends, relationships, or comparisons over time

Like bar graphs, **line graphs** can illustrate trends, relationships, or comparisons over time. In a speech on incarceration in the United States, one student used a line graph to make the point that while violent crime has abated, harsher sentencing for less serious crimes has caused a dramatic increase in the national prison population.[23] The line graph, in addition to showing the numbers of people in the prison population, also illustrates a perceptible upward trend. If a line graph contains more than one line, the presenter should color-code each line for clarity, as did the speaker in a speech on the growing influence of minorities in the United States (see Figure 13.8). When well designed, the line graph is one of the easiest types for audiences to read and follow.

pictographs

graphs that use sketches to represent concepts

Pictographs use sketches of figures to represent concepts (see Figure 13.9). During your research, you may discover sketches or pictures that could be integrated into a pictograph to help vitalize your content.

In the speech on incarceration referred to earlier, the speaker also incorporated a pictograph (see Figure 13.9) to compare and contrast the percentages of males and females, Whites, Hispanics, and Blacks currently in prison. As you research your speech, keep a look out for material you can turn into pictographs that may help audience members visualize your message, as did a speaker delivering a speech on the global implications of nuclear power plants (see Figure 13.10).[24]

The general rule to follow in making and using graphs is that a single graph should be used to communicate only one concept or idea. Consider the line graph in Figure 13.11. This graph is far too cluttered for an audience to read easily and quickly. Your goal in devising a graph is to eliminate extraneous information and to focus, rather than diffuse, the audience's attention. Emphasize the essentials.

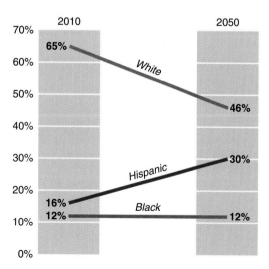

FIGURE 13.8   Growing Minority Influence.

Source: USA Today August 14, 2008. Reprinted with permission.

Photographs and Drawings   Drawings, like photographs, can help generate a mood, clarify, or identify. In explaining a sequence of plays that led to a success for his football

Of every 100 inmates in prison or jail:

9%
are female

91%
are male

40.3
are black

36.2
are white

20.5
are Hispanic

3.0
are other

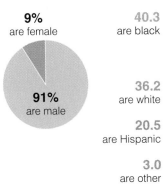
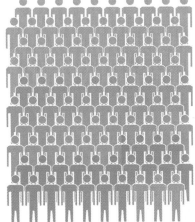

1 in 9

are black men age 20 to 34

1 in 36

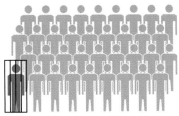
are Hispanic men age 18 or older

1 in 106

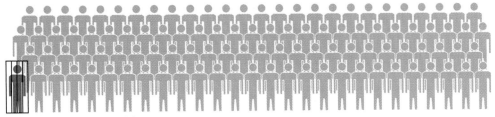
are white men age 18 or older

1 in 100

are black women age 35 to 39

1 in 355

are white women age 35 to 39

FIGURE 13.9   Pictograph of Who Is in Prison.

Source: Time March 17, 2008.

FIGURE 13.10

Pictograph of Percentage of Nuclear Power Plants Globally.

Source: USA Today July 17, 2008. Reprinted with permission.

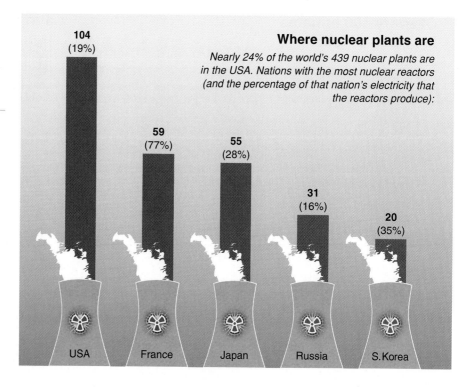

Where nuclear plants are

Nearly 24% of the world's 439 nuclear plants are in the USA. Nations with the most nuclear reactors (and the percentage of that nation's electricity that the reactors produce):

FIGURE 13.11 Poorly Designed Line Graph.

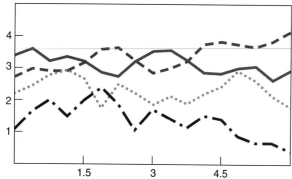

team, one speaker used a drawing like the one in Figure 13.12. Would you recommend simplifying this sketch?

You may find photographs or drawings that can add interest to your presentation and provide greater reality. For example, one student used drawings taken from her local newspaper to help illustrate her speech on the danger of rip currents (see Figure 13.13).[26]

If possible, use a variety of dark, rich colors, such as red, black, blue, and green, to add contrast to a drawing. But remember, unless a drawing is large

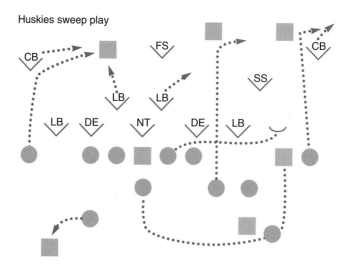

Huskies sweep play

FIGURE 13.12 Drawing.

Rip currents are powerful, channeled currents of water. They typically extend from the shoreline, through the surf zone and past the line of breaking waves. They can extend as far as 3,000 feet offshore, reach 90 feet in width and travel up to 8 feet per second.

How rip currents are formed*

1. Incoming waves cause the water to pile up between the shore and sandbars.

2. A section of a sandbar collapses from the increased water pressure.

3. The excess water is forced through the gap created by the collapsed sandbar and creates a strong, narrow current that can take a swimmer away from the shore.

How to escape a rip current

- Stay calm to conserve energy and think clearly.
- Never fight the current.
- Swim out of the current in a direction following the shoreline. When out of the current, swim at an angle away from the current and toward shore.
- If you are unable to swim out of the rip current, float or calmly tread water. When out of the current, swim toward shore.
- If you are still unable to reach shore, draw attention to yourself by waving your arm and yelling for help.

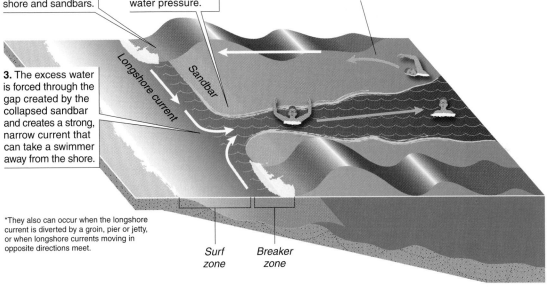

*They also can occur when the longshore current is diverted by a groin, pier or jetty, or when longshore currents moving in opposite directions meet.

Longshore current

Sandbar

Surf zone

Breaker zone

FIGURE 13.13   Drawing.

Sources: National Weather Service, U.S. Coast Guard.

---

enough to be seen, it will not increase your audience's attention or strengthen your presentation.

Computer Graphics   Speech makers commonly use computer-generated visual aids in their presentations. Years ago the tradition was for college speakers to use poster board and marking pens to enlarge charts and graphs so that audience members could see them easily. Now, however, computer graphics make it possible for students to develop professional-looking charts and graphs.

To prepare a computer graphic, begin by organizing your data. Then select the type of graphic you want—for example, pie chart, bar chart, or some other graphic. Many programs automatically generate legends for the visual.

The leading graphics program available is PowerPoint. Figure 13.14 shows a sample of a

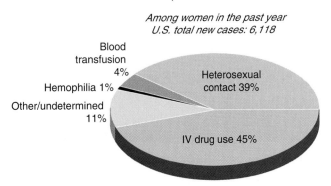

Who Gets AIDS, and Where?

*Among women in the past year
U.S. total new cases: 6,118*

Blood transfusion 4%

Hemophilia 1%

Other/undetermined 11%

Heterosexual contact 39%

IV drug use 45%

FIGURE 13.14   Computer-Generated Graph.

FIGURE 13.15 Computer-Generated Image.

Source: Howard Sochurek-Medichrome-stock shop.

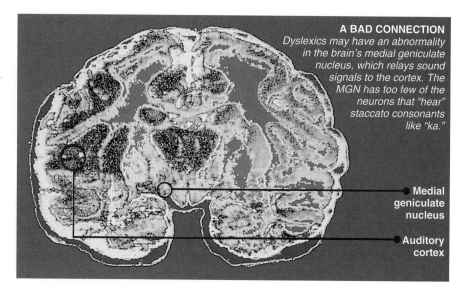

A BAD CONNECTION
Dyslexics may have an abnormality in the brain's medial geniculate nucleus, which relays sound signals to the cortex. The MGN has too few of the neurons that "hear" staccato consonants like "ka."

Medial geniculate nucleus

Auditory cortex

computer-generated graph. You can use PowerPoint to produce such a graph. When using PowerPoint to strengthen or help communicate ideas, the presenter is free to select or create backgrounds, colors, formats, layouts, and sounds. The speaker can also animate text and graphics to fade in or out or to dissolve, as he or she desires. In addition, the presenter can scan in other appropriate photographs or relevant visuals, including film clips. (We discuss PowerPoint-assisted presentations in greater detail a little later in this chapter.) You can also use graphics generated by a professional, as one student did when delivering a speech on dyslexia (see Figure 13.15), and as another student did when explaining how the Ebola virus works (see Figure 13.16).[27]

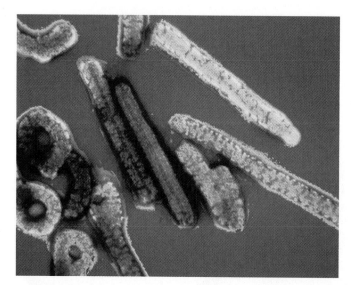

FIGURE 13.16 Speakers Often Use Professional Graphics.

The Ebola virus at work.

Guidelines for Using Visual Aids

Speakers can justify the use of visual aids by showing how they contribute to audience understanding of the message.

Criteria When evaluating visuals, remember that they must be appropriate to the audience, the occasion, the location, and the content of your speech—and to you yourself.

In developing visual materials, keep three criteria in mind: (1) simplicity, (2) clarity, and (3) visibility. *Simplicity* means that the visuals should be as transportable as possible (so that you can easily take them with you to the presentation) and as easy as possible to use. Give careful consideration to the size and weight of large items. Ask yourself if a visual can be displayed without disrupting the environment. Ask yourself if it can be set up and taken down in a minimal amount of time. With regard to clarity, remember that the purpose of a visual aid is to enhance understanding, not to cause confusion. Ideally, each visual should depict only one idea or concept, or at least should be displayed so that only the relevant portions are visible at the appropriate point in your speech. Visibility is the third criterion. Since a visual aid obviously serves no purpose if it cannot be seen and read, you must determine if your audience will be able to see and read it. Make sure that the lettering is tall enough (3 by 4 inches high or larger) and that photographs or pictures are large enough.

Methods and Equipment If you are not using a computer or in a "smart class-room," one way to present flat visuals is to display them on a chart board or on oaktag. With variously colored markers, a yardstick, and a little time, you should be able to create appealing and functional visuals. You may also use more sophis-ticated equipment to present visuals—overhead projectors, film, videotape, and 35 mm slides. Overhead projectors are often used by training professionals and salespeople. Transparencies can be created from almost any 8½- by 11-inch original of a photograph, an illustration, or a graph. Then the image can be projected onto a screen or a light-colored wall (if no screen is available). The room need not be completely darkened to use an overhead projector, but you should rehearse with transparencies to be sure they are clearly visible. (Setup time is about 10 minutes.)

Film clips can also be used to add life and motion to a presentation. For film, you need a screen or light-colored wall in a room that can be darkened. It will take about 15 minutes to prepare the room and equipment. Without adequate setup time, a film clip can become more of a hindrance than a help.

Slides are easier to use than film. However, unless you have been trained in multimedia or multi-image production, the number of slides you use should be kept to a minimum. (Also, be prepared to deal with jammed slide trays and burned-out bulbs.)

DVD recorders have improved greatly in recent years and are easy for speakers to use. Video stores have many DVDs that can be used to arouse an audience's interest. One speaker used a clip of Abbott and Costello's "Who's on First?" routine to introduce the topic of language. A company president regularly uses clips from the various *Rocky* films to motivate the sales force. The cable channel C-Span makes it convenient to incorporate current events into speeches. If your topic is current, check the C-Span listings—if C-Span is available in your area—to determine if and when the topic will be covered. Then, in addition to quoting a public official, you can actually have him or her as a video guest to briefly illustrate a point.

Work It Out

What type of visual aid do you consider the most overused? The most underused? The most effective? The least effective? Why?

In your mind, what is the difference between a visual aid and visual notes?

Skill Builder

Using Many Eyes

Do you currently share videos on YouTube or photos using Flickr? Now an experimental Web site designed to help people publish and discuss graphics in a group, Many Eyes (www.many-eyes.com), lets people share graphs, charts, and other visuals with one another to help interpret data. The theory is that collaborative interpretation of visual in-formation will spur insight and protect against bias.

Access the Many Eyes Web site. Identify the different ways data are presented. Which visuals do you find particu-larly interesting? Which do you think a public speaker might find useful? Discuss a visual that you believe could be used to tell at least two different stories.

What is this cartoon suggesting about the use of visuals? Visuals should enhance a presentation.

When using DVDs, cue up the DVD before you begin the speech. Far too many speakers press the Play button only to find that they have no picture or sound on the monitor. One speaker had scarcely begun his presentation before he had to call a coffee break while repairs were done on the video equipment. Audiences today are simply not willing to sit while you and others tinker with electronic gadgetry. Prepare it carefully in advance, and rehearse.

Audio Aids

Audiotape is readily available and easy to use as an accompaniment to a speech. Cassette and CD players come in a variety of forms and sizes, many of which are easily portable. Since speech makers often find it advantageous to integrate a brief excerpt from a song or a segment from an interview or a newscast into their presentations, audiotape has become a popular support medium. One student, for example, reinforced an informative presentation entitled "The Speech Capabilities of Dolphins" with a few moments of dolphin sounds that she had recorded during a visit to an aquarium.

If you decide to use audiotape, cue the tape to the precise point at which you want to begin. Do this before you arrive at the front of the room, so that finding the right spot on the tape will not bring your presentation to an untimely halt.

Computer-Assisted Presentations: PowerPoint

Of all the visual aids mentioned, computerized presentations have increased the most in popularity.[28] You can not only create various types of charts but also build effective online slide shows from your speech outline. You can also use a computer to display video clips, text, photographs, drawings, and charts. PowerPoint, for example, contains a clip art library that enables you to select images that enhance the meaning of your words. It also allows you to generate backgrounds, formats, layouts, and colors that you believe best reflect the purpose of your presentation. The computer-generated visuals you create can be run directly from a computer projector, converted to 35 mm slides, printed out in handout form, or blown up for display to the audience. (See the sample computer-assisted slide presentation on page 349.)

When planning a PowerPoint presentation, you need to think in bullets (see sample slide presentation). Supporting your spoken speech, PowerPoint slides illustrate your talk. Pictures and charts, as well as animated graphics and talking points, are projected onto a screen, which both you and receivers use.

Work It Out

In what ways does the visual stimulation of a PowerPoint presentation enhance or detract from one's ability to think critically about a presentation?

Although computerized presentations are the standard in business and education, you do need to be selective when deciding whether or not to create one. If not prepared with care or if allowed to upstage the speaker and overpower the message, computer presentations can drain a speech of its vitality.[29] Reflecting the growth in PowerPoint presentations, a chairman of the Joint Chiefs of Staff issued the following order, although not in these exact words, to U.S. military bases around the globe: "Enough with the bells and whistles—just get to the point."[30] To what extent do you agree or disagree with this advice? Whatever your position, the point is that a piece of technology that is supposed to facilitate communication should not be used in such a way that it becomes an obstacle to it.

One fear is that dazzling PowerPoint presentations can be used to cover up weak content.[31] The role of technology is not to elevate format over content but to facilitate communication. Although fiddling with fonts may be fun, it is more important to do adequate research. Another fear is that the number of words and slides used will be out of control. In fact, one U.S. computer company has distributed guidelines to its employees about PowerPoint presentations that require them to adhere to the "Rule of Seven": seven bullets or lines per slide, seven words per line.[32] PowerPoint gets a bad rap when a speaker forgets that its role is to *enhance* a speech, not to *be* the speech. By limiting the number of slides you use, taking pains to ensure that your spoken words are not merely what receivers see on your slides—that nothing that comes out of your mouth is replicated word for word in the slides that you display—your slides will enhance rather than overshadow you and your presentation.[33] According to MIT psychology professor Steven Pinker, when used effectively PowerPoint gives visual shape to an argument. Says Pinker, "Language is a linear medium: one damn word after another. But ideas are multidimensional. . . . When properly employed, PowerPoint makes the logical structure of an argument more transparent. Two channels sending the same information are better than one."[34]

Sample Computer-Assisted Slide Presentation

PowerPoint has been dressing up ideas and contributing to the delivery of crisp presentations for over 20 years.[35] For an example of one such PowerPoint presentation, see below.

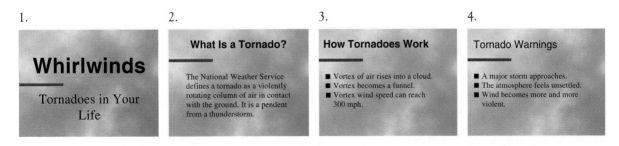

1. 2. 3. 4.

1. The first slide introduces the topic to the audience. Speakers usually keep the title slide simple but provocative to draw receivers into the presentation. The speaker's task is to find a background for the slide that reflects the tone of the presentation. What do you think of the background provided here?

2. The second slide introduces the first main point of the speech. The speaker uses the slide to ask and answer a question, clarifying the subject

for receivers. How did the speaker add credibility to the definition provided? In your opinion, should the speaker have done more to orient receivers visually to the topic prior to defining this key term?

3. The third slide introduces the second main point of the speech by summarizing how tornadoes work. In your opinion, will this slide help sustain receiver interest? Why or why not?

4. The fourth slide introduces the third point of the speech by revealing the warning signs of an approaching tornado.

5.

The Fujita Scale
Wind Speed

- F0–Up to 72 mph. Broken tree limbs and signs.
- F1–Up to 112 mph. Trailer homes flipped.
- F2–Up to 157 mph. Roofs torn off; trailer homes demolished.

6.

The Fujita Scale
Wind Speed

- F3–Up to 206 mph. Roofs and walls torn down; trains thrown from tracks.
- F4–Up to 260 mph. Frame homes leveled.
- F5–Over 260 mph. Homes and buildings completely destroyed.

7.

How Large Are Tornadoes?

- Average 500 feet in width
- Travel 5 miles on ground
- Last only a few minutes

8.

Where Do Tornadoes Occur Most Often?

- South in early spring
- Midwest in May
- The Texas and Oklahoma Panhandles are sometimes known as Tornado Alley in the spring and early summer.
- Later in the summer, tornadoes are found in the eastern part of the country.

5. In the fifth, sixth, and seventh slides, the speaker develops the fourth main point of the speech by describing how tornadoes are rated, explaining the size of the average tornado, and offering dramatic examples of tornado damage.

6. In the eighth and ninth slides, the speaker develops the fifth main point of the speech by summarizing where and when tornadoes are likely to occur and the kind of people who track them. In your opinion, are these slides too wordy? What should the speaker do to enhance receiver involvement in this phase of the speech?

7. The tenth and eleventh slides focus on the speaker's last main point—what receivers can do to protect themselves from tornadoes.

8. The final slide wraps up the speech by supporting the speaker's concluding words. It also provides a sense of closure by reflecting the first slide the speaker used in the presentation. In your opinion, did the speaker need to use a slide prior to this one, summarizing what the speech had accomplished? If so, what should that slide have contained?

9.

Who Chases Tornadoes?

- People who work for the National Weather Service
- Tourists
- A travel agency in Amarillo, Texas, plans two-week tours every summer for amateur tornado chasers.

10.

Protection from Tornadoes

- Listen to weather reports.
- Get inside a building away from glass.
- Basements are the safest places.

11.

AVOID!

- TRAILER HOMES
- OVERPASSES ON THE HIGHWAY
- TRYING TO CHASE A TORNADO

12.

WHIRLWINDS

DON'T LET THEM CAUSE TURBULENCE IN YOUR LIFE!

9. Are there any other slides you think the speaker should have added to this presentation, or are there any that you feel the speaker could have done without?

10. How many slides did the speaker use that you believe contain too many words or bullets? Shorten these slides to make them more effective.

Ethics and Communication

Information Overload, Plagiarism, and Visual Manipulation

1. David Shenk, the author of *Data Smog: Surviving the Information Glut*, observes, "With a majority of American workers now paid to churn out data, we have generated a morass of expert information that has started to undermine logical approaches to deliberation and problem solving."[36] Well over 100,000 studies now exist on depression. What this produces is not only an overabundance of information, but also so many competing expert opinions that it becomes virtually impossible for the receiver of this magnitude of information to draw a conclusion, leading one to suffer the consequences of "paralysis by analysis." Thus, we ask, How much information is too much information? What obligation does a speaker have to avoid overwhelming audience members with data? What advice would you offer a speaker regarding the steps to take to minimize the effects of "data smog"?

2. As countless scandals have shown, when it comes to deception, computer graphics make it simple for someone to distort an actual image. Unethical speakers, much like magicians create illusions, manipulate what we see by altering their visuals to conform to the point they are trying to make. For example, a university admitted to doctoring a photo on its brochure cover by inserting Black students into a crowd of White football fans because it was seeking an image of diversity in its recruitment literature.[37] Because speech makers now have the technological ability to doctor their visuals to make their points, the question that needs to be answered is, At what point does the touching up or alteration of a visual put a speaker on ethical thin ice?

COMMUNICATION IN PRACTICE
IMPROVING YOUR ABILITY TO EVALUATE SUPPORTING MATERIALS

How credible is the support you include in your speech? Use the following supporting material analysis system to test the effectiveness of the information and evidence in your speech. Simply ask yourself each of the following questions about your speech-building material:

> **Work It Out**
>
> What do the experts think? Is nuclear power safe? Does affirmative action work? Do vitamins prevent cancer? Using one of the preceding controversial issues or another of your choice, surf the Internet in search of studies and arguments on both sides of the question. Does your search lead you to agree or disagree with the *New York Times*, which noted that the "volleys of data" result in endless argumentation but no decision? Explain. How can the public speaker solve such a dilemma?

☑ How Recent Is the Information and Evidence?

Determine if the information is recent enough to be valid.

☑ How Accurate Is the Information and Evidence?

Ask the following questions to assess accuracy: Do other sources contain similar data? Does each information source provide specific information, or does he or she make unsupported claims?

☑ How Reliable Is the Information and Evidence?

Did the information cited appear in a major book, newspaper or news show, magazine, or Web site? If, for example, the source is a Web site, determine who is responsible for information that appears on that site. Your goal is to decide if the site's administrators or founders are biased or unbiased, supportive of particular social or political agendas, or neutral.

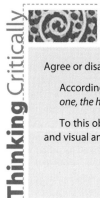

Reflect and Respond

Agree or disagree with the following observation. Give reasons and examples that support your position.

According to Aristotle: *"Of the three elements in speech making—speaker, subject, and person addressed—it is the last one, the hearer, that determines the speech's end and object."*

To this observation, we can also add that it is the last one, the hearer, that also determines the supporting materials and visual and audio aids to be used.

Focus on Service Learning
Using information contained in your text and in Web sites such as http://eduscapes.com/tap/topic20.htm or images.google.com, work with a community group such as Big Brothers Big Sisters or Habitat for Humanity to create a visually effective presentation designed to help the group raise funds. Be sure to learn as much as possible about your chosen group before beginning your work.

☑ How Sufficient Is the Information and Evidence?

Determine whether you have enough data to support the point(s) you are making.

☑ How Appropriate Is the Information and Evidence?

Evaluate whether the information you offer is supportive of your topic and is used in good taste.

☑ How Effective Are the Audio and Visual Aids?

Decide if they stir interest, enhance motivation, and promote understanding and retention

---

Revisiting Chapter Objectives

1. **Identify and use the various online and offline research resources available to you.**   The first step in the development stage of preparing a speech is to gather a variety of effective research materials to integrate into your presentation. The materials you gather may come from online or offline sources. For example, when working offline, you may consult published works, including books, journals, magazines, and newspapers available in the library. When working online, you have the Internet and its many resources, including e-mail, listservs, newsgroups, and the World Wide Web at your disposal.

2. **Conduct an informal survey and a personal interview.** In addition to online and offline resources, you may be able to draw on your personal observations and experiences. You can, for example, conduct informal surveys or personal interviews. Informal surveys consist of approximately 5 to 10 questions that you ask people affected by or familiar with your topic. Interviews are similar to surveys except that they are more detailed and assume that the persons whom you interview are experts on your topic.

3. **Identify various types of supporting material.** You can make your research interesting and understandable to audience members by using a variety of verbal support: definitions (an explanation of what a word or concept means), statistics (facts expressed in numerical form), examples (representative cases), illustrations (stories and narrative pictures), and testimonials (someone else's opinions or conclusions; quotations). You can also increase the impact and memorability of your speech by using comparisons that express similarities and contrasts that express differences, as well as repetition (the same words repeated verbatim) and restatement (the same idea in different words).

4. **Explain how visual and audio aids can enhance a presentation.** Many speeches can be enhanced with visual and audio support. Objects, models, graphs, photographs, drawings, slides, videotapes, and audiotapes can be incorporated into the presentation to reinforce, clarify, and dramatize concepts. Computer graphics programs are now making professional-looking graphics available even to student speakers.

5. **Evaluate the effectiveness of supporting materials.** Using guidelines to identify effective supporting materials is key is building an outstanding speech.

Resources for Further Inquiry and Reflection

To apply your understanding of how the principles in Chapter 13 are at work in our daily lives, consult the following resources for further inquiry and reflection. Or, if you prefer, choose any other appropriate resource. Then connect the ideas expressed in your chosen selection with the communication concepts and issues you are learning about both in and out of class.

 Listen to Me

"Fight," "Have You Seen Me?" and "The Morality Squad" from *Live from Antarctica* (GWAR)
"Stupid Girls" (Pink)
"Warrior" (Kid Rock)
"Change" (Taylor Swift)

What topics are explored in the music of GWAR, Pink, Kid Rock, or Taylor Swift? For example, how does the explicitness and threatening nature of the band's rhetoric affect you? What meanings do receivers derive from the violent language and profane imagery contained in GWAR's songs? What means of support are used to target the central negative force in the band's message? How does Pink support her premise of "stupid girls"? What support does Kid Rock use to express the life of the warrior? What does Taylor Swift mean by "Change"?

 View Me

Other People's Money
The Net
Syriana
Traitor

What means of support does Danny DeVito's, Sandra Bullock's, George Clooney's, or Don Cheadle's character use to make his or her case?

THE WRAP-UP

Read Me

David Slayden and Rita Kirk Whellock, eds. *Soundbite Culture: The Death of Discourse in a Wired World.* Thousand Oaks, CA: Sage, 1999.

James Risen. *State of War.* New York: Free Press, 2006.

Peggy Noonan. *We Will Prevail.* New York: National Review, 2003.

Ron Suskind. *The Way of the World.* New York: Harper, 2008.

What do the insights provided by the author(s) of any chapter in these books reveal about the state of reasoned discourse and use of evidence in our society?

Tell Me

Share with the class the insights you gained from your chosen Listen to Me, View Me, or Read Me selection.

Imagine that you have started late on preparing a speech on the topic of affirmative action. Because time is of the essence, you ask a friend if you can borrow a research paper that your friend wrote on the same subject. You reason that it probably contains the kind of research you would find if you only had the time to investigate the topic yourself. Explain why you would or would not use the paper your friend provides. Also indicate, if you decide to use it, whether you consider your use of your friend's paper to be plagiarism.

www.mhhe.com/gamble10e

Key Chapter Terminology

Use the Online Learning Center at www.mhhe.com/gamble10e to further your knowledge of the following terminology.

bar graph 341	listserv 330
Boolean search 329	pictographs 342
definitions 335	pie, or circle, graph 340
examples 336	statistics 336
illustrations 336	testimony 337
line graphs 342	

Idioms in Translation

being drawn into — being fascinated by or interested in	***leave no stone unturned*** — thoroughly research
blown call — wrong call	***piling on*** — adding
driving blind — being without direction	***snapshot of persons*** — quickview of persons
flesh out — develop	***touching*** — affecting

Culture Cue

People from Asian cultures are less likely to use their hands when speaking than are those from individualistic cultures.

Test Your Understanding

Go to the *Self Quizzes* on the book's Online Learning Center at www.mhhe.com/gamble10e.   **www.mhhe.com/gamble10e**

CHAPTER 14

After finishing this chapter, you should be able to

1. Identify main and subordinate ideas.

2. Create a full sentence outline.

3. Identify five methods of ordering ideas.

4. Use internal previews and summaries, transitions, and signposts effectively.

5. Develop an effective introduction and conclusion.

6. Use a checklist to refine the design and organization of your speech.

Designing Your Speech: Organizing Your Ideas

Our lives are so busy and cluttered that many of us turn to consultants and technology to achieve a sense of order and control. We hire closet experts to organize our closets, and we use personal digital assistants (PDAs) to organize our days. Public speakers also need to be organized. You can have the best ideas in the world, the most impressive support, and eye-opening presentation aids, but unless you organize your ideas, integrating your support and presentation aids so that your audience is able to follow what you are trying to communicate, your effort will fall short. Since receivers learn more from an organized speech than from a disorganized one, organization is one of your main challenges and your next step as you make your way through the speech development phase of preparation (see Figure 14.1).

Every speech ought to be put together like a living creature, with a body of its own, so as to be neither without head nor without feet, but to have both a middle and extremities, described proportionately to each other and to the whole.

—*Plato*

What is your goal when organizing ideas? Primarily, you want to facilitate communication with your audience. How can you accomplish this? You must plan. Just as an architect develops a plan for a building, so you must develop a plan for your speech. Your plan shows the structure you will adhere to—the developmental sequence you think will work best. Of course, just as an architect considers numerous designs before selecting one, you should test potential patterns to determine which one will best clarify and amplify your ideas. Fortunately, you do not have to grope your way through a thicket of possibilities. Communication theorists have developed guidelines to help you with this phase.

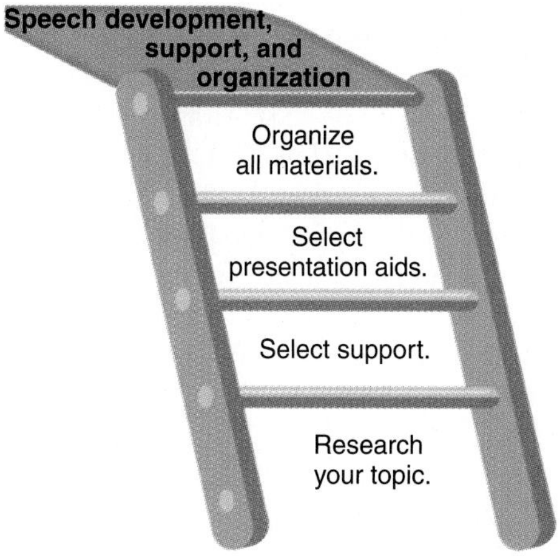

FIGURE 14.1 The Second Landing.

ORGANIZE MATERIALS: BUILDING A SPEAKING FRAMEWORK

An audience has to be able to follow your speech for it to be effective. Without good organization, a speech's message remains fuzzy and hard to follow. Since receivers rarely interrupt speakers during a speech to seek clarification, and because they do not usually have access to transcripts or tapes of presentations, speakers need to

FIGURE 14.2   Framework for a Speech.

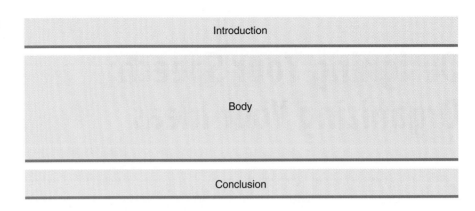

Online Learning Center

Go to the Online Learning Center at www.mhhe.com/ gamble10e and answer the questions in the *Self Inventory* to evaluate your understanding of speech outlining.

speech framework

a skeleton for speech development

organize the ideas of their speeches so that receivers comprehend them the first time they hear them. Receivers have no rewind button to push if they become distracted or confused. Thus, speakers must structure their messages so that confusion is kept to a minimum.[1]

As we saw in Chapter 7, not everyone is a skillful listener. For this reason, you should base your organization on the *principle of redundancy*. In other words, to ensure comprehension, you will need to build a certain amount of repetition into your speech. Only if this is done will listeners be able to follow your ideas easily. This basic developmental principle is often expressed as follows: *Tell them what you are going to tell them, then tell them, and finally, tell them what you have told them.*

One of the best ways to organize a speech is the introduction-body-conclusion format (see Figure 14.2), called a **speech framework** because it provides a frame, or skeleton, on which any speech or other formal presentation can be built.

Any speech you develop should be organized according to this framework. Your introductory remarks and your concluding statements should each take up approximately 10 to 15 percent of the total presentation. That leaves 70 to 80 percent of your time for developing the ideas contained in the body of your speech. Since the body will be the main portion of your presentation, it is often advisable to begin by preparing this part of the speech; once the body is set, you can move on to develop the introduction and the conclusion. Let's consider the three key parts of a speech in that order: body, introduction, and conclusion.

ORGANIZE THE BODY OF YOUR PRESENTATION

As you begin to outline the body of your speech, you will want to build a suitable structure onto which you can place your ideas. You develop this structure in stages. During the first stage of outline development, you create a *preliminary working outline*. This sparse outline has points containing one or two words that eventually will achieve fuller form in the second stage, the full sentence outline. You develop the *full sentence outline* only after you have researched and fully developed the ideas of your speech. Ultimately, during the third stage of outline preparation, you will transform your full sentence outline into an *extemporaneous outline, or speaker's notes,* that you will then use as your guide when you deliver your speech.

Work It Out
Generate guidelines to use when outlining a speech.

Outlining Principles: Identifying Main and Subordinate Ideas

Let's imagine that you have created the following working plan, or outline, for a speech about affirmative action:

I. Definition
II. Purposes
III. Outcomes
IV. Why under attack

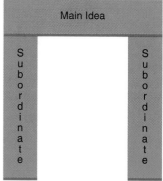

FIGURE 14.3   Construction of an Idea.

Your next task is to develop those topics. As you begin the development process, keep in mind that your audience is unlikely to recall a long, wandering, unstructured collection of data. Thus, after you have conducted your research, you will need to develop a full sentence outline that distinguishes between your **main ideas**—your speech's subtopics that directly support your thesis—and your **subordinate ideas**—those ideas that function as support or amplification for your main ideas or subtopics.

In many ways, subordinate ideas are the foundation on which larger ideas are constructed (see Figure 14.3). Consequently, you should begin the organizational process by arranging your materials into clusters of main and subordinate ideas. As you do this, you will be able to determine which evidence supports the main ideas and which supports the subordinate ideas. Your main ideas will be, say, two to five major points that you want the audience to remember.

If you are developing a speech on affirmative action programs, you might begin as follows:

Purpose: To inform the audience about affirmative action

Behavioral objective: After listening to my speech, audience members will be able to define affirmative action, identify its uses and results, and explain why it is a policy under fire.

Thesis: The definition, uses, and results of affirmative action have contributed to its being a policy under fire. (See Figure 14.4.)

You are now off to a good start. Next, you need to develop these major points into complete sentences using parallel structure—that is, using sentences with similar or matching styles.

I. Affirmative action can be defined as any action taken to ensure or affirm equal opportunity for oppressed or previously disadvantaged groups.
II. Affirmative action is used in hiring and college admissions decisions.
III. Affirmative action has benefits and drawbacks.
IV. Affirmative action is under fire for being reverse discrimination.

main ideas

the main points of a speech; the subtopics of a speech

subordinate ideas

ideas that amplify the main ideas or subtopics of a speech

Work It Out

Work in groups to develop working outlines on the following topics: stress and the college student, space exploration, cheating, green living and the college student, or a topic of your choice.

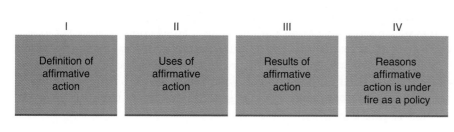

FIGURE 14.4

Dividing a Thesis into Major Points.

Many people find it helpful to pull together clusters of information that support their main ideas, as follows:

I. Main idea
  A. Subordinate idea
    1. Support for subordinate idea
    2. Support for subordinate idea
  B. Subordinate idea
    1. Support for subordinate idea
    2. Support for subordinate idea

Work It Out
Evaluate the organizational strengths and weaknesses of your most and least favorite Web pages. Or choose one of the following Web sites to evaluate: www.infoplease.com, www.cnn.com, or www.greenpeace.org.
Pay attention to your first impression of the site, the difficulty or ease you experience in trying to make sense of it, and the last impression you are left with before exiting the site. Compare and contrast the organizational framework of a Web site with the organizational framework of a speech.

When you take the time to prepare an easy-to-follow structure for your speech, in addition to enhancing receiver perceptions of your competence and adding to the personal credibility you have in their eyes, your efforts also help fulfill receiver expectations. That is, the main points of a speech alert receivers to listen for supporting information. Because they are not struggling to give order to a disordered array of information, they can focus instead on the thesis of your speech and the support you offer to build your presentation. Taking time to develop an outline has a third benefit, as well. Because you know what information you are using to support each main point of your speech, your delivery of the speech will be improved. Since your ideas are carefully laid out before you, instead of having to concentrate on what to say next, you free yourself to focus on establishing a good relationship with your receivers.

If you have taken notes on cards, you can lay out or pattern the body of your speech in the following way:

Purpose:
  I. Main idea
    A. (Supports I)   B. (Supports I)
      1. (Supports A)   1. (Supports B)
      2. (Supports A)   2. (Supports B)
      3. (Supports A)
  II. Main idea
    A. (Supports II)
    B. (Supports II)

Notice that the outline you develop indicates the relative importance of each item included in it. The main points—roman numerals I, II, III, and so on—are the most important items you want your audience to remember. Your subpoints—capital letters A, B, C, and so on—are supportive of but less important than the main points. Likewise, items beginning with arabic numerals 1, 2, 3, and so on are supportive of but less important than subpoints. Remember to line up the entries in your outline correctly. Locate the main ideas closest to the left margin. The subpoints underlying the main points should begin directly underneath the first letter of the first word of each main point. Keep in mind that a traditional rule of outlining is that at least two subpoints must support every main point.

Items that support the subpoints begin directly underneath the first letter of the first word of each subpoint. Indicate the supporting materials for these with lowercase letters (a, b, c, and so on). In this way, the full sentence outline functions as a visual representation of the supportive underpinnings for ideas. In general, there should be at least a 3 to 1 ratio between the number of words in your speech and the number of words in your outline.

An outline on avian flu, using the symbols and indentions just discussed, might be built as follows:

Purpose: To inform audience members about the fears and questions concerning the H5N1 avian flu (bird flu)

I. Several fears about H5N1 avian flu are prevalent in society today.

II. Many questions remain regarding future efforts to protect against a pandemic strain of avian flu.

> How could you use this model to organize a speech on stem-cell research?

Looking at this example, we have in plain sight the central features of what will become a speech. Because the speaker identifies two aspects of the subject, there will be two main points in the speech. It is important for the ordering of main points to flow logically if receivers are going to be able to follow the presentation easily. In this speech, to guide the receiver in processing the speech, the speaker chose to first confront existing fears about the avian flu, and then to discuss the questions revolving around the disease's control and potential treatment should it develop into a pandemic. Here is how the speaker developed the speech's main points:

1. Several fears concerning the H5N1 avian flu are prevalent in society today.
    A. Many people fear that H5N1 avian flu is the next pandemic.
        1. Cases of human infection of H5N1 avian flu have been reported in a number of countries, including China, Cambodia, Turkey, and Iraq, among people who handled infected birds.
        2. There is concern that the H5N1 avian flu virus will mutate spontaneously, giving it greater ability to jump from human to human.
        3. There is concern that travel, especially by air, will accelerate transmission of the disease around the world.
    B. Currently, chances of contracting H5N1 avian flu are small for people who do not have intimate contact with birds.
        1. Not a single bird in the United States has been found to suffer from avian influenza.
        2. Casual contact with birds will not spread flu because of the species barrier.
II. Many questions remain regarding future efforts to protect against a pandemic strain of avian flu.
    A. Developing a vaccine to attack a pandemic avian flu virus is problematic.
        1. Whether Tamiflu and Relenza will be effective against the pandemic version of the avian flu virus is unclear.
        2. Because scientists do not know what the pandemic flu virus will look like, a vaccine cannot yet be made.

     3. Scientists hope that the H5N1 vaccines now in trials will provide at least some protection in a pandemic.

  B. Improving international cooperation is critical.

     1. We need to increase awareness of the threat.

     2. We need to improve surveillance and diagnosis of the disease in birds.

  C. Biosecurity is key.

     1. The president signed an executive order adding pandemic influenza to the list of quarantinable diseases.

     2. The N95 mask provides aerosolization protection from the droplets that spread the virus.

     3. Discouraging personal stockpiling, the government is calling for the maintenance of national and regional supplies.

Giving Order to Your Ideas Using Traditional and Nontraditional Formats

> Do you prefer listening to speeches that are organized using traditional or nontraditional formats? Why?

Speeches have either a linear or a nonlinear format. Western cultures favor a linear organization, while non-Western cultures favor organizational nonlinear formats. As Richard Nisbett notes, there appears to be a geography of thought when it comes to both the development of a worldview and the frameworks of thinking that support it.[2] In his book *The Geography of Thought: How Asians and Westerners Think Differently . . . and Why,* Nisbett notes that human cognition and reasoning preferences differ, depending on whether you were brought up in a Western or an Eastern culture. According to Nisbett, East Asians are more holistic and contextual in their perceptions, while Westerners have more of a tunnel-vision perceptual style that depends more on identifying with what is prominent in a situation and remembering it. Persons from Eastern cultures tend to tolerate subtleties and deal in relationships (the stress is placed on intuitive thinking and informal logic, not the use of categories—for example, the practice of feng shui is not atomistic but extraordinarily complex). On the other hand, persons from Western cultures tend to be analytic, prefer absolutes, and deal in categories (the stress is placed on categorization and rational, logical thinking—for example, delivering a speech entitled "Six Ways to Increase Your Self-Esteem"). East Asian persons start out by focusing on the context, not zeroing in on an object of interest. Westerners begin by focusing on a central object.

    These preferences affect how persons from Eastern and Western cultures prefer to organize their ideas. According to Nisbett, in the West, we start out with a general statement and give suggested solutions. We present the evidence in favor of our position. We argue against the reasons that others might not accept the position we have taken. We summarize and offer a conclusion. In the East, they do not do it this way. Instead, they cycle back into the same topic from different directions.[3] Nisbett suggests that the following example—offered by an English professor, which focuses on writing but could equally focus on public speaking—reveals this difference in methodology:

> I was surprised when one of my students who had been a teacher in China before coming here told me that she didn't understand the requirements of essay structure. I told her to write a thesis statement and then prove its three points in the following paragraphs. She told me if she wrote this way in China she would be considered stupid. "In China," she said, "essays were written in a more circular fashion moving associated ideas closer and closer to the center."[4]

While we need to be cautious about overgeneralizing, especially since persons from one culture who spend time in another culture tend to tune their thinking style into the culture in which they are interacting, we will see these differences surface as we explore both linear and nonlinear organizational formats. You need to order the ideas in your speech in a way that will make sense to your audience.

Traditional Organizational Formats

Traditional organizational formats display a linear logic and are typical of the prototypes many North American speakers use to make sense of information. A speech has a linear organization if its main points develop and relate directly to the thesis or topic sentence that comes early in the presentation. We will look at five traditional approaches to ordering material: (1) chronological, or time, order; (2) spatial order; (3) cause-and-effect order; (4) problem-and-solution order; and (5) topical order.

Chronological Order   **Chronological, or time, order** involves developing an idea or a problem in the order it occurs or occurred in time.

One student, for example, used chronological order to inform receivers about the evolution of the right to privacy in the United States:

Purpose: To inform the audience about the evolution of the right to privacy.
Thesis: Americans believe they have a fundamental right to privacy.

I. More than a century ago, Justice Louis D. Brandeis called privacy "the right to be let alone."
II. Within a decade, the courts began to recognize the right to privacy.
III. The Supreme Court relied on a privacy rationale in reaching its famous and controversial decisions on birth control and abortion.
IV. Threats to privacy abound today.

As you can see, this student has considered the steps leading to the present situation in the order they occurred. In addition, each main point the speaker used covers a particular time period. Since the main points describe a sequence of happenings, they help the audience keep track of where the speaker is in time.

Any event that has occurred in time can be examined chronologically. When using a time-ordered presentation, you decide where to begin and end your chronology and what events to include. As you might expect, time order is used most often in informative speeches. Why do you think the following speaker decided to use a reverse chronology? Do you find it more or less effective than a chronology proceeding from earliest to latest?

Work It Out
Design criteria for evaluating speeches that are organized using traditional formats and nontraditional formats.

Work It Out
Brainstorm topics that would best be developed using each of the traditional and nontraditional patterns described in this section.

chronological, or time, order
an organizational format that develops an idea using a time order

Think of three topics you could develop using chronological order. Why do they lend themselves to that arrangement?

Visuals, like the one held by this attorney, reinforce presented information—would you find this visual effective if you were on the jury?

spatial order
an organizational format that describes an object, a person, or a phenomenon as it exists in space

Purpose: To inform the audience about the development of euthanasia.

Thesis: Euthanasia has an interesting history.

   I. Today euthanasia is considered mercy killing.

  II. During the nineteenth century, the concept of euthanasia was associated with the acceleration of the death process.

 III. The ancient Greeks were the first to espouse euthanasia as a concept.

Spatial Order **Spatial order** describes an object, a person, or a phenomenon as it exists in space. An object, for example, might be described from

top to bottom
bottom to top
left to right
right to left
inside to outside
outside to inside

With spatial order, you must select one orientation and carry it through.

One student used spatial order to explain the appearance and functioning of a beehive:

  I. Outside the hive

 II. Inside the hive

Another student used a spatial pattern to discuss the different kinds of natural disasters that plague different sections of the United States:

   I. States along the East Coast of the United States are hurricane-prone.

  II. States in the central region of the United States are tornado-prone.

 III. States along the West Coast of the United States are earthquake-prone.

Like chronological order, spatial order is used most frequently in informative speeches.

Here is an example of how a speaker used a spatial pattern in talking about Stonehenge.

How could you use spatial order to describe yourself? (For practice, try it.)

Purpose: To inform the audience of the appearance of the mysterious monuments of Stonehenge.

Thesis: The mystery of Stonehenge is revealed in its five circles of stones.

   I. The outermost circle of Stonehenge is called the Outer Sarsen Circle.

  II. The first circle is called the Outer Bluestone Circle.

 III. The second circle is the Inner Sarsen Trilithons.

 IV. The third circle is the Inner Bluestone Horseshoe.

  V. The innermost circle is the Altar Stone.

Skill Builder

Speaker's Choice

1. Find a rock, a shell, a piece of driftwood, or some other natural object.
2. Describe the object to a partner, a group of students, or the entire class, using spatial order.
3. Explain why your spatial ordering took the form it did.
4. Would approaching the object from a different angle have altered your audience's understanding and appreciation? How?

Visuals can help reinforce information contained in a spatially ordered presentation—whether you are discussing the components of a computer, the terrain of a national park, the design of an electric car, or the floor plan of a presidential library. What visuals might you incorporate with each of the preceding examples? Using spatial order involves organizing ideas according to an area concept, which should also be reflected in the main points of your outline.

Cause-and-Effect Order **Cause-and-effect order** requires you to categorize your material into things related to the causes of a problem and things related to its effects. It is then up to you to decide which aspect you will explore first. Thus, in a speech on drunk driving, you might begin by discussing the percentage of drivers during a certain period who were drunk when involved in car accidents (cause). You might then discuss the number of deaths each year that are attributed directly to drunk driving (effect). You might, for example, use cause-and-effect order when speaking about the causes and effects of high blood pressure, the causes of Alzheimer's and its impact on the victim and family members, or the causes and consequences of metal fatigue in airplanes.

You can vary this approach by discussing the effect before the cause. In the following example, a student used effect-and-cause order to reveal the causes of excessive stress among students:

I. The number of students suffering from stress-related ailments is increasing at an alarming rate.
II. Experts on such ailments have identified four major explanations for this increase.

Cause-and-effect order and effect-and-cause order are quite versatile. They are used in both informative and persuasive speeches.

cause-and-effect order
an organizational format that categorizes a topic according to its causes and effects

How could you use cause-and-effect order to explain a recent disagreement you had with an instructor, an employer, a friend, or a family member?

Problem-and-Solution Order **Problem-and-solution order** requires you to (1) determine what problems are inherent in a situation and (2) present a solution to remedy them. Thus, you might discuss the problems that develop when many students entering college are deficient in writing skills. The second portion of your speech can then suggest a number of ways the identified problem might be alleviated (perhaps, for example, by expanding tutoring programs or offering noncredit remedial courses).

One student who focused on carjackings in shopping mall parking lots used a problem-solution order, beginning her speech by referring to the number of carjackings that had occurred recently in local malls. She then discussed a solution that combined increased lighting with additional security patrols. The next example also illustrates a problem-solution pattern. Notice how the emphasis is on how the problem can best be resolved.

problem-and-solution order
an organizational format that identifies the problems inherent in a situation and presents a solution to remedy them

Ethics and Communication

Sound Bites

Are sound bites—public presentations of positions that usually last no more than 90 seconds—an effective way of informing the electorate? Why or why not?

How organized must a speaker be to present ideas or urge action in this manner? What organizational format do you believe lends itself best to this type of presentation? Is 90 seconds or less enough time to deliver a message designed not just to inform but also to influence? Explain your position.

"Hey, do you want to be on the news tonight or not? This is a sound bite, not the Gettysburg Address. Just say what you have to say, Senator, and get the hell off."

Purpose: To convince my audience that national health insurance can help solve our health care problems.

Thesis: National health insurance will solve many of the problems caused by rising health care costs.

   I. Rising health care costs have resulted in an uninsured class of people.

  II. Implementing national health insurance will solve this problem.

When using a problem-and-solution format, you may discuss the advantages of the solution as well. In that case, the body of the speech would include three main points:

I. The problem
II. The solution
III. The advantages of adopting the solution

The following example demonstrates how to develop the problem-and-solution format.

Purpose: To convince my audience that we should act now to revise the way we report poverty statistics

Thesis: We should act now to solve the problem caused by the way we currently report poverty statistics.

I. The poverty level is currently understated to keep people off welfare rolls.
  A. Poverty levels for families of four are absurdly low.
  B. Poverty levels for single-parent families are even more outrageous.
II. Minimally acceptable income levels must be raised.
  A. Government levels must be raised for families.
  B. Additional help must be given for single parents.
III. These increases will solve some of the problems of the poor.
  A. They will make life easier for families.
  B. Additional aid to single parents will help them help themselves and their children.

Problem-and-solution order is most frequently employed in persuasive speeches.

Topical Order At times, a speech may not fit neatly into any of the patterns described previously. When this happens, you may choose to develop or cluster your material by arranging it into a series of appropriate topics. This is **topical order.** Examples of topical order include the following categorical arrangements: advantages and disadvantages of a proposal; social, political, and economic factors that contribute to a problem; perceptions of upper-class, middle-class, and lower-class people on an issue. When you use topical order, you may find that you can intermingle cause-and-effect, time, problem-and-solution, or spatial order within the topical order.

topical order
an organizational format that clusters material by dividing it into a series of appropriate topics

One student used topical order to speak about the pros and cons of using animals for medical and product research.

Purpose: To inform audience members of the advantages and disadvantages of using animals for medical and product research.

Thesis: Using animals for medical and product research presents both advantages and disadvantages.

I. There are two advantages to using animals as research subjects.
  A. Using animals is more effective than simply using results of test tube experiments.
  B. During the early stages of research, using animals is more effective than using human subjects.

Work It Out
For practice, for each of the main points in the preceding examples, conduct research in an effort to identify two to four sub-points to support each main point.

II. There are two disadvantages to using animals in research.

    A. Animals are often mutilated and experience pain.

    B. Animals do not respond in precisely the same manner that human subjects do.

Support All Main Points   In a developed outline, each point is supported by information, including examples, definitions, and visuals aids pertaining to the subject in the main point they support, enabling the audience to understand why the main point is true. Usually, two to four subpoints are offered in support of a main point.

Connecting Your Ideas: Using Internal Previews and Summaries, Transitions, and Signposts

Audience members who rely on linear logic will expect you to transmit your ideas with clarity and fluidity. They will count on your using transitional tools as you move from one idea to the next. The devices that speakers using linear logic use to create a sense of presentation coherence and unity are internal previews, **internal summaries,** transitions, and signposts.

An *internal preview* precedes information the speaker will discuss, helping to prepare the audience for important information to follow as well as what to look for as the speech progresses. For example, in a presentation on genetic engineering, a speaker told her audience: "We will next consider a technique that allows biologists to transfer a gene from one species to another. It is called recombinant DNA technology."

Internal summaries follow information the speaker has presented and are designed to help receivers remember the content. The following are examples: "Thus far we have examined two key housing problems. Let us now consider a third" and "The four characteristics we have discussed thus far are. . . ." Besides helping the audience recall the material, **transitions**—connective words and phrases—facilitate the speaker's movement from one idea to another; in effect, they bridge gaps between ideas so that there are no abrupt switches.[5]

Speakers use *signposts*, signaling cues such as "equally important" or "furthermore," to indicate that additional information is forthcoming. They also use them to make receivers aware that they are about to explain something, share an important idea, or let the audience know where they are in the progression of a speech. Commonly used signposts include the words *first*, *second*, and *third*; phrases that focus attention, such as "you'll especially want to keep this in mind" or "above all else, remember this"; phrases that indicate an explanation is forthcoming, such as "for example" or "to illustrate what I mean"; or rhetorical questions (questions you ask and also answer), such as "What steps can we take to make things better?" To signal that you will be discussing a cause-and-effect relationship, you can use the expressions "as a result" and "consequently." To indicate that there is a contrasting view to the one being elaborated, you could use "after all," "and yet," "in spite of," and "on the other hand." Signposts also signal the end of a speech. When a speaker says something like "finally," or "to sum up," he or she is signaling that the speech is about to conclude. So, in addition to moving a speech forward, signposts also draw it to a close.

Nontraditional Formats

In developing an outline, you can use a number of organizational patterns in place of a linear framework. You should use one of the nontraditional patterns discussed in this section if you believe the cultures and dispositions of the persons in your

---

internal summaries
rhetorical devices designed to help listeners remember content

transitions
connective words and phrases

> While few in number, transitions help the audience follow a speech. Do you consciously plan good transitions?

audience warrant it. While a number of us prefer to use **linear logic** to develop our ideas, others of us—including some persons from Native American, Asian-American, or Latino cultures—do not. As we deduce from the preceding proto-types, linear logic develops ideas step-by-step, relying on facts and data to support each main point. In contrast to formats that depend on linear logic are formats that are more indirect and less explicit in offering hard evidence and proof in defense of a point. These patterns are called **configural formats.**

Instead of previewing, spelling out, and discussing each key point, one at a time, persons who prefer configural thinking approach their subject from a variety of perspectives and rely on examples and stories to carry the crux of their message; they also rely on receivers to understand the messages implied by the examples and stories used. Because they believe the explicit stating of a message is unnecessary, speakers who use a configural style do not bluntly tell receivers their conclusion or call on them to make a specific response; instead of ensuring that the conclusion is obvious to receivers, the speakers lead them to their conclusion indirectly and by implication. Thus, configural frameworks require receivers to do more work.

While persons in cultures who favor the use of configural patterns might not categorize them in this way, Westerners do identify three kinds of configural systems of organization. First is the *deferred-thesis pattern,* in which the main points of a speech gradually build to the speaker's thesis, which he or she does not indicate until the speech is nearly over. Second is the *web pattern,* in which threads of thought refer back to the speaker's central purpose; while to Western ears the speaker may seem to be "off topic" at points, to receivers in other cultures the tangents the speaker explores are connected to the speaker's topic and make it more meaningful. Third is the *narrative pattern,* in which the speaker tells a story without stating a thesis or developing it with main points. When using a narrative pattern, the speaker uses a series of illustrations and parables to uncover or help receivers discover the speech's main points. The speaker uses indirection and implication rather than bridges or transitions to circle and connect ideas, establish their point, and ultimately help the audience members arrive at their conclusion.[6]

The following speech outline is organized configurally. As such, it requires the audience to participate more actively in interpreting what the speaker implies.

Purpose: To persuade my audience that E. coli presents problems for our food supply

   I. A hypothetical food worker, Jake, who is employed in a meat-packing plant, inadvertently infects the plant's meat supply with E. coli.
   II. Jake's carelessness contributes to the infection of a number of persons in an array of cities across the United States.
   III. The plant is closed because of E. coli contamination.
   IV. Today, members of the families of those who were sickened by E. coli ask the federal government, "How can our food supply be made safe?"

Looking at the preceding example you can see that it has four main points, a format typical of narration. First, the speaker sets the scene for receivers, intro-ducing the subject and the situation. The speaker next describes the sequence of events as they occurred. Then, she or he discusses the situation's effects. Finally, the narrator points to a solution. If you choose to use narration, tell a solid story, use descriptive language, intersperse dialogue when possible, build interest or sus-pense, and help your audience identify with the people involved. When serving

linear logic
the step-by-step development of ideas; the reliance on facts and data to support main points

configural formats
organizational patterns that are indirect and inexplicit

Can you think of speech topics that lend themselves to these kinds of configural sys-tems of organization?

Exploring **Diversity**

Is Paying Attention Cultural?

Edward T. Hall suggests that "culture . . . designates what we pay attention to and what we ignore." If this is so, how can speakers ensure that audience members who belong to other cultural groups will pay attention to the right things? In other words, how can speakers target crucial ideas and emphasized points? How can a speaker be sure that listeners are not paying attention to the wrong thing and screening out what they should be concentrating on?

_____

Source: Edward T. Hall. *The Hidden Dimension.* New York: Doubleday, 1966.

as a narrator, you can place yourself there and tell the story in the first person, use the second person and help audience members imagine themselves in such a situation, or use the third person, as the speaker in the provided example did, and describe what happened.

As the speaker embellishes each of the ideas identified in the outline during his or her presentation, it is up to the receivers to interpret the meaning of the speaker's narrative from the stories, examples, and testimony offered. The speaker will not state directly what receivers should think or do but will rely on them to draw their own conclusions and come up with their own solutions.

Recall from Chapter 2 that members of low-context cultures, such as the United States, are usually more direct in how they convey information to others than are members of high-context cultures, such as Latin America, Japan, and Saudi Arabia. To low-context receivers, the speaker from a high-context culture may come off as vague or deceptive because of his or her reluctance to be direct, explicit, or obvious. In contrast, high-context receivers prefer to receive information through examples, illustrations, and other indirect means of expression.[7]

> **Should speakers match the organizational format they use to the preferred perceptual system of the receivers?**

According to most intercultural communication theorists, English is primarily a speaker-responsible language, but other languages, including Japanese, Chinese, and Arabic, are more listener responsible. Native users of speaker-responsible languages typically believe it is up to the speakers to tell receivers exactly what they want them to know. In contrast, native speakers of listener-responsible languages typically believe that speakers need indicate only indirectly what they are speaking about and what they want receivers to know. They believe it is up to audience members, not the speaker, to construct the message's meaning.[8]

BEGINNINGS AND ENDINGS

Once you have outlined the body of your speech and considered the need for transitional devices, you are ready to "tell them what you are going to tell them" and "tell them what you have told them." In other words, it is time to develop your introduction and conclusion.[9]

> **What techniques would you like someone to use when introducing you to a group of unfamiliar people?**

The Introduction

All too frequently, the introduction is overlooked or neglected because speakers are in too much of a hurry to get to the heart of the matter. However, in public speaking, just as in interpersonal communication, first impressions count. Thus, it is essential that you make the first few minutes of your speech particularly interesting.

Functions of the Introduction

The functions of your introduction are to gain the attention of the audience members, to make them want to listen to your speech, and to provide them with an overview of the subject you will be discussing. The art of designing introductions is much like any other art; that is, it requires creative thinking. You will need to examine your purpose, the speech itself as you have developed it, your analysis of the audience, and your own abilities.

The opening moments of contact, with one person or with a multitude, can affect the developing relationship either positively or negatively. Unquestionably, the first few moments of your speech—the introduction—will affect your audience's willingness to process the remainder. It is at this point that people will decide whether what you have to say is interesting and important or dull and inconsequential. If your introduction is designed poorly, your audience may tune you out for the remainder of your speech. On the other hand, a well-designed introduction can help you develop a solid rapport with the audience and thus make it easier for you to share your thoughts.

The material you include in your introduction must be selected with care. Since in all likelihood your listeners have not been waiting in line for several days to hear you speak, you will need to work to spark their interest; you will need to motivate them to listen to you. Student speakers sometimes go overboard in trying to accomplish this objective. Some have been known to yell or throw books across the room. Such devices are certainly attention-getters, but startling an audience can turn your listeners against you. Other speakers look for a joke—any joke—to use

In the introduction, one of the speaker's goals is to build rapport with the audience.

Work It Out

Brainstorm a number of ways you could introduce yourself to a group of people you don't know.

as an attention-getter. Unfortunately, a joke chosen at random is seldom related to the topic and thus can confuse or even alienate listeners rather than interest and involve them. (A well-chosen anecdote, however, can be very effective.) Some speakers insist on beginning with statements like "My purpose here today is . . . " or "Today, I hope to convince you. . . ." Such openings suggest mainly that the speech maker has forgotten to consider motivation and attention.

Years ago, television shows began simply by flashing the title of the program onto the screen. Today, however, it is common to use a teaser to open a show. The teaser usually reveals segments of the show designed to arouse the interest of potential viewers—to encourage them to stay tuned. Without this device, many viewers would probably switch channels. Your listeners, of course, cannot switch speakers, but they can decide not to listen actively to what you have to say. Therefore, you, too, must design a teaser to include in your introduction—material that will interest and appeal to your audience.

Types of Introductions

Effective speech makers begin in a number of different ways. They may relate an unusual fact, make a surprising statement, or cite shocking statistics. Or they might ask a question, compliment the audience, or refer to the occasion. Sometimes they use a humorous story or an illustration as a lead-in. Sometimes they rely on a suspenseful story or a human interest story to capture their listeners' attention. Audiences respond to stories about people. For this reason, the plight of a family left homeless by a fire might be used effectively to open a speech on fire prevention, and a description of people severely injured in an automobile accident might introduce a speech supporting the use of air bags. If you have selected a topic because you have a personal interest in it, you can use a personal anecdote to begin your presentation. Let us examine a few examples of these approaches.

Some of the most effective introductions use *humor,* as in the following example from a speech by Cal Ripken, Jr., retired professional baseball player, upon his induction into the Baseball Hall of Fame:

> I've really appreciated all the people who have congratulated me in the months since my election to the Hall of Fame. It sure helped me get over a conversation I had recently with a 10-year-old boy I was instructing. I was teaching him hitting and he was starting to have success and feeling quite proud of himself. And he asked me, "So, did you play baseball?" I said, "Yes, I played professionally." And he goes, "Oh, yeah, for what team?" I said, "I played with the Baltimore Orioles for 21 years." And he said, "What position?" And I said, "Mostly shortstop but a little third base at the end." And he began to walk away and he looked back and said, "Should I know you?" That certainly puts all this in perspective.[10]

When used in introductions, *illustrations,* more detailed than examples, can add even more drama, as is seen in the following introductory remarks of Brittany Young of Shepherd University:

> Tarek Dergoul, a British citizen raised in east London, sustained shrapnel wounds when a bomb exploded while he was on business in Afghanistan. He lay among the ruins for at least a week, drinking from a tap that still worked, and living on biscuits and raisins he had in his pocket. Exposed to the freezing weather, his toes turned black from frostbite. At last, he was found by troops loyal to the Northern Alliance who took him to a hospital where he received food and three operations. After five weeks, he was driven to an airfield and handed over to Americans who

arrived by helicopter. They flew him to the U.S. detention camp at Bagram airbase, near Kabul. While imprisoned, Dergoul said that violence and sexual humiliation was routine. Then in February, Dergoul was taken south to another camp at Kandahar. Due to his treatment, his memories of this time are hazy. On May 1, he was dressed in goggles and an orange jump suit, injected with a sedative and flown to Guantanamo Bay, where he sustained further abuse. Dergoul was one of the fortunate ones. He was able to go home. . . .[11]

Students Erin Gallaher and Adrienne Hallett both used *suspense* to make their points. Which of the introductions do you think is more effective? Erin's speech began this way:

Flip through any furniture catalog, and you'll be sure to note descriptions of color, style, fabric, and texture. When deciding to purchase a new sofa or armchair, most likely you'll carefully weigh options like "to recline or not to recline"—that is the question.

But there is something that most people never even consider when they're shopping for upholstered furniture. What is this hidden feature? It's the extremely flammable polyurethane foam found in the cushions of virtually every piece of upholstered furniture in your home.[12]

Adrienne's speech began this way:

He showed all of the classic symptoms. His response time was slowed, his judgement was impaired, but he thought he could handle it. As he drove home along the Interstate, his car swerved onto the shoulder of the road, running over and killing a man who was trying to change a flat tire. When the police questioned him later, he didn't remember a thing. What caused this Ohio man's actions is something we have all been guilty of, yet we won't readily admit it. Although the U.S. Department of Transportation estimates that it kills 13,000 people annually, no one will be taking the keys, calling a cab or taking a stand on this issue. Whenever we get into the driver's seat, we must be prepared for the risk presented by an impaired driver— surprisingly, not from alcohol but from a lack of sleep.[13]

Another student began a speech by asking a rhetorical question:

Do you know who you voted for in the last presidential election? I bet you don't. I bet you think you voted for the Democratic, Republican, or Independent candidate. But you didn't. You voted to elect members of the electoral college. In the course of my speech, I will explain why this practice is undemocratic, un-American, and unacceptable.

Another student used *frightening facts* to jolt her audience:

In the time it takes me to complete this sentence, a child in America will drop out of school. In the time it takes me to complete this sentence, a child in this country will run away from home. Before I finish this presentation, another teenage girl will have a baby.

We have a country [that] is gripped by a lost generation. This is an invisible group of kids lost and alone on the streets. On their own, they are hungry, sick, and scared. They are victims of our society. They are victims who desperately need help.

In this presentation I will show you how we can all help these kids.

Finally, many speakers use *startling statistics* to capture the audience's interest. The following example from a speech entitled "Protecting the Vulnerable: Restructuring the Mental Health System" was included in its introduction:

The current U.S. Census reports over 800,000 people reside in government institutions and privately owned group homes. The August 5, 2006, *Washington Post* reports that over 80,000 group home residents in the U.S. died as a result of neglect and abuse in the last two years. If these deaths aren't shocking enough, the federal government is investigating group homes for fraudulently underreporting the numbers.[14]

The Preview

If your speech is organized in a linear fashion, after you have used your introduction to spark interest and motivate your audience to continue listening, it is necessary for you to preview your speech. That is, you need to let your audience know what you will be discussing. Consider the following example of a preview:

> There are three "weight classes" of people in our society: the overweight, the underweight, and those who are the right weight. Unfortunately, many people fail to understand the role weight plays in their lives. Your weight affects how your body functions. Let's explore how.

Your preview should correspond to your purpose statement. It should let your audience know what to listen for. Additionally, by presenting it after you have gotten your listeners' attention and motivated them to continue paying attention, you ensure that your purpose statement will get a fair hearing.

The Conclusion

The conclusion summarizes the presentation and leaves your listeners thinking about what they have just heard. It provides a sense of completion.

Functions of the Conclusion

The conclusion's summary function may be considered a preview in reverse. During your preview, you look ahead, revealing to your listeners the subject of your efforts. During the summary, you review for them the material you have covered.

For example, a summary might begin, "We have examined three benefits you will derive from a new town library." During the remainder of this summation, the three benefits might be restated, to cement them in the minds of the listeners.

Work It Out
What might a speaker do in the conclusion of a speech that limits its impact? What could he or she do to enhance its impact?

Inexperienced speech makers sometimes say that the summary appears to be superfluous ("After all, I've just said all of that not more than two minutes ago"). However, it is important to remember that you are speaking for your listeners, not for yourself. The summary provides some of the redundancy mentioned earlier; it enables audience members to leave with your ideas freshly impressed on their minds. In addition to refreshing your listeners' memory, the conclusion can help clarify the issues or ideas you have just discussed.

Besides serving as a summary, your conclusion should be used to heighten the impact of the presentation. You can do this in a number of ways. One popular technique is to refer to your introductory remarks; this gives your speech a sense of closure. If, for example, you are speaking about child abuse and you begin your presentation by showing pictures of abused children, you might paraphrase your opening remarks and show the pictures again, to arouse sympathy and support. Quotations and illustrations also make effective conclusions. For example, if you are speaking about the problems faced by veterans of the war in Iraq, you could provide a moving conclusion by quoting some veterans or retelling some of the challenges they face. You are also free to draw on your own experiences when designing a conclusion. Keep in mind that, as they do with introductions, audiences

An effective conclusion heightens the impact of a presentation.

respond to conclusions that include personal references, surprising statements, startling statistics, or relevant humor.

Types of Conclusions

Let's examine how some conclusion techniques work in practice. A senior care provider, Paul Hogan, used an illustration to end a speech he gave titled "The 'Age Wave'":

> Just a few weeks ago, I was at church and a lovely woman by the name of Miriam stopped me. Miriam is a 78 year old who was widowed about five years ago. She told me that her cousin was using Home Instead Senior Care in North Carolina and loved her caregiver. She then said, with a sparkle in her eye, that she did not need us yet, but when she does she knows just how to reach me. To me, that sparkle in her eye was the new face of aging. It was almost as if Miriam was looking forward to getting older. Our goal is for every senior in the world to see aging as Miriam sees it, not from a perspective of fear and loneliness, but from one of hope and optimism.[15]

In a speech on skin cancer, University of Northern Iowa student Jesse Ohl concluded with a startling statistic:

> And finally, be informed patients. Regularly examine your body for skin cancer. Skin cancer usually begins in oddly shaped moles that often bleed or don't heal. If you see something like this, do yourself and your family a favor, and ask your physician. Be the first line of defense, and do not assume that your doctor will check for skin cancer. The *Journal of Dermatology* reports that, unless asked, physicians provide skin cancer examinations to only 1.5 percent of patients.[16]

Recognizing the effectiveness of statistics and *rhetorical questions*, Brian Swenson, a student at Dakota Wesleyan in South Dakota, ended a speech on guns and children with these words:

> Today we have looked at a few cases of child shootings, some facts and statistics about child shootings, and what you should do if you own a gun to prevent this

What advice would you offer this speaker?

from happening to your children or other children. Now, maybe you still think that you don't need to lock up your gun and that this won't happen to you; but I have one more figure for you. One child is killed every day with a handgun, and for every child killed ten others are injured. Now, I have a question for you. Is your child going to be one of the ten that are injured, or is it going to be the one that is killed? The choice is yours.[17]

Quotations can increase the impact of a conclusion. Former attorney general Robert Kennedy often ended his speeches with the following words by the playwright George Bernard Shaw.

Some men see things as they are, and ask, "Why?" I dare to dream of things that never were, and ask—"Why not?"[18]

Humor, when used appropriately, can help keep people on your side. One student ended a speech directed at first-year students with the following "letter":

Dear Mom and Dad:

Just thought I'd drop you a note to clue you in on my plans.

I've fallen in love with a guy named Buck. He quit high school between his sophomore and junior years to travel with his motorcycle gang. He was married at 18 and has two sons. About a year ago he got a divorce.

We plan to get married in the fall. He thinks he will be able to get a job by then. I've decided to move into his apartment. At any rate, I dropped out of school last week. Maybe I will finish college sometime in the future.

Mom and Dad, I just want you to know that everything in this letter so far is false. NONE OF IT IS TRUE.

But it is true that I got a C in French and a D in math. And I am in need of money for tuition and miscellaneous.

Love, _____[19]

A SAMPLE OUTLINE

The following is a student's full sentence outline, containing an introduction, body, transitions, and a conclusion. What do you think are its strengths and weaknesses?

Granny Dumping

Specific purpose: To explore why "granny dumping" is on the rise

Thesis: Increased family stresses and a lack of government assistance are causing families to abandon their older relatives.

Would you have phrased the thesis similarly? Why or why not?

Introduction

I. Over 45 years ago playwright Edward Albee wrote *The Sandbox*, a play in which a family brings their grandmother to a playground and dumps her in a sandbox.

II. Over 45 years ago this idea was labeled as absurd.

III. Now this idea is all too real.

IV. Today, I would like to talk to you about the growing problem of granny dumping, a form of elder abuse.

(Transition: Let's begin by examining the plight of growing numbers of older Americans.)

> What do you think of the speaker's introduction?

Body

I. Older Americans are being abandoned by their families.

A. John Kingery, 82, was abandoned outside a men's room in Post Falls, Idaho.

1. His clothes were stripped of their labels.

2. An Alzheimer's sufferer, Kingery was not able to remember his name.

B. Thousands of older Americans face similar situations.

1. The American College of Emergency Physicians estimates that 70,000 people are abandoned each year.

2. Most are from families that cannot pay for the necessary care.

(Transition: In addition to the pain that is being inflicted on the elderly, pain is also being inflicted on those who should care for them.)

II. Caregivers are overwhelmed by their responsibilities.

A. Millions of Americans carry the burden of caring for one or more older adults.

1. One in five families takes care of an older adult.

2. Caregivers are besieged with bills.

3. Caregivers receive little government assistance.

(Transition: So much for the problem; what about solutions?)

III. There are a number of solutions.

A. Families themselves can work together more effectively.

1. They can avoid placing all of the responsibilities on one person.

2. Relatives can help out with the nonending stack of paperwork required by government agencies.

B. The government needs to do more.

1. Programs need to be added so that patients can be cared for outside the home at least part of the time.

a. This would provide variety for the patient.

b. Such programs would also give a rest to the family so they could avoid burnout.

> Can you come up with an alternative transition?

> What strategies did the speaker use to develop the first main idea?

> How do you assess this transition?

> How did the speaker develop the second main idea?

> What functions does this transition serve?

> To what extent, if any, do you think the speaker developed the last main idea of the outline?

2. A holistic approach to elder care needs to be adopted.
   a. Caregivers need help in coping with the increased stresses that caring for an aged relative creates.
   b. Patients need help so that they are treated with respect.
   c. Both caregivers and patients need help to maintain their dignity.

> **What functions does the conclusion serve?**

Conclusion

I. We have seen that there is much that can be done to help people who must help their aging parent.

II. While Edward Albee's *The Sandbox* was labeled as an example of absurdism 45 years ago, granny dumping has become an all too real and all too tragic way of life for tens of thousands of American citizens.

> **What do you think of the outline's Works Consulted?**

Works Consulted

"Abuse Underreported in Many States," *USA Today*, April (from The Society for the Advancement of Education) 2004, p. 3.

Edward Albee, *The Sandbox* (New York: New American Library, 1961).

Rachel Boax, "Why Do Some Caregivers of Frail Elderly Quit?" *Healthcare Financing Review* 30(2): winter 1991, pp. 41–47.

Robert Butler, "Health Care for All: A Crisis in Cost Access," *Geriatrics* 47(9), September 1992, pp. 34–48.

"Elder Abuse: A Hidden Tragedy," *Biotech Week*, October 20, 2004, p. 195.

Paul Krugman, "Does Getting Old Cost Society Too Much?" *New York Times Magazine*, March 9, 1997, pp. 58–60.

"Granny Dumping by the Thousands," *The New York Times*, March 29, 1992.

"Avoiding 'Granny Dumping'," *Daily Utah Chronicle*, January 10, 2008, accessed at www.dailyutahchronicle.com/news/2008/01/10/News/Avoiding.Granny.Dumping3148735.shtml.

National Center on Elder Abuse, "2004 Survey of Adult Protective Services: Abuse of Adults 60 Years of Age and Older."

National Committee for the Prevention of Elder Abuse, "What Is Elder Abuse?" www.preventelderabuse.org/elderabuse.

Thinking Critically

Reflect and Respond

Agree or disagree with each of the following quotations. Give reasons and examples that support the position you take.

A bad beginning makes a bad ending.
　　　—Euripides

A speech is like a love affair. Any fool can start it, but to end it requires considerable skill.
　　　—Lord Mancroft

COMMUNICATION SKILLS IN PRACTICE
SPEECH DESIGN AND ORGANIZATION CHECKLIST

At this point, in order to review your progress in designing and organizing your speech, answer these questions:

- Is the specific purpose of my speech clear? If not, how can I increase its clarity?

- Have I expressed the main idea or thesis of my speech as effectively as I can? Does everything I include in my speech support my thesis? If not, what alterations should I make?

- Does my speech contain an introduction that includes both an attention-getter and a preview? Is each one of my introduction's components expressed as effectively as possible? If not, what can I do to enhance its expression?

- Have I developed a clear outline of my presentation, one that clearly delineates each one of my main points? If not, how can I make my outline clearer?

- In developing each main point, do I present sufficient verbal or visual support? Which of my main points is currently the most fully developed? What can I do to bring the others up to its level?

- Have I taken the cultural backgrounds of receivers sufficiently into account? If not, what can I do to broaden my speech's interest and appeal?

- Do I offer sufficient internal previews and summaries, as well as transitions and signposts, to facilitate comprehension and recall in my audience members? If not, what can I do to accomplish this?

- Does my speech contain a conclusion that summarizes it? Does the conclusion also use psychological appeals to promote receiver interest and heighten my speech's impact? Is each of my conclusion's components as effective as it can be? If not, what changes should I now make?

By assessing your progress toward your goal and making whatever revisions you discover are needed now, you will save yourself time and extra work during rehearsal, a topic we explore in Chapter 15.

Focus on Service Learning

Locate a community agency that helps persons from another country acclimate to the United States. How can understanding the worldview of people new to the United States enable you to prepare a speech for delivery that uses an organizational framework favored by the members of this group? What would you teach these persons about your worldview so that they could organize a presentation for delivery to members of your culture? Use resources such as, but not limited to, www.idex.org and www.cyborlink.com/default.htm to facilitate answering these questions. More specifically, what advice about organizational formats would you give a speaker from an Eastern culture who needed to address a predominantly Western audience and vice versa?

Revisiting Chapter Objectives

1. **Identify main and subordinate ideas.** Organization is one of the main challenges facing the speech maker. Part of the organizational challenge is to distinguish between main and subordinate ideas. Main ideas are the primary points of a speech. Subordinate ideas amplify the main ideas.

2. **Create a full sentence outline.** One of the best ways to organize your speech is to build its framework and prepare a full sentence outline using the introduction-body-conclusion format. Since the body of the speech is the main part of your presentation, it should be prepared first.

3. **Identify five methods of ordering ideas.** There are five generally accepted ways based on linear logic to order the ideas in a speech: (1) chronological order,

THE WRAP-UP

(2) spatial order, (3) cause-and-effect order, (4) problem-and-solution order, and (5) topical order. Speakers from a number of cultural groups prefer to use configural logic to structure their ideas.

4. **Use internal previews and summaries, transitions, and signposts effectively.** When you use linear logic, the body of your presentation must have internal previews and summaries as well as transitions and signposts to help listeners follow and recall the content. (Professional speakers today must be prepared to give very short synopses—sound bites—to the media if they want to appear on the air.)

5. **Develop an effective introduction and conclusion.** After you complete the body of the speech, you are ready to prepare the introduction and conclusion. The introduction should gain the attention of the audience members, make them want to listen to your speech, and provide them with an overview of the subject to be discussed. Devices used to enhance introductions include humor, illustrations, questions, surprising statements, and statistics.

    The purpose of the conclusion is to summarize the material covered, heighten the impact of the presentation, and enable the audience to leave the occasion with your ideas freshly impressed on their minds. Devices used to increase the effectiveness of conclusions include surprising statements, rhetorical questions, quotations, and humor.

6. **Use a checklist to refine the design and organization of your speech.** Once you have completed the outline for your speech, you should become a judge of its integrity. Go back and look at each of your speech's parts to determine whether you are ready to begin rehearsing the presentation. Be sure to take into account any cultural barriers that might affect your presentation so that your presentation will be clear to your entire audience.

Resources for Further Inquiry and Reflection

To apply your understanding of how the principles in Chapter 14 are at work in our daily lives, consult the following resources for further inquiry and reflection. Or, if you prefer, choose any other appropriate resource. Then connect the ideas expressed in your chosen selection with the communication concepts and issues you are learning about both in and out of class.

 Listen to Me

"The Scientist" (Coldplay)
"Say" (John Mayer)
"Cats in the Cradle" (Harry Chapin)
"Scenes from an Italian Restaurant" (Billy Joel)
"Paper Planes" (MIA)
"Since You've Been Gone" (Kelly Clarkson)
"You'll Think of Me" (Keith Urban)
"I Kissed A Girl" (Katy Perry)

What organizational schema does the speaker use to tell the song's story? Why do you think that this story structure was selected? Could the song have been organized using another approach? Why or why not?

 View Me

The American President   *Independence Day*
Mars Attacks!   *Commander-in-Chief*
The West Wing   *W*
Dave

Compare and contrast a key speech of the chief executive in each film or episode from the TV series. How does each commander-in-chief structure his or her address? Which do you evaluate as more effective and why?

Read Me

Vincent Bugliosi. *The Prosecution of George W. Bush for Murder*. New York: Vanguard, 2008.

First outline the case presented by Bugliosi. Then identify and evaluate the support for any one of his main points. Finally, analyze both his introduction and conclusion. Based on your assessment, explain why you believe the case he makes either does or does not hold together.

Jerome Lawrence. *Inherit the Wind*. New York: Random House, 1955.

How do both sides on the evolution-creationism debate begin, develop, and end their presentations to the court?

George Jonas. *Vengeance: The True Story of an Israeli Counter-Terrorist Team*. New York: Simon & Schuster, 2005.

How do the spokespersons for the Israelis and for the Palestinians use organization to advance their positions?

Tell Me

Share with the class the insights you gained from your chosen Listen to Me, View Me, or Read Me selection.

Find examples that enable you to support or negate the following: It is equally effective to develop a speech using formal rules of logic as it is using a holistic approach.

Key Chapter Terminology

Use the Online Learning Center at www.mhhe.com/gamble10e to further your knowledge of the following terminology.

cause-and-effect order 365
chronological, or time, order 363
configural formats 369
internal summaries 368
linear logic 369
main ideas 359

problem-and-solution order 365
spatial order 364
speech framework 358
subordinate ideas 359
topical order 367
transitions 368

www.mhhe.com/gamble10e

Idioms in Translation

drafting an outline — creating an outline
get to the heart of the matter — make a point
off topic — lose focus
in plain sight — visible

jumping-off point — starting point
prototype — model
thicket of possibilities — array of choices

Culture Cue

Unlike Chinese people, who point with an open hand, people in the United States tend to point with one finger.

Test Your Understanding

Go to the *Self Quizzes* on the book's Online Learning Center at www.mhhe.com/gamble10e.

www.mhhe.com/gamble10e

CHAPTER 15

After finishing this chapter, you should be able to

1. Assess your level of speech anxiety.

2. Use deep-muscle relaxation, thought stopping, visualization, and other techniques to reduce speech anxiety.

3. Discuss four styles of delivery: manuscript, memorized, impromptu, and extemporaneous.

4. Identify how the speaker can use visual and vocal cues to advantage.

5. Analyze a speech maker's performance (including your own) in terms of content, organization, language, and delivery.

Delivering Your Speech: Presenting Your Ideas

Let's continue stepping up to speech making. You are almost prepared to present your speech—just a few steps stand between you and success. By now, you have chosen a topic and adapted that topic to your audience. You have also conducted research, selected support and presentation aids, and outlined your speech. You probably have been assigned a presentation date. What happens next? You shift your focus to thinking about delivering your presentation. If you are like most people, as your focus shifts, you begin to feel more anxious. Maybe you feel tired or suffer from indigestion. Your back may hurt or you may feel a headache coming on. There are a host of ailments correlated with anxiety.[1] You feel so anxious that you wonder if you will really gather the courage to stand and speak before an audience. The answer is, Of course, you will! You can overcome whatever anxiety you feel by understanding its sources, learning to cope with your fears, using strategies to handle both the physical and mental symptoms of anxiety, and finally, methodically rehearsing your presentation, because the greatest fear that many speakers have is forgetting what they are going to say.[2]

The goal of this chapter is to give you the information you need to calm your fears and rehearse effectively so that you deliver a first-rate presentation (see Figure 15.1).

The human brain is a wonderful thing. It operates from the moment you're born until the first time you get up to make a speech.
—*Howard Goshom*

The greatest mistake you can make in life is to be continually fearing you will make one.
—*Elbert Hubbard*

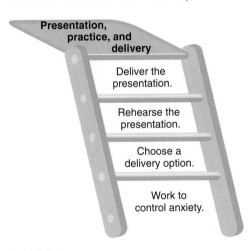

FIGURE 15.1   The Third Landing.

DEALING WITH ANXIETY AND SPEECH FRIGHT

One prominent motivational speaker begins his presentations as follows:

> I couldn't sleep last night. I finally got up at 4 this morning. I got dressed and went through this presentation 37 times. And guess what? You loved it. [Gentle laughter.] And let me tell you one thing I'll never forget about this group. That is, when I got introduced, everyone was standing. [More laughter.] Tell you what I'm going to do. I'm going to reintroduce myself, and what I want you to do is just give me the welcome you gave

Rehearsal is an integral part of speech preparation. It also helps decrease anxiety.

public speaking anxiety

fear of speaking to an audience

communication apprehension

fear of communication, no matter what the context

me this morning. Just pump it up, OK? Are you ready? [Music pulses.] Ladies and gentlemen, all the way from Atlanta, GA. If you forget everything I say, don't forget this. . . . You are the best at what you do because of one main thing: Attitude. [The audience stands and cheers.][3]

What attitude do you have toward speaking in public? Fear, or anxiety, is something that affects most public speakers.[4] It is so common that, when queried, many persons answer that they would rather be in the casket at a funeral than be delivering the eulogy. Thus, if you experience a certain amount of apprehension before, during, or after presenting a speech, rest assured that you are not alone.[5] Students sometimes allow their fears to get the better of them. Instead of using anxiety as a positive force, they let it overwhelm them. To combat this, let's look at how to make **public speaking anxiety** (fear of speaking to an audience), a form of **communication apprehension** (fear of communicating with others no matter what the context) actually work for you.

Approximately 20 percent of the U.S. population is "trait" communication apprehensive. This means that they exhibit a predisposition to being apprehensive and display escalated nervousness levels in most, if not all, communication situations. On the other hand, nearly all of us experience occasional "state" communication apprehension. This means that when facing a specific situation, such as public speaking, we display a somewhat elevated nervousness level.[6] To determine your communication apprehension score, you can take the self-analysis quiz included in the section "Self-Analysis: How Anxious Are You?" or access the Perceived Report of Communication Apprehension (PRCA) developed by James McCroskey, cited on his Web page (www.jamesmccroskey.com) under Communication Research Measures.

Understanding Your Fears

Self-Analysis: How Anxious Are You?

How anxious are you about delivering a speech? Use the following inventory to find out. Although this inventory is not a scientific instrument, it should give you some indication of your level of fear. Note that you must display some level of anxiety to be categorized as "normal." If you had no anxiety about speaking in public, you would not be considered normal; what's more, you would probably not be a very effective speech maker.

For each statement, circle the number that best represents your response:

1. I am afraid I will forget what I have to say.

   Not afraid   1   2   3   4   5   Extremely afraid

2. I am afraid my ideas will sound confused and jumbled.

   Not afraid   1   2   3   4   5   Extremely afraid

3. I am afraid my appearance will be inappropriate.

   Not afraid   1   2   3   4   5   Extremely afraid

We are largely the playthings of our fears.
—Horace Walpole

Ethics and Communication

Is Compulsory Speech Making Fair?

Studies show that many people fear public speaking more than they fear death. When informed they must give a speech, their bodies do all kinds of unpleasant things to them: hands sweat; mouths go dry; knees shake; voices quiver; hearts race; heads pound. All people with extreme fear of public speaking want to do is get out of the spotlight and sit down. Is it fair to demand that all students face up to their fear and take a course that requires them to deliver at least one speech? Are there other options that could provide the same skills without actually involving standing in front of an audience? Explain your answers.

4. I am afraid the audience will find my speech boring.

Not afraid 1 2 3 4 5 Extremely afraid

5. I am afraid people in the audience will laugh at me.

Not afraid 1 2 3 4 5 Extremely afraid

6. I am afraid I will not know what to do with my hands.

Not afraid 1 2 3 4 5 Extremely afraid

7. I am afraid my instructor will embarrass me.

Not afraid 1 2 3 4 5 Extremely afraid

8. I am afraid audience members will think my ideas are simplistic.

Not afraid 1 2 3 4 5 Extremely afraid

9. I am afraid I will make grammatical mistakes.

Not afraid 1 2 3 4 5 Extremely afraid

10. I am afraid everyone will stare at me.

Not afraid 1 2 3 4 5 Extremely afraid

Online Learning Center

Go to the Online Learning Center at www.mhhe.com/gamble10e and answer the questions in the *Self Inventory* to evaluate your understanding of speech anxiety.

Next, add the numbers you chose and rate yourself as follows:

41–50 Very apprehensive 11–20 Overconfident

31–40 Apprehensive   10 Are you alive?

21–30 Normally concerned

Sources of Public Speaking Anxiety

Why are we afraid to speak in public? Why do many of us fear speaking before an audience more than we fear snakes, heights, bee stings, or death? Before we can cope with our fears, we need to understand what causes them. The sections that follow discuss some of the more common causes of public speaking apprehension.

> Is public speaking among your top ten fears? Why or why not?

Who do you think fears speaking in public more, men or women? Why?

Fear of Failure   Many of us fear failing. The idea of speaking in public makes us feel inadequate. We worry that we won't be able to cope with the challenges. This concerns us even more if we suffer from ESL (English as a second language) anxiety, the kind of anxiety experienced by ESL students. Visualizing ourselves failing, rather than succeeding, we try to maintain a low profile. Do you ever avoid risks because you imagine your performance will not be good enough? When you disagree with something you have read or heard, are you more comfortable swallowing hard and sitting quietly than speaking up for what you think is right? Do you find it easier to go along with a group than to voice your objections? If you fear failure, you are more likely to play it safe, trying not to put yourself in situations that might cause you to feel even more inadequate.

Fear of the Unknown   A new job may cause us to feel fearful because our co-workers, the situation, and our responsibilities are unfamiliar, unknown, or still unclear. We may fear delivering a speech for the same reasons. Each new event has a threatening, unknown quality—a quality that many people prefer not to deal with. When such an event involves speaking, we may be afraid because we do not know how people will react to what we say. Although we have a cognitive understanding of what is and is not likely to happen before an audience, we let our feelings take charge, causing us to react emotionally and behave irrationally.

Fear of Being Judged   How sensitive are you to the judgment of others? Are you concerned about a friend's opinion of or judgment about you? An instructor's? Do you believe that what an audience, a reader, or an instructor concludes about you is necessarily true? Sometimes we become so sensitive to the judgments of others that we try to avoid judgment altogether. Public speaking is one situation in which such an attitude is common.

Fear of Consequences   Basically, one of two things can result from giving a speech: The audience may like it or may dislike it. That is, it will be a success or a failure. This basic result may then have further consequences. In the classroom, for example, an unsatisfactory speech may result in a failing grade. In a business situation, it may result in the loss of an important account. Whatever the consequences, the speaker needs to prepare to deal with them.

What advice would you give to a speaker about how to control fear and anxiety?

Learning to Cope with Your Fears: Controlling Anxiety

One of the best ways to cope with the fear of speech making is to design and rehearse your presentation carefully. The systematic approach suggested in this chapter covers both design and rehearsal and should—at least in theory—decrease your anxiety by increasing your self-confidence. However, theory and reality do sometimes diverge and, preparation notwithstanding, you may still find that you experience some anxiety about your speech. Let us now see how such anxiety can be controlled.

The first thing you need to do is recognize the actual bodily sensations and thoughts that accompany and support your feelings of nervousness. Make a list of the physical symptoms and fear-related thoughts that contribute to your anxiety. Then examine the symptoms and thoughts that you and others in your class identified. Do the lists include any of these physical symptoms?

rapid or irregular heartbeat	stiff neck
stomach knots	lump in the throat
shaking hands, arms, or legs	nausea
dry mouth	dizziness

When people are asked about fear-related thoughts, they often make statements like the following. Were any of these included on your lists?

"I just can't cope."

"I'm under such pressure."

"This is a nightmare."

"I know something terrible is going to happen."

Once you have identified the physical and mental sensations that accompany fear, your next step is to learn how to control these reactions.[7] The next sections describe behavior modification techniques that can help you.

Deep-Muscle Relaxation: Overcoming Physical Symptoms

Muscle tension commonly accompanies fear and anxiety. However, a muscle will relax after being tensed. Deep-muscle relaxation is based on this fact.

Try this: Tense one arm. Count to 10. Now relax your arm. What feelings did you experience? Did your arm seem to become heavier? Did it then seem to become warmer? Next, try tensing and relaxing one or both of your legs. When you examine what happens, you'll see why it is reasonable to expect that you can calm yourself by systematically tensing and relaxing various parts of your body in turn.

Try using the Skill Builder "Tense and Relax" several times before you actually present a speech. Many students report that butterflies or tensions tend to settle in particular bodily sections. Thus, it can be helpful to check the bodily sensations

Skill Builder

Tense and Relax

1. Imagine that your body is divided into four basic sections:

   a. hands and arms

   b. face and neck

   c. torso

   d. legs and feet

2. Sit comfortably. In turn, practice tensing and relaxing each of these four sections of your body.

   a. *Hands and arms.* Clench your fists. Tense each arm from shoulder to fingertips. Notice the warm feeling that develops in your hands, forearms, and upper arms. Count to 10. Relax.

   b. *Face and neck.* Wrinkle your face as tightly as you can. Press your head back as far as it will go. Count to 10. Relax. Roll your head slowly to the front, side, back, and side in a circular movement. Relax.

   c. *Torso.* Shrug your shoulders. Count to 10 in this position. Relax. Tighten your stomach. Hold it. Relax.

   d. *Legs and feet.* Tighten your hips and thighs. Relax. Tense your calves and feet. Relax.

"Calm"

1. Work through the procedure described in the text for releasing tension.
2. As soon as you experience the warm feeling throughout your body, say to yourself, "calm." Try this several times, each time working to associate the "de-tensed" feeling with the word *calm*.
3. The next time you find yourself in a stress-producing situation, say "calm" to yourself and attempt to achieve the de-tensed state.

you feel when anxious, and personalize "Tense and Relax" to deal with your individual symptoms.

Thought Stopping: Overcoming Mental Symptoms

Think you can or think you can't; either way you will be right.

—Henry Ford

Anxiety is not simply a physical phenomenon; it also manifests itself cognitively—that is, in thoughts. Thus it is important to work to eliminate the thoughts associated with anxiety, as well as the bodily symptoms.

Many people use the word *relax* to calm themselves. Unfortunately, *relax* doesn't sound very relaxing to some people. You can substitute the word *calm*. Try the Skill Builder "Calm."

A variation on the "calm technique" is to precede the word *calm* with the word *stop*. When you begin to think upsetting thoughts, say to yourself, "Stop!" Then follow that command with "Calm"—for example,

> "I just can't get up in front of all those people. Look at their cold stares and mean smirks."

> "Stop!"

> "Calm."

You may find that you can adapt this thought-stopping technique to help you handle symptoms of anxiety in interpersonal situations.

Visualization: A Positive Approach

Sports psychologists use a technique called visualization to help athletes compete more effectively. The athletes are guided in visualizing the successful completion of a play or a game. They are asked to imagine how they will feel when they win. Eventually, when they go out on the field to compete, it is almost as if they have been there before—and have already won.

You may want to try this technique to boost your confidence as a speaker. Sit in a quiet place. Picture yourself approaching the podium. See yourself delivering your presentation. Then hear your audience applaud appreciatively. After you have delivered the speech, answer these questions: Did the experience help you control your anxiety? Did it help you succeed?

Work It Out

Work in groups to develop a visualization experience to use when preparing to speak in public.

Other Techniques

Speakers report that other techniques can also help reduce speech apprehension. Some try to include a bit of humor early in the speech to get a favorable response from the audience right away. They say that such a reaction helps them calm their nerves for the remainder of the presentation. Others look for a friendly face and talk to that person for a moment or two early in the speech. Others use charts, graphs, and other visuals to help them organize the material. In this technique, the visual shows the next major point to be covered, eliminating the necessity for the speaker to remember it or refer to notes. Still others report that they rehearse a speech aloud, standing in front of an imaginary audience and "talking through" the material again and again. What other techniques have you found helpful?

Remember, no matter how you choose to deal with it, fear is a natural response to public speaking and can probably never be eliminated completely. But you do need to learn to cope with fear; only in this way will you be able to deliver a successful, well-received presentation.

OPTIONS FOR DELIVERY

When you create a speech, you write it to be heard, not merely read. Therefore, you should use an oral rather than a written style. What are the differences?

First, an oral style is more *personal*. When you deliver a speech, you are able to talk directly to your audience, invite participation, and adapt to reactions in ways a writer typically cannot. Second, an oral style is more repetitive. Because listeners cannot rehear or replay what you have said, you will need to use repetition and reinforcement, repeating and restating important ideas. Third, an oral style is *less formal*. Whereas written discourse often contains abstract ideas, complex phrasing, and a sophisticated vocabulary, simpler sentences and shorter words and phrases characterize the oral style.

Like athletes, speakers can use a variety of techniques to reduce apprehension.

The public speaker's language is less like the language of an essayist and more like the language of a skilled conversationalist. Filling your speech with everyday colloquial expressions, clear transitions, personal pronouns, and questions that invite participation is more effective than using abstract language, complex sentences, and impersonal references.

Thus, when wording your speech, remember to do the following:

- Speak in short units.
- Avoid using jargon or technical language when talking to audience members unfamiliar with your subject.
- Keep your words simple, concrete, appropriate, and vivid.

By following these guidelines, you won't sound like you are reading an essay or a manuscript, which as you will soon see, under most circumstances, you will not be doing.

Four general styles of delivery are available to you as a speech maker: (1) manuscript, (2) memorized, (3) impromptu, and (4) extemporaneous. We briefly examine all four options.

Manuscript Speeches

A **manuscript speech** is written out word for word and then read aloud by the speech maker. Manuscript speeches are most common when it is imperative that precise language be used. For example, since presidential addresses are likely to be

manuscript speech
a speech read from a script

If you were given a choice, which delivery style would you use? Why?

under close scrutiny not only in this country but also throughout the world, they often are read from a typed page or a TelePrompTer.

Unfortunately, the use of a manuscript tends to reduce eye contact between speaker and audience. Furthermore, speakers reading aloud often sound as if they are reading to, rather than talking to, the audience, and thus it is difficult to establish the much-needed conversational tone.

Memorized Speeches

memorized speech
a manuscript speech committed to memory

A **memorized speech** is a manuscript speech that the speaker commits to memory. It often takes on a canned tone. Also, speakers who memorize their lines are less able to respond to audience feedback. Additionally, of course, there is the problem of retention. Speech makers who insist on memorizing their presentations word for word often find themselves plagued by memory lapses, leading to long, awkward silences, during which they valiantly attempt to recall forgotten material. You may want to memorize certain key words, phrases, or segments of your speech, but at this point in your career there is little reason for you to commit the entire presentation to memory.

Impromptu Speeches

impromptu speech
a speech delivered spontaneously, or on the spur of the moment

An **impromptu speech** is a speech you deliver spontaneously, or on the spur of the moment without formal preparation. An impromptu speaker often has no more than a few seconds or minutes to gather his or her thoughts. An impromptu speaking situation may arise, for example, when a boss unexpectedly asks an employee to discuss the status of a project that is still in its developmental stages. If you are faced with such a request, you will need to rely on what you have learned about patterning your ideas; using the introduction-body-conclusion format will facilitate your task.

Extemporaneous Speeches

extemporaneous speech
a speech that is researched, outlined, and delivered after careful rehearsal

An **extemporaneous speech** is researched, outlined, and then delivered after careful rehearsal. Extemporaneous speaking is more audience centered than any of the preceding options. Since the speaker prepares and rehearses in advance, she or he is free to establish eye contact with the members of the audience and to respond to feedback. In addition, because extemporaneous speakers may use notes, they are not constrained by a need to commit the entire presentation to memory. Nor are they handicapped by a manuscript that must be read word for word, inhibiting their adaptability.

Thus, before delivering an extemporaneous speech, take time to create speaker's notes, also known as an *extemporaneous outline*. The extemporaneous outline contains brief reminders of the key parts of your speech as well as references to support you will use to develop each of your main points.

The extemporaneous outline you prepare should include reminder phrases for your speech's introduction; a statement of your central idea or thesis; brief notes on your main points and subpoints, including the complete names of sources or citations for references; transition reminders; and reminder phrases for your speech's conclusion. Also feel free to include delivery cues in the margins of your outline, such as "emphasize" or "hold up the visual aid," much as an actor marks up a script to facilitate speaking smoothness.

Keep the extemporaneous outline as brief as possible so that you will not be tempted to read your notes instead of maintaining eye contact with your audience.

A key to using the extemporaneous outline effectively is to begin practicing your speech using the more detailed outline you developed previously. Once you rehearse a few times using that outline and are comfortable and familiar with the content of your speech, make the switch and rely only on the extemporaneous outline during remaining practice sessions. (For a sample of a card containing brief speaker's notes, see Figure 15.2.)

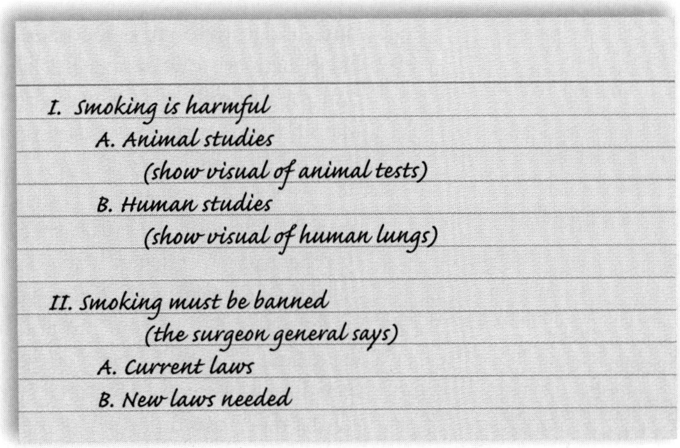

FIGURE 15.2

Sample Speaker's Notes.

Unfortunately, many speakers confuse manuscript, memorized, and impromptu speeches with extemporaneous speeches. Although asked to give an extemporaneous speech, they may insist on writing it out word for word and then either memorizing or reading it. Or they may spend too little time preparing the speech and deliver what is essentially a poorly developed impromptu presentation. Such misconceptions defeat the speakers' purpose and decrease their effectiveness as speech makers. The extemporaneous speech has been found most effective for most public speakers. Above all, do not turn extemporaneous speaking into something it is not.

REHEARSING: USING TRYOUTS AND SPEAKERS' TOOLS

In the theatre, playwrights, producers, directors, and performers never open an important show without first holding a series of tryouts or preview performances. These performances give the cast and backers an opportunity to experience audiences' reactions and, if necessary, make needed alterations in the script or actors' performance. As a speech maker, you can benefit by giving yourself the same opportunities. At your disposal are three basic speech-making tools—(1) visual, (2) vocal, and (3) verbal—which, if mastered during rehearsals, will reinforce your message.

In addition to your ideas, what qualities in you do you want to communicate to your audience? If you are like most speakers, you want your audience to accept you as a credible source. As we will see in Chapter 17, this means that you want your listeners to consider you competent, trustworthy, and dynamic.

How is credibility communicated? Obviously, it is conveyed, verbally, through the content and structure of language. However, far too frequently, speakers forget that credibility is also conveyed through visual and vocal cues. As we noted in Chapter 6, the nonverbal components of a message account for at least 65 percent of the total meaning transmitted to listeners. Thus, during rehearsals, the visual and vocal dimensions of your speech merit careful attention.

Conduct Tryouts: Rehearse, Rehearse, Rehearse

Once your extemporaneous outline is complete, it is time to become your own audience and explore the sound and feel of your speech before you present it to others. You will need three essential ingredients for your first tryout: (1) your speaker's notes, (2) a clock or wristwatch, and (3) a recording device (audio or visual) so that you can review the exact words you use to express your ideas. Before starting, check the time and turn on the recorder. Then stand up, face an imaginary audience, and begin delivering your speech. In effect, you are now in the process of preparing an oral rough draft of your presentation. Many speakers find it helpful to commit the first and last sentences of the speech to memory. If you do not memorize your opening and closing sentences, you should at the least become very familiar with them. (As one student put it, "That way I know that I'll be able to start and stop the speech.") Present the entire speech a number of times, conducting a series of tryouts or rehearsals over several days, sometimes alone, at other times before a small group of friends or relatives. During your rehearsals be sure to incorporate all your audio and visual aids into your presentation. Also practice delivering the speech in several locations. This will help you get used to the foreign feel of the room where the speech will be given. Your goal is to develop a flexible delivery—one that will enable you to meet the unique demands of the live audience.

What will you discover and do during rehearsals? First, you want to know if your presentation consumes too much or too little time. If your run-through takes 25 minutes and your time limit is 5 minutes, you have to make some serious revisions. If, on the other hand, you have designed a "60-second wonder," you may find that need to go back to the library for more material. Second, as you listen to your speech, be alert for ideas that you have not expressed as clearly as you would like. This is your opportunity to fix them. Third, you may find that you express the same thoughts again and again and again—more than is necessary for redundancy. This is your opportunity to edit. Fourth, you may realize that your speech's structure is confusing because of missing or inappropriate transitions, or that you need to remind yourself to stress certain points because of their importance. Add needed transition and delivery reminders to your notes.

Just as a playwright reworks a scene, you may also rework sections of your speech. If, when conducting a tryout, you find that your main attention getter is not as effective as it could be, improve it. If the supporting material under, say, the second main point in the body of your speech is confusing, rewrite it. If an illustration is too long and drawn out, shorten it. Your goal during tryouts is to refine your speech until it is as close as possible to the one you will present to your audience.

The clothing a speaker wears should reinforce, not detract from, the presentation.

Conduct a Visual Tune-up

Let's consider visual cues. How do you think a speech maker should look standing before an audience? Close your eyes and picture his or her clothing, posture, gestures, movements and facial expressions, and use of eye contact.

Clothing

In deciding what to wear when you deliver your speech, you should consider the topic, the audience, and the occasion. Sometimes speakers make thoughtless errors in dress. For example, one student delivered a very serious tribute to a well-known leader while wearing a shirt emblazoned with a huge Mickey Mouse emblem. (When asked why he wore that shirt, he responded, "I didn't think anyone would notice.") The clothes you wear should not distract receivers from focusing on the ideas of your speech.

Be aware that it is up to you to choose what you will wear. Your clothing does not choose you.

Posture

As a public speaker, you will almost always be expected to stand when addressing your audience. Thus, unless you are physically challenged, you should expect to be on your feet. Although this may seem obvious, the problem is that standing is something many of us do not do very well. Your posture communicates; it sends potent messages to the audience. Speakers often seem to forget this, assuming a stance that works against them rather than for them. For example, some speakers lean on the lectern or actually drape themselves over it as if unable to stand without its assistance. Some prop themselves against the wall behind them, giving the impression that they want to disappear into it.

To prepare yourself to stand properly in public, assume your natural posture and ask others to evaluate it. Are you too stiff? Do you slouch? Do you appear too relaxed? Feedback can help you put your best posture forward when you rise to speak.

> ### Work It Out
> Bring in magazine and newspaper ads with examples of models dressed appropriately to deliver a speech and of those dressed inappropriately. Identify the audience, the occasion, and the nature of the presentation before giving your judgment.

Gestures

As we noted in Chapter 6, gestures are movements of a speaker's hands and arms. The gestures you use when speaking in public may be purposeful, helping reinforce the content of your speech, or purposeless, detracting from your message. A problem most of us encounter is that we have certain favorite gestures that we are unaware of doing—things like scratching our neck, putting our hands into and out of our pockets, jingling our keys or jewelry, or smoothing our hair. Such mannerisms often become intensified when we find ourselves faced with a stressful situation such as speaking in public. In fact, when people are nervous, it is not unusual for them to add new gestures to their repertoire of annoying mannerisms. Speakers will sometimes tap a pencil or ring on the lectern or even crack their knuckles—things they would never do in normal circumstances.

Gestures can, however, serve a number of useful purposes. They can help you emphasize important points, enumerate your ideas, or suggest shapes or sizes. Thus, your job with regard to gestures is really twofold. First, you need to work to eliminate annoying gestures; second, you need to incorporate appropriate gestures that can be used to enhance the ideas contained in your speech.

Movements and Facial Expressions

It is important to understand that your presentation begins as soon as you are introduced or called on to speak—that is, before you have spoken your first syllable. The way you rise and approach the speaker's stand communicates a first impression to your listeners. Similarly, your facial expressions as you complete your speech and your walk as you return to your seat also send important signals to your audience. Far too many speech makers approach the lectern in inappropriate ways. For example, they may walk in a way that broadcasts a lack of preparation. Some even verbalize this by mumbling something like "I'm really not ready. This will be terrible." Others apologize for a poor showing all the way back to their seats.

> ### Work It Out
> Standing before the class, recite the alphabet. As you do so, make as many annoying gestures as you can. Recite the alphabet again. During this second recitation, make gestures that are as appropriate as possible.

Consider carefully your way of moving to and from the speaker's stand. The way you move communicates whether or not you are in control. You may have noticed that confident people walk with head erect, follow a straight rather than

Eye contact draws receivers into a presentation.

a circuitous path, proceed at an assured rather than a hesitant or frenetic pace, and use open rather than closed arm movements.

Eye Contact

Eye contact also communicates. Unfortunately, some speakers "talk" to walls, chalkboards, windows, trees, or the floor rather than to their listeners. Some speakers seem embarrassed to look at any audience members; others seek the attention of one person and avoid looking at anyone else. Some student speakers avoid meeting the eyes of the instructor during a speech; others focus on him or her exclusively.

Be sure that your gaze includes all the members of the audience. Look at each individual as you deliver your speech. Such contact will draw even the most reluctant listeners into your presentation.

Conduct a Vocal Tune-up

Obviously, the voice is one of our main tools in speech making. In Chapter 6, we considered four basic vocal dimensions: volume, rate, pitch, and quality. Review this material during your rehearsals, keeping in mind that your goal is to use your voice to reinforce the content of your speech.

To respond to your ideas, your audience must, of course, first hear them. Maintaining your voice at an appropriate volume is your responsibility. If you are to address a group in a large auditorium, a public-address system will probably be provided. If you are addressing a group in a smaller room, you will probably be expected to speak without amplification. By observing the people in the rear, you should be able to determine if you are speaking loudly enough for them to hear you easily. If you notice that any of the audience members look confused or upset, speak up. On the other hand, if your voice is normally loud and you notice that those seated nearest to you are cringing, turn down your volume a bit.

With regard to pitch, try not to fall into the monotone trap. If you maintain one predominant tone throughout your presentation, you will create a sense of boredom in the audience. Use pitch to reflect the emotional content of your material; use it to create interest.

Like volume and pitch, rate also communicates. Speaking too quickly or too slowly can impede understanding. Thus, respond to feedback from your audience and speed up or slow down your pace as appropriate.

Nonfluencies are a problem every public speaker needs to consider. "Uhs" and "ums" are normal in communication encounters, but they are not expected in speech making. During person-to-person conversations, we realize that people are thinking about or planning what they are going to say next. In contrast, we expect public speakers to have prepared their remarks carefully, and thus we are less tolerant of their nonfluencies. Attempt to eliminate nonfluencies from your delivery as much as possible.

Conduct a Verbal Tune-up

Although we have already focused on developing the verbal aspects of your speech (see Chapter 14), when rehearsing, be sure to use language that is clear and vivid.

As you rehearse your speech, ask yourself if it contains any unnecessary or confusing words or expressions. If so, eliminate them. For example, instead of saying "a sufficient supply of," say "enough." In general, choose simpler and more familiar words over those that could cause audience members difficulty in deciphering their meaning. Thus, say "plan" rather than "strategize." This especially holds true for idioms when addressing audiences composed of people from diverse cultures. Also remember to use transitions to guide your audience from one point to the next.

How do you make your words live in the minds of audience members? As you rehearse, ask yourself if your speech contains vivid words, including strong and active verbs, and figures of speech and images to enliven your presentation by helping audience members form mental pictures. Avoid using tired words such as "very interesting," or "world-class" or clichés such as "cool as a cucumber" or "sly as a fox." Phrases like these are used so often that audiences find them trite and meaningless. Language that helps audience members not only understand but also see, hear, and feel your message is your goal.

The Rehearsal-Confidence Connection

Rehearsal—careful practice of your presentation—gives you the confidence you need to deliver an effective speech. Now that you have prepared and tried out your extemporaneous outline, integrating appropriate presentation (both visual and audio) aids, do you find that you are more confident? Rehearsal is your key to synthesizing all you have done into a polished presentation. During rehearsals you make final revisions based on whether

- your speech is the right length or you need to delete or add material to it
- the words of your speech flow smoothly or you need to spend more time on phrasing

Work It Out

Keep a log of your progress during rehearsals. Each time you rehearse, note the location of the rehearsal, the problems you encountered, the changes you made, and any progress you observed.

What would you tell this speaker about his approach to speech making?

"It's a good speech—just a couple of points that need obfuscation."

Exploring Diversity

Culture and Delivery

Cultural background and conditioning affect a speaker's nonverbal repertoire and how members of the audience interpret nonverbal cues. Consider the following:

When it comes to eye contact, we know that speakers of Arabic, Latino, and Southern European descent tend to look directly into the faces of audience members, while Chinese, Japanese, Northern European, and Pakistani speakers are more likely to avoid focusing directly on receivers' faces. Similarly, in Native American culture, direct eye contact could be construed as insulting, whereas Caucasian Americans consider it a sign of respect. What is more, while in the West a speaker placing his or her hands on his or her hips may suggest confidence, among Asians it reflects obstinacy. Similarly, Asians are likely to interpret a speaker's folding his or her arms across the chest as arrogant. And whereas scratching one's lip in the United States probably means it itches, in China, it is an invitation to sexual intimacy.

Cultural norms also govern the intensity of a speaker's nonverbal cues. For example, speakers from Mediterranean cultures are known to amplify emotional displays, whereas Asians are likely to conceal emotional intensity by masking it with a smile. Asian speakers also tend to make less use of their arms and hands to underscore a point than do Westerners. Their constrained use of nonverbal cues may suggest a lack of involvement when that is not the case.

Vocal cues also vary from culture to culture. For example, Asians are likely to use a lower voice to express emphasis rather than a louder one. Additionally, the higher pitch and intonation pattern used by Arabic speakers is apt to convey extreme emotion to North Americans. Thus, some North American audience members may conclude that Arabic speakers are angry or agitated when neither is the case. And for similar reasons, an Arabic receiver may interpret the speech patterns and emotions of North American speakers as indicating a lack of commitment to expressed positions when this also is untrue.

Given these cultural practices, in your opinion, what adaptations in the use of nonverbal cues, if any, should a speaker from a culture different from most members of an audience make when delivering a speech?

If you have eight hours to cut down a tree, you should spend six hours sharpening your saw.

—Joey Ashner, Speaking Consultant

- your visual and audio aids work effectively or you need to troubleshoot technical problems
- you control your apprehensiveness or need to use more relaxation techniques
- you master using speaker's notes or need even more practice

GIVING THE SPEECH: SOME FINAL TIPS

If you follow the developmental plan outlined in this book, you should find yourself ready and eager to deliver your speech. Not only will you have carefully prepared and rehearsed your address, you will also have at your disposal tested techniques to help you control your nerves. At this juncture, you should need only a few additional pointers:

1. Arrive at your speaking location with ample time to spare. Be sure that you have prepared equipment to hold your notes and presentation aids.
2. If you are going to use a public-address system or other electronic equipment, test it so that you will not have to adjust the volume or replace bulbs or batteries unnecessarily during your presentation.
3. Give ample consideration to your clothing and appearance. Your confidence and believability will increase if you look the part. (But do not distract yourself with worries about your appearance while you are speaking.)
4. Let your audience know you are prepared by the way you rise when introduced and by walking confidently to the podium.
5. While speaking, work to transmit a sense of enthusiasm and commitment to your listeners.

Online Learning Center

Go to the Online Learning Center at www.mhhe.com/gamble10e and view clip 13 to see an example of presentation skills.

6. Complete your speech before returning to your seat. You have worked hard to communicate your credibility to audience members; don't ruin it in the last few seconds. Last impressions, like first impressions, count.

AFTER THE SPEECH: EVALUATING YOUR EFFECTIVENESS

As soon as you have completed your presentation, the first question you will ask yourself is, How did I do? No doubt you will also want to know what your peers and your instructor thought of your performance. You and your listeners can evaluate your speech by analyzing how effectively you were able to handle each of the following: content, organization, language, and delivery.

Content

Was the subject of your speech appropriate? Was it worthwhile? Was your purpose communicated clearly? Did you research the topic carefully? Were your audiovisual aids helpful? Did you use a variety of support? Were your main points adequately developed? Were the main divisions of your speech effectively bridged by transitional words and phrases?

Organization

How effective was your organizational approach? Did you begin with material that gained the attention of the audience? Did you preview each main point? Were your main points arranged in a logical sequence? Was the number of main points appropriate for the time allotted? Was your organizational design easily discernible? Did your conclusion provide a logical wrap-up of your main parts? Did it motivate listeners to continue thinking about your presentation?

Language

Did you use clear language to explain your ideas? Was it vivid? Did your speech sound as if it should be listened to rather than read? Could any of the words or phrases you used have been considered offensive to any audience members?

Delivery

Did you maintain effective eye contact with the members of the audience? Did you approach the speaking situation confidently? Were you able to use an extemporaneous style of delivery? Could you be heard easily? Was your speaking rate appropriate? Did you articulate clearly? Were you able to convey a sense of enthusiasm as you spoke? Did your gestures help reinforce your content?

Focus on Service Learning
Visit the following Web sites: www.school-for-champions.com/speaking/fear.htm, www.speeches.com, and www.owl.english.purdue.edu/owl/resource/544/01/. How can you use them or similar sites, as well as what you know about speech apprehension, delivery, and credibility, to prepare a volunteer for a community group to take his or her message "on the road"?

COMMUNICATION SKILLS IN PRACTICE
A SELF-EVALUATION CHECKLIST

When it is time for the audience members to comment on your presentation, they, like you, should consider the positive dimensions of your performance before making recommendations for improvement. Speaker and audience alike should remember that analysis is designed to be constructive, not destructive. It should help build confidence. It should not destroy the speaker's desire to try again.

Your instructor will probably provide you with a more formal analysis of your work, using an evaluation form similar to the one shown in Figure 15.3.

Work It Out

Develop variations and improvements of the evaluation form in Figure 15.3.

Name: _____   Speech: _____

Specific purpose: _____

1. Content
   ____ Based on accurate analysis of speaking situation.
   ____ Specific goal of speech was apparent.
   ____ Subject appropriate, relevant, and interesting to intended audience.
   ____ All material clearly contributed to purpose.
   ____ Had specific facts and opinions to support and explain statements.
   ____ Support was logical.
   ____ Handled material ethically.
   ____ Used audio and/or visual aids when appropriate.
   ____ Included a variety of data—statistics, quotations, etc.
   ____ Moved from point to point with smooth transitions.

2. Organization
   ____ Began with effective attention-getter.
   ____ Main points were clear statements that proved or explained specific goals.
   ____ Points were arranged in logical order.
   ____ Each point was adequately supported.
   ____ Concluded with memorable statement that tied speech together.

3. Language
   ____ Ideas were clear.
   ____ Ideas were presented vividly.
   ____ Ideas were presented emphatically.
   ____ Language was appropriate for intended audience.

4. Delivery
   ____ Was prepared to speak.
   ____ Stepped up to speak with confidence.
   ____ Maintained contact with audience.
   ____ Sounded extemporaneous, not read or memorized.
   ____ Referred to notes only occasionally.
   ____ Sounded enthusiastic.
   ____ Maintained good posture.
   ____ Used vocal variety, pitch, emphasis, and rate effectively.
   ____ Gestured effectively.
   ____ Used face to add interest.
   ____ Articulation was satisfactory.
   ____ On finishing, moved out with confidence.
   ____ Fit time allotted.

Additional comments:

FIGURE 15.3   Evaluation Form.

Whether or not your instructor uses the form in Figure 15.3, you will find it helpful as a personal guide.

Another means of evaluating your own effectiveness as well as the effectiveness of other speakers is to evaluate the credibility of the evidence included in a presentation. See the evaluation checklist at the end of Chapter 17.

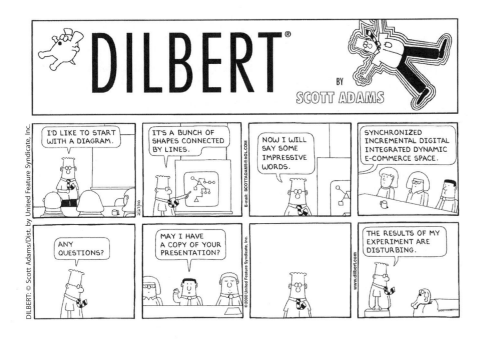

Reflect and Respond

According to poet e. e. cummings, "Most people are perfectly afraid of silence." Do you agree with cummings? Provide reasons and examples to explain your position.

Which do you believe most people fear *more* and why—silence or speaking in public?

Finally, what do the quote by e. e. cummings and the following one, by Daniel Webster, have in common?

If all my talents and powers were suddenly taken from me by some inscrutable providence, and I were allowed to keep only one, I would unhesitatingly ask to be allowed to keep my power of speaking for with that one, I would quickly regain all the others.

Thinking Critically

THE WRAP-UP

Revisiting Chapter Objectives

1. **Assess your level of speech anxiety.**   Anxiety, or fear, affects all speech makers. One of the best ways to cope with speech fright is to design and rehearse your presentation carefully. In addition, you should learn to recognize the causes of fear, as well as the physical and mental sensations that accompany it, so that you can learn to control your reactions with appropriate behavior modification techniques.

2. **Use deep-muscle relaxation, thought stopping, visualization, and other techniques to reduce speech anxiety.**   Among the techniques you can use to reduce speech anxiety are deep muscle relaxing, thought stopping, and visualization. These three techniques help eliminate the tension, thoughts, and symptoms associated with fear—the first by eliminating stress, the second by stopping the fear-inducing process, the third by boosting confidence.

3. **Discuss four styles of delivery: manuscript, memorized, impromptu, and extemporaneous.**   There are four general options for delivery: (1) A manuscript speech is written out word for word and then read aloud; (2) a memorized speech is a manuscript speech committed to memory; (3) an impromptu speech is delivered on the spur of the moment; (4) an extemporaneous speech is researched, outlined, and delivered after careful rehearsal.

4. **Identify how the speaker can use visual and vocal cues to advantage.**   In delivering the speech, you have three basic kinds of tools at your disposal: verbal, visual, and vocal. Far too often, the verbal component is overemphasized, while the nonverbal aspects are underemphasized. Effective speech making requires that you pay attention to the visual aspects of your delivery, such as your clothing, posture, gestures, movements, and use of eye contact, and that your vocal cues including volume, rate, pitch, and quality reinforce—rather than sabotage— the content.

5. **Analyze a speech maker's performance (including your own) in terms of content, organization, language, and delivery.**   Careful rehearsal of your presentation can help you develop the confidence and competence required to deliver an outstanding speech. To ensure continued improvement, you should conduct postpresentation analyses focusing on content, organization, language, and delivery, which will enable you to profit from each speaking experience.

Resources for Further Inquiry and Reflection

To apply your understanding of how the principles in Chapter 15 are at work in our daily lives, consult the following resources for further inquiry and reflection. Or, if you prefer, choose any other appropriate resource. Then connect the ideas expressed in your chosen selection with the communication concepts and issues you are learning about both in and out of class.

Listen to Me

"Help!" (The Beatles)
"I Shall Believe" (Sheryl Crow)

How do the pleas of the speakers in the songs reflect your own when you are asked to give a speech? How can you use other people to help you improve both your speech-making effectiveness and readiness to speak?

Read Me

Philip G. Zimbardo. *Shyness*. New York: Jove, 1987.
Ron Huff. *I Can See You Naked*. Kansas City: Andrews & McMeel, 1992.
Pauline Woodruff Titus. *How to Conquer Shyness*. New York: Kessinger Publishing Co., 2007.

How can combating shyness prepare you to be a better speaker?

View Me

Dave   Maid in Manhattan
Bulworth   Anchorman: The Legend of Ron Burgundy
                    The Truth About Cats and Dogs

What lessons can you derive from the presentations of the title or supporting character? How would you evaluate the public performances of Dave, Bulworth, the 10-year-old son in *Maid in Manhattan*, Ron Burgundy, or Dr. Abby Barnes? Explain.

Tell Me

Share with the class the insights you gained from your chosen Listen to Me, View Me, or Read Me selection.

Advertisements and public speakers have a number of characteristics in common. Both aim to inform as well as persuade. Their effectiveness depends on whether they are able to attract the interest of receivers, arouse their needs, and motivate them to listen and respond. The delivery of the characters in the ad, the images they project, together with the credibility of the spokespersons also affect an ad's overall impact. The same holds true for a speaker: delivery, image, and credibility interact to enhance or detract from the speaker's effectiveness. Those are the similarities. What differences do you see between public speakers and advertisements?

Key Chapter Terminology

Use the Online Learning Center at www.mhhe.com/gamble10e to further your knowledge of the following terminology.

communication apprehension 384	manuscript speech 389
extemporaneous speech 390	memorized speech 390
impromptu speech 390	public speaking anxiety 384

www.mhhe.com/gamble10e

Idioms in Translation

not up to par — ineffective

play it safe — avoid taking a risk

stomach knots — tightness in your stomach

Culture Cue

In the United States, direct eye contact demonstrates sincerity.

Test Your Understanding

Go to the *Self Quizzes* on the book's Online Learning Center at www.mhhe.com/gamble10e.

www.mhhe.com/gamble10e

CHAPTER 16

After finishing this chapter, you should be able to

1. Define *informative speaking*.

2. Distinguish among four types of informative discourse.

3. Explain how to create information hunger and increase listeners' comprehension.

4. Develop and present an informative speech.

Informative Speaking

How does it feel to have more access to information than ever before? Information not only has value today, it also confers power. Once in possession of the *right* information, we can understand things we otherwise might not have been able to, and accomplish things we otherwise would not have done. But is it possible that we now have *too much* information? According to *Living in the Information Age,* because our capacity to absorb information has not increased while we daily face deluges of new and sometimes conflicting data, we have a greater need to filter, process, and edit the information we receive.[1] We also have an increasingly important need to conceptualize. In fact, while information remains essential, we are now transitioning—moving out of the information age and into the *conceptual age*—a time when people with the ability to understand and interpret meaning, think differently, detect patterns, recognize opportunities, and edit and put the pieces together in new ways will be in demand.[2] Do you have these skills?

Informative speakers face three primary challenges: (1) to identify information important to others; (2) to put themselves in the position of their receivers and make the information they deliver understandable to them; and (3) to communicate information in ways that create interest, enhance learning, and help audience members remember their message.

Being able to convey information and meaning to others is among the most useful skills you can acquire. That is what this chapter prepares you to do—to share information you have with people who lack it but need it, or who possess it but do not fully understand it. Let's get started.

We now face the prospect of information obesity.
—David Shenk

There are things that are known and things that are unknown; in between are doors.
—Anonymous

Why do you believe the age of information was given this name? What is causing the transition into the age of conceptualization?

SPEAKING INFORMATIVELY

What's happening? How does it work? What's going on? What is it? What does it mean? These are the kinds of questions that an **informative speech** answers. Whenever you prepare an informative speech, your goal is to offer your audience members more information than they already have about a topic. Your objective is to update and add to their knowledge, refine their understanding, or provide background.[3]

How does the informative speech relate to your life? Our world is filled with informative messages that we depend on. Many of these messages are informal, but others are carefully planned, structured, and rehearsed to achieve maximum impact. In today's world, it is important to develop the ability to share information with other people. Some three-quarters of the U.S. labor force hold jobs that require the production, storage, or delivery of information. Educators in schools and businesses, sales

informative speech
a speech that updates and adds to the knowledge of receivers

professionals, medical practitioners, and consultants and managers in a wide array of fields depend on their skill in giving and receiving information for their livelihoods. They all share the need to make their messages clear, relevant, and useful to receivers.

TYPES OF INFORMATIVE PRESENTATIONS

Let's now consider four types of informative speeches: (1) messages of explanation (speeches of demonstration that explain the how or how-to of a subject), (2) messages of description (speeches that describe what a person, an object, or an event is like), (3) messages of definition (speeches that define what something is), and (4) narrative messages (speeches that tell a story).

Explanations

If your purpose is to explain how to do something (for example, how to motivate employees), how to make something (for example, how to make glass), how something works (for example, how a slot machine works), or how something develops or occurs (for example, how tornadoes form, how insider trading works), then you are preparing to deliver an explanation of a process. Your primary goal is to share your understanding of the process or procedure with your listeners and, in some instances, to give them the skills they need to replicate it. A speech of explanation deepens understanding by answering an interesting question, helping receivers get the answer(s) they need to facilitate their understanding or skill development.[4]

When organizing a message of explanation, be especially careful to avoid overcondensing the data. It is not uncommon for an inexperienced speaker to merely enumerate the steps involved in a process. This kind of perfunctory outline is hard for an audience to follow. Instead, use meaningful information groups. For example, grouping information under such headings as "Gathering Ingredients," "Blending Ingredients," and "Adding the Garnish" would be considerably more effective than simply relaying 15 steps involved in preparing a chocolate mousse. Besides facilitating understanding, this grouping system also helps the audience retain the material.

It is also important to consider the length of time it will take to accomplish your objectives in a process speech. Take a tip from televised cooking shows. Notice how an on-the-air chef always demonstrates some parts of the process live but has other parts of the dish prepared in advance to save time. This technique can be of great value to you, too.

Descriptions

One of your responsibilities as a speaker is to be able to describe a person, place, or thing for your listeners. For instance, if you were a

How many people do you know whose job requires them to deliver speeches? What percentage of their time is devoted to preparing and delivering speeches?

Online Learning Center

Go to the Online Learning Center at www.mhhe.com/gamble10e and answer the questions in the *Self Inventory* to evaluate your understanding of speech topics.

What processes are you equipped to speak about?

What techniques is this coach using to share information with his players?

Assessing Informative Speaking Skills

Sales professionals need to introduce products and services to the public. Small business owners need to promote their businesses to potential clients and customers. Virtually every job requires some skill in public speaking, and for many people it is a daily job requirement, including among other things the delivery of presentations in various forms (for example, reports, management briefings or meetings, forums, training sessions, or public relations speeches). Therefore, should recruiters for businesses, educational institutions, government, and other organizations make assessment of public speaking skills a requirement for being hired?

If your answer is yes, what form should such a skill and character assessments take? If your answer is no, what steps, if any, would you take to ensure that needed information is delivered to those who need it? Should they also make an assessment of the reputation and trustworthiness of the potential employees, including the ability to project a powerful image?

site-location specialist for a fast-food chain, you would have to describe potential store locations to the management. If you were a spokesperson for a nuclear plant that had experienced a radiation leak, you would have to describe the location and extent of the mishap to the media. Your aim is to help your listeners form mental close-ups of places, people, or things. To do this, you need to find ways to describe condition, size, shape, color, age, and so on to make your subject come alive for your audience.

Speakers tend to use either a spatial or a topical organizational pattern when describing a person, place, or thing. Thus, a speaker might use a spatial pattern when describing the Clinton Presidential Library, but opt to use a topical organization when describing the scientific contributions of Galileo.

Of course, visual aids are particularly relevant to a descriptive presentation. For example, photographs, maps, and drawings can make it easier for you to describe a significant archaeological dig, the pathos of a homeless person, the appearance of a high-tech artificial limb, or the blight of an inner-city slum.

Whatever your topic, you will want to ensure that your words and phrases evoke the appropriate sensory responses in your listeners. To do this, communicate how your subject looks, tastes, smells, feels, and sounds. In a descriptive speech, you paint with words.

Work It Out

Keep track of all the informative messages you deliver and receive in a single day.

Definitions

"What do you mean?" is a common question. In most cases, the questioner asks it when seeking clarification or elaboration of ideas from a speaker. Sometimes a satisfactory answer can be supplied in a sentence or two. At other times, however, it takes a speech, or even a book, to define a concept adequately. For example, books with titles such as *Data Smog, The Age of Paradox, Emotional Intelligence, Leader Effectiveness Training, The Age of Missing Information,* and *Happiness Is . . .* are actually extended definitions: The authors are discussing their meaning for a particular concept or idea. An informative speech of definition likewise provides an audience with an explanation of a term. "Shyness," "The Grief Cycle," "ESP,"

What kinds of informative messages do you think you are best at delivering? Why? Do you think men and women differ in the mastery of skills required to deliver the different kinds of informative presentations? Who would you rather listen to delivering a narrative message, for example, a man or a woman? Why?

and "Muscular Dystrophy" are among the topics for which a definitional presentation would be appropriate.

Can you think of others? Many students find that topics such as "Racial Profiling," "The Meaning of Obscenity," "Prejudice," "Friendship," and "Sexual Harassment" give them the freedom they need to develop effective speeches of definition.

Since many of the concepts you may choose to define will have connotative, or subjective, meanings not traditionally found in dictionaries, not all members of your audience will agree with the definition you present. On one television talk show, for example, two experts on shyness were unable to agree on what it means to be shy. It is necessary, therefore, to organize a definitional speech in a way that will be clear and persuasive. For example, how would you define *shyness*? To explain your meaning for the term, you might offer examples of what it feels like to be shy, describe how a shy person behaves, and then go on to discuss the consequences of shyness. Perhaps you would explain shyness by comparing and contrasting a shy person with an extrovert. Or you might choose to discuss the causes of shyness and then focus on different types or categories of shyness. No matter how you choose to order your ideas, your organization should be suggested by the topic and grow out of it.

Narratives

Extended stories, or narratives, function as "teaching moments" and are an alternative means of providing information. They are often more entertaining and involving than more traditional approaches to informative speaking. Speakers who use the narrative format need to convey clearly the message contained in the story they tell so that audience members perceive its relevance. "Post-Traumatic Stress Syndrome: A Soldier's Story," "The Story of My Brother's Death: My Travels through the Cycle of Grief," "My Adoption," and "How I Used a Defibrillator to Save a Life" are the titles of informative speeches in which speakers could benefit from using a narrative approach to tell audience members more about their subject. Personal stories interest receivers who are drawn to someone they can relate to. Stories help audience members identify with your topic. When delivering a narrative, fill your story's plot with action and conflict—opposing ideas or forces in opposition—with one side pitted against another. Your story may also contain humor or drama to hold the audience's attention, and suspense to heighten and maintain interest. Speakers can use temporal, topical, and spatial patterns to develop informational personal narratives.

EFFECTIVE INFORMATIVE SPEECHES: INCREASING YOUR LISTENERS' INTEREST AND COMPREHENSION

An effective informative speech accomplishes several tasks: (1) makes your listeners want to learn more about the topic; (2) communicates the information clearly by providing information balance; (3) emphasizes key points; (4) involves audience members in your presentation; and (5) provides information in ways that make it memorable, perhaps through novelty, creativity, and audiovisuals. Let's look at these tasks.

Create Information Hunger

Your primary goal in an informative speech is to deliver a message of explanation, description, definition, or narrative, but it is equally important that audience members find your presentation interesting, intellectually stimulating, and relevant (that is, significant or personally valuable). In other words, you need to work to increase each listener's need to know and hunger to receive your message.

You will be more adept at creating information hunger if you have analyzed your audience carefully (see Chapter 12). Then, by using appropriate vehicles, you will be able to generate the interest that will motivate audience members to listen to the information you want to share. Remember to use the attention-getting devices discussed in Chapter 14. For example, you can relate your own experiences or the experiences of others; you can ask rhetorical questions; you can draw analogies for your listeners to consider. You can also arouse the audience's curiosity, and you can incorporate humor or use eye-catching visual aids.

Obviously, your effectiveness as a speaker will increase to the extent that you present your information creatively and succeed in arousing the desire and the need to know among audience members.

Thus, if you addressed an audience on how the changing demographics in the United States will affect the workforce in the next decade, your speech would likely interest them because it would add to their knowledge and better prepare them to respond to changing times. In similar fashion, one speaker addressing a meeting of young Republicans pointed out that during the 2008 Republican National Convention, few people of color (some 36) were included among the over 2,000 delegates in attendance, cautioning that if the Republican Party wants to survive, it will have to find a way for its convention to be more reflective of the nation's demographics.

Seek Information Balance

Your speech will inform receivers only if they are capable of processing the information you deliver. A common danger in informative speaking is that the audience experiences information overload. **Information overload** occurs when (1) the speech maker delivers far more data about the topic than the audience needs or wants, confusing listeners and causing them to tune out what is being communicated; and (2) the speech maker presents ideas in words the listeners do not understand. Instead of using clear language and speaking at a level the audience comprehends, the speaker creates frustration among audience members by using unfamiliar jargon or words that soar beyond the reach of the listeners' vocabulary.

A speaker who tries to avoid information overload will often overcompensate and create a situation of information underload. **Information underload** occurs when the speaker underestimates the sophistication or intelligence of the audience members and tells them little that they do not already know.

As a speech maker, you need to strike a balance, providing neither too little information nor too much. As a rule, effective speech makers neither underestimate nor overestimate the capabilities of the audience. Instead, they motivate their listeners to want to fill in any information gaps.

Remember this: Pace, don't race. When you are delivering an informative speech, your task is to communicate so that audience members understand you, not to race to see how much new information you can cram into their brains in

---

Which speakers you have listened to succeeded in increasing your hunger for knowledge about a topic? What did they do to accomplish this?

Focus on Service Learning
Develop a list of Web sites you could visit to prepare a presentation on the Medicare prescription drug plan or another topic of interest to senior citizens. Then using information provided on Web sites such as www.seniorjournal .com/seniorlinks.htm, www .noodletools.com, and www .medicare.gov, work with the leader(s) of a community group composed primarily of seniors to help the group's members deal more effectively with the challenges seniors face.

information overload
the situation that occurs when the amount of information provided by a speech maker is too great to be handled effectively by receivers

information underload
the situation that occurs when the information provided by a speech maker is already known to receivers

Conveying Information across Cultures

When preparing to deliver an informative speech, should the information you include depend on the cultural makeup of your audience? Should you always work to exhibit divergent thinking by approaching your topic from a variety of perspectives? Before answering, consider this.

An African proverb says, "The earth is a beehive; we all enter by the same door, but live in different cells," meaning that people share a basic capacity to look at the same world of ideas (a hive), focus on a particular topic (a door), and strive for a similar goal (a cell). Yet in spite of having similar access to the same information, people are individually motivated and they head for different destinations. Thus the same information can take a different course when delivered to several audiences.

Consider an informative topic such as how to avoid contracting AIDS. The scientific and social information on this topic are the same everywhere in the world, yet no two groups will have the same approach to it. An informative talk on the subject addressed to a group of prison inmates might be aimed at specific remedies for a high-risk group. (The speech would contain very basic biological data regarding channels of transmission and specific physical methods of preventing exposure.) The same talk addressed to a group of apprehensive parents in a middle-class suburb might focus on the effects of presenting such information to children of various ages. A speech on the subject to a group of Chinese health professionals visiting the United States might aim at their concerns for minimizing the impact of the disease in their country.

The question: Should a speech be a global mosaic that cuts across cultures to develop common understandings, or should a speaker who belongs to a specific racial or ethnic group speak to the interests of his or her own group? What advantages and disadvantages do you see in each approach?

5 or 10 minutes. Your real challenge is to know not only what to include but also what *not* to include.

Emphasize Key Points

As we discussed in Chapter 13, emphasis can be created through repetition (saying the same thing over again) and restatement (saying the same thing in another way). As long as you do not become overly repetitious and redundant, these devices will help your listeners process and retain the main points of your speech.

The organization of your speech can also reinforce your main ideas. Remember that you can use your introduction to preview ideas in your conclusion and to help make those ideas memorable. Transitions and internal summaries also help create a sense of cohesiveness.

Involve Your Listeners

The relationship between audiences and speakers is changing. Contemporary audiences are restless. Public speakers need to work to channel the nervous energy of their audience members, who will learn more if they become involved with the material presented to them.[5] Effective speech makers do not view the audience as a passive receptacle; rather, they work to find ways to let the audience take an active part in the presentation. For example, the audience may be called on to perform an activity during the presentation. If you are giving a speech on how to reduce stress, you might have your listeners try one or two stress-reducing exercises. Or if your speech topic is "How to Read an EKG," you might pass out sample EKGs for audience members to decipher.

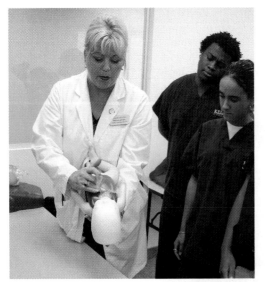

Receivers learn more when directly involved in a presentation.

Provide Information Memorably

Remember that people want to understand and remember information that they perceive as relevant to their own lives. Few of us would have much interest in a speech on the development of bees. If, however, we found that the bees we are hearing about are a new species of killer bee that is extremely resistant to common insecticides, and that droves of these bees are on the way to our community and will arrive within the next two weeks, we would develop an intense interest very quickly.

Audiences also want to listen to new information. In this case, the term *new* means "new to them." A historical blunder may be new in this sense, and it may be relevant to a college or business audience today. The cable television industry has found that weather is worthy of its own channel; the weather forecast is constantly being updated and is therefore considered new.

Repetition can help as well; audiences respond to information that is repeated. Martin Luther King, Jr., understood the value of repetition in his "I have a dream" speech. As you prepare your informative speech, look for ways to let repetition augment your message by adding emotional involvement.

Work It Out

Brainstorm ideas for involving an audience composed mainly of people under age 65 in a speech on the Medicare prescription drug plan.

Novelty and Creativity

An effective speaker looks constantly for ways to approach information from an unusual direction. If you are the fifth speaker that your audience will hear on the homeless, you must find a different slant or approach to the topic, or the audience may be bored from the outset. You might try taking a different point of view— through the eyes of a child, for example. Look for analogies that bring topics home to an audience: "The number of people entering teaching today is diminishing. The teaching profession is like a stream drying up." Try other ways to complete this analogy. As you prepare your presentation, remember that you are looking for creative ways of bringing your topic to life for the audience.

Take your mind out every now and then and dance on it. It is getting all caked up.
—Mark Twain

Audiovisual Aids

You will want to include audiovisual aids in an informative presentation. Remember first, though, that you are your primary visual aid. The way you stand, walk, talk, and gesture is extremely important to the effectiveness of your presentation.

Take objects, or make simple models if you cannot take the objects themselves. Use PowerPoint charts and graphs when appropriate.

Thinking Critically

Reflect and Respond

Agree or disagree with the following statement; supply reasons and examples that support your stance.

All information is persuasive. Thus, there is no such thing as an informative speech.

Then examine the sample informative speech outline and speech transcript that follow. Discuss how each sample can be used in defense of the position you have taken.

Also consider using video and audio clips to create interest. You can use camcorders to conduct interviews or show processes at work. One student showed a brief tape of a chemical reaction that could not have been demonstrated safely in the classroom.

The Internet is another source of visuals. On various Web sites, you will find images, charts, and graphs that you can incorporate into your presentation to help communicate your message.

SAMPLE INFORMATIVE SPEECH OUTLINE

FULL SENTENCE OUTLINE

The purpose statement and central idea guide the speaker in developing the outline.

Topic: Food contamination

Purpose: To inform the class about three sources of contamination in the human food chain.

Central idea: It is important to understand the sources of contamination in the human food chain.

A number of rhetorical questions and a visual aid draw receivers into the speech.

Introduction

I. Are you familiar with the food pyramid? (Hold up visual of food pyramid.) It's a nutritional advisory prepared by the government containing suggestions of foods we should eat to ensure a healthy diet. Of course, grains, vegetables, fruits, cheese, and meat all have their place on the food pyramid. Over the past few years, however, tainted food products have formed their own peculiar food pyramid. In the United States, food increasingly is coming under suspicion and has even sickened thousands. What foods have recently made people like you and me ill? I'll name just a few: tomatoes, peppers, beef, scallions, and spinach. These ingredients don't just comprise parts of the food pyramid—they make a great salad. (Show salad bowl.)

II. 76 million people in the United States come down with cases of foodborne disease annually.

The speaker reveals the speech's purpose.

III. Today I would like to tell you about the nature, means of transmission, and effects of three sources of contamination in our human food chain: salmonella, E. coli, and mad cow disease.

(Transition to main point I: First let's explore the nature of each of these sources of food contamination.)

Body

I. Salmonella, E. coli, and mad cow disease are food contaminants.

    A. According to the U.S. Department of Agriculture, salmonella is a rod-shaped bacterium that leads to foodborne illness.

        1. Two types of salmonella bacteria, Salmonella enteritidis and Salmonella typhimurium, are the most common, contributing to over half of all human infections.

        2. The salmonella bacteria live in the intestinal tracts of infected animals and humans.

        3. Salmonella contributes to about 1.4 million cases of illness, causing approximately 600 deaths in the United States each year.

    B. E. coli is a bacterium that lives in the digestive tracts of animals and humans.

        1. The most common type of E. coli is E. coli O157-H7, the kind contributing to most human outbreaks.

        2. E. coli afflicts approximately 70,000 people a year in the United States.

    C. Mad cow disease, formally known as bovine spongiform encephalopathy, is a fatal disease that enters and destroys the brains of cattle, sheep, deer, and elk and then us if we eat an afflicted animal.

        1. The disease's cause is a deformed prion, a mutant protein that kills the brain by literally poking holes in it, causing the brain to look like a Swiss cheese.

        2. Though few mad cow cases exist in the United States, the incubation period for the disease could extend for decades.

(Transition to main point II: Now that we have discussed the nature of each of the three food contaminants, let's explore their means of transmission.)

II. Salmonella, E. coli, and mad cow disease are transmitted through the food supply.

    A. Salmonella is usually transmitted to humans when they eat foods contaminated with animal feces or by the unwashed hands of an infected food handler.

        1. Salmonella can originate in meat, poultry, milk, dairy products, eggs, seafood, and fruits and vegetables that carry the bacteria.

        2. Salmonella survives if the product is not cooked to a safe minimum internal temperature.

        3. It can also be transferred through cross-contamination.

    B. E. coli are transmitted to humans when they consume food containing tiny amounts of human or animal feces—including milk that has not been pasteurized; water that has not been disinfected; soft cheese; undercooked meat; seafood including lobster; or contaminated lettuce, green onions, or spinach—or through contact with people infected with the disease.

        1. E. coli gets into food during processing.

        2. E. coli gets into lakes, pools, and water supplies if the water has not been properly treated.

continued

The speech's body is organized into three main points, each with a number of subpoints. Note that every entry in the body is a complete sentence and contains only a single idea.

The speaker uses a series of definitions and statistics to develop the first main point.

The speaker provides an easy-to-understand series of explanations to develop the second main point of the speech.

3. E. coli also spreads from food to food when they are combined before shipping.

4. E. coli spreads from person to person when an infected person fails to wash his or her hands.

5. Because there are so many potential sources, often the infection source remains unknown.

C. Mad cow disease is spread through infected feed, blood transfusions, and infected food.

1. Mad cow is caused by healthy cows eating ground-up parts of deceased animals.

2. Mad cow spreads to humans when they eat infected cows, receive a transfusion from an already infected person, or ingest a dietary supplement or receive a vaccine containing ingredients from infected cows.

(Now that we have looked at the means of transmission of these food contaminants, let's discuss how you know if you're afflicted with the disease.)

Personalizing symptoms for receivers helps the speaker develop the third main point of the speech.

III. Salmonella, E. coli, and mad cow disease sufferers present symptoms.

A. Salmonella's symptoms include diarrhea, abdominal cramps, and fever within 8 to 72 hours after eating the contaminated food.

1. Most people recover quickly.

2. Some develop Reiter's syndrome.

B. E. coli's symptoms include bloody diarrhea, stomach cramps, nausea, and vomiting.

1. Children are more likely to experience the bacteria's effects.

2. Some people never notice any symptoms.

3. Serious cases can affect the blood or kidneys.

B. Mad cow disease symptoms show up in both cows and humans.

1. Cows lose weight, are skittish, behave belligerently, appear confused, and may not be able to walk.

2. People experience paranoia, suffer from lack of coordination, and lapse into a coma.

The speaker summarizes what the speech has accomplished and uses a visual that refers receivers to the speech's introduction, providing a sense of closure.

Conclusion

I. Today we have explored the nature, means of transmission, and symptoms of three food contaminants: salmonella, E. coli, and mad cow disease.

II. Food safety experts believe regulation will allow better tracking of contaminants in the food chain.

III. From killer tomatoes of a recent salmonella outbreak, to spinach and fresh vegetables tainted with E. coli, to that juicy hamburger you ate yesterday—eating has become a challenge. So study the food pyramid, and prepare that well-washed salad, well-cooked hamburger, or tasty snack, and all the while, think carefully about what you're eating, and critical links in the food chain, including where the food came from, how it was shipped, whose hands may have touched it, and most important, how it was prepared and may affect you. Salad anyone? (Refer again to visual of the food pyramid and hold up salad bowl with steak.)

SAMPLE INFORMATIVE SPEECH

Topic:	Food contamination
Purpose:	To inform the class about three sources of contamination in the human food chain.
Central idea:	It is important for us to understand the sources of contamination in the human food chain.

Are you familiar with the United States Department of Agriculture's food pyramid? Do you follow its guidelines and try to eat healthy foods? The food pyramid (hold up visual of food pyramid) is a nutritional advisory prepared by the government containing suggestions of foods we should eat to ensure a healthy diet. Of course, grains, vegetables, fruits, cheese, and meat all have their place on the food pyramid. Over the past few years, however, tainted food products have formed their own peculiar food pyramid. In the United States, food increasingly is coming under suspicion and has even sickened thousands. What foods have recently made people like you and me ill? I'll name just a few: tomatoes, peppers, beef, scallions, spinach, and peanut butter. Foods like these don't just comprise key parts of the suggested food pyramid—they also make great salads or snacks. (Show salad bowl.)

On a serious note, this is not a joke. Unfortunately, according to the Centers for Disease Control and Prevention, increasing numbers of us are being sickened by contaminated food. In fact, Centers for Disease Control estimates are that some 76 million people living in the United States come down with cases of foodborne disease annually. Here's a description of just one of those cases, taken from an article by Annys Shin titled "Scientists Take on Food Poisoning's Long-Term Effects" that appeared in the Wednesday, September 17, 2008, issue of *The Record.* Shin's article told of the problems one young adult, Sarah Pierce, faced after eating contaminated food. Sarah experienced kidney failure numerous times, spent three years on dialysis, had to have her blood plasma replaced twice, suffered a broken engagement, lost friends, and lost her job just because a food she ingested had infected her with a toxic strain of E. coli. While today she has a healthy kidney because her brother donated her one of his, she has to take medicines to keep her body from rejecting it. "I would have liked to have children," she said, but because the medicines she now has to take carry a high risk of causing birth defects, having children is no longer an option for Sarah and her husband. E. coli is one food toxin, but it is far from the only culprit. Unfortunately, there are many. I will focus on three of them. Today, I would like to tell you about the nature, means of transmission, and effects of three sources of contamination in our human food chain: salmonella, E. coli, and mad cow disease.

First let's explore the nature of each of these sources of food contamination, starting with salmonella.

According to the U.S. Department of Agriculture, salmonella is a rod-shaped bacterium that leads to more cases of foodborne illness than any other bacteria. Microscopic living creatures, salmonella bacteria pass from the feces of people or animals to other people or animals. Two types of salmonella, Salmonella enteritidis and Salmonella typhimurium,

continued

Does the speaker succeed in gaining your attention? Do you believe the topic of the speech has relevance?

Do you find the use of this visual effective? Is there any other visual you might have considered using in the introduction?

How effective do you find the speaker's orientation? Does it prepare you for what is to come?

How effective is the speaker's change in tone? Does the speaker provide an effective transition?

Do you believe the illustration helps spark receiver interest?

What is the speaker aiming to accomplish with the first main point?

Is the speaker's use of rhetorical questions effective?

Is the speaker's choice of experts appropriate?

Does the speaker's use of statistics advance the speech's purpose?

How do you respond to the speaker's choice of a visual aid? Does it advance the speaker's goal?

Would you alter this transition in any way?

are the most common forms of the bacteria, contributing to over half of all human infections. Where does salmonella reside? I'll give you a clue—somewhere very close to you. Salmonella lives in the intestinal tracts of infected animals and humans. The bacteria usually are transmitted to humans when they eat foods contaminated with animal feces. You eat it because you can't see it, smell it, or taste it. Could any salmonella be hiding inside of your intestinal tract right now? The Surveillance Report from the Food Diseases Active Surveillance (FoodNet) identifies salmonella as the most commonly reported bacterial infection. Centers for Disease Control and Prevention statistics reveal that salmonella contributes to about 1.4 million cases of foodborne illness annually and causes about 600 deaths in the U.S. every year. According to food safety expert Tom Chestnut, interviewed on the June 10, 2008, airing of National Public Radio's *Morning Edition,* simply cleaning food appropriately does not get rid of the salmonella bacteria. While cleaning food reduces bacteria on the outside, Chestnut affirms that "it's very difficult to get a total elimination" of the salmonella bacteria.

Salmonella, as I noted, is not the only source of food contamination. Like salmonella, E. coli, the second of the food contaminants we will discuss, is also a bacteria that lives in the digestive tracts of both animals and humans. The most common type of E. coli is E. coli O157-H7, the strain that causes the most human outbreaks of the disease. E. coli afflicts large numbers of us but fewer than salmonella, causing approximately 70,000 people a year in the U.S. to become ill. Thoroughly cooking meat kills E. coli. Washing produce contaminated with E. coli removes the surface bacteria. However, according to food toxicologist Michele Norris, who appeared on the September 26, 2006, airing of National Public Radio's *All Things Considered,* rinsing the bacteria out of some foods, like sprouts, is impossible.

In contrast to salmonella and E. coli, the third foodborne illness we are exploring, mad cow disease, formally known as bovine spongiform encephalopathy, does not just make its victims ill. Mad cow, in contrast to salmonella and E. coli, which cause more illnesses than deaths, is a fatal disease that enters and destroys the brains of cattle, sheep, deer, elk, and humans if we are so unfortunate as to eat food from an afflicted animal. The emergence of mad cow disease is traced to a deformed prion, a mutant protein, that kills the brain by literally poking holes in it, leaving it to look like a piece of Swiss cheese. So this is likely what your brain will look like if you end up sickened by mad cow disease. (Hold up visual of Swiss cheese.) Dr. Robert Gallo, a scientist who has researched mad cow disease, tell us that, unfortunately, nothing is as indestructible as a prion, an organism that can survive temperatures upwards of 600 degrees Centigrade. Thus, even cooking meat thoroughly does not kill the prion. Neither do antibiotics. Though few mad cow cases have afflicted people in the U.S., the incubation period for the disease could extend for decades, so we're really uncertain about how many people are actually at risk—not a very comforting thought.

Now that we have discussed the nature of each of these three food contaminants, let's explore their means of transmission. Salmonella, E. coli, and mad cow disease are each transmitted through the food supply. Salmonella is usually transmitted to humans when they eat foods that have been contaminated with animal feces or by the unwashed hands of an infected food handler. Salmonella can originate in meat, poultry, milk, dairy products, eggs, seafood, and fruits and vegetables that carry the bacteria. Just a few months ago, as reported in the *New York Times* and other media outlets, a salmonella scare attributed to jalapeño peppers, cilantro, or some brands of salsa, made over 1,000 people in the U.S. ill. Salmonella is also a resilient bacterium and survives if the food product is not cooked to a safe minimum internal temperature. Fear of contracting salmonella is one reason that food experts offer advisories telling us to cook food thoroughly. Salmonella can also be transferred through cross-contamination that causes bacteria to spread beyond its original source.

As is true of salmonella, E. coli may be transmitted to humans when they consume food containing tiny amounts of human or animal feces. Among the prominent sources of E. coli are milk that has not been pasteurized and water that has not been disinfected, soft cheese, undercooked meat, seafood including lobster, lettuce, green onions, and spinach. E. coli is also spread through contact with people already infected with the disease. How does E. coli get into both the food supply and people? E. coli gets into food during processing, especially if meat is not cooked to at least 160 degrees Fahrenheit. E. coli gets into lakes and pools in which people swim, and into the water supply if the water is not properly treated. E. coli also spreads from food to food when a contaminated food is combined with one or more other foods before shipping. E. coli also spreads from person to person when an infected person fails to wash his or her hands after moving his or her bowels. Because there are so many potential sources of E. coli poisoning, often the infection source remains unknown.

In contrast to how salmonella and E. coli spread, mad cow disease is spread through infected animal feed, infected animals we consume, and blood transfusions. Caused by healthy cows eating the ground-up parts of deceased animals, mad cow spreads to humans when they eat beef from mad-cow-infected cows, receive a transfusion from an already infected person, ingest a dietary supplement, or receive a vaccine containing ingredients from mad-cow-infected cows. So if you've received a blood transfusion, take a dietary supplement, or been given a vaccine—you may be at some risk because, since 1986, over 200,000 cows are known to have been stricken with mad cow disease.

Now that we have looked at both the nature and the means of transmission of these three food contaminants, let's discuss how you'll know if you're unfortunate enough to become afflicted with one of the diseases attributed to them. Like the symptoms of a number of diseases, some of the symptoms of salmonella, E. coli, and mad cow disease are similar, and some are unique, so listen carefully. Salmonella's symptoms include diarrhea, abdominal cramps, and fever within 8 to 72 hours after eating a contaminated food. Luckily, most people who come down with salmonella recover quickly. However, if you are among the unlucky minority of salmonella victims, you may develop Reiter's syndrome, a disease caused by salmonella acquired through the digestive tract that leads to inflammation throughout the body and could cause you to develop arthritis.

E. coli's symptoms, while akin to salmonella's, also include bloody diarrhea, stomach cramps, nausea, and vomiting. Children are more likely to experience this bacterium's effects. Fortunately, some people who have E. coli never notice any symptoms. So you may have had it, but not know it. However, serious cases can also affect the blood or kidneys.

continued

> **What does the speaker do to add credibility to the information being provided to receivers?**

> **Does the speaker's warning enhance the speech's impact? Do you believe the speaker is exaggerating the dangers receivers face?**

> **Does this transition work?**

> **Is the speaker's description of symptoms vivid enough for you?**

How would you evaluate the speaker's use of research? In your opinion, does the research add to the speaker's credibility?

In contrast to salmonella and E. coli, the symptoms of mad cow disease present themselves differently, with symptoms manifesting themselves in both animals, typically cows, and humans. When afflicted, cows lose weight, become skittish, behave belligerently, appear confused, and may not even be able to walk. You've probably heard the term *downer cow*, referring to a cow that's no longer mobile. When humans come down with mad cow disease, they experience paranoia, suffer from lack of coordination like downer cows, and lapse into a coma.

Now that you are informed about salmonella, E. coli, and mad cow disease, you also have more knowledge of foodborne contaminants. As noted in the July 31, 2008, issue of the *New York Times,* food safety experts like Mike Doyle, director of the Center for Food Safety at the University of Georgia and former FDA official Michael Taylor, now a professor at George Washington University, believe that stronger regulation and a better system for tracking food throughout the food chain will facilitate the traceability of contamination and help segregate any sources of contamination.

Does the speaker effectively summarize the speech? What does the speaker do to give the speech a sense of closure? How else might the speaker have ended the speech?

In conclusion, today we have explored the nature, means of transmission, and symptoms of three increasingly common food contaminants: salmonella, E. coli, and mad cow disease. From the killer tomatoes of a recent salmonella outbreak, to the spinach and fresh vegetables tainted with E. coli, to that juicy hamburger you ate yesterday that might have come from a mad-cow-suffering steer—eating food safely is increasingly becoming a challenge. So study the food pyramid, prepare that well-washed salad, well-done hamburger, or tasty snack, and all the while, think carefully about what you're eating, and the critical links in the food chain, including where the food came from, how it was shipped, whose hands may have touched it, and most important, how it was prepared and may affect you. After all, only time will tell if you become sick from what you eat. Is anyone hungry? How about a salad? (Visual: Hold up salad.)

In your opinion, did the speaker provide you with information that you need and can use? Do you think the speaker sought to provide too much, too little, or just the right amount of information?

WORKS CONSULTED

Allison Aubrey, "Health Officials Track Salmonella, Suspect Tomatoes," *Morning Edition,* June 10, 2008.

Marian Burros, "You Are What You Eat: 2006 and the Politics of Food," *New York Times,* December 27, 2006, p. F2.

Amanda Gardner, "Home-Grown Problems Threaten U.S. Food Safety," *USA Today.*

Melissa Jane Kronfeld and Andy Geller, "Attack of the Killer Tomatoes," *New York Post,* pp. 1, 5.

Paul Krugman, "Bad Cow Disease," *New York Times,* June 13, 2008, p. A29.

Eric Schlosser, "Has Politics Contaminated the Food Supply?" *New York Times,* December 11, 2006, p. A27.

Annys Shin, "Scientists Take on Food Poisoning's Long-Term Effects," *The Record,* September 17, 2008, p. F6.

Bina Venkataraman, "6 More States Report Illnesses from Tomatoes," *New York Times,* June 13, 2008, p. A21.

Bina Venkataraman, "Amid Salmonella Case, Food Industry Seems Set to Back Greater Regulation," *New York Times,* July 31, 2008, accessed at www.nytimes.com/2008/07/31/health/policy/31outbreak.html.

Jane Zhang, "Salmonella May Be Tied to a Death," *Wall Street Journal,* June 13, 2008.

Associated Press, "Taco Bell Removes Scallions Following Outbreak of E. coli," *Wall Street Journal,* December 7, 2006, p. D6.

"Human Mad-Cow Case Confirmed," *Wall Street Journal,* December 7, 2006, p. D6.

"New Test Scans Beef for Mad Cow Disease," *U.S. News & World Report,* health.usnews.com/articles/health/healthday/2008/08/12/new-test-scans-beef-for-mad-cow-disease_print.htm. www.cdc.gov/ncidod/dvrd/bse/.

"MyPyramid.gov access point," U.S. Department of Agriculture.

en.wikipedia.org/wiki/Food_guide_pyramid.

www.about-salmonella.com.

"E. coli Shouldn't Dampen Appetite for Vegetables," *All Things Considered,* September 26, 2006.

Morbidity and Mortality Weekly Report, 2006.

www.aolhealth.com

www.cdc.gov

www.fsis.usda.gov/factsheets/salmonella_questions_&_answers/index.asp

SAMPLE SPEAKER'S NOTES

Topic:	Food contamination
Purpose:	To inform the class about three sources of contamination in the human food chain.
Central idea:	It is important for us to understand the sources of contamination in the human food chain.
Introduction	I. Foods in the food pyramid including tomatoes, peppers, scallions, spinach, and beef are increasingly coming under suspicion.
	II. CDC statistic: 76 million cases of foodborne disease in U.S.
	Story of Sarah Pierce as told by Annys Shin in 9/17/08 Record.
	III. Today I'd like to tell you about the nature, means of transmission and effects of salmonella, E. coli, and mad cow disease.
Body	I. What salmonella, E. coli, and mad cow diseases are.
	U.S. Dept. of Agriculture description of salmonella
	Two types of salmonella—Salmonella enteritidis and Salmonella typhimurium; 1.4 million cases and 500 deaths
	Where it lives
	Refer to Tom Chestnut, Food Safety Expert, NPR, *Morning Edition,* June 10, 2008
	E. coli—O157-H7; 70,000 people made ill
	Michele Norris, Director of Food Safety Program on NPR, *All Things Considered,* September 26, 2006
	Mad cow disease, bovine spongiform encephalopathy—number of cases unknown.
	Dr. Robert Gallo—resilience of prion
	II. Means of transmission
	Salmonella: contaminated food supply
	food handlers
	food preparation

continued

E. coli: feces, food processing
    shipping
    handling
    unknown sources, too
Mad cow: contaminants in feed
    person-to-person transmission

III. Symptoms
    Salmonella—diarrhea, abdominal cramps, fever, Reiter's syndrome
    E. coli—bloody diarrhea, cramps, nausea, vomiting
    Mad cow—downer cows
    lack of coordination

Conclusion

I. Now you have important information about salmonella, E. coli, and mad cow disease; you are also more knowledgeable about foodborne contaminants.

II. Today we have explored the sources, nature of transmission, and symptoms of three kinds of food chain contamination.

III. Reference to killer tomatoes, spinach and fresh vegetables, and beef.

IV. Salad anyone??? (Visual: Food pyramid and a salad bowl with steak.)

THE WRAP-UP

Revisiting Chapter Objectives

1. **Define *informative speaking*.** The goal of the informative speaker is to offer audience members more information than they presently have about a topic. Informative speaking aims to update and add knowledge, refine understanding, or provide background.

2. **Distinguish among four types of informative discourse.** Four kinds of informative speaking with which you need to be familiar are (1) messages of explanation, which explain the what or how-to of a subject; (2) messages of description, which describe what a person, an object, or an event is like; (3) messages of definition, which define what something is; and (4) narrative messages, which tell a story.

3. **Explain how to create information hunger and increase listeners' comprehension.** A primary goal of the informative speech is to increase each listener's need to know and hunger to receive a message. To do this, speakers need to analyze the audience and use appropriate attention-getting devices to generate receiver interest in their topics. At the same time that speakers work to create interest in receivers, they also need to avoid overloading or underloading receivers with information.

4. **Develop and present an informative speech.** Being able to design and deliver an effective informative speech has important implications for both your career and your life. An effective informative speech makes listeners want to learn more about the topic, communicates information clearly, involves audience members, and delivers information in a way that makes the speech memorable.

Resources for Further Inquiry and Reflection

To apply your understanding of how the principles in Chapter 16 are at work in our daily lives, consult the following resources for further inquiry and reflection. Or, if you prefer, choose any other appropriate resource. Then connect the ideas expressed in your chosen selection with the communication concepts and issues you are learning about both in and out of class.

 ### Listen to Me

"You Talk Too Much" (Joe Jones)
"The Wreck of the Edmund Fitzgerald" (Gordon Lightfoot)
"How to Dismantle an Atomic Bomb" (U2)

What lesson(s) can a speaker deduce from the laments of these songs' singers?

 ### View Me

Flight Plan   *Silkwood*
Munich   *The Dark Knight*
All the President's Men   *Religilous*
Erin Brockovich

To what extent did information hunger drive the investigations in each of these films? What did the investigator do to enhance comprehension of his or her discoveries?

 ### Read Me

Peter Morville. *Ambient Findability: What We find Changes Who We Become.* New York: O'Reilly Media, 2005.
Daniel Pink. *A Whole New mind: Moving from the Information Age to the Conceptual Age.* New York: Riverhead Books, 2005.

Can we receive too much information? If yes, what are our options? If no, what steps should we take to facilitate our powers of information processing?

 ### Tell Me

Share with the class the insights you gained from your chosen Listen to Me, View Me, or Read Me selection.

Large quantities of spam with deceptive titles are clogging the information arteries of our computers. Should spam be regulated or censored to keep it out of our e-mail boxes? Should the sender of spam be assessed a fee?

What should we do to keep the information arteries of our mind clear of information clutter? With the voluminous amounts of information being created daily, what guidelines can we use to filter in, not out, what we need to know?

Key Chapter Terminology

Use the Online Learning Center at **www.mhhe.com/gamble10e** to further your knowledge of the following terminology.

information overload 407   informative speech 403
information underload 407

www.mhhe.com/gamble10e

Idioms in Translation

bring topics home — find topics that interest

encyclopedic — voluminous

information balance — the right amount of information

strike a balance — achieve balance

Culture Cue

In the United States an up-and-down nodding of one's head signals agreement. In Asian countries it signals only politeness.

Test Your Understanding

Go to the *Self Quizzes* on the book's Online Learning Center at **www.mhhe.com/gamble10e**.

www.mhhe.com/gamble10e

CHAPTER 17

After finishing this chapter, you should be able to

1. Define *persuasive speaking*.

2. Define and distinguish between *attitudes* and *beliefs*.

3. Distinguish between logical and fallacious reasoning.

4. Explain the concept of credibility.

5. Develop and present a persuasive speech.

Persuasive Speaking

"**V**ote for me," demands the candidate. "Buy me," reads the ad. "Support my cause," cajoles the lobbyist. "Attend my rally," cries out the advocate. "Give money to our movement," pleads the fund raiser. How do you respond? Would you rally to protect freedom of speech on the Internet, or do you support government controls? Do you favor opening our borders to increased numbers of immigrants or closing them? Do you support a woman's right to choose, or are you an advocate of the right-to-life movement? Would you march against the death penalty, or do you believe in capital punishment?

Choice and change characterize our times.[1] With information and knowledge exploding, and multiple alternatives held out to us by persons competing for our attention and support, how we make decisions matters. Do we take shortcuts, or do we make reasoned choices? Do we look for easy answers, or are we skilled at seeing nuance and possibilities others may not notice? And most important, do we want to make a difference in our world (or in our community, our college, or the like)? **Persuasion,** the attempt to change or reinforce attitudes, beliefs, values, or behaviors, permeates our lives. Advertisers, public relations professionals, politicians, religious leaders, and numerous others have the same primary goal—persuading you.

Our aim in this chapter is to increase your ability to prepare, present, and process persuasive speeches by showing you how to apply your general knowledge and skills to this special type of discourse.

Man is the only animal that laughs and weeps; for he is the only animal that is struck with the difference between what things are and what they ought to be.
—William Hazlitt

It is not enough to identify the gene that predetermines the prospect of Alzheimer's disease if we go through the prime of life with a closed mind.
—Tom Brokaw

persuasion
the attempt to change or reinforce attitudes, beliefs, values, or behaviors

SPEAKING PERSUASIVELY

When you deliver a **persuasive speech,** your goal is to modify the thoughts, feelings, or actions of your audience. You hope that your listeners will change attitudes or behaviors you do not approve of and adopt attitudes and behaviors that are compatible with your interests and the way you see the world. Persuasive discourse is becoming increasingly important; more than ever, we are concerned with being able to influence others.[2]

Today's communication environment demands effective persuasion skills. In fact, with the exception of class lectures, a majority of the presentations others direct at you are likely persuasive. So are the majority of presentations you make to others. When was the last time you tried to change someone's mind at home, at school, or at work? Maybe you wanted to be given the opportunity to improve a grade on a paper

persuasive speech
a speech whose primary purpose is to change or reinforce the attitudes, beliefs, values, and/or behaviors of receivers

"I found the old format much more exciting."

and had to develop reasons why your instructor should allow you a "do over." At work, you may have sought to persuade your employer to give you a raise or a more responsible position. Whatever your objective, it is the attitudes, beliefs, and values of the person(s) on the receiving end of your persuasive appeal that you use to frame and support your case. So, whether you are negotiating to buy property, arguing that the jury should acquit your client, working in support of Amnesty International, or making an appeal for any one of thousands of other causes, understanding your receivers enables you to decide how to approach persuasive discourse.

proposition

a statement that summarizes the purpose of a persuasive speech

Online Learning Center

Go to the Online Learning Center at www.mhhe.com/gamble10e and answer the questions in the *Self Inventory* to evaluate your understanding of fallacious reasoning.

PURPOSES OF PERSUASION: THOUGHT AND ACTION

A speaker may believe that flying saucers exist, even though most of the audience may not; oppose bilingual education, while others support it; or want audience members to become organ donors, while audience members feel reluctant to make that commitment. The speaker's objective, sometimes referred to as the **proposition** of the speech, indicates what type of change the speaker would like to create in audience members. Typically, speakers want one or both of two general outcomes: They want to convince listeners that something is so (that is, to change the way audience members think), or they want to cause audience members to take an action (that is, to change the way they behave). Whatever the general nature of the proposition, it most likely will reflect at least one of the following persuasive goals: adoption, discontinuance, deterrence, or continuance.[3]

When your goal is *adoption*, you hope to persuade the audience to accept a new idea, attitude, or belief (for example, that genetically engineered food is hazardous to health), with the hope that in time, that belief will also be supported by action (your listeners will eliminate genetically engineered products from their diet). When your goal is *discontinuance*, you hope to persuade audience members to stop doing something they are now doing (stop drinking alcohol while pregnant, for example). When your goal is *deterrence*, you want to persuade the audience to avoid an activity or a way of thinking (for example, "If you believe that every woman has the right to exercise control over her own body, don't vote for candidates who would make abortions illegal."). Finally, if your goal is the *continuance* of a way of believing or acting, you want to encourage people to continue to think or behave as they now do (for instance, keep limiting our sun exposure).

Adoption and discontinuance goals involve asking listeners to alter their way of thinking or behaving, whereas deterrence and continuance goals involve asking them not to alter the way they think or behave but, rather, to reinforce or sustain it. In general, persuaders find it easier to accomplish deterrence and continuance objectives. That does not mean, however, that accomplishing adoption or discontinuance goals is impossible. They may be more difficult to achieve, but if the speaker uses a variety of appeals and a sound organizational scheme and has credibility, these goals can also be realized.

> How many attempts at persuading others have you made during the past 24 hours? Who do you think engages in more persuasive efforts, men or women?

> Many theorists contend that, to persuade audience members to act differently, you must first persuade them to think differently. Do you agree?

TYPES OF PERSUASIVE SPEECHES

Persuasive speeches focus on questions of fact, value, or policy. Selecting which kind of speech to present is among the first tasks you need to complete. By choosing one type over the others, the speaker formally decides to speak on what is or what is not (**proposition of fact**), how good or bad something is (**proposition of value**), or what ought to be (**proposition of policy**).

proposition of fact
a persuasive speech with the goal of settling what is or is not so

proposition of value
a persuasive speech that espouses the worth of an idea, a person, or an object

proposition of policy
a persuasive speech on what ought to be

Propositions of Fact

The following are sample propositions of fact:

> DNA is the ultimate fingerprint.
> High-fiber diets prevent cancer.
> Internet use decreases interpersonal skills.
> The United States is addicted to oil.
> The federal deficit is a threat to our economic security.
> Natalee Holloway was murdered in Aruba.

The last example was a proposition of fact that consumed the attention of commentators on a number of 24-hour news channels, such as Fox News and MSNBC. Various "experts" appeared on network programs in the effort to convince viewers of the persuasiveness of their evidence.

Good propositions of fact cannot be resolved with just a yes or a no answer. Instead, they are open to debate, and settling them typically requires close examination and careful interpretation of evidence, usually from a number of documents or sources. When speaking on a proposition of fact, the speaker must provide enough evidence to convince receivers of the factual nature of the statement.

Work It Out
Brainstorm topics for speeches that have goals focusing on the adoption, discontinuance, deterrence, or continuance of something. After the brainstorming sessions, develop propositions of fact, value, or policy for each topic.

Propositions of Value

The following are examples of propositions of value:

Same-sex high schools are better than co-ed high schools.

Sex education belongs in school.

Using persons in developing nations as guinea pigs for drug testing is unethical.

The use of chemical weapons is immoral.

Grade inflation decreases the value of a college education.

Finding alternative sources of fuel is a worthwhile endeavor.

Propositions of value explore the worth of an idea, a person, or an object. Like questions of fact, they require more than a simple answer, or in this case, a true or false response. When speaking on a proposition of value, the speaker must convince receivers that the evaluation contained in the proposition is valid. This usually requires that the speaker also explore one or more propositions of fact. For example, you probably will not be effective advocating for the premise that fetal tissue research is morally justifiable until you establish that such research is necessary.

Propositions of Policy

The following are sample propositions of policy:

Gay and lesbian partners should be permitted to marry.

Embryonic stem cell research should receive the full support of the federal government.

Colleges should limit financial support for athletes.

The United States should encourage investment in alternative fuel sources.

Consumers should boycott companies that use child labor to manufacture products.

The U.S. government should repudiate torture as a means to fight terrorism.

Assisted suicide should be legal.

When speaking on a proposition of policy, the speaker goes beyond questions of fact or value. Instead, the speaker must demonstrate a need for the policy and earn audience approval or support for the policy in question. When you ask audience members to support a proposition of policy, you ask them to support a course of action. Such a request often needs to be supported with statements of fact and value as well

In conclusion, if given the option, we may approach a topic by speaking on a proposition of fact, value, or policy. For example, let's say we selected as our topic the effects of corporate influence on U.S. foreign policy. Our three options might read as follows:

Proposition of fact: Corporations influence U.S. foreign policy positively and negatively.

Proposition of value: It is wrong for corporations to influence U.S. foreign policy.

Proposition of policy: Write your representatives and express your displeasure regarding corporate influence over U.S. foreign policy.

PERSUADING STRATEGICALLY

What makes one person more persuasive than another person? Countless books and articles address this question. However, over 2,000 years ago, the Greek philosopher Aristotle first identified three tools that contemporary theorists still believe persuaders use to achieve goals: ethos, logos, and pathos.

Ethos is the audience's judgment of the speaker's character or credibility. The more credible your audience believes you to be, the greater your chances of having them accept you as a source and your message as true. **Logos** is logical proof. The more effective your proof—the more reasonable your arguments and the more convincing your reasons—the greater the chances your message will make rational sense to receivers and the more likely they are to accept it. **Pathos** is emotional proof. Pathos develops empathy and passion in receivers, touching them by arousing their feelings, often through the use of expressive and emotional language and the telling of stories high in human interest. Such stories may contain testimony; recount suffering; arouse fear, anger, or compassion; or use humor. When moved by pathos, audiences are more likely to agree with your message because they believe what you are sharing could also affect them or a loved one personally.

We will refer to these tools as we talk about what it means to persuade responsibly, effectively, and ethically.

ethos
audience's judgment of speaker's character or credibility

logos
logical proof

pathos
emotional proof

> **Who do you think would be most receptive to speakers that rely primarily on logos for their persuasiveness, men or women? Who do you think would be most receptive to speakers who rely on pathos, a native of the United States, a native of Saudi Arabia, or a person from Asia? Who would find the ethos of a speaker to be most significant in evaluating a persuasive effort, a child or an adult? Why?**

PERSUADING RESPONSIBLY

Whenever we try to cause others to change their beliefs, attitudes, or behaviors, or whenever others try to influence us, we are participating in the persuasive process.[4] Understanding what persuasion *is not* will enable us to use it responsibly.

Persuasion Is Not Coercion

Imagine this: Someone puts a gun to your head and says, "Your money or your life." Such a person is acting illegally and coercively. You follow the individual's demands only because you fear for your life. Persuasion is different. When someone is successful at persuading you to do or believe what she or he asks, you choose to think or act differently because you *want to* not because you think you *have to*.

Persuasion Is Not Manipulation

When someone manipulates you to do or believe something, he or she usually uses unethical means to take advantage of you so that you do what is in *his or her* but not necessarily *your* best interest. Ethical persuasion is honest and in the best interests of receivers. Its success does not depend on spreading false or misleading information. For example, one politician used deception to convince voters of his honesty by re-editing newspaper articles written about him so that receivers were manipulated into processing the information he presented about himself favorably, when in fact it was highly unfavorable.[5] When this unethical act was uncovered, it cast a cloud over the candidate.

GUIDELINES FOR PERSUADING EFFECTIVELY

Persuasion usually occurs in steps. Audience members do not usually surrender current ways of thinking and behaving easily or all at once. However, if you offer convincing arguments, solid evidence, and a clear message in persuasive messages that you plan incrementally and deliver over time, receivers may gradually alter their positions.

Your persuasive goal needs to be based on an accurate analysis of the current beliefs and attitudes of receivers. For example, if your goal is to convince members of the National Rifle Association (NRA) that the nation's gun-control laws need overhauling, rather than advocating against the sale of all guns to the public, you might start your persuasive campaign by working to convince receivers that there are some problems with existing gun laws. Simply reducing the strength of their current stance on gun control would be a step forward that repeated persuasive efforts could then build on. Let's examine what you can do to increase your persuasiveness as a speaker.

Identify Your Goal

Acting on a good idea is better than just having a good idea.
—Robert Half

To be a successful persuader, you must have a clearly defined purpose. You must, in fact, be able to answer these questions:

> What response do I want from audience members?
> Would I like them to think differently, act differently, or both?
> Which of their attitudes or beliefs am I trying to alter? Why?

Unless you know what you want your listeners to think, feel, or do, you will not be able to realize your objective.

Know the Receivers You Are Trying to Reach

How do audience members feel about your proposal? Do they favor the change? How important is it to them? What is at stake? The more ego-involved the members of your audience are, the more committed they will be to their current position; hence, the harder it will be for you to reach them.[6] The information here builds on Chapter 12 (the second rung on the ladder).

Understand the Factors Affecting Your Listeners' Attitudes

attitudes
predispositions to respond favorably or unfavorably toward a person or subject

To be able to influence others, you need to understand the favorable and unfavorable mental sets, or predispositions, that audience members bring to a speech; that is, you need to understand **attitudes**—how they are formed, how they are sustained, and how they may be changed by you. The following forces or factors are among the most important influences on our attitudes.

If you say it enough, even if it ain't true, folks will get to believing it.
—Will Rogers

Family

Few of us escape the strong influence exerted by our families. Many of our parents' attitudes are communicated to us and are eventually acquired by us. "It is the family that bends the tender twig in the direction it is likely to grow."[7]

Religion

Not only believers but also nonbelievers are affected by religion. In fact, the impact of religion is increasing as religious organizations strive to generate and guide attitudes on politics and such social issues as abortion, civil rights, the death penalty, child abuse, and divorce.

Education

More people than ever are attending school; they start young (sometimes before the age of 5), and many attend until they are in or beyond their twenties. Moreover, the traditional role of the school has expanded, since large numbers of adults are now returning to complete their education. The courses taught, the instructors who teach them, the books assigned, and the films shown all help shape attitudes.

Socioeconomics

Economic status and social status also shape our attitudes. Our economic status helps determine the social arena we frequent. Our view of the world is likewise affected by the company we keep and the amount of money we have.

Culture

As seventeenth-century poet John Donne wrote, "No man is an island, entire of itself." From the crib to the coffin, we are influenced by others—in person and through the media. The groups we belong to, our friends, and the fabric of the society in which we find ourselves all help mold us. We shape our social institutions and are reciprocally shaped by them.

Understand Your Listeners' Beliefs

Your persuasive effectiveness will improve if you understand not only your listeners' attitudes but also their beliefs—and if you understand how audiences might respond when their important beliefs are challenged.[8]

Attitudes and beliefs are, of course, related—in fact, the two terms are sometimes used interchangeably—but they are not the same thing. Attitudes and beliefs are related to each other as buildings are related to bricks, beams, boards, and so on. That is, in a sense, **beliefs** are the building blocks of attitudes. Whereas we measure attitudes on a favorable–unfavorable scale, we measure beliefs on a probable–improbable scale. Thus, if you say that you think something is true, you are really saying that you believe it. According to psychologist Milton Rokeach, your belief system is made up of everything you agree is true. Your disbelief system, which is composed of all the things you do not think are true, develops along with your belief system. Together, the two significantly affect the way you process information.[9]

The more central or important a belief is, the harder audience members will work to defend it, the less willing they will be to change it, and the more resistant they will be to your persuasive efforts.

Use Two Principles of Influence: Consistency and Social Proof

When you are speaking persuasively, you should be aware of two significant principles. First, we all have a desire to be consistent with what we have already done.

> Which of the factors affecting attitude development are most influential in your own life? Why?

> How do you react when someone questions your position on what you consider a critical issue? Why?

beliefs
confidence in the truth of something

Work It Out

Work in groups to develop one list of statements you believe are true and another list of statements you believe are false. Identify what a speaker would need to do to persuade you to move a statement from the belief ("true") list to the disbelief ("false") list and vice versa.

consistency

the desire to maintain balance in our lives by behaving according to commitments already formed

social proof

the determination of what is right by finding out what other people think is right

In other words, once we take a stand, consistency theory tells us that our tendency is to behave consistently with that commitment.[10] Therefore, it is important to determine how your speech can engage this tendency toward **consistency.** If you can find a way to get audience members to make a commitment (to take a stand or go on record), you will have set the stage for them to behave in ways consistent with that stand.

Second, we all respond to **social proof.** That is, one method we use to determine what is right is to find out what other people think is right.[11] You can use the actions of others to convince your listeners that what you are advocating is right. As motivation consultant Cavett Robert notes: "Since 95 percent of the people are imitators and only 5 percent initiators, people are persuaded more by the action of others than by any proof we can offer."[12]

Reason Logically

Rational or logical proof (logos) includes arguments, reasoning, and evidence that add substance to a claim. Evidence is quotations or testimony from authoritative sources, conclusions from relevant studies and reports (sometimes presented in the form of statistics), and examples and illustrations in support of a proposition. You increase your chances of persuading others if you offer logical reasons why they should support what you advocate.

Talk show hosts are known for taking a social or political issue and turning it into an argument with a guest. Although such transformations may entertain us, when we analyze them critically, the arguments made are often illogical and lack sound principles of reasoning.

Effective persuaders reason with the audience, presenting evidence and arguments to help receivers move closer to their point of view. In his book *The Uses of Argument*, Stephen Toulmin identified the elements of a persuasive argument:

claim

debatable conclusion or assertion

reasons

facts or evidence for making the claim

warrant

explanation of the relationship between the claim and the data

backing

support that answers concerns of others

qualifier

indication of the strength of the connection

rebuttal

potential counterarguments

1. A **claim,** a debatable conclusion or assertion, the proposition or thesis you hope to prove and want receivers to accept (for example, "The Electoral College should be abolished.").

2. Data or good **reasons,** facts and evidence for making the claim (for example, "The Electoral College should be abolished because it makes it possible for a candidate for president of the United States to lose the popular vote but win the Electoral College vote and become president.").

3. A **warrant,** a logical and persuasive relationship that explains how you get to your claim from the data you offer (for example, "Democracy depends on all the people having their votes count rather than allowing the influence of small states to count more than the voices of a majority of the voters."). The purpose of the warrant is to legitimize the claim, making it more persuasive.

4. The **backing,** support that gives the warrant more strength by answering other questions of concern.

5. The **qualifier,** an indication of the strength of the connection between the data and the warrant, usually containing words such as *most, sometimes,* or *always.*

6. **Rebuttal,** potential counterarguments, sometimes offered during the presentation of the initial argument.

In diagram form, the Toulmin model looks like this:

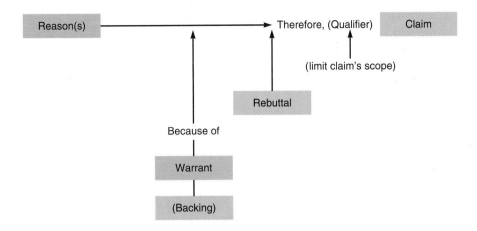

Thus, if you state your claim clearly and qualify it by limiting its applicability so that it is not overly broad, support it with reasons, and connect it to the evidence you offer via the warrant, you improve your chances of persuading the audience to accept your claim. By anticipating opposing arguments and preparing counterarguments that rebut them, you increase your chances of success. The most common forms of logical reasoning are deduction, induction, causal reasoning, and reasoning from analogy.

Deduction

When we reason deductively, we move from the general to the specific. When using **deduction,** you present a major premise (a generalization) and a minor premise (a specific instance) that leads you to deduce a conclusion. The argument you make looks like this:

> *Major premise:* People who study regularly instead of cramming usually get better grades.
>
> *Minor premise:* You want to get better grades.
>
> *Conclusion:* Therefore, you should study regularly instead of cramming.

deduction

reasoning that moves from the general to the specific

Wrong premises lead to faulty conclusions. For example:

> All protestors are liberal.
> James Dobson is a protestor.
> James Dobson is a liberal.

If you choose to use deductive reasoning in support of your ideas, be sure your premises are true and defensible.

You can evaluate deductive reasoning by asking the following two questions:

1. Are the major premise and the minor premise (or minor premises) true?
2. Does the conclusion follow logically from the premises?

Be sure to give the necessary evidence to buttress your major and minor premises.

Induction

When we reason inductively, we move from specific evidence to a general conclusion. Because we cannot examine the whole, we *sample* it by examining a number

induction

reasoning that moves from specific evidence to a general conclusion

of specific instances and then drawing a generalization about them. The following is an example of **induction;** it moves from the specific to the general—from a series of facts to a conclusion:

> *Fact:* One of every three children violates the "no drinking before the age of 21" law by the age of 12.
>
> *Fact:* Businesses benefit from violations of the "no drinking before the age of 21" law.
>
> *Fact:* Parents commonly violate the "no drinking before the age of 21" law.
>
> *Conclusion:* The "no drinking before the age of 21" law is disregarded widely in our society.

Whenever speakers use what is true in particular cases to draw a general conclusion, they are reasoning by induction.

You can evaluate inductive reasoning by asking the following two questions:

1. Is the sample of specific instances large enough to justify the conclusion drawn from them?
2. Are the instances cited representative, or typical, ones?

Causal Reasoning

causal reasoning

speculation about the reasons for and effects of occurrences

When we reason from causes and effects, we either cite observed causes and hypothesize effects or cite observed effects and hypothesize causes. We use **causal reasoning** every day. Something happens, and we ask ourselves, Why? Similarly, we speculate about the consequences of certain acts; that is, we wonder about what effects they have. The following statements illustrate causal reasoning:

> The stereotype of the successful minority hurts Asian Americans.
>
> Focusing on *average* Asian Americans and their success stories hurts Asian Americans.
>
> The fact that many organizations no longer consider Asians a disadvantaged minority hurts Asian Americans.
>
> The problems faced by the majority of Asian Americans are not being taken seriously enough.

To evaluate the soundness of causal reasoning, ask the following questions:

1. Is the presumed cause real or false?
2. Is the presumed cause an oversimplification?

Reasoning from Analogy

To convince his audience of what was wrong with our political environment, one speaker quoted this analogy, saying:

> John Tierney, a political columnist, made the following observation in a column he wrote that appeared in the *New York Times* on February 4, 2006: "Take a good look during the Super Bowl at the Steeler fans with their Terrible Towels. Imagine what's happening inside their minds as they wave the gold rags. This is your brain on partisan politics."[13]

reasoning from analogy

reasoning by comparison

When we use **reasoning from analogy,** we compare like things and conclude that since they are alike in a number of respects, they are also alike in some respect that until this point has not been examined. For example, if you wanted to argue that the methods used to decrease the high school dropout rate in a nearby city would also work in your city, you would first have to establish that your city is similar to the other city in a number of important ways—number of young people, number of schools, skill of personnel, financial resources, and so on. If you said that the two cities were alike except that your city had not instituted such a program, and that its dropout rate was therefore significantly higher, you would be arguing by analogy.

To check the validity of analogical reasoning, ask the following questions:

1. Are the two things being compared alike in essential respects? That is, do the points of similarity outweigh the points of difference?

2. Do the differences that do exist matter?

When you reason logically, you not only back up your persuasive arguments with solid evidence, but also cite your sources carefully. When quoting or using a source, share the source's credentials with audience members, as did the student who quoted from the John Tierney op-ed piece. Careful citation is critical to the development of well-reasoned arguments.

Reason Ethically

Ethical speakers do not employ logical fallacies. A fallacy is an error in logic; it is flawed reasoning. When a speaker attempts to persuade using flawed reasoning, in addition to misusing the reasoning process, he or she is also abusing the persuasion process. The following are among the most common fallacies that speakers should avoid. (Other logical fallacies are noted in Ethics and Communication, "Illogical Reasoning.")

Argumentum Ad Hominem

When you present your audience with an **argumentum ad hominem,** you inject name-calling into your speech. It is literally an "argument against the man" (or

argumentum ad hominem
the use of name-calling in an argument

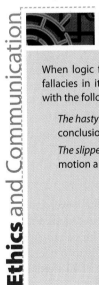

Ethics and Communication

Illogical Reasoning

When logic fails, speakers sometimes substitute logical fallacies in its place. Speakers may flaw their speeches with the following additional reasoning fallacies:

The hasty generalization: being too quick to jump to a conclusion

The slippery slope: asserting that one action will set in motion a chain reaction

The appeal to tradition: telling receivers that things have always been done a certain way

Using the Internet, books of published speeches, or issues of *Vital Speeches of the Day,* locate examples of fallacious reasoning. Explain why you believe the logic is flawed in each example.

woman). You appeal to receivers to reject an idea because of a flaw in a person associated with that idea. You attack a person's character instead of his or her stand on an issue. "She's just a left-wing liberal" and "He's just a member of the radical right" focus attention on the person and not his or her ideas.

Red Herring

red herring
a distraction used to lead the receiver to focus on an irrelevant issue

The term **red herring** derives its meaning from an act performed during English fox hunts, in which hunt masters would drag red herrings across trails in an effort to divert the hunting dogs from chasing the foxes. When you use a red herring in your speech, your goal is to send the audience on a wild goose chase. By causing receivers to focus on one or more irrelevant issues, you prevent them from considering the issue under discussion. For example, in an effort to negate the right of women to have abortions, one speaker attempted to deflect the focus of receivers by concentrating instead on the cost of health insurance.

False Division

false division
the polarization of options, when, in fact, many options exist

When you use a **false division** in your speech (a false dichotomy, dilemma, or either-or argument), you require audience members to choose between two options, usually polar opposites, when in reality there are many options in between. The following are examples of the false division at work: "If you believe in flag burning, you don't believe in the country." "If you don't like the policies of the United States, go back to your native country." "If you are not part of the solution, then you are part of the problem." "Either we eliminate gun control, or only outlaws will have guns."

post hoc, ergo propter hoc
the identification of a false cause

Post Hoc, Ergo Propter Hoc (False Cause)

argumentum ad populum
a bandwagon appeal; an appeal to popular opinion

argumentum ad verecudiam
an appeal to authority

When your argument is based on the assumption of **post hoc, ergo propter hoc,** you identify a false cause; that is, you lead your receivers to assume mistakenly that one event causes another merely because they occur sequentially. For example, one speaker pointed out that a decrease in abortions in the United States began about the same time as increased opportunities in sports for women. While a causal link may exist, the speaker has to supply evidence to establish a definitive link between the two phenomena. Correlation is not causation.

Argumentum Ad Populum (Bandwagon Appeal)

An **argumentum ad populum** is a bandwagon appeal—that is, an appeal to popular opinion. The speaker who uses such a fallacy tells receivers that, because "everyone is doing or supporting it," they should, too. Widespread acceptance of an idea, however, does not mean the idea is sound. Rather than rush to judgment based on what everyone else is saying or doing, you should consider the facts carefully and decide for yourself.

Argumentum Ad Verecudiam (Appeal to Authority)

When you inject an **argumentum ad verecudiam** fallacy into your speech, you use the testimony of someone who is not an expert on your subject and does not possess the credentials that would permit him or her to make a claim or an endorsement. Name recognition and expertise are not synonymous. For instance, while Coldplay may be well-known performers and experts on music, when it comes to talking about U.S. foreign policy, their value as a source decreases.

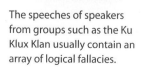

The speeches of speakers from groups such as the Ku Klux Klan usually contain an array of logical fallacies.

Gain Your Listeners' Attention

Before you can persuade or convince other people, you must first get their attention. In his book *The Art of Persuasion*, Wayne Minnick relates how a 9-year-old girl succeeded in getting the undivided attention of a male guest at her party. It seems that all the boys had gathered at one end of the room, talking to each other and ignoring the girls. "But I got one of them to pay attention to me, all right," the little girl assured her mother. "How?" inquired the mother. "I knocked him down!" was the undaunted reply.[14]

You should not knock down your listeners to get their attention, but you will need to find ways to encourage them to listen to you. It is your responsibility to put them into a receptive frame of mind. You can do this in several ways. You can compliment your listeners. You can question them. You can relate your message directly to their interests, or you can surprise them by relating to them in an unexpected way. Once you have the attention of your listeners, you must continue to work to hold it.

Make Your Listeners Feel as Well as Think

Appeals to emotion (pathos) add to a speech's impact. Following is an excerpt from a student's speech on the issue of Palestinians jailed without trial in Israel. In it, the student quotes from a letter written by a Palestinian prisoner to an Israeli officer who was sentenced to jail himself for refusing to serve as a jailer for the political detainees because of his belief that the practice of administrative detentions was wrong. Why do you think that the use of this passage in the student's speech is effective?

> Who are you, officer?
>
> I want to write to you, but first I have to know who you are. I have to know the reasons that moved you to act as you did. I have to know how you arrived at this principled decision of conscience; how you chose such a unique rebellion, so unexpected.
>
> What's your name? Where do you live? What do you do? How old are you? Do you have children? Do you like the sea? What books do you read? And what are you doing now in the cell where you are held? Do you have enough cigarettes? Is there someone who identifies with you over there? Do you ask yourself, "Was it worth paying the price?"
>
> Can you see the moon and stars from the cell window? Have your ears grown accustomed to the jangle of the heavy keys, to the creak of the locks, to the clang of the metal doors? . . . Do you see in your sleep fields of wheat and kernels moving in the wind? Do you see expanses of sunflowers, and are your eyes filled with yellow, green and black hues, and the sun tans you, and you smile in your sleep, and the walls of the cell tumble and fall, and an unknown person waves his hand to you from afar? . . .
>
> Don't you have regrets? Didn't you have doubts when they told you: "They're dangerous; they belong to Hamas, to Islamic Jihad and the Popular Front? Don't you trust our security services? Do you really believe that we are ready to throw innocent people in jail?"
>
> Why do I feel as if I know you? . . .
>
> Anonymous lieutenant, whatever your name is, sleep well; sleep the peaceful slumber of someone whose conscience is clear.

Many changes in human behavior have resulted from messages that combined emotional appeals with rational reasons. Since few people will change their attitudes or take action if they are unmoved or bored, effective speakers develop emotional appeals that are designed to make listeners feel.[15] Whether the feeling evoked is

To what extent must friends, co-workers, politicians, and advertisers compete to get your attention? Which strategies are the most effective? Why?

Effective speakers develop emotional appeals designed to make audience members feel.

Is it reasonable for speakers to cause receivers to experience dissonance to get them to believe something or do something? Is causing receivers to feel at risk, insecure, or vulnerable by manufacturing dissonance unethical? What if the speaker exaggerates the risk receivers face just to accomplish a goal? What if the risk is not really there at all?

balance

a state of psychological comfort in which one's actions, feelings, and beliefs are related to each other as one would like them to be

Maslow's hierarchy of needs

a model that depicts motivation as a pyramid with the most basic needs at the base and the most sophisticated at the apex

sadness, anger, fear, sympathy, happiness, greed, nostalgia, jealousy, pride, or guilt depends on the speaker's topic and the response desired.

As a speaker, you must appeal not just to your listeners' heads but also to their hearts. Thus, although your speech should be grounded in a firm foundation of logic and fact, it should also be built on feelings.

Evoke Relevant Needs and Issues

Balance is a state of psychological health or comfort in which our actions, feelings, and beliefs are related to each other as we would like them to be. When we are in a balanced state, we are content or satisfied. Thus, we engage in a continual struggle to keep ourselves in balance. What does this imply for you as a persuasive speaker? If you want to convince your listeners to change their attitudes or beliefs, you must first demonstrate to them that a current situation or state of affairs has created an imbalance in their lives and that you can help restore their balance. The simple introduction of imbalance, or dissonance (whether that imbalance, or dissonance, is experienced by receivers for real or created vicariously by the speaker) motivates change in receiver thinking or behaving. Thus, speakers may deliberately create dissonance in receivers and then suggest what receivers need to think or do in order to be able to alleviate their dissonance and restore their sense of balance. It is our inner drive for balance that helps explain our positive responses to an array of persuasive appeals.

Remember that human behavior depends on motivation. If you are to persuade people to believe and do what you would like them to do, you must make your message appeal to their needs and goals.

One popular device used to analyze human motivation is a schematic framework devised by the famous psychologist Abraham Maslow.[16] In **Maslow's hierarchy of needs,** motivation is seen as a pyramid, with our most basic needs at its base and our most sophisticated needs at its apex (see Figure 17.1). Maslow defined survival (physiological) needs as the basic necessities of life: shelter, food, water, and procreation. Safety needs include the need for security and the need to know that our survival requirements will be satisfied. At the third level are love and belonging

FIGURE 17.1

Maslow's Hierarchy of Needs.

From Abraham Maslow, *Toward a Psychology of Being.* Copyright © 1962. Reprinted by permission of John Wiley & Sons, Inc.

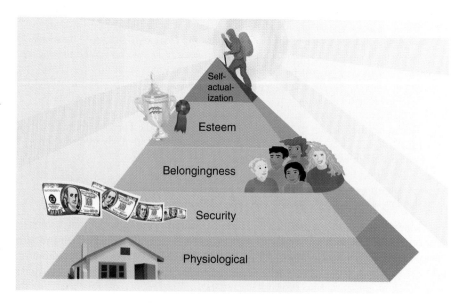

Climbing the Motivation Pyramid

For each of the following situations, identify the types of appeals you could use to persuade audience members to believe or behave as you would like them to. First, consider the nature of the particular audience. Second, aim a part of your persuasive effort at each level of Maslow's hierarchy pyramid. For each audience, which level and which appeal do you think would be most effective? Explain your reasons.

1. You want to persuade high school seniors not to drink and drive.

2. You want to convince college students to use debit, not credit, cards.

3. You want to persuade the members of your hometown to donate blood.

4. You want to convince veterans not to support an amendment making burning the flag unconstitutional.

5. You want to convince voters to support the passing of a law prohibiting former members of Congress or the president's cabinet from becoming lobbyists.

needs. Once these are met, our esteem needs can be addressed. Esteem needs include self-respect and the respect of others. Our efforts to succeed are often attempts to satisfy our esteem needs, because success tends to attract respect and attention. At the peak of Maslow's hierarchy is the need for self-actualization. When we satisfy this, we have realized our potential; that is, we have become everything we are capable of becoming.

How does Maslow's hierarchy relate to you as a persuasive speaker? Find out by trying the Skill Builder "Climbing the Motivation Pyramid" above. Remember that salient needs make salient motives. Your goal is to make your receivers identify your proposal with their needs. Whenever you attempt to do this, you will probably have to involve personal feelings.

Promise a Reward

When you are speaking persuasively, demonstrate how your listeners' personal needs can be satisfied by your proposal. You should stress how your ideas can benefit the people you are trying to persuade. Make them believe that your proposal will supply a reward.

Remember, however, that different audiences value different types of rewards. For practice, think of three different types of audiences and identify the most important needs of each. Imagine that you are a salesperson trying to persuade each of those audiences to buy one of the following items: (1) guitar, (2) plant, (3) dog, (4) hat, (5) attaché case. Describe the strategies you would use with each group. What adaptations would you make? To what extent would you display your awareness of individual differences?

It is important to remember that people are usually preoccupied with how something will benefit them personally. Your listeners, whoever they are, will want something in return for behaving as you would like them to behave.

> What are your own most important needs? How might someone use this information to persuade you to buy one of the items listed in the text?

MONROE'S MOTIVATED SEQUENCE: A FRAMEWORK FOR PERSUASIVE SPEAKING

One organizational framework that persuasive speakers have found particularly effective in motivating receivers to respond positively to their purpose is **Monroe's motivated sequence.**[17] Based on the psychology of persuasion, Monroe's framework

Monroe's motivated sequence
a speech framework composed of five phases—attention, need, satisfaction, visualization, and action

is composed of five phases, which sequentially move receivers toward accepting and acting on a speaker's proposition. Its persuasive structure especially meets the needs of speakers who desire to move audience members to action.

Phase One: Attention. At the outset of a speech, the speaker's primary task is to gain the audience's attention. (In effect, you say, "Pay attention." Perhaps you enhance receivers' interest by asking a question, referring to their experiences, using an illustration or a dramatic story, supplying startling statistics, or providing an eye-catching visual. As a result of what you say or do, your audience members should realize why your message is important to them and why they should listen to what you have to say.)

Phase Two: Need. The speaker demonstrates for receivers that the present situation poses serious problems. He or she explicitly states the need and illustrates it with a variety of supporting materials. By revealing what is wrong to receivers and relating the need to their interests and desires, the speaker prepares them for the problem's solution. (In this stage, you say, "This is wrong, and here is what we need to do about it." In addition to identifying the problem or need, you illustrate it with specific examples. In addition, you support the need's existence with illustrations, statistics, testimony, or other forms of support. Your objective is to show how the identified need has an impact on the lives of audience members and how it affects their personal or professional goals, health, happiness, and/or financial security, for example.)

Phase Three: Satisfaction. Having shown the audience members that a need exists, the speaker's next task is to satisfy their desire for a solution. (Here, you tell receivers, "I have a way to solve the problem." You present your plan, explain it fully to receivers, and help them recognize that solving the problem will satisfy their interests and desires. By using examples and illustrations to flesh out what you want audience members to believe or do, and explaining why you are asking them to believe or do this, you help them understand how they can satisfy the need you described previously.)

Phase Four: Visualization. The speaker visualizes the plan's benefits for receivers, describing how things will improve when the plan is put into action. (In this phase, you say, "This is how my plan will meet your needs, alleviate the problems you face, and help make things better." You demonstrate the benefits audience members will receive once they act upon your ideas; if desired, you also explore the negative effects receivers will suffer if they fail to act on your plan.)

Phase Five: Action. The speaker's next task is to move receivers in a particular direction by telling them what they should do to ensure that the need is satisfied. In effect, the speaker asks receivers to support the policy and act on it. (In this phase, you say, "Here's what I would like you to do." You conclude with an appeal that reinforces their commitment to putting your solution to work. You are telling them to act.)

The following outline illustrates how the motivational sequence can be used to design a presentation advocating that we should not drive when drowsy.

Focus on Service Learning

Using information found on sites such as www.speech-topics-help.com/motivational-speech-topics.html and www.bluegrass.kctcs.edu/LCC/communications/monroespeecheval.doc, write a persuasive speech that supports the fund-raising efforts of your college or a local charity.

Introduction (Attention)	I. It was after midnight when six students walking to a fraternity party were killed when Brandon Kallmeyer fell asleep at the wheel of the pickup truck he was driving, veered off the road, and hit them. II. Over 100,000 accidents occur every year because drivers fall asleep at the wheel. III. The problem of people driving while drowsy is increasing. IV. Today I would like to explore why it is important to us to examine this problem, why it continues to escalate, and what steps we can take to help alleviate it.

Body
 	
(Need)
	I. We have put sleep on the back burner.
	  A. Everyone needs approximately eight hours of sleep a day to function effectively the next day, but we average only about six hours of sleep a day.
	  B. The most important sleep hour is the REM stage, which occurs between the seventh and eighth hour.
	II. Sleep-deprived persons pose serious dangers on the road.
	  A. Highway patrol officers report stopping motorists who appear drunk, only to discover they are fatigued.
	  B. Drowsy driving is approaching a national epidemic.
	III. The drowsy driving problem can be alleviated once we fully understand its causes.

(Satisfaction)	A. We are poor judges of our own sleeplessness.
	  B. Alcohol consumption contributes to becoming sleepy behind the wheel.
	  C. Boredom is a contributing factor to becoming tired.
	IV. Tragedy can be prevented if we take the proper steps.

(Visualization)	A. Imagine what would happen if the Federal Highway Administration added more rumble strips designed to wake us up when we began to veer off the road. B. Imagine what would happen if cars were equipped with Auto-Vue cameras that emit rumble strip–like sounds when a driver drifts out of a lane. V. There are some steps we can take personally to protect ourselves.
(Action)	A. We can take naps to fight fatigue. B. We can sleep the recommended seven to eight hours a night.
Conclusion	I. Six innocent students were killed because someone didn't take action to avoid the tragedy. II. It is time to get the sleep that could save our lives and the lives of others.[18]

BECOMING A MORE CREDIBLE PERSUADER

According to attorney Gerry Spence, your success as a persuader will be determined in part by what your "targets" think of you—in other words, by your **credibility** (ethos).[19]

When we use the term *credibility*, we are talking not about what you are really like but about how an audience perceives you. If your listeners accept you as

credibility
the receiver's assessment of the competence, trustworthiness, and dynamism of a speaker

For some groups of people, the Dalai Lama is considered a highly credible speaker.

credible, they probably believe that you are a person of good character (trustworthy and fair) and are knowledgeable (trained, competent to discuss your topic, and reliable as a source of information) and personable (dynamic, charismatic, active, and energetic). As a result, your ideas are more likely to get a fair hearing. However, if your listeners believe that you are untrustworthy, incompetent (not sufficiently knowledgeable about your topic), and passive (lacking in dynamism), they are less likely to respond as you desire.

It is entirely possible—even probable—that your listeners may consider you more credible about some topics than others. For example, the following are two pairs of imaginary statements. Which statement in each pair would you be more inclined to accept?

The United States must never negotiate with terrorists. Strength is the only language they will understand.

—Condoleezza Rice

The United States must never negotiate with terrorists. Strength is the only language they will understand.

—Madonna

****

The world of contemporary music has room in it for everyone. The message music sends is tolerance.

—Bono

The world of contemporary music has room in it for everyone. The message music sends is tolerance.

—Hillary Rodham Clinton

Exploring Diversity

Persuasion and Assumed Similarity

LaRay M. Barna, an intercultural communication theorist, points out that we are all influenced by our cultural upbringing, and, while we tend to assume that other people's needs, desires, and basic assumptions are the same as our own, often they are not. How can assumed similarity—the belief that we all have similar thoughts, feelings, attitudes, and nonverbal codes—cause problems for persuasive speakers? For example, while Americans tend to value materialism, success, and rationality, Arabs are more likely to value self-respect, courage, and honor. Arabs also value storytelling, eloquence, and the ability of words to spark emotional responses in others. To this end, they use emphatic assertions to convey their seriousness. When such assertions are missing, others may assume that an Arab speaker means the opposite of what was said.[20]

On the basis of this realization, is it more beneficial for a persuasive speaker to assume *differences* rather than similarity? Explain.

What should the speaker do if members of the audience come from a variety of cultures, some who expect a more formal style of delivery than the speaker is used to, some who expect the speaker to begin by humbling himself or herself and making respectful references to the audience, some who expect the speaker to be restrained rather than overly expressive, some who expect the speaker to rely on narratives rather than formal logic or standard inductive or deductive structures, and so on?

Ethics and Communication

Big and Little Lies

What kinds of communication choices do you make when attempting to accomplish a goal? What would you do to get others to comply with your wishes? Would you lie? Would you cheat? Is it acceptable for a speaker to manipulate receivers?

Our society has been criticized for being a "culture of cheating."[21] From the school yard to the White House, from the boardroom to the war room, from the ball field to the farm field, cheating appears to go on everywhere. We saw it with the presentation of the reasons for going to war against Iraq, and we saw it with the alleged "rescue" of Private Jessica Lynch and the ensuing accusation that "the Pentagon tried to pull a fast one."[22] We saw it with Enron. We saw it with ImClone. We saw it with *A Million Little Pieces*. Politicians, CEOs, and some authors of books, such as James Frey, fudge statements, exaggerate

the value of evidence, and fabricate claims. Some lies are told "to protect national security," some to protect the president's skin; some are just boasting. What is more, it appears that the "cheaters prosper until they get caught."[23] Some, like Frey, prosper even after getting caught.

What damage, if any, do you believe is done to a speaker's credibility when receivers discover that he or she has lied to them? Is a speaker's tendency to exaggerate as harmful as committing a lie of omission or telling an outright lie? Do the ends ever justify the means? In other words, is it acceptable for a speaker to make up facts if his or her goal is a worthy one?

Would you ever lie to receivers? Would you make up statistics, pass off as true a narrative you knew to be hypothetical, or tamper with visuals if you knew that doing so would help you realize the objective(s) of your speech?

If you're like most people, you find the first statement in each pair more credible. The source cited for the first statement seems obviously more knowledgeable about the subject.

Regardless of the circumstances, however, it is up to you to build your credibility by giving audience members reasons to consider you competent, trustworthy, and dynamic.[24] To help them see you as competent, you can describe your own experiences with the subject and suggest why you feel you've earned the right to share your ideas. You can help receivers see you as trustworthy by demonstrating respect for different points of view and communicating a sense of sincerity. To help them see you as dynamic, speak with energy, use assured and forceful gestures, and create vocal variety.[25]

Note that the audience's assessment of your credibility can change during your presentation or as a result of it. Thus, we can identify three types of credibility:

Initial credibility is your credibility before you start to speak.

Derived credibility is your credibility during your speech.

Terminal credibility is your credibility at the end of your speech.

initial credibility
a measure of how an audience perceives a speaker prior to the speech-making event

derived credibility
a measure of a speaker's credibility during a speech-making event

terminal credibility
a measure of a speaker's credibility at the end of a speech-making event

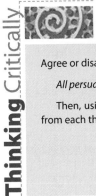

Thinking Critically

Reflect and Respond

Agree or disagree with the following statement; give reasons and examples that support your stance.

All persuasive speaking is informative. There is no such thing as a purely persuasive speech.

Then, using both the outline and the transcript of the persuasive speech that follows in the text, provide examples from each that support the position you have taken.

Of course, if your initial credibility is high, your task should be easier. But keep in mind that your speech can lower your initial credibility—and that it can also raise your initial credibility. What you say and how you say it are important determiners of credibility.

DELIVERING A PERSUASIVE SPEECH

Online Learning Center

For an example of a persuasive speech, go to the Online Learning Center at *www.mhhe.com/ gamble10e* and view clips 8 and 9. In clip 8, identify the errors the speaker makes. Then note in clip 9 how the speech was improved.

As a persuasive speaker, you must show a great deal of interest in and enthusiasm for your topic. At the moment of presentation, it must become the most important issue in the world for both you and your listeners.

Be aware that audience members may object to what you say. As a persuader, you need to be able to handle objections in an effective manner. First, be prepared for opposing points of view. Anticipate your audience's concerns and rehearse possible answers. Second, consider the source of objections. For example, audience members may dispute your facts. If you make a statement about the number of millionaires in your state and an audience member has just completed a study on wealth in the United States and has up-to-date statistics, you will need to agree, restate your findings, or suggest that this is a good point, which you both should explore. An effective way to handle opposing views is to agree with them as much as possible. "I agree that life insurance may not be the best investment . . ." is a disarming technique often used by sales representatives to counter objections to purchasing insurance.

Answer any argument in a professional manner. Do not become angry that anyone would dare question your reasoning. Remember that your credibility is at stake while you are speaking in front of others. Respond to the question or objection in an authoritative manner and move on to other questions. Maintain control.

SAMPLE PERSUASIVE SPEECH OUTLINE

By starting with a story involving undocumented students, the speaker attempts to draw receivers into the speech.

Having aroused the interest of receivers, and established that a problem exists, the speaker reveals the speech's subject and identifies clear objectives for the speech.

	FULL SENTENCE OUTLINE
Topic:	Undocumented students[26]
Purpose:	To persuade the audience that undocumented students should be allowed to attend college.
Thesis:	Undocumented students should be permitted to attend college.
Introduction	I. The scene is the third annual underwater robotics competition hosted by NASA.
	A. An unlikely team of four students from an inner-city high school was able to build a robot to compete against schools like MIT and do what was thought to be impossible—win.
	B. The four students were undocumented immigrants.
	II. Undocumented students are regularly denied the opportunity to attend college.
	A. While the 1982 Supreme Court decision *Plyler v. Doe* established that K–12 elementary schools could not bar undocumented children, colleges and universities have no such obligation.

B. The systematic exclusion affects a total of over one million students, most brought to the United States as children and who didn't intend to break the law.

III. To understand the problems facing undocumented students, we'll first explore the extent of institutional discrimination against undocumented students, next, address the criticism leveled against undocumented students, and finally put forth solutions to ensure undocumented students are allowed to enroll in college.

Body

I. Undocumented students are unable to attend college for two key reasons.

A. Undocumented students face a legal obstacle.

1. In a March 4, 2007, interview, college admissions counselor Carolyn Tweedie of St. Paul's Preparatory Academy noted that many universities and community colleges will not accept a student without a valid Social Security number.

2. Undocumented students do not have valid Social Security numbers.

B. Undocumented students face financial obstacles.

1. Forty states prohibit undocumented students from paying in-state tuition rates, forcing them to pay the higher out-of-state tuition rates, and making it financially impossible for them to attend college.

2. Undocumented students are barred from obtaining federal grants, loans, or institutional scholarships.

3. A 2006 report by the U.S. Census Bureau reveals that the wage difference between high school and college graduates is $23,000, meaning that undocumented students will be condemned to legalized poverty.

II. The three criticisms leveled at undocumented students—involving taxes, displacement, and legality—are unwarranted.

A. The belief expressed in the *Salt Lake Tribune* of February 8, 2007, that Americans will have to subsidize the education of undocumented students because they don't work and don't pay taxes is untrue.

1. The *Los Angeles Times* of April 17, 2006, argues that many undocumented students obtain phony Social Security numbers and work.

2. Many undocumented students also pay Social Security, Medicare, state, and federal taxes, along with sales, consumption, and property taxes.

B. The argument made on March 8, 2007, in the *Denver Post* by the Federation of Americans for Immigration Reform, FAIR, that undocumented immigrants would displace American students by siphoning away critically needed financial aid is inaccurate.

1. These students are not less American.

2. Their identity and right to a better life should not be contingent on a label.

continued

> The speaker identifies the problems undocumented students face, explaining each problem with reasons.

> The speaker identifies and refutes the criticisms leveled at undocumented students, supporting each position with references.

C. The position criminalizing undocumented students, expressed by U.S. congressman J. D. Hayworth in his 2006 book *Whatever It Takes,* and withholding access to higher education for that reason is unfair.

   1. According to the 2006 book *Targeting Immigrants,* legality does not assume morality.

   2. The 13th Amendment, women's suffrage, and the civil rights movement show it is common to fight against things codified into law.

III. There are a number of solutions to the problem of undocumented students.

> The speaker explains how the undocumented student problem can be solved, supplying both institutional and personal solutions.

A. Institutionally, our government needs to stop criminalizing children brought here by their parents by passing the DREAM Act.

   1. The act would grant residency to undocumented students who seek to attend college.

   2. The act would allow undocumented students to legally obtain employment upon graduation.

B. Personally, we need to become involved by taking actions aimed at helping undocumented students.

> The speaker involves receivers by telling them their help is needed.

   1. I've started a blog, *breakingdownborders.org.*

   2. I've partnered with on-campus organizations to collect over 3,000 letters addressed to Arizona representatives.

   3. I'm soliciting your help in finding out if your admissions department requires a Social Security number.

   4. We need to stop describing undocumented students as illegal.

   5. We need to promote dialogue and discourse about the plight of undocumented students.

Conclusion

I. It's time to move beyond the shallow reasoning the law provides regarding undocumented students.

> The speaker reminds receivers that sometimes unfair laws need to be broken to restore fairness.

II. Today's law is often tomorrow's injustice. Should we call Susan B. Anthony "wrong" for illegally voting in the 1872 election? Rosa Parks "disorderly" for refusing to give up her seat? Gay couples "immoral" for coming together in marriage?

III. By looking at the problem and overcoming the objections, we see that all the most driven, dedicated, and patriotic Americans lack is the label and the title.

SAMPLE PERSUASIVE SPEECH

Speech Title:	Breaking Down Borders: Allowing Immigrants to Obtain a Higher Education[27]
Topic:	Undocumented students
Purpose:	To persuade the audience that undocumented students should be allowed to attend college.
Thesis:	Undocumented students should be permitted to attend college.

The scene is the third annual underwater robotics competition hosted by NASA. The players are teams from some of the top engineering universities across the nation and four inner-city high school students with a robot that they built. They called the robot "Stinky." This very unlikely team of engineers was able to build a robot to compete against schools like MIT and do what was thought to be impossible—win. But even more amazing than the underwater war the robots were waging was the political battle that the students faced even to enter the competition. You see, all four students were undocumented immigrants who didn't let their status dictate what they could do.

As undocumented students, they don't have citizenship, residency, or any sort of legal status and, because of current immigration laws, cannot be put on the path to residency—and that's just the start. The American Immigration Foundation Web site, updated daily, argues that these students are regularly denied the opportunity to attend college. While the 1982 Supreme Court decision *Plyler v. Doe* established that K–12 elementary schools couldn't bar undocumented children, colleges and universities have no such obligation. The *San Jose Mercury News* of March 3, 2007, reveals that this systematic exclusion affects the 65,000 undocumented immigrants who graduate from high school each year for a total of over one million students. The article further comments that the overwhelming majority were brought here as children. They didn't choose to break the law and yet they're still being punished. So today, we'll first explore the extent of this institutional discrimination. Next, we will overcome the objections associated with undocumented students. Finally, we will embrace solutions to ensure that these students are allowed to be just that—students.

So, why can't undocumented students attend college? Well, the issue is twofold: discriminatory admissions and a multitude of financial obstacles. First, in a March 4, 2007, interview with college admissions counselor Carolyn Tweedie of St. Paul's Preparatory Academy, she states that many universities and community colleges will not accept a student without a valid Social Security number. But even if they do, the *Pioneer Press* of February 29, 2007, puts forth that undocumented students are prohibited from obtaining in-state tuition in forty states even though most have lived in-state for most their lives. These students are forced to pay out-of-state tuition that regularly costs thousands of dollars more—making it financially impossible for them even to attend college.

Second, regardless of your residency status, I've ingested enough Ramen to know that college costs a lot of money. Traditionally, applicants can turn to financial aid to help defer the cost, but as the *Pioneer Press* further comments, undocumented students are barred from obtaining federal grants, loans, and even institutional scholarships. This lack of financial aid makes attending college a financial burden that many immigrant families simply cannot overcome. Even more sobering, a 2006 report by the United States Census Bureau states that the wage difference between college and high school students is an average of $23,000, which means that these prohibitions are condemning these students to legalized poverty.

This past November, Arizona became the latest state to pass laws denying in-state tuition and financial aid to undocumented students. Now, this sentiment exists because of three main reasons: taxes,

continued

Do you think that starting with a story is a good idea? Does the speaker's opening capture your attention and motivate you to want to hear more? How else might the speaker pull you in to the speech? Is there a visual aid that the speaker might use in the speech's opening?

How effective do you find the speaker's orientation? Does it clearly establish the major parts of the speech?

How would you describe the speech's structure?

Does this transition facilitate the speech's progression?

Do you find the speaker's use of contemporary sources effective?

Does a signpost work here?

Are the problems the speaker cites convincing? Is the speaker supplying sufficient evidence to build a case?

> Does the speaker do a good job of handling objections?

displacement, and legality. First, the *Salt Lake Tribune* of February 8, 2007, outlines a common argument—undocumented immigrants don't pay taxes, and Americans would therefore be subsidizing their education. The *Los Angeles Times* of April 17, 2006, argues otherwise: undocumented immigrants can't legally work in America so most use made-up Social Security numbers. Here's the kicker—the government checks the validity of these numbers to dispense benefits but not to collect taxes. This means that Social Security, Medicare, and state and federal taxes are withheld from every check, regardless of residency status, leading to over $7 billion in surplus taxes every year. Undocumented immigrants also pay sales, consumption, and property taxes, all of which directly contribute to state funding for universities, and millions more even file tax returns using specially assigned IRS numbers.

Next, the Federation of Americans for Immigration Reform, FAIR, for short—that's ironic—argues on its Web site *fairus.org,* updated daily, that undocumented immigrants would displace American students and siphon away critically needed financial aid. The *Denver Post* of March 8, 2007, delineates that this argument assumes that these students are somehow less American. They grew up in our culture, succeeded in the same institutions, and abided by the same standards as everyone else. Their identity and therefore their right to a better life shouldn't be contingent on a label.

Finally, former U.S. congressman J. D. Hayworth argues in his 2006 book *Whatever It Takes* that these students shouldn't be granted a higher education because they are in violation of our rules. As one person put it, "It's hard to feel sympathy for someone that broke the law." The 2006 book *Targeting Immigrants* interjects that this argument not only stifles critical analysis but also puts the issue to rest without any consideration for context or extenuating circumstances. Obviously, we shouldn't disregard legality, but at the same time it shouldn't be our only argument. History has repeatedly shown us that legality in no way assumes morality. The 13th Amendment, women's suffrage, and the civil rights movement each fought against things that were codified into law and we're a better nation for it.

> What might the speaker do to further illustrate the problem?

> In your opinion, does the speaker do a competent job of personalizing problems? What do you think of the suggestions the speaker offers for action? Are they sufficient?

Undocumented students have been completely criminalized. They can't vote, work, or even legally drive a car—the least we can do is let them learn. So let's take a look at solutions on both the institutional and personal level. Institutionally, our government needs to stop criminalizing children who are brought here at a very early age, because as dangerous as they might be, two year olds probably shouldn't be classified as federal criminals. Next, Congress needs to pass the DREAM Act. This bipartisan legislation would grant residency to undocumented students seeking to attend college. It would also allow undocumented students to legally obtain employment after graduation.

On the personal level, to help these students I've started a blog focused on immigration at *breakingdownborders.org* that keeps track of pending legislation, tuition developments, and has links to immigrant-friendly colleges and scholarships. We've also partnered with other on-campus organizations to collect over 3,000 letters addressed to Arizona representatives. What I need from you is information. Ask your admissions department if it requires a Social Security number and shoot me an e-mail at jose@breakingdownborders.org, and I'll post whatever you find. Finally, don't use legality as an excuse for dismissing this issue. Instead, go beyond labels and critically analyze the

> In closing, does the speaker provide receivers with a summary?

context in order to form your own opinion. You may have noticed that I have not once used the word "illegal" to describe these students—this is why. And this is something that all of us can do because dialogue and discourse are essential to understanding any plight. You can even help do the same. For example, I asked my school newspaper to do a story on these students. When published, it triggered a two-week wave of response letters—some for, many against—but this is just the sort of critical discussion that needs to take place, and it all got started because of a single phone call. Surely, the educational advancement of over a million students is worth a single phone call.

It's time to move beyond the shallow reasoning the law provides for us on this issue. Should we call Susan B. Anthony "wrong" for illegally voting in the 1872 election? Rosa Parks "disorderly" for refusing to give up her seat? Gay couples "immoral" for coming together in marriage? All of these actions were "illegal." Yet, let's not forget that oftentimes today's law is tomorrow's injustice. By looking at the problem and overcoming the objections, we've seen that, in the case of these immigrants, less than a century removed from our ancestors stepping through the open doors of Ellis Island, it is essential to realize that, sometimes, the most driven, dedicated, and patriotic Americans simply lack the label and the title.

> Do the examples offered in the conclusion advance the speaker's purpose?

> Does the conclusion provide a sense of closure?

> Were you the speaker, what would you have done differently in the speech?

WORKS CONSULTED

Plyler v. Doe, 1982

Report by the U.S. Census, 2006

Interview with admissions counselor Carolyn Tweedie, March 4, 2007

Pioneer Press, February 9, 2007

San Jose Mercury News, March 3, 2007

Salt Lake Tribune, February 8, 2007

Los Angeles Times, April 17, 2006

Denver Post, March 8, 2007

J. D. Hayworth, *Whatever It Takes: Illegal Immigration, Border Security, and The War on Terror.* Regnery Publishing, 2006

Jonathan Xavier Inda, *Targeting Immigrants: Government, Technology, and Ethics.* Wiley-Blackwell, 2006.

Fairus.org

> How would you organize the *Works Consulted* page?

SAMPLE SPEAKER'S NOTES

Topic:	Undocumented students[27]
Purpose:	To persuade the audience that undocumented students should be allowed to attend college.
Thesis:	Undocumented students should be permitted to attend college.

continued

I. The scene is the third annual underwater robotics competition hosted by NASA.

   A. Competing against schools like MIT, an unlikely team of four students from an inner-city high school was able to build a robot and do what was thought to be impossible—win.

   B. The four students were undocumented immigrants.

II. Undocumented students don't have citizenship, residency, or any legal status and as a result are regularly denied the opportunity to attend college.

   A. 1982 Supreme Court decision *Plyler v. Doe* established that, unlike grades K–12, colleges and universities have no obligation to admit undocumented students.

   B. The systematic exclusion affects over one million students, most who came to the United States as children, not intending to break the law.

Body

I. Reasons undocumented students can't attend college

SS #

Financial issues

   Out-of-state tuition rate

   Lack of financial aid

   Experiencing legalized poverty (2006 Census report earnings figures)

II. Issues of taxes, displacement, and legality

   Salt Lake Tribune of February 8, 2007—regarding no work & taxes

   Los Angeles Times of April 17, 2006—received phony SS cards

   March 8, 2007 *Denver Post* report on FAIR

   Congressman J. D. Haworth, *Whatever It Takes* (2006)—criminalize undocumented students

   Targeting Immigrants (2006)—legality is not morality

III. Solutions

   Institutionally. Pass DREAM Act

   Personally

      Blog

      3,000 letters

      You can help

      Not illegal

Conclusion

I. Move beyond law.

II. Today's law = tomorrow's justice.

III. Get over label and title.

EVALUATING THE PERSUASIVE SPEECH

Although the evaluation form featured in Chapter 15 can be used to evaluate persuasive speeches, there are a number of criteria to keep in mind when evaluating persuasive discourse. Use the following checklist as a guide.

Rate the following criteria from 1 to 5; 1 represents "not at all" or "barely accomplished" and 5 represents "fully accomplished."

_____ Did the speaker's introduction fulfill its purpose?

_____ Was the speaker's proposition clearly understood?

_____ Were the reasons the speaker offered in support of the proposition clear?

_____ Was the speaker's use of testimony effective?

_____ Was the organizational pattern used by the speaker appropriate and easy to follow?

_____ Was the speaker's use of language vivid, appropriate, and motivating?

_____ Was the speaker effective in establishing his or her own credibility?

_____ Did the speaker's conclusion accomplish its purpose?

_____ Did the speaker conduct himself or herself ethically?

_____ Was the speaker's delivery effective?

Check *one* of the following:

The speech was _____ superior _____ above average _____ average
_____ below average _____ poor

Revisiting Chapter Objectives

1. **Define *persuasive speaking*.**   Persuasive speaking is the means a speaker uses to modify the thoughts, feelings, or actions of receivers so that they change the attitudes or behaviors that the speaker does not approve and, instead, adopt attitudes and behaviors compatible with the speaker's interests and worldview. The proposition of the speech indicates the kind of change the persuasive speaker would like to create in receivers.

2. **Define and distinguish between *attitudes* and *beliefs*.**   To influence receivers, speakers need to address their attitudes and beliefs. Attitudes are the mental sets, or predispositions, receivers bring to a speech. Beliefs are the building blocks of attitudes. A receiver's belief system is composed of everything the receiver believes to be true. Whereas attitudes are measured on a favorable–unfavorable scale, beliefs are measured on a probable–improbable scale. The more central a belief, the harder it is to change.

3. **Distinguish between logical and fallacious reasoning.**   Speakers who give their receivers logical reasons to support their propositions improve their chances of realizing their speech-making goals. By using deductive and inductive reasoning, causal reasoning, and reasoning from analogy, speakers can build their case and earn receiver support. Ethical speakers do not rely on fallacious reasoning to win the support of receivers. Among the logical fallacies unethical speakers use are argumentum ad hominem, red herring, false division, false cause, the bandwagon appeal, and the appeal to authority.

4. **Explain the concept of credibility.**   A speaker's success as a persuader is in part determined by his or her credibility—or how an audience perceives him or her. To find a speaker credible, receivers need to believe the speaker is a person of

good character, is knowledgeable, and is personable. The assessment of a speaker's credibility can change during or as a result of a speech.

5. **Develop and present a persuasive speech.**   The job of the persuader is to build an effective case, which includes well-supported reasons and appeals for accepting a speaker's proposition. The audience members must be drawn into the speech, sense the speaker's conviction and belief in the position he or she is advocating, and be reminded at the conclusion of the speech of what they need to believe and/or do.

Resources for Further Inquiry and Reflection

To apply your understanding of how the principles in Chapter 17 are at work in our daily lives, consult the following resources for further inquiry and reflection. Or, if you prefer, choose any other appropriate resource. Then connect the ideas expressed in your chosen selection with the communication concepts and issues you are learning about both in and out of class.

Listen to Me

"Boulevard of Broken Dreams" (Green Day)
"Burn" (Usher)
"Let It Be" (The Beatles)
"Truth No. 2" (Dixie Chicks)
"We Didn't Start the Fire" (Billy Joel)
"Let's Roll" (Neil Young)
"Shattered" (O.A.R.)
"Re-Education (Through Labor)" (Rise Against)

Compare and contrast the attitudes toward persuasion and change expressed in any of these songs with your own attitudes. What does the song you chose suggest about potential subjects for a persuasive speech?

View Me

North Country	*Good Night, and Good Luck*
The Constant Gardener	*Wall Street*
Syriana	*Malcolm X*
Munich	*Bowling for Columbine*
Frost/Nixon	*W*

What do we learn about the ethics and persuasive approaches favored by featured characters from their own words and actions?

Read Me

Stephen M. R. Covey. *The Speed of Trust.* New York: Free Press, 2008.
Robert B. Cialdini. *Influence: The Psychology of Persuasion,* rev. ed. New York: Quill, 2000.
Anthony Pratkanis and Elliot Aronson. *Age of Propaganda: The Everyday Use and Abuse of Persuasion,* rev. ed. New York: Friedman, 2000.
Naomi Klein. *The Shock Doctrine.* New York: Picador, 2008.

In what ways, if any, do tactics of persuasion influence the susceptibility of receivers?

Tell Me

Share with the class the insights you gained from your chosen Listen to Me, View Me, or Read Me selection.

Do you think the current U.S. president is an effective persuasive speaker? Explain why or why not.

Key Chapter Terminology

Use the Online Learning Center at www.mhhe.com/gamble10e to further your knowledge of the following terminology.

www.mhhe.com/gamble10e

argumentum ad hominem 431
argumentum ad populum 432
argumentum ad verecudiam 432
attitudes 426
backing 428
balance 434
beliefs 427
causal reasoning 430
claim 428
consistency 428
credibility 437
deduction 429
derived credibility 439
ethos 425
false division 432
induction 430
initial credibility 439
logos 425

Maslow's hierarchy of needs 434
Monroe's motivated sequence 435
pathos 425
persuasion 421
persuasive speech 421
post hoc, ergo propter hoc 432
proposition 422
proposition of fact 423
proposition of policy 423
proposition of value 423
qualifier 428
reasoning from analogy 430
reasons 428
rebuttal 428
red herring 432
social proof 428
terminal credibility 439
warrant 428

Idioms in Translation

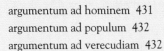

building blocks — foundation

fight fatigue — become less tired

framing — shaping

move audience members — motivate audience members

targets — audience members

wild goose chase — futile pursuit

Culture Cue

People in the United States expect speakers to base arguments on logic and objective facts, not just emotional appeals.

Test Your Understanding

Go to the *Self Quizzes* on the book's Online Learning Center at www.mhhe.com/gamble10e.

www.mhhe.com/gamble10e

LOOKING BACK AND AHEAD

Consider This Case: The Town Meeting Blues

"I don't know why you need to go through with this speech if it's making you so nervous," Mihwah said to her friend Daniel one evening.

"Because I really believe in what I'm going to say," said Daniel. "I just can't help being nervous about it, but I'm not going to let that stop me. At least, I'm going to try not to."

Mihwah and Daniel were housemates in a building near campus. Daniel was determined to speak at the upcoming town meeting in their community about an issue that was sure to be divisive. Mihwah had agreed to help him prepare and rehearse his speech, but as the day of the meeting drew closer, he was growing more apprehensive about his plan.

Daniel had been living off-campus for a year, and he'd become aware of a building boom that was taking place around the town. Private developers and contractors were busier than ever with home renovations and new commercial construction, and there was a shortage of workers for them to hire. At the same time, immigrants looking for work had begun gathering in the early morning hours, waiting on street corners for the contractors' trucks and vans to drive by. Often the contractors would stop, pick out a few men, hire them for the day, and drive on. An informal labor market had sprung up, and although it wasn't a perfect solution to the labor problem, or to the problems faced by the immigrant workers, it solved an immediate need, and local government hadn't made any attempt to interfere in it.

But a group of citizens had called a town meeting to try to force an end to the practice. They were mostly local business owners who claimed the small groups of men waiting for work were loitering in front of their stores, begging or scaring their customers away, and creating a public nuisance.

Daniel disagreed. As he'd explained to Mihwah, he believed the workers were sincerely looking for work. He'd never seen one of them begging, and he'd often observed how they kept quietly to themselves each morning until the contractors arrived. Anyone not hired for the day usually disappeared within a few minutes, and no disruptions or disorderly behavior had ever occurred that he knew of.

Daniel believed that a solution to the shopkeepers' objections could be found. He planned to speak at the town meeting to propose his solution—designating a small park in the center of town as the accepted gathering place for the workers and contractors to meet each morning. It would mean the drivers would have to go a little out of their way to find the men, but it would keep the workers away from the storefronts and allow them to continue finding the work they needed. And the contractors would benefit too, by having continued access to the informal labor pool.

Daniel knew he would have to be very persuasive to convince the business owners to consider his proposal. He thought the contractors would agree to it because it would benefit them, too, but he wasn't sure. He was even less sure about what the local government would do if it were finally forced to make some kind of decision in the matter. And he wondered what any of the meeting participants would think about his speaking out. After all, he was only a student. He suddenly wondered whether anyone else would be speaking on behalf of the immigrant workers.

"Well," said Mihwah, breaking in on his thoughts. "Since you're determined to speak, let's go over your outline again. Ready?"

DISCUSSION QUESTIONS

1. How many diverse parties are involved in the situation Daniel has observed in town? Has he considered all their possible interests?
2. What should Daniel do to make himself a more credible speaker at the town meeting? What advantages and disadvantages does he have as an observer, not a participant, in the immigrant labor situation?
3. What does he need to find out about his audiences, and how can he research this?
4. What kind of supporting material do you think Daniel will need to make his speech a success?
5. What kinds of questions should Daniel anticipate being asked at the meeting, and how can he prepare himself to answer them?

LET'S GO TO THE DVD

Investigating *The Great Debaters*

The Great Debaters, set in the 1930s, tells the story of the debate team at historically Black Wiley College. After viewing the film, and considering the hurdles overcome by the debaters (Samantha Booke, Henry Lowe, Hamilton Burgess, and James Farmer) and their coach (Melvin Tolson), answer these questions, drawing specific examples from the film:

1. Why was the team's debate training so rigorous?
2. What roles did research, self-analysis, and audience analysis play in debate preparation?
3. What does the film teach about the power of words?
4. Why is it important to be able to think on your feet?
5. How important were support, organization, credibility, and delivery in the debates?
6. Were the debaters informative? Where they persuasive?
7. Provide a speech evaluation for each of the team's debaters.

Interviewing and Developing Professional Relationships

After finishing this appendix, you should be able to

1. Define *employment interview*.

2. Describe the stages of an employment interview.

3. Distinguish between closed, open, primary, and secondary questions.

4. Perform the roles and responsibilities of an interviewee.

What does a job interview have to do with communication? A lot. In fact, when it comes to the kinds of skills that job recruiters look for, interpersonal skills top the list.[1] An employment interview is like an interaction on Match.com. However, instead of two people seeking to determine if they have what it takes to make a love connection, during a job interview, the candidate and the employer usually meet face-to-face to figure out if the organization's corporate culture and needs are a good match with the applicant's values and abilities.

During the course of our lives we all take part in interviews. From our vantage point, an interview incorporates many of the topics and principles of communication we have already discussed. Culture, self-concept, perception, listening, feedback, language and meaning, nonverbal cues, and assertiveness have parts to play in determining your interviewing success. Let us explore the interview process and what you can do to succeed as an interviewee.

Dear_____:

We enjoyed having you visit us here (last week) (last month) (recently). Everyone who talked with you was most impressed, and I personally feel that you are one of the most promising young (men) (women) I've seen in a long time. We all wish we could make you an offer at this time. However, . . .
—From a corporation's form letter

Twenty years from now, the typical American worker will have changed jobs four times and careers twice and will be employed in an occupation that does not exist today.
—Jeffrey Hallet

THE EMPLOYMENT INTERVIEW: MORE THAN CASUAL CONVERSATION

In comparison to ordinary conversations, the conversations we enact during employment interviews are planned and designed to achieve specific objectives. Thus, an **employment interview** is the most common type of purposeful, planned, decision-making, person-to-person communication. The person(s) hiring and the candidate(s) seeking to be hired engage in a process of personal contact and behavior exchange, giving and receiving information, to make educated career-related decisions.

employment interview
the most common type of purposeful, planned, decision-making, person-to-person communication

Media Wise

Piquing Career Interest

Have you found that you or your friends are taking more of an interest in criminal justice and forensics? If so, you are not alone. Even a large number of universities report having increased the scope of courses they offer in criminal justice. To what is this surge in interest attributed? Many people believe it is due to television.

The public appears fascinated with investigation and the justice system, as evidenced by the popularity of television shows such as *The Mentalist, Law and Order, Without a Trace,* and *CSI.* Their popularity has spilled over into the real world, sparking an increasing interest in criminology careers. Even the Nevada law enforcement agency Field Services Division has responded to popular interest in forensic science, changing its name to Crime Scene Investigations.[2]

In your opinion, to what extent, if any, is the portrayal of criminology careers on television and film contributing to unrealistic career expectations in those who now seek to become criminologists? For example, most of the crimes featured on *CSI*-type shows are solved in an hour, while they might take months or even years to solve in the real world. In addition, the programs on television rarely show the boring days, they reveal the staff working with state-of-the-art equipment that many cities cannot afford, and they have a crimes-solved rate that actual criminologists could never attain.

The employment interview offers a unique opportunity for the potential employer and employee to share meaningful information that will permit each to determine whether their association would be beneficial and productive. It gives both participants a chance to test each other by asking and answering relevant questions. Employers hope to gather information about you during the interview that your résumé, references, and any personality tests you may have been asked to take do not provide. They also believe the person-to-person approach is an effective way to sell their organization to you. As an applicant, you seek information about the employer and the job during the interview. You can deduce from your interaction with the interviewer what your long-term relationship might be and what life in that organization might be like if you are hired.

Some interviews are over before they begin. Why? Because the interviewer asks a question that he or she thinks is easy but that the interviewee cannot answer. For example, on being asked what she had to offer the company, all one interviewee could respond was, "Hmmmmm, that's a toughie." Then she added, "I was more wanting to hear what you could do for me." The candidate did not get the job. How would you have replied to that question?

It is as a result of a hiring or selection interview that we find ourselves accepted or rejected by a prospective employer—an individual, a small business, a large corporation, and so on. The better prepared you are for an employment interview, the better your chances will be of performing effectively and realizing your job objectives. Remember, an interview is not "just talk."[3]

Common Fears

How do you feel about interviewing for a job? Listed here are some fears that interviewees express frequently. Do you share them? Circle the numbers that most accurately reflect your level of interview apprehension: 0 = completely unconcerned; 1 = very mild concern; 2 = mild concern; 3 = more apprehensive than not; 4 = very frightened; 5 = a nervous wreck.

1. I will be asked questions I cannot answer.

   0   1   2   3   4   5

2. I will not dress properly for the interview.

   0   1   2   3   4   5

3. I will appear very nervous.

   0   1   2   3   4   5

4. I will not appear competent.

   0   1   2   3   4   5

5. The interviewer will cross-examine me.

   0   1   2   3   4   5

6. I will be caught in a lie.

   0   1   2   3   4   5

7. I will talk too much or too little.

   0   1   2   3   4   5

8. I will have poor rapport with the interviewer.

   0   1   2   3   4   5

9. I will undersell or oversell myself.

   0   1   2   3   4   5

10. I won't be hired.

   0   1   2   3   4   5

Total the numbers you circled to arrive at your "interviewee's anxiety" score.

Your scores indicate how frightened you are of assuming the role of interviewee. If you accumulated 45 to 50 points, you are a nervous wreck; if you scored 35 to 44 points, you are too frightened; if you scored 20 to 34 points, you are somewhat apprehensive; if you scored 11 to 20 points, you are too casual; if you scored 0 to 10 points, you are not at all concerned—that is, you simply do not care.

Contrary to what you might assume, not being concerned at all about participating in an interview is just as much of a problem as being a nervous wreck, and being too casual can do as much damage as being too frightened. An interviewee should be apprehensive to a degree. If you are not concerned about what will happen during the interview, then you will not care about making a good impression and, as a result, will not perform as effectively as you could.

Preliminary Tasks: Preparing the Cover Letter and Résumé

The job of the applicant is to prepare fully for the interview. By completing two documents—a cover letter and a résumé—that are well written and register a positive impression, you provide the interviewer with a preview of who you are and why you are qualified for the position.

The Cover Letter

The cover letter introduces you to the interviewer. It is a brief (usually one-page), well-written letter that fulfills the following six criteria: (1) It expresses your interest in a position; (2) it tells how you learned of the position; (3) it reviews your primary skills and accomplishments; (4) it explains why these qualify you for the job; (5) it highlights any items of special interest about you that are relevant to your ability to perform the job; and (6) it contains a request for an interview. A résumé is always included with a cover letter. Keep the cover letter to one page. The only chance you have to persuade the person opening it to read your résumé can vanish if the reader sees a lengthy letter.

The Résumé

The résumé summarizes your abilities and accomplishments. It details what you have to contribute that will meet the company's needs and help solve the employer's problems. Although formats differ, the résumé typically includes the following:

1. contact information—your name, address, telephone number, and e-mail address
2. job objective—a phrase or sentence that focuses on your area of expertise
3. employment history—your job experience, both paid and unpaid, beginning with the most recent
4. education—schools attended, degree(s) completed or expected, dates of completion, and a review of courses that relate directly to your ability to perform the job
5. relevant professional certifications and affiliations
6. community service
7. special skills and interests you possess that are revelent to the job
8. references—people who agree to elaborate on your work history, capabilities, and character; reveal only that references are available on request unless you are asked to provide specific references at the time you submit your résumé

> In your résumé, do you have the most important information first?

Since the average resume gets about 15 seconds of the reader's time, creating an effective one is essential.[4] Also, although sending a video resume may intrigue you, most companies still do not accept them.

Structure: Stages of the Interview

Most effective interviews have a clear structure. The beginning, or opening, is the segment of the process that provides an orientation to what will come. The middle, or body, is the longest segment and the one during which both parties really get down to business. The end, or close, is the segment during which the participants prepare to take leave of one another.

Just as the right kind of greeting at the start of a conversation can help create a feeling of friendliness, so the opening of an interview can help establish rapport between interviewer and interviewee.[5] The primary purpose of the opening is to make it possible for both parties to participate freely and honestly by creating an atmosphere of trust and goodwill and by explaining the purpose and scope of the meeting. Conversational icebreakers and orientation statements perform important functions at this stage. Typical icebreakers include comments about the weather, the surroundings, and current events—or a compliment. The idea is to use small talk to help make the interview a human encounter rather than a mechanical one. Typical orientation remarks include an identification of the interview's purpose, a preview of the topics to be discussed, and statements

Ethics and Communication

Résumé Padding and Résumé Poaching

1. Résumé padding has been around for a long time. Would you lie on your résumé to get your foot in the door? Would you "fix up" your résumé to help you look better on paper than you really are?

   Not too long ago, Notre Dame's football coach, George O'Leary, had to step down from his head coach position after admitting that he had falsified the academic and athletic credentials listed on his résumé. In your opinion, should O'Leary have been fired for his résumé misrepresentations? Why or why not?

2. It is not merely some résumé writers who are ethically challenged. So are some recruiters. In fact, résumés posted on Internet job boards are not necessarily private or restricted to recruiters and other employers who pay a fee for access. While some sites may sell their résumés, résumé poaching also threatens the privacy of job seekers. The employees of competitive sites have been known to pose as recruiters in order to download thousands of résumés without permission. Persons who post their résumés on supposedly secure sites find themselves harassed by readers who object to their professions. For example, one job seeker in chemistry found herself harassed by activists against animal research.[6] In your opinion, should Internet job search sites be billboards for all to see, or should they be kept private, with recruiters and employers being screened adequately before being given access?

that motivate the respondent and act as a conduit, or transition, to the body of the interview.

In the body of the interview, the parties really get down to business. At this point, the interviewer and interviewee might discuss work experiences, including the applicant's strengths, weaknesses, major accomplishments, difficult problems tackled in the past, and career goals. Educational background and activities or interests are relevant areas to probe during this phase of the interview. Breadth of knowledge and the ability to manage time are also common areas of concern.

During the close of the interview, the main points covered are reviewed and summarized. Since an interview can affect any future meetings the parties may have, care must be taken to make the leave-taking comfortable.[7] Expressing appreciation for the time and effort given is important; neither interviewee nor interviewer should feel discarded. In other words, the door should be left open for future contacts.

Work It Out

For the next few days, keep track of the verbal and nonverbal messages people use when they say hello or good-bye. Which beginnings and endings were particularly communicative? Which were ineffective? Did you observe any false starts or false endings? How could they have been avoided?

Skill Builder

Wake-up Calls

1. According to one résumé expert, "The biggest mistake that people are making is that their résumés have no real impact. . . . A good résumé won't get you a job, but it will get you in the door."[8]

   What steps can you take to ensure that your résumé doesn't end up as origami? Describe how you would market yourself so that the person who receives your résumé actually opens it and spends some time reading it. For example, one applicant for a marketing position included her résumé in a package of gourmet coffees that she sent to the potential interviewer with the slogan "Lindsay will wake up your marketing" affixed to the package. Do you think the interviewer read her résumé?

2. Once your résumé gets you in the door, give yourself an interview wake-up call. By exhibiting the following behaviors during your interview, you can help ensure you make the final cut: (1) Refer to the company you are interviewing with by name; (2) make it clear that you have researched the company; (3) respond enthusiastically to information the interviewer shares; (4) back up your answers to questions you are asked with specific examples; (5) use questions to demonstrate your knowledge of the industry and the company.

The only way to get the accurate answers is to ask the right questions.

—Kevin J. Murphy,
Effective Listening:
Your Key to Career Success

Each party has questions in the interview—both you and the employer. The essence of the interview is to find out the answers to those questions.

—Richard N. Bolles

Questions: The Heart of the Interview

Questions are the primary means of collecting data in an interview. Not only do questions set the tone for an interview, but they also determine whether the interview will yield valuable information. Using the interrogatives *what, where, when, who, how,* and *why* throughout an interview lays a foundation of knowledge on which to base decisions or conclusions.

During the course of an interview, closed, open, primary, and secondary questions may all be used, in any combination.[9] **Closed questions** are highly structured and answerable with a simple yes or no or in a few words. Following are examples of closed questions:

Where do you live?

Did you graduate in the top quarter of your class?

What starting salary do you expect?

Open questions are broader than closed questions and are less restricting or structured; hence, they offer more freedom with regard to the choice and scope of an answer. Following are examples of open questions:

Tell me about yourself.

How do you judge success?

Why did you choose to interview for this job?

Describe a time you failed.

Describe a time when you failed to solve a conflict.

closed questions

highly structured questions answerable with a simple yes or no or in a few words

open questions

questions that offer the interviewee freedom with regard to the choice and scope of an answer

Open questions give you a chance to express your feelings, attitudes, and values. For example, let's consider the first question above. "Tell me about yourself" is not a request for your life story. The interviewer is really asking, "Why should I hire you?" Thus, your task when answering a question like this is to showcase your communication skills by crafting a statement shorter than two minutes, or about the length of an elevator ride, that lets the interviewer know more about you and what you can do for the company, that is, the benefits you will bring to your employer.[10]

Open and closed questions may be either primary or secondary. **Primary questions** introduce topics or begin the exploration of a new area. "What is your favorite hobby?" and "Tell me about your last job" are examples of primary questions—the first is closed; the second is open.

Interviewers use **secondary questions**—sometimes called probing questions—to follow up primary questions. They ask for an explanation of the ideas and feelings behind answers to other questions, and they are frequently used when answers to primary questions are vague or incomplete. Following are examples of secondary questions:

Go on. What do you mean?

Can you give me an example?

Work It Out

Craft a two-minute response to the question, Why should I hire you? Try out responses on your peers.

primary questions

questions used to introduce topics or explore a new area

secondary questions

probing questions that follow up primary questions

Interviewee Roles and Responsibilities

An interviewer uses your interview in three ways: (1) to assess your probable performance if hired, (2) to determine if you and the organization's team can work well together, and assuming the first two goals result in a yes, then (3) to persuade you that the organization is a good one to work for.

What are your roles and responsibilities during this process? You need to speak and listen, and to provide information to help convince the interviewer that you are the right person for the job. At the same time, you need to collect information that will help you decide whether to accept the job if offered it. To accomplish these goals you need to research the organization to which you are applying and try to anticipate the questions the interviewer will ask. In addition, to help control the interview's direction and content, you also need to plan to ask questions. As your questions are answered, you will learn about work conditions and prospects for advancement.

Effective interviewees work hard at self-assessment. In effect, they take stock of themselves to determine who they are, what their career needs and their goals are, and how they can best sell themselves to an employer.

As a prospective interviewee, you will find it useful to prepare by thinking about and answering the following questions:

1. For what types of positions has my training prepared me?
2. What has been my most rewarding experience?
3. What type of job do I want?
4. Would I be happier working alone or with others?
5. What qualifications do I have that make me feel I would be successful in the job of my choice?
6. What type or types of people do I want to work for?
7. What type or types of people do I not want to work for?
8. How do I feel about receiving criticism?
9. What salary will enable me to meet my financial needs?
10. What salary will enable me to live comfortably?
11. What will interviewers want to know about me, my interests, my background, and my experiences?

In addition to conducting a self-survey, the interviewee needs to work to withstand the pressure of the interview situation. Are you prepared to maintain your composure while being stared at, interrupted, spoken to abruptly, or asked difficult questions? Have you practiced enough to keep cool when on the interview hot seat? How do you think you would react if you were asked tough questions? The following questions are favorites among interviewers. How would you answer them?

1. Tell me about yourself.
2. What do you think you're worth?
3. What are you good at?
4. If we hired you, what about this organization would concern you most?
5. What attributes do you think an effective manager should possess?
6. What are your short-term goals? How are they different from your long-term goals?
7. How has your background prepared you for this position?
8. What are your major strengths and weaknesses?
9. How would a former employer or instructor describe you?
10. Why did you leave your last job?
11. What do you consider your greatest accomplishment?
12. What's wrong with you?

Work It Out

Role-play asking and answering the questions listed here.

13. What would you do if I told you that I thought you were giving a very poor interview today?

14. How long do you plan to remain with us if you get this job?

15. What would you like to know about us?

Some interviewers prefer to ask even more searching questions, such as the following:

Tell me about how you handled the last mistake you made.

Are there things at which you aren't very good?

At your weekly team meetings, your boss unexpectedly begins aggressively critiquing your performance on a current project. What would you do?

You're in a situation in which you have two very important responsibilities that both have deadlines that are impossible to meet. You cannot accomplish both. How do you handle that situation?[11]

Practice in answering questions like these—under both favorable and unfavorable conditions—is essential.[12] It is important that you know what you want to say during the interview and that you use the questions you are asked as an opportunity to say it. Along the way, you can flatter the interviewer by offering comments such as "I think you've touched on something really important."

The interviewer can, of course, consult a résumé to ascertain information about the applicant—about educational background and previous positions held, for example. However, gathering enough information to evaluate the personal qualities of an applicant is more difficult. Following is a list of personal qualifications, with the questions interviewers typically ask to evaluate them:

1. *Quality:* Skill in managing one's own career

   Question: What specific things have you done deliberately to get where you are today?

2. *Quality:* Skill in managing others

   Question: What are some examples of things you do and do not like to delegate?

3. *Quality:* Sense of responsibility

   Question: What steps do you take to see that things do not fall through the cracks when you are supervising a project?

4. *Quality:* Skill in working with people

   Question: If we assembled in one room a group of people you have worked with and asked them to describe what it was like to work with you, what would they be likely to say? What would your greatest supporter say? What would your severest critic say?

When it comes to answering questions about items listed on your résumé, one career coach suggests using the acronym S.T.A.R. (situation, task, action, result) as a guide. For example, let's say your résumé notes that you turned around a sales territory in decline, ultimately increasing sales by 10 percent in your first year. The interviewer asks: "How did you do that?" Your job is to walk the interviewer through the process by revealing the situation you faced, how you assessed your task, the action you took, and the result you achieved.[13]

> **What other qualities do you believe interviewers look for in interviewees? If you were an interviewer, what questions would you ask to determine if a person possessed those qualities?**

> *Work It Out*
> Bring five copies of your résumé to class. Working in groups, take turns using the S.T.A.R. system to respond to group members' questions about your resume.

Most employment interviews can be grouped into one of three categories: the behavioral, the case, and the stress interview. In the **behavioral interview,** an employer is looking for specific examples from the prospective employee of times when he or she has exhibited specific skills. When asked a question such as "Tell me about a time you acted in a leadership role," the interviewee might respond, "I was the director of a fund-raising group," or "I was an officer in Women in Communication." In the **case interview,** a company presents the interviewee with a business case and asks for him or her to work through it. To help prepare yourself for such an interview, check out the company Web site beforehand. Some companies post sample cases on their sites. The third type of interview, the **stress interview,** typically includes more than one interviewer firing questions at the interviewee to see how that person handles himself or herself during a stressful situation.

Because the interview is a conversation and not an interrogation, during the course of the interview, the interviewee should ask questions of the interviewer as a means of demonstrating interest in the job and the company.[14] When the interviewee asks questions, the interview becomes more balanced. What kinds of questions should you ask when in the interviewee role? You should not ask questions that you can answer easily by visiting the company's Web site. You should, however, ask questions that seek clarification; for example: "I read on your site that you will be introducing new products. Could you tell me more about how you plan to roll them out?"

In general, interviewees ask questions about the company and corporate culture (rather than about salary or benefits), the industry, the position, and the people in the company. Following are some examples:

Why is this position open?

What would you say are the main challenges of this job?

What will be the priorities in the first 90 days?

With whom will I be working?

How is the department organized, and what will my role be?

How will performance be measured and evaluated?

How are conflicts resolved?

behavioral interview

an employment interview in which an employer looks for the employee to provide specific examples of specific skills

case interview

an employment interview in which the interviewee is presented with a business case by the employer and asked to work through it

stress interview

an employment interview in which more than one person fires questions at an interviewee

Work It Out

1. Enumerate the qualities and skills that would make you a good investment for an employer.

2. Enumerate the qualities and skills you need to develop further and plan how to do this.

3. Compose a "Position Wanted" advertisement for yourself.

Skill Builder

Let's Get Tough

Human relations consultant and interviewer trainer Justin Menkes helps employment recruiters learn how to gather a lot of information in a brief period of time. To accomplish this, he suggests they ask questions like those identified in the text. Try your hand at answering one of those questions: You have two very important responsibilities that both have deadlines that are impossible to meet. You cannot accomplish both. How do you handle that situation?

Which of the following possible responses does your answer most resemble?

1. I'd focus on the project I'm most comfortable with and give it my all.

2. I'd plan carefully, assign segments of the project to others, and multitask so that I could complete both.

3. I'd ask my supervisor which project is most important to the company.

According to Menkes, the first response suggests that the interviewee's focus is on himself or herself, the second response does not answer the question asked, and the third response reveals an interest in the needs of the company and an interest in developing a collaborative relationship.[15]

How are decisions made?

Why do you like working here?[16]

To be effective, both interview participants need to work hard. Questioner and respondent constantly exchange information. While one speaks, the other conveys nonverbal information through posture, facial expression, gestures, and so on. You may stop talking during an interview, but that does not mean that you stop communicating. Know what you want to accomplish with your verbal and nonverbal messages.

Impression Management: Effective Interviewing

How well do we need to know someone before we believe we understand him or her? Experience says not very long. According to psychologists Nalini Ambady and Frank Bernieri, the power of first impressions arms us with a kind of prerational ability or intuition for making judgments about others that color the other impressions we gather over time.[17] It becomes a self-fulfilling prophecy. We assume that the way someone behaves in an interview is indicative of the way that person always behaves.

> What can you do to convey to interviewers that you possess the qualities they seek?

The adage that first impressions count apparently holds true for job interviews.[18] In fact, the word *interview* is derived from the French word *entrevoir,* meaning "to see one another" or "to meet." What happens when an interviewer and an interviewee meet for the first time? What variables influence the impressions the interviewer forms of the interviewee? Most interviewers make their decisions about an applicant during the course of the interview. In fact, although most decide in the last quarter of the interview whether or not to invite the applicant back, a bias for or against the candidate is established earlier in the interview, often during the first four to six minutes.

What can you do to help the interviewer judge you positively from the outset? Among the steps you should take are the following: (1) Look like the professional the interviewer wants to hire. Keep in mind that you're going on an interview, not a date. (2) Be smart going in. Know about the company, the competition, and industry trends. (3) Be enthusiastic and show that you are happy to be there. Smile, sit up, lean slightly forward, and maintain eye contact. Communicating a high level of energy works in your favor. (4) Vary your pitch and volume. The interviewer will view you more positively if you do not speak in a monotone, whisper, or shout, or if you speak without exhibiting vocal hesitations or signs of physical tension.[19]

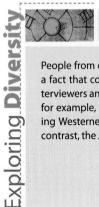

Exploring Diversity

Voices and Impression Management

People from different cultures use their voices differently, a fact that could lead to misunderstandings between interviewers and interviewees. People from the Middle East, for example, tend to speak louder than Westerners, causing Westerners to perceive them as overly emotional. In contrast, the Japanese tend to be much more soft-spoken, leading Westerners to believe that they are extremely polite and humble.

How could such habitual ways of speaking affect the interview process? What can interviewers and interviewees do to diminish such perceptual barriers?

According to researcher Lois Einhorn, the amount of time allotted for an interview also sends an important message.[20] She found that interviewees who were not hired had participated in interviews shorter than those of successful applicants. She also found that successful interviewees spoke a greater percentage of the time than their unsuccessful counterparts. In fact, the successful applicants spoke for some 55 percent of the total interview time, whereas the unsuccessful applicants spoke only 37 percent of the time. Seeming to control the interview also leaves an impression. In Einhorn's research, successful applicants initiated 56 percent of the comments made during their interviews, whereas unsuccessful applicants were viewed as followers—they initiated only 37 percent of the comments. It is important for you to send messages that you are active, not passive.

The interviewer's assessment of you will determine whether or not you get the job. The following are some of the negative factors that turn off the interviewer and lead to applicant rejection:

Believe in yourself.
—The Wizard of Oz, to Dorothy

arrogance

lack of motivation or enthusiasm

immaturity

poor communication skills

unclear goals

unwillingness to relocate or travel

deficient preparation for the interview

lack of experience

too sloppy or too slick an appearance[21]

Among the factors leading to your receiving job offers are the following:

a pleasant personality (likableness)

enthusiasm

interpersonal skills

ability to function as part of a team

knowledge of the field

computer literacy

creativity

clear purpose and goals

flexibility and the ability to handle change

confidence in what you are doing and who you are

integrity and moral standards

global perspective

sense of humor[22]

You can cement a positive image in three ways. (1) Never ask about vacation, company benefits, and personal days during your first interview. Work, instead, to display your knowledge of the company, understand its goals, and identify how you fit in by asking questions that touch on strategic and tactical issues. (2) End an interview by reaffirming your interest in the position and restating why you believe you will be an asset to the company.[23] View this as your sales opportunity; that is, ask for the order. Saying something like, "I am very interested in the position.

I would welcome the opportunity to work with you and your team," helps communicate that you really want the job. (3) Remember to send a thank you note to the person or persons who interviewed you. An essential step in the job-seeking process, this is also the one job seekers most often forget.[24] One successful job candidate sent her thank you via overnight carrier. Another who had interviewed for a job with Google delivered a handwritten thank you along with cupcakes for the recruiter and five other officials who interviewed him. One letter of the Google name appeared atop each cupcake.[25] Do you think he was hired?

DIVERSITY AND THE INTERVIEW

Culture influences how we conduct ourselves during interviews. For example, in collectivistic cultures such as those in China, Japan, and Korea, interviewees habitually display modesty. If Americans, who are used to stressing their positive qualities, were interviewing in any of those countries, they could be perceived as arrogant and self-centered. On the other hand, if persons from a collectivistic culture were to interview in the United States, they could be perceived as unassertive, lacking in confidence, and unprepared to assume leadership. While Western culture encourages people to be assertive and showcase strengths, Eastern culture traditionally teaches members to be more modest and humble about their personal achievements, qualifications, and experience. Similarly, Native American culture teaches that cooperation is a benefit and that one leads through deeds, not words. Thus, not wanting to appear boastful, Native Americans could also be hesitant to discuss their personal strengths.[26]

There are gender differences in what employees seek in a job. Survey results reveal that most men value compensation above all else, while most women put employee benefits first. Compensation is ranked third on most women's lists, after opportunities for skill development.[27]

Age also correlates with what employees want most in a job. In contrast with all other groups, the under-thirties do not even rank benefits among their top five concerns. What is important to most persons in this age bracket are opportunities to develop skills, chances for promotion, compensation, vacations, and an appealing culture and colleagues.[28]

Interviewers need to be sensitive to and demonstrate their respect for all cultures. Not hiring someone on the basis of age, sexual preference, national origin, or religion is illegal. Despite this, many Muslim workers report having thought about changing their last names to avoid alienating potential employers.[29] Would you ever change your name if you thought doing so would help you get the job you want? Why or why not?

TECHNOLOGY AND THE JOB SEARCH

The Web has changed the way we search for and find jobs. Regularly search online classified ads for job opportunities. In addition to Monster.com, aggregate sites such as Indeed.com and SimplyHired.com link you to job ads all over the Internet, including companies' career pages. Additionally, networking Web sites such as LinkedIn.com and Ryze.com can help you connect with business professionals in your field without your knowing them well or at all.[30]

Applicants should use a company's home page to get background information on the organization and its culture or to e-mail a résumé and cover letter. Following are some Web sites you can consult for information on companies and jobs:

Company Information

www.wsj.com

www.nytimes.com

www.bizweb.com

Job Information

http://stats.bls.gov   The Bureau of Labor Statistics Web site, which offers information on positions by state, listing the average salary being paid per position

www.careerbuilder.com

www.NowHiring.com

www.monster.com

Usenet newsgroups, listserv mailing lists, and blogs are three other Internet resources you can use to learn about employment possibilities and company cultures. Of the three, blogs are becoming increasingly popular in electronic recruiting, functioning as a prime means that applicants use to find out about companies. Often they contain information such as what it is like to work at a company as well as what is going on in an industry.[31]

Job seekers also create their own home pages, featuring both their online résumé and business card.[32] A variety of online resources and computer programs exist to help you prepare your résumé. Many provide you with templates that you can complete as is or customize. You can also post your résumé on the Net by e-mailing it to a server.

In fact, more and more companies now request that potential employees submit an electronic résumé (a résumé that is obtained and analyzed electronically by the employer).[33] An electronic résumé includes keywords that describe the person's competencies and skills. Once the employer scans the résumé into the company's computer tracking system, when a job becomes available, the employer can efficiently search the résumés contained in the database by the keywords that describe the characteristics a person qualified for the position should have. Electronic résumés require standard formats and block letters that are plain and simple. A résumé that is going to be scanned should not use boldface type, underlining, or bullets, because these special effects interfere with the scanning process. To facilitate the initial résumé screening, which will be done by a bias-free computer, an electronic résumé typically contains a block paragraph of keywords, which immediately follows the identification information centered above it. Unlike your traditional résumé, which probably contains action verbs such as *communicates well*, your electronic résumé should contain nouns, such as *organizational skills*. A number of Internet sites can help you prepare an electronic résumé. By posting your résumé on a home page, you increase the likelihood that an employer looking for someone with your background and qualifications will access your résumé and contact you directly.

Employers also use computers to add flexibility to currently available interviewing channels. By conducting a computer-assisted interview, for example, employers are able to conduct preliminary conversations with people geographically dispersed from them. In increasing numbers, in addition to telephones and videoconferences, employers are also conducting interviews via e-mail and chat groups. Although these channels do not enable interviewer and interviewee to shake hands with each other, and despite the fact that such interviews will probably not replace face-to-face interviews, they do expand the information resources used by organizations and can be used to supplement face-to-face interviews.[34]

You will want to avoid the following five blunders commonly made by people who use the Internet to search for a job.[35]

1. *Mismerged cover letters.* The interviewee sends a letter that expresses the desire to put skills to work for one company when applying for a job with another company.

2. *Goofy personal e-mail addresses.* Using a name like Snickerdoodle @pastrylover.com or egotisticalking@sold.com can make you look like a less than serious candidate. Use a business-sounding e-mail address instead.

3. *Fun with fonts.* It is a mistake to use bright colors and exotic fonts in résumés or e-mails. Use a plain-text format instead.

4. *Playing out of your league.* Because the Internet makes applying for a job so easy, many applicants apply for jobs for which they are not qualified.

5. *Thinking Send is the end.* Your work is not done when you click Send. Networking and follow-up remain essential components of any job search. Indeed, 61 percent of people surveyed report that networking and referrals remain the best sources for new jobs.[36]

Finally, here are some other warnings.

1. Do not post anything online, including in blogs and discussion boards, that you would not want an employer to see.

2. Do not request an interview or follow up using the too-casual tone of text-speak. Managers who were interviewed believe that text-speak, including the use of emoticons, has no place in interview communications.[37]

Getting a job today has much in common with reality-show contests. Hundreds of job candidates compete, but there will be only one winner.

LOOKING AT THE LAW: ILLEGAL QUESTIONS IN INTERVIEWS

How would you handle being asked an illegal question?

We have seen that some interview questions are tough and probing. Others concerning age, race, marital status, and other personal characteristics are protected under antidiscrimination statutes and are illegal to ask. The Equal Employment Opportunity Commission (EEOC) is the arm of the federal government responsible for monitoring discriminatory practices in hiring decisions. The guidelines are updated periodically and the laws of the EEOC apply in all 50 states.

According to the EEOC, criteria that are legally irrelevant to job qualifications are discriminatory. Interviewees in all states are protected from answering questions about race, ethnicity, marital status, age, sex, disability, and arrest records. It is important for both interviewers and interviewees to realize which questions are legally impermissible in employment interviews. Both parties to the interview have to be well versed in their rights to be able to protect them. The determining factor in whether a question is lawful is simple: Is the information sought relevant to your ability to perform the job? The following are among the most commonly asked illegal questions:

1. Are you physically disabled?
2. How old are you?
3. Are you married?
4. Do you have or are you planning to have a family?
5. What political party do you belong to?
6. Have you ever served time in prison?
7. Is English your native language?
8. What is your religion?
9. Will you need to live near a mosque?
10. Is it hard for you to find child care?
11. Are you a United States citizen?
12. Where were your parents born?
13. Who lives with you?
14. When did you graduate from college?
15. What was the date of your last physical exam?
16. To what clubs or social organizations do you belong?
17. Have you had any recent or past illnesses or operations?
18. How is your family's health?
19. Have you ever been arrested?
20. If you have been in the military, were you honorably discharged?

On the other hand, it is legal to ask the following questions:

1. Are you authorized to work in the United States?
2. What languages do you read or speak fluently (if relevant to the job)?
3. Are you over 18?
4. Would you relocate?
5. Would you be willing to travel as needed?
6. Would you be able and willing to work overtime as necessary?
7. Do you belong to any groups that are relevant to your ability to perform this job?
8. What education do you have?
9. Have you ever been convicted of [fill in the blank]? (The crime must be reasonably related to the performance of the job.)
10. In what branch of the armed forces did you serve?[38]

What if an interviewer asks you an illegal question? You can object diplomatically and remind the interviewer that the question is inappropriate. Doing so, however, can make that interviewer defensive and less willing to select you for the job. Another option is to respond to the illegal question with only information that the interviewer could have legally sought from you. That is, you handle the question by answering the part you do not object to without providing any information you do not wish to provide. For example, if the interviewer asks whether English is your native language, you can respond, "I am fluent in English." If he or she asks whether you belong to a political group, you can respond, "The only groups with which I affiliate that are relevant to this job are the Public Relations Society of America and the American Society for Training and Development."

COMMUNICATION SKILLS IN PRACTICE

GUIDELINES FOR INCREASING YOUR INTERVIEWING EFFECTIVENESS

As you can see, an interview, like any other interpersonal relationship, requires the cooperation, skill, and commitment of both participants to be effective. Interviewees can benefit from the following guidelines:

☑ Be Prepared

Understand the purpose of the interview; plan or anticipate the questions you will ask and be asked; understand your goals; and be able to communicate those goals clearly.

☑ Practice Sending and Receiving Messages

By its very nature, an interview demands skill at sending and receiving verbal and nonverbal messages. Not only must the parties clearly encode their messages, but they must also be skilled at reading the reactions and checking the perceptions of the other.

☑ Demonstrate Effective Listening Skills

Problems occur in interviews when either the interviewer or the interviewee fails to listen closely to what the other is saying. If participants listen carefully—rather than thinking about what they plan to say next—the interview has a better chance of being productive.

☑ Have Conviction

Ask and answer questions and express your opinions with enthusiasm. If you are not excited by your ideas, skills, and abilities, why should anyone else be?

☑ Be Flexible

Do not overprepare or memorize statements. Think things through thoroughly, and be prepared to handle questions or answers you did not anticipate. Be able to adjust to the other person's style and pace.

☑ Be Observant

Pay attention to the nonverbal signals sent to you and by you. Be sure that the signals you send are positive, not negative. Give the other person your total attention.

☑ Consider the Offer

Both interviewer and interviewee need to consider the ramifications of a job offer. A typical 40-hour-a-week job done for approximately 50 weeks a year adds up to 6,000 hours in only three years. Be sure that your choice is one both you and the organization can live with.

Focus on Service Learning

Using information provided on the EEOC's (Equal Employment Opportunity Commission's) Web site, www.eeoc.gov, and other Web sites, such as http://career-advice.monster.com/home.aspx, share with persons currently unemployed your understanding of how to conduct yourself during interviewing, including how to manage illegal questions.

☑ Chart Your Progress

Each time you participate in an interview, fill out a copy of the following evaluation. Circle the number that best describes your response to each question.

a. How prepared were you for the interview?

Not at all prepared   1   2   3   4   5   Fully prepared

b. What kind of climate did you help create?

Hostile climate   1   2   3   4   5   Friendly climate

c. Were the questions you asked clear?

Not clear   1   2   3   4   5   Clear

d. Were the responses you offered complete?

Incomplete   1   2   3   4   5   Complete

e. How carefully did you listen to the other person?

Not at all   1   2   3   4   5   Very carefully

f. How carefully did you pay attention to nonverbal cues?

Not at all   1   2   3   4   5   Very carefully

g. To what extent were you distracted by external stimuli?

Very much   1   2   3   4   5   Not at all

h. How self-confident were you during the interview?

Not at all   1   2   3   4   5   Very confident

i. How flexible were you during the interview?

Not flexible   1   2   3   4   5   Very flexible

j. Would you like to change or improve your behavior for your next interview?

Very much   1   2   3   4   5   Little, or not at all

If your answer to the last question is 1, 2, 3, or 4, consider how you would like to change.

Thinking Critically

Reflect and Respond

Agree or disagree with each of the following statements. Supply reasons and examples that support your stance.

Interviewers care less about what you say than how you say it.
The hiring process is a negative process.
The goal of the interviewer is to find out what's wrong with you.

What do your responses tell you about how you feel about and approach interviews?

Revisiting Objectives

1. **Define *employment interview*.**   During the course of our lives, we all take part in a number of different types of interviews, as either interviewee or interviewer. The interview is the most common type of purposeful, planned, decision-making, person-to-person communication.

2. **Describe the stages of an employment interview.**   Effective interviews are well-structured interactions. They have a beginning, which provides an orientation to what is to come; a middle, when the participants get down to business; and an end, when the main points are reviewed and the participants take leave of one another.

3. **Distinguish between closed, open, primary, and secondary questions.**   Questions are the heart of the interview and the primary means of collecting data. Four basic types of questions are asked in an interview: closed, open, primary, and secondary. Closed questions are highly structured and can be answered with a simple yes or no or in a few words; open questions are broader and offer the interviewee more freedom in responding. Primary questions introduce topics or begin exploring a new area; secondary questions (probing questions) follow up primary questions by asking for further information. Whatever the type of question, an interviewee must maintain honesty in answering.

4. **Perform the roles and responsibilities of an interviewee.**   Good interviewees work hard during an interview, functioning simultaneously as information seekers, information givers, and decision makers. To be a successful interviewee requires specific preparation. Honest self-assessment, practice in answering typical questions, and mastery of the techniques of impression management are of prime importance. To avoid misunderstanding, you need to be aware of how cultural differences can affect the interview.

Resources for Further Inquiry and Reflection

To apply your understanding of how the principles in this appendix are at work in our daily lives, consult the following resources for further inquiry and reflection. Or, if you prefer, choose any other appropriate resource. Then connect the ideas expressed in your chosen selection with the communication concepts and issues you are learning about, both in and out of class.

 Listen to Me

"Working Girls" (10cc)
"From 9 to 5" (Dolly Parton)
"Let the River Flow" (Carly Simon)
"Working Class Hero" (John Lennon)

Each of these songs revolves around the world of work. What do the attitudes expressed in the song suggest about our eagerness and/or preparedness to interview for a job?

 View Me

A Few Good Men   *Kramer vs. Kramer*
Bowling for Columbine   *Roger and Me*
Goodnight and Good Luck *The Smartest Guys*
Kinsey   *in the Room*
Disclosure   *Religulous*

Interviews play a key role in each of these films. How does the knowledge gleaned through one or more interviews advance the plot?

Read Me

Moises Kaufman. *The Laramie Project.* New York: Dramatists Play Service, 2001.
Studs Turkel. *Working.* New York: Avon Press, 1992.
John Patrick Shanley. *Doubt.* New York: Theatre Communication Group, 2005.

Interviews play a key role in each of these works. Identify the kinds of questions raised by the interviewer(s) that elicited the most useful information from the interviewee(s).

 Tell Me

Share with the class the insights you gained from your chosen Listen to Me, View Me, or Read Me selection.

Discuss the most unusual thing that you are aware of happening during an interview to either the interviewer or the interviewee.

Key Terminology

Use the Online Learning Center at www.mhhe.com/gamble10e to further your knowledge of the following terminology.

www.mhhe.com/gamble10e

behavioral interview 461
case interview 461
closed questions 458
employment interview 454

open questions 458
primary questions 458
secondary questions 458
stress interview 461

Idioms in Translation

a toughie — something difficult

cover letter — the letter that precedes a résumé

door should be left open — possibility should be kept open

get you in the door — get you an appointment

provide a platform — give a public forum

telecommute — work from home using a computer or other technology

things do not fall through the cracks — things are not forgotten or overlooked

to roll them out — to introduce [new products]

touched on something — spoke about something

walk the interviewer through — explain to the interviewer

Test Your Understanding

www.mhhe.com/gamble10e

Go to the *Self Quizzes* on the book's Online Learning Center at www.mhhe.com/gamble10e.

LET'S GO TO THE DVD

Investigating *Frost/Nixon*

The film *Frost/Nixon* demonstrates how the finesse of the interviewer can lead to unintended revelations on the part of the interviewee. After viewing the film answer these questions with reference to examples taken from it:

1. How does information derived from an interview influence perception and belief?

2. What role does preparation play in an interviewee's performance?
3. In what ways is an interviewee's effectiveness impacted by the assumptions made about the interview?
4. How do nonverbal cues affect judgments made about the interviewee?
5. What lesson from the film can you use when interviewing?

Blindering Problem

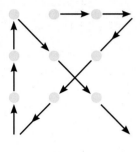

The Detective

1. ?
2. ?
3. F
4. ?
5. ?
6. T
7. ?
8. ?
9. ?
10. ?
11. ?

A

accommodation the means by which co-culture members maintain their cultural identity while striving to establish relationships with members of the dominant culture

accommodator a person who, when faced with a conflict, overvalues the maintenance of relationships and undervalues the achievement of his or her own goals

achieved leader a person who exhibits leadership without being appointed

acquaintanceships relationships with persons we know by name and with whom we converse when the chance arises

affection the need to experience emotionally close relationships

aggressiveness the expressing of one's own thoughts and feelings at another's expense

allness the erroneous belief that any one person can know all there is to know about anything

allocentric exhibiting a collectivistic orientation

appreciative listening listening for enjoyment or relaxation

argumentum ad hominem the use of name-calling in an argument

argumentum ad populum a bandwagon appeal; an appeal to popular opinion

argumentum ad verecudiam an appeal to authority

artifactual communication the use of personal adornments

assertiveness the expressing of one's thoughts and feelings while displaying respect for the thoughts and feelings of others

assimilation the means by which co-culture members attempt to fit in with members of the dominant culture

attitudes predispositions to respond favorably or unfavorably toward a person or subject

autistic society a society at home with computers but disadvantaged when it comes to establishing human intimacy

autocratic, or authoritarian, leaders directive leaders

avoider a person who, when faced with a conflict, uses the unproductive strategy of mentally or physically fleeing the situation

avoiding the relationship stage during which the participants intentionally avoid contact

B

backing support that answers concerns of others

balance a state of psychological comfort in which one's actions, feelings, and beliefs are related to one another as one would like them to be

bar graph a graph used to show the performance of one variable over time or to contrast various measures at a point in time

beliefs confidence in the truth of something

blind area the part of the self known to others but not known to oneself

blindering the process by which one unconsciously adds restrictions that limit one's perceptual capabilities

bonding the relationship stage in which two people make a formal commitment to each other

Boolean search a keyword search

brainstorming a technique designed to generate ideas

breadth the number of topics one discusses with another person

bypassing miscommunication that occurs when individuals think they understand each other but actually miss each other's meaning

C

causal reasoning speculation about the reasons for and effects of occurrences

cause-and-effect order an organizational format that categorizes a topic according to its causes and effects

channels media through which messages are sent

chronemics the study of the use of time

chronological, or time, order an organizational format that develops an idea using a time order

circumscribing the relationship stage in which both the quality and the quantity of communication between two people decrease

civil inattention the polite ignoring of others so as not to infringe on their privacy

claim debatable conclusion or assertion

closure the tendency to fill in missing perceptual pieces in order to perceive a complete world

co-cultures groups of persons who differ in some ethnic or sociological way from the parent culture

collectivistic cultures cultures in which group goals are stressed

communication the deliberate or accidental transfer of meaning

communication apprehension fear of communication, no matter what the context

communication privacy management theory theory that describes the establishment of the boundaries and borders that we decide others may or may not cross

comparison level an expectation of the kinds of rewards and profits we believe we ought to derive from a relationship

comparison level for alternatives　the comparing of rewards derived from a current relationship with ones we expect to get from an alternative relationship

competitive forcer　a person who, when faced with a conflict, adopts a win–lose orientation in which the attaining of personal goals is paramount

competitive goal structure　a goal structure in which members hinder one another's efforts to obtain a goal

competitive set　a readiness to perceive a conflict in all-or-nothing terms

complementarity　the attraction principle that states that opposites attract

comprehensive listening　listening to gain knowledge

compromiser　a person who, when faced with a conflict, tries to find a middle ground

configural formats　organizational patterns that are indirect and inexplicit

conflict　perceived disagreement

conflict grid　a model portraying the styles individuals use to resolve conflicts

connotative meaning　subjective meaning; one's personal meaning for a word

consistency　the desire to maintain balance in our lives by behaving according to commitments already formed

contact cultures　cultures that promote interaction and encourage displays of warmth, closeness, and availability

content conflict　a disagreement over matters of fact

context　the setting

control　the need to feel we are capable and responsible and are able to exert power and influence in our relationships

cooperative goal structure　a goal structure in which the members of a group work together to achieve their objectives

cooperative set　a readiness to share rewards to resolve conflicts

cost–benefit/social exchange theory　the theory that we work to maintain a relationship as long as the benefits we receive outweigh the costs

credibility　the receiver's assessment of the competence, trustworthiness, and dynamism of a speaker

critical listening　listening to evaluate the worth of a message

critical thinking　the careful and deliberate process of message evaluation

cultivation theory　a theory propounded by George Gerbner and colleagues focusing on the mass media's ability to influence users' attitudes and perceptions of reality

cultural imperialism　the expansion of dominion of one culture over another culture

cultural nearsightedness　the failure to understand that we do not all attribute the same meanings to similar behavioral clues

cultural pluralism　adherence to the principle of cultural relativism

cultural relativism　the acceptance of other cultural groups as equal in value to one's own

culturally confused　lacking an understanding of cultural difference

culture　a system of knowledge, beliefs, values, customs, behaviors, and artifacts that are acquired, shared, and used by members during daily living

cyberbole　exaggerated claims about the effects new technologies have on society

D

decision by consensus　a decision that all members understand and will support, reached as a result of members' voicing feelings and airing differences

deduction　reasoning that moves from the general to the specific

defensive behavior　behavior that occurs when one perceives a threat

definitions　explanations of what a stimulus is or what a word or concept means

democratic leaders　leaders who represent a reasonable compromise between authoritarian and laissez-faire leaders

denotative meaning　dictionary meaning; the objective or descriptive meaning of a word

depth　a measure of how central the topics you discuss with another person are to your self-concept

derived credibility　a measure of a speaker's credibility during a speech-making event

designated leader　a person given the authority to exert influence within a group

dialectical tensions　tensions that occur when opposing goals meet

dialogic listening　listening that focuses on what happens to people as they respond to each other

differentiating　the relationship stage in which two people identified as a couple seek to regain unique identities

digital divide　information gap

disclaimers　remarks that diminish a statement's importance

distance relating　relating with persons via e-mail, chat rooms, and instant messages

distinctiveness theory　the theory that states that a person's own distinctive traits are more salient to him or her than are the more prevalent traits possessed by others in the immediate environment

diversity　the recognition and valuing of difference

dominant culture　the culture in power; the mainstream culture

E

effect   the communication outcome

ego conflict   a disagreement in which persons believe that winning or losing is tied to their self-worth, prestige, or competence

emoticons   symbols that replace nonverbal cues during machine-assisted communication

emotional contagion   the catching of another person's mood

emotional intelligence   the ability to motivate oneself, to control impulses, to recognize and regulate one's moods, to empathize, and to hope

emotional isolationists   persons who seek to avoid situations that may require the exchange of feelings

empathic listening   listening to help others

equivocate   use purposefully vague language to finesse a response

essentials of communication   those components present during every communication event

ethnocentrism   the tendency to see one's own culture as superior to all others

ethos   audience's judgment of speaker's character or credibility

euphemism   a pleasant word that is substituted for a less pleasant one

evaluative feedback   a positive or negative judgment

examples   representative cases

experimenting   the relationship stage during which we begin to probe the unknown, often through the exchange of small talk

extemporaneous speech   a speech that is researched, outlined, and delivered after careful rehearsal

external feedback   a response from another

F

facework   the means used to present a public image

facial management techniques   the means we use to control the expressions we reveal to others

fact   that which is known to be true based on observation

false division   the polarization of options, when, in fact, many options exist

feedback   information returned to a message source

feminine cultures   cultures that value tenderness and relationships

figure–ground principle   a strategy that facilitates the organization of stimuli by enabling us to focus on different stimuli alternately

first impressions   initial judgments about people

fixed-feature space   space that contains relatively permanent objects

flames   online insults

formative feedback   timed negative feedback

friendly relations   the friendship stage in which we explore whether we have enough in common to continue building a relationship

friendships   relationships characterized by enjoyment, acceptance, trust, respect, mutual assistance, confidences, understanding, and spontaneity

functional theory   the leadership theory suggesting that several members of a group should be ready to lead because various actions are needed to achieve group goals

G

Galatea effect   the principle that states that we fulfill our own expectations

gender-lects   Deborah Tannen's term for language differences attributed to gender

globalization   the increasing economic, political, and cultural integration and interdependence of diverse cultures

glocalization   how globalization affects and merges with local interests and environments

gossip mill   the network through which unverified information is spread

grapevine   a type of informal, conversational network existing in organizations

grief process   a mourning process composed of five stages: denial, anger, guilt, depression, and acceptance

group   a collection of individuals who interact verbally and nonverbally, occupy certain roles with respect to one another, and cooperate to accomplish a goal

group climate   the emotional atmosphere of a group

group communication   interaction with a limited number of persons

group goals   a group's motivation for existing

group norms   informal rules for interaction in a group

group patterns of communication   patterns of message flow in a group

group role-classification model   a model that describes functions participants should seek to assume and to avoid in groups

group structure   group member positions and roles performed

groupthink   an extreme means of avoiding conflict that occurs when groups let the desire for consensus override careful analysis and reasoned decision making

H

habitual pitch   the characteristic pitch one uses

halo effect   the perceiving of qualities that are primarily positive

haptics   the study of the use of touch

hearing   the involuntary, physiological process by which we perceive sound

hidden area   the part of the self that contains information about the self known to oneself but that is hidden from others

high self-monitors   people highly attuned to impression management efforts

high-context communication   a tradition-bound communication system that depends on indirectness

high-intensity conflict   A conflict in which one person intends to destroy or seriously hurt the other

high-power-distance cultures   cultures based on power differences in which subordinates defer to superiors

high-tech–high-touch society   a technologically advanced society that values interpersonal relationships

horn effect   the perceiving of qualities that are primarily negative

HURIER model   a model of listening focusing on six skill areas or stages

hurtful messages   messages designed to upset or to cause emotional pain that further hampers trust

hyper-competitive culture   the contention that one needs to defeat another to achieve one's goals

I

"I" messages   nonevaluative responses that convey our feelings about the nature of a situation

idiocentric   exhibiting an individualistic orientation

illustrations   stories; narrative pictures

impression management   the creation of a positive image designed to influence others

impromptu speech   a speech delivered spontaneously or on the spur of the moment

inclusion   the need for social contact

individualistic cultures   cultures in which individual goals are stressed

induction   reasoning that moves from specific evidence to a general conclusion

inference   an assumption with varying degrees of accuracy

informal space   space that is highly mobile and can be quickly changed

information overload   the situation that occurs when the amount of information provided by a speech maker is too great to be handled effectively by receivers

information underload   the situation that occurs when the information provided by a speech maker is already known to receivers

informative speech   a speech that updates and adds to the knowledge of receivers

initial credibility   a measure of how an audience perceives a speaker prior to the speech-making event

initiating   the relationship stage during which contact is first made

integrating   the relationship stage in which two people are identified as a couple

intensifying   the relationship stage during which two people become good friends

intercultural communication   interaction with individuals from different cultures

interethnic communication   interaction with individuals of different ethnic origins

internal feedback   a response one gives oneself

internal summaries   rhetorical devices designed to help listeners remember content

international communication   communication between persons representing different nations

interpersonal communication   the relationship level of communication

interpersonal conflict   conflict between two or more people

interpersonal relationship   a meaningful connection, such as friendship, between two persons

interracial communication   the interpreting and sharing of meanings with individuals from different races

intimate distance   a distance ranging from the point of touch to 18 inches from a person

intracultural communication   interaction with members of the same racial or ethnic group or co-culture as one's own

intrapersonal communication   communication with the self

intrapersonal conflict   internal conflict

J

Johari window   a model containing four panes that is used to explain the roles that self-awareness and self-disclosure play in relationships

K

kaleidoscope thinking   the taking of existing data and twisting it or looking at it from another angle

killer looks   looks that discourage or inhibit the generation of ideas

killer phrases   comments that stop the flow of ideas

kinesics   the study of the relationship between human body motion, or body language, and communication

L

laissez-faire leader   a nondirective leader

language   a unified system of symbols that permits the sharing of meaning

leadership the ability to influence others

line graphs graphs used to illustrate trends, relationships, or comparisons over time

linear logic the step-by-step development of ideas; the reliance on facts and data to support main points

linguistic determinism the belief that language influences how we interpret the world

linguistic prejudice the use of prejudiced language

linguistic relativity the belief that persons who speak different languages perceive the world differently

listening the deliberate, psychological process by which we receive, understand, and retain aural stimuli

listserv an e-mail list of people who have interest in and knowledge of a particular topic

logos logical proof

loneliness the perceived discrepancy between desired and achieved social relationships

low self-monitors people who pay little attention to responses others have to them

low-contact cultures cultures that maintain more distance when interacting

low-context communication a system that encourages directness in communication

low-intensity conflict a conflict in which the persons involved work to discover a solution beneficial to all parties

low-power-distance cultures cultures that believe that power should be used only when legitimate

M

main ideas the main points of a speech; the subtopics of a speech

maintenance roles group roles designed to ensure the smooth running of a group

manuscript speech a speech read from a script

markers items that reserve one's space

masculine cultures cultures that value aggressiveness, strength, and material symbols of success

Maslow's hierarchy of needs a model that depicts motivation as a pyramid with the most basic needs at the base and the most sophisticated at the apex

mass communication the transmission of messages that may be processed by gatekeepers prior to being sent to large audiences via a channel of broad diffusion

medium-intensity conflict a conflict in which each person feels committed to winning, but winning is seen as sufficient

melting-pot philosophy the view that different cultures should be assimilated into the dominant culture

memorized speech a manuscript speech committed to memory

message the content of a communicative act

mindfulness emptying one's mind of personal concerns and interfering emotions, and choosing to focus on the person and the here and now

mixed message message that occurs when words and actions contradict each other

Monroe's motivated sequence a speech framework composed of five phases—attention, need, satisfaction, visualization, and action

moving toward friendship the friendship stage in which we make small personal disclosures demonstrating the desire to expand our relationship

multiculturalists persons respectful of and engaged with people from distinctly different cultures

MYGLO an acronym for "my eyes glaze over"

N

nascent friendship the friendship stage that finds us considering each other friends

need for affection the need to express and receive love

need for control the need to feel we are capable and responsible

need for inclusion the need for social contact

negative feedback a response that extinguishes behavior in progress

noise anything that interferes with or distorts the ability to send and receive messages

nonassertiveness the hesitation to display one's feelings and thoughts

nonevaluative feedback nondirective feedback

nonfluencies meaningless sounds or phrases that disrupt the flow of speech

nonverbal communication the kinds of human messages and responses not expressed in words

O

olfactics the study of the sense of smell

online, or machine-assisted, communication the building of relationships using computers and the Internet

onlinespeak the informal communication style that marks electronic communication

open area the part of the self containing information known to both the self and others

P

paralanguage vocal cues that accompany spoken language

paraphrasing restating in one's own words what another person has said

pathos   emotional proof

perceived self   the self we believe ourselves to be

perception   the process by which we make sense out of experience

perceptual constancy   the desire to perceive experience exactly as we have perceived it in the past

perceptual sets   expectations that produce a readiness to process experience in a predetermined way

personal distance   a distance ranging from 18 inches to 4 feet from a person

persuasion   the attempt to change or reinforce attitudes, beliefs, values, or behaviors

persuasive speech   a speech whose primary purpose is to change or reinforce the attitudes, beliefs, values, and/or behaviors of receivers

phatic communication   communication designed to open the channels of communication

pictographs   graphs that use sketches to represent concepts

pie, or circle, graph   a circle with the various percentages of the whole indicated by wedges; a means of showing percentage relationships

pitch   the highness or lowness of the voice

pop language   words and phrases used to sell oneself as hip or cool

positive feedback   a behavior-enhancing response

post hoc, ergo propter hoc   the identification of a false cause

prejudice   a biased, negative attitude toward a particular group of people; a negative prejudgment based on membership in a social category

prejudiced language   sexist, ageist, or racist language; language disparaging to the members of a co-culture

primacy effect   the ability of one's first impression to color subsequent impressions

probing   a nonevaluative technique in which we ask for additional information

problem-and-solution order   an organizational format that identifies the problems inherent in a situation and presents a solution to remedy them

problem-solving collaborator   a person who, when faced with a conflict, adopts a win-win orientation, seeking to satisfy his or her own goals as well as those of others

proposition   a statement that summarizes the purpose of a persuasive speech

proposition of fact   a persuasive speech with the goal of settling what is or is not so

proposition of policy   a persuasive speech on what ought to be

proposition of value   a persuasive speech that espouses the worth of an idea, a person, or an object

proxemics   the study of the use of space

pseudoconflict   the situation that results when persons mistakenly believe that two or more goals cannot be achieved simultaneously

public communication   communication designed to inform, persuade, or entertain audience members

public distance   a distance of 12 feet and farther from a person

public speaking   the act of preparing, staging, and delivering a presentation to an audience

public speaking anxiety   fear of speaking to an audience

Pygmalion effect   the principle that states that we fulfill the expectations of others

Q

qualifier   indication of the strength of the connection

qualifiers   tentative phrases

quality circles   small groups of employees who meet regularly to discuss organizational life and the quality of their work environment

questions of fact   questions involving the truth or falsity of a statement

questions of policy   questions designed to help determine future actions

questions of value   questions involving subjective judgments

R

racial code words   words that are discriminatory but not literally racist

rate   speaking speed

reasoning from analogy   reasoning by comparison

reasons   facts or evidence for making the claim

rebuttal   potential counterarguments

receivers   persons who receive, decode, and interpret a message

red herring   a distraction used to lead the receiver to focus on an irrelevant issue

red-flag words   words that trigger emotional deafness, dropping listening efficiency to zero

reflective-thinking framework   a system for decision making and problem solving that is designed to encourage critical inquiry

role reversal   a strategy in which persons in conflict each act as the other in order to understand the other's position

role-limited interaction   the beginning stage of friendship

S

Sapir–Whorf hypothesis   the belief that the labels we use help shape the way we think, our worldview, and our behavior

selective attention   the tendency to focus on certain cues and ignore others

selective exposure   the tendency to expose oneself to information that reaffirms existing attitudes, beliefs, and values

selective perception   the means of interpreting experience in a way that conforms to one's beliefs, expectations, and convictions

selective retention   the tendency to remember those things that reinforce one's way of thinking and forget those that oppose one's way of thinking

self-awareness   the ability to reflect on and monitor one's own behavior

self-concept   everything one thinks and feels about oneself

self-conflict   the type of conflict that occurs when a person has to choose between two or more mutually exclusive options

self-directed teams   autonomous groups of employees empowered to make decisions and supervise themselves

self-disclosure   the process of revealing to another person information about the self that he or she would not otherwise know

self-efficacy   an optimistic belief in one's own competence

self-esteem   how well one likes and values oneself

self-fulfilling prophecy   a prediction or an expectation that comes true simply because one acts as if it were true

self-image   the sort of person one perceives oneself to be

self-serving roles   group roles that impede the functioning of a group by preventing members from working together effectively

semi-fixed-feature space   space in which objects are used to create distance

senders   persons who formulate, encode, and transmit a message

separation   the means co-culture members use to resist interacting with members of the dominant culture

serial communication   a chain-of-command transmission

silence   the absence of both paralinguistic and verbal cues

situational theory   the theory of leadership that asserts that leadership depends on the situation

social capital   social connections or networks

social distance   a distance ranging from 4 feet to 12 feet from a person

social penetration theory   the theory that states that our relationships begin with relatively narrow breadth and shallow depth and develop over time

social proof   the determination of what is right by finding out what other people think is right

spatial order   an organizational format that describes an object, a person, or a phenomenon as it exists in space

speech framework   a skeleton for speech development

speech–thought differential   the difference between speaking and thinking rates

stabilized friendship   the friendship stage in which we decide that our friendship is secure and will continue

stagnating   the relationship stage during which communication is at a standstill

statistics   facts expressed in numerical form

stereotype   a generalization about people, places, or events held by many members of a society

stereotypes   mental images or pictures that guide our reactions to others

subordinate ideas   ideas that amplify the main ideas or subtopics of a speech

supportive feedback   a nonevaluative response indicating that the receiver perceives a problem as important

symbol   that which represents something else

T

tag questions   questions that are midway between outright statements and yes–no questions

task roles   group roles designed to help the group achieve its goals

technopoly   a culture in which technology monopolizes the thought-world

terminal credibility   a measure of a speaker's credibility at the end of a speech-making event

termination   the relationship stage during which the relationship ends

territoriality   the need to demonstrate a possessive or ownership relationship to space

testimony   someone else's opinions or conclusions

tolerance of vulnerability   the degree of trust we place in another person to accept information we disclose without hurting us or the relationship

topical order   an organizational format that clusters material by dividing it into a series of appropriate topics

toxic communication   the consistent use of verbal abuse and/or physical or sexual aggression or violence

trait theory   the theory of leadership that asserts that certain people are born to lead

transformational leader   a leader who gives a group a new vision, strengthening its culture or structure

transitions   connective words and phrases

triangle of meaning   a model that explains the relationship that exists among words, things, and thoughts

type X leader   a leader who does not trust group members to work and is unconcerned with the personal achievements of group members

type Y leader   a leader who displays trust in group members and is concerned with their sense of personal achievement

U

understanding   a nonevaluative response that uses restatement to check comprehension

unknown area   the part of the self that is unknown to oneself and others

V

value conflict   a disagreement that arises when persons hold different views on an issue

virtual neighborhoods and communities   online, surrogate communities

virtual reality   an environment that exists as data in a computer system

visual dominance   a measure calculated by comparing the percentage of looking while speaking with the percentage of looking while listening

volume   the degree of loudness of the voice

W

waning friendship   the friendship stage during which friends begin to drift apart

warrant   explanation of the relationship between the claim and the data

Y

"you" messages   responses that place blame on another person

Chapter 1

1. Robert D. Putnam, *Bowling Alone: The Collapse and Revival of American Community*. New York: Simon & Schuster, 2000.

2. Alan Murray, *The Wealth of Choices*. New York: Crown Business, 2000.

3. An idea attributed to Leonard Lauder, as described in Della Bradshaw, "Old-World Leader, New World Vision," *Financial Times*, February 4, 2008, p. 8.

4. See, for example, Stephen R. Covey, *The 7 Habits of Highly Effective People*. New York: Simon & Schuster, 1989, pp. 236–260.

5. See Deborah Tannen, *That's Not What I Meant!* New York: Morrow, 1986.

6. Frank E. X. Dance, "Toward a Theory of Human Communication," in Frank E. X. Dance, ed., *Human Communication Theory: Original Essays*. New York: Holt, Rinehart & Winston, 1967.

7. See, for example, Alan E. Ivey and James C. Hurse, "Communication as Adaptation," *Journal of Communication*, 21 (1971), pp. 199–207. Ivey and Hurse reaffirm that communication is adaptive, like biological evolution—not an end in itself, but a process. Also see J. F. Nussbaum, ed., *Life-Span Communication: Normative Processes*. Hillsdale, NJ: Lawrence Erlbaum Associates, 1989.

8. O. Wiio, *Wiio's Laws and Some Others*. Espoo, Finland: Welin Goos, 1978.

9. C. Wade and C. Tarvis, *Learning to Think Critically: The Case of Close Relationships*. New York: HarperCollins, 1990.

10. Marshall McLuhan, *Understanding Media*. Cambridge: MIT Press, 1994.

11. Neil Postman, *Technopoly: The Surrender of Culture to Technology*. New York: Vintage, 1992.

12. For a detailed discussion of the complex relationship between the Internet and face-to face interaction, see Barry Wellman and Caroline Haythornthwaite, eds., *The Internet in Everyday Life*. Malden, MA: Blackwell Publishing, 2002.

13. Norman H. Nie and D. Sunshine Hillygus, "The Impact of Internet Use on Sociability: Time Diary Findings," *IT & Society*, 1:1 (Summer 2002), pp. 11–20.

14. Norman H. Nie, D. Sunshine Hillygus, and Lutz Erbring, "Internet Use, Interpersonal Relations, and Sociability: Findings from a Detailed Time Diary Study," in Wellman and Haythornthwaite, 2002.

15. BurstMedia, "Online Insights," July 2007, p. 1.

16. Ibid., p. 2.

17. See, for example, Hector Jose Huyke, "Technologies and the Devaluation of What Is Near," *Technq* 6:3 (2003), pp. 57–70.

18. J. E. Katz and M. Aakhus, *Perpetual Contact: Mobile Communication, Private Talk, Public Performance*. Cambridge, U.K.: Cambridge University Press, 2002.

19. See, for example, K. Y. A. McKenna, A. S. Green, and M. E. J. Gleason, "Relation Formation on the Internet: What's the Big Attraction?" *Journal of Social Issues*, 58 (2002), pp. 9–31.

20. See, for example, www.theworldjournal.com/2003/realitycheck.htm.

21. William Schutz, *The Interpersonal Underworld*. Palo Alto, CA: Science & Behavior Books, 1966.

22. National Association of Colleges and Employers. *Job Outlook*. 2008; and Sherwyn P. Morreale and Judy C. Pearson, "Why Communication Education Is Important: The Centrality of the Discipline in the 21st Century," *Communication Education*, 57:2 (April 2008), pp. 224–240.

23. John Markoff, "A Newer, Lonelier Crowd Emerges in Internet Study," *New York Times*, February 16, 2000, p. 1.

Chapter 2

1. See Walter Lippman, *Public Opinion*. Macmillan: New York, 1957, pp. 79–103; and C. S. Abbate, S. Boca, and P. Bocchiaro, "Stereotyping in Persuasive Communication: Influence Exerted by Disapproved Source," *Journal of Applied Social Psychology*, 34 (2004), p. 1192.

2. Neil MacFarquhar, "Abandon Stereotypes, Muslims in America Say," *New York Times*, November 4, 2007, p. A12.

3. Pamela Constable, "Racial Survey Unearths Tensions," *The Record*, December 11, 2007, p. A6.

4. James Flanigan, "Passports Essential for These M.B.A.'s," *New York Times*, February 21, 2008, p. C5.

5. Marshall McLuhan, *The Medium Is the Message*. New York: Bantam Books, 1967; Marshall McLuhan, *Understanding Media*. New York: Mentor, 1964.

6. Pew Research Center, "American Mobility," December 29, 2008, http://pewsocialtrends.org.

7. Robert D. Putnam, *Bowling Alone: The Collapse and Revival of American Community*. New York: Simon & Schuster, 2001.

8. See, for example, Christopher Caldwell, "Diversity Is Not Black and White," *Financial Times*, August 12, 2007, p. 7; and Michael Skapinker, "Why the

Workplace is Diversity's Best Bet," *Financial Times*, September 18, 2007, p. 11.

9. See William B. Gudykunst and Young Yun Kim, eds. *Readings on Communicating with Strangers*. New York: McGraw-Hill, 1991.

10. Larry A. Samover and Richard E. Porter, *Communication between Cultures*, 4th ed. Belmont, CA: Wadsworth, 2001, pp. 5, 46–47.

11. Judith Cornelia Person and Edward Nelson. *Understanding and Sharing: An Introduction to Speech Communication*, 6th ed. Dubuque, IA: Brown & Benchmark, 1994, p. 193.

12. Wendy Griswold. *Cultures and Societies in a Changing World*. Thousand Oaks, CA: Pine Forge, 1994, p. 57.

13. M. P. Orbe, "Laying the Foundation for Co-Cultural Communication Theory: An Inductive Approach to Studying 'Nondominant' Communication Strategies and the Factors That Influence Them." *Communication Studies*, 47 (1996), pp. 157–176.

14. Edward T. Hall, *The Silent Language*. New York: Fawcett, 1959.

15. Griswold, pp. 22–24.

16. Carley H. Dodd, *Dynamics of Intercultural Communication*, 3rd ed. Dubuque, IA: Brown, 1991, p. 3.

17. Thomas Keneally. "Racism's as Human as Love." *The Sunday Record*, February 6, 1994, p. R-1.

18. William B. Gudykunst, *Bridging Differences; Effective Intergroup Communication*, 3rd ed. Thousand Oaks, CA: Sage, 1998, pp. 106–110; also see 4th ed., 2003.

19. W. Lippmann, *Public Opinion*. New York: Macmillan, 1922.

20. For more on prejudice, see M. L. Hecht, ed., *Communicating Prejudice*. Thousand Oaks, CA: Sage, 1998.

21. U.S. Census Bureau; Haya El Nasser, "39 Million Make Hispanics Largest Minority Group." *USA Today*, June 19, 2003, pp. 1A, 2A.

22. Larry A. Samovar and Richard E. Porter. *Intercultural Communication: A Reader*, 11th ed. Belmont, CA: Wadsworth, 2006, p. 5.

23. See, for example, G. Hofstede, *Culture's Consequences: International Differences in Work-Related Values*, 2nd ed. Beverly Hills, CA: Sage, 2001; F. R. Kluckhohn and F. L. Strodtbeck, *Variations in Value Orientations*. New York: Row & Peterson, 1960; and E. T. Hall, *Beyond Culture*. New York: Doubleday, 1976.

24. See Judith N. Martin and Thomas K. Nakayama, *Intercultural Communication in Contexts*, 2nd ed. Mountain View, CA: Mayfield, 2000, pp. 265–266. Also see 3rd ed., 2003.

25. G. Hofstede, *Cultures and Organizations*. London: McGraw-Hill, 1991.

26. See G. Hofstede, *Masculinity and Femininity: The Taboo Dimension of National Cultures*. Thousand Oaks, CA: Sage, 1998.

27. Robert R. Harris and Robert T. Moran, *Managing Cultural Differences*, 3rd ed. Houston, TX: Gulf, 1991.

28. As reported in Larry A. Samovar and Richard E. Porter. *Communication between Cultures*. Belmont, CA: Wadsworth, 1991, p. 154.

29. Gudykunst, *Bridging Differences*, 4th ed., pp. 12–13.

30. "Unhappy Meal for Muslims," *The Record*, June 8, 1994, p. C-3.

31. Griswold, p. 1.

32. Margaret H. DeFleur and Melvin L. DeFleur, "The Next Generation's Image of Americans: Attitudes and Beliefs Held by Teen-Agers in Twelve Countries," October 3, 2002, www.bu.edu/news/releases/2002/defleur/report.pdf.

33. Guo-Ming Chen and William Starosta, "A Review of the Concept of Intercultural Sensitivity." *Human Communication*, 2 (1997), p. 5.

34. Deborah Tannen, *You Just Don't Understand: Women and Men in Conversation*. New York: Morrow, 1990.

35. Josh Meyrowitz, "Media Theory," in Erik P. Bucy, ed. *Living in the Information Age*. Belmont, CA: Wadsworth, 2002, p. 32.

36. Clifford Stoll, "Further Explorations into the Culture of Computing," in Erick P. Bucy, ed., *Living in the Information Age*. Belmont, CA: Wadsworth, 2002, pp. 210–215.

37. BBC News, "How Governments Censor the Web," March 22, 2007, news.bbc.co.uk/2/hi/technology/6475911.stm.

Chapter 3

1. K. G. Wilson and S. C. Hayes, "Why It Is Crucial to Understand Thinking and Feeling: An Analysis and Application to Drug Abuse," *Behavior Analyst*, 23 (Spring 2000), pp. 25–43.

2. C. Mruk, *Self-Esteem: Research, Theory, and Practice*. New York: Springer, 2005.

3. See Maureen Stout, *The Feel-Good Curriculum: The Dumbing Down of America's Kids in the Name of Self-Esteem*. New York: Perseus Books, 2000; and Mary Amorose, "Is Self-Esteem Overrated?" *The Record*, April 27, 2000, pp. HF-1, HF-3.

4. Adam Bryant, "America's Latest Fad: Modesty It's Not." *New York Times*, February 9, 1997, p. E-3.

5. Virginia Satir, *The New Peoplemaking*. 2nd ed. Palo Alto, CA: Science and Behavior Books, 1988.

6. Roy F. Baumeister, Jennifer D. Campbell, Joachim I. Krueger, and Kathleen D. Vohs, "Exploding the Self-Esteem Myth," *Scientific American*, January 2005, pp. 84–91.

7. Michele Orecklin, "Beware of the Crowd." *Time*, August 21, 2000, p. 69.

8. R. Baumeister, L. Smart, and J. Boden. "Relation of the Threatened Egotism to Violence and Aggression: The Dark Side of High Self-Esteem." *Psychological Review*, 103 (1996), pp. 5–33.

9. B. Bushman and R. Baumeister. "Threatened Egotism, Narcissism, Self-Esteem, and Direct and Displaced Aggression: Does Self-Love or Self-Hate Lead to Violence," *Journal of Personality and Social Psychology*, 75 (1998), pp. 219–229.

10. Roy F. Baumeister, Jennifer D. Campbell, Joachim I. Krueger, and Kathleen D. Vohs, "Does High Self-Esteem Cause Better Performance, Interpersonal Success, Happiness, or Healthier Lifestyles?" *Psychological Science in the Public Interest*, 4:1 (May 2003), pp. 1–44.

11. Sharon Jayson, "Yep, Life'll Burst That Self-Esteem Bubble," *USA Today*, February 16, 2005, p. L-7.

12. Marlene Zuk, "A Case of 'Unwarranted Self-Regard,'" *The Record*, May 30, 2005, p. L-7.

13. See Roseabeth Moss Kanter, *Confidence: How Winning Streaks and Losing Streaks Begin and End*. New York: Crown, 2004.

14. Sharon Begley, "Real Self-Esteem Builds on Achievement, Not Praise for Slackers," *The Wall Street Journal*, April 18, 2003, p. B1.

15. See D. Hamacheck, *Encounters with the Self*, 3rd ed. Fort Worth, TX: Holt, Rinehart & Winston, 1992, pp. 5–8.

16. S. I. Hayakawa and Alan R. Hayakawa, *Language in Thought and Action*, 5th ed. San Diego: Harcourt Brace Jovanovich, 1990, pp. 217–218.

17. See Jean Piaget, *The Construction of Reality in the Child*. New York: Free Press, 1954.

18. Judith Martin and Thomas Nakayama, *Experiencing Intercultural Communication: An Introduction*, 3rd ed. New York: McGraw-Hill, 2008, p. 95.

19. See, for example, J. F. Nussbaum, T. Thompson, and J. D. Robinson, *Communication and Aging*. New York: Harper & Row, 1989, p. 21.

20. Justine Coupland, John F. Nussbaum, and Nikolas Coupland. "The Reproduction of Aging and Ageism in Intergenerational Talk," in Nikolas Coupland, Howard Giles, and John Wiemann, eds., *Miscommunication and Problematic Talk*. Newbury Park, CA: Sage, 1991, p. 85.

21. A. Gerike, *Old Is Not a Four Letter Word: A Midlife Guide*. Watsonville, CA: Papier Mache, 1997.

22. See A. Bandura, *Self-Efficacy: The Exercise of Control*. New York: Freeman, 1997.

23. Martin E. P. Seligman, interview in *Success*, July-August 1994, p. 41. Used by permission of *Success* magazine.

24. Johnathan Goldberg, "Our Gold-Star World," *USA Today*, December 4, 2007, p. 11A.

25. See, for example, Jean Twenge, *Generation Me: Why Today's Young Americans Are More Confident, Assertive, Entitled—and More Miserable Than Ever Before*. New York: Free Press, 2006; and Stephanie Rosenbloom, "Generation Me vs. You Revisited," *New York Times*, January 17, 2008, p. G-1, G-6.

26. "Welcoming the New Millennials," *Wall Street Journal*, December 4, 2007, p. B-9.

27. Martin and Nakayama, p. 89.

28. Carl Sandburg, *The People, Yes*. New York: Harcourt Brace Jovanovich, 1936.

29. Robert Rosenthal and Lenore Jacobson, *Pygmalion in the Classroom*. New York: Holt, Rinehart & Winston, 1968.

30. R. Rosenthal, "The Pygmalion Effect and Its Mechanisms," in J. Aronson, ed., *Improving Academic Achievement: Impact of Psychological Factors on Education*. San Diego: Academic, 2002, pp. 25–36.

31. "First, Dispel All the Myths," *USA Today* editorial, October 12, 2007, p. 8A.

32. See, for example, P. Watzlawick, "Self-Fulfilling Prophecies," in J. O'Brien and P. Kollock, eds., *The Production of Reality*, 3rd ed. Thousand Oaks, CA: Pine Force, 2001, pp. 411–423.

33. J. Sterling Livingston, cited in video, *The Self-Fulfilling Prophecy*. CRM Films, 1992.

34. David Firestone. "While Barbie Talks Tough, G.I. Joe Goes Shopping," *New York Times*, December 31, 1993, p. A-12.

35. Peggy Orenstein, "Girls Will Be Girls," *New York Times Magazine*, February 10, 2008, p. 17–18.

36. Julia T. Wood, *Gendered Lives: Communication, Gender, and Culture*, 7th ed. Belmont, CA: Wadsworth, 2007.

37. Dave Barry, "Beauty and the Beast," *Miami Herald*, January 30, 1998.

38. Diane Hales, *Just Like a Woman*. New York: Bantam, 1999, p. 136.

39. See, for example, Susan Faludi, *Fear and Fantasy in Post-9/11 America*. New York: Metropolitan Books, 2008; and Wood, 2007.

40. Flan Finder, "Giving Disorganized Boys the Tools for Success and Multitasking," *New York Times*, January 1, 2008, p. A9.

41. Martin and Nakayama, p. 91.

42. Richard Breslin, *Understanding Culture's Influence on Behavior*. Orlando, FL: Harcourt Brace Jovanovich, 1993, p. 47.

43. "Hey, I'm Terrific," *Newsweek*, February 17, 1992, p. 48.

44. Steven J. Heine, "Self as Cultural Product: An Examination of East Asian and North American Selves," *Journal of Personality*, 69:6 (December 2001), pp. 881–906.

45. Ibid.

46. Larry Samovar and Richard Porter, *Communication between Cultures*. Belmont, CA: Wadsworth, 1991, p. 91.

47. W. B. Guykunst and S. Ting Toomy, *Culture and Interpersonal Communication*. Newbury Park, CA: Sage, 1988.

48. H. C. Triandis, K. Leung, and F. Clark, "Allocentric v. Idiocentric Tendencies," *Journal of Research in Personality*, 19, pp. 395–415.

49. Osei Appiah, "Americans Online: Differences in Surfing and Evaluating Race-Targeted Web Sites by Black and White Users," paper presented at the annual meeting of the Association for Education in Journalism and Mass Communication, Miami, FL, August 2002.

50. Peggy Orenstein, *School Girls: Young Women, Self-Esteem, and the Confidence Gap*. New York: Anchor Books, 1994.

51. "In Truth, Most of Them May Not Be Lonely," *New York Times*, May 9, 1991, p. A-24. Copyright 1991 by the New York Times Co. Reprinted with permission.

52. Robert A. Bell and Michael E. Roloff, "Making a Love Connection: Loneliness and Communication Competence in the Dating Marketplace," *Communication Quarterly*, 39:1 (Winter 1991), p. 58.

53. See Eric Berne, *Games People Play*. New York: Grove, 1964.

54. Joseph Luft, *Group Processes: An Introduction to Group Dynamics*, 2nd ed. Palo Alto, CA: Mayfield, 1970.

55. John Powell, *Why am I Afraid to Tell You Who I Am?* New York: Tabor, 1982.

56. Liz Funk, "Women on Facebook Think Provocative Is Empowering," *USA Today*, September 19, 2007, p. 11A.

57. See E. Goffman, *The Presentation of Self in Everyday Life*. Garden City, NY: Doubleday, 1959; and *Relations in Public*. New York: Basic Books, 1971.

58. A. Markham, *Life Online: Researching Real Experience in Virtual Space*. Walnut Creek, CA: Alta Mira, 1998, pp. 202–203. Also see Don Tapscott, *Grown Up Digital: How the Net Generation is Changing Your World*. New York: McGraw-Hill, 2008.

59. Alan Fram and Trevor Tompson, "Many Teens Take IM Route to Dating, Breaking Up," *The Record*, November 21, 2007, p. A19.

60. For an early work discussing this possibility, see Sherry Turkle, *Life on the Screen*. New York: Simon & Schuster, 1995.

61. A. Lenhart, L. Rainie, and O. Lewis, *Teenage Life Online*. Washington, DC: Pew Internet and American Life Project, 2001.

62. Turkle, p. 12.

63. John A. Bargh, Y. A. Katelyn McKenna, and Grainne M. Fitzsimons, "Can You See the Real Me? Activation and Expression of the 'True Self' on the Internet," *Journal of Social Issues*, 58:1 (January 2002), pp. 33–49.

64. See, for example, Larry M. Gant, "In Defense of the Internet: The Relationship between Internet Communication and Depression, Loneliness, Self-Esteem, and Perceived Social Support," *CyberPsychology and Behavior*, 5:2 (April 2002), pp. 157–172.

65. Turkle, p. 179.

Chapter 4

1. Ron Alsop, "The 'Trophy Kids' Go to Work," *Wall Street Journal*, October 21, 2008, pp. D1, D4.

2. Steven R. Covey, *7 Habits of Highly Effective People*. New York: Simon & Schuster, 1990, p. 281. Also see Mark P. Orbe and Etsuko Kinefuchi, "*Crash* under Investigation: Engaging Complications of Complicity, Coherence, and Implication through Critical Analyses," *Critical Studies in Media Communication* 25:2 (June 2008), pp. 135–156.

3. For an in-depth discussion of how race affects perception, see M. L. Hecht, R. L. Jackson II, and S. A. Ribeau, *African American Communication*, 2nd ed. Mahwah, NJ: Erlbaum, 2003.

4. Natalie Augier, "Blind to Change, Even as It Stares Us in the Face," *New York Times*, April 1, 2008.

5. William V. Haney, *Communication and Organizational Behavior*. Homewood, IL: Irwin, 1973, p. 55.

6. Sara Reistad-Long, "Older Brain Really May Be a Wiser Brain," *New York Times*, May 20, 2008, p. F5.

7. E. Rubin, "Figure and Ground," in D. Beardslee and M. Werthimer, eds., *Readings in Perception*. Princeton, NJ: Van Nostrand, pp. 194–203.

8. Sharon Begley, "People Believe a 'Fact' That Fits Their Views Even If It's Clearly False," *Wall Street Journal*, February 4, 2005, p. Bl.

9. Benedict Carey, "Forgetting May Be Part of the Process of Remembering," *New York Times*, June 5, 2007, p. F5.

10. See, for example, Steve Freiss, "Memory Does Not Always Serve, and That's No Lie," *USA Today*, September 14, 2004, p. 9D; and Daniel L. Schacter, "The Fog of War," *New York Times*, April 5, 2004, p. A21.

11. Larry A. Samovar and Richard E. Porter, *Communication between Cultures*. Belmont, CA: Wadsworth, 1994, p. 81.

12. Paul Chance, "Seeing Is Believing," *Psychology Today*, January–February 1989, p. 26.

13. See Charles G. Russel, "Culture, Language and Behavior: Perception," *ETC*, 57.2 (Summer 2000) pp. 189–218.

14. Barry Arons. "A Review of the Cocktail Party Effect," MIT Media Lab, 1992. Retrieved on February 22, 2008.

15. M. Sunnafrank, A. Ramirez, and S. Metts, "At First Sight: Persistent Relational Effects of Get Aquainted Conversations," *Journal of Social and Personal Relationships*, 21:3 (February 2005), pp. 361–379.

16. Jerry Bembry, "The Pain That Whites Don't See," *The Record*, January 23, 1994, p. E-3. From Jerry Bembry, "Black's Anguish Gives 'Rage' Its Strength," *Baltimore Sun*, December 30, 1993, p. 8D. © 1993, reprinted by permission of the Baltimore Sun.

17. Chance.

18. Sheryl McCarthy, "Blinded by Prejudice," *USA Today*, December 12, 2007, p. 11A.

19. Maria T. Padilla, "Studying Sterotypes among Minority Groups," *The Record*, July 19, 1998, p. L-l.

20. Ralph Ellison, *Invisible Man*. New York: Random House, 1989.

21. Padilla, p. L-3.

22. See, for example, I. V. Blair, "The Malleability of Automatic Stereotypes and Prejudice," *Personality and Social Psychology Review*, 6:3 (2002), pp. 242–262; and P. C. Hughes and J. R. Baldwin, "Communication and Stereotypical Impressions," *Howard Journal of Communication*, 12, pp. 153–171.

23. Ira Berkow, "Rower with Muslim Name Is an All-American Suspect," *New York Times*, February 21, 2003, pp. Dl, D4.

24. Sharon Begley, "Racism Studies Find Rational Part of Brain Can Override Prejudice," *Wall Street Journal*, November 19, 2004, p. Bl.

25. Maria T. Padilla, "Studying Stereotypes among Minority Groups," *The Record*, July 19, 1998, p. L-l.

26. Irving J. Lee, *How to Talk with People*. San Francisco: International Society for General Semantics, 1980.

27. Alfred Korzybski, *Science and Sanity*, 4th ed. San Francisco: International Society for General Semantics, 1980.

28. As told on *20/20*, ABC Television, June 30, 2000.

29. Marshall Singer, "Culture: A Perceptual Approach," in Larry A. Samovar and Richard E. Porter, eds., *Intercultural Communication: A Reader*, 4th ed. Belmont, CA: Wadsworth, 1985, pp. 62–69.

30. Samovar and Porter, p. 105.

31. J. W. Bagby, "A Cross-Cultural Study of Perceptual Predominance in Binocular Rivalry," *Journal of Abnormal and Social Psychology*, 54 (1957), pp. 331–334.

32. H. A. Elfenbein and N. Ambady, "Is There an Ingroup Advantage in Emotion Recognition?" *Psychological Bulletin*, 128, pp. 243–249; M. D. Weather, E. M. Frank, and I. A. Spell, "Difference in the Communication of Affect: Members of the Same Race versus Members of a Different Race," *Journal of Black Psychology*, 28, pp. 66–77.

33. "Textbooks Show Students' Conflicting Views of Past," *Wall Street Journal*, August 6, 2007.

34. Julia T. Wood, *Gendered Lives*. Belmont, CA: Wadsworth, 1994, pp. 21, 131.

35. See Judy Cornelia Pearson, *Gender and Communication*. Dubuque, IA: Brown, 1995.

36. Kristen Homstedt, *Band of Sisters: American Women at War in Iraq*. New York: Stackpole Books, 2007.

37. J. Long, "Symbolic Reality Bites: Women and Racial Ethnic Minorities in Modern Film," *Sociological Spectrum*, 22:3 (July–September 2002), pp. 299–335.

38. See Steven D. Strak, *Glued to the Set: The 60 Television Shows and Events That Made Us Who We Are Today*. New York: Free Press, 1997.

39. Barbara Mueller, *Communicating with Multicultural Consumers: Theoretical and Practical Perspectives*. New York: Peter Lang, 2008, pp. 12–13.

40. Erin Texeira, "Multicultural Socializing in Ads Doesn't Reflect Reality in U.S.," *The Record*, February 18, 2005, p, A24.

41. V. Rohan, "Defining the Face of Evil," *The Record*, January 23, 2005, p. El.

42. G. Gerbner, L. P. Gross, M. Morgan, and N. Signorielli, "The 'Mainstreaming' of America: Violence Profile No. 11," *Journal of Communication*, 30, pp. 10–29; J. Shanahan and M. Morgan, *Television and Its Viewers:*

Cultivation Theory and Research. New York: Cambridge University Press, 1999.

43. Stevenson Swanson, "Has Late Night Made Our Democracy a Joke?" *The Record,* April 18, 2008, p. A29.

44. Russell Peterson, *Strange Bedfellows: How Late-Night Comedy Turns Democracy into a Joke*. New Brunswick, NJ: Rutgers University Press, 2008.

45. Wood, p. 238.

46. Autumn Miller and Susan Dente Ross, "They Are Not Us: Faming of American Indians by the *Boston Globe*," paper delivered at the annual convention of the Association for Education in Journalism and Mass Communication, Miami, FL, August 7–10, 2002.

47. See Daniel Goleman, "Hidden Rules Often Distort Ideas of Risk," *New York Times,* February 1, 1994, pp. C-l, C-10.

48. Ibid.

49. Joel Kotkin and Thomas Tseng, "The New Post-Ethnic Reality," *The Record,* July 13, 2003, pp. O1, O4.

50. Michael Medved, "Hollywood Finally Moves beyond Race Obsession," *USA Today,* June 10, 2003, p. 13A.

51. Leon E. Wynter, *American Skin: Pop Culture, Big Business and the End of White America*. New York: Crown, 2002.

52. Medved.

53. Kennether Gergen, *The Saturated Self: Dilemmas of Identity in Contemporary Life*. New York: Basic Books, 1991, p. 6.

54. Andrew F. Wood and Matthew J. Smith, *Online Communication: Linking Technology, Identity and Culture*. Mahwah, NJ: Erlbaum, 2001, p. 18.

55. Susan B. Barnes, *Online Connections: Internet Interpersonal Relationships*. Cresskill, NJ: Hampton, 2001, p. 102.

56. Sherry Turkle, *Life on the Screen: Identity in the Age of the Internet*. New York: Simon & Schuster, 1995, p. 267.

57. Lawrence Aaron, "Paying Tribute to a Courageous Publisher," *The Record,* August 17, 2005, p. L9.

58. Don Tapscott, *Growing Up Digital: The Rise of the Net Generation*. New York: McGraw-Hill, 1998, p. 100.

59. Andrew Adam Newman, "3 Magazines Are Accused of Retouching Celebrity Photos to Excess," *New York Times,* May 28, 2007.

60. "The Camera Lies," *Financial Times,* August 25/26, 2007, p. 6.

61. David Carr, "Not to See the Fallen Is No Favor," *New York Times,* May 28, 2007, pp. Cl, C6.

62. Osei Appiah, "Americans Online: Difference in Surfing and Evaluating Race-Targeted Web Sites by Black and White Users," paper presented at the annual convention of the Association for Education in Journalism and Mass Communication, Miami, FL, August 2002.

63. "Boy Who Shot Teen Ordered to Spend Time in Wheelchair," *Sunday Record,* January 9, 1994, p. A16.

64. See, for example, Marco Iacoboni, *Mirroring People*. New York; Farrar, Straus & Giroux 2008; and Giacomo Rizzolatti and Corrado Sinigaglia, *Mirrors in the Brain*. New York: Oxford University Press, 2008.

Chapter 5

1. C. K. Ogden and I. A. Richards, *The Meaning of Meaning*. Orlando, FL: Harcourt Brace Jovanovich, 1993.

2. Michael Agar, *Language Shock: Understanding the Culture of Conversation*. New York: Morrow, 1994.

3. Steven Pinker, *The Stuff of Thought: Language as a Window into Human Nature*. New York: Viking, 2007.

4. Charles F. Vich and Ray V. Wood, "Similarity of Past Experience and the Communication of Meaning," *Speech Monographs,* 36, pp. 159–162.

5. For a discussion of how the mindless use of language affects behavior, see Ellen Langer, "Interpersonal Mindlessness and Language," *Communication Monographs,* 59:3 (September 1992), pp. 324–327.

6. Loretta Breuning, "Networking with Yourself: How the Brain Uses Information (Part 1)," *ETC,* 47:2 (Summer 1990), p. 106.

7. Steven Lee Myers, "A Kinder, Gentler Rogues' Gallery," *New York Times,* June 27, 2000.

8. Kate Schuman, "Green Words Get Oxford Nod," *The Record,* September 21, 2007.

9. Michiko Kakutani, "When the Geeks Get Snide," *New York Times,* June 27, 2000, p. E1.

10. See, for example, S. I. Hayakawa and Alan R. Hayakawa, *Language in Thought and Action*, 5th ed. Orlando, FL: Harcourt Brace Jovanovich, 1990.

11. "'Hi, Jack' Greeting to Co-Pilot Causes Stir," *The Record,* June 8, 2000, p. A-13. Used by permission of the Associated Press. Copyright © 2000. All rights reserved.

12. See William V. Haney, *Communication and Organizational Behavior*, 3rd ed. Homewood, IL: Irwin, 1973, pp. 247–248.

13. For a discussion of names and how they affect us, see Mary Marcus, "The Power of a Name," *Psychology Today,* October 1976, pp. 75–76, 108.

14. Thomas N. Robinson, Dina L. G. Borzekowski, Donna M. Matheson, and Helena C. Kraemer, "Effects of Fast Food Branding on Young Children's Taste Preferences,"

Archives of Pediatrics and Adolescent Medicine, 161 (2007), pp. 792–797.

15. "Washington Wire," *Wall Street Journal*, October 14, 1994.

16. William Lutz, *The New Doublespeak: Why No One Knows What Anyone's Saying Anymore*. New York: Harper Collins, 1996.

17. Jennifer Lee, "A Call for Softer, Greener Language," *New York Times*, March 2, 2003, p. 24.

18. See William Lutz, *Doublespeak Defined*. New York: Harper Resource, 1999; and National Council of Teachers of English, "The 1999 Doublespeak Awards," *ETC*, 56:4 (Winter 1999–2000), p. 484.

19. Lisa Bannon, "The Vision Thing," *Wall Street Journal*, July 31, 1997, p. A1.

20. Henry Beard and Christopher Cerf, *The Official Politically Correct Dictionary and Handbook*. New York: Villard Books, 1992.

21. Diane Ravitch, "You Can't Say That," *Wall Street Journal*, February 13, 2004, p. W15.

22. Donald G. McNeil, Jr., "Like Politics, All Political Correctness Is Local," *New York Times*, October 11, 1998, p. WK-5.

23. John Zeaman, "There's Way Too Much Katakarktanq," *The Record*, February 15, 2004, pp. F1, F4.

24. Nicholas D. Kristof, "Chinese Relations," *New York Times Magazine*, August 18, 1991, pp. 8–10.

25. R. Lewis, *When Cultures Collide: Managing Successfully across Cultures*. London: Nicholas Brealey, 1996, p. 16.

26. Liz Sly, "In China, the Right Name Is Crucial," *The Record*, October 6, 1996, p. A-31.

27. Elizabeth Llorente and Ovetta Wiggins, "Human Services Agency to Correct Letter," *The Record*, February 7, 1997, p. A-3.

28. See, for example, Deborah Tannen, *Talking from 9 to 5: How Women's and Men's Conversational Styles Affect Who Gets Heard, Who Gets Credit, and What Gets Done at Work*. New York: Morrow, 1994.

29. Tannen.

30. Michael Slackman, "The Fine Art of Hiding What You Mean to Say," *New York Times*, August 6, 2006, p. WK-5.

31. See, for example, Carolyn Calloway-Thomas, Pamela J. Cooper, and Cecil Blake, *Intercultural Communication: Roots and Routes*. Boston: Allyn & Bacon, 1999, pp. 154–155; and William B. Gudykunst, *Bridging Differences: Effective Intergroup Communication*, 2nd ed. Thousand Oaks, CA: Sage, 1994, p. 83.

32. "Work Week," *Wall Street Journal*, p. A1.

33. J. J. Hemmer, Jr., "Exploitation of Native American Symbols: A First Amendment Analysis," paper presented at the National Communication Association annual convention, New Orleans, LA, November 22, 2002.

34. Suzanne Daily, "In Europe, Some Fear National Languages Are Endangered," *New York Times*, April 16, 2001, pp. A1, A10.

35. Steven Komarow, "Some Germans Fear Language Is Being Infected by English," *USA Today*, May 16, 2001, p. 6A.

36. B. Kitwana, *The Hip Hop Generation: Young Blacks and the Crisis in African American Culture*. New York: Basic Books, 2002.

37. Associated Press, "Congress Looks at Hip-Hop Language," *New York Times*, September 25, 2007.

38. Jeff Leeds, "Hearing Focuses on Language and Violence in Rap Music," *New York Times*, September 26, 2007, p. A24.

39. Monica Davey, "Fighting Words," *New York Times*, February 20, 2005, pp. ARI, 34.

40. Judy Rosen, "Rap: A Celebration of Language," *The Record*, December 2, 2002, p. L15.

41. A. Nilsen, "Sexism as Shown through the English Vocabulary," in A. Nilsen, H. Bosmajian, H. Gershuny, and J. Stanley, eds., *Sexism and Language*. Urbana, IL: National Council of Teachers of English, 1977.

42. Ibid.

43. Sam Kean, "What's in a Name?" *New York Times Magazine*, October 28, 2007, p. 25.

44. Simon Romero, "A Culture of Naming That Even a Law May Not Tame," *New York Times*, September 5, 2007, p. A4.

45. Thomas Fuller, "In Thai Cultural Battle, Name-Calling Is Encouraged," *New York Times*, August 29, 2007, p. A4.

46. Michael Wines, "In a Land of Homemade Names, Tiffany Doesn't Cut It," *New York Times*, October 1, 2007, p. A4.

47. Alexander Alter, "The Baby-Name Business," *Wall Street Journal*, June 22, 2007, pp. W1, W12.

48. A. Mulac, J. Bradac, and S. Mann. "Male/Female Language Differences and Attributional Consequences in Children's Television," *Human Communication Research*, 11 (1985), pp. 481–506.

49. C. Kramer, "Stereotypes of Women's Speech: The Word from Cartoons," *Journal of Popular Culture*, 8 (1974), pp. 624–630.

50. Frank Luntz, *Words That Work: It's Not What You Say, It's What People Hear*. New York: Hyperion, 2007, p. 108.

51. C. Kramer, "Male and Female Perceptions of Male and Female Speech," *Language and Speech*, 20 (1978), pp. 151–161.

52. Patricia Hayes Bradley, "The Folk-Linguistics of Women's Speech: An Empirical Examination," *Communication Monographs*, 48, pp. 73–90.

53. Nancy M. Henley and Cheris Kramarae, "Gender, Power and Miscommunication," in Nickolas Coupland, Howard Giles, and John Weimann, eds., *Miscommunication and Problematic Talk*. Newbury Park, CA: Sage, 1991, p. 42.

54. Deborah Tannen, *You Just Don't Understand*. New York: Ballantine, 1991, p. 42.

55. M. Hiller and F. L. Johnson, "Gender and Generation in Conversational Topics: A Case Study of Two Coffee Shops," paper presented at the annual meeting of the Speech Communication Association, San Diego, CA, November 1996.

56. Cited in Craig Johnson and Larry Vinson, "Placement and Frequency of Powerless Talk and Impression Formation," *Communication Quarterly*, 38:4 (Fall 1990), p. 325.

57. "When Cheers Turn to Abuse, Colleges Need to Take Action," *USA Today*, March 7, 2008, p. 12A.

58. Melanie B. Glover, "Experts See Epidemic of Foul-Mouthed Kids," *The Record*, February 28, 2008, p. A6.

59. Rachel Emma Silverman, "On the Job Cursing: Obscene Talk Is the Latest Target of Workplace Ban," *Wall Street Journal*, May 8, 2001, p. B12.

60. See, for example, James O'Connor, *Cuss Control: The Complete Book on How to Curb Your Cursing*. New York: Three Rivers, 2000.

61. "The Informed Reader; Swearing Is the Best Way to Capture Connotations," *Wall Street Journal*, October 9, 2007, p. B14.

62. Randall Kennedy, *Nigger: The Strange Career of a Troublesome Word*. New York: Pantheon, 2002.

63. Anahad O'Connor, "In Bid to Ban Racial Slur, Blacks Occupy Both Sides," *New York Times*, February 25, 2007, pp. 23, 26.

64. Amy Harmon, "Internet Changes Language for :-) & :-(." *New York Times*, February 20, 1999, p. B-7.

65. Laura M. Holson, "Text Generation Gap: UR2 Old (JK)," *New York Times*, March 19, 2008, pp. BU1, BU9.

66. Hayakawa and Hayakawa.

67. For more information, see Richard Lacayo, "Mixed Signals on Sanctions," *Time*, December 17, 1990, p. 114.

Chapter 6

1. Ann Davis, Joseph Pereira, and William M. Bulkeley, "Security Concerns Bring New Focus on Body Language," *Wall Street Language*, August 15, 2002, pp. A1, A6.

2. See, for example, H. A. Elfenbein and N. Ambady, "Predicting Workplace Outcomes from the Ability to Eavesdrop on Feelings," *Journal of Applied Psychology* (October 2002), pp. 963–972.

3. Marilyn Daniels, *Dancing with Words: Signing for Hearing Children's Literacy*. Wesport, CT: Bergin & Garvey, 2001.

4. Ray Birdwhistell, *Kinesics and Context*. Philadelphia: University of Pennsylvania Press, 1970; Mark L. Knapp and Judith A. Hall, *Nonverbal Communication in Human Interaction*, 6th ed. Belmont, CA: Wadsworth, 2005; and Albert Mehrabian, *Silent Messages*, 2nd ed. Belmont, CA: Wadsworth, 1981.

5. For some practical advice, see Dale G. Leathers. *Successful Nonverbal Communication: Principles and Applications*. New York: Macmillan, 1992.

6. Knapp and Hall.

7. See, for example, Judith N. Martin and Thomas K. Nakayama, *Intercultural Communication in Contexts*, 2nd ed. Mountain View, CA: Mayfield, 2000, p. 181.

8. Kathleen Fackelmann, "Look Who's Talking with Gestures," *USA Today*, July 5, 2000, p. 7D.

9. Quoted in Daniel Goleman, "Sensing Silent Cues Emerges as Key Skills," *New York Times*, October 10, 1989.

10. M. D. Licke, R. H. Smith, and M. L. Klotz, "Judgements of Physical Attractiveness: The Role of Faces and Bodies," *Personality and Social Psychology Bulletin*, 12 (1986), pp. 381–389.

11. T. R. Levine et al., "The Lying Chicken and the Avoidant Egg: Eye Contact, Deception, and Causal Order," *Southern Communication Journal*, 71:4 (December 2006), pp. 401–411; and D. S. Berry, "What Can a Moving Face Tell Us?" *Journal of Personality and Social Psychology*, 58 (1990), pp. 1004–1014.

12. Helmut Morsbach, "Aspects of Nonverbal Communication in Japan," in Larry Samovar and Richard Porter, eds., *Intercultural Communication: A Reader*, 3rd ed. Belmont, CA: Wadsworth, 1982, p. 308.

13. V. Richmond, "Teacher Nonverbal Immediacy: Use and Outcomes," in J. L. Chesebro and J. C. McCroskey, eds., *Communication for Teachers*. Boston: Allyn & Bacon, 2002, pp. 65–82.

14. See Julie Woodzicka, "Sex Differences in Self-Awareness of Smiling during a Mock Job Interview,"

Journal of Nonverbal Behavior, 32:2 (June 2008), pp. 109–121.

15. Warren St. John, "They're Not Just Saying Ah," *New York Times*, October 2, 2005, p. 13.

16. Nancy Henley, *Body Politics: Power, Sex and Nonverbal Communication* New York: Simon & Schuster, 1986.

17. Christina Binkley, "Heelpolitik: The Power of a Pair of Stilettos," *Wall Street Journal*, August 2, 2007, p. D8.

18. Del Jones, "The Bald Truth about CEOs," *USA Today*, March 14, 2008, pp. 1B, 2B.

19. Malcolm Gladwell, *Blink*. New York: Little, Brown, 2005.

20. Del Jones, "Does Height Equal Power?" *USA Today*, July 18, 2007, pp. 1B, 2B.

21. For a summary of Mehrabian's work in this area, see his article "Significance of Posture and Position in the Communication of Attitude and Status Relationship," *Psychological Bulletin*, 71(1969), pp. 359–372.

22. Paul Ekman, W. V. Friesen, and J. Baer, "The International Language of Gestures," *Psychology Today*, May 1984, pp. 64–69.

23. L. Samovar, R. Porter, and E. McDaniel, *Communication between Cultures*. Belmont, CA: Wadsworth, 2006.

24. See L. K. Guerrero, J. A. DeVito, and M. L. Hecht, eds., *The Nonverbal Communication Reader: Classic and Contemporary Readings*, 2nd ed. Prospect Heights, IL: Waveland, 1999; and Joseph Kahn, "Chinese People's Republic is Unfair to Its Short People," *New York Times*, May 21, 2004, p. A13.

25. "Cold Shoulder for Fat Customers," *New York Times*, April 5, 2005, p. F6.

26. V. Ritts, M. L. Patterson, and M. E. Tubbs, "Expectations, Impressions, and Judgments of Physically Attractive Students: A Review," *Review of Educational Research*, 62 (1992), pp. 413–426.

27. See, for example, J. Kilbourne, "The More You Subtract, the More You Add: Cutting Girls Down to Size," in J. Spade and C. Valentine, eds., *The Kaleidoscope of Gender*, Belmont, CA: Wadsworth, 2004, pp. 234–244.

28. Ruth La Ferla, "Generation E. A.: Ethnically Ambiguous," *New York Times*, December 28, 2003, pp. ST1, ST9.

29. Karin Nelson, "What's Vision Got to Do With It?" *New York Times*, September 27, 2007, p. G9.

30. John T. Molloy, *New Dress for Success*. New York: Warner, 1990.

31. See, for example, M. S. Singer and A. E. Singer, "The Effect of Police Uniforms on Interpersonal Perception," *Journal of Psychology*, 119 (1985), pp. 157–161.

32. See, for example, Scott Shane, "Language Help from, Um, Almost-Words," *Sunday Record*, September 12, 1999, pp. L3, L7.

33. Cited in Peter Jaret, "My Voice Has Got to Go." *New York Times*, July 21, 2003, p. G1.

34. Mehrabian.

35. For background on how culture affects rate, see Hyun O. Lee and Franklin J. Boster," Collectivism-Individualism in Perceptions of Speech Rate: A Cross-Cultural Comparison," *Journal of Cross Cultural Psychology*, 23:3 (September 1992), pp. 377–388.

36. F. Goldman-Eisler, "Continuity of Speech Utterance, Its Determinance and Its Significance," *Language and Speech*, 4 (1961), pp. 220–231.

37. Adam Jaworski, *The Power of Silence: Social and Pragmatic Perspective*. Thousand Oaks, CA: Sage, 1993.

38. Edward Hall, *The Hidden Dimension*. New York: Doubleday, 1969.

39. Lizette Alvarez, "Where the Healing Touch Starts with the Hospital Design," *New York Times*, pp. F5, F10.

40. See J. K. Burgoon, "Privacy and Communication," in M. Burgoon, ed., *Communication Yearbook 6*. Beverly Hills, CA: Sage, 1982, pp. 206–249; J. K. Burgoon and L. Aho, "Three Field Experiments on the Effects of Violations of Conversational Distance," *Communication Monographs*, 49 (1982), pp. 7l–88; and J. K. Burgoon and J. B. Walther, "Nonverbal Expectations and the Evaluative Consequence of Violations," *Human Communication Research* 17:2 (1990), pp. 232–265.

41. See, for example, A. G. White, "The Patient Sits Down: A Clinical Note," *Psychosomatic Medicine*, 15 (1953), pp. 256–257.

42. D. Diamond, "Behind Closed Gates," *USA Today*, January 31, 1997, pp. 4–5.

43. Cathy Horyn, "A New Year, A New Color. But Are We Blue?" *New York Times*, December 20, 2007, pp. C1, C11.

44. Horyn, p. C11.

45. Horyn, p. C11.

46. Max Luscher, *The Luscher Color Test*. New York: Simon & Schuster, 1980. See also Luscher, *The Four-Color Person*. New York: Simon & Schuster, 1980.

47. Susan Carey, "More U. S. Companies Are Blue, and It's Not Just the Stock Market," *Wall Street Journal*, August 30, 2001, pp. A1, A2.

48. Robert Levine, *A Geography of Time, or How Every Culture Keeps Time Just a Little Differently*. New York: Basic Books, 1997.

49. Del Jones, "I'm Late, I'm Late, I'm Late," *USA Today*. November 26, 2003, p. B1.

50. Hall.

51. Alex MacKenzie, *The Time Trap*. New York: McGraw-Hill, 1975.

52. See Robert J. Samuelson, "The Sad Fate of the Comma," *Newsweek*, July 23, 2007, p. 41.

53. Ibid.

54. J. Burgoon, J. Walther, and J. Baesler, "Interpretations, Evaluations, and Consequences of Interpersonal Touch," *Human Communication Research*, 19 (1992), pp. 237–263.

55. Marilyn Elias, "Study: Hugging Warms the Heart, and Also May Protect It," *USA Today*, March 10, 2003, p. 7D.

56. An especially persuasive argument is made by Ashleu Montagu in *Touching: The Human Significance of the Skin*. New York: Harper & Row, 1971.

57. Marilyn Elias, "Hugs Can Do a Heart Good," *USA Today*, March 8, 2004, p. 7D.

58. See D. F. Fromme, W. E. Jaynes, D. K. Taylor, E. G. Harold, J. Daniell, J. R. Roundtree, and M. Fromme, "Nonverbal Behaviors and Attitudes toward Touch," *Journal of Nonverbal Behavior*, 13 (1989), pp. 3–14.

59. Barbara Bales, *Communication and the Sexes*. New York: Harper & Row, 1988, p. 60.

60. See, for example, R. Heslin and T. Alper, "Touch: A Bonding Gesture," in J. M. Wiemann and R. P. Harrison, eds., *Nonverbal Interaction*. Beverly Hills, CA: Sage, 1983, pp. 47–75.

61. See, for example, J. T. Wood, *Interpersonal Communication in Everyday Encounters*, 5th ed. Belmont, CA: Wadsworth, 2009.

62. Henley.

63. James L. Lynch, *The Broken Heart*. New York: Basic Books, 1979. See also James L. Lynch, *The Language of the Heart*. New York: Basic Books, 1986.

64. Jim Beckerman, "A Whiff of Vanilla Seems to Please Us All," *The Record*, September 16, 2003, pp. F1, F2.

65. N. Wade, "Scent of a Man Is Linked to a Woman's Selection," *New York Times*, January 22, 2002, p. F2.

66. N. Wade, "For Gay Men, Different Scent of Attraction," *New York Times*, May 10, 2005, pp. A1, A14.

67. Lauran Neergaard, "Researchers Find Bad Times Really Do Stink," *The Record*, March 28, 2008, p. A6.

68. M. G. Millar and K. U. Millar, "The Effects of Suspicion on the Recall of Cues to Make Veracity Judgments," *Communication Reports*, 11 (1998), pp. 57–64.

69. R. G. Riggio and H. S. Freeman, "Individual Differences and Cues to Deception," *Journal of Personality and Social Psychology*, 45 (1983), pp. 899–915.

70. D. B. Buller and J. K. Burgoon, "Deception: Strategic and Nonstrategic Communication," in J. Daly and J. M. Wiemann, eds., *Interpersonal Communication*. Hillsdale, NJ: Erlbaum, 1994.

71. Paul Ekman and Mark G. Frank, "Lies That Fail," in Michael Lewis and Carolyn Saarni, eds., *Lying and Deception in Everyday Life*. New York: Guilford, 1993, pp. 184–200.

72. David J. Lieberman, *Never Be Lied to Again*. New York: St. Martin's, 1998.

73. See, for example, L. Case et al., "The Impact of Deception and Suspicion on Different Hand Movements," *Journal of Nonverbal Behavior*, 30:1 (Spring 2006), pp. 1–19.

74. B. Veland, "Tell Me More: On the Fine Art of Listening," *Utne Reader*, 1992, pp. 104–109; A. Mulac, "Men's and Women's Talk in Same Gender and Mixed Gender Dyads: Power or Polemic?" *Journal of Language and Social Psychology*, 8 (1989), pp. 249–270.

75. J. F. Dovidio, S. L. Ellyson, C. F. Keating, K. Heltman, and C. E. Brown, "The Relationship of Social Power to Visual Displays of Dominance between Men and Women," *Journal of Personality and Social Psychology*, 54 (1988), pp. 233–242.

76. Shelly Branch, "Forget Standing Tall, Female Models Make Slouching Look Good," *Wall Street Journal*, pp. A1, A9.

77. Julia T. Wood, *Gendered Lives*. Belmont, CA: Wadsworth, 1994, p. 154.

78. N. G. Rotter and G. S. Rotter, "Sex Differences in the Encoding and Decoding of Negative Facial Emotions," *Journal of Nonverbal Behavior*, 12:2 (1998), pp. 139–148.

79. P. Anderson, "Exploring Intercultural Differences in Nonverbal Communication," in L. Samovar and R. Porter, eds, *Intercultural Communication: A Reader*, 3rd ed. Belmont, CA: Wadsworth, 1982, pp. 272–282.

80. E. R. McDaniel, "Japanese Nonverbal Communication: A Review and Critique of Literature," paper presented at the annual meeting of the Speech Communication Association, Miami Beach, FL, November 18–21, 1993.

81. Rebecca Knight, "Interactions Speak Louder than Words," *Financial Times*, July 2, 2007, p. 12.

82. Neil MacFarquhar, "A Kiss Is Not Just a Kiss to an Angry Arab TV Audience," *New York Times*, March 5, 2004, p. A3.

83. Kaet Saks, "In Perfect Harmony," *The Record*, August 19, 1999, pp. HF1, HF3.

84. Steven G. Jones, *Cybersociety: Computer-Mediated Communication and Community*. Thousand Oaks, CA: Sage, 1995, p. 116.

85. Jina Yoo, "To Smile or Not to Smile:)   : Defining the Effects of Emoticons on Relational Outcomes," paper presented at the annual meeting of the International Communication Association, 2007; and C. Constantin, S. Kalyanaraman, C. Stavrositu, and N. Wagoner, "To Be or Not to Be Emotional: Impression Formation Effects of Emoticons in Moderated Chatrooms," paper presented at the annual meeting of the Association for Education in Journalism and Mass Communication, Miami Beach, FL, August 7–10, 2002.

86. Jones, p. 172

87. Karen De Witt, "So, What Is That Leather Bustier Saying?" *New York Times*, January 1, 1995, p. 2E.

88. Bret Lortie, "Your Lying Eyes," *Bulletin of the Atomic Scientists*, 58:6 (November/December 2002).

Chapter 7

1. Karen Arenson, "The Fine Art of Listening," *New York Times Education Life*, January 13, 2002, pp. 34–35.

2. Cesar G. Soriano, "News Flash: Teen Stops Speaking!" *USA Today*, August 9, 2000, p. 1D.

3. Brendan Schurr, "Teenager Vows Not to Speak for a Year," *The Record*, August 16, 2000, p. A-5.

4. See Jane Allan, "Talking Your Way to Success (Listening Skills)," *Accountancy*, February 1993, pp. 612–663; and John W. Haas and Christina L. Arnold, "An Examination of the Role of Listening in Co-Workers," *Journal of Business Communication*, April 1995, pp. 123–139.

5. The Office Team Survey, 2000, was cited in *Sssh! Listen Up!* HighGain, Inc. Newsletter, June 2000, p. 4.

6. K. W. Hawkins and B. P. Fullion, "Perceived Communication Skill Needs for Work Groups," *Communication Research Reports*, 16 (1999), pp. 167–174.

7. J. T. Wood, "Buddhist Influences on Scholarship and Teaching," *Journal of Communication and Religion*, 2004, pp. 32–39.

8. See, for example, M. Levine, "Tell the Doctor All Your Problems but Keep It to Less Than a Minute," *New York Times*, June 1, 2004, p. F6; and M. Nichols, "Listen Up for Better Sales," *Business Week Online*, September 15, 2006, p. 12.

9. Jared Sandberg, "Bad at Complying? You Might Just Be a Very Bad Listener," *Wall Street Journal*, September 25, 2007, p. B1.

10. Jim Adams et al. "How College Students Spend Their Time Communicating," *International Journal of Listening*, 22:1 (2008), pp. 13–28.

11. See Tory Rankin, "The Measurement of the Ability to Understand Spoken Language," Ph.D. dissertation, University of Michigan, 1926, p. 43; Larry Barker, R. Edwards, C. Gaines, K. Gladney, and F. Hally, "An Investigation of Proportional Time Spent in Various Communication Activities by College Students," *Journal of Applied Communication Research*, 8 (1981), pp. 101–109.

12. Brigitta R. Brunner, "Listening, Communication & Trust: Practitioners' Perspectives of Business/Organizational Relationships, *International Journal of Listening*, 22:1 (2008), pp. 73–82.

13. See A. D. Wolvin and C. G. Coakley, "A Survey of the Status of Listening Training in Some Fortune 500 Corporations," *Communication Education*, 40 (1991), pp. 152–164.

14. For a detailed discussion, see Ralph G. Nichols and Leonard A. Stevens, *Are You Listening?* New York: McGraw-Hill, 1956. See also K. Watson and L. Barker, "Listening Behavior: Definition and Measurement," in R. Bostrom, ed., *Communication Yearbook 8*. Beverly Hills, CA: Sage, 1984, pp. 178–197; and Andrew Wolving and Carolyn Gwynn Coakly, *Listening*, 4th ed. Dubuque, IA: Brown, 1988.

15. John R. Freund and Arnold Nelson, "Distortion in Communication," in B. Peterson, G. Goldhaber, and R. Pace, eds., Chicago: Science Research Associates, 1974, pp. 122–124.

16. Gerald Goldhaber, *Organizational Communication*, 4th ed. Dubuque, IA: Brown, 1988.

17. See L. Wheeless, A. Frymier, and C. Thompson, "A Comparison of Verbal Output and Receptivity in Relation to Attraction and Communication Satisfaction in Interpersonal Relationships," *Communication Quarterly*, Spring 1992, pp. 102–115.

18. See, for example, Judi Brownell, *Listening: Attitudes, Principles, and Skills*. Boston: Allyn & Bacon, 1996.

19. Janel Beavin Bavelas, Linda Coates, and Trudy Johnson, "Listener Responses as a Collaborative Process: The Role of Gaze," *Journal of Communication*, 52:3 (September 2002), pp. 566–579.

20. For insight into empathic listening, also see Judi Brownell, *Listening: Attitudes, Principles, and Skills*, 3rd ed. Boston: Allyn & Bacon, 2006.

21. B. L. Omdahl, *Cognitive Appraisal, Emotion, and Empathy*. Mahwah, NJ: Erlbaum, 1995.

22. T. Holtgraves, *Language as Social Action: Social Psychology and Language Use*. Mahwah, NJ: Erlbaum, 2002.

23. See, for example, J. B. Weaver III and M. B. Kirtley, "Listening Styles and Empathy," *Southern Communication Journal*, 60 (1995), pp. 131–140.

24. Karen S. Peterson, "Sharing Memorable Moments Can Calm the Soul, Heal the Body," *USA Today*, February 15, 1999, p. 4D.

25. Angela Delli Santi, "N.J. Doctors to Learn Cultural Sensitivity," *The Record*, April 11, 2005, p. A3.

26. Nissa Simon, "Can You Hear Me Now?" *Time*, August 18, 2003; and Kim Painter, "Getting Bad Reception?" *USA Today*, October 3, 2005, p. 6D.

27. C. Crosen, "Blah, Blah, Blah," *Wall Street Journal*, July 10, 1997, pp. 1A, 6A; and Betsy A. Lehman, "Getting an Earful Is Just What the Doctor Needs," *The Record*, March 21, 1994, p. B4.

28. See also Judi Brownell, *Listening: Attitudes, Principles, and Skills*, 2nd ed. Boston: Allyn & Bacon, 2004.

29. Ralph G. Nichols and Leonard A. Stevens. *Are You Listening?* New York: McGraw-Hill, 1956.

30. Harry Jackson, Jr., "Fear of Forgetting," *The Record*, April 5, 2005, pp. F1, F12.

31. See A. Vangelisti, M. Knapp, and J. Daly, "Conversational Narcissism," *Communication Monographs*, December 1990, pp. 251–271.

32. Alfie Kohn, "Girl Talk, Guy Talk," *Psychology Today*, February 1988, pp. 65–66.

33. Christine Kenneally, *The First Word: The Search for the Origins of Language*. New York: Viking, 2007.

34. Deborah Tannen, *The Argument Culture: Moving from Debate to Dialogue*. New York: Ballentine, 1998.

35. Don Tosti, "Operant Conditioning," speech presented at Operant Conditioning Seminar, New York, Fall 1983.

36. David W. Johnson, *Reaching Out: Interpersonal Effectiveness and Self-Actualization*. Englewood Cliffs, NJ: Prentice-Hall, 1972; and Thomas Gordon, *Leader Effectiveness Training*. New York: Wyden, 1977.

37. For a discussion of the benefit of questioning, see John F. Monoky, "Listen by Asking." *Industrial Distribution*, April 1995, p. 123.

38. Quoted in "Making TLC a Requirement," *Newsweek*, August 12, 1991, p. 56.

39. For a discussion of the kinds of information conveyed by verbal and nonverbal feedback, see Dale G. Leathers, "The Informational Potential of the Nonverbal and Verbal Components of Feedback Responses," *Southern Speech Communication Journal*, 44 (1979), pp. 331–354.

40. Harold Leavitt and Ronald Mueller, "Some Effects of Feedback on Communication," *Human Relations*, 4 (1951), pp. 401–410.

41. See R. Boostrom, *Developing Creative and Critical Thinking*, Lincolnwood, IL: National Textbook, 1992.

42. Teri Gamble and Michael Gamble, *Public Speaking in the Age of Diversity*. Boston: Allyn & Bacon, 1994, p. 18.

43. Deborah Tannen, *You Just Don't Understand: Women and Men in Conversation*. New York: Morrow, 1990.

44. S. Petronio, J. Martin, and R. Littlefield, "Prerequisite Conditions for Self-Disclosing: A Gender Issue," *Communication Monographs*, 51 (1984), pp. 282–292.

45. See also Michael Purdy and Deborah Borisoff, *Listening in Everyday Life: A Personal and Professional Approach*, 2nd ed. Lanham, MD: University Press of America, 1997.

46. Judi Brownell, *Listening*, 2nd ed.

47. B. R. Burleson, "Emotional Support Skills," in J. O. Green and B. R. Burleson, eds., *Handbook of Communication and Social Interaction Skills*. Mahwah, NJ: Erlbaum, 2003.

48. See, for example, Deborah M. Saucier et al. "Are Sex Differences in Navigation Caused by Sexually Dimorphic Strategies or by Differences in the Ability to Use the Strategies?" *Behavioral Neuroscience*, 116:3 (2002), pp. 403–410; and Bia Kim, Sewon Lee, and Jaesik Lee, "Gender Differences in Spatial Navigation," *Proceedings of the World Academy of Science, Engineering and Technology*, 25 (November 2007), pp. 297–300.

49. C. Y. Cheng, "Chinese Philosophy and Contemporary Communication Theory," in D. I. Kincaid, ed., *Communication Theory: Eastern and Western Perspectives*. New York: Academic Press, 1987.

50. Documented by T. S. Lebra in *Japanese Patterns of Behavior*. Honolulu: University Press of Hawaii, 1976.

51. C. Kiewitz, J. B. Weaver III, H. B. Brosius, and G. Wiemann, "Cultural Differences in Listening Style Preferences: A Comparison of Young Adults in Germany, Israel, and the United States," *International Journal of Public Opinion Research*, 9:3 (Fall 1997), p. 233.

52. John Stewart and M. Thomas, "Dialogic Listening: Sculpting Mutual Meanings," in J. Stewart, ed., *Bridges, Not Walls: A Book about Interpersonal Communication*, 6th ed. New York: McGraw-Hill, 1995, pp. 184–201.

53. Larry A. Samovar and Richard E. Porter, *Communication between Cultures*. Belmont, CA: Wadsworth, 1995, pp. 211–212.

54. For more information on this topic, also see Julia T. Wood, *Gendered Lives: Communication, Gender and Culture,* 7th ed. Belmont, CA: Wadsworth, 2007.

55. D. A. Christakis, F. J. Zimmerman, D. L. DiGuiseppe, and C. A. McCarty, "Early Television Exposure and Subsequent Attentional Problems in Children, *Pediatrics,* 113 (2004), pp. 707–713.

56. See, for example, "Personality Typing," *Wired,* July 1999, p. 71.

57. See, for example, Gui Qing Koh et al., "Presence and Podcasting: The Role of Contextual and Formal Attributes," paper presented at the annual meeting of the International Listening Association, 2007.

58. Sharon White Taylor, "Wireless and Witless," *New York Times,* July 5, 2000, p. A-17; and "Cell Phone Rage: Helpful Hints," *New York Times,* July 8, 2000, p. A-14.

59. Rita Rubin, "Merely Listening on Phone Shown to Distract Drivers," *USA Today,* March 10, 2008, p. 5D.

60. David Shenk, *Data Smog.* New York: Harper-Edge, 1997.

61. Todd Gitlin, "Supersaturation, or the Media Torrent and Disposable Feeling," in E. Bucy, ed., *Living in the Information Age: A New Media Reader,* 2nd ed. Belmont, CA: Thomson Wadsorth, 2005, pp. 139–146.

62. Sheila C. Bentley, "Listening in the 21st Century," paper presented at the annual convention of the National Communication Association, Chicago, November 1999.

63. Michael Fitzgerald, "The Coming Wave of Gadgets That Listen and Obey," *New York Times,* January 27, 2008, p. BU4.

64. Cynthia B. Leshin, *Internet Investigations in Business Communication.* Upper Saddle River, NJ: Prentice Hall, 1997, pp. 53–56.

65. Stephen R. Covey, *The 7 Habits of Highly Effective People.* New York: Simon & Schuster, 1990, pp. 239–240.

Chapter 8

1. Virginia Satir, *The New Peoplemaking.* Palo Alto, CA: Science and Behavior Books, 1998, p. 51.

2. John L. Locke, *The De-Voicing of Society: Why We Don't Talk to Each Other Anymore.* New York: Simon & Schuster, 1998.

3. Bruce Headlam, "Awash in All These Words, Will We Forget How to Talk?" *New York Times,* December 17, 1998, p. G-12.

4. John Naisbitt, *Megatrends.* New York: Warner, 1984, pp. 35–52. See also *Mind Set! Reset Your Thinking and See the Future.* New York: Collins Business, 2006.

5. See Debra Lynn Veal, "Electric Friendship, Information—Even Love," *Sunday Record,* April 3, 1994.

6. See Duane Stoltzfus, "Meeting a la Modem: Personal Computer Goes Interpersonal," *Sunday Record,* December 19, 1993.

7. Catherine Greenman, "From Yakety-Yak to Clackety-Clack," *New York Times,* November 5, 1998, pp. G-l, G-7.

8. See Judy Jeannin, "Sister Can You Spare a Moment?" *Sunday Record,* January 30, 1994.

9. J. O'Neil, "Help Others for a Longer Life," *New York Times,* November 12, 2002, p. F6.

10. Lori Oliwenstein, "Marry Me," *Time,* January 28, 2008, pp. 73–76.

11. "Sick? Lonely? Genes Tell the Tale," September 15, 2007, accessed at www.theage.com.au/news/World/Sick-Lonely-Genes-tell-the-tale/2007/09/15/11892; and Kathleen Fackelmann, "For Lonely Hearts, 1 Can Be an Unhealthy Number," *USA Today,* August 27, 2007, p. 8D.

12. William C. Schutz, *The Interpersonal Underworld.* Palo Alto, CA: Science and Behavior Books, 1966, pp. 18–20.

13. Steve Duck, *Human Relationships,* 3rd ed. Thousand Oaks, CA: Sage, 1999, p. 57.

14. *Time,* December 20, 1993, p. 15.

15. See, for example, Robert A. Bell, "Conversational Involvement and Loneliness," *Communication Monographs,* 52 (l985) pp. 218–235.

16. Robert A. Bell and Michael Roloff, "Making a Love Connection: Loneliness and Communication Competence in the Dating Marketplace," *Communication Quarterly,* 39:1 (Winter 1991), pp. 58–74.

17. Schutz, p. 24.

18. Andrea Heiman, "Flirting Still Has Its Attractions," *Sunday Record,* March 20, 1994.

19. Robert E. Nofsinger, *Everyday Conversation.* Newbury Park, CA: Sage, 1991, p. 1.

20. See Deborah Cameron, *Good Talk? Living and Working in a Communication Culture.* Thousand Oaks, CA: Sage, 2000.

21. Anita L. Vangelisti and Mary A. Banski, "Couples' Debriefing Conversations: The Impact of Gender, Occupation, and Demographic Characteristics," *Family Relations,* 42:2 (April 1993) pp. 149–157.

22. Karen Shafer, "Talk in the Middle: Two Conversational Skills for Friendship," *English Journal,* 82:1 (January 1993) pp. 53–55.

23. Bob Smith, "Care and Feeding of the Office Grapevine," *Management Review*, 85 (February 1996), p. 6; and Lisette Hilton, "They Heard It through the Grapevine," *South Florida Business Journal*, 21 (August, 2000), p. 53.

24. See Joann Klimkiewicz, "Society Has Become Addicted to Gossip," *The Record*, April 29, 2007, p. F4; Graeme Turner. *Understanding Celebrity*. London: Sage, 2004; and F. T. McAndrew, E. K. Bell, and C. M. Garcia, "Who Do We Tell and Whom Do We Tell On? Gossip as a Strategy for Status Enhancement," *Journal of Applied Social Psychology*, 37:7 (July 2007), pp. 1562–1577.

25. M. M. Turner, M. A. Mazur, N. Wendel, and R. Winslow, "Relational Ruin or Social Glue? The Joint Effect of Relationship Type and Gossip Valence on Liking, Trust, and Expertise," *Communication Monographs*, 70 (June 2003), pp. 129–141.

26. I. Altman and D. A. Taylor, *Social Penetration: The Development of Interpersonal Relationships*. New York: Holt, Rinehart & Winston, 1973.

27. Sandra Petronio, *Boundaries of Privacy: Dialectics of Disclosure*. Albany: State University of New York Press, 2003. See also Sandra Petronia, "Translational Research Endeavors and the Practices of Communication Privacy Management," *Journal of Applied Communication Research*, 35:3 (August 2007), pp. 218–222.

28. Mark L. Knapp and Anita L. Vangelisti, *Interpersonal Communication and Human Relationships*, 2nd ed. Boston: Allyn & Bacon, 1992, p. 33.

29. Alan Garner, *Conversationally Speaking*. New York: McGraw-Hill, 1981, p. 69.

30. Knapp and Vagelisti.

31. Michael Korda, "Small Talk," *Signature*, 1986, p. 78.

32. See Lawrence B. Rosenfield and Daniella Bordaray-Sciolino, "Self-Disclosure as a Communication Strategy during Relationship Termination," paper presented at the national meeting of the Speech Communication Association, Denver, CO, November 1985.

33. Rosenfield and Bordaray-Sciolino.

34. Steve Duck, "A Topography of Relationship Disagreement and Dissolution," in *Personal Relationships 4: Dissolving Personal Relationships*. New York: Academic Press, 1982.

35. Leslie Kaufman, "When the Ex Writes a Blog, the Dirtiest Laundry Is Aired," *New York Times*, April 18, 2008, pp. Al, A23; and Emily Gould, "Exposed," *New York Times Magazine*, May 25, 2008, pp. 32–40, 52, 56.

36. See S. W. Duck and J. T. Wood, "What Goes Up May Come Down: Sex and Gendered Patterns in Relational Dissolution," in M. A. Fine and J. H. Harvey, eds., *The Handbook of Divorce and Relationship Dissolution*. Mahwah, NJ: Erlbaum, pp. l69–187; and J. T. Wood, *Gendered Lives: Communication, Gender and Culture*, 7th ed., Belmont, CA: Wadsworth, 2007.

37. See, for example, Harold S. Kushner, *When Bad Things Happen to Good People*. New York: Schocken Books, 1981.

38. Erica Goode, "Experts Offer Fresh Insights into the Mind of the Grieving Child," *New York Times*, March 28, 2000, pp. F7, F12.

39. N. Stevens, "Re-engaging: New Partnerships in Late-Life Widowhood," *Aging International*, 27:4 (Spring 2003), pp. 27–43.

40. J. W. Thibaut and H. H. Kelly, *The Social Psychology of Groups*. New York: Wiley, 1959.

41. See Richard West and Lynn H. Turner, *Introducing Communication Theory: Analysis and Application*. Mountain View, CA: Mayfield, 2000, pp. 180–190.

42. L. A. Baxter and B. M. Montgomery, *Relating Dialogues and Dialectics*. New York; Guilford, 1996; and L. A. Baxter, "Dialectical Contradictions in Relationship Development," *Journal of Social and Personal Relationships*, 7 (1990), pp. 69–88.

43. See also Sandra Petronio, ed., *Balancing the Secrets of Private Disclosures*. Mahwah, NJ: Erlbaum, 1999.

44. C. A. VanLear, "Testing a Cyclical Model of Communicative Openness in Relationship Development," *Communication Monographs*, 58 (1991), pp. 337–361.

45. J. T. Wood, L. Dendy, E. Dordek, M. Germany, and S. Varallo, "Dialectic of Difference: A Thematic Analysis of Intimates' Meanings for Differences," in K. Carter and M. Presnell, eds., *Interpretive Approaches to Interpersonal Communication*. New York: State University of New York Press, 1994, pp. 115–136.

46. See, for example, L. Anolli, M. Balconi, and Rita Ciceri, "Deceptive Miscommunication Theory (DeMiIT): A New Model for the Analysis of Deceptive Communication," in A. Luigi, R. Ciceri et al., eds., *Say Not to Say: New Perspectives on Miscommunication. Studies in New Technologies and Practices in Communication*. Amsterdam, Netherlands Antilles: IOS Press, pp. 73–100.

47. See Mark L. Knapp, *Lying and Deception in Human Interaction*, Boston: Penguin Academics, 2008.

48. C. Camden, M. T. Motley, and A. Wilson, "White Lies in Interpersonal Communication: A Taxonomy and Preliminary Investigation of Social Motivations," *Western Journal of Speech Communication*, 48 (1984), pp. 309–325.

49. See, for example, J. B. Bavelas, A. Black, N. Chovil, and J. Mullett, *Equivocal Communication*. Newbury Park, CA: Sage, 1990, p. 171.

50. Benedict Carey, "I'm Not Lying, I'm Telling a Future Truth. Really," *New York Times*, May 6, 2008, p. F5.

51. Sissela Bok, *Lying*. New York: Pantheon, 1978. See also Sissela Bok, *Secrets*. New York: Random House, 1989.

52. J. K. Rempel and J. G. Holmes, "How Do I Trust Thee?" *Psychology Today*, February 1986.

53. A. L. Vangelisti and L. P. Crumley, "Reactions to Messages That Hurt: The Influence of Relational Contexts," *Communication Monographs*, 65 (1998), pp. 173–196.

54. Virginia Rohan, "Have We No Shame?" *The Record*, September 26, 2004, pp. El, E4.

55. Natalie Angier, "Laughs: Rhythmic Bursts of Social Glue," *New York Times*, February 27, 1996, pp. C-1, C-5.

56. Angier. See also Regina Barreca, *They Used to Call Me Snow White . . . but I Drifted: Women's Strategic Use of Humor*. New York: Penguin Books, 1991.

57. Seth Borenstein, "Why Have Sex?" *The Record*, August 1, 2007, p. A8.

58. L. A. Rudman and J. E. Phelan, "The Interpersonal Power of Feminism: Is Feminism Good for Romantic Relationships?" *Sex Roles*, 2007.

59. Heiman.

60. Heiman.

61. ScienceDaily.com, "Women More Perceptive Than Men in Describing Relationships," www.sciencedaily.com/releases/2008/02/080213111055.htm.

62. N. M. Punyanunt-Carter, "An Analysis of College Students' Self-Disclosure Behavior on the Internet," *College Student Journal*, 40 (2006), pp. 329–331.

63. Liz Funk, "Women on Facebook Think Provocative Is Empowering," *USA Today*, September 19, 2007, p. 11A.

64. Stephanie Rosenbloom, "Sorry, Boys, This Is Our Domain," *New York Times*, February 21, 2008, pp. G1, G8.

65. J. D. Ragsdale, "Gender, Satisfaction Level, and the Use of Relational Maintenance Strategies in Marriage," *Communication Monographs*, 63 (1996), pp. 354–369.

66. A. M. Sherman, H. E. Lansford, and B. L. Volling, "Sibling Relationships and Best Friendships in Young Adulthood: Warmth, Conflict, and Well-Being," *Personal Relationships*, 13 (2006), pp. 151–165.

67. Julia T. Wood and C. Inmam, "In a Different Mode: Recognizing Male Modes of Closeness," *Journal of Applied Communication Research*, August 1993.

68. Julia T. Wood, *Gendered Lives*, 3rd ed. Belmont, CA: Wadsworth, 1999, p. 201.

69. Deborah Tannen, *The Argument Culture: Moving from Debate to Dialogue*. New York: Random House, 1998, pp. 186–187.

70. See M. Hecht, S. Ribeau, and J. Alberts, "An Afro-American Perspective on Interethnic Communication," *Communication Monographs*, 56 (1989), pp. 385–410; and M. Hecht, S. Ribeau, and M. Sedano, "A Mexican-American Perspective on Interethnic Communication," *International Journal of Intercultural Relations*, 14 (1990), pp. 31–55.

71. H. C. Triandis, *Culture and Social Behavior*. New York: McGraw-Hill, 1994, p. 30.

72. M. J. Collier, "Communication Competence Problematics in Ethnic Friendships," *Communication Monographs*, 63 (1996), pp. 314–336.

73. See Ann S. Wildemuth, "Love on the Line: Participants' Descriptions of Computer Mediated Close Relationships," *Qualitative Research Reports in Communication*, 2 (2001), pp. 89–95.

74. Karen S. Peterson, "Dating Game Has Changed," *USA Today*, February 11, 2003, p. 9D.

75. J. McQuillen, "The Influence of Technology on the Initiation of Interpersonal Relationships," *Education*, 1123 (2003), pp. 616–624.

76. Sherry Turkle, *Life on the Screen: Identity in the Age of the Internet*. New York: Simon & Schuster, 1995; and Katie Hafner, "At Heart of a Cyberstudy, the Human Essence," *New York Times*, June 18, 1998, p. G-9.

77. Scott McCartney, "Society's Subcultures Meet by Modem," *Wall Street Journal*, December 8, 1994, p. B1.

78. "Living a Second Life Online," *Newsweek*, July 28, 2008, p. 10.

79. Marie Puente, "Blogger Gives Dark Secrets the First-Class Treatment," *USA Today*, March 15, 2006, pp. 1A, 6A.

80. Alex Mindlin, "Girl Power Is in Full Force Online," *New York Times*, December 24, 2007, p. C3.

81. Charles McGrath, "The Pleasures of the Text," *New York Times Magazine*, January 22, 2006, pp. 15, 19.

82. Steve Duck, *Understanding Relationships*. New York: Guilford, 1991, pp. 1–2.

83. Keith E. Davis, "Near and Dear: Friendship and Love Compared," *Psychology Today*, February 1985, pp. 22–30.

84. For a discussion of how to enhance the teaching of relationships in a basic course, see Diane Tkinson Gorcyca, "Enhancing the Instruction of Relationship

Development in the Basic Communication Course," paper presented at the annual meeting of the Speech Communication Association, Miami Beach, FL, November 18–21, 1993.

Chapter 9

1. Daniel Goleman, *Emotional Intelligence*. New York: Bantam, 1995, p. 34. See also *Social Intelligence: The New Science of Human Relationships*. New York: Bantam, 2006.

2. See, for example, Julie Yingling, *A Lifetime of Communication*. Mahwah, NJ: Erlbaum, 2004.

3. See Katherine C. Maguire, "Will It Ever End? A (Re) Examination of Uncertainty in College Student Long-Distance Dating Relationships," *Communication Quarterly*, November 2007, pp. 415–432; and Charles Berger, "Uncertainty and Information Exchange in Developing Relationships," in Steve Duck, ed., *Handbook of Personal Relationships*. New York: Wiley, 1988, p. 244.

4. C. R. Berger and R. J. Calabrese, "Some Explorations in Initial Interactions and Beyond: Toward a Developmental Theory of Interpersonal Communication," *Human Communication Research*, 1 (1975), pp. 98–112.

5. See, for example, W. Gudykunst, "Uncertainty and Anxiety," in Y. Y. Kim and W. Gudykunst, eds., *Theories in Intercultural Communication*. Newbury Park, CA: Sage, 1988, pp. 123–156.

6. M. Sunnafrank, "A Communication-Based Perspective on Attitude Similarity and Interpersonal Attraction in Early Acquaintance," *Communication Monographs*, 51 (1984), pp. 372–380.

7. See, for example, Keith E. Davis, "Near and Dear: Friendship and Love Compared," *Psychology Today*, 19 (1985), pp. 22–30; and Rosemary Blieszner and Rebecca G. Adams, *Adult Friendship*. Newbury Park, CA: Sage, 1992.

8. Keith J. Winstein, "Ability to Quit Smoking Is Affected by Friendships," *Wall Street Journal*, May 22, 2008, p. D6.

9. See W. Samter, "Friendship Interaction Skills across the Lifespan," in J. O. Freene and B. R. Burleson, eds., *Handbook of Communication and Social Interaction Skills*. Mahwah, NJ: Erlbaum, 2003; Daniel Goleman, "'Friends for Life': An Emerging Biology of Emotional Healing," *New York Times*, October 10, 2006; and Alan K. Goodby and Scott A. Myers, "Relational Maintenance Behaviors of Friends with Benefits: Investigating Equity and Relational Characteristics," *Human Communication*, 11:1 (Spring 2008), pp. 71–85.

10. W. K. Rawlins, "Friendship as a Communicative Achievement: A Theory and an Interpretive Analysis of Verbal Reports," doctoral dissertation, Temple University, Philadelphia, 1981.

11. Robert J. Sternberg, "A Triangular Theory of Love," *Psychological Review*, 93 (1986), pp. 119–135; and Robert L. Sternberg, *The Triangle of Love: Intimacy, Passion, Commitment*. New York: Basic Books, 1988.

12. See Sally A. Lloyd and Beth C. Emery, *The Dark Side of Courtship: Physical and Sexual Aggression*. Thousand Oaks, CA: Sage, 2000; and J. D. Cunningham and J. K. Antill, "Current Trends in Nonmarital Cohabitation: The Great POSSLQ Hunt Continues," in Julia Wood and Steve W. Duck, eds., *Understanding Relationship Processes, 6: Off the Beaten Track: Understudied Relationships*. Thousand Oaks, CA: Sage, 1995, pp. 148–172.

13. D. Holmberg, "So Far So Good: Scripts for Romantic Relationship Development as Predictors of Relational Well-Being," *Journal of Social and Personal Relationships*, 19:6 (December 2002), pp. 777–796.

14. Julia T. Wood, *Gendered Lives*, 3rd ed. Belmont, CA: Wadsworth, 1999, p. 340.

15. Virginia Satir, *The New Peoplemaking*. Mountain View, CA: Science and Behavior Books, 1988, p. 79; and A. Vangelisti, K. C. Maguire, A. Alexander, and G. Clark, "Hurtful Family Environments: Links with Individual and Relationship and Perceptual Variables," *Communication Monographs*, 74:3 (September 2007), pp. 357–385.

16. See the 2000 U.S. Census Report.

17. Sharon Jayson and Anthony DeBarros, "Young Adults Delaying Marriage," *USA Today*, September 12, 2007, p. 6D.

18. D. Gibbons and P. M. Olk, "The Individual and Structural Origins of Friendship and Social Position among Professionals," *Journal of Personality and Social Psychology*, 84:2 (February 2003), pp. 340–352; and "The Power of Nice," *Workforce*, 82:1 (January 2003), pp. 22–24.

19. See, for example, Susan A. Wheelan, *Creating Effective Teams: A Guide for Members and Leaders*. Thousand Oaks, CA: Sage, 1999; and James R. Barker, *The Discipline of Teamwork: Participation and Concertive Control*. Thousand Oaks, CA: Sage, 1999.

20. Alan V. Horwitz, Jerome C. Wakefield, and Robert L. Spitzer, *The Loss of Sadness: How Psychiatry Transformed Normal Sorrow into Depressive Disorder*. Boston: Oxford University Press, 2007.

21. Eric G. Wilson, *Against Happiness*. New York: Farrar, Straus & Giroux, 2008.

22. John Cloud, "When Sadness Is a Good Thing," *Time*, August 27, 2007, p. 56.

23. Carroll E. Izard, *Human Emotions*. New York: Plenum, 1977, p. 10.

24. For example, Ellen Berscheid and Elaine Hatfield Walster, *Interpersonal Attraction*, 2nd ed. Reading, MA: Addison-Wesley, 1978.

25. Emily Prager, "The Science of Beauty," *New York Times*. April 17, 1994.

26. Berscheid and Walster.

27. Eliot Aronson, *The Social Animal*, 3rd ed. San Francisco: Freeman, 1980, p. 239.

28. Izard.

29. Earl Ubell, "The Deadly Emotions," *Parade*, February 11, 1990, pp. 3–5; and Jane E. Brody, "Controlling Anger Is Good Medicine for the Heart," *New York Times*, November 20, 1996, p. C15.

30. See *The Record*, June 20, 2004, p. B1; and Thomas Sancton, "Oedipus, Schmoedipus," *Time*, December 9, 1996, p. C15.

31. Emily Nussbaum, "My So-Called Blog," *New York Times Magazine*, January 11, 2004, pp. 33–37.

32. E. Nagourney, "Blow a Gasket, for Your Heart," *New York Times*, February 11, 2003, p. F6.

33. See Daniel Goleman, "A Feel-Good Theory: A Smile Affects Mood," *New York Times*, July 18, 1989, pp. C1, C9.

34. Ellen O' Brien, "Moods Are as Contagious as the Office Cold," *The Record*, November 15, 1993, p. B3.

35. John Powell, *Why am I Afraid to Tell You Who I Am?* Niles, IL: Argus, 1969. For a more recent discussion, see Katherine J. Miller and Joy Koesten, "Financial Feeling: An Investigation of Emotion and Communication in the Workplace," *Journal of Applied Communication Research*, 36:1 (February 2008), pp. 8–32.

36. Sandra Petronio, ed., *Balancing the Secrets of Private Disclosures*. Mahwah, NJ: Erlbaum, 1999.

37. Theodore Isaac Rubin, *The Angry Book*. New York: Macmillan, 1970; and *Emotional Common Sense*. New York: Harper & Row, 1986.

38. Rubin, *The Angry Book*.

39. Marilyn Elias, "The Traits of Wrath in Men and Women," *USA Today*, August 11, 1994, p. 1D.

40. Elias, p. 2D.

41. See Stephanie A. Shields, *Speaking from the Heart: Gender and the Social Meaning of Emotion*. New York: Cambridge University Press, 2002; and Stephanie Armour, "Tears at Work Not Recommended," *USA Today*, January 18, 2008, p. 9B.

42. Kay Deaux, *The Behavior of Women and Men*. Belmont, CA: Brooks/Cole, 1976.

43. See, for example, Michael Ryan, "Go Ahead—Cry!" *Parade*, January 5, 1997, p. 22.

44. Paul Ekman and Wallace Friesen, *Unmasking the Face*. Los Angeles: Consulting Psychology, 1984. For an intercultural perspective, see Stella Ting-Toomey, *The Challenge of Facework*. Albany: State University of New York Press, 1994.

45. Jerry Gillies, *Friendship: The Power and Potential of the Company You Keep*. New York: Coward-McCann, 1976.

46. Sidney Jourard, *The Transparent Self*. New York: Van Nostrand, 1971; and Sidney Jourard and Ted Landsman, *Health Personality*. New York: Macmillan, 1980.

47. See, for example, Denise H. Cloven and Michael E. Roloff, "The Chilling Effect of Aggressive Potential on the Expression of Complaints in Intimate Relationships," *Communication Monographs*, 60:3 (September 1993), pp. 199–219.

48. David Johnson, *Reaching Out: Interpersonal Effectiveness and Self-Actualization*. Englewood Cliffs, NJ: Prentice-Hall, 1972.

49. Susan Chira, "Study Finds Benefits in Emotional Control," *New York Times*, May 26, 1994.

50. See Myra Warren Isenhart and Michael L. Spangle, *Collaborative Approaches to Resolving Conflict*. Thousand Oaks, CA: Sage, 2000.

51. J. M. Gottman, *The Marriage Clinic: A Scientifically Based Marital Therapy*. New York: Norton, 1999.

52. Cited in Mireya Navarro, "We're Friends, Right?" *New York Times*, February 10, 2008, pp. ST 1–2.

53. J. M. Gottman and R. W. Levinson, "Observing Gay and Lesbian Heterosexual Couples' Relationships: Mathematical Modeling of Conflict Interaction," *Journal of Homosexuality*, 45:1 (2003), pp. 711–720.

54. Ibid.

55. Lori Oliwenstein, "Marry Me," *Time*, January 28, 2008, pp. 73–76.

56. Also see J. W. Pennebaker, B. Rime, and V. E. Blankenship, "Stereotypes of Emotional Expressiveness of Northerners and Southerners: A Cross-Cultural Test of Montesquieu's Hypotheses," *Journal of Personality and Social Psychology*, 70 (1996), pp. 372–380.

57. See F. E. Jandt, *Intercultural Communication: An Introduction*, 3rd ed. Thousand Oaks, CA: Sage, 2001; and L. A. Samovar, R. E. Porter, and E. R. McDaniel, *Communication between Cultures*, 4th ed. Belmont, CA: Thomson Wadsworth, 2007.

58. For additional information, see J. D. Pearson, *Gender and Communication*, 2nd ed. Dubuque, IA: Brown, 1991, pp. 183–184; and Stella Ting-Toomey, "Managing Intercultural Conflict Effectively," in Larry A. Samovar and Richard E. Porter, eds., *Intercultural Communication: A Reader*, 7th ed. Belmont, CA: Wadsworth, 1994, pp. 360–372.

59. Alan C. Filley, *Interpersonal Conflict Resolution*. Glenview, IL: Scott, Foresman, 1975.

60. Philip G. Zimbardo and Shirley L. Radl, *The Shyness Workbook*. New York: A&W, Visual Library, 1979.

61. Ibid.

62. Lynn Z. Bloom, Karen Coburn, and Joan Pearlman, *The New Assertive Woman*. New York: Dell, 1975.

63. Arthur J. Lange and Patricia Jakubowski, *Responsible Assertive Behavior*. Champaign, IL: Research Press, 1976.

64. Sherwin B. Cotler and Julio J. Guerra, *Assertive Training*. Champaign, IL: Research Press, 1976, pp. 15–22.

65. For exercises related to the topics covered, see Danny Saunders, "Exercises in Communicating," *Simulation/Games for Learning*, 21:2 (June 1991), pp. 186–200.

66. Alan Wright, "Friending, Ancient or Otherwise," *New York Times*, December 2, 2007, p. WK 4.

67. Craig Wilson, "Suddenly, You've Got a Friend—Tons of Them," *USA Today*, February 6, 2008, p. 1D.

68. Steven Levy, "How Many Friends Is Too Many?" *Newsweek*, May 26, 2008, p. 15.

69. Lee Siegel, *Against the Machine: Being Human in the Age of the Electronic Mob*. New York: Spiegel & Grau, 2008.

70. S. B. Barnes, *Computer-Mediated Communication: Human-to-Human Communication across the Internet*. Boston: Allyn & Bacon, 2003.

71. See Nicholas Negroponte, *Being Digital*. New York: Vintage Books, 1995.

72. John Tierney, "Hitting It Off, Thanks to Algorithms of Love," *New York Times*, January 29, 2008, pp. F1, F4.

73. Lisa Takeuchi Cullen and Coco Masters, "We Just Clicked," *Time*, January 28, 2008, pp. 84, 88–89.

74. See Noam Cohen, "The Global Sympathetic Audience," *New York Times*, November 4, 2007, pp. 2ST, 8ST.

75. Angel Jennings, "What's Good for a Business Can Be Hard on Friends," *New York Times*, August 4, 2007, pp. C1, C2.

76. Ibid.

77. Stephanie Armour, "Boss: It's in the E-Mail," *Wall Street Journal*, April 10, 1999, p. B3.

78. Goleman, *Emotional Intelligence*, p. 28.

Chapter 10

1. D. Johnson and F. Johnson, *Joining Together: Group Theory and Group Skills*, 9th ed. Boston: Allyn & Bacon, 2006.

2. Andrea Coombes, "Survey Finds Few Feel True Love for Their Jobs," *Wall Street Journal*, February 20, 2008.

3. See www.creativity-engineering.com/client.html for a list of current companies providing training in team building.

4. Henry Jenkins, "From YouTube to YouNiversity," *The Chronicle of Higher Education*, February 16, 2007, B10; and Association of American Colleges and Universities, *College Learning for the New Global Age*, Washington D.C.: Association of American Colleges and Universities, 2007.

5. See, for example, G. Lumsden and D. Lumsden, *Communicating in Groups and Teams*, 4th ed. Belmont, CA: Wadsworth, 2004; and T. E. Harris and John C. Sherblom, *Small Group and Team Communication*. New York: Addison Wesley, 2007.

6. Natalie Angier, "Why We're So Nice: We're Wired to Cooperate," *New York Times*, July 23, 2002, pp. F1, F8.

7. See, for example, H. Lancaster, "The Team Spirit Can Lead Your Career to New Victories," *Wall Street Journal*, January 14, 1996, p. B1; and "Work Week," *Wall Street Journal*, November 28, 1995, p. A1.

8. See www.organizedchange.com/selfdir.htm (2008); Daniel S. Iacofano, *Meeting of the Minds*. New York: MIG Communication, 2001; M. A. Verspeij, "When You Put the Team in Charge," *Industry Week*, December 1990, pp. 30–32; A. Versteeg, "Self-Directed Work Teams Yield Long-Term Benefits," *Journal of Business Strategy*, November/December 1990, pp. 9–12; and R. S. Wellins, C. W. Byham, and J. M. Wilson, *Empowered Teams: Creating Self-Directed Workgroups That Improve Quality, Productivity, and Participation*. San Francisco: Jossey-Bass, 1991.

9. Different texts offer different definitions. See, for example, Lumsden and Lumsden, 4th ed., and Thomas E. Harris and John C. Sherblom, *Small Group and Team Communication*. Boston: Allyn & Bacon, 1999.

10. J. Hackman, "The Design of Work Teams," in J. Lorsch, ed. *Handbook of Organizational Behavior*. Englewood Cliffs, NJ: Prentice-Hall, 1987, pp. 315–342.

11. Charles Redding, *Communication within the Organization*. New York: Industrial Communication Council, 1972.

12. Douglas McGregor, *The Human Side of Enterprise*. New York: McGraw-Hill, 1960.

13. B. Tuchman, "Developmental Sequence in Small Groups," *Psychological Bulletin*, 63 (1965), pp. 384–399; and S. A. Wheelen and J. M. Hockberger, "Validation Studies of the Group Development Questionnaire," *Small Group Research*, 27:1 (1996), pp. 143–170.

14. See, for example, J. Keyton, "Group Termination: Completing the Study of Group Development," *Small Group Research*, 24 (1993), pp. 84–100.

15. See, for example, Marshall Scott Poole, "Do We Have Any Theories of Group Communication?" *Communication Studies*, 41:3 (1990), p. 237.

16. Dave Logan, John King, and Hale Fischer-Wright, *Tribal Leadership: Leveraging Natural Groups to Build a Thriving Organization*. New York: Collins, 2008.

17. Kenneth Benne and Paul Sheats, "Functional Roles of Group Members," *Journal of Social Issues*, 4 (1948), pp. 41–49.

18. For a discussion of supportive leadership, see Peter G. Northouse, *Leadership: Theory and Practice*, 2nd ed. Thousand Oaks, CA: Sage, 2001.

19. Linden L. Nelson and Spencer Kagen, "Competition: The Star Spangled Scramble," *Psychology Today*, September 1972, pp. 53–56, 90–91.

20. Morton Deutsch, "A Theory of Cooperation and Competition," *Human Relations*, 2 (1949), pp. 129–152.

21. Jack R. Gibb, "Defensive Communication," *Journal of Communication*, 2 (1961), pp. 141–148.

22. Gibb.

23. See Y. Otsubo, A. Masuchi, and D. Nakanishi, "Majority Influence Process in Group Judgment: Test of the Social Judgment Scheme Model in a Group Polarization Context," *Group Process and Intergroup Relations*, 5:3 (July 2002), pp. 249–262; and D. G. Meyers, *Social Psychology*, 7th ed. New York: McGraw-Hill, 2002, pp. 302–303.

24. John Dewey, *How We Think*. Boston: Heath, 1910.

25. Jay Cocks, "Let's Get Crazy!" *Time*, June 11, 1990, p. 40.

26. Betty Edwards, *Drawing on the Right Side of the Brain*. New York: St. Martin's, 1979.

27. See James Webb Young, *A Technique for Producing Ideas*. New York: McGraw-Hill, 2003; and Luke Johnson, "How to Find Ideas for Challenging Times," *Financial Times*, June 18, 2008, p. 10.

28. Alex Osborn, *Applied Imagination*. New York: Scribner's, 1957.

29. Kelly K. Spors, "Productive Brainstorms Take the Right Mix of Elements," *Wall Street Journal*, July 24, 2008, p. B5.

30. Sidney Parnes, *A Source Book for Creative Thinking*. New York: Scribner's, 1962.

31. Leslie Dorman and Peter Edidin, "Original Spin," *Psychology Today*, July 8, 1989, p. 46.

32. Rosabeth Moss Kanter, "How to Be an Entrepreneur without Leaving Your Company," *Working Woman*, November 1988, p. 44. See also Rosabeth Moss Kanter, *When Giants Learn to Dance*. New York: Touchstone, 1990.

33. G. Hofstede, *Culture and Organizations: Software of the Mind*. New York: McGraw-Hill, 1997.

34. Paul B. Brown, "A Defense of the Boss' Pay," April 12, 2008, p. C5.

35. Francesco Guerrera, "Women Crack Glass Ceiling from Above," *Financial Times*, July 23, 2008, p. 3.

36. See, for example, L. P. Stewart, P. J. Cooper, A. D. Stewart, and S. H. Friendley, *Communication and Gender*, 4th ed. Boston: Allyn & Bacon, 2003, p. 44–50.

37. S. Helgesen, *The Female Advantage: Women's Use of Leadership*. New York: Doubleday, 1990.

38. Julia T. Wood, *Gendered Lives*, 7th ed. Belmont, CA: Wadsworth, 2006; and Iris Aaltio and Pila Lapisto, "Discursive Practice in Ways Male and Female Managers Talk about Careers," www.mngtworkato/ac/nz .ejrot.conference2003/proceeding/gender/Aaltio.pdf.

39. See, for example, S. B. Paletz, K. Peng, M. Erez, and C. Maslach, "Ethnic Composition and Its Differential Impact on Group Processes in Diverse Teams," *Small Group Research*, 35 (2004), pp. 128–157.

40. J. T. Materson, *Communication in Small Groups: Principles and Practices*, 8th ed., Boston: Allyn & Bacon, 2006.

41. Delores Cathcart and Robert Cathcart, "The Group: A Japanese Context," in Larry A. Samovar and Richard E. Porters, eds., *Intercultural Communication: A Reader*, 8th ed. Belmont CA: Wadsworth, 1997, pp. 329–339.

42. Harry C. Triandis, Richard Brislin, and C. Harry Hul, "Cross-Cultural Training across the Individualism-Collectivism Divide," *International Journal of Intercultural Relations*, 12 (1988), pp. 269–289.

43. Cathcart and Cathcart.

44. Michiyo Nakamoto, "Modernisers Span a Cultural Divide," *Financial Times*, May 22, 2008, p. 14.

45. Erin White, "Making the Generation Gap Work for You," *The Record*, July 27, 2008, pp. J1–J2.

46. Stefan Stern, "Y's and Wherefores of a Multi-Generational Workplace," *Financial Times*, April 15, 2008, p. 12.

47. Laurie J. Flynn, "MySpace Mind-Set Finally Shows Up at the Office," *New York Times*, April 9, 2008, p. 7.

48. Clive Thompson, "Close Encounters," *Wired*, August 2008.

49. Brad Stone, "At Social Site, Only the Businesslike Need Apply," *New York Times*, June 18, 2008, pp. C1, C2.

50. "Being Lifelike Makes the Virtual World So Compelling," *Financial Times*, June 18, 2008, p. 8.

51. Jefferson Graham, "Twitter Took Off from Simple to 'Tweet' Success," *The Record*, July 21, 2008, pp. 1B, 2B.

52. Caroline Winter, "Is the Vertical Pronoun Really Such a Capital Idea?" *New York Times Magazine*, August 3, 2008.

53. Bobby R. Patton and Kim Griffin, *Decision Making: Group Interaction*. New York: Harper & Row, 1978.

Chapter 11

1. Katherine Q. Seelye and Julie Bosman, "Critics and News Executives Split over Sexism in Clinton Coverage," *New York Times*, June 13, 2008, p. A1, A24.

2. Mark Rudov, guest on "Your World with Neil Cavuto," Fox News, January 4, 2008.

3. Chrystia Freeland, "Clinton's Real Lesson for Women," *Financial Times*, June 4, 2008, p. 11.

4. For creative ideas on how to use film to better understand leadership, see Roy V. Leeper, "Mutiny on the Bounty: A Case Study for Leadership Courses," paper presented at the joint meeting of the Southern States Communication Association, Lexington, KY, April 14–18, 1993; and Michael Z. Hackman and Craig E. Johnson, *Leadership: A Communication Perspective*, 4th ed., Long Grove, IL: 2004.

5. Paul B. Brown, "What Sets Leaders Apart from the Pack?" *New York Times*, February 5, 2006, p. BU8.

6. For a historical perspective and a summary and critique of 114 studies on small groups, focusing on leadership, discussion, and pedagogy, see John F. Cragan and David W. Wright, "Small Group Communication Research of the 1970s: A Synthesis and Critique," *Central States Speech Journal*, 31 (1980), pp. 197–213; and Michael S. Frank, "The Essence of Leadership," *Public Personnel Management*, 22:3 (Fall 1993), pp. 381–389.

7. For a discussion on how to develop leadership skills, see Stephen S. Kaagan, *Leadership Games*. Thousand Oaks, CA: Sage, 1999; and Lois B. Harle and Charlotte S. Waisman, *The Leadership Training Activity Book*, New York: Amacom, 2004.

8. Craig L. Pearce, "Follow the Leaders," *Wall Street Journal*, July 7, 2008, pp. R8, R12.

9. Douglas McGregor, *The Human Side of Enterprise*. New York: McGraw-Hill, 1960.

10. Norman Augustine and Kenneth Adelman, *Shakespeare in Charge*. New York: Hyperion, 1999.

11. For a classic study on leadership style, see K. Lewin, R. Lippit, and R. K. White, "Patterns of Aggressive Behavior in Experimentally Created Social Climates," *Journal of Social Psychology*, 10 (1939), pp. 271–299.

12. For an early study on trait theory, see Frederick Thrasher, *The Gang: A Study of 1313 Gangs in Chicago*. Chicago: University of Chicago Press, 1927.

13. Marvin Shaw, *Group Dynamics: The Psychology of Small Group Behavior*, 3rd ed. New York: McGraw-Hill, 1981.

14. See Fred Fiedler, *A Theory of Leadership Effectiveness*. New York: McGraw-Hill, 1967.

15. Keith Davis, *Human Relations at Work*. New York: McGraw-Hill, 1967.

16. See, for example, F. E. Fiedler, "Personality and Situational Determinants of Leadership Effectiveness," in D. Cartwright and A. Zander, eds., *Group Dynamics: Research and Theory*, 3rd ed. New York: Harper & Row, 1968, pp. 389–398.

17. P. Hersey and K. Blanchard, *Management Organizational Behavior: Utilizing Human Resources*. Englewood Cliffs, NJ: Prentice Hall, 1988.

18. See Stephen R. Covey, *The 7 Habits of Highly Effective People*. New York: Simon & Schuster, 1989.

19. See, for example, M. Z. Hackman and C. E. Johnson, *Leadership: A Communication Perspective*, 4th ed. Long Grove, IL: Waveland, 2004.

20. For an interesting discussion of how conformity pressures can hamper decision making, see Russel F. Proctor, "Do the Ends Justify the Means? Thinking Critically about 'Twelve Angry Men'," paper presented at the annual meeting of the Central States Communication Association, Chicago, April 11–14, 1991.

21. John Schwartz and Matthew L. Wald, "NASA's Curse?" *New York Times*, March 9, 2003, p. WK5.

22. Irving Janis, *Victims of Groupthink: A Psychological Study of Foreign Policy Decisions and Fiascos*. Boston: Houghton Mifflin, 1972.

23. Benedict Carey, "How to Turn a Herd on Wall St." *New York Times*, April 6, 2008, pp. WK1, WK4.

24. See Ori Brafman and Rom Brafman, *Sway: The Irresistible Pull of Irrational Behavior*. New York: Doubleday, 2008; and Robert Thaler and Cass Sunstein,

Nudge: Improving Decisions about Health, Wealth, and Happiness. New Haven: Yale University Press, 2008.

25. Joseph Nye, "Good Leadership Is Deciding How to Decide," *Financial Times*, April 1, 2008, p. 13.

26. M. T. Claes, "Women, Men, and Management Styles," in P. J. Dubeck and D. Cunn, eds., *Workplace/Women's Place: An Anthology*, 2nd ed. Los Angeles: Roxbury, 2002, pp. 121–125; and A. H. Eagly and S. J. Karau, "Role Congruity Theory of Prejudice Toward Female Leaders," *Psychological Review*, 109:3 (2002), pp. 573–598.

27. J. K. Fletcher, "The Paradox of Post Heroic Leadership: Gender Matters" (Working Paper No. 17). Boston: Center for Gender in Organization, Simmons Graduate School of Management, 2003.

28. R. I. Kabacoff, "Gender Difference in Organizational Leadership: A Large Sample Study," paper presented at the meeting of the American Psychological Association, San Francisco, CA, 1998.

29. See, for example, T. D. Daniels, B. K. Spiker, and M. J. Papa, *Perspectives on Organizational Communication*, 4th ed. New York: McGraw-Hill, 1997.

30. Jennie Yabroff, "Betas Rule," *Newsweek*, June 4, 2007, pp. 64–65.

31. Deborah Tannen, *The Argument Culture: Moving from Debate to Dialogue.* New York: Random House, 1998, pp. 170, 194.

32. J. F. Benenson, S. A. Ford, and N. H. Apostoleris, "Girls' Assertiveness in the Presence of Boys," *Small Group Research*, 29 (1998), pp. 198–211.

33. See, for example, Daniel Canary, William R. Cupach, and Susan J. Messman, *Relational Conflict.* Thousand Oaks, CA: Sage, 1995.

34. Majaana Lindeman, Tuija Harakka, and Liisa Keltikangas-Jarvinen, "Age and Gender Differences in Adolescents' Reactions to Conflict Situations: Aggression, Prosociality, and Withdrawal," *Journal of Youth and Adolescence*, 26 (1997), pp. 339–351.

35. Canary, Cupach, and Messman.

36. Anthony De Palma, "It Takes More Than a Visa to Do Business in Mexico," *New York Times*, June 26, 1994.

37. Lea P. Stewart, "Japanese and American Management: Participative Decision Making," in Larry A. Samovar and Richard E. Porter, eds., *Intercultural Communication: A Reader.* Belmont, CA: Wasdworth, 1985, pp. 186–189.

38. Delores Cathcart and Robert Cathcart, "Japanese Social Experience and Concept of Groups," in Samovar and Porter, pp. 293–304.

39. Marie Brennan, "Mismanagement and Quality Circles: How Middle Managers Influence Direct Participation," *Employer Relations*, 13 (1991), pp. 22–32.

40. Pearce, 2008.

41. Pearce, 2008.

42. John Gapper, "Corporate Culture Shock Is a Big Deal," *Financial Times*, July 31, 2008, p. 9; and Geoffrey A. Fowler, "In China's Offices, Foreign Colleagues Might Get an Earful," *Wall Street Journal*, February 13, 2007, p. B1.

43. Paul B. Brown, "Boardroom Types," *New York Times*, May 3, 2008, p. C5.

44. Phred Dvorak, "Firms Push New Methods to Promote Diversity," *Wall Street Journal*, December 18, 2006, p. B3.

45. Adapted from Aesop's Fables.

46. See, for example, Larry K. Leslie, *Mass Communication Ethics: Decision Making in Post Modern Culture.* Boston: Houghton Mifflin, 2000, pp. 263–266; Barbara Ehrenreich, "In Defense of Talk Shows," *Time*, December 4, 1995, p. 92; and Howard Kurtz, *Hot Air.* New York: Basic Books, 1997.

47. For a description of how to promote a win-win approach to conflict, see Deborah Weider-Hatfield, "A Unit in Conflict Management Communication Skills," *Communication Education*, 30 (1981), pp. 265–273; Joyce L. Hocker and William W. Wilmot, *Interpersonal Conflict*, 3rd ed. Dubuque, IA: Brown, 1991; and Herb Cohen, *Negotiate This!* New York: Warner Business Books, 2003.

48. Robert Blake and Jane Mouton, "The Fifth Achievement," *Journal of Applied Behavioral Science*, 6 (1970), pp. 413–426.

49. Alan Filley, *Interpersonal Conflict Resolution.* Glenview, IL: Scott, Foresman, 1975.

50. Morton Deutsch, "Conflicts: Productive and Destructive," *Journal of Social Issues*, 25 (1969), pp. 7–43; H. Whitteman, "Group Member Satisfaction: A Conflict-Related Account," *Small Group Research*, 22 (1992), pp. 24–58; and R. C. Pace, "Personalized and Depersonalized Conflict in Small Group Discussion: An Examination of Differentiation," *Small Group Research*, 21 (1991), pp. 79–96.

51. See Deborah L. Duarte and Nancy Tennant Snyder, *Mastering Virtual Teams*, 3rd ed. San Francisco: Jossey Bass, 2007.

52. T. Silverman, "Expanding Community: The Internet and Relational Theory," *Community, Work, and Family*, 4 (2001), pp. 231–237.

53. A. Lantz, "Meetings in a Distributed Group of Experts: Comparing Face-to-Face, Chat, and Collaborative Virtual Environments," *Behavior and Information Technology,* 20 (2001), pp. 111–117.

54. B. R. Patton and T. M. Downs, *Decision-Making Group Interaction,* 4th ed. Boston: Allyn & Bacon, 2003.

55. Eric Timmerman and Craig Scott, "Virtually Working: Communicative and Structural Predictors of Media Use and Key Outcomes in Virtual Work Teams," *Communication Monographs,* 73 (2006), pp. 108–136.

56. Deborah Tannen, *Talking from 9 to 5.* New York: Morrow, 1994.

Chapter 12

1. David Wallechinsky, Irving Wallace, and Amy Wallace, *The Book of Lists.* New York: Morrow, 1977, p. 469.

2. Elie Wiesel, *Souls on Fire.* New York: Summit, 1982.

3. Gretchen Morgenson, "Given a Shovel, Digging Deeper into Debt," *New York Times,* July 20, 2008, pp. 1, 14, 15.

4. See Charles Francis, "How to Stop Boring Your Audience to Death," *Vital Speeches of the Day,* February 15, 1996, p. 283.

5. Michael Skapinker, "Chief Execs Should Learn the Art of Oratory," *Financial Times,* January 29, 2008, p. 11.

6. Wynton C. Hall, "Do Effective Speakers Make Effective Presidents?" *USA Today,* February 28, 2008, p. 11A.

7. Roger Ailes, *You Are the Message.* New York: Doubleday, 1989.

8. Robert Orben, "Speech Writing for Presidents," presentation delivered to the Speech Communication Association in Washington, DC, April 1983.

9. Q. McGuire, "Attitudes and Attitude Change," in G. Lindsley and E. Aronson, eds., *The Handbook of Social Psychology,* vol. 2. New York: Random House, 1985, pp. 287–288.

10. Thomas M. Scheidel, "Sex and Persuasability," *Speech Monographs,* 30 (1963), pp. 353–368.

11. Larry A. Samovar, Richard E. Porter, and Edwin R. McDaniel, *Communication between Cultures,* 6th ed. Belmont, CA: Thomson, 2007; and Barbara Mueller, *Communicating with the Multicultural Consumer: Theoretical and Practical Perspectives.* New York: Peter Lang, 2008.

12. See Jill Givson and Trudy L. Hanson, "The Breakfast of Champions: Teaching Audience Analysis Using Cereal Boxes," *Texas Speech Communication Journal,* 31:1 (Winter 2007), pp. 49–50; and Lawrence R. Wheeless, "The Effects of Attitude Credibility and Homophily on Selective Exposure to Information," *Speech Monographs,* 41 (1974), pp. 329–338.

13. For a look at the topics treated recently in public speeches by the leaders of the largest corporations in the United States, see 2006–2009 issues of *Vital Speeches of the Day.*

14. Thomas Leech, *How to Prepare, Stage, and Deliver Winning Presentations.* New York: Amacom, 1982, p. 11.

Chapter 13

1. Randy Reddict and Elliot King, *The OnLine Student.* Fort Worth: TX: Harcourt Brace College, 1996, p. 3. Information on conducting research, pp. 161–179, is particularly valuable.

2. Danny Sullivan, "Nielsen Net Ratings Search Engine Ratings," August 27, 2006, accessed on August 11, 2008, at Searchenginewatch.com.

3. Russ Juskalian, "Video Search Engines Help Sort It All Out," *USA Today,* July 30, 2008, p. 3B.

4. For a more comprehensive treatment of supporting materials see Teri Gamble and Michael Gamble, *Public Speaking in the Age of Diversity,* 2nd ed. Boston: Allyn & Bacon, 1998, chaps. 7 and 8.

5. Paul Starbuck, "Exercise Anorexia: The Deadly Regimen," in *Winning Orations.* Mankato, MN: Interstate Oratorical Association, 2007, p. 5.

6. Megan Solan, "Serving Those Who Serve," in *Winning Orations 2004.* Mankato MN: Interstate Oratorical Association, 2005.

7. Solan.

8. Paula Rawlins, "GI Schmo," in *Winning Orations.* Mankato, MN: Interstate Oratorical Association, 2007, p. 15.

9. Amy Solomito, "Untitled," in *Winning Orations.* Mankato, MN: Interstate Oratorical Association, 2007, p. 73.

10. Lev Grossman, "The Off-Line American," *Time,* August 25, 2008, p. 52.

11. For a discussion of the power of examples in public speaking, see Gamble and Gamble; and Scott Consigny, "The Rhetorical Example," *Southern Speech Communication Journal* 41 (1976), pp. 121–134.

12. Solomon D. Trujillo, "Two Lives: The One We Make Defines Our Legacy," *Vital Speeches of the Day* 66:6 (January 1, 2000), p. 169. Reprinted with permission.

13. Nancy H. Nielsen, "Designing America's Bridge," *Vital Speeches of the Day* (August 2008), pp. 375–376.

14. Harvey Mackay, "Postgraduate Life," *Vital Speeches of the Day* (August 2008), p. 359.

15. Theresa McGuiness, "Greeks in Crisis," in *Winning Orations*. Mankato, MN: Interstate Oratorical Association, 2000, p. 75. Reprinted by permission.

16. William L. Laurence, "Eyewitness Account: Atomic Bomb Mission over Nagasaki," *New York Times*, September 9, 1945.

17. Jillian Collum, "Toxic Forces: How the United States Military Is Polluting Our Communities," in *Winning Orations*. Mankato, MN: Interstate Oratorical Association, 2007, p. 84.

18. "I Have a Dream," by Martin Luther King, Jr. Reprinted by arrangement with the Estate of Martin Luther King, Jr., c/o Writers House as agent for the proprietor, New York, NY. Copyright 1963 Dr. Martin Luther King, Jr., copyright renewed 1991 Coretta Scott King.

19. Mary Panzer, "Photojournalism for the Web Generation," *Wall Street Journal*, July 8, 2008, p. D7.

20. Jerry Weissman, *Presenting to Win: The Art of Telling Your Story*. New York: Prentice-Hall, 2006.

21. Jae Yang and Kari Gelles, "USA Today Snapshots," *USA Today*, August 13, 2008, p. 1B.

22. Carla K. Johnson, "30% of Americans Abuse Alcohol," *The Record*, July 3, 2007, p. A7.

23. "America Incarcerated," *Time*, March 17, 2008, p.14.

24. Anne R. Caarey and Julie Snider, "Where Nuclear Plants Are," *USA Today*, July 17, 2008, p. 1A.

25. "In Memoriam," *New York Times*, May 28, 2007, p. A1.

26. Karen Sudo, "Deadly Riptides," *The Record*, August 1, 2008, p. A1.

27. *Discover*, June 2003, pp. 42–47.

28. W. I. Ringle and W. D. Thompson, *TechEdge: Using Computers to Present and Persuade*. Needham Heights, MA: Allyn & Bacon, 1998.

29. L. Zuckerman, "Words Go Right to the Brain, But Can They Stir the Heart," *New York Times*, April 17, 1999, pp. A17–A19.

30. Greg Jaffe, "What's Your Point, Lieutenant? Just Cut to the Pie Charts," *Wall Street Journal*, April 26, 2000, pp. A1, A6.

31. June Kronholz, "PowerPoint Goes to School," *Wall Street Journal*, November 12, 2002, pp. B1, B6.

32. Jan Parker, "Absolute PowerPoint," *New Yorker*, May 28, 2001, pp. 76–87.

33. Frances Cole Jones, *How to WOW*. New York: Ballentine Books, 2008, p. 132; also see Dale Cyphert, "Presentation Technology in the Age of Electronic Eloquence: From Visual Aid to Visual Rhetoric," *Communication Education* 56:2 (April 2007), pp 168–192.

34. Parker; also see Mark R. Stoner, "PowerPoint in a New Key," *Communication Education* 56:3 (July 2007), pp. 354–381.

35. Lee Gomes, "PowerPoint Turns 20, as Its Creators Ponder a Dark Side to Success," *Wall Street Journal*, June 20, 2007, p. B1.

36. David Shenk, *Data Smog: Surviving the Information Glut*. San Francisco: Harper Edge, 1997, p. 93.

37. "College Faked Photo in Pitch for Diversity," *The Record*, September 21, 2000, p. A13; for more on this subject see David D. Perlmutter and Nicole Smith Dahman, "(In)Visible Evidence in the Apollo Moon Landings," *Visual Communication* 7:2 (May 2008), pp. 229–251.

Chapter 14

1. For decades, studies revealed how organization affects reception, For example, see Christopher Spicer and Ronald E. Bassett, "The Effect of Organization on Learning from an Informative Message," *Southern States Communication Journal* 41 (1976), pp. 290–299; and Johen E. Baird, Jr., "The Effects of Speech Summaries upon Audience Comprehension of Expository Speeches of Varying Quality and Complexity," *Central States Speech Journal* 25 (1974), pp. 119–127.

2. Richard Nisbett, *The Geography of Thought: How Asians and Westerners Think Differently . . . and Why*. New York: Free Press, 2003.

3. National Public Radio, "Analysis: Geography of Thought," *Talk of the Nation* broadcast of interview of Richard Nisbett by Neal Conan, March 3, 2003. © 2003 National Public Radio, Inc. Used with permission.

4. Ibid.

5. D. L. Thislethwaite, H. DeHaan, and J. Kamenetsky suggest that a message is more easily understood and accepted if transitions are used: see "The Effect of 'Directive' and 'Non-Directive' Communication Procedures on Attitudes," *Journal of Abnormal and Social Psychology* 51 (1955), pp. 107–118. Also of value on this aspect of speech organization is E. Thompson, "Some Effects of Message Structure on Listeners' Comprehension," *Speech Monographs* 34 (1967), pp. 51–57.

6. See for example, Arran Gare, "Narratives and Culture: The Role of Stories in Self-Creation," *Telos* (Winter 2002); and Jessica Lee Shumake, "Reconceptualization Communication and Rhetoric from a Feminist Perspective," *Guidance & Counseling* (Summer 2002).

7. Myron W. Lustig and Jolene Koester, *Intercultural Competence: Interpersonal Communication across Cultures*, 3rd ed. New York: Longman, 1999.

8. See R. S. Zaharna, "Rhetorical Ethnocentrism," for example, http://nw08.american.edu/~zaharna/rhetoric.htm.

9. For a more comprehensive treatment of introductions and conclusions, see Gamble and Gamble, *Public Speaking in the Age of Diversity*, 2nd ed. Boston: Allyn & Bacon, 1998, chap. 10.

10. Cal Ripken Jr., "There Are No Endings," *Vital Speeches of the Day* 73 (October 2007), p. 444.

11. Brittany Young, "Prisoner Abuse: The Stain on American Democracy," in *Winning Orations*. Mankato, MN: Interstate Oratorical Association, 2007, p. 89.

12. Erin Gallaher, "Upholstered Furniture: Sitting in the Uneasy Chair." *Winning Orations*. Mankato, MN: Interstate Oratorical Association, 2000, p. 99. Reprinted with permission.

13. Adrienne Hallett, "Dying in Your Sleep," in *Winning Orations* Northfield, MN: Interstate Oratorical Association, 1995, p. 27. Reprinted with permission.

14. Melissa Benton, "Protecting the Vulnerable: Restructuring the Mental Health System," in *Winning Orations*. Mankato, MN: Interstate Oratorical Association, 2007, p. 53.

15. Paul Hogan, "The 'Age Wave'," *Vital Speeches of the Day* 73 (December 2007), pp. 557–558.

16. Jesse Ohl, "Rising Sun, Rising Cancer," in *Winning Orations*. Mankato, MN: Interstate Oratorical Association, 2007, p. 31.

17. Brian Swenson, "Gun Safety and Children," in *Winning Orations*. Mankato, MN: Interstate Oratorical Association, 1990, p. 101. Reprinted with permission.

18. This Kennedy quote has been attributed to G. B. Shaw, as well as the poet Robert Browning.

Chapter 15

1. See, for example, Camille D. Smith, Chris R. Sawyer, and Ralph R. Behnke, "Physical Symptoms Associated with Worrying about Giving a Public Speech," *Communication Reports* 18 (2008); and "Ailments Correlated with Anxiety," *USA Today*, June 3, 2003, p. 1A.

2. J. B. Donovan, "Power to the Podium: The Place to Stand for Those Who Move the World," *Vital Speeches of the Day* 58 (1991), pp. 149–150.

3. Ellen Joan Pollock, "The Selling of a Golden Speech," *Wall Street Journal*, March 12, 1999, p. B1. The Wall Street Journal Eastern Edition by Robert L. Bartley. Copyright 1999 By Dow Jones & Co. Inc. Reproduced with permission of Dow Jones & Co. via the Copyright Clearance Center.

4. See, for example, Betty Horwitz, *Communication Apprehension: Origins and Management*. Florence, KY: Cengage

Learning, 2001; Timothy L. Sellnow, "Controlling Speech Anxiety," paper presented at the annual meeting of the Speech Communication Association, Chicago, IL, October 29– November 1, 1992; Marianne Martin, "The Communication of Public Speaking Anxiety: Perception of Asian and American Speakers," *Communication Quarterly* 40 (Summer 1992), pp. 279–288; James McCroskey, Steven Booth Butterfield, and Steven K. Payne, "The Impact of Communication Apprehension on College Student Retention and Success," *Communication Quarterly* 37 (Spring 1989), pp. 100–107; and Judy C. Pearson and Jeffrey Child, "Preparation Meeting Opportunity: How Do College Students Prepare for Public Speakers," *Communication Quarterly* 54 (August 2006), pp. 351–366.

5. Eleanor Blau, "Taking Arms against Stage Fright," *New York Times*, September 20, 1998, p. AR-33; and Holina Ablamowicz, "Using a Speech Apprehension Questionnaire as a Tool to Reduce Students' Fear of Public Speaking," *Communication Teacher* 19 (July 2005), pp. 98–102.

6. J. D. Mladenka, C. R. Sawyer, and R. R. Behnke, "Anxiety Sensitivity and Speech Trait Anxiety as Predictors of State Anxiety during Public Speaking," *Communication Quarterly* 46 (1998), pp. 417–429; and Penny Addison, Elc Clay, Shuang Xie, Chris R. Sawyer, and Ralph R. Behnke, "Worry as a Function of Public Speaking State Anxiety Type," *Communication Reports* 16 (2003).

7. For a more detailed guide to fear-control training, see Joe Ayres and Tim Hopf, "Visualization: Reducing Speech Anxiety and Enhancing Performance," *Communication Reports* 1:1 (winter 1992), pp. 1–10.

Chapter 16

1. See Francis Cairncross, "The Roots of Revolution and the Trendspotter's Guide to New Communications," in Erik P. Bucy, *Living in the Information Age: A New Media Reader*. Stamford, CT: Wadsworth/Thompson Learning, 2002, pp. 3–10.

2. Daniel Pink, *A Whole New Mind: Moving from the Information Age to the Conceptual Age*. New York: Riverhead Books, 2005; and Garr Reynolds, *Presentation Zen*. New York: New Ridges Press, 2008.

3. Although compiled years ago, a valuable source to consult is Charles Petrie, "Informative Speaking: A Summary and Bibliography of Related Research," *Speech Monographs* 30 (1963), pp. 79–91.

4. See, for example, Katherine E. Rowan, "Informing and Explaining Skills: Theory and Research on Informative Communication," in John O. Greene and

Brant R. Burleson, eds., *Handbook of Communication and Social Interaction Skills*. Mahwah, NJ: Lawrence Erlbaum Associates, 2003, pp. 403–438.

5. See, for example, Brendan Lemon, "Audiences Today Are Getting in on the Act," *New York Times*, October 8, 2000, pp. AR-5, AR-22.

Chapter 17

1. Robert B. Cialdini, *Influence: Science and Practice*, 4th ed. Boston: Allyn & Bacon, 2001, p. 239.

2. For an excellent explanation of why we study persuasion, see Deirdre D. Johnston, *The Art and Science of Persuasion*. Dubuque, IA: Brown & Benchmark, 1994. For an analysis of key theories of persuasion, see Dominick A. Infante, Andrew S. Rancer, and Deanna F. Womack, *Building Communication Theory*, 3rd ed. Prospect Heights, IL: Waveland, 1997. An interesting discussion also occurs in Jay A. Conger, "The Necessary Art of Persuasion," *Harvard Business Review* 76:3 (May–June 1998), pp. 84–95.

3. See Wallace Folderingham, *Perspectives on Persuasion*. Boston: Allyn & Bacon, 1966, p. 33; and James Price Dillard, "Persuasion Past and Present: Attitudes Aren't What They Used to Be," *Communication Monographs* 60:1 (March 1993), pp. 90–97.

4. For an interesting definition and discussion of persuasion, see Anthony Pratkanis and Elliot Aronson, *The Age of Propaganda*, rev. ed. New York: Freeman, 2000; and Cialdini, 2000.

5. Patrick D. Healy, "Weld Aides Find a Way to Deal with Negative Press: Re-edit It," *New York Times*, February 4, 2006, pp. B1, B4.

6. For a discussion of now-classic studies, see M. Sherif and C. Hovland, *Social Judgment*. New Haven, CT: Yale University Press, 1961; and C. Sherif, M. Sherif, and R. Nebergall, *Attitude and Attitude Change*. Philadelphia: Saunders, 1965. For a very understandable explanation, see also E. Griffin, *A First Look at Communication Theory*, 4th ed. New York: McGraw-Hill, 2000.

7. Scott Cutlip and Alan Center, *Effective Public Relations*. Englewood Cliffs, NJ: Prentice-Hall, 1985, p. 122.

8. A framework for understanding the importance of beliefs is provided by Martin Fishbein and Icek Ajzaen, *Belief, Attitude, Intention and Behavior: An Introduction to Theory and Research*. Reading, MA: Addison-Wesley, 1975. See especially Chapters 1 and 8.

9. Milton Rokeach, *The Open and Closed Mind*. New York: Basic Books, 1960.

10. Prominent theorists such as Leon Festinger, Fritz Hieder, and Theodore Newcomb consider the desire for consistency a central motivator of behavior. For a more contemporary discussion of the topic, see Robert B. Cialdini, *Influence*, rev. ed. New York: Quill, 2000.

11. Cialdini, p. 116.

12. Cialdini; see also Mike Allen, "Determining the Persuasiveness of Message Sidedness: A Prudent Note about Utilizing Research Summaries," *Western Journal of Communication* 57:1 (Winter 1993), pp. 98–103.

13. John Tierney, "Smells Like Team Spirit," *New York Times*, February 4, 2006, p. A13.

14. Wayne Minnick, *The Art of Persuasion*. Boston: Houghton Mifflin, 1968.

15. For a discussion of the role of affect, see, for example, Mary John Smith, *Persuasion and Human Action*. Belmont, CA: Wadsworth, 1982.

16. Abraham Maslow, *Motivation and Personality*. New York: Harper & Row, 1954, pp. 80–92.

17. Bruce E. Gronbeck, Rayme E. McKerrow, Douglas Ehninger, and Alan H. Monroe, *Principles and Types of Speech Communication*, 15th ed. New York, Allyn & Bacon, 2002.

18. Based on a speech by Amanda Taylor, "Drowsy Driving: A Deadly Epidemic," in *Winning Orations*. Mankato, MN: Interstate Oratorical Association, 2000, pp. 12–15.

19. Credibility has received much attention from researchers. See, for example, James M. Kouzes and Barry Z. Posner, *Credibility*. San Francisco: Jossey-Bass, 1993.

20. J. W. Anderson, "A Comparison of Arab and American Conceptions of 'Effective' Persuasion," *Howard Journal of Communications* 2:1 (Winter 1989–1990), pp. 81–114.

21. Bob Ivry, "From White Lies to the White House," *The Record*, June 8, 2003, pp. A-1, A-16.

22. Mark Bowden, "Sometimes Heroism Is a Moving Target," *New York Times*, pp. WK1, WK4.

23. Bowden.

24. Speakers can establish credibility early in a speech. For example, see R. Brooks and T. Scheidel, "Speech as Process: A Case Study," *Speech Monographs* 35 (1968), pp. 1–7.

25. Nonverbal aspects of credibility are discussed in more detail in Chapter 16.

26. Developed as part of a class exercise by students in communication courses at the College of New Rochelle in New Rochelle, New York, and at the New York Institute of Technology in New York City, using a transcript made of the videotaped speech by Jose

Magana, "Breaking Down Borders: Allowing Immigrants to Obtain a Higher Education," in *Winning Orations*. Mankato, MN: Interstate Oratorical Association, 2007, pp. 1–2.

27. Transcribed from a speech by Jose Magana of Arizona State University appearing in *Winning Orations*. Mankato, MN: Interstate Oratorical Association, 2007, pp. 1–2.

Appendix Notes

1. Eli Amdur, "How Workers Should Prepare for the World in 2050," *The Record*, May 23, 2008, pp. J1, J2.

2. Rick Bentley, "Interest in Forensic Science Has Surged during 'CSI'," (Rock Hill, SC) *Herald*, January 12, 2002, www.heraldonline.com.

3. Melinda Ligos, "Young Job Seekers Need New Clues," *New York Times*, August 8, 2001, p. G1; and Lois J. Einhorn report in "An Inner View of the Job Interview: An Investigation of Successful Communicative Behavior," *Communication Education* 30 (1981), pp. 217–228, that successful candidates were able to identify with the employer, support their arguments, organize their thoughts, clarify their ideas, and speak fluently.

4. Eli Amdur, "On a Resume, There's Nothing Like a Good Opening," *The Record*, January 27, 2008, pp. J1, J2.

5. Leonard Zunin and Natalie Zunin, *Contact: The First Four Minutes*. Los Angeles: Nash, 1972, pp. 8–12.

6. Adam Geller, "Problem Postings," *The Record*, March 17, 2003; and Kris Maher, "Resume Rustling Threatens Online Job Sites," *Wall Street Journal*, February 25, 2003, pp. B1, B10.

7. See Mark L. Knapp, Roderick P. Hart, Gustav W. Friedrich, and Gary M. Schulman, "The Rhetoric of Goodbye: Verbal and Nonverbal Correlates of Human Leave-Taking," *Speech Monographs* 40 (1973), pp. 182–198.

8. David Koeppel, "On a Resume, Don't Mention Moon Pies or Water Cannons," *New York Times*, November 24, 2001, Section 10, p. 1.

9. Charles J. Stewart and William B. Cash, Jr., *Interviewing: Principles and Practices*, 6th ed. Dubuque, IA: Brown, 1991.

10. Arlene Hirsch, "Tell Me about Yourself Doesn't Mean 'Tell It All'," *The Record*, November 28, 2004, pp. J1, J2; and Anthony DePalma, "Preparing for 'Tell Us about Yourself'," *New York Times*, July 27, 2003, p. NJ1.

11. Malcolm Gladwell, "What Do Job Interviews Really Tell Us?" *New Yorker*, May 29, 2000, p. 84.

12. Ibid.

13. Eli Amdur, "Train Yourself to Be a S.T.A.R. during the Job Interview," *The Record*, September 4, 2005, p. J1.

14. Eli Amdur, "An Interview Is a Two-Way Deal, So Ask Questions," *The Record*, April 17, 2005, pp. J1, J2.

15. For a study confirming that employers use a candidate's speech characteristics to judge competence and likability, see Robert Hopper, "Language Attitudes in the Employment Interview," *Speech Monographs* 44 (1974), pp. 346–351.

16. Eli Amdur, "Be the Person Companies Will Want to Hire," *The Record*, October 24, 2004, pp. J1, J2.

17. Gladwell, pp. 68–86.

18. "Initial Minutes of Job Interview Are Critical," *USA Today*, January 2000, p. 8.

19. Eli Amdur, "The 10 General Rules to Help You Be a Good Interviewee," *The Record*, August 5, 2007, pp. J1, J2.

20. Einhorn.

21. Rachel Emma Silverman and Kemba J. Dunham, "Even in a Tight Market, Job Hunters Can Blunder," *Wall Street Journal*, June 20, 2000, p. B12.

22. Also see Gladwell, pp. 68–72, 84–86; and C. J. Stewart and W. B. Cash, Jr., *Interviewing Principles and Practices*, 7th ed. Dubuque, IA: Brown, 1994.

23. Marvin Walberg, "Interviewing: Expected the Unexpected," *The Record*, September 4, 2009, p. A9.

24. Joann S. Lublin, "Notes to Interviewers Should Go Beyond a Simple Thank You," *Wall Street Journal*, February 5, 2008, p. B1.

25. Lublin.

26. See, for example, F. Mahoney, "Adjusting the Interview to Avoid Cultural Bias," *Journal of Career Planning and Employment* 52 (1992), pp. 41–43.

27. Mary Williams Walsh, "Money Isn't Everything," *New York Times*, January 30, 2001, p. 10.

28. Ibid.

29. Marjorie Valbrun, "More Muslims Claim They Suffer Job Bias," *Wall Street Journal*, April 15, 2003, pp. B1, B8.

30. Sarah E. Needleman, "Job Seekers: Put Your Web Savvy to Work," *Wall Street Journal*, September 9, 2007, p. B3.

31. Kris Maher, "Blogs Catch on as Online Tool for Job Seekers and Recruiters," *Wall Street Journal*, September 28, 2004, p. B10.

32. For a discussion of online search techniques, see Cynthia B. Leshin, *Internet Investigations in Business Communication*. Saddle River, NJ: Prentice Hall, 1997, pp. 95–134.

33. See Zane K. Quible, "Electronic Resumes: Their Time Is Coming," *Business Communicaiton Quarterly* 58 (September 1995), pp. 5–9.

34. Wallace V. Schmidt and Roger N. Conaway, *Results-Oriented Interviewing: Principles, Practices, and Procedures.* Boston: Allyn & Bacon, 1999, p. 11.

35. Mark Cendella, "Top 10 Blunders of Online Job Hunters," *The Record*, September 5, 2004, p. Jl.

36. David Koeppel, "Web Can Help, but a Job Hunt Still Takes Lots of Hard Work," *New York Times*, September 12, 2004, pp. MB1, 3.

37. Sarah E. Needleman, "Thx for the Iview! I Wud (Heart) to Work 4 U!!" *Wall Street Journal*, July 29, 2008, pp. Dl, D4.

38. From David Kirby, "Selling Yourself: There Are Questions You Shouldn't Answer." Adapted from *The New York Times*, January 30, 2001, p. 2. Copyright © 2001 by the New York Times Co. Reprinted with permission.

Online Chapter

1. See W. James Potter, *Media Literacy*, 4th ed. Thousand Oaks, CA: Sage, 2008.

2. B. Haring, "Internet Vet Wary of Superhighway's Direction," *USA Today*, April 6, 1995, p. 7D.

3. J. Hancock and P. Dunham, "Impression Formation in Computer-Mediated Communication Revisited: An Analysis of the Breadth and Intensity of Impressions," *Communication Research* 28 (2001), pp. 325–332; and L. Pratt, R. Weisman, M. Cody, and P. Wendt, "Interrogative Strategies and Information Exchange in Computer-Mediated Communication," *Communication Quarterly* 47 (1999), pp. 36–66.

4. Roger Fidler, "New Media Theory," in Eric P. Bucy, ed., *Living in the Information Age.* Belmont, CA: Wadsworth, 2002, pp. 21–29.

5. Neil Postman, *Amusing Ourselves to Death.* New York: Viking, 1985.

6. See, for example, "The Veronis Suhler Stevenson Communications Industry Forecast, 2007–2011."

7. Ibid.

8. See "Television and Health" accessed at www.csun.edu/science/health/docs/tv&health.html.

9. "Nielsen Reports TV, Internet, and Mobile Usage among Americans," July 8, 2008, www.nielsen.com/media/2008pr 080708.html.

10. Ellen Graham, "The New Living-Room Détente," *Wall Street Journal*, June 27, 1997, p. R4.

11. Douglas Foster, "Burdened with Being Everywhere," *New York Times*, August 19, 2000, p. Al5.

12. Richard Soklos, "I Cannot Tell a Lie (from an Amplification)," *New York Times*, February 5, 2006, p. BU3.

13. Andrew Keen, *The Cult of the Amateur: How Today's Internet Is Killing our Culture.* New York: Doubleday, 2007.

14. James Alexander Thom, "The Perfect Picture," *Reader's Digest*, August 1976, p. 113. Reprinted with permission.

15. Clarence Page, "Someone's Watching Your Web Searches," *The Record*, January 26, 2006, p. L-9.

16. Ken Belson, "Lipstick on Your Caller," *New York Times*, February 5, 2006, p. WK4.

17. Janice Kaplan, "Are Talk Shows Out of Control?" *TV Guide*, April 1, 1995, pp. 10–15.

18. Thomas E. Weber, "Privacy Concerns Force Public to Confront Thorny Issues," *Wall Street Journal*, June 19, 1997, p. B6.

19. Joshua Quittner, "Invasion of Privacy," *Time*, August 25, 1997, pp. 28–35.

20. Albert Bandura, *Social Learning Theory.* Englewood Cliffs, NJ: Prentice Hall, 1977.

21. U.S. Department of Health and Human Services, *Youth Violence: A Report of the Surgeon General, 2001*, retrieved from www.surgeongeneral.gov.

22. American Academy of Pediatrics, "Children, Adolescents, and Television," *Pediatrics* 107 (2001), pp. 423–426.

23. Wilbur Schramm, Jack Lyle, and Edwin Parker, *Television in the Lives of Our Children.* Palo Alto, CA: Stanford University Press, 1961.

24. Ibid., p. 13.

25. Lee Siegel, *Against the Machine: Being Human in the Age of the Electronic Mob.* New York: Spiegel and Grau, 2008.

26. David Browne, "On the Internet, It's All about 'My'," *New York Times*, April 30, 2008, p. ST7.

27. Jean M. Twenge, *Generation Me: Why Today's Young Americans Are More Confident, Assertive, Entitled—and More Miserable Than Ever Before.* New York: Free Press, 2007.

Chapter 1

Chapter 2

Chapter 3

Chapter 4

Chapter 5

Chapter 6

Chapter 7

Chapter 8

Chapter 9

210: © PHOTOSINDIA.COM LLC/ALAMY;

213: © MASTERFILE;

214: (TOP) © ROYALTY-FREE/CORBIS, (BOTTOM) © BANANASTOCK/AGE FOTOSTOCK;

217: © IMAGE SOURCE/PUNCHSTOCK;

219: © PAULA BRONSTEIN/GETTY;

220: © BANANASTOCK/PUNCHSTOCK;

221: © JOHN CARTER/PHOTO RESEARCHERS;

227: © ROBERT BRENNER/PHOTO EDIT;

230: © BRIAN SNYDER/REUTERS/CORBIS;

237: © 24/7 DIGITAL/IMAGESTATE.

Chapter 10

244: © ANTHONY BRADSHAW/GETTY;

247: © KEITH BROFSKY/GETTY;

250: © BLEND IMAGES/ALAMY;

253: © PETER CAVANAGH/ALAMY;

256: © IMAGE SOURCE PINK (RF);

259: © RABH IMAGES/ALAMY;

268: © RAYES/GETTY.

Chapter 11

276: © CORBIS;

278: © STEVE SKJOLD/ALAMY;

280: © CBS VIA GETTY;

286: © JOSE CARILLO/PHOTOEDIT.

Chapter 12

300: © MICHAEL NEWMAN/PHOTOEDIT;

306: © RODERICK SMITH/ALAMY;

308: THE MCGRAW-HILL COMPANIES, INC./CHRISTOPHER KERRIGAN, PHOTOGRAPHER;

310: © CHUCK SAVAGE/CORBIS;

312: © MARIA TEIJEIRO/GETTY IMAGE;

316: © BOB DAEMMRICH/PHOTOEDIT.

Chapter 13

326: © COMSTOCK IMAGES (RF)/JUPITER;

332: © MICHAEL NEWMAN/PHOTOEDIT;

339: © THINKSTOCK IMAGES (RF)/JUPITER;

341: © MARIO TAMA/GETTY NEWS;

346: (TOP) © HOWARD SOCHUREK/MEDICHROME STOCK SHOP, (BOTTOM) © CENTER FOR DISEASE CONTROL/PHOTOTAKE.

Chapter 14

356: © ANDERSEN ROSS/GETTY;

362: © BOB DAEMMRICH/PHOTOEDIT;

364: (TOP) © ROYALTY-FREE/CORBIS, (BOTTOM) © INGRAM PUBLISHING/AGE FOTOSTOCK;

371: © DAVID YOUNG-WOLF/PHOTOEDIT;

375: © ANDY SACKS/GETTY.

Chapter 15

382: © ALEX WONG/GETTY;

384: © DWAYNE NEWTON/PHOTOEDIT;

386: © DIGITAL VISION LTD./SUPERSTOCK;

389: © POLKA DOT IMAGES (RF)/JUPITER;

392: © SYRACUSE NEWSPAPERS/THE IMAGE WORKS;

394: © STEWART COHEN/PHOTODISC RED/GETTY.

Chapter 16

402: © BANANASTOCK LTD.;

404: © MICHAEL J. DOOLITTLE/THE IMAGE WORKS;

408: THE MCGRAW-HILL COMPANIES, INC./JAN L. SAEGER, PHOTOGRAPHER.

Chapter 17

420: © JONATHAN NOUROK/PHOTOEDIT;

432: © ROBERT W. GINN/PHOTOEDIT;

433: © PETER TURNLEY/CORBIS;

438: © AP PHOTO/HELGE O. SOMMER.

Boldface numbers indicate pages on which glossary definitions appear; page numbers followed by *f* indicate figures; and page numbers followed by *t* indicate tables.